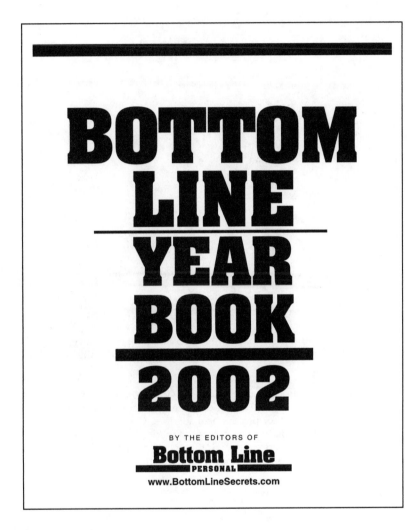

BOTTOM LINE YEAR BOOK 2002

BY THE EDITORS OF

Bottom Line
PERSONAL

www.BottomLineSecrets.com

Contents

PART THREE: YOUR FINANCIAL FUTURE

11 • PLANNING YOUR RETIREMENT

12 • ESTATE PROTECTION

PART FOUR: YOUR LEISURE

13 • SAVVY TRAVEL

14 • ENJOYING YOUR LEISURE

15 • CAR SMARTS

16 • HOME AND FAMILY

17 • THE WINNING EDGE

PART FIVE: YOUR LIFE

18 • BUSINESS AND CAREER

19 • EDUCATION SMARTS

20 • SELF-DEFENSE

21 • VERY, VERY PERSONAL

1

Staying Healthy

Cancer Survival Secrets

Almost from the minute a diagnosis of cancer is confirmed, advice begins pouring in—from your doctor…your parents… your spouse…your friends.

But perhaps no one is better equipped to tell you how to beat the disease than cancer survivors themselves. Recently, we polled several survivors to get their strategies for making it through the difficult times…

● **Get a second opinion as soon as possible after your initial diagnosis.** Ideally, you will get opinions from several specialists, including a medical oncologist, a radiation oncologist and a surgeon.

Lung cancer survivor Richard Bloch was such a believer in this approach that he founded a free, multidisciplinary second-opinion panel staffed by more than 100 physicians in his native Kansas City, Missouri. "I believe that one out of every four patients the panel

saw had his or her life saved because of the panel," Bloch says.

● **Commit yourself to doing everything in your power to beat the disease.** "This might sound silly," says Bloch, "but some people just turn everything over to their doctors and expect them to fix it." You must become intimately involved in all aspects of your cancer treatment. It's tempting, of course, to leave the details to the doctors. But to maximize your chances of survival, you have to muster all of your resources and exhaust every option open to you.

● **Expect the first three months after the diagnosis to be awful.** That advice comes from Daniel Kohn, a therapist who was diagnosed with a brain tumor four years ago.

"You're going to be in shock and in denial, no matter how well-equipped you are," he says. "Just ride it through. It gets better."

Richard Bloch, a philanthropist in Kansas City, Missouri, and cofounder of the tax-preparation firm H&R Block, Inc. In 1978, Bloch was diagnosed with terminal lung cancer and given three months to live.

•**Pick doctors who are affiliated with a major hospital.** Fight for your right to have the doctor you choose, no matter what your insurance company says.

•**Look beyond your family for emotional support.** When Bloch was diagnosed, the few cancer survivors he knew didn't seem interested in talking with him. So he launched the Cancer Hot Line (800-433-0464, *www. blochcancer.com*), a volunteer group of cancer patients who take phone calls from newly diagnosed cancer patients.

Many cancer patients find support groups especially helpful. It certainly doesn't hurt to meet people who were given death sentences 10 years ago...and are still alive.

•**Have an advocate.** This is someone who accompanies you to doctor appointments, takes notes, keeps track of paperwork and argues for you when you're hospitalized.

A good advocate can also research the particular cancer and filter his/her findings to you so you aren't overwhelmed by all the information.

•**Get a fax machine.** Having one at home will make it much easier to send, receive and make copies of all your medical records (many fax machines do double duty as a copier).

If you have access to a fax machine at work or someplace else outside your home, think twice before using it. You may not want others to see all your medical records.

•**Make use of the Internet.** You're going to need information and explanations. But trying to get that from numerous sites can just add to the confusion.

If you don't have a home computer, make use of a friend's or one at a nearby library, copy shop or "cybercafe." *Especially helpful:* National Cancer Institute, *rex.nci.nih.gov.*

•**Make friends with your doctor's staff.** That way, when you call with a question or problem, they'll treat you as an individual— and make sure you get what you need.

Drop off cookies, chocolates or even gift certificates to thank them.

•**Ask your doctor's office to schedule the appointments** when you are referred to specialists. They can line up an appointment sooner than you can.

•**Buy a wig *before* undergoing chemotherapy**—if the drugs to be used are likely to cause hair loss. Your doctor can probably prescribe a wig for you. That's a good idea because it means that part or even all of the cost might be covered by health insurance.

•**Indulge yourself.** When Kohn took steroids as part of his treatment, he craved fatty foods like chicken wings and french fries. That's not unusual.

Kohn's wife was horrified. She thought he wasn't taking care of himself. But the food provided one of his few sources of pleasure during this time.

•**If you don't have cable television, get it.** You'll often be too sick to read or write. A funny movie or TV show can do wonders for your mood—and it's critical that you keep your mood up.

•**Plan for depression.** Bloch notes that "everything about cancer is depressing. Expect down days and plan things that cheer you up at those times."

Ask your doctor about anti-depressant therapy to ease the feelings of hopelessness that often accompany cancer.

Cancer Breakthrough

Treating tumors with heat boosts the effect of radiation and chemotherapy. Patients undergoing *hyperthermia* lie for 90 minutes with a water bag on the skin near the tumor. High-frequency radio waves raise the tumor temperature to about 106°F. *Possible side effects:* Temporary rise in blood pressure and pulse...skin burns. Hyperthermia may shrink tumors by enhancing the effects of radiation and chemotherapy. Selected research centers are using it to supplement treatment for breast, ovarian and rectal cancer and soft-tissue sarcomas. Consult with your oncologist.

Ellen Jones, MD, PhD, radiation oncologist, Duke University Medical Center, Durham, NC.

Up to 70% of Cancers Can Be Avoided... Here's How to Improve Your Odds

Melanie Polk, MMSc, RD, director of nutrition education, American Institute for Cancer Research, 1759 R St. NW, Washington, DC 20009.

People often assume that cancer is out of their hands because it is "genetic." In fact, lifestyle decisions are much more important in determining who gets cancer—and who doesn't.

Even if your genes place you at risk for cancer, 60% to 70% of all malignancies can be avoided by paying attention to four lifestyle factors—diet, weight control, physical activity and not smoking.

IF YOU MAKE JUST ONE CHANGE...

Eating a plant-based diet is the single most important thing you can do to lower your cancer risk.

Foods should be minimally processed and as close to their natural state as possible. Processed foods may have lost some of their nutritional value.

Example: Eat a potato rather than potato chips.

Also limit intake of foods with added sugar, such as soft drinks and sweetened cereals.

If you eat red meat, have no more than three ounces per day.

Eating at least five servings—about one-half cup each—of fruits or vegetables every day can decrease your risk of cancer by 20%.

OTHER IMPORTANT STEPS

•**Maintain a healthful weight,** and be physically active. Try not to gain too much weight after reaching your full height (at about age 18 for women...24 for men).

Start by walking every day—working your way up to a brisk, one-hour walk daily. In addition, work up a sweat by engaging in some form of vigorous physical activity for at least one hour each week.

•**Drink alcohol in moderation**—if at all. There is no evidence that alcohol reduces cancer risk, though some evidence suggests that moderate alcohol consumption helps prevent coronary artery disease in men and possibly women. If you do drink, limit your consumption to one drink a day for women ...two drinks a day for men.

Avoid alcohol entirely if you are a woman with an increased risk of breast cancer.

•**Select foods that are low in fat and salt.**

Limit your intake of fatty foods. Use a moderate amount of monounsaturated oils, such as olive and canola.

Avoid animal fat and hydrogenated fat, which is commonly found in shortening, margarine and bakery items.

Watch those snack foods, salty condiments and pickles.

•**Prepare and store foods safely.** Keep cold foods cold and hot foods hot.

If you eat meat, avoid charring it. Limit cured or smoked meat. Take precautions when grilling—trim fat from meat, marinate it, microwave it for half the cooking time before grilling.

•**Avoid tobacco in any form.**

CANCER RISK FACTORS

Anticancer precautions are particularly important for individuals at increased risk for cancer. *These risk factors include*...*

•**Family history of genetically linked cancers,** such as breast, ovarian and colon cancers.

•**Inflammatory bowel disease**.

•**Human papillomavirus (HPV) infection.**

•**Alcoholism.**

•**Hepatitis B or C virus (HBV/HCV).**

Additional risk factors for women...

•**First menstrual period before the age of 12.**

•**First child born after age 30.**

•**Childless and over age 50.**

•**Postmenopausal and on hormone-replacement therapy.**

*This information is based on a major study by the American Institute for Cancer Research that reviewed more than 4,500 studies to determine the relationships among diet, lifestyle and cancer risk.

Vitamins and Colon Polyps

Multivitamins and calcium supplements fight precancerous polyps. Use of vitamins and calcium also makes it less likely that colorectal polyps will return in patients who have already had them removed. Nearly all cases of colon and rectal cancer start as benign polyps.

Richard Whelan, MD, assistant professor of surgery and director of colon and rectal surgery, Columbia University College of Physicians and Surgeons, New York City.

Lutein vs. Colon Cancer

Cut colon cancer risk by consuming more lutein. Lutein is a carotenoid pigment found in plants. *Recent study:* Eating a lutein-rich diet cut colon cancer risk by 17%. Consumption of other carotenoids, such as beta-carotene and lycopene, had no impact on risk. *Theory:* Lutein protects colon cells from damage caused by highly reactive compounds called free radicals. Good sources of lutein include tomatoes, carrots, oranges, broccoli, kale, Romaine lettuce and spinach.

Martha Slattery, PhD, MPH, professor of family and preventive medicine, University of Utah Medical School, Salt Lake City.

Treating Prostate Cancer

Sheldon Marks, MD, a urologic oncologist in private practice in Tucson, Arizona. He is author of *Prostate & Cancer: A Family Guide to Diagnosis, Treatment and Survival.* Fisher.

In years past, 30% of men diagnosed with prostate cancer already had an advanced form of the disease. Last year, of 179,000 men diagnosed, only 5% had advanced cancer.

Reason: More men now routinely get a blood test for levels of *prostate specific antigen* (PSA). Prostate cells produce this enzyme in high quantities when the gland is irritated or damaged. A normal PSA level is less than 4.0. A higher level suggests cancer.

PSA tests clearly help detect early-stage tumors. Yet doctors keep debating whether men should have a yearly PSA test.

Case against: Prostate cancer often grows so slowly that it poses little threat. Treating it early with surgery or radiation—which can cause impotence and incontinence—could cause worse effects than the disease.

Case for: Each year, 37,000 men die of prostate cancer, making it the second-leading killer of men. Treatment *before* the disease spreads can save thousands of lives.

Who should get a yearly PSA test? Men over age 40 who have a family history of the disease…and all men over age 50.

The yearly checkup should include a digital rectal exam (DRE). By inserting a gloved finger into the rectum, the doctor can detect prostate abnormalities.

If the PSA and/or DRE are abnormal, the next step is an ultrasound test with a prostate biopsy. If this confirms cancer, the goal is to find treatment that maximizes survival time while minimizing side effects.

STAGES AND GRADES

Prostate cancer severity is categorized by stage and grade.

The four stages—A, B, C and D—indicate a tumor's size and the likelihood that it is still confined to the prostate or the extent to which it may have spread.

Low-grade prostate cancers are slow-growing…high-grade cancers are fast-growing.

"STAGE A" TUMORS

Most of these tumors are discovered during surgery to relieve urinary problems caused by *benign prostatic hyperplasia* (BPH)—noncancerous, age-related prostate enlargement.

●A1. Small, low-grade tumor. An excellent option—especially for men over age 65—is "watchful waiting." Every six months, a PSA test, DRE and urinalysis are done to see if the cancer is growing. If so, it's time for treatment.

Men under age 65 should consider treatment sooner. Surgical removal of the prostate (radical prostatectomy) is often the best option.

Downside I: Surgery can damage nerves that control erections and blood vessels that supply the penis. After surgery, men tend to experience impotence. Potency often takes six to 12 months to return. But in 50% of cases, impotence is permanent.

Good news: The prescription impotence drug *sildenafil* (Viagra) is helpful for two-thirds of these men. Other treatments for impotence include the intraurethral medication *alprostadil* (Muse), vacuum erection devices, penile self-injections of *alprostadil* (Caverject) and penile implants.

Downside II: Many men experience weeks or months of incontinence after surgery. For a few, the problem is permanent.

Kegel exercises before and after surgery can help control incontinence. Repeatedly squeeze the pelvic muscles, as if trying to stop urine flow, for five minutes every waking hour until you stop experiencing incontinence.

Two radiation methods are alternatives to surgery…

●External beam. Radiation is directed at the prostate in one 10- to 15-minute treatment daily. Typically, there are five sessions a week over seven weeks.

●Interstitial seed therapy. Tiny radioactive seeds are implanted in the prostate.

Up to 50% of men who undergo external beam radiation become impotent. The rate can be much lower with seed therapy.

●**A2. High-grade, aggressive cancer.** Patients under age 70 should consider radical prostatectomy…men over 70 radiation.

Men age 75 or older and in poor health should skip treatment or opt for hormone therapy.

Male hormones (androgens)—which can spur cancer growth—are eliminated by removal of the testicles…or by injections of hormone-blocking drugs.

In the majority of men, hormone therapy causes permanent impotence. But a new hormone medicine—*bicalutamide* (Casodex)—blocks the body's ability to use androgen while preserving potency.

●**A3. Tumor discovered through a high PSA.** Surgery or radiation is usually best if the patient is expected to live 10 years or longer.

"STAGE B" TUMORS

These cancers, discovered by DRE, are confined to the prostate.

●**B1. Cancer on one side of the prostate.** For those whose life expectancy is more than seven years, radical prostatectomy is often the best choice.

Second choice: *Radiation.* But men in their 80s and in poor health may prefer watchful waiting or hormone therapy.

●**B2. Cancer on both sides of the prostate, with no evident spread outside the gland.** *Best treatment:* For men under age 70—usually surgery. For men over 70, radiation is usually better.

If you choose radiation, ask your oncologist about pretreatment with hormone shots. Eight or nine months of these shots followed by radiation is more effective than radiation alone.

"STAGE C" TUMORS

The cancer is growing outside the gland, in surrounding fat or other nearby areas. It has not spread to lymph nodes or bone.

Men under age 65: Surgery is often best because it may remove almost all the cancer. "Step therapy"—surgery, followed by radiation if cancer returns—is also an option.

Men age 65 or older: Radiation is often best. It can stop cancer in both the prostate and surrounding tissue. Hormone therapy is an alternative for men predicted to live five years or less.

"STAGE D" TUMORS

The cancer has spread to lymph nodes or bones. In *D1*, cancer is still within the pelvis. In *D2*, it has moved beyond.

In Stage D, the goal is to control the spread of disease. *Best way:* Hormone therapy. For men under age 65, it should be accompanied by "debulking"—surgically removing as much tumor as possible.

For men 65 or older, hormone therapy alone is usually better.

NUTRITIONAL STRATEGIES

●**Avoid beef and other fatty meats, as well as whole-fat dairy products.** They can stimulate cancer growth. Beef can also increase pain in advanced cancer.

•**Consume tomatoes,** red grapes, red grape juice, red wine (one glass a day), red bell peppers, watermelon and strawberries. They contain lycopene, a red pigment that can slow cancer growth.

•**Emphasize soy foods.** They contain phytoestrogens, compounds that may slow cancer.

•**Drink green tea.** It contains cancer-fighting antioxidants. Have four or five cups per day…or the equivalent in green tea extract capsules.

•**Ask your doctor about taking a daily supplement** containing 200 micrograms of *selenium.* This may slow the cancer. Also ask about *PC-SPES.* This combination of eight Chinese herbs may slow growth of prostate tumors that don't respond to hormone therapy. *Downside:* Potential for blood clots and other side effects.

USEFUL RESOURCES

Prostate Forum is the most accurate, up-to-date newsletter on nutrition and prostate cancer. 800-305-2432. *Cost:* $36 for 12 issues.

Three helpful Web sites…

•*www.afud.org.* The site of the American Foundation for Urologic Disease contains comprehensive information on prostate cancer and updated research.

•*http://rattler.cameron.edu:80/prostate.html.* "Gary Huckaby's Prostate Pointers" is a thorough resource for newly diagnosed patients.

•*http://comed.com/prostate.* The Prostate Cancer Infolink provides information on every aspect of prostate cancer.

Aspirin Slows Prostate Cancer Growth

In a recent study, aspirin blocked the action of *COX-2,* a protein present in human prostate cancer tissue at higher levels than in healthy tissue. New aspirin derivatives, known as *COX-2 inhibitors*—including *celecoxib*

(Celebrex)—were just as effective. Long-term use of aspirin may cause side effects, such as stomach bleeding. But the new drugs have fewer side effects, so they are good alternatives. COX-2 inhibitors are used to treat arthritis. Their effectiveness for treating and preventing prostate cancer will be tested soon.

El-Nasir Lalani, PhD, professor of molecular and cellular biology, Imperial College of Medicine, London.

The Many Benefits Of Garlic

Garlic's health benefits may go beyond lowering blood pressure and cholesterol levels. In studies conducted recently at Memorial Sloan-Kettering Cancer Center, antioxidant compounds in an over-the-counter aged garlic product (Kyolic) inhibited growth of human prostate cancer cells. Most previous research focused on garlic's ability to prevent cancer—this is among the first studies to suggest that garlic may halt progression of prostate tumors. *Helpful:* Taking a daily aged garlic supplement (600 mg twice a day) may be beneficial not only for all prostate cancer patients, but also for all men age 40 or older who have a family history of the disease. Ask your doctor.

Carmia G. Borek, PhD, professor of community health, Tufts University School of Medicine, Boston. She is author of *Maximize Your Health-Span with Antioxidants.* Keats.

Herbicides and Cancer

Non-Hodgkin's lymphoma may be caused by exposure to herbicides and fungicides. *Recent finding:* Patients exposed to herbicides containing *phenoxyacetic acid* were most likely to come down with the disease—up to 20 years after exposure. Other chemicals linked to the lymphatic system malignancy included the herbicide *glyphosate* and certain fungicides. Exposure to insecticides and organic solvents did not increase risk.

Lennart Hardell, MD, PhD, associate professor of oncology, Örebro Medical Center, Örebro, Sweden.

Lung Cancer Test Breakthrough

New 20-second lung cancer test potentially could save 100,000 lives annually. In a recent study, a new cancer-detection technique, called spiral computed tomography (CT), was used to screen 1,000 smokers and former smokers over age 60. It detected 23 cases of early-stage lung cancer, of which only four were visible on chest X rays. *Impact:* Detecting lung cancer this much earlier might significantly increase the five-year survival rate above the dismal 14% it is now. *Best:* If you are a smoker, quit. Better yet—never start.

Robert Smith, PhD, director of cancer screening, American Cancer Society, 1599 Clifton Rd. NE, Atlanta 30329.

400,000+ Deaths Per Year…Everyone Knows the Dangers…Why They Smoke… How to Quit!

David Wetter, PhD, associate professor of behavioral science at University of Texas MD Anderson Cancer Center, Houston. Research-based strategies and information on quitting smoking can be found at *www.surgeongeneral.gov/tobacco/default.htm.*

Despite the known health risks, forty-seven million Americans still smoke cigarettes. *The big reasons…*

•**Cultural norms.** Caucasian teens smoke more than African-American and Asian teens. The latters' families are more disapproving of smoking.

•**Smoking beliefs.** Having positive beliefs about smoking can make you more inclined to smoke.

Examples: Thinking smoking reduces stress or keeps weight down.

•**Genes.** We believe there is no single smoking gene…but thousands of gene alterations that increase your risk for becoming a smoker.

BEST WAYS TO QUIT

•**Nicotine replacement.** Patches and gum curb withdrawal symptoms. In conjunction with behavioral changes, they can double the likelihood you'll quit. If patches and gum don't work, your doctor can prescribe a nicotine-replacement inhaler or spray…or *bupropion* (Zyban), which reduces cravings for cigarettes and limits weight gain.

•**Counseling.** It can be as effective as drug therapy. Costs are often covered by insurance. *Useful resources…*

•American Cancer Society, 800-227-2345.
•American Lung Association, 800-586-4872.

•**Identify times** you are inclined to smoke and find smoke-free alternatives.

Example: If you like a cigarette with coffee, take a walk instead of drinking coffee.

•**Once you quit, vow never to have another cigarette.** Ninety percent of smokers who have just one go back to smoking.

•**Don't be discouraged by failures.** Most people quit five times before succeeding.

Cut Cigarette Cravings

Self-massage can be a big help for people trying to withstand cigarette cravings.

In a recent study, the average number of cigarettes smoked per day fell from 16 to 12 in would-be ex-smokers who performed self-massage three times a day for one month. Self-massage also reduced feelings of anxiety.

•**Ear massage.** Pinch the ear, working from the top to the earlobe. Stroke the back and the inside of your ear with your index finger. Gently tug the earlobe. Massage it gently with your thumb and index finger.

●**Hand massage.** Massage the palm of one hand with the thumb of the other. Massage each finger, from base to tip, with thumb and index finger. Gently stretch each finger by pushing it up and back with the palm of the other hand. Firmly press the web between thumb and index finger and hold for 30 seconds.

Caution: Self-massage is *not* a substitute for nicotine supplements, hypnosis and other smoking-cessation measures. It should be considered an adjunct to these strategies.

Maria Hernandez-Reif, PhD, director of research, Touch Research Institute, University of Miami School of Medicine. Her study of 20 smokers was published in *Preventive Medicine*, 525 B St., Suite 1900, San Diego 92101.

Nicotine and the Sexes

Nicotine's effect on mood differs greatly between the sexes. In women, it tends to be calming and reduce aggression. In men, it provokes aggression and triggers anxiety. These differences explain why many women find it more difficult than men to quit smoking. *Self-defense:* Instead of smoking, women under stress or suffering from depression or anxiety should seek medical help. When trying to quit smoking, women should consider relaxation techniques, psychotherapy or other strategies to reduce stress. Men should be aware that smoking increases aggression.

Sandra File, PhD, DSc, professor of psychopharmacology, Centre for Neuroscience, King's College, London. Her study of 32 nonsmoking college students was presented at a recent meeting of the British Pharmacological Society.

Psoriasis Trap

People who smoke more than 15 cigarettes a day double their risk for psoriasis, compared with nonsmokers. Smokers' risk for *pustular psoriasis*—a severe form of the skin condition—rises tenfold. Ex-smokers also have a higher rate of psoriasis than individuals who have never smoked.

Luigi Naldi, MD, dermatologist, Riuniti Hospital, Bergamo, Italy. His study of 1,020 psoriasis patients was published in the *Archives of Dermatology*, Beth Israel Hospital, 330 Brookline Ave., Boston 02215.

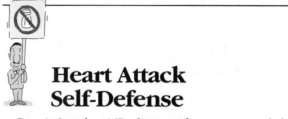

Heart Attack Self-Defense

Dennis Sprecher, MD, director of preventive cardiology and rehabilitation at the Cleveland Clinic Foundation. He is a contributing author of *The Cleveland Clinic Heart Book*. Hyperion.

You've cut back on dietary fat and cholesterol. You've started exercising and lost weight. If you ever smoked, you've stopped. Perhaps you've even taken to drinking green tea.

What else can you do to reduce your risk of heart disease?

Quite a lot, actually. These eight suggestions come from Dr. Dennis Sprecher, a heart attack specialist at the world-renowned Cleveland Clinic...

●**Consume more apples, onions and green beans**...and more purple grape juice. These foods are rich in the heart-protective antioxidants called *flavonoids*.

Flavonoids benefit the heart by inhibiting oxidation of cholesterol—a chemical process that promotes artery blockages.

Flavonoids also help dilate the arteries that supply oxygen-rich blood to the heart.

Caution: Unsweetened grape juice—at 154 calories per eight ounces—is too calorie-dense to be consumed on a daily basis.

Like purple grape juice, red wine contains flavonoids. But given the risks associated with alcohol, men should have no more than two five-ounce glasses a day...women no more than one five-ounce glass a day.

●**Boost your intake of omega-3 fatty acids.** Fish oil is a good source of omega-3 fatty acids, which are believed to account for the lower incidence of heart-related deaths among people who eat at least some fish.

Omega-3s boost levels of HDL (good) cholesterol and reduce blood pressure by relaxing arteries…stabilizing heartbeats…and inhibiting formation of artery-clogging blood clots. Try to eat fish high in omega-3s, such as salmon and trout, twice a week.

Caution: Fish oil is a highly concentrated source of fat calories. Consuming too much of it raises LDL (bad) cholesterol levels.

If you don't like fish, ground flaxseed—sold in health-food stores—is an alternative source of omega-3s. Add it to cereal.

Another little-known source of omega-3s is arugula lettuce.

•Eat more beans and other low-fat foods—and less meat. One cup of black beans provides as much protein as two ounces of lean ground beef. But the beans contain only 1 g of total fat, compared with 12 g for the meat.

Also, beans contain no saturated fat or cholesterol. The meat contains 4 g of saturated fat and 43 mg of cholesterol.

•Eat more soy- and oat-based foods. Both protect the heart by encouraging excretion of cholesterol circulating in the bloodstream.

Use soymilk instead of cow's milk on high-fiber bran or oat cereal. Low-fat soy cheese and tofu—found in the dairy section of many supermarkets—are other good sources of soy. Or have oatmeal or oat bread instead of sugary cereals.

•Cut *way* back on salt. It's well known that sodium—found in table salt and many processed foods—can damage the heart by raising blood pressure. Yet the average American still consumes 6,000 mg a day—far more than the recommended 2,400 mg.

To lower your salt intake, follow the diet developed as part of a landmark study known as Dietary Approaches to Stop Hypertension (DASH). *More information: http://dash.bwh. harvard.edu.*

The DASH diet consists primarily of fruits, vegetables, whole-grains and low-fat dairy products. People who followed the DASH diet experienced a 15% reduction of atherosclerosis (stiff, clogged arteries), a cause of heart attack.

The DASH diet also reduces blood pressure about as much as medications do.

•Eat six small meals a day. Small, frequent meals make it less likely that the body will turn the calories you consume into fat.

If you plan to eat at a restaurant, have an apple or another low-fat snack beforehand. This takes the edge off your hunger so you are less likely to load up on calorie-laden breads or appetizers.

•Work out more frequently. In addition to burning excess calories, physical activity boosts levels of HDL cholesterol.

Although most experts recommend exercising 30 minutes three times a week, new research confirms that *daily* activity yields the greatest benefits.

Jog, walk, run, dance or do some other moderately vigorous exercise for at least 30 minutes a day. If you cannot manage a 30-minute workout, do three 10-minute sessions.

•Curb psychological stress. In response to a stressful situation—be it a traffic jam or a difficult boss—your body produces two key hormones. *Epinephrine* increases heart rate. *Cortisol* raises blood pressure.

If your body constantly generates these hormones, you overwork your heart—and that increases your risk for heart attack.

When we are under stress, our breathing becomes rapid and shallow. That deprives the heart of oxygen.

To reverse this oxygen-robbing tendency, inhale deeply through your nose for a count of 10 when you feel stress. Then exhale for a count of 10. Repeat twice more.

Ask your doctor about heart-protecting medication. A daily aspirin helps reduce the blood's tendency to clot. That makes heart attack less likely.

Caution: Do not take aspirin to protect your heart without talking to your doctor first. In some people, regular use can cause internal bleeding.

If your total cholesterol is 200 or higher and/or you have a strong family history of heart disease, you should probably take *pravastatin* (Pravachol) or another prescription "statin" drug.

Heart Attack Symptoms... Gender Differences

Symptoms of heart attack differ according to gender. The classic symptom—crushing chest pain—is common mostly among men. Women may feel pain in the upper abdomen, arm, neck, jaw, teeth or back. They may become dizzy and weak...and may experience sweating, nausea or shortness of breath. If you suspect you're having a heart attack, seek immediate medical attention—even if you're not suffering the classic symptom.

Marianne Legato, MD, director, Partnership for Women's Health, Columbia University, New York City.

Niacin and Your Cholesterol

Niacin (nicotinic acid) may help improve your cholesterol. Studies using specific brands of high-quality niacin show that taking 1,000 mg to 2,000 mg daily can boost "good" HDLs by 15% to 35%, lower "bad" LDLs by 5% to 15% and reduce triglycerides by 20% to 30%. Careful combination by your physician of low-dose, brand-specific niacin with a statin to regulate blood cholesterol may mean taking lower doses of the statin—a potential health and cost benefit. *Caution:* Niacin intake can be toxic. Its use alone or combined with other drugs must be carefully initiated and monitored by your doctor. *Very important:* OTC generic brands, particularly slow-release forms, are especially prone to cause liver damage and other toxicity.

David M. Capuzzi, MD, PhD, director of the Cardiovascular Disease Prevention Center, Thomas Jefferson University Hospital, Philadelphia.

Syndrome X... The Little-Known Cause Of Many Heart Attacks

Gerald M. Reaven, MD, professor of medicine at Stanford University School of Medicine in Stanford, CA. He is coauthor of *Syndrome X: Overcoming the Silent Killer That Can Give You a Heart Attack.* Simon & Schuster.

It's well known that a high cholesterol level—especially a high level of LDL (bad) cholesterol—is a major risk factor for heart attack. Now, another risk factor is finally getting the attention it deserves as a major contributor to heart disease. That factor is insulin resistance.

Insulin—produced by the pancreas—is the hormone that ushers blood sugar (glucose) into cells. Cells can become resistant to insulin's action. When they do, the pancreas pumps out more insulin in an attempt to "force" sugar into the cells.

Excess insulin directly damages coronary arteries. It also triggers an array of metabolic abnormalities that contribute to the development of artery-clogging fatty plaques and to blood clots.

The constellation of abnormalities, which affects 70 million Americans, is called "syndrome X." *It includes...*

•**Excess fibrinogen,** a substance that promotes blood clots.

•**Excess plasminogen activator inhibitor-1** (PAI-1), a substance that slows clot breakdown.

•**High levels of triglycerides,** the body's main fat-storage particles.

•**Low levels of HDL (good) cholesterol,** which sweeps fat out of arteries.

Many people with syndrome X also have high blood pressure. And they're likely to have glucose intolerance—a condition characterized by slightly elevated blood sugar levels.

Important: Glucose intolerance is *not* diabetes. But up to 5% of people with syndrome X go on to develop type 2 diabetes annually. That's the form that occurs when, due to insulin resistance, blood sugar levels rise into the diabetic range.

DIAGNOSING SYNDROME X

The results of five simple tests point to a diagnosis of syndrome X. Risk for heart attack rises with each out-of-bounds test score.

- **Fasting triglyceride** level in excess of 200 milligrams per deciliter (mg/dl).
- **Fasting HDL cholesterol** level under 35 mg/dl.
- **Blood pressure** higher than 145/90.
- **Being overweight** by 15 pounds or more.
- **Fasting blood sugar** level higher than 110 mg/dl...or a level higher than 140 two hours after drinking a glucose solution.

FIGHTING SYNDROME X

- **Eat the right diet.** Americans are besieged by a glut of high-concept diets, all of them purporting to be best for weight loss and health.

The American Heart Association diet counsels cutting down on fat and boosting consumption of carbohydrates. *The Zone* diet advises boosting protein intake and lowering fat.

These diets may work for people who don't have syndrome X. But protein and carbohydrates stimulate insulin production—which is a dangerous outcome for people with the syndrome.

The Atkins diet counsels consumption of low levels of carbohydrates and as much fat as desired. But that diet is too high in artery-clogging saturated fat.

The ideal diet to combat syndrome X supplies 45% of calories from carbohydrates... 15% from protein...and 40% from fat.

Key: Emphasize beneficial mono- and polyunsaturated fats. These should supply 30% to 35% of the diet. Only 5% to 10% should come from saturated fats.

Good sources of healthful fats include avocados...fatty fish (such as sea bass, trout, sole and salmon)...natural peanut butter...nuts and seeds...canola, corn, olive, safflower, peanut, soybean, sesame and sunflower oils.

- **Lose weight.** Shedding pounds improves insulin resistance. *Recent study:* Insulin resistance fell an average of 40% in overweight individuals who lost 20 pounds.
- **Exercise.** People who exercise daily use insulin 25% more efficiently than those who do not exercise. Forty-five minutes of aerobic exercise a day is ideal.
- **Stop smoking.** Smoking promotes insulin resistance.

MEDICATION

If lifestyle changes alone don't overcome syndrome X, medication can help....

- **Triglyceride-lowering medication.** Three drugs can lower triglyceride levels. They also lower PAI-1 levels and raise HDL cholesterol.

One of them—niacin—has the added benefit of lowering LDL cholesterol. A common side effect of nicotinic acid is facial flushing.

Self-defense: To minimize flushing from nicotinic acid, increase the dose gradually.

Two other effective drugs are *gemfibrozil* (Lopid) and *fenofibrate* (Tricor). In rare cases, however, they can cause liver damage.

Self-defense: Talk to your doctor about testing liver function periodically.

- **Blood pressure medication.** Fifty percent of people with high blood pressure have syndrome X. But some blood pressure drugs can worsen the condition.

Talk to your doctor about the potential risks of high-dose diuretics and beta-blockers if you have syndrome X.

Because syndrome X is caused by insulin resistance, it's logical to ask whether *thiazolidinediones*—drugs that increase insulin sensitivity—might be helpful.

Such drugs are currently used to treat type 2 diabetes.

Ongoing research will determine if thiazolidinediones improve syndrome X. Until the studies are completed, these drugs should *not* be used to treat the condition.

The Beans/ Supple Arteries Connection

A recent study of more than 100 women showed that those who had higher blood levels of phytoestrogens, reflecting a higher dietary bean intake, had more-flexible arteries than non-bean eaters—suggesting they had a lower risk of hypertension and heart disease. Phytoestrogens—hormones of plant origin—are found in soy and other beans. *Action:* Substitute beans for high-cholesterol foods, such as fatty meat.

C. Noel Bairey Merz, MD, director, department of preventive and rehabilitative cardiac care, Cedars–Sinai Medical Center, Los Angeles.

Flu Shot Benefits

Flu shots may fight more than influenza. Recent research suggests that the shots also help prevent second heart attack. *Theory:* Influenza inflames coronary arteries, promoting formation of fatty deposits that can trigger heart attack. *Self-defense:* Heart patients should ask their doctor about flu shots.

Morteza Naghavi, MD, instructor of medicine, University of Texas–Houston Health Science Center.

Radiation and Coronary Arteries

Coronary arteries zapped with radiation stay open longer following angioplasty. That's the procedure in which a balloon-tipped catheter is used to open clogged arteries. *Background:* Vessels cleared by angioplasty often narrow again, necessitating a second procedure. *Recent study:* Twenty-six angioplasty patients received low-dose radiation to the arteries, delivered by pellets inserted into the vessel for up to 45 minutes. Twenty-nine patients were treated with "dummy" pellets. Three years later, only one-third of the irradiated vessels had renarrowed, compared with two-thirds of the vessels treated with the sham procedure.

Paul S. Teirstein, MD, director, interventional cardiology, Scripps Clinic, La Jolla, CA.

Vitamin C and Stress

Vitamin C may help prevent illness in people who are under severe psychological stress. A dose of vitamin C equal to several grams a day in humans reduced levels of corticosterone in rats stressed by being immobilized. High levels of *corticosterone* and other stress hormones have been linked to heart disease, ulcers and other illnesses. It is likely that vitamin C has the same effect in people. *When under stress:* Consume more orange juice, citrus fruits and other vitamin C-rich foods...or take a daily 500-mg vitamin C supplement.

P. Samuel Campbell, PhD, chairman, department of biological sciences, University of Alabama, Huntsville. His study was presented at a recent meeting of the American Chemical Society.

Vitamin Danger

Otherwise beneficial vitamin and mineral supplements can have serious consequences for some people...

●**Smokers.** Synthetic beta-carotene may raise lung cancer risk, according to one study. *Better:* Get your daily dose from carrots, spinach and other food sources...or take a natural *mixed* carotenoid supplement.

●**People with kidney disease or hyperparathyroidism.** Avoid getting too much calcium, as these ailments can disrupt calcium metabolism. Limit supplemental intake of calcium to 300 mg a day.

●**Adult men and menopausal women.** Too much iron can lead to heart disease and other illnesses. *Better:* Enough foods are fortified with iron, so iron supplements make sense only for premenopausal women, children under age 13 and anyone who is iron deficient.

●**People with the metabolic disorder hemochromatosis,** or a history of kidney stones. Limit supplemental intake of vitamin C to 250 mg a day.

•**People on blood-thinning medication and/or daily aspirin therapy.** Vitamin E, ginger, ginkgo biloba, St. John's wort and garlic can all intensify the blood-thinning effect. *Better:* Ask your doctor about adjusting your medication and your supplement intake.

Bradley Bongiovanni, ND, a naturopathic physician in private practice in Cleveland.

Safer Supplements

The National Nutritional Foods Association, the largest dietary supplement trade group in the US, grants a seal to manufacturers that get an A grade for quality control and cleanliness during independent inspections. The seal gives some assurance that a supplement contains what is indicated on the label. *Also helpful:* The Food and Drug Administration shares complaints it receives about supplements and brands it pulls off the market. *Catch:* The FDA itself does *not* test supplements. *Information:* 888-463-6332...*www.fda.gov*.

Andrew L. Rubman, ND, professor of clinical medicine, College of Naturopathic Medicine, Bridgeport, and director, Southbury Clinic for Traditional Medicines, both in Connecticut.

Use Melatonin Wisely

Use melatonin *only* on the advice of your doctor. Marketing campaigns urge older people to take melatonin supplements to make up for its decline as they age. Melatonin is touted for resetting the biological clock and fighting jet lag and insomnia. *Reality:* The level of melatonin, which is produced by the pineal gland, does not automatically drop as people age. It is lower in many older people because of illness, not aging. *Trap:* Melatonin's sale is unregulated, and its long-term effects are unknown.

Martin Scharf, PhD, director, Tri-State Sleep Disorders Center, Cincinnati.

Unexpected Side Effects From Common Drugs

Jay Sylvan Cohen, MD, associate professor of family and preventive medicine, University of California, San Diego, School of Medicine. He is author of Make Your Medicine Safe: How to Prevent Side Effects from the Drugs You Take. Morrow.

About 40% of the people who take prescription drugs experience side effects ...yet many don't make the connection between their symptoms and medications they are taking.

SUBTLE SYMPTOMS

Antidepressants, such as Paxil and Prozac, cause diminished desire for sex. This symptom is often mistakenly blamed on stress, lack of sleep or relationship problems.

Zocor and Lipitor, which are taken to lower cholesterol, can produce symptoms that mimic the flu. Doctors can easily miss the connection, but muscle aches may signal tissue breakdown. That can lead to serious kidney damage.

Be suspicious of any changes in your behavior or in the way you feel after starting a new prescription, especially if the drug you are taking has only recently been approved by the Food and Drug Administration.

THE UNCERTAINTY FACTOR

Product information sheets list common side effects, but that information may not be the whole story...

•**Limited data.** Initial side effects are based on the experiences of people who have taken the drug before it was approved for widespread use. Preapproval studies include a relatively small number of people over a limited period of time.

Many drug side effects, therefore, are discovered only after a drug is put on the market.

Additional consideration: The population studied is often not representative of the general public. People who are very ill or who must take several medications, for instance, are often not included in clinical studies. Women are also often underrepresented in drug studies.

•**Unexpected side effects.** These may be serious.

Example: The drug Rezulin, recently approved for use in treating diabetes, was found—before approval—to cause a small amount of liver irritation in some cases. After the drug was in widespread use, however, it caused at least 80 deaths and hundreds of cases of severe liver damage before it was taken off the market.

● **Unique response.** Drug companies anticipate certain side effects based upon reactions of the sample population. But—every individual is a special case. So your experience may not be the same as that of another person.

DOSAGE DANGERS

As many as 80% of side effects are dose-related.

If you begin taking a new drug, ask your doctor if it is possible to start with a small dose. You can always step up the dosage later if necessary. But for many people, a lower dose is just as effective as a higher dose...and with minimal side effects.

Better Sleep On Down

Allergy sufferers often sleep better on down pillows. In recent tests, synthetic pillows had up to eight times more pet allergens and five times more dust-mite allergens than down or feather pillows. *Theory:* The covers of down pillows—more tightly woven to keep pointy feathers from working their way out—are more effective barriers to allergens.

Ashly Woodcock, MD, consultant respiratory physician, North West Lung Centre, Wythenshawe Hospital, Manchester, England.

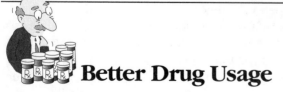 # Better Drug Usage

Consider avoiding a new drug until at least *five years* after its release, unless it is a rare, documented "breakthrough" drug. Serious adverse effects and drug interactions may go undetected until a drug has been taken by

hundreds of thousands of people. *To find out how old a drug is:* Ask your pharmacist...or visit the FDA Web site, *www.fda.gov/cder.* Popular new drugs that you may want to avoid for now: Relenza *(zanamivir)* and Tamiflu *(osteltamivir)* for flu...Avelox *(moxifloxacin)* for diarrhea predominantly from irritable bowel syndrome...Mobic *(meloxicam)* for arthritis.

Sidney M. Wolfe, MD, director of Public Citizen's Health Research Group, Washington, DC.

Emergency Warning: Know Your Medications

If you take medication regularly, make sure emergency medical personnel have fast access to this information. *Reason:* Emergency procedures can harm people using certain drugs. *Examples:* Nitrate drugs used during anesthesia can be dangerous to people who take Viagra...drugs used to dissolve blood clots can harm people who take blood-thinning *warfarin* (Coumadin) or aspirin daily. *Lifesaver:* Carry a card listing medications in your wallet, next to your driver's license. It should also list dietary supplements ...chronic conditions...allergies...contact lenses. *Alternative:* Use an emergency medical information service. MedicAlert (800-432-5378) sells bracelets and necklaces engraved with health information and a number to call for your medication information.

Charles Inlander, president of People's Medical Society, the largest US nonprofit consumer health advocacy organization, Allentown, PA.

Antibiotic Therapy Warning

Antibiotic therapy can be sabotaged by the minerals found in nutritional supplements and over-the-counter antacids. Iron, magnesium, aluminum and calcium can bind to *quinolone* antibiotics in the stomach, preventing them from being absorbed. Quinolones include *ciprofloxacin* (Cipro), *gatifloxacin* (Tequin) and *levofloxacin* (Levaquin). *Self-defense:* Avoid products containing iron, magnesium, aluminum or calcium if you're being treated with a quinolone.

Paul Ament, PharmD, clinical pharmacy coordinator, Latrobe Area Hospital, Latrobe, PA.

Penicillin Allergies Can Go Away

As many as 90% of people who believe they are allergic to penicillin test negative for the allergy after avoiding the medicine for 10 years. This retest may be worthwhile because penicillin and related antibiotics are often the least expensive, most effective ways to treat infections. *Caution:* Even if a penicillin allergy disappears, it could return if penicillin is used.

Harold Nelson, MD, senior staff physician, National Jewish Center for Immunology & Respiratory Medicine, Denver.

Migraine Myths

Myth: **Strong headaches require strong medications.**

Reality: Acetaminophen, ibuprofen and other over-the-counter (OTC) products relieve migraine pain in many people—and have fewer side effects than prescription drugs. Try an OTC drug several times before concluding that it will not work for you. Check with your doctor regarding appropriate dosage—it may exceed package instructions.

Myth: **If one OTC drug doesn't relieve your migraines, none will.**

Reality: Different people respond differently to the same drug. Try a variety of OTC pain-relief

medications before asking your physician about a prescription.

Frank T. Vertosick, MD, staff neurosurgeon, Western Pennsylvania Hospital, Pittsburgh, and author of *Why We Hurt: The Natural History of Pain.* Harcourt. The OTC medication he uses for his migraines is children's chewable acetaminophen.

Blood Clotting Danger

Clot-busting medication may endanger people over age 75. *Tissue plasminogen activator* (Activase) and *streptokinase* (Streptase) are used to clear arteries and improve blood flow during and after heart attack. But in patients over age 75, they can cause internal bleeding and stroke. *Recent study:* Twenty percent of patients over age 75 who received the drugs died while still in the hospital. That rate is 4% higher than among patients who didn't get the drugs.

Stephen B. Soumerai, ScD, professor of ambulatory care and director, Drug Policy Research Group, Harvard Medical School, Boston. His analysis of 2,659 heart patients' medical records was presented at a recent meeting of the Society of General Internal Medicine.

Throw Out Old Sunscreen

Sunscreen that is three years old or older—or past the expiration date should be discarded. The active ingredients lose effectiveness over time, and do so more quickly if stored in a warm environment. So sunscreen left over from prior years may not provide the degree of protection described on its label.

David J. Leffell, MD, professor of dermatology and surgery, Yale University School of Medicine, New Haven, CT.

☼ How to Avoid Stroke... And Get the Right Life-Saving Help If it Strikes

Harold P. Adams, Jr., MD, professor and director, division of cerebrovascular diseases at the University of Iowa College of Medicine in Iowa City, and chairman of the advisory committee of the American Stroke Association. For more on strokes, contact the association at 888-478-7653 or at *www.strokeassociation.org*.

Stroke is the leading cause of disability in this country—and the third leading cause of death.

Strokes are sometimes called "brain attacks." Like heart attacks, they result from interrupted blood flow to critical tissue. *There are two kinds of stroke...*

●**Ischemic stroke** is by far the more common type. It is caused by a blood clot that forms within the brain's arteries or is carried by the blood to the brain from elsewhere in the body.

Ischemic stroke can also occur when fatty deposits (plaques) rupture inside an artery in the brain or neck.

●**Hemorrhagic stroke** is more likely to result in death. It occurs when a blood vessel in the brain ruptures, allowing uncontrolled bleeding into the brain or surrounding spaces.

AN OUNCE OF PREVENTION

In addition to quitting smoking and keeping blood sugar in check, follow these guidelines...

●**Keep your blood pressure down.** Check pressure annually—more often if you have borderline numbers. Blood pressure should be 120/80 or below.

People who develop high blood pressure in midlife have higher stroke risk. Most require medication, but stroke risk can be reduced by changes in diet, weight and exercise.

One effective strategy was developed as part of an ongoing study known as Dietary Approaches to Stop Hypertension (DASH). The DASH diet, which emphasizes fruits, vegetables and low-fat dairy products, appears to help reduce blood pressure.

●**Control cholesterol.** Regular exercise and a healthful diet can help you maintain the proper ratio of LDL (bad) cholesterol to HDL (good) cholesterol—which reduces formation of artery-narrowing plaques.

The same DASH diet that controls blood pressure helps keep cholesterol down. So does the Mediterranean Diet, which emphasizes grains, fruit, vegetables and olive oil.

If diet and exercise aren't sufficient, your doctor may prescribe cholesterol-lowering medication.

●**Relax.** Chronic psychological stress elevates stroke risk in two ways. It raises blood pressure and can lead to overeating, smoking or heavy drinking.

Helpful: Meditation. A recent study showed that transcendental meditation can reduce both stroke and heart attack risk.

●**Drink alcohol in moderation.** Moderate alcohol use seems to lower stroke risk. But don't exceed two glasses of wine daily. And since alcohol can cause other health problems, nondrinkers should not start drinking to reduce stroke risk.

●**Use aspirin—maybe.** Taking aspirin daily may prevent stroke and heart attack by keeping clot-forming platelets from clumping together. Most patients take one 81-mg tablet daily or a 325-mg tablet every other day. But the data are stronger for prevention of heart attack.

Discuss the matter with a doctor before starting aspirin therapy. Aspirin can cause bleeding in the stomach and other problems.

Aspirin is especially beneficial for people who have experienced a *transient ischemic attack* (TIA). A TIA is often a warning sign that a full-blown stroke is imminent.

Symptoms: TIA symptoms are similar to those of stroke—sudden weakness or numbness of the face, arm or leg, especially on one side of the body...sudden confusion...trouble speaking or understanding speech...vision loss...sudden severe headache...or sudden trouble walking, accompanied by dizziness and loss of balance or coordination.

Seek immediate treatment for these symptoms even if they resolve quickly.

Some patients can't tolerate aspirin or have TIA symptoms despite taking aspirin. In such cases, doctors often prescribe other anti-platelet agents, such as *ticlopidine* (Ticlid) or *clopidogrel* (Plavix).

THE GOLDEN WINDOW

Treatment within three hours offers the best chance of full recovery. Like heart attack, stroke is a 911 emergency. Before emergency strikes, ask your doctor the location of the nearest "stroke center"—where stroke experts are always on hand.

Using a computed tomography (CT) brain scan or ultrafast magnetic resonance imaging (MRI), a stroke team determines if a stroke is ischemic or hemorrhagic. Clot-busting tissue *plasminogen activator* (TPA) cannot be given to patients with hemorrhagic stroke. If the stroke is ischemic, TPA given within three hours can be a lifesaver. Delivered by injection into a vein—or via catheter directly into the brain—TPA breaks up blood clots, restoring normal circulation to the brain.

The treatment of hemorrhagic stroke is more difficult, but surgery is sometimes helpful.

Ambulance crews are starting to get sophisticated stroke-treatment tools that until recently were available only in emergency rooms. So, it's usually best to go to the hospital by ambulance.

Prayer Heals

A total of 466 heart patients who were the object of other people's prayers during their hospital stay had 11% fewer complications than did 524 patients who were not prayed for. Patients did not know prayers were said for them. Those who did the praying knew only the patients' first names...and prayed only for "a speedy recovery with no complications." The researchers note that, statistically, such a difference between the groups would occur by chance only one in 25 times.

William S. Harris, PhD, heart researcher, Lipids and Diabetes Research Center, Saint Luke's Hospital, Kansas City, MO. His study of 990 coronary care unit patients was published in the *Archives of Internal Medicine*, 515 N. State St., Chicago 60610.

Magnet Dangers

Magnets used to treat arthritis and other joint problems can cause implanted pacemakers and defibrillators to malfunction.

Placed in mattress pads by arthritis sufferers to ease joint pain during sleep, a magnet can change a pacemaker's settings so that it delivers a jolt that can cause cardiac arrest. A magnet can even turn off a defibrillator—with potentially deadly results.

If you have a pacemaker or defibrillator: Talk to your doctor before using magnets for any condition. Be careful around stereo speakers, too—some contain strong magnets.

Good news: Magnets worn around the lower arms, legs or waist—at least six inches from the pacemaker or defibrillator—are not close enough to the devices to cause problems.

Thomas A. Mattioni, MD, director of electrophysiology, Arizona Heart Institute, Phoenix.

How to Beat Osteoporosis

George J. Kessler, DO, clinical instructor of medicine and an attending physician at Weill Medical College of Cornell University and an osteopathic physician in private practice in New York City. He is author of *The Bone Density Diet: Six Weeks to a Strong Body and Mind*. Ballantine Books.

Who should be concerned about osteoporosis? The short answer is everyone. Your body builds all the bone density it will ever have by your late 20s. Bone density starts to decline after age 30, and this process accelerates as the body's synthesis of sex hormones slows.

Osteoporosis is especially prevalent among women, although 20% of its victims are men.

Until recently, it was thought that osteoporosis affected mostly Caucasian women, but new evidence suggests that these women are simply more likely to *report* breaks due to osteoporosis. All races are at risk.

NUTRITION AND EXERCISE

Bones *seem* stable as rock. In fact, they're made up of living cells. These are constantly being broken down and replaced by new ones.

Osteoporosis develops when breakdown accelerates and/or rebuilding slows. *But lifestyle strategies can keep the process in balance...*

●**Minerals.** Most of us are well aware that calcium is necessary for bone health. Premenopausal women and men under age 65 need 1,000 mg per day. For postmenopausal women and men over age 65, 1,500 mg is better.

Dairy foods are the classic source of calcium. One cup of milk contains 300 mg, one cup of plain yogurt 450 mg. But you can also get calcium from beans (100 mg to 200 mg per cup)...kale (90 mg per cup)...and collard greens (350 mg per cup).

Calcium-fortified orange juice contains 300 mg per cup, fortified grapefruit juice 280 mg per cup. Fortified breakfast cereals typically contain 250 mg per serving.

Soy milk, tofu and other soy products may contain supplemental calcium and also *phytoestrogens* and other nutrients. These natural plant estrogens promote growth of new bone tissue and slow bone loss.

Bones need other minerals, too—notably magnesium and phosphorus—as well as vitamin D. Fortunately, plant sources of calcium also contain the other minerals. You can get all the vitamin D you need from 32 ounces of fortified milk...or from just 20 minutes of sunlight a day. (Skin makes vitamin D upon exposure to sunlight.)

●**Exercise.** The physical stresses to which bones are subjected during exercise stimulate new bone growth. Get at least 30 minutes of walking, weight lifting or another weight-bearing exercise, three times a week.

BONE ROBBERS

To slow the excretion of calcium from your body, it's essential to cut back on certain foods and activities. *Keep an eye on...*

●**Protein.** Each ounce of animal protein you eat causes elimination of roughly 25 mg of calcium. Most Americans get far more protein than they need.

●**Alcohol.** Have no more than three drinks per week.

●**Cigarettes.** Smoking doubles your risk for osteoporosis-related hip fracture.

●**Salt.** An eight-ounce serving of canned soup contains up to 3,000 mg of sodium chloride. Every 500 mg of sodium leaches 10 mg of calcium from your bones.

●**Caffeine.** Each cup of coffee pulls out 40 mg of calcium.

●**Soft drinks.** Phosphorus in sodas promotes calcium excretion.

DO YOUR BONES NEED HELP?

Bone densitometry is a 15-minute outpatient procedure that gauges bone strength. Most women should have the test at menopause—men, at ages 55 to 60. If it indicates a problem, doctors use one of the cross-linked collagen tests—N-Telopeptide (NTx) or deoxypyridinoline (Dpd)—to measure the rate of bone loss. Your doctor will use information from both tests to determine whether you need treatment for osteoporosis.

Depending on the degree of bone thinning, the rate of bone breakdown, your age, gender and other issues, your treatment may include hormones, bone-building drugs and/or medication for an underlying condition (such as an overactive thyroid).

HOW ABOUT HORMONES?

A woman who has significant bone thinning is a candidate for hormone-replacement therapy (HRT). It's the most effective way to slow bone loss. Even if bone loss was minimal up to menopause, HRT may be a good idea. Bone loss accelerates in the first three to five years after onset of menopause.

Whether or not to go on HRT is a personal decision. A woman with a family history of osteoporosis may want to remain on HRT. A woman at high risk for breast cancer may wish to avoid it. Some women may benefit from a long course of HRT, others from a short course. Women should take HRT only if benefits outweigh risks.

Three alternatives to the synthetic hormones are used...

●**Estriol.** This weak natural estrogen protects bone without increasing cancer risk. Sold by prescription as a pill or cream, it is not widely available. You may have to ask your doctor to find it for you. If he/she can't help, ask your pharmacist.

●**Natural progesterone.** Another bone-building hormone that declines at menopause or before, progesterone is less likely than estrogen to cause breast cysts, uterine fibroids and insomnia. It's sold over the counter.

●*Raloxifene* (**Evista**). This prescription drug and other *selective estrogen receptor modulators* are similar to estrogen. They have a real but smaller effect on bone density—and none of the cancer risk. In fact, they can *lower* your risk for breast cancer.

HORMONE ALTERNATIVES

For people who want to avoid hormones, four drugs are worth asking a doctor about...

●*Alendronate* (**Fosamax**). Available by prescription, alendronate is the drug of choice for men and for bone loss linked to steroid drugs. It slows bone loss.

●*Resedronate* (**Actonel**). This new prescription drug is similar to alendronate but is less likely to cause digestive problems.

●*Calcitonin* (**Miacalcin**). This prescription drug is often the best choice for people who cannot tolerate alendronate or who prefer a natural rather than a synthetic product. It slows bone loss and decreases bone pain.

●*Ipriflavone.* This over-the-counter derivative of soy protein resembles estrogen. It can be used by women and men and is the only drug that slows bone loss *and* builds new bone.

Signs of Osteoporosis

Unexplained foot fractures are often the first sign of osteoporosis. Feet and toes are especially vulnerable to fracture because they contain many small bones and bear so much weight. Bone scans of 21 men and women with foot fractures not caused by accident or obvious injury revealed that all but one had low bone density. *Self-defense:* If you suffer an unexplained foot fracture, ask your doctor to test you for osteoporosis.

Rod Tomczak, DPM, EdD, assistant clinical professor of orthopedics, Ohio State University Medical Center, Columbus. His study was published in *The Journal of Foot and Ankle Surgery,* 515 Busse Hwy., Park Ridge, IL 60068.

Osteoporosis Trap

Seemingly normal bone scans can hide advanced osteoporosis.

In older women who have calcium deposits around the spinal bones, a *dual energy X-ray absorptiometry* (DEXA) scan can appear normal despite bone loss. These deposits can lead to false-negative readings—delaying treatment that could prevent fractures.

For accurate diagnosis: Insist on a DEXA scan of the hips as well as the spine. Request a spinal X ray, too—especially if you are age 70 or older and have back stiffness, numbness, pain down your arms and legs and/or trouble with your balance.

John P. Bilezikian, MD, director, metabolic bone disease program, Columbia–Presbyterian Medical Center, New York City.

Protect Yourself from Bone Loss

People taking corticosteroids, such as prednisone, for more than three months should have a bone-density scan every six to 12 months...take calcium supplements and 400 IU to 800 IU of vitamin D daily. Ask your doctor what is best. Monitoring and preventing bone loss are easier than the years of therapy needed to rebuild bone that steroids may weaken.

Barbara Lukert, MD, director, Osteoporosis Clinic, University of Kansas Hospital, Kansas City, KS.

Salt Weakens Bones

The sodium in salt causes the body to excrete calcium, which is necessary for strong bones. *Troubling:* Most people are not aware of the top dietary salt sources—bread, cheese, most luncheon meats, tomato products, salad dressing, mayonnaise, beef, cereal, cakes and baked goods, margarine and sausage.

Connie Weaver, PhD, nutritionist, Purdue University, West Lafayette, IN.

Hypnosis Heals

Hypnosis helps broken bones heal more quickly. A study of 12 people with broken ankles found that those who received hypnotherapy in addition to the normal treatment of casts and crutches healed more quickly, felt less pain and were better able to walk than those who were given only standard treatment. Researchers advise people who want to benefit from hypnosis to consult a licensed psychologist or other professional with formal training in medical hypnosis.

Carol S. Ginandes, PhD, clinical instructor in psychology, department of psychiatry, Harvard Medical School, Boston, principal investigator of the study.

Dangerous New Infectious Diseases

Mohammad N. Akhter, MD, MPH, executive director of the American Public Health Association and clinical professor of family and community medicine at Georgetown University Medical School, both in Washington, DC. For more information, see "Emerging Infectious Diseases: A Peer-Reviewed Journal Tracking and Analyzing Disease Trends" at the US Centers for Disease Control Web site, *www.cdc.gov.*

Nowadays, it's very easy for people to travel to and from places that used to be too remote to visit. When people travel, infectious diseases travel with them.

From dengue fever, West Nile virus and Ebola virus to Marburg virus and hantavirus infection, new diseases can crop up anytime, anywhere.

We're also threatened by Lyme disease and variants of "old" diseases, such as tuberculosis. Even influenza remains a major threat. Each flu epidemic kills 20,000 to 40,000 people in the US.

DENGUE FEVER

This mosquito-borne viral illness is sometimes brought into the US by travelers returning from the tropics. If infected individuals entering the US are then bitten by a mosquito that can transmit dengue fever, the illness could be introduced into this country.

Symptoms: Fever, intense headache, joint and muscle pain and a red rash. Dengue hemorrhagic fever, a severe reaction, can be fatal.

Treatment: None for the disease itself. Complications, such as shock, can usually be controlled.

Prevention: Avoid mosquitoes whenever possible, especially when visiting places where dengue fever has occurred—Mexico, South and Central America, and some US states, including Arizona and Texas.

HANTAVIRUS INFECTION

This potentially lethal virus is contracted through contact with feces of infected rodents. It first appeared in the southwest US in 1993 and has shown up in a dozen states since.

The people most likely to contract hantavirus include workers who enter the crawl spaces under houses...and anyone who spends time in places where they could touch or inhale rodent droppings.

Many victims say they didn't even *see* rodents or droppings.

Symptoms: Fatigue, fever and muscle aches in the beginning. Later on, coughing and shortness of breath.

Treatment: None for the hantavirus itself. But people who seek emergency care have a better chance of surviving respiratory distress—the deadliest problem associated with this infection.

Prevention: Protect yourself against rodents. Keep your kitchen clean. Whenever possible, stay out of barns and sheds. Clear away brush that could provide nesting places. If rodents are a problem in your neighborhood, alert your local public health department at once.

INFLUENZA

New flu strains emerge every year. A flu shot provides some protection—but it's not foolproof.

Symptoms: Headache, runny nose, sore throat, fever and fatigue. Serious complications, such as pneumonia, can be fatal.

Treatment: Liquids, good nutrition, bed rest and aspirin help control symptoms. Ask your doctor about the antiviral drugs that are now available for influenza—*amantadine* (Symmetrel), *rimantadine* (Flumadine), *oseltamavir* (Tamiflu) and *zanamivir* (Relenza).

Prevention: Get an annual flu shot as soon as it becomes available (typically in October).

Especially if the vaccine is in short supply—as it may be this flu season—wash your hands frequently…stay in good physical shape…get adequate sleep…and eat healthfully to support your immune system.

LYME DISEASE

This tick-borne viral illness is a growing problem in the Northeast, mid-Atlantic and upper Midwest.

Symptoms: A rash that resembles a bull's-eye and swollen lymph glands near the bite. If not treated early, the disease can progress with such symptoms as joint pain, facial palsy and fever. In the worst cases, arthritis, heart problems, personality changes and memory loss may also occur.

Treatment: Oral antibiotics can usually cure Lyme disease if it has been caught early. Once the infection has progressed, intravenous antibiotics are used—but may not always be effective.

Prevention: Before going into wooded areas, use insect repellent containing DEET. Wear closed-toe shoes, a long-sleeved shirt and long pants. Choose light-colored clothing, which makes it easier to spot ticks.

Walk in the center of trails to avoid brushing against vegetation that might harbor ticks. Avoid sitting on the ground. Once a day, do a full-body "tick check."

You might also consider getting the Lyme vaccine. Lymerix appears to prevent the illness, but there have been reports of severe reactions, including arthritis.

WEST NILE VIRUS

Over the past few years, this mosquito-borne illness has caused a potentially deadly brain inflammation known as West Nile encephalitis in 71 people in the northeast US.

Symptoms: Flu-like illness, headache, rash, neck stiffness, muscle weakness, incoherence and paralysis.

Treatment: None for the illness itself. Anyone who exhibits suspicious symptoms should seek immediate medical help.

Prevention: During warm weather, protect yourself against mosquitoes when outdoors. Apply insect repellent containing DEET. Wear long pants and a long-sleeved shirt.

Remove any standing water, which attracts mosquitoes. Stay inside at dawn and dusk, when mosquito populations are at their highest.

New Cellular Phone Danger

Avoid *attached earphones.* According to one study, the wire in some earpieces acts like an antenna and channels up to three times as much electromagnetic radiation to the head as does a cell phone held next to the ear. Few scientists believe that there is any danger from cell phone radiation, but one recent study found a link between cell phone use and brain tumors. *Self-defense:* Use a regular phone instead of a cell phone whenever possible… keep the cell phone turned off whenever you don't need it. Since children have thinner skulls than adults, they may be even more vulnerable to radiation—so restrict their use of cell phones.

Timothy McCall, MD, a Boston internist and author of Examining Your Doctor: A Patient's Guide to Avoiding Harmful Medical Care. *Citadel Press.*

How to Get the Best Diabetes Treatment

Irl B. Hirsch, MD, medical director of the Diabetes Care Center at the University of Washington Medical Center in Seattle. He is author of *12 Things You Must Know About Diabetes Care Right Now!* American Diabetes Association.

Dramatic improvements in diabetes treatment are now becoming available for the 10 million Americans diagnosed with the condition.

Recently, the Food and Drug Administration (FDA) approved *insulin glargine* (Lantus), a more effective, longer-lasting drug that is injected once a day instead of the standard once- or twice-daily insulins.

Soon, the FDA is expected to approve a fast-acting insulin powder that can be administered via an inhaler—not injections.

In the meantime, diabetes treatment remains tricky.

For 90% of cases—people with adult-onset (type 2) diabetes—treatment means careful control of blood sugar (glucose) levels through diet, exercise and sometimes oral or injected medication.

For the remaining 10% of the cases—people with juvenile-onset (type 1) diabetes—a complicated regimen of daily insulin injections is required.

Problem: When treating diabetes patients, few physicians adhere to professional guidelines set by the American Diabetes Association (ADA).

Some fail to perform thorough physical exams or order vital tests. Others don't prescribe necessary medications, such as cholesterol-lowering drugs. That puts people with diabetes at risk for blindness, kidney problems, heart disease, nerve damage and other complications.

To learn more about effective diabetes care, we spoke to diabetes specialist Irl B. Hirsch, MD…

●How often should the necessary tests be performed? People with diabetes should measure their own blood glucose levels with a blood glucose meter. All meters sold today have met FDA criteria for accuracy.

If you take insulin, check your glucose levels four times a day—before meals and at bedtime. If you don't take insulin, do it twice daily, varying the time of day.

Whether you take insulin or not, measuring glucose levels one to two hours after meals can also be helpful in identifying glucose "spikes."

Blood glucose levels should measure 80 to 120 before a meal…and 100 to 140 at bedtime.

Blood pressure should also be monitored. If you are being treated for hypertension, take your own blood pressure with a cuff at least once a week. If your blood pressure is 130/85 or below, you can have your blood pressure taken at your usual doctor's visits.

People with diabetes also need the *glycated hemoglobin* blood test to measure blood glucose control over the previous 12 to 16 weeks. The reading should be below 7%. If you take insulin, have the test quarterly. If you treat your diabetes with oral medication or through diet alone, have the test performed twice a year.

A foot exam should be performed twice a year to check for calluses and sores that could lead to infection or even amputation.

All diabetes patients also need an annual dilated eye exam…a urine protein test…and a cholesterol and fasting triglycerides profile, measured by a blood test.

Levels of HDL (good) cholesterol should be above 45…LDL (bad) cholesterol below 100…triglycerides below 200.

●When is it appropriate to consult a specialist? If you have problems controlling your blood glucose, cholesterol and/or blood pressure, see an endocrinologist. That's a medical doctor specializing in diseases of the endocrine system, including diabetes.

An ophthalmologist (a physician specializing in eye disease) or optometrist (a non-physician who checks for common eye problems) should perform your eye exam to monitor for damaged blood vessels.

A podiatrist should custom-fit orthotics—shoe inserts—if your feet become swollen and red from ill-fitting shoes.

A nephrologist (a physician specializing in the kidneys) should treat you if you have kidney disease.

If you see a specialist or take medication prescribed by another physician, be sure to tell your primary-care doctor.

•Are diabetes patients at higher risk for heart disease? Yes. About two-thirds of them die as a result of heart disease—three times more than people without diabetes.

Additional risk factors include smoking...an LDL cholesterol level above 160...a total cholesterol level above 240...blood pressure above 140/90...obesity...protein in the urine...family history of high cholesterol or premature heart attack.

More serious risk factors include an abnormal electrocardiogram (ECG)...atherosclerosis (hardening of the arteries)...or chest pain on exertion. If you have two or more of these three risk factors, ask your doctor about undergoing a *nuclear stress test.*

During this procedure, a radioactive material is injected and the heart is viewed, often while you are exercising.

To lower your risk, lose weight, if necessary...follow a low-fat, low-calorie, high-fiber diet...and exercise.

Many cholesterol-lowering drugs, such as *pravastatin* (Pravachol), *simvastatin* (Zocor) and *atorvastatin* (Lipitor), may help. The ADA also recommends one baby or adult aspirin daily to thin the blood and lower heart attack risk.

•Why is high blood pressure so dangerous for people with diabetes? High blood pressure is common in type 2 diabetes patients. Type 1 patients, especially before age 40, generally have hypertension only if they also have kidney disease.

Hypertension increases your risk for kidney disease, eye problems, heart attack and stroke.

To lower your risk, lose weight, if necessary...don't add salt to your food...stop smoking...limit daily alcohol intake to two ounces of hard liquor, two glasses of wine or two beers...and exercise regularly.

If diet and lifestyle changes do not lower your blood pressure, your doctor may prescribe an angiotensin-converting enzyme (ACE) inhibitor, such as *ramipril* (Altace).

This class of drugs—which also protects the kidney and heart—is the first line of defense against hypertension.

•What's the best exercise for people with diabetes? It depends on your age and health. Aerobic activities, such as walking and swimming, are good choices for most people.

Exercise 20 to 45 minutes three times a week. Avoid weight lifting. It requires "bearing-down" movements that may cause retinal damage.

Diabetes–Pizza Trap

In a recent study, blood sugar (glucose) levels remained elevated into the next morning in type 1 (insulin-dependent) diabetics who had pizza for dinner. Levels also rose in those who ate a nonpizza meal, but they returned to normal by morning.

Pizza seems to have a unique propensity to raise glucose levels for six to 12 hours.

If you are diabetic: Ask your doctor about taking long-acting insulin before eating pizza— or other Italian dishes, such as manicotti or ravioli, which may also elevate glucose.

Jo Ann Ahern, RN, coordinator, pediatric program, Yale–New Haven Hospital, New Haven, CT. Her study of type 1 diabetics was published in *Diabetes Care*, 3705 Fifth Ave., Pittsburgh 15213.

Beware! Six Healthy Foods That Can Be Very Dangerous... *to You*

Julie Avery, RD, nutrition projects manager, Preventive Cardiology Program at the Cleveland Clinic Heart Center in Ohio.

Foods that are universally recognized as "good" can cause problems in some people. *It is important to be aware of the risks...*

GRAPEFRUIT JUICE

Medical researchers discovered that the digestion of grapefruit juice utilizes the same liver "pathway" as some drugs. So if you drink grapefruit juice and take these medications at the same time, the effects of the drugs may be increased or decreased.

Drugs that may be affected by grapefruit juice: Blood pressure medications… antihistamines…cholesterol-lowering drugs… some antidepressants.

Bottom line: Ask your pharmacist if any of the drugs you're taking may be affected. If the answer is yes, avoid grapefruit and grapefruit juice for at least four hours before and after taking medication.

Otherwise, enjoy it. It is rich in vitamin C and fiber. Pink and red grapefruits also contain *lycopene*, an antioxidant that protects against heart disease and cancer.

AVOCADOS

Avocados are loaded with nutrients and fiber but are also high in fat. One medium avocado has 30 grams of fat—more fat than six teaspoons of oil. Ounce for ounce, avocados are loaded with calories, too—more than five times the calories of most other fruits.

Bottom line: Avocados are healthful in moderation. A safe limit would be one thin slice a day. If you use avocado to make guacamole (add diced tomato, chopped onion and garlic), have no more than three tablespoons.

GREEN LEAFY VEGETABLES

Broccoli, spinach, Swiss chard and other leafy greens are rich in vitamin K, which is involved in blood clotting. If you're taking a blood-thinning medication, such as Coumadin *(warfarin)*, eat consistent amounts of these foods.

Eating a lot more—or a lot less—leafy greens than usual can alter the effects of these drugs, resulting in abnormal clotting.

Bottom line: Leafy greens are loaded with vitamin C, folate and other essential nutrients. Everyone should have at least two servings daily. If you're taking a blood thinner, be sure to eat the same amount all the time.

WINE

Red wine contains *flavonoids*, which appear to keep cholesterol from accumulating in the arteries. Moderate amounts of red wine reduce the risk of heart disease and stroke.

Downside: Drinking too much alcohol can interfere with certain medications. It also increases the risk of liver disease, depression and other health problems.

Bottom line: Women should limit wine consumption to five ounces daily…men, 10 ounces daily. Or for other alcoholic beverages, the upper limit is one drink daily for women and two for men. These amounts provide the benefits without as much risk.

RAW FISH

Raw fish is sometimes contaminated with parasites. This is true of the raw fish served in sushi bars as well as raw oysters and clams. Raw shellfish also may transmit hepatitis.

For a healthy person, the parasites aren't a problem—they're destroyed in the intestine. For those with weak immune systems, however, parasites may cause digestive discomfort—and even illness.

Bottom line: Anyone with weakened immunity—such as the elderly…very young children…those undergoing chemotherapy, etc.—should avoid raw fish and shellfish.

Cooked fish is fine—heat destroys the parasites.

TOMATOES

Tomatoes, a great source of vitamin C and lycopene, can occasionally cause food allergies. Tomatoes can also cause hives and/or difficulty breathing in those who are allergic to aspirin, since they contain *salicylates*, compounds similar to aspirin.

Bottom line: Eating tomatoes is unlikely to cause problems for most people. But food allergies are potentially serious, so talk to your doctor about any food to which you suspect you may be sensitive.

Odd Food Cravings

Bizarre food cravings sometimes signal iron-deficiency anemia. A strong desire to eat dirt, ice, paint, chalk or wood is called *pica* (PIE-kuh) and should be reported to a doctor.

Other symptoms of anemia include fatigue …pallor…cracks in the sides of the mouth… brittle nails.

A simple blood test can confirm an iron deficiency. If anemia is due to an iron deficiency, it is treated with iron-rich foods, such as beef and beans, and iron supplements.

Connie M. Weaver, PhD, distinguished professor and head, department of foods and nutrition, Purdue University, West Lafayette, IN.

Coffee Scare

A study of more than 250 women found that those who consumed more than four cups of coffee a day were more than twice as likely to have an unstable bladder as those whose daily coffee consumption was less than one cup. Researchers report that more than one-third of women older than 65 suffer from urinary incontinence due to an unstable bladder, and suggest that women cut their coffee intake—to below two cups a day if they already have bladder problems.

Lily A. Arya, MD, assistant professor, department of obstetrics/gynecology, Hospital of the University of Pennsylvania, PA.

Home Remedies for Embarrassing Ailments

Richard Firshein, DO, author of *The Nutraceutical Revolution* (Riverhead) and *Reversing Asthma: Breathe Easier with This Revolutionary New Program* (Warner). Dr. Firshein is director of Firshein Center for Comprehensive Medicine, a complementary medicine practice in New York. He answers health questions at *www.drcity.com.*

Many of us suffer from embarrassing health problems because we don't get the information to resolve them.

Good news: Many problems can be managed easily with simple home care.

FOOT ODOR

Blame it on heat and moisture. Feet are loaded with sweat glands, which are especially active when you wear shoes all day. It's an ideal environment for odor-causing bacteria and yeast.

Quick fixes: Change socks twice a day. This will keep your feet dry, making them less hospitable to germs. Also let shoes air out for at least 24 hours between wearings. If you can't wait that long, dry the insides with a hair dryer.

Helpful: Rub your feet with a pumice stone twice a week to remove dead skin, which absorbs moisture and provides a favorable environment for germs. This is easiest to do in the shower. Pumice stones are sold in drugstores.

BELCHING

In some cultures, it is polite to belch. In the US, of course, it is a major faux pas. You can't eliminate belches entirely. They are essential for venting excess gas from the digestive tract. Those who belch a lot, however, may be swallowing too much air—called *aerophagia.*

Quick fixes…

● **Give up chewing gum.** It is one of the main reasons we swallow air.

● **Avoid carbonated beverages.**

● **Don't drink anything with a straw,** which mixes a lot of air in with the liquid.

Also: People tend to gulp air when they're under stress. I've found that once they realize that they're doing it, it's easier for them to stop.

Caution: Sudden excessive belching may be due to a gastroesophageal reflux disease or an ulcer. These require medication or surgery in severe cases.

HEMORRHOIDS

These distended blood vessels in and/or around the rectum can cause severe itching and intense pain.

Quick fixes: Over-the-counter topical remedies containing cortisone, such as *Anusol* and *Preparation H,* may help shrink hemorrhoids. To relieve itching and burning, moisten a washcloth with witch hazel and apply it to the area twice a day. Also eliminate spicy foods.

Long-term: High-fiber foods add bulk and moisten stools and reduce straining. Eat more fruits, vegetables, whole grains and beans.

Flaxseed powder is a particularly healthful form of fiber. Start with one-quarter teaspoon daily in food or water. Increase gradually to one teaspoon daily.

Also consider taking 2,000 mg of *rutin* daily for two weeks. This antioxidant seems to help strengthen blood vessels, including those in the rectum. It is sold in pharmacies and health food stores.

Cautions: Fiber may increase irritation—so add it to your diet gradually. And any rectal bleeding should be checked by a physician.

EARWAX

This waxy, yellowish substance is created during the ears' self-cleaning process. Occasionally it builds up in the outer ear, causing pain or hearing loss. It can also cause unsightly deposits.

Quick fix: Mix equal amounts of hydrogen peroxide and warm water. Use a dropper to put a few drops of the mixture in the ear. Hold your head sideways and wait a few minutes. This will help loosen wax and float it out of the ear canal.

Important: Don't use a cotton swab to clean the ear canal—the delicate eardrum is easily damaged.

Check for food sensitivities and allergies: People tend to produce more earwax when they eat certain foods or are exposed to certain allergens. Avoid meat, dairy products and fatty snack foods for three weeks. That may be all that is needed to diminish earwax. If this works, you may want to avoid these foods permanently. If in doubt, keep a food diary.

FLATULENCE

Passing gas is the equivalent of a belch—except air and gases go in the other direction.

The average adult passes gas eight to 20 times a day. Some people, however, produce excessive amounts. This occurs when they have trouble digesting certain foods—particularly beans or dairy products. Undigested food in the intestine is eaten by bacteria, which then produce excess gas.

Quick fix: Once a day, eat a container of yogurt containing live *Lactobacillus acidophilus.* These bacteria aid digestion. Or take acidophilus supplements (follow label instructions). This is helpful for *everyone*—even those without a flatulence problem.

Also helpful: Beano, an over-the-counter enzyme product, breaks down gas-causing carbohydrates in the intestine.

About 70% of adults don't produce enough lactase, an enzyme needed to digest lactose (a sugar in dairy foods). You can take lactase supplements or buy dairy foods with added lactase.

Hint: If you've been eating more fiber in order to improve digestion or lower cholesterol, you may have a temporary increase in gas. To prevent this, increase your fiber intake gradually over several weeks.

DANDRUFF

Those little white specks are simply skin cells that are shedding more quickly than they should.

Quick fix: Apply an antidandruff shampoo at the beginning of your shower. Leave the lather on your hair until you're almost done. Then rinse it out. Antidandruff shampoo works best when the lather is allowed to soak into the scalp.

Dietary solution: Eating too little fatty acids—the types of fats found in fish—can cause dandruff. Therefore, take 3 g of fish oil daily...or eat fish four times a week.

OILY SKIN

Those slick spots on the forehead and around the nose are caused by *sebum,* the oily substance produced by sebaceous glands in the skin.

Some people have an inherited tendency toward oily skin. Dietary factors may be involved as well.

Quick fixes: Wash your face several times a day with a mild soap. If you have dry patches, use a soap that includes a moisturizer. Don't use alcohol to remove the oils—it will make the skin too dry.

Skin reflects what is happening in the body. One of the first things I recommend for mildly oily skin is a change of diet. Avoid eating fatty foods for two to three weeks...and pare down your diet to the basics—fish, raw vegetables, grains, etc.

If your skin becomes less oily, start adding foods back into your diet, just one at a time.

This will help you identify which foods may be contributing to the problem.

Viagra Warning

Viagra can be dangerous when taken in combination with other medications, particularly nitroglycerin-related drugs. It also can be hazardous for people with coronary artery disease. *Safety:* Consult your doctor before using Viagra. Do not buy it by mail or over the Internet and risk a dangerous drug interaction.

Patrick Walsh, MD, urologist in chief, Johns Hopkins Hospital, Marburg Bldg., Rm. 134, Baltimore 21287.

Laser Surgery vs. Night Driving

Vision-correcting laser surgery can make driving at night dangerous. Two to seven years after undergoing *photo-refractive keratectomy* (PRK), 56% of patients failed a contrast sensitivity test that measured their ability to see clearly at night. *Theory:* Laser surgery damages the *stroma*, the corneal layer that is responsible for night vision. Researchers fear that the reduced night vision is permanent. LASIK, a vision-correcting procedure similar to PRK, could cause comparable problems.

William Jory, MD, consultant eye surgeon, London Centre for Refractive Surgery.

Sodium and Cataract Risk

Too much sodium in the diet can lead to cataracts. Adults consuming the most sodium were twice as likely to develop *posterior subcapsular cataracts*—a type of cataract that covers the back of the eye lens—as those

consuming the least. *Self-defense:* Limit sodium intake to 2,400 mg a day, as recommended by federal guidelines.

Robert B. Cumming, MPH, PhD, associate professor of public health and community medicine, University of Sydney, Australia.

New Vision Drug

Breakthrough drug treatment for vision loss slows progress of macular degeneration, the leading cause of blindness in the elderly. The FDA has approved the prescription medicine *Visudyne*, which is injected into the arm and then light-activated, so it should act only in the eye and have limited side effects. Visudyne is for the *wet form* of macular degeneration—not for the more common, but less serious, dry form.

Jennifer I. Lim, PhD, is associate professor of ophthalmology, Keck School of Medicine, University of Southern California, Los Angeles.

Senior Self-Defense

Most falls by seniors at home are not caused by household hazards but by weak muscles, bad eyesight and bad shoes. A study of 1,000 people over age 72 living at home analyzed the causes of home falls not caused by loss of consciousness. Very few of the falls were associated with any of 13 common potential hazards, such as loose rugs and slippery bathtubs. They concluded that the best way for seniors to avoid falls is to strengthen muscles, improve balance, preserve vision, wear appropriate footwear, monitor the effects of medication—and remove potential hazards.

Thomas M. Gill, MD, associate professor of medicine and geriatrics, Yale University, New Haven, CT.

Chewing Fights Memory Loss

Chewing increases activity in the hippocampus, the brain region where new memories are temporarily stored.

With age, hippocampal cells deteriorate... and memory declines.

Recent study: Older mice lost short-term memory faster when they lacked a set of teeth.

Implication: Healthy teeth—or good dentures—may help preserve memory in older people by preserving the ability to chew.

Minoru Onozuka, PhD, assistant professor of anatomy, Gifu University School of Medicine, Gifu, Japan. His study of molarless mice was published in *Behavioural Brain Research,* University of Michigan, 525 E. University St., Ann Arbor, MI 48109-1109.

Cold Defense

Avoid colds by being active. A study of middle-aged adults found that those who were most active throughout the day had fewer colds.

Men with the highest levels of physical activity accumulated at work, at home and in regular exercise experienced a 35% reduction in risk of colds compared with less active men. Highly active women experienced a 20% reduction in risk.

Any kind of activity, as long as it was at least moderately intense and performed for two to three hours per day, provided cold-reducing benefits—from structured exercise to gardening and yardwork to brisk walking.

Chuck Matthews, PhD, research assistant professor, department of epidemiology and biostatistics, University of South Carolina, Columbia.

2

Physicians and Hospitals

How to Get Much Better Hospital Care

Managed care and rampant cost-cutting have left many hospitals understaffed. Doctors are constantly rushed. Fewer nurses must care for more patients.

Result: Patients buzz for help with no response...get diagnostic tests by mistake... receive medication with no explanation.

You can still get superb care in the hospital—if you become your own health-care "manager." *Seven things you must do...*

●**Have a friend or relative stay with you.** A caring companion can get you water when you need it...help you to the bathroom...and command the attention of doctors and nurses when necessary.

Your companion can also look after your interests at a time when you may be too weak to protect them yourself. Your advocate can ask questions, take notes and clarify exactly what's being done—and why.

If possible, call on more than one person for help. That's because round-the-clock company is best. Posted visiting hours are only guidelines—and they are meant for visitors, not health advocates. In fact, nurses often appreciate having an extra set of hands when they're too busy to help you.

Exception: Space is always tight in intensive care units. Having an extra person in the ICU may prevent other patients from getting the care they need.

●**Identify a point person.** On an average day, a hospital patient might talk with his/her primary-care doctor...surgeon and/or anesthesiologist...and an ever-changing cast of interns and residents.

It's not uncommon for patients to get conflicting information from all these professionals.

Marie Savard, MD, clinical associate professor of medicine at the University of Pennsylvania School of Medicine and an internist in private practice, both in PA. She is author of *How to Save Your Own Life* (Warner Books) and *The Savard Health Record* (Time Life).

29

You need a point person who can sort everything out and answer your questions.

Typically, that will be the attending physician. He's the doctor on record at the hospital as being in charge of your case.

The attending physician coordinates your care. Depending on your medical problem, he might be your surgeon, cardiologist or internist.

As soon as you've settled in your room, ask the nurse assigned to your case to identify your point person. Get his name, telephone number and pager number.

●**Obtain your daily schedule.** Each day, the nurses on your floor receive a "plan of care" listing tests you're scheduled for...meals ordered...and special instructions from your doctor. They also receive a separate list of all medications that have been ordered for you.

Each morning, ask the nurse in charge of your care to let you see both lists. Take notes on all important entries. It's the best way to ensure that mistakes don't occur, such as undergoing the wrong test or getting the wrong medication.

●**Get to know the staff.** You want the nurses, technicians and other staff members to see you as a real person—not just another face on the ward.

Make small talk when staff members come to your room. Ask about their weekends... families...interests. Introduce your friends and family to them. Above all, let them know that you appreciate their care.

●**Get the sleep you need.** Sleeping in the hospital is hard. The environment is noisy and unfamiliar. Even worse, staff members from different teams and services usually awaken patients every few hours for medication...blood pressure checks...IV adjustments.

Ask your assigned nurse if all these tasks can be combined in one visit. Making arrangements ahead of time permits better coordination of your care and less interruption of your sleep.

●**Don't put up with pain.** Adequate postsurgical pain management speeds healing and helps prevent stress and depression. Yet doctors often skimp on pain medication because they fear the possibility of side effects and addiction.

The concern about addiction is misplaced. Adequate pain medication during hospitalization does *not* lead to subsequent abuse of painkillers.

If you're in pain, alert the medical staff. Otherwise, they'll assume that the medicine you're receiving is effective. If your doctor or the nurses decline to help, request a consultation with the hospital's pain specialist if available.

●**Get a copy of your discharge summary.** After your stay, the hospital provides a summary of your treatment to your attending physician and any other doctors he designates. You should get a copy of this summary, too.

The report will provide important information for any physician who treats you in the future. It lists the reason for your hospital admission, important test results and surgical findings, all medications prescribed and the recommended future plan of care.

The summary is usually sent to your physicians two to three weeks after your discharge. Before you leave the hospital, give your primary-care physician a self-addressed, stamped envelope. Ask him to send you a copy of the report when it arrives at his office.

In the meantime: Before you leave the hospital, get copies of the results of all tests specifically related to your condition.

If you were hospitalized for a heart attack, for example, this would include a copy of your final electrocardiogram (EKG).

Safer ICU Stay

Intensive care unit (ICU) infections are less likely when patients stay semireclined instead of lying flat. Infections are commonly picked up in ICUs—in as many as 30% of ICU patients in one Europe-wide study. More than half are respiratory infections. In many cases, the infection—not the underlying disease—is fatal. *Self-defense:* If a relative is in an ICU, insist that his/her bed be kept in a semireclined position, as long as there is no medical reason why this can't be done.

Nigel R. Webster, PhD, professor of anaesthesia and intensive care, University of Aberdeen, Scotland, writing in *The Lancet,* 42 Bedford Sq., London, England WC1B 3SL.

Guarding Against X Ray Mistakes

To prevent diagnostic mistakes when an X ray is taken, make sure the doctor has your previous X ray for comparison.

●**Help the technologist take a clear X ray** by not wearing anything metallic and staying as still as possible.

●**Ask the radiologist or another doctor to review the X ray** with you and discuss findings that support his/her reading.

●**Get a second reading if you are not confident.**

Michael Linver, MD, clinical associate professor of radiology, University of New Mexico, X-Ray Associates, Albuquerque.

Everything You Wanted to Know About All the Scary Errors in Medical Tests

Richard Podell, MD, MPH, clinical professor, family medicine, UMDNJ–Robert Wood Johnson Medical School, New Brunswick, NJ. Dr. Podell's private practice in New Providence, NJ, integrates traditional medical and holistic therapies. He is author of *The G-Index Diet.* Warner.

No medical test is perfect. Even when performed by a skilled technician and analyzed at a reliable laboratory, what you do *before* the test can significantly alter the results.

No news: At least 2% of test paperwork gets lost and never reaches the doctor's attention. So—don't assume all is well if your doctor doesn't contact you. Always call for results a week or two after having a test.

Here are practical guidelines for the most common tests to ensure your results are as accurate as possible…

BIOPSY

Biopsy is vital for people with suspicious results on preliminary cancer tests. It is also used to diagnose skin ailments.

Procedure: Tissue is removed with a "punch" biopsy device or with a scalpel …then analyzed under a microscope. Depending on the location of the suspicious tissue, you may require sedation and/or stitches.

Accuracy: Results can be ambiguous. A pathologist's judgment and experience are critical for an accurate assessment.

Results: One to two weeks.

BONE DENSITY

Women should have this painless test for osteoporosis within one year of menopause… and every 12 to 24 months thereafter. Appropriate frequency varies by individual. Have the test earlier if there is a family history of the disease or if you've ever had a bone fracture—especially an "easy break" that occurs in low-trauma situations, such as falling on grass and breaking a wrist.

Men should have the test if they've ever suffered a severe fracture or have a family history of osteoporosis.

Patients taking corticosteroids, such as those for asthma, lupus or rheumatoid arthritis, should be tested at the start of therapy and every one to two years thereafter (frequency varies by individual). These drugs make bones brittle.

Procedure: You lie fully clothed on a special table or stick your heel, wrist or finger into an ultrasound or dual-energy X-ray absorptiometry (DEXA) machine.

Preparation: None is necessary.

Accuracy: Varies depending on the site measured and the test used. DEXA is the most accurate test, especially when performed at the spine or hip.

Results: One week.

CHOLESTEROL TEST

Every five years, men and women over age 20 should have a blood test to measure their total HDL (good) and LDL (bad) cholesterol levels. This test is especially important for women after menopause, when LDL tends to rise and HDL tends to fall. If the level of LDL cholesterol is elevated, the test should be performed more often.

Procedure: Blood is taken from your arm.

Preparation: None prior to total and HDL tests. Before LDL and triglyceride testing, fast for 12 hours and don't drink alcohol for three days.

Accuracy: Very precise if guidelines are followed.

Results: Within two days.

COLON CANCER TESTS

Both men and women should have an annual test for hidden (occult) blood in the stool starting at age 50—earlier if there is a family history of colon cancer. Also see your doctor for a rectal exam every year beginning at age 40.

Accuracy: There are many benign causes of blood in the stool, such as hemorrhoids and ingestion of certain foods or medications. False-positive results can occur.

Better: Have a sigmoidoscopy every three years or a colonoscopy every five years. These tests are far more accurate than a stool test.

Procedure: For the stool test, your doctor will likely give you a kit to obtain a stool sample. You'll collect the sample at home and then bring it to the office or lab for evaluation.

Colonoscopy is performed at a hospital or an outpatient medical facility. Sigmoidoscopy is usually done in the doctor's office.

For either procedure, you'll lie on your side on a table and the doctor will insert a scope into your anus.

Sedation—either general or local—is needed for colonoscopy, which examines the entire length of the colon.

There is usually mild to moderate discomfort—fairly brief—during sigmoidoscopy,

which only examines the lower third of the colon. Anesthesia is usually not given.

Preparation: Four days prior to having a stool test, don't take aspirin, ibuprofen or vitamin C supplements. Don't eat red meat for three days before the test.

Stay on a liquid diet for 24 to 36 hours before a colonoscopy or sigmoidoscopy. You will also have to take medications or perform enemas the night before the test to clean out the bowel.

Results: Three days for the stool test... immediately for the other tests.

MAGNETIC RESONANCE IMAGING (MRI)

MRIs are important for those who may have disorders of the brain, spinal cord, other organs or blood vessels.

Procedure: You lie inside a narrow tube for 30 minutes or more. During this time, you'll hear the loud clicking noises of the MRI scanner.

Preparation: If you are claustrophobic, request a sedative prior to the procedure...or ask your doctor about having an open MRI, which has a less-confining tube but is not quite as sensitive.

Accuracy: The clarity of the image varies depending on the body site scanned. MRIs require the radiologist's interpretation and judgment.

Results: Within one week.

MAMMOGRAM

All women age 40 and over should undergo annual mammography and clinical breast exams. Schedule the mammogram during the two weeks after your menstrual period.

Reasons: Just prior to and during menstruation, breasts may be tender, making the test more painful. Breast tissue is also more dense at this time, making it harder to spot abnormalities.

Procedure: A technician positions your breast on a plate, compresses it and takes X-ray images.

Preparation: Don't wear any aluminum-containing antiperspirant on the day of the test. It can produce specks on the X ray that look like abnormalities. Be sure to shower if you wore antiperspirant the day before.

Accuracy: 10% to 15% of breast cancers are missed by mammograms—but most of these may be detected on physical exam by a doctor or during self-examination. Almost any mass that is found will require further evaluation, often a biopsy.

Results: Federal guidelines require that negative results be mailed to patients within two weeks of the test. Suspicious or positive results must be conveyed even more quickly.

PAP SMEAR

All women age 18 and over should have an annual Pap smear to screen for cervical cancer. The risk of this cancer is greatly increased for women with multiple partners or who became sexually active at a young age. Tests can be performed anytime except during a menstrual period.

Procedure: You sit on an examining table and place your feet in stirrups at the end of the table. The doctor inserts a speculum into the vagina to prop it open. He/she inserts either a long cotton swab or a brush into the vagina to scrape off a few cells from your cervix. These cells are smeared on a slide for analysis. The test may be mildly uncomfortable.

Preparation: Don't douche, have sex or use vaginal medication for 24 hours before the test.

Accuracy: After a normal test, the chance of developing cervical cancer within the next three years is less than one in 20,000.

Important: A Pap smear detects only cervical cancer—not uterine or ovarian cancer. Endometrial biopsies to screen for uterine cancer are offered to women who have irregular vaginal bleeding or postmenopausal women on estrogen therapy. A pelvic ultrasound can be used to screen for ovarian cancer, as can a CA-125 blood test, but they are not routinely given.

Results: One to two weeks.

PROSTATE CANCER TESTS

All men over age 40 should have an annual rectal exam, in which the doctor feels for lumps or enlargement of the prostate.

All men over age 50 should have a prostate-specific antigen (PSA) blood test. Men with a family history of prostate cancer should begin testing at least five years before the age at which the relative developed cancer.

Procedure: Blood is drawn from your arm.

Preparation: Avoid sexual activity and rectal exams for 24 hours prior to the test. Either may falsely raise the PSA level.

Accuracy: At very high levels, it strongly suggests prostate cancer. Lesser elevations can be caused by either prostate enlargement or prostate cancer.

Results: Within two days.

STRESS TEST

This test is important for men and women with suspected or known heart disease, such as those with chest pain. It is also important for those with risk factors for heart disease, such as a family history of heart attack at a young age.

Procedure: Blood pressure and electrical heart activity are measured while you walk or run on a treadmill or pedal a stationary bike. The test detects whether blood flow to the heart is compromised.

Preparation: Wear gym shoes and comfortable clothing. Don't eat for six hours prior to the test.

Accuracy: Relatively high false-positive rate in people with a low risk of heart disease. It is much less useful to screen for heart disease in people who do not have symptoms or risk factors.

In those with symptoms, a stress test can provide an estimate of the risk of dying in the next five years. If you develop any discomfort during the test, tell your doctor promptly.

Results: Available immediately.

Doctors' Mistakes and Older Patients... Self-Defense Strategies

Robert N. Butler, MD, professor of geriatrics at Mt. Sinai School of Medicine and president of the International Longevity Center–USA, both in New York City. He is the former director of the National Institute on Aging in Bethesda, MD. In 1976, Dr. Butler won a Pulitzer Prize for his book Why Survive? Being Old in America. *HarperCollins.*

As we grow older, we're more likely to have health problems that require first-rate medical care.

Unfortunately, as many seniors have learned, it can be hard to find a doctor suited to care for *their* special needs.

How can older people be sure to get good medical care? Dr. Robert Butler, a well-known crusader for elder rights, explains how important it is to watch out for mistakes doctors sometimes make when treating elderly patients...

Mistake: **Failing to appreciate the physical changes that come with age.** A disease that causes one set of symptoms in a young person may manifest itself quite differently in an older person. Not all doctors realize that. And an unwary doctor can easily miss the diagnosis.

Example I: If a 30-year-old man suffers a heart attack, he is likely to experience severe chest pain. But chest pain affects fewer than 20% of older heart attack victims. Instead, older victims may simply seem weak or confused.

Example II: An older person suffering from an overactive thyroid may exhibit apathy instead of hyperactivity, the classic symptom.

Mistake: **Urging older people to "take it easy."** Even if you've been disabled by a stroke or another medical problem, leading an active lifestyle helps keep you healthy—and happy.

Even people in their 80s and 90s can develop big, powerful muscles with a program of weight lifting. Such a program can literally put a bedridden patient back on his/her feet.

Mistake: **Being too quick to blame health problems on old age.** Doctors often assume that health problems are inevitable in older people, exhibiting a defeatist "what-can-you-expect-at-your-age?" attitude.

They order fewer diagnostic tests and generally treat disease less aggressively in old people than in young people.

Example: An elderly woman seems confused and disoriented. Assuming that she has Alzheimer's disease, her doctor neglects to order tests that might show the real culprit to be an easily correctable drug reaction.

Mistake: **Not giving the patient enough time.** A good physician takes the time to ask about your work status and lifestyle as well as your medical problems...and, in general, makes you *feel* taken care of.

At each office visit, the doctor should ask about symptoms you have reported in the past. He should also review your response to medications...and ask about new problems.

Your first visit to a new doctor should be devoted to giving a thorough medical history and undergoing a physical exam and lab tests. This can take more than an hour. Once this comprehensive exam is completed, you probably won't need another exam for a year—unless there's a health crisis.

Mistake: **Failing to advocate preventive measures.** Some doctors seem to think, "Why bother trying to lower an elderly patient's cholesterol level. He's just going to decline anyway."

We now know that heart patients of *any* age can benefit from a program of dietary modification, lifestyle change and—if necessary—medication or surgery.

Mistake: **Giving inappropriate prescriptions.** Doctors are too quick to order tranquilizers and antidepressants for their older patients, thinking—incorrectly—that psychotherapy is of no use. And they often fail to realize that older bodies respond differently to drugs.

Example: It can take an older person twice as long to "clear" *diazepam* (Valium) from his body as a young person. A dose that would be appropriate for a young person could make an older person drowsy.

If you're not sure that your doctor knows about all the drugs you're taking, put all of your medications (including nonprescription drugs and herbal remedies) in a paper bag and bring them with you to your next office visit.

For referral to a certified geriatrician in your area, call the American Geriatrics Society at 800-247-4779.

Children and Surgery

If a child needs surgery, tour the hospital before checking in. Many hospitals offer preoperative tours for kids up to age 18. *Aim:* To familiarize them with the hospital environment and make it less impersonal and frightening. Tours may include visits to the admitting area, preoperative section, waiting rooms and several spots in the pediatric unit. Some parents fear their children may be scared during a tour, making it harder to bring them in for the operation. *Reality:* Tours usually relax children—and parents, too.

Katie Crocco, certified child life specialist, pediatric department, Bridgeport Hospital, Bridgeport, CT.

Don't Take Viagra Before Surgery

Viagra dilates blood vessels so blood flows easily to the penis. But dilation affects the rest of the body, too—lowering blood pressure. This can be dangerous during surgery because some anesthetics have the same effect on blood pressure. Do not use Viagra within 24 hours of surgery—and tell your doctor and anesthesiologist when you last took it.

Patrick C. Walsh, MD, urologist-in-chief, Johns Hopkins Medical Institutions, Baltimore.

Herbs and Surgery

Herbs and supplements can complicate surgery...

•**Licorice**—an herbal cough and sore throat remedy—taken two weeks before surgery can lead to irregular heartbeat during and after surgery.

•**Ephedra**—an herb used for cough, asthma and weight loss—may cause irregular heartbeat and high blood pressure.

•**Kava**—an herbal sedative—can cause severe drowsiness after surgery if certain anesthetics are used.

•**St. John's wort**—the herbal antidepressant—can cause confusion and agitation in postsurgical patients.

Also: Many herbs can interfere with blood clotting.

Self-defense: Tell your doctor at least two weeks prior to surgery about each herb and supplement you take.

Carol L. Norred, certified registered nurse anesthetist, clinical instructor of anesthesiology, University of Colorado Health Sciences Center, Denver.

How Much Do You Think The Average Patient Is Overcharged Each Year?

Pat Palmer, founder and president of Medical Billing Advocates of America in Salem, VA. She is coauthor of *The Medical Bill Survival Guide: What You Need to Know Before You Pay a Dime.* Warner.

On average, each patient is overcharged $1,300 per year on medical bills. Hospital bills especially are often studded with errors and inflated charges. More than 90% of medical bills contain errors. *Recent examples...*

•**A couple was billed for their newborn girl's circumcision.**

•**A heart patient was charged for use of the delivery room.**

•**A patient woke up after surgery with a teddy bear under his arm.** It was billed as a $57.50 "cough support device."

Insurance companies and HMOs usually pay without ferreting out such errors because they can't afford the staff needed to scrutinize every bill.

Result: All medical consumers wind up with higher insurance costs.

COMMON BILLING ERRORS

•**Billing "accidents."** Some billing mistakes may be mere clerical errors—a mistyped number...a misspelled code...a repeated entry. In these instances, alerting the hospital's billing department should get the mistake rectified.

It's not an accident if the hospital insists you pay the full amount even though you have brought the error to their attention… shown them multiple charges for the same item…proved that you did not use or need what you were billed for.

●**Bundled charges.** Hospital bills for major procedures, such as surgery or obstetrical care, may have some disguised double- charges. *The rip-off:* They include a "bundled" charge for a group of items or services, in addition to separate charges for each item or service.

Example: You're given a charge for a "Chem-7" blood test and also charged for several of the seven parts of the test individually.

Buzzwords to watch out for: "Trays" and "packs"—as in "C-section tray" and "cataract eye pack." If you see these buzzwords by a charge, be aware that redundant charges may follow.

●**Monstrous markups.** Why should you be charged $30 for gauze that costs the hospital less than $1? The markup should never be more than 300%.

To find out how much the hospital paid, call its purchasing department and ask who the medical supplier is. Then call the supplier. Or go to *www.medmarket.com* to search for specific products and who supplies or manufactures them. Then call the supplier/manufacturer and ask what their typical prices are.

TO FIGHT BACK

●**Demand an itemized statement.** You may not know that you've been double-charged for a "maternity pad" and "cord clamp" that appear on your bill until you see the detailed list.

If you ask for this statement, it will probably be mailed to you after you leave the hospital. Do not pay your bill until then.

●**Question everything.** Read your *entire* bill. Ask about any charge that you don't understand…or that seems illogical or suspicious.

If there's a problem, call the hospital department where the service was performed. If the problem is not settled, fax or mail a letter explaining the problem to the hospital's business office.

If you need help deciphering the bill, consult your doctor, pharmacist or any friend who happens to be a health-care provider. Or search medical information sites on the Internet for answers.

Example: Medical Dictionary, *http://medical-dictionary.com.*

●**Be persistent.** When you call to ask about a charge, the billing department may stonewall you in the hope that you'll give up and go away. Some workers are *trained* to evade questions. Don't let them get away with it.

Give the billing department one more call and allow the staff a few more days to reply.

No response? Call and ask for the department supervisor. Still no action? Call the hospital administrator or chief financial officer (CFO).

If that goes nowhere, threaten to call a medical billing advocate…or the media.

To locate a medical billing advocate in your area, look in the Yellow Pages under "insurance claims processing services" or "billing services." Or contact the Medical Billing Advocates of America in Salem, Virginia, at 540-387-5870 or *www.billadvocates.com.*

How to Protect Your Full Rights As a Patient

Charles Inlander, president, People's Medical Society, 462 Walnut St., Allentown, PA 18102. He is author of *This Won't Hurt (And Other Lies My Doctor Tells Me).* People's Medical Society.

Being ill or injured is a stressful experience—some injuries/illnesses, of course, are more stressful than others. The general feeling is one of being out of control—at the mercy of the "system."

You want answers…information…state-of-the-art treatment. You want to be treated with respect. And you want your medical information kept confidential.

Knowing your rights as a patient can protect you from abuse by the system.

GETTING COMPLETE INFORMATION FROM YOUR DOCTOR

In the past, many doctors viewed patients as unable to understand diagnoses, and so shared little about patient conditions and treatment alternatives (beyond what was required to obtain "informed consent").

Today, patients are savvier and demand more from their doctors. *How to proceed...*

●**Demand the time that is needed to tell your doctor about your symptoms.** And—demand the time to hear his/her explanation of possible diagnoses and courses of treatment.

Helpful: Write down your symptoms so you don't overlook them in conversation with your doctor.

If you don't think your doctor is listening to you or giving you the time you need—*speak up!*

●**Get a second opinion before surgery or other invasive treatment.** Most insurers are willing to pay for this—since a second opinion may indicate a less drastic and less costly course of action.

●**Do your own research.** While you aren't licensed to practice medicine (even on yourself), there's plenty of easy-to-understand medical information available on the Internet (try *www.ivillage.com* and *www. wellweb.com*). Also check InteliHealth at *www.intelihealth.com.* Of course, don't rely solely on any information you find. Discuss it with your doctor.

PATIENT BILL OF RIGHTS

Most hospitals nationwide have adopted some or all of the 12 rights enumerated in the *Patient Bill of Rights* approved by the American Hospital Association in 1992. *These rights include...*

●**Right to receive considerate and respectful care.**

●**Right to obtain relevant, current and understandable information** about diagnosis, treatment and prognosis from doctors and other caregivers. This includes disclosure of the financial implications of the alternatives presented.

●**Right to make decisions about the plan of care.** This includes the right to refuse a recommended treatment.

●**Right to have an advance medical directive**—a living will or a durable medical power of attorney. These documents permit you to express the kind of care you want and don't want.

●**Right to every consideration of privacy.** This extends not only to a patient's body during examination and treatment, but also to case discussions.

●**Right to expect confidentiality** for all communications and records pertaining to treatment.

●**Right to review records** pertaining to personal medical care. This includes the right to have such information explained.

●**Right to expect a reasonable response** from a hospital to a request for appropriate and medically indicated care. That may require transfer to another medical facility.

●**Right to be informed about business relationships among the hospital, doctors and others** that may influence a patient's treatment and care.

Example: The urologist owns an interest in the lithotripsy center, where kidney stones are sonically blasted. The urologist will be inclined to send you there even though there may be alternative treatments.

●**Right to consent or decline to participate in clinical studies** of an ailment that you suffer from.

●**Right to expect reasonable continuity of care.** You don't want a different doctor every other day.

●**Right to be informed of hospital policies and practices**—such as how to resolve billing disputes.

WINDOW DRESSING?

These rights sound great but they're only "window dressing." Hospitals that say they support these rights might not. *Instead...*

●**Doctors may not adequately inform patients of a prescribed drug's side effects.**

●**Hospitals may not prepare itemized bills.**

●**Hospitals may not even have a doctor in the emergency room 24 hours a day.**

Reality: No one else will be looking out for your rights.

If you're a patient and believe your rights have been or are being violated, you can take action.

Ask to speak with the hospital's patient advocate, a person employed by the hospital to be a go-between for patients and the hospital's administration.

You'll find the name and number of the patient advocate (sometimes called a patient representative) on your hospital admission papers or posted in your hospital room.

Vocal objections to treatment you've received or failed to receive may be necessary.

REVIEW YOUR MEDICAL RECORDS

Review your medical records to ensure that there are no mistakes that could produce problems for you down the line.

The best course of action: Ask your doctor for a copy of your records. About half the states have statutes that give you the right to review your records. However, even in states without such statutes, you still have this right. Hospitals that have adopted the *Patient Bill of Rights* are supposed to provide your records upon request.

Note: Federal law ensures that nursing home residents in Medicare and Medicaid facilities can gain access to their records. Similar protection is provided to patients in federal facilities such as Veterans' Administration hospitals.

PRIVACY ISSUES

Many states have laws designed to ensure privacy of a person's medical records by preventing their dissemination. Depending on your state, release of your medical information may be possible only if you give written consent.

Today, though, medical records may be stored on computers and information may be sent to doctors, hospitals and insurers over the Internet.

Doctors and hospitals try to ensure confidentiality of medical records by limiting access to their own computer files. But, there's always a danger that a "hacker" can gain access to this information.

What's more, doctors, hospitals and insurers routinely share medical information without your consent, particularly if it's for treatment or payment.

The federal government is currently grappling with exactly how to ensure privacy of medical records while allowing access when necessary.

Example: Should a drugstore filling a prescription have access to a patient's records so it can check for potentially adverse reactions to other prescriptions? Proposed federal regulations on the topic have resulted in a wide range of comments. Expect that we haven't heard the last on this issue.

Also from Charles Inlander...

When Doctors Don't Agree

If doctors' opinions conflict, ask each for the source of his/her advice. Research your condition, and discuss the results with each doctor. Tell them you have conflicting opinions. If you still can't decide, get a third opinion. Consider paying for it yourself if your insurance will not cover it—a small, but important, investment in your health.

More from Charles Inlander...

Is Your Doctor Board Certified?

Family practitioners are increasingly likely to fail their board-recertification tests. Doctors must be recertified every five to 10 years—depending on the specialty—to make sure their skills and knowledge are up to date. In 1998, the failure rate for family practitioners jumped from 4% to 8%. *Self-defense:* To verify a doctor's board certification, contact the American Board of Medical Specialties, 866-275-2267, *www.abms.org.*

How to Do Your Own Medical Research

Your own medical research may lead you to the latest treatments or new options that your doctor may not know about—and the facilities best equipped to treat your condition.

•**Learn basics about the disease** from a good medical dictionary or textbook at a library.

•**Ask a medical librarian** to help locate summaries and abstracts of journal articles that you can print out.

•**Computer users at home can get free access to journal references and abstracts from the National Library of Medicine databases** through PubMed on its Web site *www.ncbi.nlm.nih.gov.*

•**Use your new knowledge to discuss treatment options with your doctor.**

Suzanne McInerney, coauthor, *Infomedicine—A Consumer's Guide to the Latest Medical Research.* Little, Brown. She credits her research with saving the life of her cancer-afflicted mother.

Get Acquainted With Your Doctor

After choosing an HMO primary-care doctor, set up a "get-acquainted" appointment. If you have a chronic ailment, ask how much experience he/she has treating it and how readily he will refer you to a specialist. Trust your instincts—if you don't have confidence in a doctor when you're healthy, odds are you won't like him when you're sick. Most HMOs will pay for the appointment.

Alan Steinberg, MD, an internist in private practice in Marina del Rey, CA. He is author of *The Insider's Guide to HMOs.* Plume.

How to See a Specialist Faster

To get an appointment with a specialist sooner, tell the receptionist at the specialist's office that you are feeling anxious about your condition. If this does not work, emphasize that your primary-care physician wants you to be seen by the specialist quickly. If this still does not work, ask your primary-care doctor to make the appointment for you. If your own doctor cannot get a prompt appointment, call the specialist and ask for a referral to someone who is more readily available. This will often work, since doctors do not want to lose patients.

Susan A. Albrecht, PhD, RN, is associate professor, University of Pittsburgh School of Nursing.

It Pays to Find a Good Chiropractor... Here's How...

Timothy McCall, MD, a Boston internist and author of *Examining Your Doctor: A Patient's Guide to Avoiding Harmful Medical Care.* Citadel Press.

When I was attending medical school in the early 1980s, I was taught to view chiropractic with a great deal of skepticism. Instructors argued that chiropractors didn't do their patients much good and that chiropractic manipulation of the neck could lead to stroke.

I now know that my instructors were off base. The truth is that chiropractic manipulation is of proven benefit for musculoskeletal problems, including neck and back pain. And in the very rare cases in which the manipulation causes stroke, the cause isn't chiropractic itself. It's a bad chiropractor. Just as MDs vary in quality, so do DCs (doctors of chiropractic). And as with MDs, you need to be on the lookout for DCs who seem primarily interested in making money.

If you're looking for a first-rate chiropractor, I recommend seeking out one who:

•**Spends enough time with each patient.** Like many medical doctors, some chiropractors shuttle rapidly from one exam room to another, spending only a few minutes with each patient. According to Dr. Scott Haldeman, a University of California professor who is both an MD and a DC, chiropractors and doctors alike should see no more than 40 patients a day. Some practitioners see double that. It's impossible to provide good care at such a rapid pace.

●**Lets you set your own schedule for treatments.** In an effort to drum up business, some chiropractors tell their patients that they must return two or three times a week—or risk permanent disability. Such scare tactics are inappropriate. There's no risk with scheduling chiropractic visits less frequently.

●**Is honest about your course of treatment.** Watch out for chiropractors who say you'll need to continue treatment indefinitely. If chiropractic is going to be helpful, Dr. Haldeman says, you should see results within the first four visits. In no case should you sign a contract for a specified number of visits. Pay for one visit at a time.

●**Takes it easy on X rays.** Some chiropractors X-ray their patients as part of each visit. Others refuse to accept X rays taken by medical doctors. Yet for most people with back pain of short duration, X rays aren't of any value. And each X ray exposes you to radiation and costs you money.

●**Does *not* sell dietary supplements.** Vitamins and other nutritional supplements are helpful for certain conditions, and many patients like the convenience of being able to buy pills directly from a chiropractor. But I don't think any chiropractor or physician should be selling supplements to his or her patients. Some patients feel pressured to buy products they don't really want just to maintain a good relationship with the practitioner.

●**Is willing to refer you to a physician when appropriate.** When the diagnosis is in doubt, when you've had unexplained weight loss or other worrisome symptoms—or if you seem to be getting worse despite treatment—your chiropractor should suggest a medical evaluation.

The above are really just rules of thumb. Some otherwise excellent chiropractors, for example, may sell supplements. But the more warning signs a chiropractor exhibits, the greater the chance you're seeing the wrong kind of manipulator.

What You Can Do to Protect Yourself and Your Family

Leo Galland, MD, director of The Foundation for Integrated Medicine, 133 E. 73 St., Suite 308, New York City 10021. He is author of *Power Healing*. Random House.

These days, doctors spend little time with patients, especially those patients who are under managed care. So there are bound to be symptoms of illness or injury doctors either miss or dismiss. Some of these symptoms, however, are signs of serious ailments.

Here are five common—and potentially serious—complaints that may signal serious disease...

FATIGUE: ANGINA

When I say "fatigue," I'm not referring to the lethargy one feels after a bad night's sleep. I mean a sudden and sustained change in your energy level.

You may first notice it when exercising—finding it hard to complete your usual regimen or possibly suffering shortness of breath. Such an episode may last 20 to 60 minutes. Episodic fatigue in someone over age 40 could be caused by silent angina—clogging of the arteries in the heart, but without the telltale pain of regular angina, when the heart muscle is deprived of blood. Silent angina can kill.

What to do: Insist on an *exercise* stress test, which can detect blockages based on changes in the electrocardiogram. If the results are unclear, request a *thallium stress test*, in which a radioactive solution is injected into your system and follows the blood flow in the heart.

Angina treatment: There are many options —the best one depends on the individual.

RECURRENT SORE THROAT: REFLUX

When recurrent sore throat, cough or hoarse voice are not linked to a cold, influenza, allergies or strep, it could be *atypical esophageal reflux.* Typically, esophageal reflux appears as indigestion. But the continued irritation of the throat and larynx could produce a persistent cough, soreness or hoarseness.

Chronic reflux increases the risk of esophageal cancer. If reflux enters the lungs, asthma may result.

What to do: Ask your doctor about taking an acid-lowering drug, such as Prilosec or Prevacid. If it helps, your problem is likely reflux.

If neither of these drugs helps, it still could be reflux—or some other problem. You may need to undergo laryngoscopy. In this outpatient procedure, a doctor examines your throat and larynx using a very tiny camera-tipped viewing tube inserted through the mouth.

Reflux treatment: Beyond acid-lowering drugs, eating small-portion, low-fat meals may help...as may taking a dose of chewable calcium, such as Tums, with meals and at bedtime. *Also:* Don't eat within three to four hours of going to bed...and relax when you eat, rather than eating on the run.

SNORING: SLEEP APNEA

Snoring is a concern if it is loud enough to disturb others...it occurs at least three times a week...you feel tired and have memory lapses during the day. It results from trying to breathe with a partially blocked passageway. Heavy snoring is associated with obesity, high blood pressure and heart disease.

If your heart is healthy, you may be suffering from obstructive sleep apnea, in which you briefly stop breathing altogether—for a few seconds—repeatedly throughout the night. It occurs when the throat relaxes too much and closes on itself—blocking the passage of air, thereby waking up the individual. The result is a lack of oxygen to the brain and heart, which increases risk of stroke.

What to do: Ask your doctor for a referral to a sleep specialist, who will monitor your breathing while you sleep.

Sleep apnea treatment: Lose weight...elevate the head of your bed...and wear a device to maintain an open airway. If necessary, there are also a variety of successful surgical techniques.

MEMORY LOSS: HYPOTHYROIDISM...DEPRESSION

Doctors may dismiss memory loss and difficulty concentrating as a result of stress or, in menopausal women, low estrogen levels. But they can be symptomatic of hypothyroidism (underactive thyroid) or depression.

Underactive thyroid can produce weight gain, raise cholesterol levels and increase heart disease risk. Severe depression can lead to suicide...and depressed people tend to take poorer care of their health, so their prognosis for various health conditions is worse than normal.

What to do: Insist on a blood test to measure the thyroid-stimulating hormone, which is elevated when the thyroid is underactive. Possible depression requires assessment by a skilled professional.

Hypothyroidism treatment: Thyroid hormone.

Depression treatment: A combination of medication and psychological therapy. Many effective antidepressants are now available.

DIGESTIVE DISORDERS: PARASITES

Diarrhea, constipation, gas and bloating are often blamed on "nervous stomach" or irritable bowel syndrome. But they may be due to an intestinal parasite, which can be lethal. The problem is more likely to be parasitic if it develops suddenly in someone who previously had normal bowel movements...or it seems to be linked to travel or an episode of food poisoning.

What to do: Don't accept irritable bowel syndrome as a diagnosis—especially if you've never had bowel problems before. Irritable bowel syndrome typically develops in adolescence or young adulthood. Ask your doctor to have a sample of your stool evaluated by a lab specializing in tropical medicine. Sometimes more than one specimen needs to be examined.

Parasite treatment: There are several types of antibiotics, depending on the parasite.

How to Keep Your Medical Records Private

Rosemary Gafner, EdD, cofounder and president of Medical Risk Management, a Houston-based consulting firm that advises doctors on risk management.

The new technologies that make communication easier also make it more likely that information about your health will wind up in the wrong hands.

Examples: Confidential lab results are faxed to a patient's office…a doctor leaves sensitive information on voice mail or an answering machine…via computer, an insurer is sent a full medical file, not just information relevant to a claim.

Every patient is vulnerable, but three sets of people face heightened risk…

●**Anyone whose medical file contains information about a family history of serious illness.** You could be fired, overlooked for promotion or lose your health insurance coverage if these data are disclosed.

●**People seeing psychiatrists or taking antidepressants.** In the wrong hands, this information could alter your company's impression of you, limit your chances for promotion or become the object of office gossip.

●**Women trying to get pregnant.** This information could be used by your company to trigger an early transfer to a less desirable job in anticipation of your maternity leave.

PRIVACY PROTECTION STEPS

●**Set privacy standards with your doctor.** Request that notes for specific treatments be kept separate from your general medical chart. This will prevent the most sensitive information from being routinely transmitted with insurance claims.

The only information a doctor is obligated to disclose to a health insurer is a diagnosis—not a patient history.

●**Review your medical record with your doctor.** Ask about anything you don't understand. Identify incorrect information…have him/her correct the record…and talk to him about what information can be disclosed—and to whom.

●**Request that lab results not be left on voice mail or answering machines.** Office voice mail can be accessed by others. Messages left on home answering machines can be overheard.

Make sure your wishes regarding notification of lab results are recorded on your medical chart.

Best: Insist that the information be given out only when you call the doctor's office.

Don't be offended if your doctor's assistant asks you to verify your identity.

●**Be wary of communicating by E-mail.** Increasingly, patients and doctors are using E-mail to discuss medical questions and to report test results. Unfortunately, this communication is not secure.

It is possible, though unlikely, that the message could be intercepted by a hacker or monitored by an employee in your company's computer department.

A more likely scenario is that a colleague or friend will pass by your computer screen and read a message that you do not want him to see.

Self-defense: Use E-mail only to make appointments or request notification when test results arrive. Provide no details about the reasons for tests or appointments in your message.

INSURANCE PROTECTION

●**Amend medical release forms at doctors' offices.** When you want your doctor to file insurance claims for you, you are asked to sign a form authorizing release of medical information.

What to do: Note on the form that your authorization is limited to one year.

That lets you review your records with your doctor annually and refresh your memory about changes in your health status over the past year. Keeping up-to-date will facilitate any explanations you may need to make to your insurer should it question a claim.

You can specifically exclude certain medical information—such as sensitive lab tests or psychiatrist's notes—and request that they not be divulged without your permission.

There are no penalties for this. If your insurer needs additional information, it will ask your doctor for the information and your doctor can contact you.

Doctor's Bill Alert

Are you on Medicare and received a bill from a doctor demanding payment? Before paying, make sure you owe the money.

Under Medicare, health-care providers are responsible for submitting timely and correct claims. If the doctor goofs—fails to submit a claim or submits a claim with your incorrect Medicare number—the doctor, not you, is responsible for the bill.

If you're dunned by the doctor for payment under these circumstances, don't be fooled into paying what you don't owe.

Added protection: Report your doctor's illegal collection activity to the Medicare Fraud hot line at 800-MEDICARE.

Note: You should be on the alert that the claim was not being processed if you haven't received a "Medicare Benefits Notice" or an "Explanation of Medicare Benefits" within 45 days of the filing of the claim. So if you haven't received one, this should tip you off to the fact that no claim (or one with an incorrect Medicare number for you) was submitted.

Charles Inlander, president, People's Medical Society, 462 Walnut St., Allentown, PA 18102. He is author of *This Won't Hurt (And Other Lies My Doctor Tells Me).* People's Medical Society.

Be Sure to Get Medical Test Results

Do not accept being told that the doctor's office will call if there is a problem. Sometimes failure to call means someone forgot. Ask your doctor to let you know when to expect test results—and follow up if you hear nothing within a reasonable time after the test.

Consumer Reports on Health, 101 Truman Ave., Yonkers, NY 10703.

EKGs and Heart Attack

After a heart attack, be sure to obtain a copy of your electrocardiogram (EKG).

Reason: Postattack, the EKG pattern permanently changes in a way that indicates where and how much of the heart has been damaged. Physicians will need to see this EKG to properly interpret a subsequent one. Comparing the two, they will be able to tell if the heart has undergone post–heart-attack changes —or if a second attack is under way.

Helpful: Ask for a wallet-sized copy of the post–heart-attack EKG when leaving the hospital. Carry it always.

Neil L. Kao, MD, an internist and allergist in private practice in Peoria, Illinois. His advice was published in the *Journal of the American Medical Association,* 515 N. State St., Chicago 60610.

Pill-Splitting Cuts Costs

Three major HMOs—Foundation Health Systems, Kaiser Permanente and United HealthCare—are asking members who use certain medications to buy higher-dose pills and split them. Savings can be considerable, since high-dose pills often cost about the same as low-dose ones. But some doctors and pharmacists warn against splitting…and not all pills can be split—only ones that are "scored." Ask your doctor or pharmacist if pill-splitting is appropriate for you.

Susan C. Winckler, RPh, group director, policy and advocacy, American Pharmaceutical Association, Washington, DC.

 # Blood Pressure Trap

Hidden high blood pressure is high at most times but reads low at the doctor's office. If office readings are 20 points or more below the "normal" cutoff of 140/90, you're probably okay. If in-office readings are 120/70 or above—and you have a family history of cardiovascular disease, are obese or sedentary or have other risk factors—ask your doctor about at-home monitoring.

Wolfgang Linden, PhD, professor of psychology, University of British Columbia, Vancouver.

Patient and Doctor Confidentiality

Many doctors bend insurance rules so patients who need treatment can have their care covered. Almost 40% of doctors confided to researchers that they have manipulated insurance rules in some way. *Example:* Some doctors exaggerate symptom severity so patients can spend extra time recovering in a hospital. The study did not deal with deception to increase doctors' revenue—only to improve patient care.

Survey of 720 doctors by *American Medical Association's Institute for Ethics*, reported in *The Journal of the American Medical Association*, 515 N. State St., Chicago 60610.

Customizing Medications

Medications can be customized with doctor's approval to meet patients' needs. *Example:* If you cannot tolerate an oral medication, such as ibuprofen, a compounding pharmacist sometimes can prepare suppositories or transdermal (skin) gels.

When compounding may help: For a dosage that is not commercially available …more natural formulation, such as for hormone-replacement therapy…better-tasting version…one that has no dye, lactose, preservative, etc. *Drawback:* Few health insurers cover compounded medications. *To find a compounding pharmacist:* Ask your doctor…or contact International Academy of Compounding Pharmacists, 800-927-4227, or Professional Compounding Centers of America, 800-331-2498.

Robert GiaQuinto, RPh, pharmacist/owner, Rye Beach Pharmacy, Rye, NY.

3

Simple Treatments for Common Ailments

Hay Fever Self-Defense... How to Stop the Misery

If you're among the 20 million Americans who suffer from sneezing, congestion, runny nose and itchy eyes—perhaps also headaches, earaches, fatigue and moodiness—the first thing you need is a diagnosis.

Your doctor should start by ruling out other causes of your symptoms, such as nasal polyps or sinus infection. After that, he/she can usually diagnose hay fever based on your medical history—when your symptoms typically appear and disappear.

Note: Hay fever doesn't normally cause fever. Hay fever symptoms plus fever could mean a sinus infection or another infection.

If you have hay fever, these proven strategies will help eliminate your symptoms...

REDUCE POLLEN EXPOSURE

The most common cause of hay fever is an allergy to ragweed pollen. But pollen from cocklebur, lamb's-quarters, pigweed and other weeds that bloom in summer and fall causes comparable symptoms. West of the Rockies, hay fever symptoms stem mainly from sagebrush, saltbush and sheep sorrel pollen.

Best defenses...

●**Keep windows closed at home**—and in your car.

●**Use an air conditioner to filter out pollen.** Change the filter as often as the manufacturer suggests...or when it looks dirty.

●**Since pollen levels peak in early morning,** save your outdoor activities for after 10 a.m. Listen for pollen counts on the news.

●**Have someone else do outdoor chores.** Even if offending plants don't grow in your vicinity, pollen can travel 500 miles.

Stuart H. Young, MD, clinical associate professor of pediatrics and internal medicine at Mount Sinai School of Medicine, and an allergist in private practice, both in New York City. He is coauthor of Allergies: The Complete Guide to Diagnosis, Treatment and Daily Management. *Plume. For more on allergies and asthma, see Dr. Young's Web site at* www.nyallergy-asthma.com.

•**Eliminate pollen-carrying plants from your yard.**

•**If you are extremely allergic and are outdoors for long periods,** shower and shampoo when you go back in. Put clothes directly into the washing machine or hamper. Washing helps keep pollen out of your house.

•**If you have severe hay fever,** consider wearing a simple filter mask while outdoors. The masks are sold at home-improvement and hardware stores. They must fit snugly over your nose and mouth.

AVOID OTHER IRRITANTS

You can also help curb hay fever by avoiding three other respiratory irritants…

•**Alcohol.** Alcoholic beverages increase nasal congestion in hay fever sufferers. During hay fever season, keep alcohol consumption to a minimum. Better yet—avoid alcohol altogether.

•**Diesel exhaust.** It contains compounds that exacerbate hay fever. Diesel exhaust plus pollen can produce an allergic response that is significantly greater than the response to ragweed alone.

Also—give trucks and buses a wide berth when you're walking on the street. Many have diesel engines.

•**Ozone.** If the air quality index—which forecasts ozone pollution—is poor, stay inside as much as possible. Ozone exacerbates hay fever.

TAKE MEDICATION

If symptoms persist despite your taking these precautions, prescription medication is often helpful…

•**Prescription antihistamines** are usually first choice. Over-the-counter allergy medications tend to make you sleepy.

Best prescriptions: *Loratadine* (Claritin) and *fexofenadine* (Allegra). They relieve all allergy symptoms except congestion—without causing drowsiness.

Caution: Women of childbearing age should request loratadine. Recent studies have shown that it may be safer than fexofenadine during pregnancy.

For mild, intermittent symptoms, take these medicines as needed. For daily symptoms, take the medicine regularly throughout hay fever season.

If you also suffer from runny nose and congestion, Claritin-D and Allegra-D may be the best prescriptions. They contain the decongestant *pseudoephedrine.*

•**Steroid nasal sprays** such as *fluticasone* (Flonase) or *budesonide* (Rhinocort) are best if your only symptom is nasal congestion.

They are sometimes used in conjunction with decongestants.

Bonus: Steroid sprays are safer than cortisone pills because they work directly on affected nasal membranes. Oral steroids cause many side effects, including high blood pressure, cataracts, ulcers and osteoporosis. They are used only in severe cases when other treatments have failed.

Downside: Irritation of nasal membranes. Point the nozzle slightly away from the delicate septum.

•**Nasal saline sprays** rinse the nose and reduce inflammation. All brands are about equal.

ALLERGY SHOTS

Most hay fever sufferers don't need allergy shots. But shots may be helpful if symptoms are so severe that you require cortisone medication regularly during the season…if your allergies last beyond ragweed season…or if you also have asthma or allergies other than hay fever that give you year-round symptoms.

Sensitivity tests generally reveal which allergens are causing the problem. The doctor applies a small drop of different allergens to the skin, scratches the skin with a tiny needle, then waits 20 minutes for a mosquito bite–like reaction.

The tests help determine appropriate treatment. You could receive small injections of an allergen (allergy-triggering substance) in gradually increasing doses weekly for up to two years. This eventually desensitizes you to that allergen.

New Cold Remedy

Proven way to help get rid of colds—zinc nasal gel. *Zicam* reduces the duration of a common cold from about nine days to two if taken at the onset. It relieves nasal congestion, coughs, etc. *Cost:* About $9 for half an ounce—enough for three colds. Available over the counter.

Michael Hirt, MD, assistant clinical professor of medicine, University of California, Los Angeles. His recent study of 213 patients was published in the journal *Ear, Nose and Throat*.

Flu Prevention

New flu drug may be a lifesaver in case of a widespread flu epidemic.

In a recent study, *oseltamivir* (Tamiflu) kept 74% of adults who did not receive a flu shot from getting the illness.

One of a class of drugs known as *neuraminidase* inhibitors, oseltamivir blocks replication of the influenza virus. Oseltamivir is already used to treat flu. It could be available for flu prevention soon.

Frederick G. Hayden, MD, professor of internal medicine and pathology, University of Virginia School of Medicine, Charlottesville.

Stop Feeling Tired: Hidden Causes of Chronic Fatigue And How to Vanquish Them

Benjamin Natelson, MD, professor of neurosciences at the University of Medicine and Dentistry—New Jersey Medical School, and director of the New Jersey Chronic Fatigue Syndrome Center (800-248-8005), both in Newark. He is author of *Facing and Fighting Fatigue—A Practical Approach*. Yale University Press.

Fatigue is one of the leading reasons why Americans see their doctors. Unfortunately, it is also one of the most undertreated ailments in the US.

Problem: If doctors cannot diagnose a specific illness as the cause of fatigue—a virus, for example—they frequently dismiss their patients' complaints.

Good news: Fatigue is typically caused by a treatable condition, such as sleep deprivation, ongoing psychological stress or depression. In rare cases, it can be caused by *chronic fatigue syndrome* (CFS).

If you eat a nutritious diet and are in otherwise good health—but still feel sapped of energy for more than six weeks—here's what to do...

IS DISEASE TO BLAME?

The first step is to rule out any underlying illness. To do this, your doctor should order blood tests for anemia...diabetes...hepatitis and other liver disorders...infectious mononucleosis...lupus...Lyme disease...rheumatoid arthritis...and thyroid deficiency.

You should also undergo a *creatine phosphokinase* (CPK) test of muscle chemistry...a test for low magnesium...and a "sed rate" (sedimentation rate) analysis to check for general inflammation of body tissues.

If the results are normal, your doctor should perform a test of *dehydroepiandrosterone* (DHEA)—a hormone produced in the adrenal glands.

Chronic sinusitis—an ongoing sinus infection that causes facial pain, nasal discharge and recurring sinus headaches—is another cause of fatigue. If you have these symptoms, ask your doctor for a CT scan of the sinuses.

COMMON CULPRITS

If no specific illness is detected, you and your doctor should focus on three key areas...

•**Sleep habits.** If you snore—or sleep lightly for much of the night—you may have a breathing disorder known as *sleep apnea*. This condition causes repeated awakenings and prevents deep, restful sleep.

If you suspect snoring is the problem, ask your doctor about breathing aids, including adhesive strips such as BreatheRight, medications and nasal sprays. If the more serious diagnosis of sleep apnea is possible, consider consulting a sleep clinic.

If you have trouble falling—or staying—asleep, you may have poor "sleep hygiene." Avoid caffeine after lunchtime and try to wake up at the same time each morning.

●**Stress.** Even minor stress—such as getting stuck at a red light when you're late—can drain your energy. If your daily activities include such stresses, you may be exhausted at the end of the day.

Your doctor should also discuss your lifestyle to detect a stress pattern. A stress-management program can help you cope.

●**Depression.** This is the most overlooked cause of persistent fatigue. Unless symptoms are severe, many people who are depressed never realize what's wrong with them.

Good news: Depression usually subsides when treated with psychotherapy and antidepressants—such as *selective serotonin reuptake inhibitors* (SSRIs), including *fluoxetine* (Prozac) and *sertraline* (Zoloft).

If both depression and insomnia are present, a sedating antidepressant, such as *amitriptyline* (Elavil), may be preferable.

DIAGNOSING CHRONIC FATIGUE

If these measures do not help, you may have CFS. This disorder, which affects approximately 2% of Americans, is suspected when a lack of energy interferes with personal, professional or social activities.

CFS is typically diagnosed if you have four or more of the following symptoms for at least six months…

Fatigue that lasts more than 24 hours following physical activity…impaired short-term memory…muscle or joint pain…recurring headaches…sore throat…tender lymph glands …waking up tired in the morning, even after a full night's sleep.

Although medical experts have not identified the causes of CFS, possible triggers include…

●**Fibromyalgia.** This illness is marked by chronic muscle and joint pain, but some fibromyalgia patients also experience severe, chronic fatigue.

Treatment: Pain management with *gabapentin* (Neurontin), *hydromorphone* (Dilaudid) or another medication.

●**Infection.** Many cases of CFS begin with fever, sore throat or swollen or tender lymph glands—all of which suggest an infection.

Treatment: Antibiotics if the infection is bacterial.

●**Premenstrual syndrome** (PMS). Eighty-five percent of CFS sufferers are female. Because PMS exacerbates fatigue, some experts believe it may contribute to CFS.

Treatment: SSRI antidepressants, such as *paroxetine* (Paxil) and *sertraline* (Zoloft).

TREATING CHRONIC FATIGUE

Regardless of what's triggering your CFS, a specialist* is likely to focus on two aspects of treatment that may surprise you…

●**Aerobic exercise.** It can enhance sleep, increase metabolic activity, reduce stress and relieve depression. Begin with easy walking —no faster than a slow stroll—three times a week for five minutes at a time. Build up to at least 20 minutes of walking each day.

●**Cognitive-behavioral therapy.** Dwelling on how tired you are actually increases stress and fatigue.

A trained cognitive-behavioral therapist can help you reduce CFS symptoms. It often takes just one or two sessions to identify "catastrophic" thinking—*My life is terrible. I can't do anything.* This therapy helps you focus on a more positive appraisal—*I can handle this. My fatigue lessens from time to time.*

Other treatments include…

●**Drug therapy.** There is no drug treatment for CFS. But *ondansetron* (Zofran), an antinausea drug that boosts levels of the neurotransmitter serotonin, is undergoing clinical trials. Some reports suggest it may help ease CFS.

●**Supplements.** Magnesium and/or DHEA supplements may also help if patients are deficient in them.

*To locate a chronic fatigue specialist, contact a university-affiliated medical center in your area to find an internist or infectious-disease physician who sees CFS patients in his/her practice. Or contact the Chronic Fatigue Immune Dysfunction Syndrome Association of America, 800-442-3437, *www.cfids.org*.

Restless Legs Relief

An unpleasant tingling sensation in the legs, *restless legs syndrome* (RLS) can make it difficult to fall asleep and stay asleep. *To ease symptoms...*

- **Massage legs before bed.**

- **Take a warm bath.**

- **Apply a heating pad.**

- **Avoid caffeine, nicotine and alcohol.**

- **Exercise regularly.**

- **Try meditation, yoga or another relaxation technique.**

If these approaches don't work, see your doctor about medication.

Barbara Phillips, MD, director, sleep apnea center, Samaritan Hospital, Lexington, Kentucky. For more on RLS, send a self-addressed, stamped, business-sized envelope to the RLS Foundation, Box 7050, Rochester, MN 55903.

New Drugs for Bone Damage

Bone and joint damage caused by rheumatoid arthritis (RA) is lessened by a newly approved combination drug therapy. After one year on both *methotrexate* (Rheumatrex) and *infliximab* (Remicade), 52% of RA patients reported a reduction in symptoms. Only 17% of those on methotrexate alone reported such an improvement. The drug combination, taken once every four to eight weeks, reduced joint tenderness and swelling and improved quality of life.

Peter E. Lipsky, MD, professor of internal medicine and microbiology, University of Texas Southwestern Medical Center, Dallas.

High Blood Pressure and Calcium Loss

High blood pressure hastens bone loss by promoting calcium excretion. A recent study of 3,676 elderly women found that those with the highest systolic pressure (the upper number) lost almost twice as much bone mass each year as did those with the lowest systolic pressure. Women with high systolic pressure should ask a doctor about implementing dietary and lifestyle changes to lower pressure. Changes include reducing salt and animal protein intake, eating more fruits and vegetables and doing weight-bearing exercise. Drugs may also be needed.

Francesco P. Cappuccio, MD, reader in preventive cardiovascular medicine, St. George's Hospital Medical School, London. His study was published in The Lancet, 42 Bedford Sq., London WC1B 3SL.

New Options for Migraine Relief

Fred Sheftell, MD, director and founder of The New England Center for Headache in Stamford, CT, and national president of the American Council for Headache Education. He is coauthor of Conquering Headache. Decker.

Twenty-eight million Americans suffer from migraines. But fewer than half receive treatment for the pain.

Trap: Because migraine symptoms are so varied, many doctors fail to give the proper diagnosis, much less prescribe appropriate treatment.

As a result, migraine sufferers often rely on over-the-counter painkillers, such as *acetaminophen* (Tylenol) or *ibuprofen* (Advil).

These may relieve mild pain, but not moderate to severe pain. Taken too frequently or at a high dosage, these pain relievers can aggravate—rather than relieve—headache pain.

Good news: If you suffer from migraines, you can lessen the frequency and severity of your attacks by avoiding certain foods and getting enough exercise. In the case of severe migraines, prescription drugs can halt or even prevent the pain.

IS IT REALLY A MIGRAINE?

Migraines affect 6% of men and 18% of women. The migraine predisposition is inherited.

Fluctuations in the brain chemical *serotonin* trigger a migraine. These changes affect blood vessel activity, resulting in swollen, inflamed blood vessels.

Migraines last from four to 72 hours and are accompanied by nausea...vomiting... and/or sensitivity to light or sound. Migraines also cause at least two of the following symptoms—they occur on one side of the head... cause throbbing or pulsating pain...interfere with or restrict activity....worsen with physical activity.

Before diagnosing a migraine, your doctor must rule out any other possible causes of your headache—particularly high blood pressure or allergies. These conditions require separate treatment.

THE ROLE OF DIET

Foods that contain the amino acid *tyramine* can trigger migraine attacks by dilating blood vessels.

Sources include red wine, beer and dark-colored alcohol, such as scotch and bourbon...chocolate...nuts...bananas...onions... pizza...avocados...processed meats...pork... sour cream...pickled and fermented foods... and aged cheese.

The food additives *monosodium glutamate* (MSG), *hydrolyzed fat* and *hydrolyzed protein* can also result in migraines by causing fluid retention and blood vessel dilation. These are found in potato chips and canned foods.

Magnesium helps reduce the frequency of migraine attacks by stabilizing nerves that, when excited, can act as triggers. Migraine sufferers should be sure to eat plenty of foods that contain this mineral. Spinach and other green, leafy vegetables are good choices.

To ensure that you get enough magnesium: Ask your doctor about taking a daily 400-mg supplement. You may need to take magnesium for four months before seeing results.

Foods rich in vitamin B-2 (riboflavin)—broccoli, fish and dairy products—also help fight migraines. Riboflavin is thought to help by increasing the efficiency of *mitochondria*, the microscopic "power plants" inside the body's cells.

Consider taking a supplement containing 400 mg of vitamin B-2 each day. This dosage has been shown to decrease the frequency of migraines by more than 50%.

A doctor should supervise vitamin treatment taken at this high dosage. It takes three to four months to see results.

EXERCISE

Aerobic exercise improves blood flow to the brain and triggers the release of painkilling compounds called *endorphins.* After four months of regular exercise, migraine sufferers have fewer attacks.

Walk, bike or do some form of aerobic exercise for 30 to 40 minutes three or four days a week.

IS IT TIME FOR DRUG THERAPY?

Moderate to severe migraines often require drug therapy. The *right* medication—used at the first sign of a migraine attack—can relieve pain quickly.

"Triptans" are the best medications to stop migraines that do not respond to lifestyle changes.

●***Zolmitriptan* (Zomig)** tablets typically relieve pain in about 60 minutes. They also help prevent recurrences.

●***Sumatriptan* (Imitrex)** is available in the form of self-injection, nasal spray or tablet. The injection stops pain in an hour. The nasal spray and tablets take longer to work but are ideal for patients who dislike injections.

●***Naratriptan* (Amerge)** tablets relieve pain more slowly than zolmitriptan or sumatriptan tablets but are more effective at preventing recurrence.

●***Rizatriptan* (Maxalt)** is a tablet or wafer that dissolves on the tongue. Migraineurs who also suffer nausea often prefer the wafer. Rizatriptan may also work faster than other triptans.

Side effects: Fatigue, mild chest discomfort and tightness of the neck and shoulders can occur with any triptan. Injections tend to be faster-acting but more troublesome than tablets or wafers.

New triptans, such as *eletriptan* (Relpax), *almotriptan* (Axert) and *frovatriptan,* should hit the market soon. These stop recurring migraines better than existing triptans.

Warning: Triptans are off limits to people with coronary artery disease, uncontrolled high blood pressure (above 140/90) and individuals who have suffered a stroke. Those who smoke or have another risk factor for heart disease—obesity or total cholesterol above 220—must be monitored closely while taking these medications.

PREVENTIVE DRUGS

If triptans don't ease migraines within four hours, or if attacks are frequent, the next step is preventive medicine.

Everyone responds differently to these drugs, so work with your doctor to find the right medication for you. *They include...*

● **Beta-blockers.** *Atenolol* (Tenormin), *nadolol* (Corgard), *propranolol* (Inderal) and *timolol* (Blocadren).

● **Calcium-channel blockers.** *Verapamil* (Calan).

● **Antidepressants.** *Amitriptyline* (Elavil) and *nortriptyline* (Pamelor). *Fluoxetine* (Prozac), *paroxetine* (Paxil) and *sertraline* (Zoloft) are excellent for depression but less effective for headache.

● **Anticonvulsants.** *Divalproex* (Depakote).

● **Seratonin-2 antagonists.** *Cyproheptadine* (Periactin).

● **Alpha-2-adrenoceptor agonists.** *Clonidine* (Catapres).

● **Pain relievers/sedatives.** Aspirin or acetaminophen, caffeine and a mild sedative (Fiorinal or Fioricet).

TRACKING MIGRAINE SYMPTOMS

Migraine symptoms and your response to treatment can vary. To help you—and your doctor—identify patterns, keep a headache diary.

Record the duration of each migraine...any medication you take...severity of the pain on a scale of 1 (least) to 10 (greatest)...and the degree of relief.

Migraines are often triggered by specific events, such as emotional upset...skipping a meal...weather changes...flickering or bright lights...sleep changes.

Record any triggers and try to avoid them.

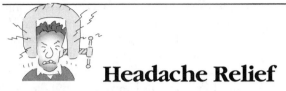

Headache Relief

When a headache starts, keep moving. Exercise produces painkilling endorphins and relieves stress. *Also:* Drink a caffeinated beverage to speed absorption of aspirin...massage your head and neck. *Guided imagery*—close your eyes...imagine water moving over you on a sunny beach, the waves easing tension. When you relax, picture your headache as an object. Turn it into liquid—and let it pour through your fingers.

Roger Cady, MD, is director of Headache Care Center, Springfield, MO.

Little-Known Causes of Stomach Upset

Charlene Prather, MD, associate professor of medicine and gastroenterology, St. Louis University School of Medicine.

● **Antacids.** Some brands contain magnesium, which causes diarrhea by shunting water into the intestines. Other brands contain aluminum, which causes constipation.

Self-defense: Take just enough antacid to ease stomach upset. Alternate between magnesium- and aluminum-based brands.

● **Fatty foods.** Fats slow the passage of food through the stomach and intestines. This can cause nausea and cramps.

Self-defense: Avoid fatty foods...chew cardamom seeds, a folk remedy for relieving an upset stomach.

● **Fruit.** Apples, mangoes, oranges, peaches, pears, etc., contain fructose, a sugar that can lead to bloating.

Self-defense: Spread your five fruit servings throughout the day—so you won't get all of your fructose at once.

●**Politeness.** Stifling a belch can cause painful gas buildup.

Self-defense: Belch when you must—quietly and away from others. Limit gas by avoiding carbonated beverages and the use of straws, which can cause you to swallow air.

●**Sugarless gum.** Many brands contain sorbitol, xylitol or mannitol, artificial sweeteners that promote growth of gas-causing colon bacteria.

Self-defense: Have no more than three sticks of gum per day.

●**Whole grains.** Too much fiber can cause constipation, intestinal gas and bloating.

Self-defense: When increasing fiber intake, do so slowly to give your body time to adjust. Drink eight to 10 glasses of water daily.

Bad Back Pain

Michael S. Sinel, MD, assistant clinical professor of medicine, University of California, Los Angeles Medical Center, and a spine specialist in private practice in Beverly Hills. He is coauthor of *Win the Battle Against Back Pain: An Integrated Mind-Body Approach.* Dell.

Back pain is often blamed on a herniated disk or another anatomical problem. Yet about 85% of all cases stem from nonanatomical causes—psychological stress, depression, anxiety or anger...or being in poor physical condition.

Consequently, the remedy for back pain usually isn't bed rest or surgery. *It's improving emotional and physical conditioning...*

●**Start a diary.** Just days after experiencing physical pain or emotions, it's hard to remember them accurately. Keeping a pain-activity-mood-medication (PAMM) diary helps.

Every waking hour, rate your pain from 0 (no pain) to 10 (worst pain imaginable). Also rate your moods from 0 (feeling great) to 10 (severe emotional distress). Simultaneously,

record any medicine you take and any activity—whether it's "fighting with spouse" or "can't sleep."

Periodically review this diary to help identify what situations and reactions lead to pain ...and act to avoid them.

●**Evaluate your personality.** Certain traits are linked to psychological stress...and to back pain. They include extreme self-discipline, strong drive to succeed, perfectionist and compulsive tendencies and harsh self-criticism. *If you have any of these traits, strive to temper them.*

●**Recognize and reprogram negative thoughts.** People under psychological stress often give in to irrational negative thoughts. These produce depression, anxiety and fear—as well as back pain.

In stressful situations, identify negative thoughts like "I'll never get better at this job," and practice changing them to coping thoughts —"I'm doing better than a week ago."

The same goes for thoughts about back pain. Change "I'll never lose this pain" to "The pain isn't so bad anymore."

●**Talk back to your brain.** Tell it that you're not going to take the pain anymore. Put up "pain gates"—defenses that shut out pain.

Examples: Distract yourself with a hobby or call a friend.

●**Feel the anger.** Hit a pillow or yell in a room by yourself. By keeping anger inside, you cause muscle tension that can lead to back pain.

●**Learn a relaxation technique.** Relaxation in any form can offer stress relief. But formal relaxation techniques are more effective for handling stressful situations. They decrease heart and breathing rates, blood pressure and muscle tension.

Learn deep breathing...progressive relaxation...meditation...or imagery (visualizing peaceful situations or enjoyable activities).

Buy a book or audiotape to master one of these techniques. Then use the technique in times of stress to fend off back pain.

●**Talk to a psychotherapist.** Counseling fosters positive attitudes that help prevent back pain.

●**Change your job.** Stress at work and job dissatisfaction can trigger back pain. Find a less stressful, more rewarding job...or improve the one you have. Alter your hours or duties.

●**Find purpose.** Don't let pain be the center of your life. The more purpose you have in life—the more things you care about—the less pain you'll have.

●**Set concrete goals.** Build short-term, achievable goals into every area of life. Daily success eases stress and builds good feelings that help prevent back pain.

Examples: Tell yourself you'll make 10 sales today...or do something nice for your spouse.

●**Improve fitness.** Regular low-impact aerobic exercise is vital. Just 30 minutes every other day of brisk walking, swimming, water aerobics or recumbent stationary bicycling (easier on the back than upright bicycling) reduces levels of stress hormones and triggers the release of pain-relieving endorphins.

Combined with weight training, aerobic exercise also strengthens muscles that support the back. If you have severe back pain, keep away from high-impact sports, like football and basketball, as well as such sports as racquetball or golf that require sudden pivoting or twisting.

●**Do back exercises.** An orthopedist, physiatrist (physician who specializes in the diagnosis and nonsurgical treatment of musculoskeletal disorders) or physical therapist can suggest exercises to strengthen back and abdominal muscles—which help support the spine.

Also ask the doctor or physical therapist for slow stretching exercises to improve flexibility.

●**Maintain proper weight.** Being overweight increases stress on every body structure, including the back.

A protruding stomach, in particular, burdens the lower back, making it more susceptible to injury.

●**Lift things properly.** We've all heard about the proper way to lift a heavy object. Bend at the knees, not at the waist...hold the object close and push straight up with your legs so that they support most of the weight ...keep your spine straight as you lift...and never twist while lifting. If you have to turn in another direction, turn your entire body.

●**Sit down and stand up correctly.** When you stand, do a "pelvic tilt." With palms on the small of your back, slightly push your lower back inward and tilt your pelvis forward as you gradually extend your back upward.

To sit, move your tailbone as far back as possible above the chair, with your upper body tilting forward. Bring your upper body upright as you sit down.

●**Change position frequently.** Don't stand or sit in one position for long periods. If you have to stand still, lean against something. If you can, rest one foot on a stool or rail. Wear shoes with cushioned soles and low heels.

Long periods of sitting tax the lower back. Driving can be especially troublesome because road vibrations are transmitted to the spine. On car trips, stretch and walk around at least once an hour.

●**Use a good chair.** It should place your back in the proper position—maintaining the curve in your spine. If you can't get such a chair, roll up a towel and place it against the small of your back. Prop your feet on a footstool or large book.

●**Sleep on your side,** with hips and knees bent toward your body—as in the fetal position. Place a small pillow between your knees. If you must lie on your back, place pillows under your knees.

Vitamin C Fights Hypertension

A study of otherwise healthy people with high blood pressure, 80% of whom received antihypertensive medication, found that when they supplemented their diet with 500 mg of vitamin C daily, their average blood pressure fell from 155/87 to 142/79. Researchers suggest that people with moderate hypertension—up to160/90—take 500 mg a day of vitamin C in addition to their regular medicine, half in the morning and half at night. *Caution:* Lowering blood pressure may require a medication adjustment. Check with your doctor.

Balz Frei, PhD, director, Linus Pauling Institute, Oregon State University, Corvallis.

What to Take When You Can't Sleep

Robert E. Hales, MD, professor and chair of the department of psychiatry at the University of California, Davis, School of Medicine. A past president of the Association for Academic Psychiatry, Dr. Hales has coauthored or coedited 28 books on mental health, most recently *The Mind/Mood Pill Book*. Bantam.

If you're among the 40 million Americans who are troubled by insomnia, you probably already know about the importance of keeping regular bedtime and wake-up hours...avoiding late-afternoon or evening caffeine and alcohol...and forsaking reading or TV viewing while in bed.

Perhaps you have gone so far as to try over-the-counter sedatives. Unfortunately, these nonprescription drugs are seldom of much benefit. And they can cause unpleasant side effects, including dry mouth, blurred vision and constipation.

In most cases, herbal and/or prescription sleep aids help you fall asleep faster and stay asleep longer. And when used appropriately, they're quite safe.

Important: Before trying any sleep aid, you should be checked for an underlying cause of your sleeplessness, such as a prescribed medication, depression, anxiety or primary sleep disorder, such as obstructive sleep apnea —a potentially serious condition that causes you to wake up repeatedly.

If you have sleep apnea, *benzodiazepine* drugs or other sleep-inducing medications may further interfere with your breathing, and that can be life-threatening.

OCCASIONAL MILD INSOMNIA

The herbal remedies *valerian* and *kava kava* are often highly effective at curbing mild insomnia, which is defined as transient periods of disturbed sleep due to a major life event, such as a wedding, a relocation or a new job.

Unlike sedative hypnotic agents, such as the benzodiazepine *temazepam* (Restoril), valerian does not cause morning-after drowsiness or stomach upset. It can, however, cause headaches and restlessness.

Kava kava can cause grogginess the following morning, but it is often the best choice if you prefer a mild, sleep-enhancing over-the-counter preparation. Neither remedy is habit-forming.

Capsules and tea bags of valerian and kava kava are sold in health-food stores. Follow label directions carefully.

Caution: The Food and Drug Administration does not regulate herbal remedies. It's best to stick with brands found effective by friends or recommended by your pharmacist or doctor.

TROUBLE FALLING ASLEEP

If you frequently have trouble *falling* asleep, your best bet may be the nonbenzodiazepine drug *zolpidem* (Ambien). It typically works within 15 minutes. Zolpidem doesn't cause next-day grogginess, though it can cause diarrhea, nausea and dizziness.

Although zolpidem is not habit-forming, it may become less effective after several weeks of use and require a larger dose.

TROUBLE STAYING ASLEEP

The benzodiazepines temazepam (Restoril), *lorazepam* (Ativan) and *clonazepam* (Klonopin) are highly effective against early-morning awakenings. They stay in the body longer than zolpidem, approximately eight to 12 hours.

Like all benzodiazepines, these three drugs are addictive. They should be used for no more than two to three consecutive weeks, and then sporadically—only when you need help with your sleep. They are off-limits to current and former substance abusers.

Benzodiazepines also can cause rebound insomnia. If you go off one of the drugs abruptly after taking it for several weeks, you may experience one or two nights in which you have trouble falling asleep, wake up frequently and have nightmares.

To avoid this, gradually reduce your dose over the course of a week or two. This should be done in consultation with your doctor.

Side effects of benzodiazepines include next-day grogginess, nausea and dizziness.

CHRONIC SLEEP PROBLEMS

Chronic sleep problems often accompany depression. Doctors have found that the prescription antidepressant *trazodone* (Desyrel) —taken at a small dosage—often helps both conditions.

Trazodone is not habit-forming, although it can cause headaches, nausea and stomach upset.

Trazodone can increase the blood levels of the heart drug *digoxin* (Lanoxin) and the anti-seizure drug *phenytoin* (Dilantin). It can also reduce the effectiveness of the anticoagulant *warfarin* (Coumadin).

If you take one of these drugs: Alert your doctor before considering trazodone.

Two related drugs—*nefazodone* (Serzone) and *mirtazapine* (Remeron)—may be better options for older people or for those taking blood pressure medication.

USING SLEEP AIDS SAFELY

Avoid alcohol for at least several hours before taking a sleep-inducing remedy or drug. Otherwise, you can become confused and/or experience problems with breathing and coordination.

Especially hazardous: Mixing a benzodiazepine with alcohol. The combination can be deadly.

Older people tend to metabolize drugs more slowly than younger people. For this reason, a sleeping pill dosage that would be safe and effective in a younger person might cause dizziness and other side effects in older people.

If you're age 60 or older, ask your doctor about taking half the usual recommended dosage.

Soothe Sensitive Teeth

Use a cotton ball to apply warm olive oil at the gum line. This creates a lasting seal that protects sensitive roots that have become exposed as a result of gum recession.

Helpful: Heat the oil in a pan until it begins to smoke. Dry your teeth with a cotton ball. Use another to dab the oil onto your teeth.

See your dentist if sensitivity persists.

Danny Bui, DDS, a dentist in private practice in Bethesda, MD.

Sinusitis Self-Defense

David A. Sherris, MD, associate professor of otorhinolaryngology at the Mayo Clinic in Rochester, MN.

Each year, 37 million Americans develop sinusitis, a painful inflammation caused when mucus becomes trapped in nasal passages. *There are two forms...*

●**Acute sinusitis** occurs when sinuses swell as a result of colds, allergies and exposure to irritants, such as smoke, industrial chemicals and dry winter air. Trapped mucus becomes a breeding ground for bacteria, causing infection.

●**Chronic sinusitis** occurs when symptoms don't respond to treatment after three months or longer. It can be caused by a bacterial or fungal infection...allergies...or an anatomical problem, such as a polyp in the nose.

Both types of sinusitis produce a runny nose with a thick yellowish or greenish discharge ...headache...congestion...fever...cough...and facial pain.

TREATMENTS

See your doctor if your sinus symptoms last more than two weeks or if they get progressively worse. Untreated infections can spread to the eyes or brain, causing serious complications. *Treatments include...*

●**Decongestants,** such as *pseudoephedrine* (Sudafed), to reduce the swelling in the nose so the mucus can drain.

●**Warm saltwater washes** to help the cilia—tiny hairs in the nose—do their job of pushing out debris and mucus. Mix one-quarter teaspoon of salt in four ounces of warm water.

Gently squirt the mixture into your nostrils using a bulb syringe. Repeat several times a day.

●**Antibiotics,** such as *amoxicillin*, to kill bacteria. *Note:* Only take antibiotics if absolutely necessary.

●**Corticosteroid nasal sprays,** such as *budesonide* (Rhinocort), to reduce inflammation—in chronic or allergic cases.

●**Sinus surgery.** This might be recommended for chronic sinusitis that doesn't respond to drug treatments. Surgery doesn't cure the disease, but it can reduce symptoms.

FUTURE THERAPY

New research at the Mayo Clinic suggests that more than 90% of chronic sinusitis might be caused by fungus—not merely 10%, as previously thought.

In preliminary research, patients have shown significant improvement using an antifungal drug. A larger study pitting the antifungal drug against a placebo is currently being planned.

4

Exercise and Nutrition

The Ultimate Antiaging Diet

Americans spend billions of dollars each year trying to eliminate wrinkles, gray hair, etc. But *true* aging happens *inside* the body.

The best way to combat it is to eat a healthful diet—one that supplies nutrients without exposing cells to harmful substances that promote aging.

Here are the eight critical elements of an antiaging diet...

●**Eat eight to 10 servings of fruits and vegetables daily.** One serving equals one piece of fruit...one cup of berries, cut fruit or cooked vegetables...or one cup of raw or leafy vegetables.

Most fruits and vegetables are fat free, fiber dense and the best source of antioxidants, which help prevent disease and may slow the aging process.

The more fruits and vegetables you eat, the lower your risk for weight gain, heart disease, cancer, diabetes and high blood pressure...and the better your chances of living a long life.

Eat fruits and veggies throughout the day. Try to include two fruits or vegetables at every meal or snack.

Examples: Add a banana and a glass of orange juice to breakfast...snack on fruit or carrot sticks...have vegetable soup, V-8 juice, a salad or fruit for lunch...and aim for two servings of steamed vegetables for dinner.

Prepackaged or frozen vegetables are fine as long as they don't contain added sauces, butter or cheese.

Whenever possible, add vegetables to foods you ordinarily prepare without vegetables.

Examples: Grate carrots or zucchini and toss into spaghetti sauce or chili...add corn or green chili peppers to muffins...add frozen vegetables to canned soup.

Elizabeth Somer, RD, a registered dietitian in Salem, Oregon, and a frequent guest on NBC's Later Today. She is author of six books, including *Age-Proof Your Body: Your Complete Guide to Lifelong Vitality.* Quill.

•**Have beans five times a week.** One serving equals three-quarters of a cup.

All beans are a good source of *saponins*. That's a family of compounds that lower cholesterol levels, thereby lowering heart attack risk.

Canned beans are fine as long as you rinse away the high-sodium liquid.

Soybeans are loaded with *phytoestrogens*, estrogen-like compounds that may lower the risk for breast and prostate cancer.

Many people find they like soybean-based products—soy milk, soy burgers and other "fake meat" products.

•**Concentrate on minimally processed foods.** Select foods that are as close as possible to their original state. These foods tend to be low in fat, calories and sugar...and high in vitamins, minerals and fiber.

Examples: Choose a baked potato over potato chips...oatmeal over a granola bar... whole-wheat bread rather than white. For vegetables, fresh is often best—then frozen and then canned.

•**Drink eight eight-ounce glasses of water each day.** At least this much is needed to keep our bodies functioning properly.

Since we tend to neglect water consumption, it's a good idea to set up a reminder system.

At home: Each morning, line up eight glasses of water on the kitchen counter. Keep drinking all day long until they're gone.

At the office: Keep a pitcher of water on your desk...or swallow 10 gulps of water each time you pass a drinking fountain.

While traveling: Keep a bottle of water in your car and refill it often.

Water and green tea are the only beverages that count toward your daily quota. Not juices, not milk and definitely not soda, coffee or tea.

•**Steer clear of excess calories.** In studies involving lab animals, drastic reductions in caloric intake increase life span. If this finding holds true for humans, the typical human life span might rise to 180 years.

The best way to cut back on calories is to avoid fat, sugar and alcohol—calories that don't supply any nutrients.

Also helpful: Substitute prune purée or applesauce for fats in baking...cut the amount of sugar specified in recipes by 25% to 50%...

instead of eating a candy bar, drizzle fat-free chocolate sauce on fruit slices.

•**Eat little meals and snacks.** People who eat mini-meals and snacks throughout the day tend to have low cholesterol levels and low blood pressure. They're also unlikely to suffer from insulin resistance, which can lead to type 2 diabetes.

The trick is to distribute your caloric intake evenly throughout the day. Go no more than four hours between meals or snacks.

•**Enjoy food.** Don't become obsessed with fat grams or calorie counts. Food is a joyful thing and should remain that way. It shouldn't only be good for you. It should also look good, taste good and make you feel good.

•**Take supplements wisely.** Many people could benefit from nutritional supplements. There's no need for megadoses or handfuls of pills—the aim is balance.

Ask your doctor about taking a daily "moderate-dose" multivitamin, such as *Centrum* or *Nature Made Essential Balance*. These multivitamins provide a broad range of nutrients in appropriate balance.

Since no single pill can contain a day's supply of calcium and magnesium, it's often a good idea to take a combination supplement containing 500 mg calcium with 250 mg magnesium.

STICKING WITH IT

When people adjust their diets too rapidly, the changes become an unpleasant chore. Plus, brain chemistry can work against you. Your taste buds are still "expecting" eggs and sausage, but you're feeding them shredded wheat.

Helpful: Set long-term goals. Where do you want to be by the end of the year? In a couple of years? Outline the steps you'll take to get there. Plan each change and slowly progress to your goal.

Simple Ways To Stop Uncontrolled Eating

Joyce Nash, PhD, a clinical psychologist in private practice in Menlo Park, California. She is author of *Binge No More*. New Harbinger. For more on binge eating disorder, contact Eating Disorders Awareness and Prevention, 800-931-2237, or go to Dr. Nash's Web site, *www.joycenashphd.com.*

Are you unable to control your eating? If so, you have plenty of company. One American in 10 suffers from *binge eating disorder** (BED), which involves frequent bouts of overeating.

BED strikes both men and women, especially obese individuals. It often goes hand-in-hand with chronic stress.

The binges can be triggered by hunger...or, more commonly, by restrictive dieting, anxiety, anger or simply boredom.

BED interferes with work and personal relationships. In addition to poor self-esteem, it can lead to persistent depression.

In severe cases, psychotherapy—alone or with prescription antidepressants—may be necessary. But there is much sufferers can do for themselves.

RECORD YOUR BINGES

Binges often seem to run on some sort of "automatic pilot." *Self-monitoring can reveal just how and why you binge...*

● **Mark the time, place and content of every meal, snack or drink.** How hungry were you before you began eating? Underline any episode you deem a binge...and record what might have provoked it.

● **Look for patterns** after two weeks— when, where and on what you binged... whether you were hungry...what decisions, thoughts or emotions preceded the binge... and how you felt about yourself afterward.

*A binge is any loss of control over eating—whether it's two hours of fast food or two days of carrot sticks. Unlike two better-known eating disorders, bulimia and anorexia nervosa, BED does not involve regular vomiting or self-starvation.

NORMALIZE YOUR EATING

Binge eaters often fall into a destructive cycle in which restrictive dieting—denying all foods or certain "forbidden" foods—is followed by a binge.

Some binge eaters skip breakfast or lunch and gorge on dinner. Others "graze" all day.

Better: Establish a regular eating schedule. That means three balanced meals a day plus two or three snacks. Plan one meal or snack every three to four hours.

Important: Limit meals to 30 minutes apiece...and snacks to 15 minutes each. Focus on *when* you eat, not on *what* you eat.

Avoid diets that prohibit certain foods. Saying that you will never again eat ice cream virtually guarantees that you will crave it.

LEARN TO CONTROL CRAVINGS

It's almost inevitable to feel some cravings. Don't panic or give in. *Instead, whenever you feel a craving coming on, invoke the "five Ds"...*

● **Delay** eating for at least 10 minutes—to let the craving pass.

● **Distract** yourself. Go for a walk, call a friend, etc.

● **Distance** yourself from temptation. Leave the kitchen, avoid the cafeteria, throw out tempting foods.

● **Determine** how important it is to satisfy the craving.

● **Decide,** if the craving persists, how much food you can prudently consume. Then *enjoy* what you have chosen to eat.

ACCENTUATE THE POSITIVE

More so than most people, binge eaters base their self-worth on their physical appearance.

Relentlessly bombarded with images of perfection—airbrushed models and actors in magazines and movies and on TV—they silently berate themselves for failing to measure up.

The result? Low self-esteem. The antidote? Set more realistic standards.

Helpful: Write down at least five positive attributes of yours that are *unrelated* to weight or body shape. Don't overlook attributes that might be considered mundane (being able to sew, for instance) or offbeat (being able to read upside down).

Review the inventory whenever you need a boost.

BANISH NEGATIVE THOUGHTS

Binge eating is fueled by negative thinking. To encourage a more constructive inner voice, write out a series of positive thoughts, one each on three-by-five index cards.

On each "reminder" card, jot down a single positive thought that rebuts a negative.

Example: If you often find yourself thinking, *No one will ever love me*, write down, *My mother, sister and best friend love me.*

The positive messages must be brief and believable. Platitudes such as *I have much to be thankful for ring false.*

Carry the cards with you to reflect on whenever you have time—first thing in the morning, when stopped at red lights, etc.

BEFRIEND YOUR BODY

Binge eaters frequently see their bodies as "the enemy." To make friends with their bodies instead, it's critical that they hold periodic "peace talks."

What to do: Stand naked in front of a mirror. Tell your body what you like about it… and what you'd like to change. Thank it for all it does for you. Apologize for mistreating or criticizing it. Ask what it needs from you now. Imagine and write down its response.

IMPROVE YOUR COPING SKILLS

Binge eaters often use food to cope with stressful situations.

Better: Practice problem-solving skills. Identify and describe every problem in detail… brainstorm possible solutions…implement the most reasonable one…assess its effectiveness.

Muscle relaxation exercises and deep breathing can help ward off cravings.

Muscle relaxation: Lie down and get comfortable. Alternately tense and relax the large muscle groups, beginning with the fists and arms, then the legs, torso, neck and head.

Deep breathing: Take a deep breath that fills your abdomen like a balloon. Exhale, letting yourself relax. Repeat until stress melts away.

SEEK OUT PLEASURE

Binge eaters often put obligations to others ahead of their own needs, leaving no time for themselves. Too many "shoulds" and not enough "wants" can cause feelings of deprivation…and the inevitable binge.

To restore balance: List all daily activities. Mark each with an "H" (*have to*), "W" (*want to*) or "M" (*mixture of the two*). Next, rank how much satisfaction each activity provides—high, medium or low.

If the Hs far outnumber the Ws or Ms—or if your satisfaction ratings are mostly medium or low—reassess your priorities. Eliminate some obligations to include enjoyable things.

Benefits of High-Fiber Cereal

High-fiber cereal reduces consumption of fat and cholesterol. *Recent finding:* Men who ate two bowls of high-fiber cereal a day lowered their average daily total fat intake from 91 g to 82 g (34% to 28% of total calories). Average saturated fat intake fell 16%, and average dietary cholesterol intake fell 31%. *Helpful:* Replace fatty breakfast foods and evening snacks with a cereal that contains at least 4 g of fiber per serving.

Brenda Davy, RD, research dietitian, department of food science and human nutrition, Colorado State University, Fort Collins. Her study of 36 middle-aged men was presented at a recent meeting of the American Heart Association.

Fruits and Vegetables Prevent Stroke

A study of the eating habits of 113,000 individuals found that each daily serving of fruits and vegetables correlated with a 6% reduction in the incidence of "ischemic"— blood clot—strokes, about 80% of all strokes. It's believed this may be because a produce-rich diet is high in healthful fiber, folate and potassium. *Most healthful:* Citrus fruits, leafy greens and crucifers (broccoli, cauliflower, cabbage and brussels sprouts).

Kaumudi J. Joshipura, ScD, BDS, assistant professor of oral health policy and epidemiology, Harvard School of Dental Medicine, 188 Longwood Ave., Boston 02115.

Three Foods that Are No Longer Taboo

Three good-for-you foods once considered unhealthful...

Nuts: 170 calories and 14 grams of fat per ounce. But people who eat them a few times a week actually consume fewer total calories than people who eat no nuts. And some nuts, such as almonds, pecans and walnuts, can help cut cholesterol.

Shellfish: Contain cholesterol—but saturated fat, not cholesterol, is the main culprit in raising cholesterol levels in humans. And shellfish are low in saturated fat.

Eggs: Also high in cholesterol, but low in saturated fat. It is all right to eat up to one a day, unless your doctor has advised otherwise.

Gene Spiller, PhD, director, Health Research and Studies Center, 340 Second St., Los Altos, CA 94022.

The Food and Nutrients That Protect the Heart... Good News About Nutraceuticals

Stephen L. DeFelice, MD, chairman of the Foundation for Innovation in Medicine (*www.fimdefelice.org*) in Cranford, NJ, and former chief of clinical pharmacology at Walter Reed Army Institute of Research in Washington, DC. DeFelice coined the term "nutraceutical" and was among the first researchers to study carnitine's effects on the heart. He is author of *The Carnitine Defense*. Rodale.

There's now compelling evidence that certain foods contain special nutrients that guard against heart disease. The most important of these so-called "nutraceuticals" is *carnitine*, an amino acid found in red meat and in smaller amounts in chicken, fish, dairy products and certain fruits and vegetables.

Carnitine's primary function in the body is to ferry fatty acids from the foods we eat into the mitochondria. These microscopic "furnaces"—found inside every cell—convert fatty acids into the chemical energy that is put to use throughout the body.

CARNITINE SUPPLEMENTS

Biologists have been studying carnitine since the 1940s. Recent studies suggest that high levels of carnitine improve cardiac function in people suffering from coronary artery disease.

Other studies have shown that carnitine given immediately before or after a heart attack helps stabilize the heart rhythm. That improves the heart's pumping efficiency.

Carnitine has also been shown to minimize damage to the heart in the aftermath of a heart attack.

No one can predict when a heart attack will strike. For this reason it's often a good idea for people age 35 or older to take a daily carnitine supplement—to ensure that carnitine levels in the body are sufficient to protect the heart. Consult your doctor.

Carnitine supplementation is especially important for individuals with one or more risk factors for heart attack—obesity, family history of heart disease, elevated cholesterol level, high blood pressure and diabetes.

Carnitine supplements are sold over the counter in drugstores and health-food stores. Check labels carefully. Animal studies suggest that carnitine *fumarate* is more cardioprotective than other forms of carnitine.

Typical daily dosage: 1,500 mg to 3,000 mg. Taking carnitine twice daily—in divided doses 12 hours apart—helps keep blood levels consistent.

At this dosage, carnitine is extremely safe. Any excess is simply excreted in the urine.

BEYOND CARNITINE

Carnitine isn't the only heart-healthy nutraceutical. Vitamin E, magnesium, folic acid and other B vitamins, chromium and ethyl alcohol *in moderation* are proven to reduce heart attack risk.

Since these compounds are present in food only in minute quantities, it can be hard to get enough of them from food alone. For this reason, supplementation is often a good idea.

VITAMIN E

Vitamin E helps neutralize free radicals, helping keep these highly reactive molecular fragments from triggering the buildup of fatty deposits in coronary arteries.

Typical daily dosage: 400 international units (IU). To get that much vitamin E from food alone, you'd have to eat 48 cups of wheat germ or 100 cups of spinach.

One recent study of patients at high risk for heart disease seemed to suggest that vitamin E supplementation did not protect the heart against a lack of oxygen. This study contradicts numerous other studies showing that the supplements are heart-protective.

It may turn out that vitamin E is more effective at *preventing* high cholesterol and high blood pressure than at reducing heart attack risk in individuals who already have these risk factors.

Decades of clinical experience suggest that vitamin E supplementation is safe.

Caution: Check with a doctor if you've had a stroke or are on daily aspirin therapy and/or are taking *warfarin* (Coumadin) or another prescription anticoagulant. In such cases, vitamin E supplementation can thin the blood to the point that hemorrhage is likely.

MAGNESIUM

Magnesium prevents platelets from clumping together and clogging coronary arteries. It also stabilizes heart rhythm, reducing the risk of damage to the heart muscle during a heart attack.

Typical daily dosage: 400 mg to 500 mg. Divide into two doses and take twice a day to keep blood levels up all day.

Dietary sources of magnesium include artichokes, beans, shellfish, nuts and whole grains.

B VITAMINS

The B vitamin folic acid cuts blood levels of *homocysteine*, a blood protein that's been linked to heart disease. Folic acid's homocysteine-busting effect is especially pronounced when it's taken in combination with vitamins B-6 and B-12.

Typical daily dosages: 400 micrograms (mcg) folic acid...400 mg vitamin B-6...500 mcg to 1,000 mcg vitamin B-12.

ALCOHOL

Moderate drinking fights heart disease three ways. It boosts levels of HDL (good) cholesterol...helps rid the body of LDL (bad) cholesterol...and helps prevent platelet clumping.

Typical daily "dosage:" The equivalent of one drink for women...one or two drinks for men. One drink equals 12 ounces of beer, four ounces of wine or 1.5 ounces of distilled spirits.

If you have a family or personal history of alcohol abuse: Consult a doctor before using alcohol. Pregnant women should not drink alcohol.

CHROMIUM

Chromium has been shown to reduce insulin resistance, in which cells' increasing insensitivity to insulin causes glucose levels to rise. This is a significant problem for people with diabetes.

Typical daily dosage: 500 to 1,000 mcg.

Dietary sources of chromium include brewer's yeast, liver, egg yolks, wheat germ and whole-grain cereal.

MAKING IT WORK

If it's too hard to keep track of which supplements to take once a day and which twice a day, divide all the doses in half and take all your supplements twice a day.

Caution: Consult a doctor before taking any nutritional supplement. Like prescription medications, supplements can interact with other drugs you take.

Your doctor should carefully monitor the effects of the supplements...and, if necessary, adjust dosages.

Cooked Carrots Are More Nutritious Than Raw Ones

Antioxidant levels increased more than 34% after carrots were cooked—and continued to increase while the vegetables were kept at 104°F for one week. Heating softens carrot tissue, allowing the release of antioxidants attached to cell walls. This phenomenon may also occur in other vegetables.

Luke Howard, PhD, associate professor of food science, University of Arkansas, Fayetteville.

Nuts vs. Cholesterol

Eating moderate amounts of pecans (three-quarters of a cup daily for eight weeks) can lower LDL (bad) cholesterol levels by 10%, a recent study has shown.

The monounsaturated and polyunsaturated fats in the nuts are responsible for this effect, especially when nuts take the place of saturated fats in the diet.

Studies with almonds and walnuts have shown similar results. Nuts are also high in heart-healthy fiber, vitamin E, copper and magnesium.

Wanda Morgan, PhD, RD, associate professor of human nutrition and food science, New Mexico State University, Las Cruces.

Is Organic Food Worth The Extra Cost? Extra Trouble?

Marion Nestle, PhD, chair of the department of nutrition and food studies at New York University in New York City. A member of the US Food and Drug Administration's science board, she also chaired the American Cancer Society committee that issued dietary guidelines for cancer prevention in 1996. Her book on food politics will be published in 2002 by the University of California Press.

Sales of organic food have been rising in the US. Last year, Americans spent $8 billion on organic produce, meat and poultry.

That's remarkable, since few of us even know what organic means. In fact, because of inconsistent standards, there's been no guarantee that food called *organic* really meets that description.

This practice should change when the US Department of Agriculture (USDA) implements standards of quality for all foods designated organic.

For the first time, we'll know precisely what the organic label means…and we'll have assurance that organic foods meet specific requirements.

The question remains, however, whether the higher cost of organic food is justified. Is it safer than standard supermarket fare? Is it more nutritious?

•How will the new organic standards affect consumers? The proposed standards will help guarantee that products classified as organic were grown without pesticides and have not been genetically engineered. Organic farmers will be forbidden to put pesticides or sewage sludge on their crops. (Sewage sludge is a fertilizer made from the contents of municipal sewer systems.) Finally, food labeled organic must not have been irradiated.

•Are pesticides and sewage sludge dangerous? No one knows, but we have reason to be cautious. Pesticides kill bugs, so obviously, they might not be good for people.

Sewage sludge is sterilized, so it contains no bacteria or viruses. It could, however, contain toxic metals, including mercury.

● **What's the concern about genetically altered foods?** There are a few concerns. Genetically modified plants contain a gene or genes from another organism. Each transplanted gene has a desirable trait, such as the ability to repel pests or resist disease. The goal is to imbue the new plant with those abilities.

Seventy-five percent of packaged foods in the US contains some genetically changed material. That's mainly due to widespread use of altered corn and soybeans for purposes of pest-, weather- and disease-resistance.

Unfortunately, the long-term effects of tinkering with nature are unknown. A disease-resistance trait might be passed from a crop into weeds, making the weeds almost unkillable. Or the transferred genes might somehow affect human health.

Another concern is food allergies. If the transplanted gene comes from something you're allergic to, you might have a life-threatening reaction after eating the modified food.

● **What criteria must meat and dairy products meet to be certifiable as organic?** They must come only from livestock fed organic food. Furthermore—contrary to standard practice in the US—the animals cannot have been treated with growth hormone or antibiotics.

There is no solid evidence that growth hormone or antibiotics in livestock are harmful to humans. Of course, many people prefer to avoid putting these substances into their bodies unnecessarily.

● **What is the concern about food irradiation?** Zapping food with gamma rays does a good job of eliminating disease-causing bacteria, including E. coli, Listeria, Salmonella and Campylobacter.

Earlier this year, the government approved irradiation of beef, pork and lamb. Poultry has been allowed to undergo irradiation since 1992.

But irradiation is not a foolproof means of preventing bacterial illness. Meat can easily become contaminated again after it is irradiated. So it is not even clear that irradiation can prevent E. coli and other outbreaks from occurring.

Organic food proponents believe that irradiation is merely a "Band-Aid" approach to protecting people from food poisoning. They assert that if livestock and poultry were kept in cleaner quarters, they would not become contaminated in the first place.

● **Does organic food taste better?** Many people think so. Good taste depends mostly on freshness, which is affected by how far produce is shipped.

Since fruits and vegetables grown organically are often more perishable than those treated with chemicals, they are usually sold close to where they are grown.

Many people believe that organic poultry tastes better than poultry from big producers. That may be because organic chickens are fed a more varied and nutritious diet.

● **Is organic produce more nutritious?** Since it tends to be fresher, it may retain more nutrients. However, the nutritional value of fruits and vegetables is determined partly by the soil in which they're grown. A non-organic apple could have more vitamins and minerals than an organic one. Or vice versa.

● **Overall, is organic food safer and more healthful?** It's hard to say for sure because so little is known about the long-term effects of the chemicals and processes that are forbidden for organic food.

But I believe that it makes sense to pay a little extra money for food that doesn't contain antibiotics, sewage sludge or pesticides.

● **Where can I buy organic food?** You can find it at health-food stores, natural food stores, farmers' markets and, increasingly, in supermarkets.

Or you can order it on the Web at Green People, *www.greenpeople.org*...or Eco-Organics, *www.eco-organics.com*, 888-326-6742.

Soy Milk and Calcium

Soy milk doesn't provide as much calcium as cow's milk.

Reason: Soy milk calcium is less easily absorbed by the body.

If you drink soy milk: Get more calcium through nonfat or low-fat dairy products. Or look for soy milk that contains 500 mg of calcium per cup—your body will absorb 300 mg, the equivalent of one cup of cow's milk.

Robert P. Heaney, MD, professor of medicine, Creighton University School of Medicine, Omaha. His comparison of calcium in cow's milk and soy beverages was published in the *American Journal of Clinical Nutrition*, 9650 Rockville Pike, Bethesda, MD 20814.

Peas Are Packed With Vitamins

Peas are super-high in vitamins, especially folate—a B vitamin that may help prevent heart disease. Bite for bite, more beta-carotene and lutein get absorbed by the body from peas than from spinach. They have more fiber than cooked broccoli and are an excellent source of vitamin C.

Karin van het Hof, PhD, head of study of vitamin content of various vegetables, Unilever Research Vlaardingen, Van den Bergh Nederland, Box 160, 3000 AD Rotterdam, The Netherlands.

When a Recipe Calls For Alcohol

Alcohol does *not* burn off completely when it's used in cooking. In fact, up to 85% of alcohol remains after it is added to a boiling liquid and then immediately removed from heat.

When alcohol is used to make a flamed dish, 75% remains. If simmering for two-and-a-half hours, 5% remains.

Bottom line: People trying to avoid alcohol should not use recipes that call for it.

Alternative: If a recipe calls for one cup of wine or spirits, substitute any of the following—⅞ cup chicken stock and ⅛ cup lemon juice or vinegar...⅞ cup fruit juice and ⅛ cup lemon juice or vinegar...one cup nonalcoholic wine made from 100% juice...one cup water and vinegar to taste.

Franca Alphin, MPH, RD, nutrition director, Duke University Student Health Services, Durham, NC.

Olive Oil vs. Blood Pressure

Twenty-three people with high blood pressure were put on a reduced-fat diet. One group got most of its fat from sunflower oil. Another got most from olive oil. After six months, those in the olive oil group needed 48% less blood pressure medication. The sunflower oil group could reduce its medication by only 4%.

L. Aldo Ferrara, MD, associate professor of medicine, Federico II University, Naples, Italy.

The Fountain of Youth Right Under Our Noses: The Foods That We Eat

Laurie Deutsch Mozian, MS, RD, Woodstock, NY–based author of *Foods That Fight Disease*. Avery. She is a nutrition consultant who lectures extensively on phytochemicals in foods.

The research is overwhelming. You may dramatically reduce risk of chronic diseases—from cataracts and cancer to heart disease and stroke—by eating more fruits, vegetables, legumes and other plant-based foods.

These foods are loaded with protective compounds called *phytochemicals*. Unlike vitamins and minerals, which are essential for preserving health, phytochemicals actually stop changes in the body that can lead to disease.

Nearly all plant foods contain phytochemicals, but these few really stand out...

CRUCIFEROUS VEGETABLES

Broccoli, cabbage, cauliflower and other crucifers, such as arugula, bok choy, collards and watercress, contain a variety of cancer-fighting compounds.

Example: Broccoli contains *sulforaphane*, which boosts the body's ability to produce cancer-stopping enzymes. It also contains *indole-3-carbinol*, which lowers levels of harmful estrogens in the body and may reduce the risk of breast cancer.

BRIGHTLY COLORED VEGETABLES

The same plant pigments that give vegetables their color also provide impressive health benefits.

Examples: The orange or yellow flesh of winter squash comes from *beta-carotene*, a phytochemical that is a precursor to vitamin A. It blocks the effects of harmful oxygen molecules called free radicals in the body. Free-radical damage is thought to contribute to many conditions associated with aging—memory loss, heart disease, cancer, cataracts, etc.

Other top choices: Sweet potatoes, spinach, kale and carrots.

TOMATOES

Tomatoes deserve special mention because they contain the exceptionally powerful phytochemical *lycopene*. Lycopene may reduce risk of cancer. It also may protect against cancers of the breast, lung and endometrium.

For the most benefit: Lightly cook tomatoes in a little oil, which enhances the body's absorption of lycopene. If you don't eat a lot of whole tomatoes, take advantage of tomato sauce. Unlike some phytochemicals, lycopene isn't damaged by the high heats used in food processing.

PEAS AND BEANS

Legumes, in addition to being excellent sources of protein and dietary fiber, contain a rich array of phytochemicals.

Examples: Soy beans and most other beans contain *genistein*, which may reduce the risk of breast cancer as well as reduce hot flashes and other types of menopausal discomfort. Legumes also contain *saponins*, compounds that help lower cholesterol and may prevent DNA in cells from undergoing cancerous changes.

Take advantage of canned beans: They contain nearly the same phytochemical payload as dried beans, without the long cooking time. Rinse to remove salt before using.

FRUITS

Let color be your guide. Pink fruits, such as watermelon and guava, contain lycopene, which is twice as effective as beta-carotene at blocking free radicals.

Bluish fruits, such as grapes and blueberries, contain *anthrocyanins*, which reduce the amount of cholesterol produced by the liver.

Few foods are better for your health than apples. Like many fruits, apples contain quercetin, which helps prevent buildup of cholesterol in arteries. Most of the quercetin is found in the apple's skin.

GARLIC AND ONIONS

These foods are members of the *allium* family, which also includes leeks, chives and shallots. Allium vegetables are incredibly rich in phytochemicals.

Examples: Garlic is loaded with allicin, which has been shown to lower cholesterol and high blood pressure. The active ingredient in garlic isn't released until the cloves are minced or crushed. If raw garlic is too overpowering for your taste, sauté or bake the cloves until they're soft. This sweetens the flavor and reduces the "bite"—but it might also reduce the effectiveness of the phytochemicals. Raw garlic also contains *ajoene*, a phytochemical that makes blood platelets less sticky. Ajoene is not found in garlic capsules.

Onions contain *diallyl sulfide*, which may protect against cancer. In Vidalia, Georgia, the "onion capital of the world," the rate of stomach cancer is about half the national average.

GINGER

Phytochemicals in ginger can help prevent nausea better than over-the-counter drugs. Some compounds in it have anti-inflammatory effects, which may help joint swelling caused by arthritis.

FLAXSEED

Grains are rich in phytochemicals, but flaxseed is unique because it is a rich source of *lignans*. These compounds help prevent free radicals from damaging healthy cells and increasing risk of cancer. Lignans help lower cholesterol.

Important: Crush seeds or grind them in a small coffee grinder. Whole flaxseed has a tough coating that isn't broken down in the digestive tract. Ground flaxseed has a nutty taste that is good when sprinkled over cereal or added to soups or salads. Or use about one tablespoon in an eight-ounce yogurt.

You might want to start with a smaller dosage and work your way up since flaxseed is high in fiber.

TEA

Tea, hot or iced, is rich in *polyphenols*, which help prevent free radicals from oxidizing cholesterol in the blood. Cholesterol that is oxidized is more likely to stick to artery walls, increasing the risk of heart disease or stroke. Tea also contains the phytochemical *EGCG*, which appears to interfere with all stages of cancer. As few as four cups of tea a day have protective benefits.

Both ordinary black and green teas contain polyphenols. Green tea undergoes less processing than black tea, so it is a better source of polyphenols.

Melon Self-Defense

Always wash melons, winter squash and pumpkins thoroughly before cutting them. All grow on the ground, so their rinds can be contaminated by bacteria. These can enter the pulpy flesh during cutting.

Unwashed melons are suspected of causing some recent cases of food poisoning.

Use a mild dish soap, such as Ivory, and running water...or try a fruit wash spray, available in many grocery stores.

Franca Alphin, MPH, RD, nutrition director, student health services, Duke University, Durham, NC.

Grapefruit Juice Drinkers, Beware!

Before you drink grapefruit juice check with your doctor. Grapefruit juice has been found to heighten the effect of many drugs, including statins, calcium channel blockers, Valium and possibly Viagra, with potentially dangerous effects. Researchers believe that grapefruit juice contains an as-yet-unidentified substance that inhibits the action of an enzyme found in the intestine that breaks down drugs. The effect can persist for up to 24 hours.

Garvan Kane, MD, internist, Mayo Clinic, Rochester, MN.

Dangerous Diets

Beware diets that claim weight losses of more than one to two pounds per week ...promote *miracle* foods or supplements ...restrict or recommend large quantities of specific foods to the detriment of a balanced diet...imply you can lose weight—and keep it off—without making any lifestyle changes or exercising...rely heavily on case histories, testimonials and anecdotes—but offer no scientific research to back up those claims...typically promise a "money-back guarantee."

Stephen P. Gullo, PhD, president, Center for Healthful Living, 16 E. 65 St., New York City 10021.

Exercise as Medicine

Mitchell Krucoff, MD, and Carol Krucoff, coauthors of *Healing Moves: How to Cure, Relieve, and Prevent Common Ailments with Exercise*. Harmony. Dr. Krucoff is a senior staff interventional cardiologist at Duke University Medical Center, Chapel Hill, NC.

Study after study has shown that physical activity enhances health while inactivity impairs it. Everyone—no matter what his/her level of ability—deserves and needs physical activity.

Our exercise prescriptions for specific ailments are low-tech, low-risk, low-cost—and easy to do.

Take an incremental approach to our "healing moves." If all you can do today is walk to your mailbox, fine. Tomorrow, walk to your neighbor's mailbox. On day three, walk a little farther.

You will improve your health as long as you make a commitment to being active every day. Little strategies—a 10-minute walk in the morning, 15 minutes of yard work, taking the stairs instead of the elevator, parking in the farthest space—add up and can make a dramatic difference in your health.

For best results—and to ensure safety—speak with your doctor and consult a qualified exercise professional who can design a program for you.

ARTHRITIS

It may seem counterintuitive, but exercise does prevent the progression of many types of arthritis.

Stationary bicycling is good for people who should avoid putting stress on their hips, knees and feet. Swimming and water aerobics are also excellent because they put little stress on joints.

New studies indicate that resistance exercises with weights may be very helpful for rheumatoid arthritis sufferers.

CANCER

A major problem for cancer patients is fatigue. Yoga, walking and other moderate exercises can boost energy levels, mood and stamina. Walking is ideal for cancer patients because it improves lung function, stimulates bone and muscle growth and is easy on joints.

COLDS

One of the most potent immune enhancers—and cold preventers—is exercise. Moderate activity can help your immune system even if you're fighting a cold—as long as your symptoms are above the neck. If you have fever, muscle aches or a hacking cough that produces phlegm, don't exercise.

Rule of thumb: Wait until the worst is over, then start activity slowly until you feel like yourself again.

DIABETES

Walking and other forms of aerobic exercise help prevent and manage diabetes because they help the body control blood glucose.

People with diabetes should work with their physicians to develop individualized programs. In general, moderate aerobic exercise, such as walking for 20 to 45 minutes at least three days per week, is recommended. Frequency is essential to moderate blood glucose. Exercising every day, or nearly every day, confers maximum benefit.

HIGH BLOOD PRESSURE

If you have mild to moderate hypertension (up to 159/99), talk with your doctor about trying moderate-intensity aerobic activity, such as brisk walking for 30 to 45 minutes a day most days of the week. This regimen may bring blood pressure into an acceptable range without medication. Meditative practices, such as yoga and tai chi, can also be very effective.

Markedly elevated blood pressure should be controlled with medication before you embark on an exercise program, since vigorous exercise can temporarily raise blood pressure even more.

HIGH CHOLESTEROL

Amid all the hoopla over oat bran and fish oil, synthetic fats and prescription drugs, one of the most effective strategies for improving cholesterol—exercise—is frequently neglected.

Regular exercise raises the level of HDL (good) cholesterol and lowers the level of LDL (bad) cholesterol.

Do some form of moderate-to-hard aerobic exercise five days a week for at least 30 minutes per session. Try to burn at least 1,000 calories a week—the equivalent of walking or running eight to 10 miles—through movement. While moderate- to high-intensity activity is most beneficial for improving cholesterol levels, even low-intensity activities—such as gardening or strolling—can help if done daily.

OBESITY

For lasting weight loss, aim to create a 300- to 500-calorie deficit each day through a combination of eating less and exercising more.

The best calorie burner is aerobic exercise—activity that demands large quantities of oxygen for long periods of time. This includes walking, running, bicycling and in-line skating.

In general, a three-mile walk five days a week, plus good eating habits, results in significant weight loss.

Creating a calorie deficit solely through diet can be dangerous. About half the weight lost on extremely low-calorie diets is from muscle and bone. And metabolism slows with excessive caloric restriction.

OSTEOPOROSIS

No matter how much calcium you consume, you won't build bone unless you exercise. *Perform exercises that put force on the skeleton...*

•**Weight-bearing exercise,** such as walking and dancing, in which your legs bear the weight of your body.

•**Resistance exercise,** such as working out with free weights or weight machines. The force of maximally challenged muscle pulling against bone stimulates bone building.

The higher the impact, the greater the bone strengthening. Stair climbing, running and racquet sports, for instance, are high-impact. Swimming and biking are not weight-bearing.

Perform weight-bearing activity for 30 minutes a day, most days of the week. Lift weights two to three times a week for 20 to 40 minutes.

REPETITIVE STRESS INJURIES

While a mouse click isn't strenuous, performing thousands of clicks for hours on end can be extremely troublesome. *Result:* Microscopic tears in tendons, nerves, muscles and other soft tissues.

People who do hand-intensive work should do a few minutes of warm-up stretches for the hands, wrists, neck, shoulders and arms. Stretch throughout the day and cool down at the end of the day. *Best stretches...*

•**Shoulder shrugs.** Lift shoulders toward ears...hold five seconds...lower.

•**Wrist curls.** With open hands, rotate wrists in circles.

•**Neck circles.** Draw imaginary circles in front of you with your nose.

•**Fist flings.** Form a loose fist, then fan out fingers as far as comfortable.

For people who keyboard: Grasp the fingers of one hand with the other hand and gently pull back until you feel an easy stretch in the wrist.

If you hunch over a desk: Once every half hour, raise arms and stretch back over your chair, looking up at the ceiling. Take a brief walk once an hour to boost circulation and give overused muscles a break.

Finally, perform exercises that strengthen the back and abdominal muscles, such as abdominal crunches and back extensions.

RESPIRATORY DISORDERS

Asthmatics are often afraid to exert themselves because physical activity can trigger an attack.

People with emphysema or chronic bronchitis are often short of breath just getting through the activities of daily living. They assume they haven't enough "wind" for even gentle exercise. In reality, inactivity promotes a vicious cycle in which muscles weaken...heart and lungs lose tone...and self-esteem deflates.

Asthmatics: Ask your doctor about appropriate medication, especially if exercise brings on symptoms. Work up to at least 30 minutes of aerobic activity, such as walking or swimming, most days of the week. Stay well hydrated to thin secretions, so they lubricate airways rather than clog them.

Emphysema sufferers: Consult your doctor, who may recommend drugs, monitors or supplemental oxygen during exercise. Walking is often the easiest exercise, although stationary cycling and water aerobics are also fine. Start slowly and progress gradually, adding a few minutes each week.

Beware of Workout Headaches

Headaches that start during exercise and disappear when resting may be a warning sign of a weak blood vessel in the brain—which could rupture and bring on a stroke. *At special risk:* People over age 50 or who have other heart disease risk factors. See your doctor.

Seymour Diamond, MD, director, Diamond Headache Clinic, Chicago, and author of several books, including *The Hormone Headache.* IDG.

Heartburn and Weight Lifting

Exercise-induced heartburn affects weight lifters three times as often as it hits other athletes. The process of lifting apparently causes excess stomach acid to enter the esophagus, creating the problem. *Self-defense:* Do not eat for one to two hours before a workout. During a session, always exhale while pushing or pulling a weight.

Philip Schoenfeld, MD, spokesperson, American College of Gastroenterology, 4900-B S., Arlington, VA 22206.

Stroke-Reducing Nutrients

Eating bananas and other foods rich in potassium and/or magnesium can reduce the risk for stroke among people with high blood pressure.

Recent finding: Men with high potassium intake faced a stroke risk 36% lower than that of men with low potassium intake. Stroke risk was also lower among men using potassium supplements—but not magnesium supplements.

Fruits and vegetables—particularly oranges, cantaloupe and tomatoes—are good sources of potassium. Foods rich in magnesium include green vegetables, whole grains and beans and peas.

Alberto Ascherio, MD, DPH, associate professor of nutrition and epidemiology, Harvard School of Public Health, Boston.

Walking Boosts Brainpower

In a recent study, sedentary adults 60 to 75 years of age started walking briskly three times a week, gradually increasing the length of the walks from 15 to 45 minutes. After six months, their mental function had improved by 15%. Similar adults who did stretching and toning exercises for one hour three days a week showed no improvement. *Theory:* By increasing oxygen flow to the brain, walking averts the earliest mental changes that occur with aging.

Arthur Kramer, PhD, professor of psychology, University of Illinois, Urbana-Champaign.

Are You Getting Enough Copper?

Multivitamins rarely provide enough copper. The daily requirement for copper is 2 mg. Most women take in half that amount from food, while men get 1.5 mg. Copper deficiency can trigger rapid tissue breakdown that accelerates aging. *Trap:* Most multivitamins contain *cupric oxide*, a form of copper that isn't readily absorbed. *Self-defense:* Eat a copper-rich diet containing nuts, whole grains, leafy greens and beans—and take a multivitamin containing copper sulfate (*cupric sulfate*). It's easily absorbed.

David Baker, PhD, nutrition researcher, division of nutritional sciences, University of Illinois, Urbana–Champaign.

Exercising Before Eating A Fatty Meal Can Save Your Life

Fatty foods cause a spike in triglyceride levels. Over time, surging triglyceride levels raise heart disease risk. *Recent finding:* In men who exercised one hour before eating a high-fat meal, triglyceride levels rose only 40% as high. Exercising *after* eating lowered the predicted spikes by only 5%. *Theory:*

Exercise boosts production of enzymes that rapidly clear triglycerides from the blood.

Tom R. Thomas, PhD, director, exercise physiology lab, University of Missouri, Columbia.

Better Bean Digestion

To stop beans from causing gas, cook them thoroughly and discard cooking water. Uncooked starch from beans is one major source of intestinal gas. Rinse canned beans well after removing them from the can, and throw away the water, which contains indigestible sugars. Build up servings of beans gradually over a few weeks, so your body has time to adjust. *If you still have gas:* Try Beano, an over-the-counter product that aids digestion of gas-causing sugars. *Reminder:* Beans are very nutritious, containing fiber, protein, potassium, magnesium and other nutrients.

Franca Alphin, MPH, RD, nutrition director, Duke University Student Health Services, Durham, NC.

Very Surprising Exercise Partner...Your Computer

Patrick Netter, known as "The Gear Guru," an independent sports and fitness equipment expert and consultant. *www.gearguru.com*.

Don't let foul weather compel you toward laziness. These on-line resources can help you get in shape and stay in shape. Nearly all are free. *My favorites...*

- **Active.com.** Follow training programs developed by top running, swimming, triathlon and walking coaches. Calendar of competitions for dozens of sports. Site features interviews with sports champions. *www.active.com*

- **Asimba.com.** Personalized fitness and weight-loss programs based on goals you set. Provides weekly progress reports, plus support and motivation. Health club locator for US, Canada and abroad.

Helpful: Training and Nutrition Log provides an at-a-glance view of performance and progress, including distance, time and calories burned. *www.asimba.com*

- **Choose to Move.org.** Twelve-week physical activity and healthful eating program for women. Sponsored by the American Heart Association. *www.choosetomove.org*

- **Getfit.com.** Allows you to create and store a workout schedule so you can access your fitness calendar anytime you want. Provides specific exercises to develop particular muscle groups. *www.getfit.com*

- **Gymamerica.com.** Depending on your goals, this site will help you tailor a specific workout...and have your questions answered by one of its health experts. *www.gymamerica. com*.

- **Stayhealthy.com.** Tracks diet and fitness progress using a pager-like device, worn on your waist, that communicates with a computer. Monitors calories burned based on body movement. Body composition analyzer works with above device to measure body fat, muscle mass and hydration. Can be downloaded to a PC-compatible computer using an Internet browser.

Cost: $330, includes both devices, software and first year's subscription. $10/month thereafter. 800-321-1218. *www.stayhealthy.com*.

Exercise vs. Stroke

It is well known that physical activity lowers the risk for heart disease.

In one of the first studies to explore exercise's effect on stroke, researchers recently found that healthy women who walk briskly for 30 minutes a day have a 40% lower risk for *ischemic* stroke, the most common form.

Exercise lowers blood pressure, which is a major stroke risk factor.

Helpful: Exercise at a moderate intensity—brisk walking or biking, for example—on most or all days of the week.

Frank B. Hu, MD, PhD, assistant professor of nutrition, Harvard School of Public Health, Boston. His eight-year study of 72,488 nurses ages 40 to 65 was published in *The Journal of the American Medical Association*, 515 N. State St., Chicago 60610.

Be Your Own Personal Trainer

Miriam E. Nelson, PhD, director of the Center for Physical Fitness at the School of Nutrition Science and Policy at Tufts University in Boston. She is coauthor of the Strong Women series of exercise books and the founder of *www.strongwomen.com*.

If you exercise regularly, then you probably already know the value of a good personal trainer.

A trainer can help you establish and maintain a regular exercise schedule...suggest appropriate workouts...push you harder for better results...and teach you proper form and technique.

But trainers typically charge $45 for a one-hour session.

Good news: It's possible to achieve all of this on your own—without a trainer. *Here's how...*

A REGULAR SCHEDULE

●**Work out with a friend.** Commit to specific times and days each week. You're less likely to miss a workout if another person is counting on you.

●**Make a realistic time commitment.** How much time can you devote to exercise each week? Thirty minutes a day? Thirty minutes three times a week? If you set unrealistic goals, you're likely to quit.

Choose the days you'll exercise, then write them in your calendar. Check them off once you've completed each workout.

Helpful: Think of each session as an "appointment" with yourself.

. Having difficulty fitting your routine into a busy schedule? Try exercising before work or during your lunch hour...getting up early two mornings a week...dropping a low-priority item from your schedule...or performing three 10-minute workouts, rather than one 30-minute session.

●**Choose a suitable location.** Look for a convenient site that offers the services and equipment you need.

If winters are severe where you live, exercise indoors. Buy a stationary bicycle or treadmill, or use an exercise video.

When traveling, stay at a hotel with a fitness center. Ask the concierge for a walking or running route. Or pack a jump rope.

●**Keep a detailed exercise log.** Charting your progress will motivate you to maintain your program.

Include the date you exercised...how long you worked out...and the routine you performed.

Note at the bottom of the log the intensity of each routine—*too easy, just right, too hard.* This helps you recognize when a routine is no longer challenging.

Example: February 15...40 minutes...running and weights...intensity—just right.

For a weight-training routine, list the type of exercise...pounds or level of the workout...and number of repetitions.

THE BEST ROUTINES

There are three basic types of workouts...

●**Aerobic exercise.** Brisk walking, jogging or bicycling increases the heart rate.

●**Strength training.** Lifting light weights preserves muscle strength and function.

●**Flexibility training.** Stretching expands your joints' range of motion.

Find a routine that satisfies your requirements for exercise, such as preventing back pain or tightening your abdomen.

Participate in aerobic exercise at least three times a week...strength or flexibility training at least twice a week. Begin each session with five minutes of easy exercise, warming up to full intensity. End with a five-minute cool-down that includes stretching.

THE RIGHT INTENSITY

Exercise won't do you much good unless you work out at an appropriate level of intensity.

To "push yourself" as a personal trainer would, ask yourself after your workout… *Could I have exercised longer? Could I have done more difficult exercises?* If so, increase your intensity next time.

Or you might be exercising too hard. Ask yourself after the routine…*Am I exhausted? Do my limbs feel heavy and sore?* If so, decrease your intensity.

Exercise physiologists have devised these exercise intensity guidelines…

•**Aerobic activity.** At least three times a week for a minimum of 20 minutes, exercise at a level that requires strenuous movement, elevating your heart rate to 60% of its maximum.* Breathing is rapid. Sweating starts within 15 minutes.

Incorporate into your daily life easy, sustainable movement that increases your heart and breathing rates slightly. *Sample activities:* Strolling…gardening…golf.

Avoid overexertion. You've overdone it if your heart is pounding to the point of discomfort or nausea or if breathing becomes too rapid for you to speak easily.

•**Strength training.** For the first four weeks—while you are learning the exercises—work out at a moderate exertion level. This causes fatigue only if prolonged, like carrying a full briefcase that gets heavier as the day goes on.

Stabilize at a level that begins at moderate intensity and gets harder after six or seven repetitions. You should be able to maintain good form while performing the movement eight times, but you will need to rest afterward.

Avoid any movements that require all your strength. These can cause injuries to bones and muscles.

•**Flexibility training.** Hold the pose and push it to the maximum stretch—but not to the point of pain. And *never* bounce.

*To measure heart rate: Find your pulse on your neck or wrist. Count the number of beats for 15 seconds and multiply by four. *To calculate maximum heart rate:* Subtract your age from 220. If you're age 50, for example, your maximum heart rate is 170.

Exercise Fights Ulcers

Men who are active are 30% to 50% less likely to develop ulcers than sedentary men. *Theory:* Exercise reduces acid secretion in the stomach, improves immune function or simply relieves anxiety. The more a man works out, the less likely he is to develop an ulcer.

Caroline Macera, PhD, researcher in a study of 11,000 people, Centers for Disease Control and Prevention, Atlanta, published in *The British Journal of Sport Medicine.*

Better Fitness Walking

Take *more* steps—not longer ones. Long strides can cause knee, shin and foot pain. A smooth, rolling stride—at a faster pace—is more effective than a long stride to speed up a walk and better for the body.

Therese Iknoian, exercise physiologist and author of *Walking Fast* (Human Kinetics), quoted in *Remedy*, 120 Post Rd. W., Westport, CT 06880.

Post-Workout Sauna Danger

Caution: A sauna after a workout delays recovery of muscles. *Reason:* Saunas can cause dehydration, cramping, nausea, dizziness and headache. *Safer:* Take a cold shower, or use ice packs to return muscles and your body to normal temperature. Consume some fluids, carbohydrates, protein and other essential nutrients right after exercise. *Also:* Check your heart rate before entering the sauna—your heart should be beating at a normal resting pace.

Eric Sternlicht, PhD, exercise physiologist and president, Simply Fit, exercise and nutrition consultants, Orange, CA.

A Shrewder Weight Loss Suggestion

Brief intervals of exercise spaced throughout the day can help you lose weight effectively.

An 18-month study put about 150 overweight, sedentary women into three groups that combined dietary control with different exercise options. One group gradually worked up to one 40-minute exercise session, five days a week...one group broke the same total amount into 10-minute segments...and the third group was given electric treadmills for home use to break the same total amount into brief segments at their convenience.

After six months, members of each group had lost an average of 26 pounds, but over the next year the first group regained six pounds on average and the second group regained nine pounds, while the treadmill group regained an average of only four pounds.

John M. Jakicic, PhD, is assistant professor of psychology at Brown University, Providence, RI.

Better Weight Lifting

Start slowly—do not extend arms or legs to their full range until the third or fourth repetition. Never extend so far that you lock your knees or elbows. When using a machine, do not let the weight stack touch the top or bottom—keep it one finger's width away. When going up, raise weights at a constant speed. Stop at the highest point you can reach without locking. Pause for one second, then start the descent. Come down more slowly than you went up—but keep the weights moving.

Wayne Westcott, PhD, strength consultant, South Shore YMCA, Quincy, MA.

5

Natural Healing

Powerful Herbal Medicines We Rarely Hear About

As a health consumer, you are probably familiar with many of the top-selling herbal medicines—the memory enhancer ginkgo biloba...the depression fighter St. John's wort...and the immunity booster echinacea. There are more than 10,000 medicinal herbs used to treat a variety of ailments, including flu, varicose veins, the bone-thinning condition known as osteoporosis and hemorrhoids.

Some herbs work just as well as conventional drugs. Herbs often have fewer side effects, and they usually cost less, too.

ASTRAGALUS
STRAGALUS MEMBRANACEOUS

This herb has been used for centuries in traditional Chinese medicine in tea or soup, typically in root form.

Also called *huang qi* (wahng chee), astragalus is used to bolster the immune system to help the body fight off colds, influenza and harmful bacteria.

Typical daily dosage: At the first sign of cold or flu symptoms, prepare a tea of one teaspoon of liquid extract or one-half teaspoon of tincture in one cup of hot water, steeped and drained. Or you can use 2 g of the root.

Caution: Certain species of astragalus are toxic. Do not try to pick and use this herb on your own. Purchase it from a reliable source.

BUTCHER'S BROOM
RUSCUS ACULEATUS

This herb is often used in Europe for relief from varicose veins and hemorrhoids.

Typical daily dosage: One 300-mg tablet ...or 7 mg to 11 mg of total ruscogenin, the active ingredient.

James A. Duke, PhD, author of 25 books, including *The Green Pharmacy.* Rodale. He recently retired as chief of the US Department of Agriculture's medicinal plant laboratory.

CELERY SEED
APIUM GRAVEOLENS

This herb's anti-inflammatory properties help ease arthritis and gout and lower blood pressure.

If you can eat celery without problems, you're unlikely to experience any side effects.

Caution: See your doctor before using celery seed for hypertension. It may augment the action of prescription antihypertensives.

Typical daily dosage: Two 500-mg capsules of standardized extract or one-half teaspoon of tincture before meals. For seeds, one tablespoon of seeds in one cup of hot water or added as a spice to soups.

ELDERBERRY
SAMBUCUS NIGRA

This herb fights viral illnesses, including flu, cold and herpes.

In a study conducted during a 1993 outbreak of flu in Israel, 90% of people who took a standardized elderberry extract were better within three days.

Typical daily dosage: At the onset of flu, cold or herpes, one-half teaspoon of liquid elder flower extract before meals or two to three cups of elder flower tea (two teaspoons of dried elder flowers in one cup of hot water, steeped and drained).

FENUGREEK
TRIGONELLA FOENUM-GRAECUM

This herb is used to treat diabetes, diarrhea and constipation.

In studies conducted in India, fenugreek was shown to contain five compounds that cause significantly reduced blood sugar levels in people with type 1 and type 2 diabetes.

Fenugreek contains *mucilage*. This soluble fiber absorbs water and provides relief from diarrhea and constipation.

Mucilage also enhances the herb's ability to lower blood sugar levels and may reduce cholesterol and triglyceride levels.

Caution: Do not take fenugreek *instead of* prescription diabetes drugs. See your doctor if you want to try it to treat diabetes.

Typical daily dosage: 620 mg of standardized extract before meals or one cup of fenugreek tea (one tablespoon mashed seeds steeped in one cup of hot water).

KUDZU
PUERARIA MONTANA

This herb may help prevent osteoporosis and reduce cravings for alcohol.

Kudzu contains *genistein* and *daidzein*—phytoestrogens that protect against bone loss.

Typical daily dosage: Three 100-mg capsules.

PUMPKIN SEED
CUCURBITA PEPO

In parts of Europe, pumpkin seeds are the standard treatment for benign prostate enlargement. The seeds are rich in zinc, selenium and other minerals that have been shown to reduce prostate cancer risk.

Typical daily dosage: Eat one-quarter cup of the seeds.

USING HERBS SAFELY

Plant medicines can intensify or block the effects of prescription drugs. Consult your doctor before taking any herb—especially if you are pregnant or take prescription medications.

If you're scheduled for surgery, tell your doctor about the herbs you take...and stop taking them three weeks prior to the procedure. Some herbs reduce—or increase—blood pressure or diminish the effects of anesthesia.

The active ingredients in herbal medicines can vary, depending on the manufacturer. Choose "standardized" brands. These indicate the amount of the active ingredient—and give recommended dosages. You can buy them at health food stores.

Tell your pharmacist about any herbs you are taking, so he/she can monitor possible interactions with prescription drugs.

To find a physician familiar with herbal treatments, contact the American Association of Naturopathic Physicians at 877-969-2267 or *www.naturopathic.org*.

Herbs and Your Eyes

Macular degeneration—the leading cause of blindness among older people—

occurs when the central area of the retina (macula) deteriorates.

In addition to eating a nutritious diet, taking *ginkgo biloba* and *bilberry* may help guard against the ailment. These antioxidant herbs boost blood flow to the eyes...and minimize free-radical damage to the retinas.

Typical dosages: Ginkgo, 40 mg to 80 mg three times a day...bilberry extract, 80 mg three times a day.

Caution: Consult your doctor before taking ginkgo if you're taking aspirin or *warfarin* (Coumadin). Ginkgo can enhance the blood-thinning effects of these drugs.

Michael T. Murray, ND, coauthor of *Encyclopedia of Natural Medicine.* Prima.

Natural Alternative to HRT

Postmenopausal women may be able to cut their risk for heart disease without hormone-replacement therapy (HRT). A recent study found that a nonprescription red clover extract (Promensil) boosted the elasticity of artery walls as effectively as HRT. Researchers believe *isoflavone* compounds in red clover are responsible for this effect. The loss of arterial elasticity—which often occurs in menopause—raises a woman's risk for heart disease.

Paul J. Nestel, MD, head, cardiovascular nutrition, Baker Medical Research Institute, Melbourne, Australia.

Natural Relief for Joint Pain

A combination of flaxseed, borage and cod liver oil is an effective alternative to aspirin, Celebrex and Vioxx for joint problems.

These products work in the same way as the drugs to suppress inflammation and pain, but they are much safer. Effects are typically seen within two weeks.

Buy the oils as separate 400-mg soft-gel capsules. Take each two or three times a day.

Alternative: Buy a high-quality combination "Perfect Oils" supplement from Nutritional Therapeutics (800-982-9158). *Cost:* $21 for 90 capsules.

Important: Consult your doctor before trying this remedy.

Andrew L. Rubman, ND, is associate professor of clinical medicine at College of Naturopathic Medicine, University of Bridgeport, CT, and director of Southbury Clinic for Traditional Medicines, Southbury, CT.

Important Alternative Therapies Too Often Overlooked

Kenneth R. Pelletier, MD, clinical professor of medicine and director of the complementary and alternative medicine program at Stanford University School of Medicine in Stanford, California. He is author of *The Best Alternative Medicine: What Works? What Does Not?* Simon & Schuster.

Even conservative doctors have started offering alternative therapies such as acupuncture to relieve pain and St. John's wort to curb mild depression.

Yet many effective alternative therapies remain underused...

BLACK COHOSH

In Germany, a black cohosh extract called *Remifemin* is frequently prescribed as an alternative to hormone-replacement therapy (HRT). Preliminary evidence suggests that black cohosh is effective at relieving premenstrual discomfort, menstrual pain and menopausal ailments.

This is good news given the evidence linking HRT to increased risk for heart attack.

Any menopausal or postmenopausal woman should ask her doctor about taking black cohosh supplements. They're sold at health food stores.

Caution: Take black cohosh no longer than six months, since no studies have established whether sustained use is safe.

GUGGUL

An extract from the *mukul myrrh* tree native to India, guggul is used in that country to lower cholesterol. Evidence is mounting that it is effective—and safe. In a recent Indian study, 40 patients with high cholesterol who took a 25-mg supplement of guggul three times a day for 16 weeks cut their total cholesterol an average of 21%. Levels of HDL (good) cholesterol rose by 35%.

If you have high cholesterol: Ask your doctor about taking guggul supplements.

MENTAL IMAGERY

Mental imagery begins with the patient entering a state of deep relaxation similar to that obtained via hypnosis. The doctor or hypnotherapist then leads the patient through images in which treatments, recovery and desired outcomes are envisioned.

Mental imagery is of proven effectiveness against chronic pain and anxiety. It has also been used successfully to lower blood pressure and heart rate in heart patients and to improve cancer patients' production of cancer-killing lymphocytes, neutrophils and killer T-cells.

Writing down thoughts and feelings can be a powerful form of mental imagery. Last year, *The Journal of the American Medical Association* published a study of 112 people with asthma or rheumatoid arthritis who all received standard care. In one group, each patient wrote an essay on three consecutive days, describing his/her reaction to a traumatic experience.

Result: Four months later, those in the writing group had markedly improved health.

MIND-BODY RELAXATION

Meditation, hypnosis, stress management and biofeedback are all effective against anxiety and depression, asthma, high blood pressure, chronic pain and carpal tunnel syndrome.

Heart disease patients treated with stress-management classes and muscle tension biofeedback have fewer fatal heart attacks and require fewer heart operations than do similar patients on a standard aerobic exercise program.

Stress-management lessons focus on teaching better coping methods for stressful situations. Methods include visualization, meditative breathing and other relaxation techniques.

Muscle tension biofeedback involves placing electrodes on the skin to measure muscle tension. The patient learns to reduce tension by monitoring a dial or another feedback device.

Anyone who wants to reduce stress or anxiety can consider these techniques. Contact the National Center for Complementary and Alternative Medicine at the National Institutes of Health, at 888-644-6226...or go to its Web site at *www.nccam.nih.org*.

PRAYER

Recent studies suggest that prayer promotes healing even when the patient is unaware of being prayed for.

In a study of 393 heart patients at San Francisco General Hospital, half the patients were prayed for, half were not. Neither patients nor doctors knew who had been prayed for.

After 10 months, the prayed-for group had required less medical care—and had lower mortality—than the group not prayed for.

REIKI

In this laying-on-of-hands technique, a practitioner sends "healing energy" through his hands into the patient's body. Reiki has proven effective in managing pain and healing wounds.

At the University of Michigan Medical School in Ann Arbor, researchers found that Reiki speeds healing of incisions.

People who have chronic pain or feel they are healing too slowly from a wound should try Reiki. Contact the International Center for Reiki Training at 800-332-8112...or go to *www.reikilinks.com*.

SOY FOODS

Soy foods are believed to slow menopause onset and prevent bone loss in menopausal women. Now a study at Stanford University School of Medicine suggests soy is effective when combined with daily supplements of vitamin D and calcium.

Soy derives its effectiveness from estrogen-like compounds known as *phytoestrogens*.

Tofu, tempeh, soy milk, edamame (baby soybeans), soy cheese and miso are all rich in phytoestrogens.

Menopausal and postmenopausal women should ask their doctors about taking soy with calcium and vitamin D supplements.

Important: Consult your doctor before taking any herbal supplement. Pregnant and lactating women should not take herbs.

Heart Attack Defense... Ordinary Black Tea

Black tea may fight heart attack more strongly than doctors had thought.

Recent finding: People who drank at least one cup of black tea a day had a 44% lower risk of heart attack.

Researchers attribute this to *flavonoids*—potent antioxidants abundant in tea, as well as in fruits and vegetables. Flavonoids help prevent blood clots that can trigger heart attack.

J. Michael Gaziano, MD, MPH, director of cardiovascular epidemiology, Brigham and Women's Hospital, Boston.

Foot Massage Helps Headaches

Reflexology—massaging specific pressure points on the feet and other extremities—helped 81% of migraine and tension headache sufferers in one recent study. Many people were able to stop taking headache medicine after using reflexology for six months. To find a reflexology practitioner, visit *www.reflexology-usa.org*.

Laila Launso, doctor of social science, department of social pharmacy, The Royal Danish School of Pharmacy, Copenhagen, Denmark.

Hand Reflexology

Bill Flocco, founder and director of the American Academy of Reflexology in Burbank, California, and past president of the International Council of Reflexologists in Richmond Hill, Ontario, Canada. He is author of *Hand Reflexology: A Wealth of Health* (818-841-7741), and three other books and numerous teaching manuals on reflexology.

The devotees of hand reflexology maintain that there is a "map" of the human body on our hands. Every part of the body is matched by a corresponding "reflex point" on the fingers, palms and backs and edges of the hands.

Applying pressure to these reflex points stimulates nerve impulses that travel indirectly to the corresponding body areas. These impulses help muscles relax, open blood vessels, increase circulation and allow in more oxygen and nutrients—key facilitators of healing.

American physician William Fitzgerald, MD, introduced this therapy in his 1917 book *Zone Therapy*. The technique soon expanded to include foot reflexology and is now used by thousands of "reflexologists."

For quick relief of pain and muscle tension, the hands remain the primary area for reflexology.

Caution: Don't do hand reflexology if you have a hand injury. If you have any medical problem, consult a doctor first.

THE BASICS

Apply gentle pressure to the reflex points on your hand, using the *thumb roll* technique.

To work the reflex points on your left palm, place the fingers of your right hand on the back of your left.

Place the pad of your right thumb on your left palm.

Squeeze gently, pressing in with the thumb. As you press, bend the thumb so that the tip slowly rolls forward and downward. Maintaining contact between the right thumb and left palm, straighten the thumb so that it moves forward about one-eighth of an inch over the reflex area. Repeat this thumb rolling movement, gradually working the entire reflex area.

Use the same technique to work the palm or fingers. To work reflex points on your right hand, perform the thumb roll with your left. If your nails are long, use the sides of your thumb rather than the tip.

Reflex areas should be worked for at least five minutes. Work a broad area around the specified reflex points. Benefits can be felt in one or two sessions.

EYESTRAIN

The eye reflex points are at the base of the index, middle and ring fingers—the meta-tarsal phalangeal joints or "big knuckles." Thumb roll directly on these knuckles—as well as just above and below the knuckles—on both sides of both hands.

SORE SHOULDERS

The shoulder reflex points are on the backs of the hands in the grooves between the long bones. To work them, use your fingertips.

If your left shoulder is the problem, work the reflex points on your left hand. Put your right thumb flat on your left palm.

On the back of your left hand, place the tips of your right index, middle and ring fingers in the grooves. Gently apply and maintain even pressure, slowly and repeatedly moving your fingertips in the direction of the wrist.

If your right shoulder is the problem, work the reflex points on your right hand.

STOMACH UPSET

The soft portion of each palm—below the big knuckles—contains many reflex points for the digestive system. The stomach reflex points are mostly on the left palm. For stomach upset and heartburn, use the thumb roll to work the palm just beneath the large knuckles at the base of the index, middle and ring fingers.

Start with light pressure and gradually increase.

NECK PAIN

The neck's main reflex points are on the lower half of the thumbs. Thumb roll the area between the two knuckles of each thumb. The rolling thumb should roll from pad to tip, so that you apply sufficient pressure all the way around the area.

CARPAL TUNNEL SYNDROME

This painful, sometimes immobilizing hand and wrist condition often results from repetitive stress on the median nerve as it passes through the wrist. Working reflex points for the forearm can reduce pain. These reflex points are on the outer edges of the hands, midway between the base of the pinkie and wrist.

Thumb roll this area on whichever arm has the problem.

Caution: Although reflexology can help ease pain for carpal tunnel syndrome, the condition is potentially serious. If you have symptoms, see a doctor.

BACK PAIN

Reflex points for the spine are on the inner edge of the hand, from the bottom of the thumb to the wrist. Thumb roll this area on both hands. Reflex points for the lower back are toward the wrist.

FINDING A REFLEXOLOGIST

Self-care with hand reflexology provides many benefits, but for long-term results, certified practitioners are best.

Search the Internet, using the key word "reflexology" and the name of your state...or look in the Yellow Pages under "reflexology." You can also call the American Reflexology Certification Board (ARCB) in Littleton, Colorado, at 303-933-6921 for a certified reflexologist in your area.

Ideally, your practitioner should be certified by the ARCB. It provides an independent testing and certification service.

Natural Remedies For Pain Relief

Jamison Starbuck, ND, a naturopathic physician in family practice and a lecturer at the University of Montana, both in Missoula. She is past president of the American Association of Naturopathic Physicians and a contributing editor of The Alternative Advisor: The Complete Guide to Natural Therapies and Alternative Treatments. *Time Life.*

F or many people, reaching for pain relievers is as instinctual as eating. Hungry? Go to the refrigerator and grab a bite. In pain? Swallow a pill. But pain pills have their costs.

Acetaminophen (Tylenol, Panadol, etc.) can cause liver damage. Nonsteroidal anti-inflammatory drugs (NSAIDs), such as *naproxen* (Aleve) and *ibuprofen* (Advil, Motrin, etc.), can cause gastrointestinal bleeding and impaired kidney function. They can also inhibit cartilage repair in the knees, hips and other joints. In addition to being addictive, Lortab, Percocet and other narcotic painkillers can cause drowsiness and clouded thinking. The muscle relaxant *cyclobenzaprine* (Flexeril) has been linked with dizziness, rash, arrhythmia and even convulsions.

In certain cases, the risks posed by these adverse reactions are offset by clear benefits. When pain is especially severe, nothing can replace the merciful relief of medication. But for run-of-the-mill discomfort—tension headache, ankle sprain, joint stiffness, back pain and post-surgical pain—it's often better to skip drugs and opt instead for natural treatments.

Ice may seem old-fashioned, but it remains one of the best natural painkillers. It's great for back pain, aching, swollen joints and headache. It reduces congestion, improves blood flow and promotes healing. A bag of frozen peas works as well as an ice pack, and it can be refrozen and reused many times. Usually a 10-minute application, two or three times each hour, is effective.

If headaches are your problem, drinking lots of water is often all that's needed. In particular, tension headaches and "toxic" headaches from drinking too much alcohol or consuming too much caffeine respond well to "hydrotherapy." Have eight ounces of water every 10 minutes for one hour. Make sure a bathroom is handy before starting this remedy!

For acute sprains, strains and scrapes, bruises and other minor trauma, nothing beats *arnica*. This homeopathic remedy—available in health food stores and now many drugstores— reduces bruising and pain. Unless you are accident-prone, a single vial costing less than $10 should last several years. I recommend arnica in 30C potency—typically two pellets one to three times daily, for up to seven days.

For tendinitis and sciatica—and to speed recovery from surgery—I often recommend *bromelain*. This natural anti-inflammatory agent—an enzyme derived from pineapple— stimulates the breakdown of inflammatory compounds at the injury site. Bromelain is available in capsules at health food stores and pharmacies. The typical dosage is 250 mg one to four times daily. Bromelain is off-limits for people with high blood pressure.

Boswellia serrata (frankincense) has a long tradition as an arthritis treatment in India and the Middle East. Though human studies on this herb are inadequate, the clinical experience of many practitioners—myself included —has been extremely promising. I routinely recommend Boswellia as a substitute for NSAIDs in cases involving back pain, arthritis, inflammatory joint pain and acute muscle and bone injuries. Even with long-term use, Boswellia does not seem to cause the gastrointestinal bleeding and pain that can be a problem with NSAID use.

Boswellia can be found in health food stores. Look for Boswellia alone, or combined with ginger and turmeric, two additional herbal pain relievers that are easy on the stomach. The typical dose is 300 mg of Boswellia, three times a day, as needed for pain.

More from Jamison Starbuck...

Adrenal Fatigue Making You Sick?

My office is often filled with people complaining of fatigue. Many of these patients have already been told by a medical doctor that nothing is wrong with them—or that their weariness is symptomatic of depression. Dissatisfied with this advice, they turn to naturopathic medicine, hoping that I have an answer. In many cases, I do.

The answer often lies with their adrenals, two strawberry-sized glands situated just above the kidneys. Through the secretion of numerous hormones, including cortisol, DHEA and aldosterone, the adrenals control the metabolism of fat, carbohydrate and protein...regulate inflammation...and influence mood, sleep, blood pressure and digestion.

Complete failure of the adrenals is rare. Lots of people, however, are troubled by what naturopathic physicians call "adrenal fatigue." Typically, this condition results from prolonged physical or psychological stress. Like the batteries of a car whose headlights are left on all night, the adrenals simply run down.

In addition to exhaustion, symptoms of adrenal fatigue include poor sleep, insomnia between 2 a.m. and 4 a.m. and increased susceptibility to infection and allergic reactions. Cholesterol is the primary building block for adrenal hormones, so a total blood cholesterol level below 160 is often a warning sign of adrenal fatigue.

Fortunately, the adrenals are pretty forgiving. Many of my patients find that they feel much better after devoting a month to stress-reduction and improved nutrition. *Here's what I typically recommend...*

●**Don't skip meals...and don't substitute sweets for "real" foods.** Each meal should include protein—a cup of lowfat or fat-free yogurt, cottage cheese, a glass of soy milk or several ounces of beans, tuna or meat. Protein reduces adrenal stress by stabilizing blood sugar levels.

●**Take vitamin B-5.** Also known as pantothenic acid, B-5 is critical for adrenal function. You can get B-5 from fish, milk, beans, peas, whole grains, broccoli, cauliflower and kale. But people with adrenal fatigue usually benefit from taking a B-5 supplement. I typically recommend 50 mg per day.

●**Spend more time relaxing.** I often recommend yoga, qi gong, deep breathing exercises or simply walking quietly in a natural setting. As much as possible, avoid situations or activities that rev you up—noisy, busy restaurants, bars or gyms, scary movies, tense family or work settings.

●**Try acupressure.** Once or twice a day, press firmly on the fibrous spot between the thumb and first finger, about one inch in from the edge of the web. Known in traditional Chinese medicine as LI4 (large intestine 4), this acupuncture point is used in a variety of treatments. Pressing on this spot is said to "tonify" the adrenals by "quieting the spirit."

●**Consider herbal medicine.** Ashwaganda is traditionally used in India to treat nervous exhaustion and stress-induced ailments. The typical daily dose is 500 mg three times per day. Licorice root helps reverse adrenal fatigue by slowing the excretion of cortisol. The typical daily dose is 500 mg. Take one or both herbs for up to three months.

Watch out—people with high blood pressure should not take licorice. Pregnant women should take herbs only with a doctor's supervision.

Finally from Jamison Starbuck...

Using Vinegar to Treat Common Ailments

Vinegar has been used medicinally for thousands of years. Hippocrates is said to have recommended a vinegar-and-honey mixture to clear up phlegm and ease breathing.

During the 10th century, vinegar was employed in hand-washing to prevent the spread of infection. Through World War I, vinegar was a staple in military medical kits—used as a wound disinfectant.

Recently, a colleague from the publishing world asked me to review a book touting the amazing powers of vinegar. Because I'm a longtime advocate of effective home remedies—and aware of vinegar's status as the most popular home remedy in America—I was happy to take a look.

Unfortunately, the book was filled with nonsense. *Here are the fallacies debunked...*

Vinegar cannot cure cancer, heart disease, high blood pressure or any other serious disease.

Nor does it promote weight loss. There is simply no truth to the belief that vinegar is a natural fat-burner. Excessive vinegar consumption over several weeks or months can lead to heartburn.

Finally, vinegar does not prevent or treat arthritis. Arthritis has a variety of causes, including heredity, lifestyle and dietary choices. If you're having symptoms, consult your doctor.

Here's the truth about vinegar…

•Vinegar can be used to treat itchy fungal infections of the skin—candida, athlete's foot, jock itch, etc. Painting white vinegar directly on the infected area helps curb the itch and eliminate the fungus. I typically recommend starting with twice-daily applications of a 25% vinegar/75% water mixture and gradually increasing this to undiluted vinegar if your skin can tolerate it. You should see results within seven days.

•Vinegar can help relieve sore throat pain. Mix one or two teaspoons of apple cider vinegar in four ounces of warm water. Gargle with this solution four times daily for up to three days at the onset of a sore throat. It soothes pain and acts as a mild antiseptic, helping to kill viruses and/or bacteria on contact.

•Vinegar makes a healthful—and tasty —addition to dark, leafy greens, such as spinach, kale, chard, collard and beet greens. These vegetables contain lots of potassium, calcium and iron. But for proper digestion of these minerals, the body requires plenty of stomach acid. Studies show that many people over age 50 just don't produce enough acid. Vinegar is acidic, so it boosts the body's ability to draw essential minerals from food.

•Vinegar offers soothing topical relief of sunburn pain. While certainly it is best to avoid too much sun exposure, many people nonetheless end up with some sunburned skin at least once a year. If that is the case for you, try applying apple cider vinegar directly to your burn.

•Vinegar is a good substitute for conventional household cleaners. Folks with multiple chemical sensitivities or anyone who wants to lower chemical exposure can substitute vinegar for harsh or strongly scented cleaning agents. Use vinegar on windows, floors and other household surfaces.

Caution: Do not consume vinegar if you have an ulcer, gastritis or an "acid stomach." It can exacerbate these conditions.

Fight Bug Bites…Naturally

To protect yourself from bug bites, take a multi–B-vitamin complex twice daily. A preliminary study indicates that riboflavin, one of the B vitamins, causes the body to emit an odor that repels mosquitoes, stinging ants, wasps, yellow jackets and bees.

Important: Use one that contains an average of 50 mg of most B vitamins.

For kids: Safest dosage is about 1 mg per three pounds of body weight. *Example:* 20 mg for a 60-pound child. Break open a tablet and add it to juice or put it in the middle of a ball of bread.

Also: Apply a sports rub or an aromatic compound that contains menthol or eucalyptus. These odors temporarily scare off bugs.

Natural remedies: Sprinkle monosodium glutamate (MSG) powder—available in supermarkets and pharmacies—on the bite as often as needed. Or use After Bite, a penlike device that delivers a safe amount of sodium hydroxide (lye).

Both penetrate the skin and break down the offending compounds that cause stinging and itching.

Andrew L. Rubman, ND, associate professor of clinical medicine at College of Naturopathic Medicine, University of Bridgeport, and director of Southbury Clinic for Traditional Medicines, Southbury, CT.

Aromatherapy… For Much More Than Just Pleasant Smells

Jane Buckle, RN, PhD, president of the Hunter, NY-based RJ Buckle Associates LLC, which teaches aromatherapy and other complementary techniques to health-care professionals. *www.rjbuckle.com.* She is author of *Clinical Aromatherapy in Nursing.* Arnold.

When you hear the word "aromatherapy," you probably think of a scented bath or a fragrant candle.

But medical practitioners in the US and elsewhere around the world are using distilled oils of aromatic plants medicinally. Essential oils activate the parasympathetic nervous system, causing relaxation, which speeds healing.

AROMATHERAPY IN ACTION

Plant oils can be used in a warm bath…a "carrier oil"—such as almond or sesame oil—for massage…or a lotion.

The oil aromas can also be sniffed from a bottle…a cotton ball…or a *diffuser*—a machine that emits the aroma into the air.

Clinical and scientific studies support the use of aromatherapy as an adjunct to medical care for treating…

●**Anxiety.** Essential oils that were inhaled for three minutes relieved anxiety in men and women, according to recent research in the *International Journal of Neuroscience.* Use rosemary, Roman chamomile or patchouli. *Typical treatment:* Sniff one to three drops when anxious.

Caution: Avoid using rosemary if you have high blood pressure.

●**Bronchitis.** Use spike lavender. *Typical treatment:* One drop of spike lavender in a bowl of three cups of boiling water. Drape a towel over your head, close your eyes and inhale the steam. Do this for five minutes, four times a day.

●**Hair loss.** In people with patchy hair loss due to *alopecia areata,* essential oils helped restore hair growth, notes a recent *Archives of Dermatology* study that used a carrier oil containing a mixture of thyme (two drops), rosemary (three drops), lavender (three drops) and cedarwood (two drops). *Typical treatment:* Massage the mixture into scalp for two minutes daily.

●**Headache.** Use peppermint. If pain isn't gone in five minutes, try Roman chamomile or true lavender. *Typical treatment:* Five drops in one teaspoon of carrier oil. Apply to temples or sniff.

●**Hot flashes.** Use clary sage, fennel, geranium or rose. *Typical treatment:* 10 drops in two cups of water in a spray bottle. Spray on face during hot flash.

●**Insomnia.** Use ylang ylang, neroli or rose. *Typical treatment:* Five drops in a diffuser placed in the bedroom.

●**Low back pain.** Use lemongrass. If you get no relief in 20 minutes, try rosemary or spike lavender. *Typical treatment:* Five drops in one teaspoon of carrier oil. Apply to the painful area every three hours.

●**Menstrual cramps.** Use geranium. *Typical treatment:* Five drops added to one teaspoon of carrier oil. Rub on the lower abdomen and low back every three hours.

●**Muscle spasms.** Use clary sage, sage or lavender. *Typical treatment:* Five drops added to one teaspoon of carrier oil. Apply to the affected muscles at least every three hours.

●**Osteoarthritis.** Use frankincense, rosemary or true lavender. *Typical treatment:* Five drops added to one teaspoon of carrier oil. Apply to the painful area every three hours.

WHAT TO BUY

Aromatherapy is most effective when the essential oils are prepared with no extraneous ingredients.

Good brands include Northwest Essence (*www.pacificmassage.com*) and Scents & Scentsibility (*www.scentsibility.com*). They are also available in health food stores.

USING AROMATHERAPY SAFELY

Some essential oils can irritate or burn skin if applied undiluted. Always dilute before using topically. If skin stings or becomes red, dilute with a plain carrier oil and wash with unperfumed soap.

The oils are flammable. Store away from candles, fires, cigarettes and stoves. Don't pour oil on lightbulbs to scent a room.

Caution: Essential oils can be lethal when ingested—even in tiny doses. Keep away from children and pets. People with asthma or epilepsy and pregnant women should consult their doctor before using aromatherapy.

Related Useful Sites

Conditions

☐ American Heart Association National Center

www.amhrt.org

The American Heart Association's official Web site has all the information you need to keep your heart healthy. Learn the warning signs, and find out if you are at risk for a heart attack or stroke.

☐ Oncology Tools

www.fda.gov/cder/cancer

This is an excellent resource from the Food and Drug Administration. It contains a variety of information related to cancer and approved cancer drug therapies. Click on *What Is New* to see which drugs have most recently been approved.

☐ CancerNet

http://cancernet.nci.nih.gov

This site is offered by the National Cancer Institute and has a world of valuable information on every aspect of the disease. Learn where clinical trials are being conducted, read about how to cope with cancer and check out the latest treatment options.

☐ Prostate Cancer InfoLink

www.phoenix5.org/Infolink/index.html

This site is extremely helpful for anyone who needs up-to-date information on this all-too-common form of cancer. There's valuable advice on screening, diagnosis and treatment of prostate cancer. There are also great support-related resources for patients and their families.

☐ Chronic Lung Disease Resource

www.cheshire-med.com/programs/pulrehab/rehinfo.html

This award-winning site highlights the best information on chronic lung disease (CLD) and is geared toward the general public. Find highly reliable information about asthma, cystic fibrosis, respiratory infection and other CLDs. You can visit the CLD forum or chat live with other sufferers.

☐ The American Lung Association

www.lungusa.org

The American Lung Association's site has a wealth of information on lung health. Learn about tobacco control, smoking and lung health, asthma remedies (for kids and adults) and lung health in diverse communities. You can also subscribe free to two on-line newsletters.

☐ Medscape

www.medscape.com

Intended for medical professionals, but a great resource for consumers, too. Latest medical news updated daily plus thousands of full-text, peer-reviewed clinical articles. Free access to Medline, the world's largest medical abstract database. You can also browse leading medical journals from around the world. Free service, but you must register.

Consumer

☐ Dr. Greene's HouseCalls

www.drgreene.com

This informative site is updated daily and answers just about every health question parents can think of. Whether your toddler has an ear infection, or you're trying to make sense of your teenager's moods, or trying to get your kids to sleep—it's all here.

☐ Dr. Koop's Community

www.drkoop.com

Very useful site created by former US Surgeon General C. Everett Koop. There's a daily health tip, up-to-the-minute health news and great advice on how to stop smoking. Or join the interactive health chat, where you can find the answers to all your questions.

☐ Mediconsult.com

www.mediconsult.com

This site provides a user friendly guide to medical conditions. There's a search engine that will lead to exactly the information you're seeking...or try *Mediconditions,* a menu with over 100 conditions to research. There's also a *Medical Directory*.

☐ The New England Journal of Medicine
www.nejm.org

The esteemed medical journal is now available on-line. You can receive each week's table of contents by E-mail and search past issues by topic, title or author. There are also links to other sources of useful medical information.

Alternative

☐ Acupuncture.com
www.acupuncture.com

Learn about this 5,000-year-old Chinese healing method, which is used by millions of people today. Choose from a list of ailments, and learn how acupuncture can help your specific problem.

☐ Ask Dr. Weil
www.drweil.com

Dr. Andrew Weil, the well-known Harvard-educated specialist in integrative medicine, answers your questions about the ever-expanding field of medical botany and mind/body interactions.

☐ Austin Nutritional Research
www.realtime.net/anr

This very informative site guides you through the world of vitamins, minerals, herbs and more.

For Women

☐ La Leche League International
http://lalecheleague.org

Information about breastfeeding. La Leche League is a world renowned non-profit organization dedicated to providing support and education to women who choose to breastfeed.

☐ Susan G. Komen Foundation
www.komen.org

The Komen Foundation is the world's leading research organization solely dedicated to breast cancer. This website provides excellent advice regarding breast health, as well as locations around the country of the annual Race for the Cure.

And More...

☐ Virtual Drugstore
www.virtualdrugstore.com

Her's a one-stop reference to the latest in pharmaceuticals. Use the searchable database to find information about a particular drug. Or select from a list of diseases and learn which drugs are being used to treat them.

☐ Depression.com
www.depression.com

Another excellent resource for people who are struggling with depression. Read about the different types of the illness as well as the newest available treatments.

☐ Healthanswers.com
www.healthanswers.com

This comprehensive site contains answers to questions on topics covering wellness and your body, plus feature articles, a free newsletter, latest health news and chat groups. Look up any drug or vitamin in a vast pharmaceutical database.

☐ Hospital Web
http://neuro-www.mgh.harvard.edu/hospitalweb.shtml

Check out hospitals in your area or anywhere in the world. Click on a state, and you'll find a list of local hospitals. More are being added every day. Each hospital has its own Web site, where you can review programs, services, doctors, etc.

☐ American Academy of Allergy, Asthma & Immunology
www.aaaai.org

This is an extremely comprehensive and easy-to-navigate site for people who suffer from all forms of allergies. Learn the symptoms, causes and latest treatments for pediatric asthma.

6

Smart Money Management

You Can Be a Millionaire Too!

You don't have to strike it rich on a TV game show to become a millionaire. Even in today's volatile, high-priced stock market, patient investors can reach $1 million by investing $50 a month in conservative blue-chip companies.

Time horizons: Assuming an average annual return of 14%—if you invest $50/month, compounded monthly, it will take 39 years to become a millionaire.

Double that to $100/month, and you'll be a millionaire in 34 years.

Double it again to $200/month, and you'll be a millionaire in 29 years. *Here's how to invest your way to $1 million...*

STARTING OUT

Income for American households now averages $38,000 a year. At least 5% of that should be invested each year—10% would be better.

Most families fall short of that investment target because they spend too much and save too little.

• **Waste less money.** That's the first goal for all families. I work as an adviser to Junior Achievement kids. These high school students tell me they waste $25 to $50 a month. If the average kid wastes that much money, the average adult is probably wasting thousands of dollars a year.

Helpful: For the next week, every time you spend more than $1 on something other than a regular household necessity, write down the amount and what it was for. At the end of the week, you'll see where the leaks are and can figure out how to plug them.

HOW TO INVEST

There are three key rules for becoming a millionaire...

Bill Staton, CFA, CPC, chairman of Staton Investment Management, a money-management firm, and founder of The Staton Institute, an investment advisory firm—both in Charlotte, NC. He is author of *The America's Finest Companies Investment Plan* (Hyperion) and the audiocassette album *Lifetime Riches—The Seven Secrets for Multiplying Your Wealth*. Nightingale-Conant.

●**Diversify wisely.** Start by investing in at least five companies—each in a different industry.

Work your way up to eight to 10 companies—with roughly equal dollar amounts invested in each. Owning more than 12 well-selected stocks is not likely to increase your investment success.

Invest in what I have identified as America's Finest Companies®. Investing in quality is the surest road to success. My list includes every US company that has increased earnings or dividends-per-share for each of the past 10 years.

Investing in common stocks has returned an average 12% a year, in dividends and capital gains, since 1945.

The companies on my list have returned nearly 15% a year on average. At that rate, given compounding, you'll double your money every five years.

●**Be patient.** With any investment, the longer your time horizon, the more likely you are to hit your goal. Invest with the idea that you will own a stock for at least 10 years—20 years is better.

You can't count on that 15% return every year. But fluctuations in the market smooth out over time. Quality companies will earn above-market returns as they have, on average, over the past 55 years.

●*Sell*...if the fundamentals that made a firm one of America's Finest Companies change for the worse.

●*Don't sell*...if the stock has a poor quarter or a poor year *if its fundamentals are still strong.* One of the first signs of serious trouble is that the dividend stops growing or is cut. Sell such a stock, and replace it with another company that fits the bill.

●**Keep investing.** Once you have the right number of stocks in your portfolio, keep your portfolio balanced by investing new money in the stock that has gone up the least. Those stocks have the greatest long-term growth potential.

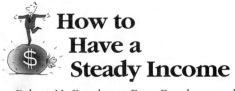

How to Have a Steady Income

Robert M. Freedman, Esq., Freedman and Fish, 260 Madison Ave., New York City 10016. Mr. Freedman is former chairman of the elder law section of the New York State Bar Association and founder of the National Academy of Elder Law Attorneys.

The peace of mind that comes from knowing you'll have a steady income for life comes at a price—your assets will decline rather than grow. *But if lifetime income is your goal, there are a number of ways to achieve it...*

RETIREMENT PLANS

When you retire, you'll likely have a choice of how to take your money from the company pension plan.

Many financial advisers suggest rolling over a company retirement plan distribution into an IRA to retain maximum flexibility. When the money is in an IRA, you can invest it as you see fit. And you'll have full access to the funds at all times.

But if a steady income for life is your primary goal, you may want to have the pension money paid to you in monthly installments. If your spouse survives you, he/she can continue to receive a monthly income for life.

Caution: Once you've made the election to take pension distributions in the form of a monthly annuity, you can't change your mind.

Alternative: Roll over pension funds to an IRA, and, in effect, create your own fixed flow of income. Simply withdraw the IRA money in regular monthly installments.

Self-defense: Sit down with a financial planner who can work out a withdrawal schedule to provide for a monthly income from the IRA (based on your life expectancy).

While distributions from your IRA must begin by April 1 of the year following the year you turn 70½—you can *start* taking your annuity payments from the IRA at any younger age you choose. (If you're under age 59½, though, you'll be assessed a 10% early withdrawal penalty, unless payments are made in a series of substantially equal periodic payments.)

BUY A COMMERCIAL ANNUITY

Those who lack the experience of handling large sums of money may want to use insurance proceeds or other lump-sum payments to buy lifetime income from an insurance company in the form of an annuity.

Commercial annuities are investment products offered by insurance companies. They are bought directly from the company or through banks and brokerage firms.

The insurance company paying on the life insurance policy can provide an annuity, but shop around to find the best one for you.

From an investment perspective, commercial annuities may not appeal to you. You must consider the fees the company charges for the annuity in relation to the return.

But if you're prepared to pay the price and the insurance company is sound, then peace of mind can be yours with a commercial annuity.

INCOME OPTION

Annuities pay a fixed monthly amount to you during your lifetime and can be tailored to provide a continued flow of income to your surviving spouse.

TURNING ASSETS INTO INCOME

•**Reverse mortgages.** Older people of moderate means can convert the equity in their home into a monthly retirement income by using a reverse mortgage. Instead of paying principal and interest monthly, you receive a monthly check.

General qualifications…

•Generally you must be age 62 or older.

•There must be little or no other mortgage on the home.

•The home must be single family (or a one-unit condominium that is FHA-approved) and owner-occupied. Owners of mobile homes don't qualify for reverse mortgages.

The monthly income you receive is fixed according to the value of your home, the area in which you live (FHA-insured reverse mortgages set maximum loan caps for various areas) and your current age. There are different payment options to choose from, one being a monthly income for life (or the joint life of the home owners).

Caution: The reverse mortgage becomes due when the owner sells the home, moves or dies.

CHARITABLE REMAINDER TRUSTS

If you have substantial assets, especially appreciated assets such as securities, you can use them to obtain a fixed income for life *and* benefit charity by setting up a charitable remainder trust. *Benefits…*

•**Fixed income.** You receive a fixed monthly income based on the value of the assets in the trust—and the type of charitable remainder trust you use.

You can even obtain inflation protection by using a charitable unitrust. It pays a monthly income based on a percentage of the value of the assets annually. If the assets' value rises, you benefit accordingly.

•**Tax deduction.** You can claim a current income tax deduction for the value of the "remainder interest" of the money that the charity will receive when you die. This deduction is determined by IRS tables, which have recently been changed.

Caution: To achieve tax benefits, the trust must be set up carefully. Consult an attorney for this purpose.

OTHER CHARITABLE OPTIONS

Instead of using a personal charitable trust, consider…

•**Pooled income funds.** Your contribution to the charity goes into a pool with gifts from other donors. The money is invested by professional money managers.

Your income is based on the size of your gift and your age. You also receive an upfront tax deduction for the gift based on the value of what the charity will get upon your death.

•**Charitable gift annuity.** Some of the country's biggest charities will provide you with a monthly income and a tax deduction— in return for a hefty donation. The monthly income payments may not be as large as those from a commercial annuity, but you're providing a benefit to society rather than to an insurance company's shareholders.

Bouncing Checks Can Cost You Dearly

Dire new consequences of bouncing a few checks: Your checking account may be closed—and you may be banned from opening one elsewhere for years.

Self-defense: Make sure you have overdraft protection, and find out your bank's policy about reporting overdrafts to a national database…don't depend on the "float"—money still in your account but against which you have written checks…balance your checkbook every month. If a check hasn't cleared within 30 days, contact the payee to move it along. Otherwise your balance may seem bigger than it really is.

If a check bounces: Contact your bank immediately. Repay the overdraft and explain any mitigating circumstances.

Catherine Williams, president of Consumer Credit Counseling Service of Greater Chicago.

Shorter Grace Periods

Credit card grace periods are getting shorter. Issuers used to make purchases interest free for at least 25 days, regardless of the previous balance. But only a few cards follow this approach. Now, if you carry over even a penny from the previous month, issuers charge interest immediately on new purchases. And some cards have *no* grace period—you always pay interest when you use them.

Bottom line: Know a card's rules before accepting it…and follow them carefully to avoid interest charges.

Janet Kincaid, credit card specialist, Federal Deposit Insurance Corporation, Kansas City, MO. *www.fdic. gov/consumers.*

Traps in Striking It Rich… Mistakes to Avoid

Ed Slott, CPA, E. Slott & Co., CPAs, 100 Merrick Rd., Rockville Centre, NY 11570. *www.irahelp.com.* A practicing CPA for more than 20 years, Mr. Slott is a nationally recognized IRA distributions expert and editor and publisher of *Ed Slott's IRA Advisor.* 800-663-1340.

There are many ways in which you can come into large sums of money. The money may come to you from good luck…your own hard work…or even bad luck.

However you come by the money, you'll want to minimize taxes on it…and maximize your opportunities for a financially secure future.

INHERITANCES AND GIFTS

There are two types of property you may inherit…

Tax-deferred property, such as traditional IRAs and qualified plan benefits, and…

All other types of property.

●**Tax-deferred property.** Inherited properties are generally free from income taxes. This doesn't apply to tax-deferred property. You must pay income tax on such property.

But there are strategies for spreading out your tax obligation. The rules are quite complex, so it's best to work with a tax adviser.

Opportunity: While you must pay income tax on distributions to you from traditional IRAs and other tax-deferred property, you can claim an itemized deduction for the federal estate tax paid on such property. This deduction, called the income in respect of a decedent (IRD) deduction (or estate tax deduction), is claimed as you report the tax-deferred property.

The IRD deduction is treated as a miscellaneous itemized deduction on Schedule A, but it's not subject to the 2% of Adjusted Gross Income (AGI) limit. And it's not subject to the Alternative Minimum Tax (AMT).

●**Other property.** When you inherit other property, you receive a stepped-up (to tax cost) basis for the property's value reported on the estate tax return.

Idea: Keep a copy of the estate tax return to have a record of your basis for purposes of determining gain or loss when you later sell inherited assets.

●**Gifts.** Like inheritances, you must keep track of the basis in any securities or other property you receive as a gift. Generally, your basis in a gift is the same as the basis of the person who gave you the gift (not necessarily its value at that time).

Ask about basis when you receive the gift and keep a record of it.

JOB-RELATED WEALTH

You may emerge as a millionaire if your company goes public. Or, you may be a young athlete who receives a huge signing bonus and a multiyear contract.

From a psychological point of view, the problem with such newfound wealth is the feeling of omnipotence or indestructibility.

Don't let your newly inflated ego cause you to go broke as quickly as you made the money—many have. Respect the fact that you are still vulnerable and ignorant financially and seek competent advisers for all major financial decisions.

If your wealth comes from your company's instant success, consider cashing out a portion of your holdings (to the extent permitted by law or contract) and hedge your bets by diversifying your investments. Don't wait until the stock goes up some more because it can go down just as well.

LADY LUCK

Lottery winnings can make you rich overnight. Unfortunately, statistics show that most winners lose all their money soon after they receive it. If you're lucky enough to win, create a plan to be sure you don't lose it.

Planning starts with a budget and a long-term investment strategy. Make sure you budget for large items, like income taxes. You'll most likely have to start paying quarterly estimated taxes even if you never did before.

Withholding on lottery installments may not cover your estimated tax obligations.

Have an investment professional work with you to make and monitor investments. Don't start day-trading. The key to holding onto your money for life is discipline.

INSURANCE SETTLEMENTS

If you receive money from an insurance settlement resulting from a personal injury or accident, it's likely that you may not be able to work because of the injury. Make sure your money will last you for the rest of your life. Seek the advice of a competent financial planner who can help you budget and make investment decisions.

GETTING YOUR FINANCIAL HOUSE IN ORDER

There's nothing wrong with having some fun with your newfound wealth, as long as you don't ignore your long-term needs.

●**Pay off debt.** Now that you have the money, you can pay off your debts.

●**Pay off the highest interest rate debt first.** For example, pay off credit cards with 18% or 20% annual interest rates first. Paying off a 20% debt is the same as earning 20% on your money.

●**Pay off expenses or past due bills that may have piled up.** These can include back taxes, medical bills, and other household bills.

Exception: Don't rush to pay off your mortgage or home equity loan. These may have low interest rates of around 5% or 6% and the money you'd use to pay them off can be earning more for you—even with a conservative rate of return. What's more, the interest you do pay is tax deductible.

But if your mortgage rate is higher than 8% or so, you may want to pay it off.

●**Plan for the future.** Make sure you provide for upcoming large expenses, such as home improvements, college and weddings for children, and your retirement. Don't think that your new wealth means you should stop contributing to IRAs and 401(k) plans if you are eligible to do so.

NEW RESPONSIBILITIES

Money may bring certain rewards, but it also brings added responsibilities. *You may now have to take actions that you never considered before...*

●**Estate planning to protect your money for your heirs.** Be sure you make a will and take other steps to provide for your beneficiaries. This may include, for example, integrating life insurance into your estate plan to pay estate taxes.

●**Insurance.** Now is the time to obtain the insurance you didn't need or couldn't afford before, such as life insurance, disability insurance and an umbrella policy for personal liability protection.

●**Advisers.** Sudden wealth does not equate with sudden financial genius.

You'll probably need the guidance of various types of experts to help you manage and protect your money. It's a good idea to work with a financial planner, attorney, accountant and an insurance professional to cover all your bases. You'll pay for this assistance but may save money in the long run by not losing your newfound fortune.

Credit Card Rebates

New credit card rebate programs are springing up—you can earn credits for college savings, charity donations and US savings bonds. But be realistic about how much the rebates are really worth. The average consumer charges $5,000 a year, and the average rebate is 1%—or $50 per year. If you charge a large amount each year—in the $100,000 range—a rebate card can work in your favor. *But:* Credit cards with rebates often charge higher interest—so if you carry a balance, rebate cards may not be worthwhile.

Robert McKinley, president, Cardweb.com, Inc., 450 Prospect Blvd., Frederick, MD 21701.

Economic Slowdown Self-Defense

Delay buying costly durable goods, such as cars and appliances. Prices will drop as the economy slows and manufacturers try to entice customers. Pay off high-rate debt as quickly as possible, then pay off other fixed-rate debt. Variable-rate debt can be paid off later because rates will drop as interest rates fall.

Gerri Detweiler, education adviser, Myvesta.org, nonprofit financial assistance organization, 6 Taft Ct., Rockville, MD 20850.

More from Gerri Detweiler...

Better Credit Card Borrowing

Borrowing more on low-rate credit cards is a bad idea. New borrowing on existing cards is often at much higher interest than the low rate you had for balance transfers or earlier borrowing. When you send in monthly checks, credit card firms apply the payments to older, lower-rate debt first. That leaves borrowers with extended payments at higher interest. *If you must borrow on a credit card:* Wait to be offered a new card at a low introductory rate.

Paying with Savings Vs. Credit

If you pay a $500 bill with a credit card that carries 17.99% interest and send in $20 a month, you will pay a total of $715 and it will take 59 months to pay off the bill. But if you simply put $20 a month into a savings account earning 2.1% interest, you will build up $500 in 24 months and can then pay cash for what you want. *Bottom line:* Saving is a cheaper and faster way to pay for what you want without debt.

Steve Rhode, president, Myvesta.org, nonprofit financial-solutions organization, Rockville, MD.

Beware! You Can't Bank on Hot New Bank Services

Edward F. Mrkvicka, Jr., former chairman and CEO of a national bank and current president of Reliance Enterprises, Inc., a national financial consulting firm, 22115 O'Connell Rd., Marengo, IL 60152. He is author of *Your Bank Is Ripping You Off.* St. Martin's.

Changes in banking laws and advances in technology have spawned new banking options—but not all of the changes are for the better...

INTERNET BANKING

Internet banks operate without retail outlets and big staffs, so they often offer higher interest rates and lower fees than traditional banks. *But consumers may pay a high price in other ways...*

•**Poor service.** Internet banks are often bad at dealing with problems.

Example: If an improperly recorded deposit causes checks to bounce, it is nearly impossible to set things straight, according to customers with whom I've spoken.

Resolving problems is a hassle at any bank—but when you have a location, you can meet with a real person.

•**Lack of insurance.** Not all Internet "banks" have FDIC insurance, yet some claim they do.

Alternative: Consider a brick-and-mortar bank that also has an Internet presence.

There are several Web sites you can use to research a bank. Both *www.bankrate.com* and *www.gomez.com* focus on E-banks.

BROKERAGE & INSURANCE

The softening of the Glass–Steagall Act allowed banks to expand into other fields—most notably investments and insurance. But don't trust a bank to be anything but a bank. *Problems...*

•**Lack of experience.** Yesterday they were pushing Christmas clubs...today mutual funds. Would you want to be the first person on whom your family doctor performed open-heart surgery?

•**Limited offerings.** Most banks have agreements to push one specific provider's insurance and offer only a very limited selection of mutual funds.

•**High fees.** Bank broker fees are typically higher than you would find elsewhere.

•**Miscommunication.** Customers often don't understand that bank-sold investments are not insured—even when they are sold by an FDIC-insured bank.

•**Legal traps.** If you have a disagreement with the bank at which you have multiple forms of business—say, a mortgage and a checking or savings account—the bank has the right to seize your other assets if there is a dispute.

Example: If you disagree about whether a mortgage payment was made on time, the bank can seize the penalty from your checking or savings account.

This right to seize could be extremely damaging in a major dispute. In these cases, consider closing accounts before the bank can attach additional funds.

AUTOMATED BILL PAYMENT

Most banks will pay regularly occurring bills for customers. That can save time and postage. *But there are traps...*

•**Credit rating risk.** If a payment is late, the biller won't care that it is your bank's fault.

Automated bill payment only makes sense for payments to the same bank that is doing the automatic bill paying—say, for your mortgage or car payment.

HIGH-FEE CHECKING

Interest-bearing checking accounts sound good—but they come with fees so high and interest rates so low, you would have to keep thousands of dollars in the account to break even. That money would produce better returns elsewhere.

Sneaky rule changes: Banks write new rules in banking jargon and bury them in small print. *Beware of fees for...*

•**Speaking to a teller.**
•**Calling to check a balance.**
•**Returning canceled checks.**
•**Not meeting account minimums,** which banks have been increasing.

Self-defense: Most banks still offer simple, low-cost checking accounts—they just won't be the accounts they try to sell you when you walk in the door. And most banks offer free basic accounts to seniors, students and disabled people—but they rarely advertise them.

More from Ed Mrkvicka...

Make Sure a CD Is Insured

Total all your accounts at the bank. FDIC insurance covers a maximum of $100,000 *per depositor.*

If you have several accounts at one bank and then buy a CD, you may exceed the limit...and lose coverage for the amount over $100,000.

Simple self-defense: Buy the CD at a different bank.

Don't Refinance Your Car

Refinancing a car loan is rarely a good idea. If you have good credit and high-rate initial financing, refinancing at a lower rate or for a shorter term can save money. But many auto refinancings lower monthly payments by stretching out the terms of the loan—so the *total* paid for the car ends up higher. And unlike homes, cars depreciate, so you end up paying more to buy something of declining value.

If you need cash: Consider a home-equity loan instead of a car refinancing.

Douglas R. Lebda, CEO, *LendingTree.com*, a Web site where banks compete for consumers' business, Charlotte, NC.

Bills It's Okay To Pay Late

Sometimes it is tough to pay all your bills on time.

Utility payments can usually be paid late—and without bad entries on your credit report. Call telephone, gas, electric and cable companies to make deferred payment arrangements.

Other options...

●**Renters can ask landlords about paying later.** There is little chance it would be reported to credit bureaus.

●**Those with good credit** may be able to transfer credit card balances to a new card with a lower interest rate—and gain 30 more days to make a payment.

●**Stores will often let customers negotiate** missed payments on their credit cards without penalty. Get a promise—in writing—that a missed payment will not be reported to credit bureaus.

Important to pay on time—mortgage, auto loans and leases, American Express bills.

David Masten, consumer finance and credit consultant, Jersey City, NJ, and author of *The Fix Your Credit Workbook.* St. Martin's.

Kids and Money

Help children learn to save money by showing them positive aspects of deferred gratification. Offer them a future reward if they start saving now...and be sure to give them the reward when earned. It should be something the child wants, not something parents think he/she should want. Find ways to make the process itself rewarding. *Example:* Offer a reward if a child practices the piano—but make sure he gets to play music he enjoys. *Very important:* Be a good role model. Children are more likely to become good savers if they see parents save regularly.

Walter Mischel, PhD, professor of psychology, Columbia University, NY, quoted in *The Wall Street Journal.*

Hidden Credit Hazards

Nancy Lloyd, former Federal Reserve Board economist and author of *Simple Money Solutions: 10 Ways You Can Stop Feeling Overwhelmed by Money and Start Making It Work for You.* Random House.

There are more minefields to managing credit these days. *Strategies for common problems...*

DEBIT CARDS

Debit cards are riskier than *credit cards.* They come with less federal protection than credit cards—even if your debit card bears a Visa or MasterCard symbol. If someone gets your card number, he/she could drain your account, even without your Personal Identification Number (PIN).

With a credit card, if you notify the issuer within 60 days of a fraudulent charge, your liability won't exceed $50.

With a debit card, under federal law, you must notify the issuer within two business days to cap your loss at $50.

After three days, the liability on a debit card increases to $500. After 60 days, you could be out your entire bank balance, plus the amount of your overdraft line—potentially tens of thousands of dollars if it is tied to your home-equity line.

Best: Get an ATM card *without* the debit feature.

ELECTRONIC BILL PAYING

Ask about delays, fees and security before signing up for any electronic bill-paying service. Most people assume that these services pay the bills as soon as the money is taken out of their accounts.

But many companies aren't equipped to accept electronic payments, so the bank ends up mailing a check, which can take another week or more. The extra time can lead to late payments, late fees and damaged credit.

Best: If a creditor does not accept payments electronically, write a check yourself.

LATE PAYMENTS

If you know you can't make loan or credit card payments on schedule, call those creditors immediately. Ask them to devise a better payment plan. If the first person you reach won't negotiate, ask to speak with a supervisor.

Request the new terms in writing. If the creditor refuses written confirmation—which is surprisingly common—type up the terms yourself and send them to the lender via certified mail. That way you have a paper trail confirming the agreement.

If a creditor is unwilling to negotiate, contact a nonprofit credit counseling service, such as Consumer Credit Counseling Services, 800-388-2227.

LOAN CONVERSIONS

Beware of lenders' promises to save you money by converting credit card debt into a home-equity loan. You are literally betting your house.

Paying a credit card bill late will hurt your credit rating. That's not a good thing...but it is better than losing your home. Few bill payers are disciplined enough to resist making new credit card charges after conversions.

SELF-DEFENSE

Review your credit report before hunting for a new job, a mortgage, an apartment, an insurance policy or a car.

To get a copy of your report, call one of the three national credit bureaus—Equifax (800-685-1111)...Experian (800-682-7654)...Trans Union (800-916-8800).

Cost: $8 to $10. Some states allow residents one free report each year.

The Right Time to Refinance

Lower mortgage rates don't always mean it is time to refinance, we hear from real estate attorney David Schechner. *When it pays:* You should be able to recover the cost of refinancing within 18 months and plan to stay in your home for five to seven years. If you don't meet the criteria, refinancing is not for you. *If refinancing doesn't make sense:* Consider making an extra payment each year on your mortgage. You'll save thousands of dollars in interest.

David Schechner is a real estate attorney in West Orange, NJ.

All About TIPS (Treasury Inflation-Protection Securities)

Lewis J. Altfest, CFP, president, L.J. Altfest & Co., Inc., a fee-only financial planning firm, 116 John St., New York City 10038. He is professor of finance at Pace University in New York.

Concern about inflation is real. The Consumer Price Index (CPI), the broadest measure of inflation, has risen from 1.7% in 1997 to 3.8% in 2000.

One way to protect your wealth from the inroads of inflation is to add Treasury Inflation-Protection Securities (TIPS) to your investment portfolio. *Basics...*

•**TIPS are issued by the US Treasury Department in various maturities.**

•**They pay interest semiannually.**

•**Your principal is adjusted to the rate of inflation.**

•**You can't lose principal.** You're guaranteed to get your full investment back at maturity.

BACKGROUND

The Treasury first issued 10-year TIPS in January 1997 following a 3.2% rise in the CPI in 1996.

But when the equities markets took off and inflation dissipated, most investors lost interest in a security yielding 4% with a total return of only 2.5% in 1997.

A conventional 10-year Treasury had a 12% total return that same year.

Now, the yields on TIPS look pretty good (currently 7.2%). This year, TIPS proved to be the best performing 10-year, fixed-income instrument.

HOW TIPS WORK

Money invested in TIPS increases with the rate of inflation. The inflation rate used for this adjustment is the Consumer Price Index for All Urban Consumers (CPI-U), which is published monthly by the US Department of Labor.

TIPS are available in five-year, 10-year and 30-year maturities. Just like traditional Treasuries, TIPS pay interest semiannually.

Unlike traditional Treasuries, the principal of TIPS is adjusted on the coupon date over the life of the bond. Thus, the principal compounds over time.

Example: You buy a $10,000, 10-year TIPS on January 15 with a 4% coupon and the CPI is 3% for the first six months of the year. Thus, on July 15 the principal of the bond will increase to $10,300 and your first interest payment will be $206 ($10,300 x 4% divided by 2 because this interest is for a six-month period).

If the CPI continues at the same 3% rate, then on the following January 15, the principal would adjust to $10,609 and the second interest payment would be $212 ($10,609 x 4% divided by 2).

Theoretically, principal can be adjusted downward. This would occur if the CPI showed a negative number (deflation).

However, you're guaranteed to recoup your initial investment ($10,000 in the example above) upon maturity, no matter how much the principal is adjusted downward.

Caution: Don't confuse TIPS with I bonds. While both are inflation-adjusted instruments of the US Treasury, I bonds are savings bonds with different tax rules and redemption rates.

TAX TREATMENT OF TIPS

The semiannual interest payments are taxed as ordinary income just like interest on traditional Treasuries.

However, the adjustments to the principal of TIPS are also currently taxable as ordinary income in the year they accrue—even though they are not received until the bond matures.

To minimize the impact of this tax rule requiring current income recognition for income to be received in the future consider...

•**Buying TIPS in tax-deferred accounts,** such as IRAs, where this "phantom" income problem is not an issue. You'll receive the principal adjustments at maturity, but need not pay income tax until withdrawals are taken from the tax-deferred accounts.

●**Buying TIPS through mutual funds.** Since mutual fund rules require current income to be distributed to shareholders, the inflation adjustment is paid as it accrues rather than at maturity. There are currently five TIPS mutual funds. The largest is PIMCO Real Return Bond Institutional Fund (PRRIX) that returned 12.98% from January 1, 2000, to December 14, 2000.

TIPS mutual funds own foreign as well as US securities, so there is some element of risk not associated with direct ownership of TIPS.

Tax break: Income from TIPS is free from state and local income taxes.

WHO SHOULD BUY TIPS

Some investment managers view TIPS as a separate asset class—neither a bond nor a stock. Why? Most bonds decrease with inflation, but TIPS don't.

Important: The coupon rate on a TIPS will be lower than the coupon rate on a Treasury bond of comparable maturity. But this differential doesn't necessarily mean that you'll receive less income from a TIPS than an ordinary Treasury bond.

In order to make an informed decision to purchase TIPS, you should look at the "break-even inflation rate." This can be determined by subtracting the yield on TIPS from the yield on the ordinary Treasury bond.

Example: If the 10-year Treasury bond is yielding 5.75% and the 10-year TIPS is yielding 3.75%, break-even inflation rate is 2%. If inflation is actually 2% and you expect it to remain at or below 2% for the next 10 years, then it doesn't matter which bond you purchase—you'll receive the same yield with either. But if you believe inflation will be above 2% annually for the next 10 years, then the TIPS is a better choice.

Note: Since the CPI in 2000 ran at about 4%, TIPS were a winning choice.

Secret of Much Better… And Cheaper…Banking Service

Malcolm Moses, Malcolm P. Moses & Associates, business and financial consultants, 3428 Hewlett Ave., Merrick, NY 11566.

If you run a small company, both large and small banks are interested in your business. But even if a bank solicits your business, the services you receive may not always match the red-carpet treatment you get at the outset—especially as lending has tightened at many banks.

For outstanding service, you need to learn about the banking services that are available—and build a banking relationship that allows you to get the most for your fees.

RELATIONSHIPS ARE KEY

A solid banking relationship is especially important today.

Reason: As credit becomes harder to get, banks may not be so eager to extend themselves for small customers. Business owners who have the best relationships with their bankers will get the best treatment as the economy slows. *Prudent tactics today…*

●**Establish a relationship with a bank in your area.** Large banks are usually able to offer a greater variety of services. But talk with smaller institutions, which often offer more personal service.

●**Show banks what they need to know.** This includes evidence that the company has good cash flow and that you and your top managers are experienced and knowledgeable about your industry. A formal business plan—including financial history and projections—is helpful.

The strength of your business is your best leverage for getting the lowest interest rate available. But today, most bank loans are made according to established formulas, so don't expect very much leeway on rates. More favorable treatment is likely to come only after your company has been with the bank for a period of time, will continue to be profitable, has good balances, no bounced checks and no surprises.

New loan approvals are also usually faster for established longtime bank customers—often a few days, as opposed to weeks or longer for newer customers.

● **Be prepared to provide a personal guarantee.** Most new customers will be asked by the bank to personally guarantee loans and may be required to pledge personal or business assets as security.

● **Be candid with your banker.** When your business has a problem, don't conceal it. As a rule, it's better to convey negative information during a personal visit to your bank.

Effective: In addition to breaking the bad news, describe your plan for solving the problem, and then make it work.

● **Share financial details.** If you're a borrower, make it a practice to provide quarterly financial reports to your banker. Be sure to respond promptly when your banker asks for information.

● **Focus on the people who can help you most.** Don't waste time trying to meet the top officers of your bank. Loan decisions are usually made by committee. A loan officer often acts as an advocate.

Exception: If your bank is a small local institution, it may benefit you to become acquainted with senior officers who may indeed participate in customer relations.

● **Give your banker an annual tour of the company.** Make sure the visit is during operating hours. Give the banker your current business plan and review it with him/her. Introduce him to key people and describe and/or demonstrate new products or services in development.

● **Invite your banker to lunch once or twice a year.** Suggest that he bring an assistant or colleague so you can develop more relationships at the bank. The more officers who know you, the better off you'll be.

IF YOU DON'T ASK...

Many business owners are so concerned about getting and servicing bank loans that they overlook other vital—often free—services that banks offer but don't always advertise. *What to ask for...*

● **Expert business advice.** More than almost anyone else in your area, bankers are likely to have up-to-date advice for small businesses.

Examples: Information on companies that are actual or potential suppliers as well as those that may be customers or prospects. Get on the mailing list for any industry surveys or newsletters that your bank publishes. They are often sources of valuable information that can affect corporate planning.

● **Help with finding new managers.** Your banker may occasionally recommend management talent, especially in the financial field. That's particularly true today, when even the best managers are squeezed out by mergers and downsizing.

Or if you're unhappy with your accountant, tell your banker. He may provide constructive advice.

● **Assistance in selling, buying or merging your company.** Many large banks have venture capital and merger-and-acquisition departments.

● **The bank's financial reports.** The bank's quarterly and annual reports, for example, may present a useful picture of the institution's own corporate strategy. Such information can give you valuable insights into the economy and the bank's current posture.

Useful: When you receive advice from your banker, follow up with a thank-you note—especially one that explains how you put the advice into practice. Information flow, even in the form of the occasional note, maintains your good relationship with the bank.

7

Insurance Savvy

How to Get the Most Out Of Managed Care

Health care is big business. In fact, it is the country's number-one form of commerce. But patients face a stacked deck. Health-care providers, such as doctors and hospitals, want to make money. Managed-care organizations want to save money. Your personal health comes third.

The key to getting quality medical care is to be assertive. You cannot entrust this crucial issue to anyone else.

Here's how to get the most out of your managed-care plan...

KNOW WHAT'S COVERED

Carefully read the plan documents provided by your employer or insurer to find out what is covered. Don't wait for a medical emergency to do this important fact-finding. Publications don't cover everything...and there may be gray areas that need clarification, such as care when traveling and some medications.

If you or someone in your family has a medical condition that doesn't seem to be covered, call the insurer's customer service number or emergency hot line. Ask what treatment options are covered. Get the answer in writing before proceeding with any treatment. Otherwise, you may end up paying for it yourself.

Example: For mental illness, many plans will pay for a certain number of days of care in the hospital and a certain number of outpatient visits with a psychologist. But many people with mental illness are now being treated on a "partial hospitalization" basis, spending six hours a day in the hospital and going home at night.

CHALLENGE BAD RULINGS

Your physician may advise against a certain procedure simply because it isn't covered by

Charles Inlander, president of People's Medical Society, a nonprofit organization that helps consumers make informed decisions about health care, 462 Walnut St., Allentown, PA 18102. He is author of many books, including *This Won't Hurt And Other Lies My Doctor Tells Me.* People's Medical Society.

your plan. Don't automatically accept that. Your medical options should be determined by what is best for you—not by what your doctor thinks the plan will pay for.

Get a second opinion to determine which procedure is best.

If there is a conflict between two doctors about a serious condition, seek a third opinion.

Important: Never tell the physician from whom you are seeking a second opinion what the first physician said. That may prejudice his/her opinion...and he may not want to disagree with a peer for fear of losing future referral business.

USE SPECIAL PROGRAMS

If you have a chronic health condition—asthma, arthritis, high blood pressure, diabetes, etc.—participate in your plan's disease-management program.

This is a multidisciplinary team approach that includes physicians, nurses, social workers and pharmacists. *Aim:* To prevent acute episodes that result in hospitalization.

Patients may receive special education about their conditions, frequent telephone monitoring and regular home visits by nurses.

Example: After one plan started a diabetes-management program, patients' emergency room visits dropped by 75%...hospitalizations dropped by 70%...and lost workdays declined by 63%. The annual savings amounted to about $1,500 per patient.

Ask if your plan has contracts with any *centers of excellence.* These are special facilities, such as the Mayo Clinic, the Cleveland Clinic and Memorial Sloan-Kettering Cancer Center, that are known for treating certain rare conditions, such as advanced heart disease or cancer.

Because they specialize in specific disorders, their staffs know better how to proceed without wasting time and money. They generally don't order unnecessary tests or perform procedures that are not needed.

CHOOSE YOUR HOSPITAL

Find the best hospital for your procedure. Don't automatically accept the facility that your plan routinely uses.

The medical support system at a specialized facility—nurses, technicians and other specialists—plays at least as big a role in your recovery as the surgeon.

MEDICAL CARE FOR CHILDREN

If your child has a serious illness, insist that he/she be seen by a pediatric specialist. Children have very different medical needs than adults. A doctor who sees only adults may not provide the best treatment for your child.

FOLLOW EMERGENCY RULES

Carefully follow the rules about emergency health care while traveling. Denials of such claims are a frequent source of consumer complaints, although many plans are relaxing their stance.

If you must go to an emergency room or be seen by a physician while away from home, get the following...

● **Detailed bill,** including the diagnosis and a list of services provided and charges.

● **Names, addresses and phone numbers of all health-care providers,** as well as the medical license number of the doctor who treated you.

● **Copy of medical record of your care.**

● **Letter from the doctor or hospital** stating that the treatment could not have waited until you returned home and that transferring you to another facility would have adversely affected your health.

KEEP GOOD RECORDS

At the first sign of a problem regarding your medical treatment—say, your plan refuses to refer you to a specialist when you believe you need one—start keeping notes.

Document each interaction with your physician or plan employees, noting the names of those with whom you spoke, the date of each conversation, what was said and by whom. This documentation is crucial if you later challenge the plan's decisions.

APPEAL IF NOT SATISFIED

Many denials are later reversed, so file an immediate written appeal if you disagree with your plan's initial decision.

Contact the claims examiner for your case, and explain why you feel your benefits were wrongfully denied. Also state what action you want your plan to take.

If your appeal is denied, ask the claims examiner to explain in writing why the plan rejected your claim. Then move up the chain of command and speak with the examiner's supervisor. Again, ask for the plan's decision in writing.

If you're still not satisfied, ask to have your case reviewed by the plan's medical director. Sometimes it may be necessary to contact your state regulatory agency or a private attorney.

Best line of defense in appeal: Your health-care providers' opinions. Ask your doctor to write to the plan explaining why he/she feels certain tests or treatment are necessary. If medical research or second opinions support his view, be sure to include them as well.

Health Insurance Savings

Coverage for contraception can be a big money-saver. Paying for prescription contraceptive techniques adds about $17 per employee to the annual cost of medical benefits. But about half of all fertile women will experience an unplanned pregnancy at some point in their lives, and the direct medical costs of each of those can range anywhere from $7,000 to more than $11,000, with significant indirect costs stemming from the new mother's maternity leave.

Women's Health Care Issues: Contraception as a Covered Benefit, report from William M. Mercer, Inc., a benefits consulting company, New York.

Smart Way to Get Disability Insurance

Reimburse your employer for disability insurance premiums and you'll get a much higher benefit if you become disabled. Disability payments are taxable if an employer pays for the policy—but tax free if you pay for

it. The typical cost per year—per employee—paid by employers is surprisingly low. *How to do it:* Write a check to your employer for the cost.

Jonathan Pond, president, Financial Planning Information, Watertown, MA.

How to Escape Common Health Insurance Traps

Paul Lerner and Julie Lerner, brother-and-sister coauthors of Lerner's Consumer Guide to Health Care: How to Get the Best Health Care for Less. *Lerner Communications. Paul is an AIDS activist. Julie is a five-year survivor of non-Hodgkin's lymphoma. For more on health insurance, visit* www.lernerhealth.com.

Health insurance does not cover *every* medical cost. The average American pays $1,200 out of pocket each year.

Here are seven of the most common traps that prevent consumers from getting the most from their health insurance...

***Trap:* Failing to appeal a denial for coverage.** If your health insurer denies a claim for service, don't assume the battle is lost. Submit an immediate appeal in writing.

Get the name of the insurance company's medical director and send your appeal—by certified mail—directly to him/her.

Save copies of all written correspondence. For phone calls, keep a diary. Record the date, the contact name and a conversation summary.

In your letter, stick to the specifics of your appeal. If possible, quote from your member contract section of your insurance plan information booklet to back up your appeal.

If your appeal is denied, don't give up. Most states guarantee an external appeal in which a third party objectively reviews your case. Contact your state insurance department for more information.

***Trap:* Failing to inquire about "UCR" limits** or fee schedules on out-of-network health services. "UCR" stands for "usual, customary and reasonable" medical charges.

These are defined as an average cost for a given medical service in your region.

A fee schedule typically assigns a reimbursement value to every service a physician provides. Most health plans use UCR limits or a fee schedule.

Unlike HMOs, which restrict your choice of doctors, preferred-provider organizations (PPOs) and point-of-service plans allow users to consult out-of-network physicians. However, the user must pay a percentage of the cost.

Beware: The percentage paid by the health plan applies only to the UCR rate or fee schedule for that service.

Example: Let's say your plan covers 80% of the cost for a visit to an out-of-network specialist. Let's also say the specialist charges $200, but your health plan has determined that the service should cost $100. The insurer will reimburse 80% of $100—only $80. You must pay the remaining $120 yourself.

Before consulting a doctor from outside of your network, find out your insurance company's UCR limit or fee schedule for the service or procedure.

If there is a significant difference between the doctor's fee and the reimbursement rate, explain your situation to your doctor. He may be willing to negotiate a lower rate.

Trap: **Failing to keep track of your requests for referrals.** Because referrals to specialists are costly for managed-care companies, some may process them slowly. To prevent a long delay, monitor your requests closely.

Do not see a specialist until the referral has been approved. Once your doctor has agreed to the referral, make sure both your doctor and your plan follow through. If you don't hear back within one week, call your doctor's office manager to follow up.

Trap: **Failing to find out which prescription drugs are covered by your plan.** Health plans typically have a list of approved medications. If your doctor prescribes a drug that isn't on this "formulary," you may wind up paying for it.

Call your insurer's customer service department to make sure a drug prescribed for you is on your plan's formulary before you order it.

If the drug is not covered, talk to your doctor about substituting another drug. If your doctor still prefers the drug, request that he call and ask the insurer to make an exception.

Trap: **Failing to ensure that your treatment is "medically necessary."** Most insurers cover only procedures and services they deem "medically necessary."

Example: *Rhinoplasty*—nose reconstruction—for cosmetic reasons typically is not covered. But the procedure may be covered if it is medically necessary to correct a breathing problem.

If you consult a doctor for any health condition, be sure he indicates on your chart the necessity for the medical service or procedure. If your plan denies reimbursement, ask your doctor to write a letter explaining the medical necessity.

Trap: **Failing to use preventive and wellness services covered by your health plan.** Many insurance companies offer preventive and wellness services at no cost. These may include flu shots…weight-loss and smoking-cessation programs…cancer screenings…and case management for diabetes, high blood pressure and other chronic health conditions.

Read your member handbook carefully and see an employee benefits person at your company.

Trap: **Failing to take advantage of your COBRA options.** Few people realize that they can maintain the health insurance they receive through an employer if they lose their job or become self-employed. This right is guaranteed for 18 months under a federal law known as the Consolidated Omnibus Budget Reconciliation Act (COBRA).

If you leave an employer that paid for your health insurance, ask the company's human resources department about COBRA coverage. You must pay the entire premium yourself, but the breadth of coverage and corporate rate almost always beat what you can purchase as an individual. You must sign up within 60 days of when your employer notifies you of your COBRA rights.

Buy Long-Term-Care Insurance Early

Buy the best long-term-care insurance policy you can afford while in your 50s.

Annual premiums are set for life when you acquire the policy, but cost rises 8% to 10% with each year that you wait to purchase a policy. Buying a policy in your 50s keeps premiums down.

Example: A typical policy providing an inflation-adjusted benefit of $200 per day costs $2,200 in premiums annually at age 50, $3,700 at age 60 and $6,620 at age 70.

A premium of $2,000 or so may seem like a lot of money—but considering the potential payoff, it may be a better investment than contributing the same amount to an IRA or 401(k).

Denise Kligman, head, life and health division, Owens Group Insurance Brokerage, 619 Palisade Ave., Englewood Cliffs, NJ 07632.

Accidental Death Policies Are a Waste of Money

These policies offer big payments if someone dies in a bus, train or airplane accident—but such types of death are rare. They pay *nothing* if someone dies of more probable causes, such as heart disease or cancer. While accidental-death policies carry low premiums and seem like a bargain, they are unlikely to provide money when it is needed.

Much better: A life insurance policy that pays a benefit regardless of cause of death.

Jerry S. Rosenbloom, PhD, professor of insurance and risk management, The Wharton School of the University of Pennsylvania, Philadelphia.

Be the Beneficiary of Your Own Life Insurance Policy

Lee Slavutin, CPC, CLU, a principal of Stern Slavutin-2 Inc., insurance and estate planners, 530 Fifth Ave., New York 10036. *www.sternslavutin.com.*

If you or a loved one have a life insurance policy you no longer need, simply abandoning it or cashing it in are possibilities. Another option, though, might have a bigger payoff. You can sell the policy to a buyer who will keep it in force.

For the past decade or so, such transactions have included what are known as "viatical" settlements. They are used by insured individuals with terminal illnesses or by chronically ill individuals to pay for long-term care. (*Viaticum*, in Latin, refers to the provisions furnished to a Roman official going on a journey.)

Recently, the market has expanded to include "lifetime settlements." In these transactions, policies are bought from people who are not terminally ill, or even chronically ill, but who might die in 10 to 12 years.

Bottom line: In either case, the policyholder gets money up-front. But, upon the insured individual's death, the proceeds go to investors rather than to the original beneficiaries.

VIATICAL SETTLEMENTS

As might be expected, insurance policies are easiest to sell in case of a terminal illness. With a short life expectancy, the purchase price will be greater, as a percentage of the policy's face value.

Example: Joan owns a $200,000 insurance policy on her life. If she has a 12-month life expectancy, a buyer might bid $120,000 (60%) for the policy. At her death, the buyer would collect $200,000.

Naturally, a thorough investigation of Joan's medical records would precede any sale.

Tax treatment: Viatical payments made to terminally ill individuals escape federal income tax. Several states also honor this exclusion, which is permitted no matter how the recipient uses the proceeds.

To qualify for this tax benefit, a physician has to certify that death is reasonably expected within 24 months. The payment must come from a "viatical settlement provider" who will report the amounts received (by the insured) to the IRS on Form 1099-LTC.

These providers must be licensed in the state where the insured resides. In states where viatical companies aren't licensed, providers must comply with standards established by the National Association of Insurance Commissioners (NAIC).

Viatical payments made to chronically ill individuals to pay for long-term-care costs are tax free only to a limited extent.

Caution: Check into a buyer's credentials before selling, in order to avoid paying tax on the payment.

LIFETIME SETTLEMENTS

Sellers without a terminal or chronic illness would receive a lower price, as a percentage of the policy's face value.

Key factors: If no terminal or chronic illness is evident, buyers prefer policies covering the life of a person over age 65 who has had some health problem (though not necessarily a chronic illness).

Example: Bob, 66, has been covered by a $1 million "key-person" policy by his company. He had a heart attack and is going to retire, so the key-person coverage is no longer necessary.

After looking at Bob's medical history and estimating his life expectancy, a buyer offers $150,000 for the policy.

Tax treatment: The tax consequences will depend on the amount paid and the seller's basis in the contract, which generally will be the amount of premiums paid.

Example: Bob's company has paid $150,000 in premiums. With a $150,000 purchase price and $150,000 in premiums paid, no taxes will be due.

On the other hand, if Bob's company had paid only $100,000 in premiums, taxes will be due on $50,000 of income.

Tax rates: What tax rates will apply to that income? *That depends on the nature of the policy...*

● **Permanent life insurance.** Such policies (whole life, universal life, variable life) have a cash value. The difference between the cost

and the cash value will be ordinary income—and taxed up to 39.6%. Any excess proceeds that you receive on the sale qualify for the 20% rate on capital gains.

Example: Suppose $100,000 had been paid in premiums, the cash value was $120,000 and the purchase price was $150,000. The first $20,000 will be taxed as ordinary income, while the excess $30,000 is a long-term capital gain.

● **Term life insurance.** Such policies have no cash value, although they do have viatical value, and it's uncertain whether ordinary income or capital gains rates apply.

Ascertain whether your tax preparer is comfortable reporting such income as a capital gain.

SELLING OUT

Older sellers with health conditions may get relatively high amounts for their policies.

Example: Bill, 73, was covered by a $1 million permanent life insurance policy. Now that he is divorced and his children are prospering, there is no loved one who needs the protection of life insurance.

Therefore, Bill does not wish to keep paying the premiums. He could turn in the policy for its $300,000 cash value.

Instead, he might be able to sell the policy for more money. A buyer, discovering that Bill has had health problems, might project a relatively short life expectancy and offer $500,000 for the policy.

Key: In many permanent life policies, premiums eventually are paid out of the cash value, which declines. The lower the cash value, the greater the advantage of a lifetime settlement.

A policy sale may provide needed cash if someone's circumstances change.

Example: Beth, 68, suffered a severe head injury in a skiing accident that left her mentally impaired. Medical and custodial-care bills were enormous.

Fortunately, she was covered by a $1 million term insurance policy, which her family was able to sell for $200,000 to help cover those costs.

GETTING HELP

So, just how do you go about selling a life insurance policy?

●**Ask if your life insurance agent or broker** has experience in viatical or lifetime settlements. If so, that individual can help you by asking for bids from several buyers.

If your agent doesn't know about these transactions, he/she might refer you to someone who does.

●**Go on the Internet.** Using your Web search engine, enter "viatical settlements" or "lifetime settlements" to get leads. My favorite search engines are Yahoo!, AOL and Altavista.

Contact the National Viatical Association (800-741-9465 or *www.nationalviatical.org*) or the Viatical and Life Settlement Association of America (202-367-1136 or *www.viatical .org*).

Vital: If you engage someone to help you sell your policy, be sure that person's fee or commission will be paid by the buyer, not by you.

If the agent's fee is based on the policy's selling price rather than its face value (death benefit), there's more incentive to negotiate on your behalf.

Once negotiations begin, you most likely will have to supply information about your medical history.

Getting the requisite medical information is not always easy because physicians' offices are overwhelmed with paperwork. You may have to insist that your doctor and staff proceed rapidly.

If you get multiple forms, find out if you can use those from only one company—sometimes other buyers will accept them.

Self-defense: Retain an attorney early in the process. A lawyer can help structure the transaction so that you'll receive cash rather than promises for your policy.

More from Lee Slavutin...

Long-Term Care: New Option

A problem with obtaining long-term-care insurance is that most people won't need long-term care, in which case the expensive premiums are wasted.

But new combined life insurance/long-term-care policies address this problem. The policies pay a standard life insurance benefit, but should you need long-term care, you can tap the policy benefit tax free. The life insurance benefit may be reduced by amounts spent on care needs. Whether you eventually need care or not, your premiums will earn a return. Ask your insurance adviser for details.

 # Insurance For Private Corporations

A private corporation should never own insurance on the life of its owner.

Reasons: Policy proceeds are subject to claims of the business's creditors...and may be subject to estate tax at rates up to 55%. A regular C corporation's proceeds may also be subject to the AMT.

Much better: Have the policy owned by a separate life insurance trust that is not liable for business claims, and that escapes both income and estate tax.

How (old policies): Buy it from the corporation for its cash surrender value, then transfer it to a trust.

How (new policies): Have the trust buy it directly. Consult an estate adviser.

Irving L. Blackman, CPA, is a founding partner, Blackman Kallick Bartelstein, LLP, 300 S. Riverside Plaza, Chicago 60606.

Data-Loss Insurance

Losing vital electronic data because of a power outage or virus is one of the worst disasters any business can face.

Good news: Courts support the contention that the costs of recovering lost business data are covered by a company's regular property insurance policy.

Bad news: Insurance companies are likely to fight the claim.

Essential first step: If you do lose data, make a claim quickly—so that your insurer at least cannot claim you forfeited your right to collect by making an "untimely" claim.

Robert L. Carter, Jr., and Donald O. Johnson, attorneys, McKenna & Cuneo, LLP, Washington, DC, citing *American Guarantee v. Ingram Micro*, USDA CentCalif., No. 99-185, in *American Bar Association Journal*, 750 N. Lake Shore Dr., Chicago 60611.

Avoid Tax on Life Insurance

Insurance death benefits can be taxed at rates of more than 50%. Any part of a person's estate that exceeds $675,000 in 2001 is taxed—by up to 55%. That includes insurance proceeds. State and local taxes can push the government's take higher. *To remove insurance payments from an estate:* Life insurance can be held in an irrevocable trust...by a family limited partnership...or by the insured's adult children. Each plan has complexities. Consult a financial adviser.

Stephen J. Silverberg, managing partner, Silverberg & Hunter, LLP, specialists in estate planning and elder law, 855 Franklin Ave., Garden City, NY 11530.

Most People Fail To Insure Their Most Important Asset: Themselves

Frank N. Darras, managing partner in the law firm of Shernoff, Bidart & Darras, 600 S. Indian Hill Blvd., Claremont, CA 91711. He has been involved in more than 5,500 disability insurance cases and is considered the nation's leading expert on the subject.

The odds are one in four that a 35-year-old man will miss more than 90 consecutive days of work due to an illness or injury.

The right disability insurance protects you and your family against the loss of your income in such situations. *To get the most for your money...*

DON'T COUNT ON YOUR EMPLOYER

Purchase your own individual disability insurance rather than settling for the coverage provided through your employer.

A privately purchased policy gives you far stronger rights and outstanding remedies against your insurance company if it denies your claim or fails to pay benefits promptly. *Other advantages...*

●**You can obtain more and broader coverage** than employer-provided policies typically provide.

●**Any benefits you receive are tax free if you pay premiums personally.** Benefits from employer-provided insurance are taxable.

●**Your company-sponsored insurance plan** will offset whatever benefits you qualify for by subtracting payments under your state disability insurance, workers' compensation and Social Security disability.

Result: The disability payments you receive under a company-paid policy can be pitifully small—sometimes as low as $50 a month.

THE BEST POLICY

Buy the maximum amount of individual disability coverage you can afford. That amount is determined by your annual income and will generally replace no more than 60% of your earnings. So if you make $100,000 a year, your maximum annual benefit would be $60,000.

Be prepared to provide income tax returns for the last three years to document your past earnings.

If you are self-employed, your benefits will be based on net earnings after business expenses, rather than gross business earnings.

Key requirements of any individual disability insurance policy...

●**Noncancellable.** The insurance company can never pull out of your state, regardless of how many of its policyholders later become disabled and file claims. The only way that you can lose this coverage is if you don't pay your premium within the policy grace period.

●**Guaranteed renewable to age 65.** The insurer can never increase your original premium, no matter how many policyholders become sick or injured...and no matter how much money the company is losing on its disability business.

●**Covers inability to work at your own occupation.** You will receive benefits if you can no longer do the important duties of your occupation at the time you became sick or injured—even if you could work full-time in a different occupation.

Example: A heart surgeon develops a tremor in his hands. If he has "own occupation" coverage and can no longer perform surgery, he would receive total disability benefits—even if he could work full-time as a general practitioner.

●**Avoid any *occupation* coverage.** Although this type of protection is much cheaper, it pays benefits only if you are unable to perform any occupation for which you have been trained or educated...or are suited.

Example: The heart surgeon would not qualify for benefits if he could work as a high school science teacher.

●**Obtain the longest benefit period in your own occupation for as long as possible.** You want this coverage to last your lifetime...or at least until you reach age 65. But be prepared to negotiate. Insurance companies may initially offer it for no more than two, five or 10 years—and sometimes for as little as one year. However, any period for which you are protected in your own occupation is better than having to meet Social Security's stricter standard of "any occupation."

●**90-day wait *(elimination period)* before collecting benefits.** Have enough financial reserves to weather four-and-a-half months without any income. It will likely be that long before you receive your first disability benefit payment.

Since benefits are paid retroactively—and on a monthly basis—you must be disabled at least 30 days in addition to the 90-day elimination period before benefits begin. It usually takes two weeks to process your first check, so the total wait before receiving any money is about 135 days (90 plus 30 plus 15). Extending the elimination period to 120 days or longer can cut premium costs, but the savings usually are not worth the longer wait.

Include residual coverage as an option—so if you become able to resume some but not all of your duties and have some loss of earnings, you will be entitled to partial disability benefits.

●**Avoid policies that have a *fraud exception.*** This allows an insurance company to cancel your policy if it discovers at any time that you fraudulently misstated any answer that affected its risk of insuring you.

I tell my clients to look for policies with a two-year contestability period. Then, after two years, the company can't cancel your policy even if there is misinformation. Options on the fraud exception vary by state.

Fraud exception or not, answer application questions honestly. Don't overstate income or conceal medical problems. Make sure you read the occupational, medical and financial questions yourself. A company with a two-year contestability clause has the right to rescind a policy within the first two years if it discovers you have made material misstatements.

●**Cost-of-living adjustment.** If you are young and expect to earn a lot, paying extra for this benefit is money well spent. If you become disabled at age 40, cost-of-living adjustments will keep you ahead of inflation for the next 25 years.

WHAT YOU'LL PAY

Premiums can equal or exceed those of life insurance.

Example: A 40-year-old white-collar professional earning $75,000 a year would pay an annual premium of $1,956 for an "own occupation" coverage. The policy would provide $3,900 per month in benefits ($46,800 a year), replacing a little more than 60% of his/her earnings, up to age 65. If he added a 3% cost-of-living adjustment, the premium would jump about $300 to $2,250 a year.

WHERE TO BUY

Purchase disability insurance from a licensed agent who has shopped the lowest rates and provided you with the most generous coverage available. Your agent can be helpful should you ever need to upgrade your coverage or file a claim.

Start by finding out who are the licensed and appointed agents in your area from these leading insurers…

●**Berkshire Life** (800-819-2468…*www.berkshirelife.com)*

●**Guardian** (800-933-3303…*www.glic.com)*

●**MassMutual** (800-272-2216…*www.massmutual.com)*

●**Northwestern Mutual** (414-271-1444…*www.northwesternmutual.com)*

●**UnumProvident** (800-421-0344…*www.unum.com)*

There are no Web sites that compare the cost of individual disability coverage from insurance carriers. Contact the agents or the companies individually. You can also get this insurance through professional and trade associations.

The Importance Of Flood Insurance

Get flood insurance—no matter where you live. Coverage for water damage is tricky. Homeowners' policies usually cover damage caused by falling water (rain). But damage caused by rising water is *flood damage*—covered only under federal flood insurance. *Troubling:* The nature of water damage can be a matter of opinion. If a tree hits your roof, an adjuster could say wind-driven rain knocked it over *or* rising groundwater weakened its roots, causing it to fall. *Cost:* About $300 per $100,000 of coverage.

Mike Beeman, public relations officer, Federal Emergency Management Agency, New York City.

8
Taxes

Tax Cuts for Individual Taxpayers Now and Tomorrow

The new tax law—*The Economic Growth & Tax Relief Reconciliation Act of 2001*—represents the largest tax cut in 20 years. It brings long-term tax relief to individual taxpayers in all tax brackets.

RATE REDUCTIONS

Tax rates for the four top income tax brackets—39.6%, 36%, 31% and 28%—are reduced by 0.5% effective July 1, 2001.

Additional rate reductions are introduced each year until the year 2006, when, for example, the top tax rate will have fallen from 39.6% to 35%.

Withholding: New wage withholding tables effective July 1, 2001, incorporate the reduced rates. Wage earners can look forward to higher take-home pay.

Reminder: File a new wage withholding statement with your employer if other changes made by the new law, such as the increased child tax credit, will further reduce the tax you expect to owe for the year. *To take advantage of rate reductions...*

●**Defer receipt of income to future years** when it will be taxed at lower rates. *Ways to defer income...*

●Enter into an agreement with your employer to delay receipt of compensation, including bonuses.

●Replace investments that mature this year with ones that mature in early 2002.

●Postpone year-end billing if you own a cash-basis business. This will push receipts to the following year.

●**Accelerate deductions into the current year,** when they will be worth more.

Caution: High-income taxpayers may not see the full rate cut they expected. That's because

Sidney Kess, attorney and CPA, 10 Rockefeller Plaza, Suite 909, New York City 10020. Mr. Kess is coauthor/consulting editor of *Financial and Estate Planning* and coauthor of *1040 Preparation, 2001 Edition.* CCH.

as the regular income tax drops, their alternative minimum tax (AMT) burden rises.

IMPACT ON INVESTING

The new law did not change the tax rates on capital gains, but rates on ordinary income were cut. This means that the gap between the tax on ordinary income and the tax on capital gains has narrowed.

Example: Under old law, there was an 8% spread between the tax rate on ordinary income and the rate on long-term capital gains, for taxpayers in the 28% bracket. The new law narrows this gap for this bracket to just 5% by 2006.

Impact: Holding investments long-term to obtain favorable tax rates becomes less important. Selling for investment results rather than tax results becomes paramount.

For kids: Children older than age 13 with only modest investment income—say $6,000—may wind up paying the same 10% tax rate on ordinary income and long-term capital gains.

MARRIAGE PENALTY RELIEF

For decades, married working couples who filed joint returns have paid more income tax than they would have paid had they stayed single. The new law reduces this well-known marriage penalty.

How: By increasing the standard deduction and the size of the low 15% tax bracket for married couples to twice that of singles. *Problems...*

●**Relief doesn't start until 2005** and takes four years to become fully effective.

●**Married couples who itemize deductions** rather than take the standard deduction will not benefit fully. They can only profit from the expansion of the 15% tax bracket.

Delay the wedding: Singles contemplating marriage may want to consider putting off the wedding date to gain another year of tax savings. *Note:* There are some special circumstances in which marriage may result in a tax break even before marriage penalty relief starts—such as when one spouse has income and the other has little or no income.

FOR HIGH-INCOME TAXPAYERS

Current law limits the dollar value of itemized deductions high-income taxpayers can take and reduces their personal exemptions.

New law: These restrictions will be phased out starting in 2006, becoming fully effective in 2010.

Making itemized deductions and personal exemptions fully deductible will slice an extra 1% to 2% off the top tax rate for some taxpayers. It will effectively lower their top tax bracket to 33%–34%.

Caution: Two new Congresses between now and the start of the phaseout in 2006 will have the opportunity to reinstate the restrictions on high-income taxpayers.

TAX CREDITS INCREASED

●**Child tax credit.** Starting this year, the credit for each eligible child rises to $600 from $500. The credit continues to grow until it reaches $1,000 by 2010. *Note:* The child credit phases out as income exceeds $75,000 for singles and $110,000 for married couples filing jointly.

●**Dependent care credit.** Starting in 2002, taxpayers will be able to claim a larger dependent care credit.

The credit increases in two ways. First, the amount of eligible expenses taken into account in figuring the credit rises to $3,000 for one dependent and $6,000 for two or more dependents (up from $2,400 and $4,800). Also, the maximum credit percentage increases to 35% (from 30%). *Result of these changes:* The top credit for one dependent in 2002 is $1,050 (up from $720).

The credit percentage is reduced by one percentage point for each $2,000 of AGI of more than $15,000. Thus, taxpayers with AGI of more than $43,000 are limited to a 20% credit. But these taxpayers will still have a larger credit because of the increase in eligible expenses.

●**Adoption credit.** This credit was set to expire at the end of 2001 for children without special needs. It has been made permanent for all adopted children. The amount of the credit has been increased to $10,000 per eligible child.

Starting in 2003, the credit can be claimed for a special needs adoption in the year the adoption becomes final, without regard to any adoption expenditures by the taxpayer.

And more from Sidney Kess...

Family Tax-Saving Opportunity

The maximum tax rate on long-term capital gains normally is 20%. The rate is 10% for persons who are in the 10% or 15% tax bracket on ordinary income.

But starting in 2001, persons who pay the 10% capital gains rate will owe only 8% gain tax on assets held for more than five years.

Family tax saver: Most children age 14 or older are in the 10% or 15% (or zero) tax bracket, so next year, they will get the benefit of the new 8% tax rate.

If you are planning to cash in securities that you have held for more than five years to pay expenses (such as college costs) for such a child or grandchild, consider instead giving the securities to the child and having the child sell them for his/her own account.

Your holding period for the gift assets will carry over to the child, so the child will get the benefit of the 8% tax rate. This will reduce tax owed on their sale from your 20% rate to the child's 8% rate—a significant difference.

Note: You can make annual gifts of up to $10,000 each to as many recipients as you wish free of gift tax. The tax-free limit on each gift is $20,000 if made jointly with a spouse.

Caution: Children under age 14 are taxed at their parents' tax rate for investment income over a set amount ($1,500 in 2001)—so have the child wait until he reaches age 14 to sell the capital gains assets.

More from Sidney Kess...

The Best Way to Help Pay for College: Section 529 Tuition Plans

If you have a college-bound child or grandchild, find out about "529 plans." Named after a section of the Tax Code, they are loaded with tax benefits and have already attracted billions of dollars, according to some estimates. They can be excellent vehicles for college funding.

HOW THEY WORK

These plans allow parents or grandparents to shift income to the children's lower tax brackets without losing control of the assets generating that income.

Under Section 529, states can set up plans that qualify for tax breaks. *These tax benefits are available to everyone, regardless of income...*

● **Any income earned inside the plan is not currently taxable.**

● **Money withdrawn from the plan to pay qualified higher education expenses** after 2001 is tax free.

● **Parents or grandparents can contribute $100,000** per couple for each child and elect to have that gift spread over five years, for gift-tax purposes.

The money saved in 529 plan accounts can be used to pay for tuition, books, fees and reasonable room and board charges.

Undergraduate and graduate school costs are eligible.

Beware: You can't use 529 plan money for pre-college education expenses.

CONTROL

Alternative way to shift income to your children: Transfer assets to a custodial account.

But, assets in custodial accounts will belong to the child when he/she comes of age, as early as age 18.

Trap: Money put into a custodial account will usually throw off taxable income each year to the child. This means someone has to prepare income tax returns for the student or pay a professional to do it.

With 529 plans, parents won't lose control of money meant to be used for college. There's no risk your child will use the cash to buy a car or take an extended vacation.

Fallback position: If an emergency arises and you need some cash, it can be withdrawn from a 529 plan, although a 10% penalty will be imposed.

If the money in a 529 plan isn't needed for college due to death, disability or a scholarship, penalty-free withdrawals are permitted.

Option available to all 529 investors: Roll over the account balance from one student to another family member's account, tax and penalty free.

Rollovers also may be made to a beneficiary's spouse, as a family member.

Bonus benefit: A 529 plan does not throw off taxable income until the year withdrawals are taken. This can be a huge relief around April 15 of each year until then.

Trap: On the other hand, each distribution from a 529 plan is deemed to be partially taxable—and partially tax free, depending on the current ratio of earnings to contributions. The IRS requires the program's investment director to send out Forms 1099G annually, indicating the taxable portion of withdrawals.

PAYING ATTENTION

In recent years, 529 plans have proliferated...

●**Forty-eight states have 529 plans in operation or under development.**

Exceptions: The states Georgia and South Dakota. (For current status, see *www.savingfor college.com.*)

●**Old-style "prepaid tuition plans"** are still offered by about a dozen states. In these plans, investment returns are guaranteed to keep pace with increases in college tuition. Such plans may have restrictions on who can invest and on the schools at which the proceeds may be used.

●**New plans**, which are actually managed investment funds, are becoming the norm. Some plans have guarantees and there is the potential for returns higher than the rate of tuition growth (which has slowed in the past decade).

Key: New plans are more flexible than prepaid tuition plans. Most may be open to anyone (not just to in-state residents) and the money can be used at virtually any accredited school in the US for approved higher-education-related expenses.

New-style 529 plans have more upside potential than prepaid tuition plans, too. Investors will share in any growth of the underlying securities. Proven money managers such as Fidelity, Merrill Lynch, Putnam,

and Salomon Smith Barney make the investment decisions.

In 11 states, 529 plans are run by TIAA-CREF, which manages billions of pension dollars for education and research employees.

TIAA-CREF has an excellent reputation as a low-cost money manager. On its Web site, *www.tiaa-cref.org/tuition,* you'll find a calculator to help you determine how much you need to invest for your children's college education.

In new-style 529 plans, preset asset-allocation guidelines are followed, with stocks giving way to bonds as the child nears college.

Downside: With these plans, you have no say about how college funds are invested—but you may now be able to choose the investment program (for example, opting for all fixed income).

Section 529 plans work particularly well for younger children, who will have many years to benefit from tax deferral. For such children, look for 529 plans that invest heavily in stocks, which likely will post hefty long-term returns.

MAKING CHOICES

●**Look at the restrictions.** Some plans have a three-year waiting period until proceeds can be used to pay for college so they don't make sense for older teenagers.

Other plans have only a 12-month waiting period.

●**Permitted use of funds.** Most plans state that the money can be used to pay for books or supplies or off-campus housing.

Other plans include all books and supplies as well as apartment rentals for students attending college at least half time.

●**Investigate the investment approach.** You may prefer a plan where the initial equity allocation for a young child's account is 80% invested in stocks rather than a plan where only 60% is. Long term, stocks are likely to pay off.

Playing the odds: Some plans allow investors to choose a 100% equity option, which likely will yield the highest returns over 10 years or longer.

•**Focus on fees.** Some plans charge much higher investment management fees than others. You should look for programs with a management fee of approximately 1%. Over long periods, this can make a sizable difference in the amount that has accumulated.

•**Do your homework.** Many states offer some form of state tax benefit, on top of the federal tax breaks...

•In-state investors may get a deduction or credit against state income tax.

•Plan earnings may be exempt from state income tax when used for college.

See if the value of these tax benefits outweighs any of the plan's disadvantages.

FROM GOOD TO EXCELLENT

Federal tax legislation to make Section 529 earnings tax exempt, rather than tax deferred, has passed Congress twice. But—it was vetoed as part of larger tax bills. Both political parties have expressed support for tax-free 529 plans.

If the earnings from 529 plans become tax exempt, that would apply to money already invested there.

Such an expanded tax benefit would make a sweet deal even more appealing.

Also from Sidney Kess...

How to Borrow Tax Free... And Interest Free

A business can serve as a source of *tax-free* funds for shareholders or key employees by providing loans to them.

Tax-free advances to shareholders can increase the rewards of business ownership—while those made to employees can enhance compensation packages without incurring income or employment taxes.

But careful planning is necessary—carelessly arranged loans can result in back tax bills and tax penalties.

Here's how to make the most of loan opportunities...

BASICS

Funds advanced by a business to an owner or employee through a loan are not taxable income to the loan recipient because the recipient must repay them.

Thus, business owners and employees can use loans to obtain funds from the business without incurring income taxes or payroll taxes.

Snag: The IRS knows that this gives those who control a business—its owners and key employees—good reason to claim that whatever they take from the business is a "loan," whether they intend to repay it or not.

So loan arrangements invite IRS scrutiny. If the IRS decides a loan isn't genuine, it will treat the funds advanced from the business as a taxable payment—a dividend to a corporate shareholder, or compensation to an employee.

Safety: To make sure a loan will stand up to IRS scrutiny...

•**It must look like a genuine loan** according to its specific terms and its documentation.

•**The parties must act in a manner consistent with the loan being genuine.**

To make a loan look genuine to an IRS auditor, fully document it and set terms that resemble those of a bank loan as closely as possible. *How...*

•**Have the borrower sign a promissory note** for the amount of the loan.

•**Set specific repayment terms** and a maturity date in the note.

•**Designate a market rate of interest.**

•**Have the borrower secure the loan** with collateral.

•**The note should be transferable to a third party,** just like any other debt owed to the business.

•**The company should be able to sue** if the borrower defaults.

•**The company's corporate minutes** should specifically authorize the loan and its terms.

•**The company's books should reflect the outstanding loan.**

Note: No one factor is determinative. For instance, a loan may be made without security—or even be interest free—and pass scrutiny. But the more of the traits a loan has, the more likely it is to avoid an IRS challenge altogether.

Important: It's not enough merely to formalize loan paperwork. The parties must act in a manner that is consistent with the loan being genuine.

This means the borrower must make repayments according to the loan's terms—and upon any failure to do so, the company should take steps to enforce the loan as it would any other.

No matter how complete the loan paperwork is, if the parties ignore the terms of the loan and treat it as a sham, the IRS will as well. Owners should also avoid taking loans that are proportionate in size to their ownership interest in their firm.

Common mistake: Owners of private businesses often are very careless with their corporate minutes and similar paperwork. They naturally focus more on running the business than bookkeeping.

But sloppy paperwork regarding a loan from the business can prove very expensive. Even when a loan is genuine, lack of paperwork can lead the IRS to conclude that it is a sham and to assess back taxes.

OTHER HURDLES

There are other obstacles that businesses may "trip" on when making a loan to shareholders…

● **The accumulated earnings penalty tax.** To borrow funds from a business, the business must first have saved them. But regular corporations that save too much in earnings that aren't used in the business are subject to this steep penalty tax. The tax may apply when a regular corporation has accumulated earnings exceeding $250,000 ($150,000 for professional corporations).

Snag: Unless the company is a bank, its regular business won't include making personal loans. So amounts loaned to shareholders will be accumulated earnings put to nonbusiness use. An excess amount of loans to its owners may open liability for the penalty tax.

● **Reasonableness.** It's perfectly permissible for a corporation to make loans to its owners in addition to paying dividends. But the IRS will want to see that loans are not being paid instead of dividends.

In one case the IRS challenged loans made by a company to its owner, saying they were disguised dividends. But the Tax Court upheld the loans as genuine—after which the company owner took out many more.

The IRS then challenged the loans again—and this time the Tax Court ruled for the IRS, saying, "There is a principle of too much; phrased colloquially, when a pig becomes a hog, it is slaughtered."

H.E. Boecking, Jr., TC Memo 1993-497.

DISCOUNT LOANS

In addition to conventional loans, a business may make interest-free or below-market-rate loans to owners or employees.

Interest-free loans provide obvious advantages to borrowers, but because of their tax-avoidance potential, Congress has enacted rules restricting their use. Under these rules, below-market-rate loans generally are treated as if they carry a market rate of interest, called "imputed interest." *Exceptions…*

● **If loans to the recipient don't exceed $10,000,** no imputed interest applies unless the loans have a tax-avoidance purpose.

● **When loans exceed $10,000 but not $100,000,** imputed interest is limited to the amount of the borrower's net investment income—and if that amount is under $1,000, there is no imputed interest.

Result: Under these limits, significant interest-free borrowing from a business remains possible without incurring "imputed interest."

But even when imputed interest is incurred on loans exceeding $100,000, below-market borrowing may still pay.

Rules: Interest is imputed on the loan at the "applicable federal rate," which is published monthly by the IRS. Rates vary with the term of the loan. Demand loans use a short-term rate.

The imputed interest is taxable interest income to the lender/recipient, and is deductible by the borrower if the interest on an interest bearing loan made under the same circumstances would be deductible.

At the same time, the lender is deemed to make an extra payment to the borrower that is sufficient to cover the imputed interest. This payment is treated as a dividend or compensation when the loan is made by a business, depending on circumstances. (It may be deemed a gift when a loan is between individuals.)

When these effects net out, a loan with imputed interest still may be attractive.

Example: A corporation makes an interest-free loan to an executive. An amount deemed to cover imputed interest is compensation to the executive, and the deemed payment of the imputed interest itself is income to the company. *Results...*

For the company: Taxable imputed interest income and deductible deemed compensation payment offset each other.

For the executive: The compensation received is taxable. But paying only tax on the amount deemed necessary to cover imputed interest probably will be less costly than paying real interest on a commercial loan.

Moreover, other terms of the loan may be more advantageous than would be available from a commercial lender.

In addition, the executive may obtain a deduction for the imputed interest he is deemed to pay, depending on how he uses the loan proceeds.

Example: If he uses them for investment or business purposes. This deduction may largely offset the compensation income he is deemed to receive under the arrangement.

Tax rules for below-market loans are complex. They can be found in IRS Publication 550, *Investment Income and Expenses,* in Chapter 1, Investment Income. This is on the IRS Web site, *www.irs.gov,* or can be obtained by calling 800-829-3676.

Be sure to review overall compensation strategies with an expert.

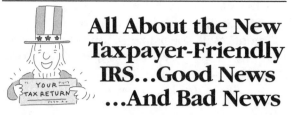

All About the New Taxpayer-Friendly IRS...Good News ...And Bad News

Edgar H. Gee, Jr., CPA, in Knoxville, Tennessee, and Willis Jackson, Esq., 602 S. Gay St., Suite 702, Knoxville, Tennessee 37902, and Michael J. Knight, CPA, Michael J. Knight & Co., CPAs, Fairfield, CT 06430. Mr. Gee is coauthor of *Guide to Worker Classification Issues.* Practitioners Publishing Co.

The IRS is going through a major structural change. For taxpayers, especially business owners, this is both good news—and bad news.

THE GOOD NEWS

There's a greater chance you'll be dealing with IRS agents who are knowledgeable about relevant tax issues.

That may mean less red tape and fewer unnecessary hassles. Although the process will take time, eventually taxpayers might not be bounced around as much when dealing with the IRS.

THE BAD NEWS

The new IRS may be able to focus more intensely on your industry—and your business.

If you try to cut corners, you might be caught by the IRS.

Bottom line: The IRS restructuring encourages you to use savvy, sophisticated tax-cutting strategies—but discourages questionable maneuvers.

SHARPENING THE FOCUS

IRS's old way of doing things: A vertically integrated, top-down structure...assignments and handling of taxpayers based on geography.

New way: A horizontally integrated structure, based on function.

The new IRS (which is partially up and running now) is arranged in four divisions...

• **Large corporations.**

• **Small businesses**—including the self-employed.

● **Tax-exempt entities.**

● **Wages and investment income.**

Agents will specialize in one area, rather than having to be broad-based Tax Code experts.

Example: The agents working on wages and investment income will have to keep up with less than 20% of the Tax Code because the other 80%-plus is not germane to their work.

SMALL-BUSINESS WORLD

Among the new operating divisions, the small-business division has the most personnel, indicating that the IRS is placing a great deal of emphasis on small-business issues.

This unit will be responsible for estate and gift tax issues, too, so you can expect scrutiny when closely held companies change hands from one generation to another.

Other issues the small-business division will be likely to emphasize...

● **Unreported income.** The IRS is aware that there are certain pockets of noncompliance, especially among small companies that do a cash business. This has been and continues to be a major concern for the agency.

● **Excess paperwork.** Business owners typically groan about the burden placed upon them by IRS filing requirements. A unit focused on the concerns of small companies may help speed the way toward more electronic filing and streamlined record keeping.

SEEING REASON

Some ongoing tax issues remain important to closely held companies and the IRS. *Example...*

● **Unreasonable compensation.** Business owners would prefer to receive deductible salaries and bonuses rather than nondeductible dividends.

The IRS, though, likes to see business owners receive some income in the form of dividends, subject to double taxation.

Trap: Frequently, the IRS will act against owner-executives, asserting that they are receiving "too much" compensation so the excess should be recast as a dividend.

Good record keeping can show that compensation was, indeed, reasonable, based upon an owner's efforts and on compensation paid to peers.

We're in an era when shortstops hitting .220 earn seven-figure salaries. And—executives of publicly held companies bring home eight figures. So, is it unreasonable that the prime mover of a successful small business be well-rewarded?

In recent cases, courts have ruled that compensation was reasonable based upon the way an independent investor would look at a company. A sufficient (over 20%) return on equity may be enough to deem compensation reasonable.

GOING SOLO

Other IRS concerns affect both large and small companies...

● **Independent contractors.** For years, the IRS has been attempting to recast independent contractors as employees, to increase payroll tax collections.

IRS backs off: Because of court decisions and federal legislation, the IRS has become more willing to concede independent contractor cases.

Historically, the IRS has looked upon people who controlled their own working conditions as independent.

New environment: "Safe harbor" provisions have been expanded significantly to provide a number of exceptions to the Internal Revenue Code's general rules.

Relying upon the advice of a qualified accountant or attorney may well provide an employer the basis for relief in independent contractor disputes.

Key: An internal IRS guide, circulated to agents, has led to a much better understanding of the independent contractor issue within the agency. Such guides will be produced for other major issues and may help IRS auditors on those topics, too.

Caution: While the IRS may be willing to acquiesce in some independent contractor cases, many states are not. They fear loss of unemployment taxes. Check with your local tax pro about your state's position.

TAXING TAX-EXEMPTS

Among the new IRS divisions is one that will cover tax-exempt entities. In addition to schools, hospitals, charities, etc., this unit will be responsible for employee benefit plans as well as state and local government tax issues.

Not-for-profit entities are attracting new attention…

●**Tax-exempt status may be questioned.** Lobbying or political activities may lead to revocation.

●**Quid-pro-quo contributions may not be fully deductible.**

Example: When donors sign up for the annual dinner dance, the value of the nondeductible meal must be revealed.

●**Unrelated business income tax may be assessed.**

Example: Souvenir sales in a museum's gift shop may generate taxable income.

Caution: The IRS has announced it is looking hard at not-for-profits' on-line operations.

If you are involved with a not-for-profit group, perhaps as a trustee or board member, be especially careful to avoid any infractions. IRS scrutiny is on the increase.

MAKE THEM AN OFFER

On the bright side, the new "kinder, gentler" IRS is more likely to accept offers in compromise. That is, the agency may settle with taxpayers for amounts less than their full tax bill.

In order to keep taxpayers in the system, financial hardship is considered in weighing taxpayers' offers. A year or two ago, that most likely would not have been the case.

A FRIEND IN NEED?

Rather than rely upon postfiling threats (audits) to sustain the system, the IRS is emphasizing prefiling and filing assistance.

Prefiling assistance may be especially valuable if IRS outreach enhances taxpayer education.

The Appeals Division will retain its autonomy, separate from the new units. That likely will maintain the objectivity and fairness of the appeals process.

NEW QUESTIONS

The probability of working with more knowledgeable agents is a plus. But—within a decentralized IRS, how will taxpayers gain access to higher authority in case of disagreements?

If agents increasingly rely on industry papers published by the IRS, will facts-and-circumstances judgment be abandoned?

How does one deal with ongoing problems? The answer is to contact the IRS's Taxpayer Advocate Service for assistance.

Outlook: Whether the IRS can reshape itself is still uncertain. Attitudes built over decades can't be overturned overnight.

Bottom line: As the Tax Code becomes increasingly complex, all taxpayers stand to gain if the IRS truly lives up to its promise of becoming a help rather than a hindrance.

How to Get The IRS to Waive Tax Penalties

Ralph Anderson, CPA, cochairman of the tax department, Richard A. Eisner & Company, LLP, 575 Madison Ave., New York City 10022.

Penalties imposed for violating the tax law can be substantial—up to 25% of unpaid tax. But in the right situations, the IRS can be surprisingly lenient.

If you know how to ask—a simple letter will do—you can have a penalty waived, though you will still have to pay the tax that you owe in addition to any accumulated interest. *Examples…*

●**First requests.** If you've never been subject to tax penalties before, simply ask the IRS to forgive the penalties—the word the IRS uses is "abate."

Penalties can be forgiven for underpayment of tax, late filing, and negligence, if handled appropriately. In my experience, waivers to first-timers are granted no matter what the reason for the penalty.

●**Newly retired/disabled taxpayers.** If you retired this year or in the prior year *after age 62* (or became disabled at any age) and underpaid your estimated taxes, the IRS is inclined to grant a waiver as long as you did not exhibit "willful neglect" to pay.

The IRS understands that retirees who formerly paid their taxes through withholding may be unfamiliar with estimated tax filing.

●**Taxpayers who change accounting firms.** If the new firm finds errors that the old one missed—and if these lead to added taxes and penalties—the IRS is likely to abate the penalties. You are, after all, voluntarily acknowledging the additional taxes and interest.

To obtain a penalty waiver in this situation, you must show that you routinely rely on professional advice. If you can prove this, the IRS will probably abate *all* penalties.

●**Insufficient records.** If you incur late-filing penalties because you don't have all the information needed to comply with tax law, abatement is generally granted.

This situation typically arises for owners or beneficiaries in pass-through entities where the entities don't provide the necessary information in time.

Example: Say you are a partner in a partnership that fails to supply you by April 15 with a Schedule K-1, which you need to complete your return. In September, you receive the form showing a sizable but unexpected income item. As a result, you've substantially underpaid your taxes and are subject to underpayment penalties. Since you lack the control over obtaining the K-1, the IRS is sympathetic and may waive the penalty.

●**Filing extensions.** Suppose you have a big tax bill due in April but don't expect to receive cash to pay the bill—a bonus or otherwise—until later. You may be able to avoid penalties for paying late.

Ask for a filing extension, and make an honest estimate of the taxes you owe and when you will be able to pay. At the same time, request abatement of late-filing penalties. You should receive it.

Example: One client of mine had a $1.7 million tax liability that he duly noted on his filing extension request, which he filed in April. He couldn't raise the money to pay the tax until October, by which time penalties of $265,000 had accrued. But since he had been accurate and honest about the taxes he owed on his filing extension request, the IRS waived *all* penalties.

HOW TO ASK FOR ABATEMENT

Abatement of penalties isn't automatic. You must ask the IRS for it and provide a reason why penalties should be waived.

For instance, if you are late in filing your return, and penalties are due, attach a letter to the return explaining that the tax and interest are being paid but that you are not paying the penalties and you wish them to be abated. *Possible explanations...*

●**You have never been liable for penalties before.**

●**You are newly retired or you have changed accountants.**

●**You made an honest mistake.**

●**You didn't have the information in time to avoid the penalties.**

●**Tax professionals steered you wrong.**

If the amount involved is $5,000 or more, it's advisable to work with a tax professional when seeking abatement. He/she can help you frame your request.

If the amount is smaller, the cost of professional fees may outweigh the penalties. Try to obtain the abatement yourself.

Great Tax Breaks For Home Owners

Laurence I. Foster, CPA/PFS, partner, personal financial planning practice, Richard A. Eisner & Company, LLP, 575 Madison Ave., New York City 10022. Mr. Foster is former chairman, estate planning committee, New York State Society of Certified Public Accountants.

When young people seek to buy their first home, they often receive help from family.

But the IRS can help too—by providing tax breaks both for the home purchase itself and for family members who assist the home buyers financially...

HELP FROM PARENTS

How parents and others can help young home buyers...

●**Tax-free gifts.** Parents or others can make tax-free gifts to a home buyer to help cover the cost of the down payment on a home.

Every individual can make gifts of up to $10,000 per recipient per year that are exempt from gift tax. So a home buyer could receive several $10,000 gifts from different family members. Married couples can jointly make tax-free gifts of up to $20,000 ($40,000 if joint gifts are made to a child and a child's spouse).

Even larger gifts can be made without incurring current gift tax by using part of your lifetime gift and estate tax credit ($675,000 in 2001).

Advantage: Such a gift may reduce future estate taxes by reducing the size of the gift maker's estate—especially if the gift funds were invested in appreciating assets.

Special help: If you are going to help a home purchaser with a gift, make a gift large enough to enable the buyer to avoid having to pay for mortgage insurance. Generally, such insurance is required when the down payment covers less than 20% of the home's value.

Avoiding the cost of the insurance premiums eliminates a charge against family wealth.

●**Interest-free loans.** In some cases, it may be better to help a home buyer with an interest-free loan rather than a gift (assuming that this doesn't prevent the buyer from obtaining a mortgage). This can provide protection against unforeseen circumstances. *Examples...*

●**Divorce.** After making a gift to your child and his/her spouse to help them buy a home, they divorce—and the house goes to the spouse who's not your child. In that case, you'll never get your gift back.

However, if you made a loan to the couple that was secured by the home, the spouse who received the home would have to repay you.

●**Hostile creditors.** A home buyer may fall into trouble with creditors who threaten to seize the home. If you assisted with the purchase of the home through a gift, that money may be lost. But if you assisted with a loan that is secured by the home, you will get your money back—because you will be the first creditor in line to be repaid, usually after the first mortgage.

Retain the option of being repaid in the future—perhaps when the home buyer is better established financially and you have greater need of the money.

If all goes well between both the home buyer and yourself, you can later forgive up to $10,000 of the loan annually as a tax-free gift (or up to $20,000 as a joint gift).

●**Co-ownership.** When a person can't qualify to buy a home alone, a parent or other family member may buy the house with the child as a co-owner.

The parent can then charge the child rent and claim the tax benefits of owning a rental property.

Depreciation and other rental expenses may shelter rental income from tax, turning the home into a tax shelter for the co-owner. And if the home appreciates in value, it may be an attractive investment as well.

For the co-owner to deduct tax losses, a fair rental must be charged to the child for the partial interest in the house that is rented. But a fair rent need not be full market rent—the Tax Court has stated that a discount of as much as 20% below market rent may be fair when renting to a family member because of the reduced risk involved. [Bindseil, TC Memo 1983-411.]

Investment rules rather than residential tax rules apply to the outside co-owner of the home. For instance, the tax exclusion for up to $500,000 of gain on a home sale won't be available to the nonresident buyer. So consult an expert before acting.

ADDITIONAL TAX BREAKS

●**IRA withdrawals.** Up to $10,000 total during the taxpayer's lifetime can be withdrawn from an IRA before age 59½ without penalty when used toward the cost of a first-time home buyer's purchase of a home.

First-time home buyer is defined as a person who has not owned a principal residence within the prior two years. A withdrawal can be made to help a spouse, child, grandchild, or parent or grandparent buy a home.

While the IRA withdrawal escapes penalty, it is still subject to income tax under normal rules.

And there's an extra cost as well—future tax deferrals are lost on the withdrawn funds. Money that is taken out of an IRA can't be replaced, and withdrawing $10,000 effectively costs five years of maximum contributions. So consider the total cost of this option before acting.

●**Loan origination fees** or "points" incurred to buy a principal residence are fully deductible (provided they are reasonable in amount in relation to normal local banking practices).

Snag: Young home buyers with few deductible items other than mortgage interest may find it does not pay to itemize deductions. That's especially important if they buy a home late in the year, so the mortgage interest deduction for the year is small. In that case, they may not be able to deduct the points currently.

Helpful: The IRS has ruled that in such a case, a home buyer can elect to amortize the points over the life of the loan—spreading the deduction over later years, when it will be more valuable. [*Letter Ruling* 199905033.]

Points also are deductible when incurred on a loan used to improve a primary residence.

Points incurred on a refinancing must be amortized—but upon a subsequent refinancing, any points that remain undeducted from a previous refinancing become deductible.

●**Home-office deduction.** This deduction can offset normal home-ownership costs—effectively providing a tax subsidy to a buyer who will qualify to claim it.

Normally nondeductible costs such as insurance and maintenance become deductible to the extent that they relate to the office. And depreciation is a no-cash-cost deduction that provides tax shelter benefits.

To qualify for the deduction: A portion of the home must be used exclusively for business. The office also must be the principal place where a business is conducted…or be used to meet with customers or clients on a regular basis…or be necessary to maintain required records for a business primarily conducted elsewhere.

The part of the home that's used as an office for more than three of the five years before a sale will be treated as business property and will not qualify for the tax exclusion.

More from Laurence Foster…

New Tax Break for Gifts to Children and Grandchildren

People in the 10% or 15% tax bracket normally pay 10% tax on long-term capital gains. But starting this year, they'll owe only 8% tax on assets held more than five years. If you are in this tax bracket, be aware of this before selling five-year-gain property this year.

Opportunity: If you're in a higher tax bracket and pay the top 20% rate on long-term capital gains, you can make a gift of five-year-gain property to children age 14 or older. But it should be a gift of a "present interest" of $10,000 or less—$20,000 or less if you are a married couple.

The children will carry over your holding period for the property—so it will be five-year property for them, too.

And if they are in the 15% tax bracket, they will be able to sell it next year and pay only 8% gains tax—compared with your 20% rate.

This can be a good way to cash in investments to pay college costs or other expenses for children.

Home-Office Snags In Home Sale Rules

It's now generally easier to avoid tax on the sale of a home, due to recent tax law changes.

Rule: Up to $250,000 of gain on a home sale is now tax free if the home has served as a primary residence for two of the prior five years. The tax-free amount is $500,000 on a joint return.

Catch: The new law also makes it more difficult to avoid tax on the part of a home that holds a home office. *How...*

•**Under the prior law, tax deferral was available for gain on a home sale,** including the home-office portion if the office did not qualify for a deduction at the time of sale.

As a result, it was easy to qualify a home office for tax deferral simply by using it for some nonbusiness purpose before the sale.

Snag: Under today's law, the "two out of five years rule" applies to a home office as well as the rest of the house. Thus, a home owner may have to go without a home office for two years prior to the sale of a home to qualify gain attributable to the part used as an office for tax-favored treatment.

•**Even if the part of a home used as an office qualifies for tax-free treatment under the "two year rule,"** gain may not be completely tax free.

The law now requires that any gain attributable to depreciation taken on the home office after May 6, 1997, be recaptured and taxed at a 25% rate.

Such depreciation may not yet amount to much in dollar terms—but it will grow each year.

Strategy: Be aware of the steps needed to get tax-favored treatment for a home office before selling a home. And beware of the tax cost before establishing one.

New Rules on Tax-Free Home Sales

New proposed regulations spell out the rules for claiming an exclusion for up to $250,000 of gain on the sale of a home ($500,000 on a joint return). Home owners should examine the rules for unexpected traps and opportunities. *Example:* One does not have to own and reside in the home at the same time. Thus, a person who owned a home for two years and resided in it for a different two years qualifies for the exclusion.

Proposed Treasury Regulations, REG-105235-99.

Joint Ownership of Property Trap

The common practice among married couples of owning property jointly can be a big mistake for estate tax purposes.

Why: When one owner dies, jointly owned property passes automatically outside the terms of the will to the surviving owner. This can cause many problems, including loss of one spouse's personal estate-tax-exempt amount.

Example: In 2001, the estate-tax-exempt amount is $675,000, so a couple can bequeath up to $1.35 million free of tax by using both their exempt amounts.

But if they own all their property jointly, upon the death of one spouse it will all pass to the survivor *without* the first spouse using his/her exempt amount. The property will pile up in the survivor's estate and be exposed to tax to the extent it exceeds the single exempt amount that remains available.

Best: Consult with an estate-planning professional about moving to separate ownership of property. With proper planning, a credit shelter trust can be used to hold separate property so that it does benefit from the estate-tax-exempt amount upon the death of the first spouse, yet can be used for the benefit of the surviving spouse for his/her entire life.

Irving L. Blackman, CPA, founding partner, Blackman Kallick Bartelstein, LLP, 300 S. Riverside Plaza, Chicago 60606.

Property Tax Trap

If you have a mortgage escrow account, call your county or town tax assessor to be sure your taxes are paid. You are legally responsible—and held personally liable on the tax roll—for delinquent taxes. *Problem:* Mortgage servicers have discretion on when they pay taxes. They pay at their own convenience—some even incur penalty costs for paying late if it's easier for their bookkeeping. *If you get a delinquency notice:* Call your servicer for an explanation. It could be an innocent mistake—or your account could have been transferred to another company. Despite some abuses, escrow is useful for many people. It serves as a forced savings account to make sure money for taxes is available when needed. And many mortgage companies require it.

Richard Roll, president, American Homeowners Association (AHA), national consumer membership organization, Stamford, CT.

Big Tax Deductions That Business Owners Too, Too Often Miss

Barbara Weltman, author of several books, including *J.K. Lasser's Tax Deductions for Your Small Business, Fourth Edition.* John Wiley & Sons. She is an attorney in private practice in Millwood, NY.

Most business owners know that the vast majority of expenses related to running the business are tax deductible. However, the tax laws keep changing and that means very few business owners take full advantage of the many tax breaks available to them.

Fortunately, most tax errors and oversights can be easily corrected with some looking ahead of your own and a session with your tax adviser early enough in the tax year to permit strategic planning. *Here are the main areas for potential tax savings...*

●**Automobile write-offs.** A frequent error is not maximizing the write-off for a car used in business. The path of least resistance is to automatically take a deduction based on the standard mileage rate—34.5¢ per mile in 2001. But if you had heavy repair costs or your insurance costs suddenly shot up or you didn't drive much, your deduction could be much bigger if you base your write-off on the actual cost method.

Strategy: Chances are you won't know until year-end which method is most advantageous. Play it safe by keeping good records all year of expenses related to the business use of the car. Otherwise, you must default to the standard mileage rate, which may not be the best way to go.

●**Expensing vs. depreciation decision.** Buying equipment raises the question of whether the new item should be expensed—written off at once—or depreciated over a period of years. Expensing the purchase generally produces the greater tax benefit, so most businesses assume that is always the better choice.

Exceptions to the rule: Expensing only pays if you have enough income to offset the expense. If your business is a start-up, you probably don't have enough income to expense. You're also probably better off depreciating rather than expensing if the business is having a bad year and you don't think profits are going to improve anytime soon.

●**Keep all the records you are supposed to.** Some business owners assume that if they just throw all their receipts into a box, that will take care of everything. In such tricky areas as travel and entertainment, the IRS sets down rigid rules about the records you must keep. If the IRS audits your return, and your records don't measure up, you lose the write-off, even if it was a legitimate business expense.

Example: Just keeping the credit card receipt from a business lunch isn't enough. The IRS will disallow the deduction if you can't show the date, the amount spent, whom you entertained at lunch and the business reason for getting together.

Keep all receipts that establish a legitimate business expense. Keep a diary or an expense log in which you enter every item the IRS wants you to record.

●**Overlooked deductions.** Small-business owners get so bogged down in day-to-day management that many tax-saving deductions never get taken. *Here are frequently overlooked deductions...*

●Business entertaining in your home. If you entertain business clients in your home, you can write off the cost of the meal, the liquor you served, even the flowers you used to brighten the table. You must be able to justify the deduction—meaning you must keep the same detailed records as you would if you entertained the person at a restaurant.

●Clothing specific to the job. You can't write off the cost of clothing you wear on the job if it also is usable on the street. You can deduct the cost of buying, cleaning and maintaining clothing specific to your business that isn't readily adaptable to street use—coveralls, for instance, or protective gear.

A recent court case held that a nurse could deduct the cost of her uniform because it was specific to her job, but not the cost of the athletic shoes she wore, because they also could be worn on the street.

●Charitable contributions. Within limits, you can deduct donations the business makes to a legitimate charity. You also gain a deduction—and a morale booster for employees—by matching the contributions they make.

Training and education costs: You obviously get to write off the cost of training your employees, but there is a potential pitfall here. Most of the time, you can expense the training costs—writing them off in the year incurred. But—the IRS and the courts have recently become more aggressive in requiring that certain types of training expenses be capitalized and written off over time.

There is not a clear line here—between expensed and capitalized training costs. In most cases, you can expense them—but there is a slim chance you might be challenged. The safest course is to consult your tax adviser about the issue before making your final decision.

●**Retirement plans.** Employee retirement plans not only offer tax advantages to the business, but also are essential in retaining quality employees in today's tight job market. Yet many small-business owners still regard retirement plans as too costly and too complicated to consider.

How to do it: A SIMPLE (Savings Incentive Match Plan for Employees)—allowing for annual contributions by participants of up to $6,500 in 2001—requires almost no paperwork to create. All you must do is make an employer contribution based on an easy-to-calculate formula.

You write off your contribution as the employer. You can contribute to the plan yourself and gain a further tax break since your contribution reduces your taxable income.

●**Home office deduction rules have been liberalized.** If you work from home, you may be entitled to a home office deduction, even if you weren't entitled to one in the past.

Old rule: In the past, you actually had to earn money from your home office. A freelance writer who spent all his/her time working at home could qualify. A plumber who operated out of a home office but made his money in the field, could not.

New rule: Going back to the 1999 tax year, you qualify for a deduction if you use your home office for substantial administrative or managerial activities—keeping your books and records, scheduling appointments, ordering supplies—and have no other fixed location for doing that kind of work.

●**Hiring family members.** The salary paid to any family member working in the business is a tax-deductible expense. The only qualifications are that the family member must be doing legitimate work and the compensation must be reasonable.

Important: There are special tax benefits if you use your children in the business. A child can earn up to the standard deduction tax free—$4,550 in 2001. Salary paid to your child under age 18 is not subject to FICA if you're self-employed. Finally, the child can use the income to fund a Roth IRA, which builds up tax free over the years and allows withdrawals of earnings not subject to taxation in the future.

More from Barbara Weltman...

New Filing Trap for Couples

Starting this filing season, if the second Social Security number on a joint return does not match the name for it in the files of the Social Security Administration (SSA), the IRS will remove the name from the return. It will then treat the return as a "single" or "head of household" filing—increasing the amount of tax due.

Example: The IRS sent warning letters to 2.4 million people who had mismatched numbers on 1999 returns. Many more were affected, including newlyweds.

If you've changed your name, inform the SSA before you file by requesting a new Social Security card. Use Form SS-5, *Application for a Social Security Card,* available at *www.ssa.gov* or by calling 800-772-1213.

More from Barbara Weltman...

Use the Copier

Do not give the IRS originals of any documents it requests. Courts have ruled that the IRS is not responsible for the consequences if it loses documents. *Bottom line:* Be sure to keep originals of anything given to tax authorities.

And from Barbara Weltman...

Social Security Tax-Saving Strategy

Social Security recipients lose a significant portion of benefits to taxes if their income exceeds certain limits. More specifically, when Modified Adjusted Gross Income (MAGI)—which is Adjusted Gross Income increased by tax-free interest on municipal bonds, certain exclusions and a portion of Social Security benefits—exceeds...

●**$32,000 on a joint return** or $25,000 on a single return, up to 50% of Social Security benefits are included in taxable income.

●**$44,000 on a joint return,** $34,000 on a single return or zero if married filing separately, up to 85% of Social Security benefits are included in taxable income.

●**Tax-saving strategy.** Reduce tax on your Social Security benefits by reducing your MAGI. *How...*

●Defer income. Invest for growth rather than income. Postpone realizing gains on investments and taking discretionary distributions from IRAs and other retirement plans.

●Make tax-free investments. Roth IRA payouts of earnings are tax free if certain conditions

are met, so fund a Roth IRA rather than a regular IRA.

Interest from tax-free municipal bonds is included in MAGI for purposes of determining tax on Social Security benefits—but municipals pay a lower interest rate than taxable bonds.

●Shift income. Make estate-tax-reducing gifts of property to younger family members by shifting income-producing property.

●Deduct losses. At year-end, take "paper" investment losses to offset income from gains and up to $3,000 of ordinary income. You can repurchase the loss investment after 31 days, or a similar but not identical one immediately.

Finally from Barbara Weltman...

How Long to Keep Old Tax Records

The IRS says taxpayers must keep old tax returns and other tax records for as long as they may be needed for the administration of any provision of the Tax Code.

Generally, this means you must keep records that support the items shown on your return until the statute of limitations for that return runs out.

Major Time Limitation Periods

Normal audit limit ....3 years

Audit limit if gross income is understated by 25% or more ....6 years

Time limit for deducting worthless securities/bad debts........7 years

Audit limit if no return is filed..........no limit

Audit limit if fraud is committed ......no limit

Important: All tax records for properties such as homes, businesses and investments should be held until you dispose of them and report the disposition on your tax return, in addition to the time limits above.

Trap: The IRS can always create a situation in which it says no time limit applies to your return by alleging that you never filed or that you committed fraud on your return.

You'll need copies of your return to refute such an allegation—so the safest practice is to keep your returns forever.

Roth IRAs Are Being Underused Because People Are Shortsighted Tax-Wise

Ed Slott, CPA, E. Slott & Co., CPAs, 100 Merrick Rd., Rockville Centre, NY 11570. *www.irahelp.com.*

Roths have an immediate tax cost compared with traditional IRAs. Contributions aren't deductible, and conversions to Roth IRAs are taxable.

But people who focus on the Roth's upfront tax costs neglect long-term tax benefits that may be much larger...

•**Future distributions of earnings** may be totally tax free instead of taxed at ordinary rates—usually enough to make up for the current tax cost.

•**There's no minimum distribution requirement,** so funds can be invested in the Roth IRA for tax-free gains longer.

•**Roth IRAs can be used to make highly tax-favored bequests.**

•**The $2,000 per year Roth IRA contributions** can be withdrawn both tax and penalty free at any time for any reason.

Also from Ed Slott...

Gift Tax vs. Estate Tax

Using an IRA to fund gifts can be better than leaving it subject to estate tax. *Why:* Gift tax is much less costly than estate tax.

Example: In the 55% gift-and-estate-tax bracket, a gift of $500,000 results in gift tax of $275,000. But to make a $500,000 bequest, an estate needs more than $1.1 million. The estate tax of $610,000 is more than twice the gift tax because it applies to the whole estate not just the gift amount.

Strategy: When an IRA faces estate tax, withdraw funds from it, pay income tax on the withdrawals and use them to fund lower-tax-cost gifts. Use the annual gift tax exclusion to shelter gifts from gift tax to the extent possible.

Even better: Use IRA withdrawals to finance life insurance that can provide even bigger tax-free benefits for heirs.

Only the IRS Can Put a Lien on a Pension Account

Federal law that governs qualified retirement plans exempts pension-plan accounts from creditor claims, except claims of the IRS. So if the IRS places a lien on a pension-plan account and its owner then declares bankruptcy, the lien will survive bankruptcy and enable the IRS to collect the pension proceeds when they become payable to the owner. And, the IRS says that, since it is the only party that can collect against the pension account in that case, the bankruptcy court should pay the account over to the IRS immediately.

IRS Legal Memorandum 200041029.

Best Ways to Write Off Worthless Securities

Richard J. Shapiro, Esq., tax partner, Ernst & Young LLP, 787 Seventh Ave., New York City 10019. Mr. Shapiro is author of *Taxes and Investing—A Guide for the Individual Investor.* Options Clearing Corporation. The book is available free from the various national stock and option exchanges.

If you determine that a security you own has become worthless—and there are many in this time of dot-com fizzles—you can write off the loss in the year of worthlessness.

Generally you can claim a capital loss—a short-term loss (on securities held one year or less) or a long-term loss (more than one year)—depending on the purchase date. The sale date is considered to be the last day of the year in which the security became worthless.

Example: You purchased a hot dot-com when it went public on November 1, 2000. The company went under in October 2001, ceasing all operations. Your loss is a long-term capital loss because your holding period runs from November 1, 2000, through December 31, 2001.

Important: A loss for a worthless security must be taken in the year it becomes worthless. If you do not claim a loss on your original return, you can file Form 1040X, *Amended US Individual Income Tax Return,* to amend your return for the year the security became worthless. You generally have seven years from the due date of your original return to file the amended return.

Note: A security must be totally worthless. You can't take a loss for a partially worthless security.

WORTHLESSNESS THE EASY WAY

You're in luck if the company was liquidated because you'll be notified of this. You will receive a Form 1099-DIV, *Dividends and Distributions,* at the end of the year showing the liquidation distribution (which may be zero).

This date of "sale" is the date of the distribution and, by using your original cost basis, you can compute your gain or loss.

But, even if the company was liquidated, you might never be notified or receive a 1099.

WORTHLESSNESS THE HARD WAY

You can claim a loss for worthless securities (stocks, bonds, notes, debentures) even if the company has not been liquidated. Even though the IRS doesn't provide a definition of "worthlessness," you must be sure the security is worthless to the satisfaction of the IRS. *To support your deduction, establish that...*

●**There is no current liquidating value of the company** and no foreseeable value in the future.

●**The liabilities of the corporation exceed its assets** and there is no expectation that the business will continue.

●**The books show balance sheet insolvency** and the business has ceased operations.

Important: Get a letter from your broker or the company noting the year the security became worthless.

Do not confuse a bankrupt company with a defunct company. There are many companies that continue to operate in bankruptcy and their stocks and bonds continue to trade—the prefix "vj" is often used in newspaper listings to note securities trading in bankruptcy.

If you have securities that you have deducted as worthless which later regain value, the IRS does not require you to amend your return. Instead, use the date you declared them as worthless as your acquisition date—and zero as your cost basis—to determine any future gain.

END RUN

The best way to take your loss and ensure its deductibility is to close your position by selling the securities. Many brokerage firms will buy your worthless securities for $1 for the lot. The sale establishes worthlessness.

If your broker holds the securities in "street name," having the broker buy them for $1 is a simple solution. If you're holding the securities yourself, sell them to someone—but not your spouse, siblings or lineal descendants.

Procedure: Sell the securities to an individual for $1, receive a check for payment in this amount and write a bill of sale. Then, sign over the certificate and have it verified by your broker or bank. Send the certificate to the transfer agent of the company and have a new certificate issued to the new owner.

OTHER WRITE-OFFS

Expenses you incur in investing activities are deductible, subject to the 2%-of-adjusted-gross-income floor on miscellaneous itemized deductions. *Deductible investment expenses include...*

●**Accounting fees** for maintaining investment records.

●**Computer and on-line services.** *Note:* You cannot claim first-year expensing for the cost of a computer but instead must depreciate its cost. You allocate the cost of the computer between investment and business use—and personal use—to find the portion you can depreciate. Software generally is depreciated over three years (or faster if the software has a shorter life).

●**Fees for investment planners.**

●**Safe-deposit box rental to store and safeguard securities.**

●**Subscriptions to investment newspapers, newsletters, and magazines.**

You cannot deduct certain expenses, even if you really do incur them in the course of your investing activities. *Nondeductible investment expenses include...*

●Broker's commissions. These are added to the cost basis of securities, thus minimizing gain or maximizing loss when the securities are sold.

●Home-office expenses.

●Trips to investment seminars.

●Trips to stockholders meetings (unless there are unusual circumstances).

How to Avoid Year-End Mutual Fund Tax Traps

Carole Gould, Esq., frequent contributor of articles on mutual fund investing to *The New York Times* and author of *The New York Times Guide to Mutual Funds.* Times Books.

As the year draws to a close, you may be tempted to dump your losing mutual funds and buy new ones.

Be careful! You can easily buy yourself a big increase in your tax bill in April.

Watch out for the following mutual fund tax traps...

Trap: Buying into a mutual fund late in the year. The problem is that most funds pay dividends in November or December. Buying shares in a fund that will soon pay dividends is a bad idea because all shareholders as of the record date receive a full year's worth of dividends...even if they've owned shares for just one day.

The tax law requires you to pay tax on a distribution even if you reinvest the dividends in the fund.

Because undistributed dividends are part of a fund's assets, when dividends are paid out to shareholders, the fund's share price drops.

Your shares will be worth less, but you will have cash or more shares if you reinvest. So the value of your holdings remains the same —except for any taxes you owe.

Example: On December 10, you buy 100 shares of ABC Fund for $2,000, at $20 per share. The fund pays a $2 per share dividend on December 20, and its price drops to $18. You now own shares worth $1,800 plus $200 cash. Taxes owed at the capital gain rate of 20% equal $40. In only 10 days, your $2,000 investment has shrunk to $1,960.

Note: If you make this investment through a tax-deferred account, such as an IRA, the value of your investment remains unchanged because there are no current taxes.

Salt in the wound: If ABC Fund suffers a big loss before year-end, you'll have lost money on your investment, but still have to pay tax on the dividends that were distributed.

Avoidance: Wait until *after the shareholder record date* to buy fund shares. Call the fund's investor services line for the exact date.

Trap: Not recognizing that switches among funds within a fund family create taxable gains. Most fund companies let you switch money among their stock, bond and money market funds with a telephone call or over the Internet. It's so easy that many investors don't realize the switch is a taxable sale.

When you move money among accounts, the IRS says you sold shares in the first account and reinvested the proceeds in the second account. You owe taxes on any gains.

Avoidance: Make sure any switches among funds make sense tax-wise (as well as investment-wise).

Caution: You can also create taxable gains by writing checks against fund holdings.

Trap: Losing tax-deductible losses by reinvesting sales proceeds in the same fund. The "wash-sale" rule prevents you from deducting a loss when you sell shares in a mutual fund and then buy shares in the same fund within 30 days before or after the original sale.

Avoidance: To claim a loss in 2000, invest the money in a similar but not identical fund.

(*Example:* Reinvest in a large-cap growth fund run by another fund family.) Or wait 31 days to buy shares of the original fund.

Trap: Not maximizing your 2000 mutual fund investing expenses. Fund investing expenses are considered "miscellaneous expenses," which are deductible to the extent they exceed 2% of your Adjusted Gross Income (AGI).

Strategy: Maximize the deduction by bunching payments and deducting them in 2000. (Delay payments till January if you expect to have a lower AGI next year.)

What's deductible: Cost of books giving investment advice...newspapers and magazines with investment advice...investment counseling and advisory service fees... postage and telephone costs related to investing...Internet access fees for on-line investing.

Filing Extension Trap for Retirement Plans

It's not true that contributions to Keogh plans and other personal retirement accounts always can be made as late as the extended due date of your tax return. Plans that have "minimum funding standards"— such as defined-benefit and money-purchase plans—must be funded by 8½ months after year-end. That is *September 15*, even when a tax return is extended to October 15.

Trap: The IRS's own publications say the "contribution deadline" is October 15 when a return is extended until then. But the Tax Court says that is for deduction purposes only. To meet minimum funding standards, contributions must be made by September 15 or penalties apply.

Phillip M. Wenger, CPA, TC Memo 2000-156.

How to Donate an IRA to Charity

If you wish to make a bequest to charity, it may be better to donate a traditional IRA instead of cash or property.

Why: When you donate cash or property to charity and leave an IRA to family members, funds in the IRA will be subject to income tax when distributed.

But if you do the reverse, leaving the IRA to charity and cash/property to family, your family will get the cash/property income tax free.

Best: Name a charity as the direct beneficiary of a separate IRA. This minimizes the negative impact that the charitable beneficiary may have on the size of your overall minimum required annual distribution.

If you later wish to reduce the bequest, take all your required IRA distributions from this IRA.

All in the Family Loans

Loans to family members—*assume you will never be paid back.* Borrowing from family is usually a last resort. *Trap:* Even well-meaning family members will put you at the bottom of their list of creditors. *Reminder:* You can give a gift of $10,000 to anyone tax free every year—$20,000 from a couple giving jointly. If you have the means, consider family loans gifts—don't expect to be paid back. This prevents hurt feelings and strained relationships when the loan is not repaid. And while from an income tax standpoint, writing off a bad loan is preferable to making a gift, it may invite IRS scrutiny, so put it in writing.

Jonathan Pond, president, Financial Planning Information, 9 Galen St., Watertown, MA 02472.

How to Tap Your Nest Egg In Very Tax-Wise Ways

Harry R. Tyler, CFP, CLU, ChFC, president, Tyler Wealth Counselors, Inc., Suite 200C, 1450 E. Boot Rd., West Chester, PA 19380. He is an accredited instructor for the Pennsylvania Institute of CPAs' continuing professional education courses.

When you retire you stop receiving paychecks. You must then rely on unearned income—Social Security, pension, 401(k), IRA, and, for a truly comfortable retirement, money from an investment portfolio you've accumulated with after-tax earnings.

Key: Circumstances vary, but most people will be able to withdraw about 5% or 6% of their invested assets each year in retirement, and still maintain the purchasing power of the balance.

Example: If you think you'll need $50,000 or $60,000 per year in retirement from an investment portfolio, you should intend to accumulate at least $1 million. Chances are you'll be able to withdraw the desired amount while watching your portfolio continue to grow—if you have invested sensibly.

TAXABLE OR TAX DEFERRED

Figuring out how much you need to accumulate and how much you can withdraw is only half the problem though.

If you have a tax-deferred retirement account (such as an IRA) as well as investments in a taxable portfolio, which do you tap first?

You might draw down taxable investments, leaving your IRA to compound tax deferred. This can go on until age 70½, when legally required minimum distributions begin.

Problem: The money may be compounding tax deferred, but higher taxes may actually be due at some point. *Result:* The tax-deferred compounding benefits the IRS, too. The longer you leave money in the account and the more you accumulate, the larger your tax obligation will be.

The money that comes out of a traditional IRA is fully taxed at ordinary income rates, which can be more than 40%, federal and state included. (Withdrawals from a Roth IRA, of course, can be fully tax free.)

After age 70½, you must begin to take minimum withdrawals from your IRA, based on the size of the account. If the account keeps growing, you may be required to take an amount so large you'll be pushed into a higher tax bracket.

Problem: If you draw down all other assets and let your IRA build up, that account may be exposed to estate, as well as income, taxes after your death and your spouse's death.

Bottom line: In your IRA, you're building up dollars that will be heavily taxed. (The IRS never intended to lose money in the long run on IRAs.)

DRAWING DOWN RETIREMENT PLANS

Better way: Draw down your IRA first, and your other investments later.

As long as you're over age 59½, you can withdraw money from your IRA without incurring a 10% early withdrawal penalty.

By taking some withdrawals between age 59½ and 70½, you may keep your tax-deferred account small enough so that when required minimum distributions begin, you won't be in a higher tax bracket.

While you draw down your IRA, you let your taxable accounts continue to grow. If those taxable investments are largely in individual growth stocks—the approach I recommend—and you don't trade heavily, you should have little taxable income each year and enjoy a kind of tax deferral on those assets in the form of unrealized appreciation.

END OF THE LINE

If you draw down your tax-deferred assets while allowing your taxable accounts to grow, you may eventually use up your entire IRA.

At that point, start to sell assets (stocks and stock funds) from your taxable account to support your retirement. If you hold a diversified portfolio, you can dispose of low-appreciation securities or even securities you're holding at a loss to manage your tax bill while providing retirement income.

Even if you have to realize some gains when you sell securities from your portfolio, they may qualify for the tax-favored 20% rate on long-term capital gains, if they've been held more than 12 months. If you're in the lowest (15%) bracket, a 10% rate may apply.

New break: As of 2001, newly acquired assets held more than five years qualify for an 18% capital gains tax rate. For low-bracket taxpayers, the capital gains rate falls to 8% for assets held more than five years regardless of when they were acquired.

Holding onto appreciated securities makes even more sense now because they may qualify for special low rates.

Estate tax loophole: At your death, you can pass on all of your securities to your heirs, who'll get a basis step-up and owe no income tax on all prior appreciation, under current law.

Note: IRAs and other tax-deferred plans won't get a step-up in basis.

FOR EARLY BIRDS

If you need income before age 59½, tapping your IRA usually means paying a 10% penalty on top of income taxes.

You can avoid the penalty by taking *substantially equal periodic payments* (SEPPs), based on one of three IRS-approved methods. Once started, these payments must continue for at least five years or until age 59½, whichever comes later.

The SEPP rules can be massaged so that you can take out virtually any amount you need, penalty free, as long as your IRA is large enough. You can select whichever of the three methods (minimum distribution, amortization, or annuitization) works in your situation.

Tactic: Split your IRA into two or more separate IRAs.

Example: You have a $300,000 IRA and you want to withdraw $1,250 per month. However, the SEPP rules (amortization method) require you to withdraw $1,875 per month from a $300,000 IRA. You'd be paying tax on an unneeded $675 a month.

Solution: Split your $300,000 IRA into a $200,000 IRA and a $100,000 IRA. You could take distributions from the $200,000 IRA, pulling out the desired $1,250 per month from that account, using the amortization method.

The other $100,000 IRA can remain untouched to continue its tax-free buildup, until you are beyond age 59½ and clear of the 10% penalty.

The 10 Most Common Tax Return Filing Mistakes

Randy Bruce Blaustein, Esq., is a senior tax partner in the accounting and auditing firm of Blaustein, Greenberg & Co., 155 E. 31 St., New York City 10016.

The most common filing mistakes on Form 1040 tax returns, as reported by the IRS...

1. Incorrect taxpayer identification numbers, resulting in *disallowed exemptions*.

2. Incorrect taxpayer identification numbers, resulting in disallowed child tax credit.

3. Earned income credit figured or entered incorrectly.

4. Dependent's last name is incorrect.

5. Primary Social Security number incorrect.

6. Incorrect Social Security numbers for children, resulting in loss or adjustment of earned income credit.

7. Nontaxable earned income from W-2s not included on returns, so earned income credit is changed.

8. Child tax credit figured incorrectly.

9. Based on information reported, IRS refigures tax using the filing status for a single person.

10. The refund amount or amount owed is figured incorrectly.

Also from Randy Blaustein...

IRS Scrutinizes Offshore Banking

The IRS is targeting credit card account records to detect persons using offshore banks to evade taxes.

The IRS says the use of offshore tax haven banks by high-income individuals has grown to the point where it is costing as much as $70 billion in taxes annually.

Key: It's perfectly legal to move funds to a foreign bank. But banks in tax havens, such as the Bahamas and Cayman Islands, often fail to report to the IRS income earned on the funds they hold—letting US residents illegally avoid tax.

That leaves the US account owners with the problem of how to get their money out. One strategy the banks have come up with is to give account owners credit and debit cards that are paid from the foreign accounts.

Now: The IRS is onto the game, and is seeking the records of credit card companies to identify the people using this strategy.

More from Randy Blaustein...

Time-Shares Have No Real Estate Tax Benefits

The reason, they are not real estate purchases. A time-share is simply the right to use property that is owned by someone else, usually a resort developer. Since you are buying only the right of temporary occupancy— and not an equity position—you get none of the tax benefits of buying a house or an apartment. And in the unlikely event that a time-share increases in value, your profits are fully taxable if you sell.

 ## Holiday Savings

Company holiday parties are fully deductible. The cost of business meals and entertainment normally is only 50% deductible. But this limit does not apply to social activities for company employees to which staff members at all levels are invited along with top executives. Employees' families may be invited to the activities as well.

Examples: Christmas parties, company outings, dinners celebrating company anniversaries or business milestones. All costs associated with such events are fully deductible.

Irving Blackman, CPA, founding partner, Blackman Kallick Bartelstein, LLP, CPAs, 300 S. Riverside Plaza, Chicago 60606.

New Tip Tax Rule

The IRS is extending "voluntary tip income compliance agreements" to all industries in which tipping is customary. Under these agreements, employers instruct employees about the need to report tips as income and establish procedures that employees can use to do so. In exchange, the IRS agrees not to conduct any tip-reporting audits of the employer.

Until now, these agreements have been available in only a handful of industries—primarily the restaurant industry. If your business has potential audit exposure regarding tip income, consult a tax adviser.

IRS News Release, IR-2000-26.

How to Protect Yourself With a Private IRS Ruling

Seymour Goldberg, Esq., CPA, Goldberg & Goldberg, PC, 666 Old Country Rd., Suite 600, Garden City, NY 11530. Mr. Goldberg is author of *J.K. Lasser's How to Protect Your Retirement Savings from the IRS* (John Wiley & Sons) and *Pension Distributions: Planning Strategies, Cases and Rulings* (New York State Society of Certified Public Accountants).

It's not necessary to take a chance with the IRS when you adopt an important new tax strategy that you fear might later be challenged.

You can protect yourself in advance by obtaining a *private* IRS ruling that will shield you from any related IRS audit challenge in the future.

UNIQUE FACTS

Every taxpayer is in a unique position compared with every other.

So when you devise a new tax strategy that is customized to your needs, you may not be able to find a favorable court precedent or published IRS ruling that is exactly consistent with your situation. This backup doesn't guarantee favorable tax treatment.

Risk: Even if your planning is done with a skilled professional adviser, the Tax Code is so technical that an overlooked detail in the rules could result in a costly tax dispute—and in possibly steep back-tax payments and penalties.

Whether your tax planning involves your personal taxes, estate plan, IRAs and retirement accounts, or business, it can be a great benefit to gain advance knowledge of how the IRS will treat your transaction.

HOW TO GET A RULING

A private letter ruling is issued by the IRS to a particular tax-payer—either an individual or a business—and specifies how the IRS will treat a transaction.

Private letter rulings can be obtained *before* transactions take place to learn how the IRS will treat them.

A favorable ruling *guarantees* favorable tax treatment according to its terms—even if the IRS decides to treat other taxpayers differently by assessing tax against other persons who are in the same position as you.

Unfavorable private rulings are very rare.

Reason: In the process of obtaining the ruling, your tax adviser will discuss it with the IRS technician who will be reviewing your request prior to issuing the ruling.

The IRS technician will disclose his/her thoughts about the request to your adviser *before* issuing the ruling. *If he...*

●**Agrees that your proposed transaction is proper and legal,** you can go ahead and obtain a formal favorable ruling.

●**Expresses some reservations about your request,** you can modify it to meet the IRS's concerns.

●**States that your proposal is improper** and that the IRS will issue an adverse ruling, you can *withdraw* your ruling request so no negative ruling is ever issued.

Results: The ruling request process can reveal any problems with your proposal before you are committed to it, enabling you to correct them. Thus, very few adverse private letter rulings are ever issued.

PROCEDURES

A request for a private letter ruling should be handled by a tax professional who is experienced in obtaining them.

For individuals, the IRS charge for issuing a private ruling generally is...

●**$500 for persons with gross income under $150,000 in the prior year.**

●**$5,000 for persons with income of $150,000 or more.**

For businesses, there is a range of charges that varies with the subject matter of the ruling and size of the business.

There are different fee schedules when a pension-related ruling request is made.

Multiple rulings: It often happens that a number of different taxpayers will be involved in the same transaction in the same matter. *Examples...*

●**An IRA will make distributions to several heirs,** each of whom wants to know the tax that will be incurred.

●**A business transaction will affect multiple employees,** shareholders, or partners.

The IRS charge for rulings that are "substantially identical" to an original ruling is $200 each.

When many taxpayers are involved in a transaction in a substantially identical way, it's not necessary to obtain a separate ruling for each. One or two rulings will be sufficient for all.

Although a private letter ruling officially binds the IRS only regarding the taxpayer who receives it, in fact the IRS is not likely to treat identically situated taxpayers in different ways.

Of course, every involved party can seek a duplicate private ruling if absolute safety is desired.

Before filing a ruling request: Examine private rulings that the IRS has released to other individuals in situations similar to yours. These are released to the public and are indexed and published by commercial tax reporting services.

Somebody else's favorable ruling may provide a "road map" to obtaining a favorable ruling of your own. And if several favorable rulings exist on transactions such as yours already, then your tax adviser may decide you don't need a ruling of your own.

Very useful: Full rules for obtaining private letter rulings are explained in *IRS Revenue Procedure* 2000-1, which can be downloaded free from the IRS Web site at *www.irs.gov.*

The Revenue Procedure indicates the specific types of issues that the IRS will not rule upon...fee schedules...a sample format for a letter ruling request...and a checklist for determining whether a ruling request is complete.

Last-Minute Refunds Allowed

IRS policy formerly was to disallow refunds claimed on late tax returns mailed just before the three-year statute of limitations expired—and delivered after the three-year date.

Why: It said the "filed when mailed" rule applies only to timely filed returns, so refund claims received by it in the mail after the three years were up were filed late. But a recent court decision overruled the IRS to hold such refund claims are timely. The IRS has announced it accepts this decision.

Result: Last-moment refunds are allowed—and such claims that previously were rejected may now be accepted. If you made such a claim, consult a tax adviser.

Faye Anastasoff, CA-8, 2000-2 USTC ¶50,705.

Alternative Minimum Tax Trap

Many small corporations mistakenly pay alternative minimum tax (AMT) that they don't owe. The corporate AMT can cause the loss of tax benefits from accelerated depreciation, tax credits and other tax-reducing "tax preference items," so that profitable businesses benefiting from these preferences will pay at least a minimum amount of tax.

But an exemption to the AMT for small corporations was created by Congress in 1997.

Snag: A recent sampling of tax returns by the IRS indicates that thousands of corporations that qualify for the exemption are overlooking it and paying AMT anyway. The IRS does not catch this and refund the tax when it processes corporate tax returns—so the tax simply goes overpaid.

Companies that have paid corporate AMT for 1998 and after should check to see if they qualify for the exemption—and a tax refund.

James E. Cheeks, attorney, 43 E. 22 St., New York 10010, and formerly adjunct professor of taxation at Pace University.

Tax Loopholes in Working Abroad

Edward Mendlowitz, CPA, partner, Mendlowitz Weitsen, LLP, CPAs, Two Pennsylvania Plaza, Suite 1500, New York 10121. He is author of nine books on taxes, including *An Introduction to Estate Planning.* Practical Programs.

Americans who work abroad run the risk of having their income taxed twice—once in the country where they work and again in their home country.

To prevent this, the tax law gives special breaks to taxpayers with overseas jobs. In some cases, these tax breaks can be used to the taxpayer's advantage. *Here are the tax breaks and the loopholes...*

FOREIGN INCOME EXCLUSION

A provision in the Tax Code permits Americans who live and work in other countries to exclude up to $78,000 of wages, salary, professional fees, and moving expenses from US income tax in 2001. The figure rises to $80,000 in 2002. The exclusion is not automatic but must be elected on Form 2555, *Foreign Earned Income.*

To qualify for the exclusion, you must be a "bona fide resident" of a foreign country for a full tax year. Whether you are a bona fide resident depends on your intention and the length and nature of your stay.

Example: If you go abroad to work for a temporary period and return to the US after you accomplish your goal, you're not a bona fide resident of that country. But if accomplishing the purpose requires an indefinite stay and you make your home there, you may be considered a bona fide resident.

Loophole: **Satisfy the physical presence test.** People who are not bona fide residents of another country may qualify for the $78,000 foreign income exclusion by meeting the Tax Code's "physical presence" test. To satisfy the test, you must be physically present in the foreign country for at least 330 days of any 12 consecutive months. To figure the minimum 330 full days, add up all the separate periods you were in the foreign country during the 12 months. The 330 days need not be consecutive.

Caution: Don't invest in the foreign company you're planning to be working for. All income from services, such as consulting work, is considered earned income if your capital is not used in the business. But, if your capital is used, no more than 30% of your net income is earned income qualifying for the foreign income exclusion.

Example: You go to Germany and consult with a manufacturing partnership. All of your compensation is earned income. Same situation, except you invest in that partnership, which hires you to do the same consulting work. Only up to 30% of your income under this working structure is considered earned income even though your compensation is identical. You lose the exclusion on 70% of your income.

FOREIGN TAX CREDIT

When you pay tax in a foreign jurisdiction on income earned in that country, you're entitled to a credit for that payment on your US tax return. To get the credit, you must file IRS Form 1116, Foreign Tax Credit, with your US tax return.

The credit is limited to the lesser of the foreign taxes paid on the foreign earned income or the US tax on that income.

Example: You paid $45,000 in foreign taxes on $100,000 that you earned abroad. US tax on that income is $35,000. Your foreign tax credit is limited to $35,000.

MORE LOOPHOLES

Loophole: **Do not pay Social Security taxes when you work abroad.** They should not be deducted from your earnings because you are not required to pay them.

Self-employment tax is treated differently. Whether you're required to pay self-employment tax depends on the tax treaty the US has with the country in which you work.

Example: The treaty with Australia does not provide for an exemption for self-employment tax. So even though the money you earn in Australia is exempt from US income tax, you'll have to pay self-employment tax to Australia on your earnings.

Loophole: **Use local law to minimize your tax bill.** Many countries, including the Netherlands and Belgium, offer "expatriate concessions" that shelter part of your earned income from local tax. Check to see whether you qualify for these tax breaks before you arrive. If you don't take steps right away to qualify for the concessions, you may lose the opportunity.

Loophole: **Deduct expenses attributable to taxable income.** Expenses attributable to foreign earned income are allocated between taxable and excludable income. You can deduct the expenses attributable to taxable income.

Loophole: **Account for overseas expenses in ways that minimize your overall tax bill.** If you account to your employer for your expenses and are reimbursed for them, the reimbursement is not included on your W-2 form. You don't have to report the expenses on your tax return.

Similarly, many companies offer housing allowances to make up for higher costs when executives are sent abroad to work. This increases their taxable income.

Strategy: Ask your company to sign the lease for your overseas housing instead of giving you a housing allowance. Under this arrangement, the company pays the rent and you don't have to worry about reporting it.

Loophole: **Maximize your deduction for travel expenses** if your company is US-based but you take extensive business trips abroad. When you work abroad temporarily, say, for several weeks or more, all of your expenses—transportation, lodging, and food—are deductible business expenses.

Even if you vacation while abroad, all travel costs generally remain deductible if the primary purpose of the trip was business and you didn't have control over the assignment.

Loophole: **Foreign dividend checks.** The US has treaties with many foreign countries limiting the tax rate that the foreign country will assess on foreign earned interest and dividend income. The tax is withheld at the source—that is, by the company paying the dividend or interest.

Example: You get a dividend check from a Dutch company, which withholds 15% in taxes. You do not have to file a tax return with the Netherlands. And you can take a US tax credit on your return for the 15% Netherlands tax.

FOR FOREIGNERS WORKING IN THE US

Loophole: **Work in the US under a visa rather than a green card.** Whether the US income of a foreign citizen is subject to US income tax depends on the person's immigration status. Legal resident aliens (green-card holders) are treated as if they were US citizens, and must pay US tax on all worldwide income.

People who hold work visas must pay US tax only on income earned in the US and do not owe any Social Security tax. The rate of tax and withholding from earnings depends on the tax treaty between the foreign country and the US government.

Loophole: **Do business in the US as a corporation.** Properly structuring the form in which you do business in the US can make a big difference in the amount of US tax you owe. Foreigners who own US businesses in the form of sole proprietorships or partnerships owe US taxes on the business income.

Foreigners who operate US businesses as corporations may be compensated solely by payment of dividends, not salaries. In this case, how the dividends are taxed depends on the tax treaty signed between the US government and your home country. However, the US corporation will be subject to US corporate taxes.

More from Ed Mendlowitz...

Living Together Loopholes

Unmarried couples can save substantial amounts of tax by carefully planning their joint finances. *They should pay special attention to the following loopholes...*

Loophole: **Transfer money to your partner completely free of gift tax.** An individual can give up to $10,000 a year each to any number of persons, including his/her partner, without owing any gift tax on the transfer.

In addition, individuals can give away during their lifetimes up to $675,000 (increasing to $1 million by 2006) free of estate and gift taxes.

Caution: Your estate tax exemption amount is reduced by any exemption used on lifetime gifts.

More: In addition to the amounts mentioned above, payments made directly to a school or college to finance an individual's education are not subject to gift tax. The same is also true of payments made directly to an organization for the purpose of paying medical expenses.

You can pay an unlimited amount for the education or medical expenses of your live-in partner—or his children—as long as you write the checks directly to the institution.

Loophole: **Name your partner as one of the executors of your will.** Executors collect fees for their services in administering estates. The fees, which are set by state statute, are deducted from the value of the taxable estate, reducing the estate tax owed.

There's no reason why your partner shouldn't collect at least a share of these fees.

Loophole: **Claim your partner as your dependent on your tax return.** Unmarried couples cannot file joint tax returns and use the beneficial joint-filing tax rates.

But one partner may be able to claim a dependency exemption for the other. *Requirements...*

●**Your partner must live with you for the entire year.**

● **You must furnish more than 50% of his support.**

● **Your partner cannot earn more than $2,900 per year (in 2001).**

● **The relationship can't violate state law.**

Note: Municipal bond income and other nontaxable income, such as life insurance or certain disability insurance proceeds, are not counted when you calculate whether your partner's earnings exceed the income limit.

Limitation: Dependency exemptions on a single tax return begin to phase out when Adjusted Gross Income (AGI) exceeds $128,950 in 2000. You forfeit the exemptions entirely when your AGI exceeds $251,450.

Loophole: **Deduct your dependent partner's medical expenses on your tax return.** When you pay medical expenses for a person you're supporting, you can deduct that person's medical expenses on your tax return even though the person earns more than the income limit of $2,800.

Loophole: **Hire your partner to work in your business**. So long as your partner's salary is reasonable in relation to the work he does, you can deduct the salary as a business expense. Remember that the company must pay the employer's share of Social Security and Medicare taxes on your partner's wages.

Tax breaks: If your companion earns less than $4,550 in 2001, he will not have to pay federal income tax. And if his salary stays under $26,250, he will be taxed at the low 15% federal income tax rate.

Loophole: **Provide for your companion with an irrevocable life insurance trust.** Use excess cash built up in your business to buy split-dollar life insurance. *Definition:* With a split-dollar insurance policy, the owner and the company together use company funds to take out a policy on the owner's life.

How it works: Set up an irrevocable life insurance trust on behalf of your live-in partner that will own the policy's death benefit, minus the amount of the premiums paid. Upon death, your company recoups what it paid for the policy and your partner receives death benefits free of estate and income taxes.

Loophole: **Name your partner beneficiary of your pension plan.** Money paid to beneficiaries of qualified plans passes outside your will directly to the people you name as beneficiaries.

Strategy: The IRS requires that you begin making minimum withdrawals from qualified plans starting April 1 of the year after you turn 70½ or in the year you stop working, if later. The withdrawals are based on your life expectancy, or the joint life expectancy of you and your beneficiary.

When your partner is younger than you, the joint life expectancy is longer and the minimum withdrawals are smaller allowing the money to continue compounding tax free in the account.

Loophole: **Use trusts to provide ongoing income to your companion. A good option...**

● **Grantor retained annuity trust (GRAT).** You can place assets—securities, real estate, shares in a business—in a GRAT and give your partner the right to receive annuity payments of income each year. After the trust term, the assets pass to the beneficiaries.

Also from Ed Mendlowitz...

Investment Loopholes

Investors may hold two types of corporate stock—publicly traded shares and shares in closely held companies. *Consider these tax-saving strategies in dealing with corporate stock...*

PUBLICLY TRADED SHARES

Loophole: **Have shares of stock in your employer's company that are held in your 401(k) plan distributed directly to you rather than rolled over to an IRA.** Employees who receive shares of corporate stock that have been contributed to their 401(k) account have two choices when it comes to taking the shares out of the plan. *They are...*

● **Roll over the shares into an IRA and pay no tax, or...**

● **Have the shares distributed to them and pay taxes**...and possibly owe an early withdrawal penalty.

When you roll over company stock into an IRA, you or your IRA beneficiaries will pay tax on the full value of the shares when they are withdrawn from the account. IRA distributions are taxed at ordinary income rates—up to 39%.

Better: Have the company stock in the 401(k) distributed directly to you and pay tax at the time of distribution. If the stock has greatly appreciated, consider paying tax on the cost of the stock to the company when it was contributed to the plan, not its fair market value.

When you then hold the shares for more than one year and sell them, the sales proceeds will be taxed at favorable long-term capital gains rates.

Loophole: **Fund a charitable remainder trust (CRT) with appreciated securities.** When you transfer appreciated securities to a CRT, the trust can sell the securities tax free and buy higher yielding, more diversified investments. The trust will pay you income for life, and the charity will receive what's left in the trust after your death.

Tax benefits: You get an immediate income tax deduction for the present value of the amount the charity will receive after your death. That's based on IRS tables. You avoid paying tax on the securities' appreciation and will receive a greater annual return than if you sold the stock yourself, paid the tax and reinvested the proceeds.

Loophole: **Donate appreciated long-term stock instead of cash to charity.** When you donate shares, you can deduct the full fair market value. Also, you owe no capital gains tax on the stock's buildup in value since you bought it.

CLOSELY HELD CORPORATE STOCK

Loophole: **Use Section 1244 stock losses to offset salary and other income.** Generally, when you lose money on the sale of closely held stock, any net capital losses can be used to offset up to $3,000 of wages, dividends, interest and other ordinary income. Any balance is carried forward to future years. But up to $100,000 in losses from sales of closely held stock that qualifies as Section 1244 stock can be used to offset ordinary income on a joint tax return ($50,000 for singles).

In order to qualify for Section 1244 treatment...

• **You must have paid cash or property to acquire the shares.**

• **The amount of capital invested in the company** would not have exceeded $1 million at the time of your investment.

Loophole: **Use a complete redemption to liquidate closely held shares.** Generally, investors take money out of a corporation in the form of dividends, which are taxed at high ordinary income rates. However, you can pay much lower capital gains tax rates by arranging for the company to redeem shares.

How this works: When shares are owned by a husband and wife (or parents and children) or other family members, one owner can sell all of his/her shares and pay capital gains rates on the profit, as long as the seller agrees to sever all relations with the company for 10 years.

Sellers must agree in writing to notify the IRS if they take a job with the company, serve on its board of directors or reacquire stock (except by inheritance) within 10 years after the sale.

Loophole: **Avoid gifts of closely held shares as you get older.** Heirs of company owners who die holding stock get a "stepped-up basis" in the shares, meaning the tax cost in the shares is advanced to their value on the date of the owner's death. *Impact:* The heirs pay no capital gains taxes on the shares' pre-death increase in value.

Strategy: Older business executives may want to sell or make gifts of other assets and retain their shares in the private company so that their heirs get a stepped-up cost basis.

Loophole: **Consider using family limited partnerships for gifts of closely held stock.** You can make gifts of closely held shares to a family limited partnership, retaining the general partnership interest and giving children the limited partnership units over time. The general partner has complete control over the partnership.

Tax impact: Gifts of family limited partnership units can be discounted—that is, reduced in value—to take into account minority interests and lack of control and marketability.

This reduces the gift tax owed on the interests. Gifts of family limited partnership interests also remove any future appreciation in the shares transferred from the estate of the original owner.

Loophole: **Use a preferred stock recapitalization to freeze the value of shares in a growing private business.** Business owners can transfer closely held common shares to their children and have the balance exchanged for newly issued preferred stock with a face value equal to the fair market value of the owner's stock.

Tax savings: No gift or income taxes are owed as long as the preferred stock is entitled to a cumulative market rate dividend, is valued at fair market value, and the value assigned to the common stock is at least 10% of the total value of all the corporate stock.

Caution: If you subsequently decided to donate some of the preferred shares to charity, you can only deduct your basis, not the value of the preferred shares.

Loophole: **Account for future taxes when transferring shares in a divorce settlement.** There are no tax consequences when stock in a closely held company is transferred as part of a divorce settlement. However, the person receiving the shares takes the same tax basis as the person transferring them... along with any built-in capital gains. So figure in taxes when valuing the shares.

Example: Jack transfers 10,000 shares in his company to Jill during their divorce. Jack paid $100 each for shares that are now worth $250 apiece. Because of the $150 per share built-in gain, the shares are worth only $1.9 million to Jill ($2.5 million market value minus $600,000 capital gains tax).

Loophole: **Create an ESOP to reduce taxes.** When a shareholder sells more than 30% of his stock to an employee stock ownership plan (ESOP), the stock sale is tax free as long as the proceeds of the sale are invested in other securities within one year.

Deducting the Interest on Business-Related Debt

Interest on business-related debt is usually tax deductible on Schedule C or C-EZ. A debt is related to business if you use the loan proceeds for business purposes—even if you take out the loan personally.

In that case, you can deduct interest as long as you are legally liable for the debt...you and the lender both expect it to be repaid...and you and the lender have a genuine debtor–creditor relationship.

If a loan made to you is partly for business purposes and partly for personal ones, you must allocate the interest. Only the business-related portion is tax deductible.

David Cooper, editor, *Small Business Tax News*, Box 42518, Washington, DC 20015.

Surprising News About IRS Audits

IRS audits are more common among people who earn less than $25,000 a year than among those who earn more than $100,000.

Reason: The IRS is scrutinizing wage earners who claim the earned income credit. That is a refundable credit for low-income workers that is reduced as income increases. Wage earners who are making $25,000 or less have a 1.36% chance of being audited.

Those with incomes over $100,000 have a 1.15% chance of an audit.

Note: Until the early 1990s, 10% of high-income tax returns were audited.

Martin Nissenbaum, national director of personal income tax planning at Ernst & Young LLP, New York City.

Earned Income Credit Fiasco

More than 25% of earned income credit (EIC) payments are erroneous or fraudulent. Congress created the EIC as a tax credit to benefit low-income working people.

But in 1997 (the most recent year for which figures are available), fully 25.6% of all EIC payments were erroneous or fraudulent, up from 21% in 1994.

Problems…

• **Congress has made the rules for claiming the EIC so complex,** and has changed them so many times, that low-income people often can't claim it correctly without professional help that they can't afford.

• **Applicants basically get the credit simply by asking for it,** and the IRS doesn't have the resources to audit so many low-income individuals.

US Treasury Report on Administration of the Earned Income Credit.

Abusive IRS Investigation

The IRS has been ordered to pay $1.5 million for an abusive investigation. *Facts:* When an IRS agent began an investigation of attorney Jerry Payne, Payne sought to cooperate and to provide the information the agent wanted. But the agent wouldn't tell Payne what he wanted. Instead he sent dozens of letters to Payne's clients, business associates, friends and relatives, saying Payne was under criminal investigation and seeking information from them. Payne sued the IRS for the damage done to his reputation.

Court: The agent could and should have gotten the information confidentially from Payne himself. The IRS owes Payne $1.5 million in damages and $1,000 in punitive damages.

Jerry S. Payne, DC S.D. Tex., No. CIV. H-93-1738; 86 AFTR2d ¶2000-5307.

Tax on Insurance Trap

The IRS may tax insurance paid out in the wake of a disaster. The insurance company may reimburse more than the original cost of your home if you have lived in it for some time and building costs have gone up. To the IRS, the higher payout means you have *profited* from the disaster and so must pay tax on that profit. *Self-defense:* Spend the benefit payment on repairs or replacement property within two years of the end of the year in which the damage occurred. When you file taxes, defer the so-called gain. When you sell the house, that gain will become part of your profit—and will not be taxed if it totals $250,000 or less for individuals …$500,000 or less for couples.

Randy Bruce Blaustein, Esq., senior tax partner, R.B. Blaustein & Co., New York City.

The IRS and Your Accountant

In the course of preparing your income tax return, you may have had conversations with your accountant about "hypothetical" situations dealing with the possibility that the IRS would be able to discover unreported income.

Warning: Even though Internal Revenue Code Section 7525 establishes a client–tax adviser privilege, the privilege is not applicable in criminal tax proceedings. What all this means is that the IRS can serve your accountant with a summons compelling the accountant to repeat the details of every conversation you ever had over the past few years.

Another warning: Don't count on your accountant telling the IRS he doesn't remember what you discussed. The IRS can gain powerful leverage by threatening to prosecute the accountant as a conspirator in your evasion of tax if he/she doesn't provide the IRS with the information it wants.

Trap: Paying Taxes by Credit Card

The IRS says it wants taxpayers to make tax payments by credit card—for taxpayer convenience and to ease its own paperwork.

But unlike businesses that accept card charges, the IRS doesn't give any "credit" for the processing fee collected by the credit card company—so the fee is charged in addition to the tax bill.

Fees vary by size of tax payment, typically from 2% to 3.5%.

This is more than the average 1% "reward" some credit card companies offer on charges—so tax payments charged on credit cards typically cost taxpayers extra money. *This table shows how much…*

Tax Payment	Fee	"Reward"	Net Cost
$1,000	$35	$10	$25
$5,000	$133	$50	$83
$10,000	$262	$100	$162
$25,000	$699	$250	$449
$50,000	$1,375	$500	$875
$99,999	$2,499	$1,000	$1,499

The result is that it is still less expensive to pay taxes the old-fashioned way—by check.

Philip J. Harmelink, Ernst & Young LLP, and William M. VanDenburgh, CPA, writing in Tax Notes.

IRS Flooded With "Innocent Spouse" Claims—Allows Few

Since the IRS Restructuring and Reform Act of 1998 made it much easier to claim "innocent spouse" relief, the agency has been flooded with claims—half of which don't meet even the most basic requirements for relief.

Example: Fully 33% of claims are made by people who didn't file joint returns.

Why: Many divorce lawyers now are automatically filing "protective" claims for clients, regardless of the facts.

To process all the claims, the IRS has been forced to more than double the number of employees handling them, from 415 to 953—with most of the extra agents shifted from examination duties.

Bottom line: The IRS has granted innocent spouse relief in 16% of cases since the law changed.

However, it points out that among those cases that meet basic legal requirements sufficiently to be considered "workable," it has granted full relief 44% of the time, and partial relief an additional 7% of the time. It says this is much more often than relief granted under old law.

Figures from Tax Analysts.

Little-Known Tax Refunds

Don't leave unclaimed tax refunds behind when returning from abroad. Each year, 12 million Americans do so upon returning from nations that charge Value Added Tax (VAT). This tax is refundable to foreigners when they leave the country. VAT rates run as high as 19%, but few travelers get refunds because they don't understand the refund process. *Information:* Global Refund, *www. globalrefund.com.*

Herbert J. Teison, editor, Travel Smart, *40 Beechdale Rd., Dobbs Ferry, NY 10522.*

Tax Traps in Divorce and Separation...How Couples Avoid Them

Harvey I. Sladkus, Esq., fellow of the American and International Academies of Matrimonial Lawyers, former adjunct professor of law, Benjamin N. Cardozo School of Law, and of counsel to the firm of Todtman, Nachamie, Spizz & Johns, PC, 425 Park Ave., NY 10022.

A marital separation or divorce is stressful enough on its own—and can be made even more stressful by mistakes that increase the tax bill.

A change in marital status has a big impact on taxes. But people going through a separation or divorce are likely to be distracted —and may make costly tax mistakes before seeing a tax adviser.

Important: When considering separation or divorce, consult a tax professional as soon as possible. With smart planning, it may be possible to shift some of the costs of the divorce to the IRS.

Discuss these key subjects with your adviser—and beware of making tax mistakes associated with them before you do...

SEPARATION STRATEGIES

•**Alimony.** The key tax trait of alimony is that it is deductible by the spouse who pays it and taxable income to the spouse who receives it.

Opportunity: If one spouse will be in a higher tax bracket than the other after separation or divorce, that spouse may pay alimony and deduct it at a higher tax bracket rate than the rate that the other spouse pays upon receiving it—creating a net tax saving for the couple.

Consider the value of this tax effect when negotiating separation terms and use it to offset other costs incident to the divorce.

Example: While separated, a high tax bracket husband pays his lower tax bracket wife alimony sufficient to cover her legal fees. The net tax benefit helps offset the cost of the fees. This net saving effectively can be shared between the spouses in the terms of their overall financial settlement.

To be deductible, alimony (maintenance) must be paid under a divorce decree, separate maintenance order, separation agreement, or a written agreement relating to a separation or divorce.

Trap: When a couple separates, one spouse may agree to support the other until they meet with their lawyers some time later to work out the details. Such support payments will not qualify as deductible alimony, since they are not made under a formal separation agreement and are considered voluntary payments.

To obtain alimony treatment from the start, meet with your lawyers as soon as possible to work out the necessary written agreement.

•**Dependency exemptions.** The lower tax bracket spouse may receive custody of the children while the higher earning spouse pays support for them.

Again, joint tax savings may be maximized by having the higher tax bracket spouse claim the dependency exemptions for the children (unless such spouse is a high income taxpayer subject to the phaseout of exemptions).

The Tax Code says exemptions for children go to the parent with custody unless he/she signs a written statement releasing the exemptions to the noncustodial parent.

The custodial parent should sign IRS Form 8332, *Release of Claim for Exemption for Child,* specifically designating the years in which each parent will or will not claim the child or children and the parent claiming the exemption should file it with his tax return.

Trap: Having a court-issued divorce decree assign the dependency exemptions to the noncustodial parent is not enough by itself for that parent to claim the exemptions.

Example: In a recent case, a divorced father attached to his tax return a copy of the divorce decree that gave him the exemptions for his children. But the Tax Court said that was not sufficient because he hadn't also filed a release signed by his former wife—so she got the exemptions nonetheless. [*Cheryl Miller,* 114 TC No. 13.]

Negotiate: The noncustodial spouse who is paying support for children should negotiate to obtain the written release for the exemptions at the beginning, when determining support levels and other financial aspects of the separation.

If the spouse overlooks this and has to go back later to ask for the release, obtaining it may cost more.

●**Joint versus separate returns.** A couple legally married at year-end may file a joint return even if formally separated. They should examine the merits of filing joint versus separate returns. The execution of an indemnification agreement in favor of the spouse with the lesser income should be negotiated, in the event of an audit, since the filing of a joint return makes each spouse jointly and severally liable for the tax deficit.

Note: The indemnification agreement won't prevent the IRS from going after either spouse, but it will allow the indemnified spouse to sue the other.

A joint return generally provides lower tax rates, but a separate return provides the tax advantage of letting a high tax bracket spouse deduct alimony paid to a lower bracket spouse.

On a joint return, alimony is *not* deductible by the spouse who pays it, and is tax free to the recipient.

Timing is important. If payments started only late in the year, so that little was paid, joint filing may be more attractive. But if alimony was paid during most of the year, separate filing may be more attractive.

Negotiate: If a couple desires to continue filing joint returns after separating, alimony will be more expensive after taxes to the spouse who pays it, and more valuable after taxes to the spouse who receives it. This should be reflected in the overall financial terms of the settlement they negotiate.

Separate filing: When spouses will file separate returns, they should carefully review all the items on their return that will be affected by switching from joint to separate filing.

Again, they should agree in advance on how every item will be handled, and reflect it in the terms of their overall agreement.

Failing to agree on how tax items will be handled, so that inconsistent positions are claimed on separate returns, can lead to audit exposure or other unexpected tax costs.

Example: When two spouses filing separate returns both claimed full credit for the estimated taxes they had paid jointly, the IRS said it could make its own allocation of the payments between them, even if that satisfied neither. [*IRS Legal Memorandum* 200011047.]

●**Pensions.** It's crucial that claims to future pension distributions be settled at the time of a divorce.

Federal law creates strong spousal rights in pension-plan assets. If spouses don't agree on how these rights will be settled as a result of the divorce, great complications may result later on.

Example: A husband who is covered by an employer's qualified pension plan divorces and then remarries. The divorce settlement neglects to cover the pension—perhaps because it won't be collected for many years. When the husband finally reaches retirement age or dies, both of his spouses may claim rights to his pension benefits, generating a lawsuit. And one of the spouses may be left without benefits that she was relying on to support her own retirement. Failure to consider this may subject the attorney to a malpractice suit.

●**Stock options.** These now represent a major portion of the wealth of many families—and present special divorce-planning problems.

In some states, stock options are considered compensation for past services, and so are deemed part of the marital property to be divided upon divorce. But other states consider options to be an incentive for future services—and thus the separate property of the spouse who earns them.

Know the legal status of stock options in your state before making any representation to your spouse about how they may be handled in a divorce settlement. Then have the issue handled by an expert.

Financial key: The value of options may be extremely volatile, and will only be finally determined in the future. This creates the risk that, no matter how options are valued when negotiating a property settlement, one spouse or the other may later consider this value far too high or too low.

When negotiating the settlement, be aware of the risk posed by the volatility of the options' value, and include terms that mitigate the risk.

●**Joint property.** A couple may jointly own property, such as a vacation home, that both wish to retain after a divorce.

Snag: Upon divorce, joint ownership is automatically converted to a tenancy in common, which gives either spouse the legal right to sell his/her interest in the property and leave the other spouse with an unwanted co-owner.

Have the divorce settlement spell out how the property will be handled after the divorce. Have it specify each spouse's right to use the property, and liability for related costs. Also include a right of first refusal for each spouse should the other decide to sell, and a means of appraising the property to determine a fair price.

●**Mortgage interest deduction.** When a couple separates, one spouse may move out of the family home but continue paying the mortgage on it.

Snag: The spouse's mortgage interest deduction may be placed at risk, since the home no longer is his residence.

Safety: Consult with an expert about the special rules that apply in this case and the steps to take to protect the deduction.

Turn Old Clothes...Appliances...Furniture And More...Into Cash

William R. Lewis, CPA, president of Client Valuation Services, Box 22031, Lincoln, NE 68542.

What do you do with those old clothes you don't wear and the household items you no longer use? Turn these items into cash by giving them to charity and taking an itemized deduction on your tax return.

Be sure to follow a few simple—but important—rules...

●**Get a dated, signed receipt from the charity.** It should list exactly what items you've given rather than something vague like "three bags of clothing" or "two boxes of small appliances."

●**Assign fair market value to each item.** The IRS allows you to claim a tax deduction for the amount that the items would likely sell for in a thrift or consignment shop. One way to determine these amounts is to check prices at a thrift shop. However, few people will visit a thrift shop to do this.

My book—*Cash for Your Used Clothing*—details the fair market value for more than 800 different items. *Examples...*

Man's dress shirt: $14	Iron: $6
Woman's dress: $40	Microwave: $60–$80
Boy's denim jeans: $12	10-speed bike: $40–$80
Girl's sweater: $14	Sofa: $120–$210
Electric blender: $8	Table/chairs: $120–$200

Someone paying 34% combined state and federal taxes would save $13.60 in taxes from a single woman's dress.

Condition does matter: Items must be in good shape and not ludicrously out of style.

●**If the total deduction exceeds $500,** file Form 8283, *Noncash Charitable Contributions.* You must itemize instead of taking the standard deduction.

●**Understand how the IRS views these matters.** Someone with an Adjusted Gross Income (AGI) of $75,000 to $100,000 typically can report an average of $2,500 in noncash donations without raising eyebrows at the IRS.

Someone reporting $20,000 in income who takes a $2,500 deduction for noncash donations should be ready to have his/her return questioned. Your total donation cannot exceed 50% of your AGI for the year. If it does, the remainder can be carried over for up to five years.

Vital: Receipts to prove the donations and proof you assigned fair market value in a reasonable way.

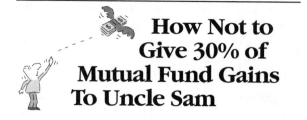

How Not to Give 30% of Mutual Fund Gains To Uncle Sam

Sheldon Jacobs, editor of *The No-Load Fund Investor*, 410 Saw Mill River Rd., Ardsley, NY 10502. He is author of *The Handbook for No-Load Fund Investors.* The No-Load Fund Investor, Inc.

Many investors focus on how much funds earn—ignoring how much they get to keep after taxes. You can't control timing of funds' stock sales or taxes the sales generate. But now that the SEC is requiring funds to report after-tax returns, it will be easier to build a tax-efficient portfolio …and reduce your tax bite from 30% or more to less than 5% of fund profits.

•**Hold tax-inefficient investments through tax-deferred accounts.** Hold funds likely to ring up big tax bills—taxable bonds, Real Estate Investment Trusts and other high-dividend stocks—in IRAs or other retirement vehicles.

•**Take advantage of tax-advantaged funds.** These are managed to enable investors to keep a very high percentage of their profits.

•*Fidelity Tax-Managed Stock.* FTXMX. 800-343-3548.

•*T. Rowe Price Tax-Efficient Balanced.* PRTEX. 800-638-5660.

•*Vanguard Tax-Managed Capital Appreciation.* VMCAX. 800-662-7447.

•*Vanguard Tax-Managed Growth & Income.* VTGIX. 800-662-7447.

•**Consider index funds.** Since index funds are not actively managed, they trade less frequently, generating few taxable gains. *Examples…*

•*Schwab 1000,* which tracks the 1,000 largest publicly traded US companies. SNXFX. 800-225-8570.

•*Vanguard 500 Index.* VFINX. 800-662-7447.

Warning: Not all index funds are tax efficient. The Vanguard Small-Cap Index Fund (NAESX) lost more than one-tenth of its recent 12-month return to capital gains taxes. The fund tracks the Russell 2000, which changes about one-third of its portfolio each year. *More stable choice…*

•*Vanguard Small-Cap Growth Index* tracks growth-oriented shares in the S&P Small-Cap 600 Index. VISGX. 800-662-7447.

•**Look for low-turnover,** low-dividend funds. *Examples…*

•*Neuberger Berman Genesis.* NBGNX. 800-877-9700.

•*Third Avenue Small-Cap Value.* TASCX. 800-443-1021.

•*T. Rowe Price Small-Cap Value.* PRSVX. 800-638-5660.

Heavy trading is often a sign of high tax bills. The same goes for funds that invest in high-dividend stocks. Dividends are taxed at ordinary income rates, rather than the maximum 20% rate for long-term capital gains.

•**Favor newer funds.** New funds will not have portfolios of highly appreciated shares, which could result in tax bills if the manager sells. Morningstar lists funds' potential capital gains exposure. Look for a fund group with a strong record with similar funds.

•**Don't rebalance frequently.** Investors often are told the importance of maintaining target allocations—say, 60% equities, 40% bonds. But selling fund shares can lead to a capital gains tax bill.

Better: To return to your allocation, use new money or take distributions in cash and use them to reallocate. If you don't have money to invest, let your allocation shift slightly instead of adding to your tax bill.

•**Hold mutual fund shares more than one year before selling.** Short-term capital gains are taxed at a higher rate depending on your bracket.

9

Savvy Investing

The Perils of On-Line Investing

The Internet has brought dramatic change to the way investors buy and sell stocks. Now anyone can get real-time stock quotes, research reports and daily investing advice—all for free.

Unfortunately, there are also new ways to get burned. Last year, the Securities and Exchange Commission (SEC) logged more than 4,000 complaints about on-line brokerage firms.

Here are five on-line investing mistakes—and how to avoid them...

Mistake: **Basing investment decisions on a bulletin-board posting** or an E-mail offering.

This is a cyber version of the old *pump and dump* scam. You see a message urging you to buy a hot small-cap stock. After gullible investors inflate the stock price, the promoter sells his/her shares...and the price plummets.

Red flags: Words such as *guaranteed... high return...safe as a CD...pre-IPO offering...* and time limitations on the offering.

To steer clear of trouble, buy only stocks you can research with the SEC. Public companies are required to file annual (10-K) and quarterly (10-Q) reports containing audited financial statements as well as discussions of investment risk. Free information is available at *www.sec.gov/edgar.shtml* or by calling 800-732-0330.

Mistake: **Choosing a broker solely on the basis of low commissions.** Decide on your needs before signing up with an on-line brokerage. *Issues to consider...*

●**Product variety.** Do you want access to banking services? Mutual funds? Foreign stocks?

Ken Johnson, licensed securities broker and coauthor of *The Sixth Market: The Electronic Investor Revolution.* Dearborn Trade. He is also founder of sixthmarket. com, a company that provides services to help electronic traders become more profitable, Austin, TX.

High-yield bonds? IPOs? Does the broker offer the mutual fund families you like? Are you willing to pay a bit more for extensive brokerage research?

● **Ease of service.** Does the broker have branches? Can you place trades by phone without paying additional fees? Are on-line screens easy to navigate? Does the broker offer free year-end statements with the cost-basis information you'll need to complete your taxes?

● **Execution of trades.** How quickly are orders filled in sharply rising or falling markets? Does the broker trade directly with stock exchanges or funnel your order to another firm, which would lead to higher execution prices?

Active traders often gravitate to firms such as www.datek.com...*www.tradecast.com*...or www.cybercorp.com for fast execution and rock-bottom commissions. Infrequent or less-seasoned traders might go with www.fidelity.com or www.schwab.com. These cost a bit more but offer advice and analysis that less experienced customers may need.

Helpful resources: These sites offer interactive tools that let you specify requirements and preferences, then suggest the best brokers. *http://onmoney.xolia.com* and *www.gomezadvisors.com.*

● **Disciplinary history.** Find out if the brokerage has been subject to disciplinary actions. All brokers are regulated by the SEC, National Association of Securities Dealers (NASD), the exchanges and their state securities regulators. Find Web sites for state regulators at www. nasaa.org.

Also helpful: The site *www.nasd.com/secindrg* contains useful information, including public disclosure about each firm and information about filing complaints and dispute resolution.

Mistake: **Trading too much.** All of this instant electronic power and information has simply made it too easy to make too many trades. That's fine for experienced traders— but for most of us, it can lead to trouble.

Groundbreaking research done by University of California, Davis, assistant professor of management Terrance Odean indicates that many inexperienced investors become over-confident, trade too much, hold riskier portfolios than seasoned investors, expend more time on trading—and still underperform those less active investors.

To trade successfully, you must learn a disciplined strategy—one that can put the odds of success in your favor. That comes from training and experience. If you have the time and the desire to learn, there are a wealth of resources available, including...

www.activetradermag.com
www.hardrightedge.com
www.manningtrading.com
www.pristine.com/aeduc
www.traderslibrary.com

If you would rather not make that commitment, stick with your full-service broker and mutual funds.

Mistake: **Putting too much faith in on-line investment advice.** On-line advice doesn't take into account your particular financial needs. That's why so much of it seems contradictory.

Important: Avoid stock tips from television and on-line media. By the time you hear the news, it is generally too late to profit from it.

Example: When the Federal Reserve cut interest rates earlier this year, many financial sites wrote about the benefits to financial stocks. But investors had boosted prices of the stocks in anticipation of rate cuts—months earlier.

Smart investors use just one or two trusted gurus for stock tips and market information. Most reputable on-line investment advisers let you try them out for free. *Examples...*

● **Merrill Lynch & Co.** offers analysts' reports free for 30 days. *www.ml.com.*

● **Salomon Smith Barney** lets guests register on its site and access its research reports for a 60-day trial period. *www.salomonsmithbarney.com.*

Helpful: Consider hiring an on-line firm to educate you in self-directed trading and provide trading ideas. If you find a good one, stick with it for the long term. *Cost:* Expect to pay anywhere from $20 to $250 a month. *My favorites...*

www.egoose.com
www.investorsadvantage.com
www.pristine.com
www.tciphl.com

Mistake: **Not planning for problems unique to on-line trading.** *These include…*

●**Trades that fail to go through** because the broker's server or your modem crashes.

●**Typographical errors** that result in your buying or selling the wrong stock.

●**Clicking on your order twice** so you end up buying or selling twice as many shares as you want to.

Good idea: Practice on-line investing before you trade for real. Most on-line brokers offer hands-on tutorials. Or you can sign up for free Internet stock market simulation games at *www.mainxchange.com* and *www.virtual stockexchange.com.*

Helpful: Create viable alternatives—as a backup plan—to protect yourself against trading delays or system crashes…

●**Open a second account with another on-line brokerage.**

●**Trade by touch-tone telephone.**

●**Fax your order or speak with a broker by phone.** Make sure your broker waives the surcharge for telephone trades during an on-line crisis.

IF YOU HAVE PROBLEMS

Call your on-line broker immediately if you make an error or a trade doesn't go through. Your broker may be able to cancel a trade that hasn't been executed.

If you don't get satisfaction from customer service, write to the firm's compliance department. Tell the firm how you would like the problem resolved. Request a response within 30 days.

If you're still dissatisfied: Send a letter of complaint and ask for an arbitration hearing from the exchange on which you traded *(www.nasdaq.com…www.amex.com…www. nyse.com),* or write to the Office of Investor Education and Assistance at the SEC, *www. sec.gov/investor.html.*

Avoiding Trading Traps On the Internet Isn't Hard… Especially Important Now!

Mary L. Schapiro, president, NASD Regulation, self-regulatory organization of the securities industry and NASDAQ Stock Market, Washington, DC.

Every day, more than a million trades are performed on-line. *But despite its popularity, on-line trading has risks, especially during extreme volatility*—as we have had *recently…*

●**System overload.** During periods of high-volume trading, on-line brokerages' Web sites can crash. Some firms may institute controls—such as the suspension of trading—to restore order.

Self-defense: Make sure you can place a call to execute a trade during busy times. And—research articles on how your brokerage fared during high-volume days.

●**Use limit orders.** A limit order is an instruction to buy or sell a security at a specific price. Unlike a market order, which is executed at the prevailing price, a limit order guarantees you will not pay more than a certain amount for a purchase or receive less than a specific amount for a sale.

During a volatile market, a stock price on the computer screen may not reflect the actual price of the stock at the time the order is executed (the price could have increased or decreased substantially). This is another good reason to place a limit order instead of a market order.

●**Monitor the status of your orders.** Buy and sell orders are not placed instantaneously. Don't assume your order has been lost and place another one. You could end up owning twice as many shares as you wanted or selling stock you don't own.

Self-defense: Ask how you can check an order's status—especially during fast markets—before placing it again.

●**Carefully track your trading.** Keep a diary in case you have a problem with a brokerage firm. Keep copies of transaction statements and confirmations.

If you have a problem: Try to work it out with the brokerage branch manager or supervisor. If this does not work, contact the firm's legal department. If you still have not received a satisfactory response, file an arbitration claim with NASD Dispute Resolution. *General information:* 301-590-6500...*www. NASDADR.com.*

Some Investments Are Best Left to the Pros

●**Biotech stocks.** Special expertise is needed to understand a company's fundamentals and the intricacies of the new-drug pipeline and testing processes...research-and-development costs are high.

●**Business-to-business technology stocks.** Tricky to analyze if no revenue is projected. Investors must understand the competitive advantages of technologies.

●**Junk bonds.** Bonds with ratings lower than BBB are risky unless you know the reasons for the poor ratings and have good justification to believe that they will be upgraded.

●**Stock options.** Few investors understand the complete strategy...so most lose their shirts.

Andrew Horowitz, CFP, president, Horowitz & Co., an investment advisory firm, Weston, FL.

Invest Small...Earn Big

Satya Pradhuman, first vice president and director of small-cap research for Merrill Lynch & Co., 4 World Financial Center, New York City 10080. He is author of Small-Cap Dynamics. Bloomberg.

Small stocks haven't been this cheap in more than 20 years. With the Federal Reserve lowering interest rates and the stock market likely to stabilize, I expect smaller stocks to gain 12% to 14% this year—significantly outperforming larger stocks, as measured by the Dow Jones Industrial Average and the S&P 500 stock index. A popular benchmark for small-cap investors is the Russell 2000 Index.

Shrewd investors should consider having at least 10% to 15% of their equity holdings in small-capitalization companies.

FORCES AT PLAY

Even after the sell-off of 2000, many of the big growth stocks—especially in technology—still haven't fallen to value stock levels. In the small-cap category, there is almost nothing *but* value.

The major theme—beyond relative valuations—that favors small-cap stocks is more stable markets. In volatile markets, investors focus on the biggest, most liquid stocks—large-cap growth issues.

I follow about 1,500 companies with market capitalizations of $250 million to $1.6 billion, which I consider small-cap.

Our quantitative models suggest market volatility will diminish over the next 12 months. As risk subsides, investors will concentrate on stocks with the best fundamentals—small-caps.

DETERMINING VALUE OF SMALL-CAPS

You can't rely on price-to-earnings ratio (P/E) to measure value in the small-cap sector. Many small-caps have erratic earnings—or no earnings at all.

Small-cap valuation measures...

●**Price to revenues.** The average small-cap is selling at 0.81 times per-share revenues. The average large-cap sells at 2.2 times per-share revenues.

●**Price to book value.** Book value is tangible assets minus current liabilities—what the company would be worth if it were liquidated. The average small-cap sells at two times book value, versus 4.3 times for the average large-cap.

●**Price to cash flow.** Cash flow includes after-tax profits and allowances for depreciation. Historically, small-caps have sold at a price-to-cash-flow ratio 60% greater than that for large-caps. Currently, they're selling at a 30% *discount* to that of large-caps.

●**Easier access to capital.** In recent years, access to capital has been very difficult for smaller companies. Fed tightening reduced the supply of capital. Anyone without a technology or telecommunications story to tell got squeezed out. The rate cuts by the Fed—and additional cuts I expect—will increase access to capital for small-caps and reduce borrowing costs.

HOW TO PICK SMALL-CAPS

●**Valuation measures.** Look for stocks selling at prices that are low relative to sales, book value or cash flow versus other stocks in their industries. These figures are available in annual reports and Wall Street analysts' reports.

●**Strong product lines.** Look for stocks with franchise value—a product or a service that promises to feed future growth.

●**Strong balance sheet.** Look for companies that can generate sufficient cash flow to support growth. High debt is dangerous in a slowing economy.

Merger & acquisition possibilities: The slowing economy isn't likely to slow the push to consolidate. Several hundred small-cap firms have already been bought out in the past few years.

Any small-cap stock you find compelling because of relative valuation, low debt load, strong franchise and strong cash flow could become a takeover target.

CURRENT FAVORITES

Three sectors look promising…

●**Energy.** This sector has more rapid earnings growth than other small-cap sectors. These stocks should do well if oil prices are at least in the $20-to-$25 range.

●**Health-care services.** Health Maintenance Organizations (HMOs) and hospitals are able to put through bigger price increases, which should mean more consistent earnings.

●**Technology.** As the slowing economy squeezes profit margins, companies will increase spending on technology to improve

productivity. Unlike large-caps, valuations among small-cap tech stocks are back to where they were in 1998—before the run-up in technology began.

DRIP News…Sound Ways To Invest and Pay No Commission

Jeff Fischer, comanager of Motley Fool's Rule Breaker DRIP Portfolio, a fund managed on-line as an educational tool. *www.fool.com*. He is author of *The Motley Fool's Investing Without a Silver Spoon*. Motley Fool.

Dividend Reinvestment Plans (DRIPs), also known as direct-purchase plans, are an easy—and usually commission-free—way to buy stock directly from companies and automatically reinvest dividends. About 1,100 companies now offer them…and that number is growing.

SYNTHETIC DRIPS

Companies that offer DRIPs are generally financially solid and well-known, such as Coca-Cola, Johnson & Johnson and Pfizer. Until now, investors seeking young, high-growth or technology companies have had to look elsewhere. New services offer programs—nicknamed *synthetic DRIPs*—for companies that don't offer the real thing.

Synthetic DRIPs effectively double—to more than 2,000—the number of companies in the DRIP universe.

Investors who enroll can buy either small numbers of shares or fractional shares in companies such as AOL Time Warner and ExxonMobil for small commissions and get most of the benefits of DRIP investing—particularly dollar-cost averaging. The services buy shares on the market and parcel them out.

One benefit you may not get: Dividend reinvestment—since many high-growth companies, such as Yahoo!, don't pay dividends.

Best synthetic DRIP services: Buy and

Hold (800-646-8212...*www.buyandhold.com*) or Sharebuilder.com (800-638-7865...*www. sharebuilder.com*).

Trap: Synthetic DRIPs let you invest more often than once a month, the limit for most DRIP plans. This lets investors take advantage of short-term opportunities—but it could lead to excessive trading.

Fees: Commissions should not be more than 2.5% of your amount invested. If you can't afford to invest at least $100 per transaction, synthetic DRIPs may not be worth the commission. But you can cut down on commissions by setting up an automatic, recurring investment.

My favorite synthetic DRIPs: AOL Time Warner...Amgen...Genentech.

FOREIGN DRIPS

Until recently, few foreign companies offered DRIPs for US investors. Now more than 250 do, including Deutsche Telekom AG, Sony and Toyota.

When you buy DRIPs in a foreign company, you're buying an American Depositary Receipt (ADR). ADRs trade on US exchanges rather than on foreign exchanges. They may also pay dividends just like regular stocks.

Foreign DRIPs are not for novice investors. Currency shifts versus the dollar can wipe out gains...and the different regulatory and compliance rules make it hard to understand what you're buying.

Limit Orders vs. Market Orders

Limit orders let you name your own price for buying or selling a stock. Limit orders are best for short-term traders, for whom every small price difference matters. They are also good for stocks whose prices may change dramatically, such as those of newly public companies, where a market order to buy could cost much more than you want to pay if the price shoots up. The more common *market orders* are filled at whatever price is currently available. *Caution:* About 40% of limit orders are never filled. If you really want to buy or sell a stock, use a market order.

Steve Bradley, former Salomon Smith Barney executive and coauthor of *The Stock Market* (John Wiley & Sons), quoted in *Business Week,* 1221 Avenue of the Americas, New York City 10020.

Costs Determine Performance

Costs determine fund performance within a given category. In general, a major criterion determining which funds do best is simply how much they charge investors. Funds with high expenses tend to do worse than funds of the same type that have low ongoing expenses. Look for annual expenses below 1% a year in most categories. In some areas, such as international funds, costs may go higher. *Exception:* In small-cap stock funds, the relationship between costs and performance is less clear.

Harold Evensky, CFP, chairman, Evensky Group, comprehensive personal financial services, Coral Gables, FL.

Past Performance May Boost Returns

Past performance *may* be helpful when deciding where to invest. Despite warnings that a fund's past performance does not predict future returns, one strategy using past performance seems to boost returns. *How it works:* At the end of the year, buy that year's top diversified stock fund. Hold it for one year...then switch to the next year's best-performing fund at the end of that year. For the past 25 years, this strategy produced annualized returns of 21.2%, compared with a 15.1% gain for the average diversified fund.

Sheldon Jacobs, editor, *The No-Load Fund Investor,* 410 Saw Mill River Rd., Suite 2060, Ardsley, NY 10502.

The Most... And Least... Tax-Efficient Mutual Funds

Bertram J. Schaeffer, CIMA, partner in the accounting firm Ernst & Young LLP and national director, investment advisory services, 2001 Market St., Philadelphia 19103.

Mutual fund investors who have been zapped in recent years by big tax bills on reinvested distributions have been looking for more tax-efficient ways to invest. In response, the securities industry has come up with a number of highly tax-efficient investment vehicles.

Here is a rundown on tax efficiency...

Mutual fund distributions are immediately taxable to investors, unless the fund is held in a tax-deferred retirement account. That's true even if the distributions are reinvested. Those fund owners owe tax without pocketing any cash.

Bigger problem: Funds that trade actively may stick investors with passed-through, short-term gains that are taxable at ordinary tax rates rather than the favorable rates on long-term gains.

BEST AND WORST

According to Morningstar Inc., value-style funds have been less tax efficient than growth funds...

• **Large-capitalization value funds** (value stocks have lower stock fundamentals than the average stock) had a 10-year tax efficiency of 80.5%.

• **Large-capitalization growth funds** (investing in large companies with superior earnings growth prospects) had a 10-year tax efficiency of 86.9%.

Note: Morningstar calculates tax efficiency by figuring what a top-bracket investor would have wound up with after tax versus a fund's reported pretax return.

It's true that most taxpayers are not in the highest federal tax bracket but, at the same time, most investors also would owe state or even local income tax. Thus, the Morningstar numbers generally are realistic.

Growth and future: There is no guarantee that growth funds will be more tax efficient than value funds in the future. A market sell-off could scare shareholders into redeeming their shares thereby forcing growth funds to liquidate appreciated holdings, triggering taxable gains for investors who stay the course with the fund.

Perspective: The average large-cap value fund returned 13.93% annually for the 10 years in the report (through January 2000). Pretax, a $10,000 investment would have grown to about $37,000.

After tax: The average large-cap value fund returned 11.22% per year—after tax. The $10,000 would have grown to around $29,000. In the average fund in this category, around 22% of the 10-year return would have been lost to taxes.

Laggards: The above numbers are averages, which means that many funds leaked even more profits to the IRS. Dreyfus Fund, for example, had a 10-year tax efficiency of only 71.8% while Vanguard Windsor Fund's tax efficiency was 72.7%.

Such tax-inefficient funds, if you want to own them, should be held in a tax-deferred retirement account.

For your taxable account, consider these types of funds...

• **Successful funds.** Mutual funds with above-average returns tend to be tax efficient. Leading funds attract new investors, so they don't have to sell appreciated holdings to meet redemptions. Also, an expanding shareholder base dilutes the impact of capital gains distributions.

Example: Legg Mason Value Trust has been a large-cap value leader, averaging annual returns of 21.32% for the past 10 years. The fund has a 95.1% tax efficiency for those 10 years, delivering a 20.26% after-tax return.

Again, the tax-efficient Legg Mason fund has benefited from success, which attracts new money and reduces investors' tax bills. Any reversal of fortune would reduce tax efficiency.

●**Tax-managed funds.** While most mutual funds aim for pretax returns, a few weigh after-tax returns as well. They take losses on individual stocks when they can and use those losses to offset realized gains.

Example: JP Morgan Tax-Aware US Equity Fund has not made a capital gains distribution since inception in 1996. Its three-year, after-tax return (22.32%) is 98.9% of its pretax return (22.57%). Investors have had to pay only a few dollars in tax on dividends passed through from companies in the portfolio.

●**Index funds.** Funds that aim to track a particular index tend to be tax efficient because they usually hold on to the same stocks, the ones in the index. If there are few changes within the portfolio, there probably won't be realized gains to pass through to investors.

Example: Vanguard's huge 500 Index Fund, which tracks the S&P 500, has an above-average tax efficiency of 93.8%.

Many index funds, as well as successful growth funds, have sizable unrealized gains among present holdings. Those gains might be realized in the future, if a downturn leads to a surge in redemptions, so investors should be wary.

Example: Vanguard 500 Index Fund has a 38% potential capital gains exposure, which means that 38% of the fund's assets may turn into taxable gains if it sells its profitable holdings.

BEYOND MUTUAL FUNDS

There are other ways to enjoy the advantages of mutual funds (diversification, professional securities selection), and some of these alternatives may offer excellent tax efficiency.

●**Exchange-Traded Funds (ETFs).** These are index funds traded on the American Stock Exchange. *Offerings include...*

●Standard & Poor's Depository Receipts (SPDRs), known as "Spiders" (ticker symbol: SPY), which track the S&P 500.

●"Mid-cap Spiders" (MDY), which track the S&P MidCap 400.

●"Sector Spiders," such as SPDR Technology (XLK), which includes the tech stocks in the S&P 500.

●Dow Jones Industrial Average Tracking Stock (DIA), known as "Diamonds."

●NASDAQ 100 Tracking Stock (QQQ), known as "Cubes."

●World Equity Benchmark Shares (WEBS). There are 17 WEBS, each of which tracks a single country's stock market, using indexes developed by Morgan Stanley.

Key: Many more ETFs are expected to be introduced to track a wide variety of indexes and sub-indexes.

Benefit: ETFs may be even more tax efficient than index mutual funds.

ETFs rarely realize capital gains because they adjust their portfolios only when a company leaves the index. What's more, ETFs are not subject to shareholder redemptions so they don't have to sell off their holdings and realize gains.

Example: In seven years since inception, the Spider has made only one $0.09/share distribution, which is much less than the distributions have been from S&P 500 index mutual funds.

●**Closed-end funds.** Don't confuse ETFs with closed-end funds, another type of publicly traded diversified portfolio. Closed-end funds generally are not index funds—they include equity and fixed-income funds, foreign and domestic funds.

Again, closed-end funds do not have to cope with investors' redemptions, which further helps tax efficiency.

On the other hand, closed-end funds are actively managed so they may realize gains, which must be passed through to investors.

Bottom line: Closed-end funds vary widely in their tax efficiency, so check on a fund's record before investing.

BUYING AND HOLDING

●**Unit Investment Trusts (UITs).** UITs aren't publicly traded but you can sell units back to the brokers that offer them (which includes most major firms). You'll have a gain or a loss, depending on the performance on the underlying securities.

UITs hold onto their securities without making any trades. Thus, there are no realized gains to pass through to investors.

Downside: UITs mature in one to six years, depending on the trust. At that time, you'll owe tax on any profits.

Fortunately, favorable long-term rates probably will apply.

Loophole: Upon maturity of one trust, investors can then roll into a new one. If the same stocks are in the new trust, any gains on those stocks can be deferred. The trust's sponsors probably will help with the tax-reporting paperwork.

If you're considering a UIT, ask if you can request in-kind distributions (you'll receive shares of the companies held in the trust) upon maturity, which would defer any tax.

•**Holding Company Depositary Receipts (Holdrs).** Pronounced "holders," these packaged products were first introduced in July 1998 by Merrill Lynch.

A few Holdrs—Telecom Holdrs and Biotech Holdrs, for example—trade on the AMEX and more are likely to follow.

Like UITs, Holdrs are buy-and-hold portfolios so there are no trading gains to be passed through to investors. They last for 40 years so you can minimize the tax consequences by simply buying and holding on.

Investors can exchange Holdrs for the underlying shares. Then, you can sell any losers to realize losses while letting any winners ride, untaxed.

Set your priorities. For any type of investment, you should focus on the potential rewards versus the risks rather than the tax consequences.

However, if you do have a particular type of fund in mind (an S&P 500 index fund, for example, or an Internet-related sector fund), you should pick a vehicle by focusing on after-tax, rather than pretax, prospects.

Better Fund Investing

Protect against tax problems that can occur when a fund takes big capital gains. Look for funds labeled *tax managed*. Avoid funds that change managers often—many new managers make heavy sales. Check funds' distribution dates so you do not buy just before a capital gains payout. Avoid funds that are losing investors but have big built-up gains that will eventually be distributed—check with Morningstar, *www.morningstar.com*.

James Poterba, PhD, associate department head, economics department, Massachusetts Institute of Technology, Cambridge, and coauthor of a study of fund tax efficiency.

Dividends and Market Downturns

Don't invest in companies that pay dividends merely to cushion your portfolio when stock prices fall. While it may seem attractive to receive a stream of dividends during a volatile market, investors should look at the big picture. Dividends are taxed as ordinary income—at a higher rate than long-term capital gains—and do not provide substantial growth. That comes from capital appreciation. Companies tend to do better if they do not pay out earnings as dividends, but invest them in developing their business or use them to repurchase their own stock. *Bottom line:* Look at a stock's *total return*. That may include dividends, but would largely consist of capital appreciation.

S. Timothy Kochis, CFP, is president of Kochis Fitz, a financial-planning and money-management firm, 450 Sansome St., Suite 1600, San Francisco 94111.

Momentum Investor's Trap

The best-performing mutual funds of one year are likely to be among the best performers of the next year—or among the worst.

Study: When all funds were studied back to 1962, it was found the top 10% of funds of one year had a greater-than-average chance to repeat among the top funds the next year—but also had an offsetting greater-than-average chance to be among the bottom 10% of funds the next year.

Why: The top-performing funds over a short period, such as a year, usually are undiversified funds that have concentrated their investments in a hot sector of the market.

Because the funds are less diversified, they are more volatile.

As long as the sectors they have invested in stay hot, they stay hot.

Trap: But when the sectors fall, they pull their undiversified investors down with them.

Study by Mark Carhart, cohead of quantitative strategies, Goldman Sachs Asset Management, 32 Old Slip, 24th Fl., New York City 10005.

Technical Champion's Most Useful Indicators

Gerald Appel, president of Signalert Corp., which manages $750 million in private investor assets. He is also publisher of *Systems and Forecasts*, 150 Great Neck Rd., Suite 301, Great Neck, NY 11021.

Technical indicators—sophisticated mathematical tools used to discern patterns in the millions of shares traded on Wall Street each day—can alert investors to major changes in the market.

Important: Since indicators are not foolproof (and sometimes conflict with each other), use them as just one part of your decision-making process.

Six technical indicators I have found useful for managing clients' portfolios...

ADVANCES/DECLINES

This measure of market breadth may be maintained on a daily or weekly basis. The Advances/Declines line is a cumulative total, calculated by subtracting the number of stocks that declined in price from the number that rose in price. The higher the Advances/Declines number, the healthier the market.

Important: If Advances/Declines is trending downward in a rising market, stock picking is trickier. Only a select group of stocks is benefiting.

NEW HIGHS/NEW LOWS

This is a weekly barometer of stocks making new 52-week highs or lows. It is a more precise gauge of the market as a whole than Advances/Declines.

To detect the bottom of a market cycle: If the overall market is declining and the number of stocks reaching new lows is also declining, it is a strong sign that a decline is nearly over.

VALUE LINE ARITHMETIC INDEX

This is a daily average of about 2,000 stock prices from Value Line, the investment advisory company. Unlike the S&P 500, this index is not weighted by market capitalization. A $100 billion company has the same percentage representation as a $100 million one.

The Value Line Arithmetic Index is a helpful indicator for timing the purchase of mutual funds or stocks. The unweighted Arithmetic Index provides a much better correlation with the market as a whole than the S&P. When it is rising, you have a better chance of making money in any type of stock or stock fund.

Caution: Often, investors buy stock funds when the S&P 500 is rising, only to be perplexed that their funds aren't going up, too. That's because in recent years, technology stocks have had such large gains that just a dozen or so make up a large proportion of this capitalization-weighted index.

SHORT-TERM BONDS

Check the rate of change in current yields of three- and five-year government bonds versus the same figures six months earlier.

If the yields are lower, trends are favorable. You can use this as an indicator to move into the stock market without fear.

Almost no serious stock market declines have taken place in the past 30 years when this indicator was positive.

If other indicators give conflicting signals, this is the one to follow.

VALUE OF THE US DOLLAR

When the dollar is weak against the euro or the yen, international stock mutual funds make good investments. When the dollar is strong—as it is now—foreigners invest their money here and international funds flounder.

MUTUAL FUND NET OUTFLOWS

This is a measure of how much money is exiting mutual funds each month. It is a great tool to spot market bottoms in stock and bond mutual funds.

When more money flows out of funds than into them, pessimism is high. Then it is a smart time to buy. These periods of net outflows are usually followed by long rallies.

Example: There were strong net outflows from bond funds in 1994...and bond funds performed well for the next four years.

WHERE TO FIND THESE INDICATORS

Newspapers: The "Market Laboratory" section of *Barron's...Investor's Business Daily ...The Wall Street Journal.*

On-line:

- *www.bigcharts.com*
- *http://moneycentral.msn.com*
- *www.ici.org*
- *http://finance.yahoo.com*

CD Buying Smarts

Caution: Broker-sold bank CDs can be riskier than ones you buy directly from a bank. *Example:* A broker may say you can sell a CD before maturity without an early withdrawal penalty, but the broker may have to sell it at a discount if interest rates have risen since your CD purchase. That could cost you more than a bank's early withdrawal penalty would. *Self-defense:* Understand all conditions before you buy one. Pay special attention to the maturity—many people get confused and don't realize they've made 20-year commitments. *And:* Deal with a reputable broker—preferably one with which you have a relationship. Call your state's consumer protection office or securities administrator to check an unfamiliar broker's credentials.

Jay Rosenstein, editor, *FDIC Consumer News*, Federal Deposit Insurance Corp., 801 17 St. NW, Rm. 100, Washington, DC 20434.

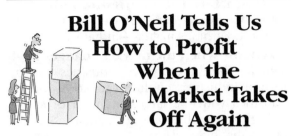

Bill O'Neil Tells Us How to Profit When the Market Takes Off Again

William J. O'Neil, founder and chairman of Investor's Business Daily, 12655 Beatrice St., Los Angeles 90066. (*www.investors.com*)...and chairman of William O'Neil & Company, which provides investment research to institutional investors. He is author of *24 Essential Lessons for Investment Success.* McGraw-Hill.

Three-quarters of all stocks are ruled by market climate. No matter which way the market is moving, the most important thing is to follow its lead.

Zero in on stocks making new highs in the top five or six industry sectors so you will be ready as the new bull market emerges. Follow the Dow, NASDAQ and S&P every day for your first clue to a market turn.

When the market does turn, there are many ways to profit. *Here are the rules I've learned over 45 years...*

- **Don't let emotions override common sense.** When emotions take over, you react to rumors or buy what experts tell you to buy—instead of doing your homework.

Avoid cheap, low-quality stocks and buy stocks that meet these conditions...

- A company that is number one or two in a strong industry.
- Earnings up 50%—or more—and accelerating for three quarters in a row.
- Sales up at least 25% a quarter or accelerating. Without strong gains in sales, earnings won't hold up.
- Return on Equity (ROE) of 20% or more.
- Profit margins that are among the highest in its industry.
- Heavy trading volume at key buy points of a stock chart's price action, indicating institutional investors are buying.
- Leaders with relative price strength in the top 20% of the market.

●**Don't buy the *profits-don't-matter* baloney.** Internet investors weren't the first to fall for it. Earnings matter—and always will.

●**Follow when the market changes leadership.** There are always industries heating up and industries cooling off. Look for the industries with the largest number of stocks hitting new highs. *Investor's Business Daily* reports that every day.

Current areas of interest: Fiber optics, full-service brokerage firms, Internet infrastructure building.

●**Don't overdiversify.** Many investors believe owning 20 to 30 stocks protects them against loss. But it is very hard to follow so many companies.

Rule: Keep your eggs in just a few baskets that you know well. If you have $10,000 to invest, spread it over three stocks. With $50,000, choose four or five. Divide $100,000 among five or six stocks.

●**Get stock ideas by watching what the best professionals are doing.**

Helpful: Investor's Business Daily rates stocks by how heavily their shares are being bought by mutual funds. Top institutional investors in stocks can also be found on the SEC Web site, *www.sec.gov,* or at *www.free edgar.com.* Also track high-performing funds and their top holdings. This information is available in financial magazines and on Web sites, such as *www.morningstar.com.*

Read interviews with fund managers to see what stocks they like.

●*Remember*—**profit comes only when you sell.** People obsess about which stocks to buy, yet ignore sell rules. Without them, you'll sacrifice paper profits on good stocks and take losses on bad ones. *Consider selling a stock when...*

●Its price-to-earnings ratio (P/E) increases by 130% from when it first began to move up.

●It drops more than 8% below your purchase price—selling will cut your loss.

●Growth in its earnings per share shows a major slow-up for two consecutive quarters.

●Performance seems too good to be true. Be wary if a stock advances almost every day—with price gains of 25% to 50% in a few weeks

—and volume accelerating. Just before the climax, it will show the biggest one-day advance. That's when to sell—when everyone else is gushing.

Perfect Time For Investing

S tocks historically have done worse in warmer months than during the rest of the year. According to the Halloween Indicator, for 73 years—from 1926 through 1998—large- and small-cap stocks have averaged significantly higher returns from November through April. In extreme form, this suggests selling all stocks at the end of April and reinvesting the money on October 31. *Reality:* Much of this indicator's success can be traced to the "January Effect"—the market's tendency to do well in the first month of the year. But even if the January Effect is ignored, stocks still tend to perform better in colder months. Recognizing this indicator still can be worthwhile even if you don't plan to follow it in its extreme form. *Example:* The best time to sell stock may be spring. If you are planning to buy, consider waiting until autumn.

Mark Hulbert, editor, *Hulbert Financial Digest,* 5051-B Backlick Rd., Annandale, VA 22003.

Direct Purchase Plans (DPPs)

D PPs let small investors buy stock directly from companies—in some cases, even if you start with as little as $10. About 600 companies now have DPPs, including such well-known firms as Allstate, Campbell Soup, ExxonMobil and Wal-Mart. But the SEC does not let companies advertise DPPs aggressively, and brokers do not tell customers about them—since the plans let you buy without paying commissions. *More information:* Direct Purchase Plan Clearinghouse, 800-774-4117 or *www.enrolldirect.com.*

Matthew Sitler, director, shareholder services, Georgeson Shareholder Communications Inc., 17 State St., 28th Fl., New York City 10004.

Portfolio Readjustment Strategy

Lewis J. Altfest, CFP, president, L.J. Altfest & Co., Inc., a fee-only financial planning firm, 116 John St., New York 10038. He is professor of finance at Pace University in New York City.

The Federal Reserve seems to have done a good job of balancing the economy, getting rid of the overexuberance of the stock market. I'm advising my older clients to be conservative, though.

In terms of overall allocation, I am recommending that they have no more than 65% in stocks—with 35% in bonds, which have actually done better so far this year than stocks.

THE SHIFT TO VALUE

The recent correction in the overvalued technology and telecommunications sectors caused major disappointments for many shareholders.

Now is a good time to look at your portfolio from a fundamental point of view. Forget "sex appeal" and take price into account. Consider shifting from tech stocks to value stocks. This shift is already beginning to happen in the marketplace, where we're seeing a resurgence of the so-called "old economy" stocks of the Dow and the S&P 500. Actually, the old and new economies are coming together as all companies adapt to new technology. There's only one economy, after all.

Of course, you want to own some growth companies, but for now, I advise clients to allocate more to value, aiming to have up to half of their stock portfolios in value-oriented stocks and mutual funds.

Guideline: Remember the 50-20 rule. Don't buy—and/or lighten up on—anything that has a price/earnings (P/E) multiple of more than 50.

Instead, favor stocks selling for less than a 20 P/E multiple—the lower the better, so long as the company has solid fundamentals in sales and earnings growth...and strong management.

I anticipate a continuing peaceful transition from stocks with high P/Es to those with low P/Es, without the market collapsing. I don't see a recession near-term. The Fed has the economy in control.

MUTUAL FUND SELECTIONS

The value-oriented no-load mutual funds that I like now are...

● **Vanguard Windsor II (VWNFX).** 800-523-1154.

● **Royce Opportunity (RYPNX).** 800-221-4268. An investment-class fund that concentrates on small- and micro-cap companies with capitalizations under $1.5 billion.

For some international representation (about 20%), which all investors should have today, I like...

● **Tweedy Browne Global Value Fund (TBGVX).** 800-432-4789. Looks for undervalued stocks throughout the world, including the US.

BOND FUND SELECTIONS

Now bonds are looking better than many stocks. Top-rated corporates (AA, A) are yielding relatively more than Treasuries than they have for a long time. But you need a good professional bond fund manager to get the most benefit from this situation. *My favorite now...*

● **Loomis Sayles Bond Fund (LSBRX).** 800-633-3330.

I don't even mind junk bonds right now because they are selling at a discount due to fears of economic slowdown or recession. Just be sure to avoid funds that have a large portion in low-rated communications industry bonds. *A conservative selection in the high-yield sector...*

•**Vanguard High Yield Corporate Fund (VWEHX).** 800-523-1154. Invests in a diversified portfolio of junk bonds, with 80% rated B or higher. Also, it can hedge up to 20% of its assets.

INTERESTING VALUE STOCKS

Some investors may be looking for interesting value selections among individual stocks right now. *I suggest two good candidates...*

•**Federated Department Stores (NYSE: FD).** A retail powerhouse with a P/E ratio of 12. That is reflecting a worst-case scenario about the consumer and the economy.

•**Waste Management (NYSE:WMI).** A turnaround situation that is not dependent on the economy. The stock is cheap on a fundamental basis. Not only is Waste Management number one in the garbage collection business, but it also owns many dumps, which are becoming more valuable because environmental considerations are restraining new facilities.

Individually Managed Account Advantages

Daily portfolio monitoring and refinement as market conditions change...ability to exclude certain types of investments, such as tobacco and alcohol stocks...tax efficiency because the investor owns the securities and can offset capital gains with losses.

A managed account features a portfolio of investments owned directly by the investor and managed by a professional money manager for a fee. *Drawback:* Typical minimum investment is $100,000, but some accounts can be opened for $50,000.

John Sharry, president, private-client group, Phoenix Investment Partners, Hartford, CT.

The Better Way to Invest In Index Funds...Costs a Lot Less, Too

David Yeske, CFP, president of the financial-planning and investment-management firm Yeske & Co., 220 Bush St., San Francisco 94104. He is a personal finance columnist for *San Francisco* magazine.

At a time when the number of critics of indexed investing is growing, there is one way to index that is gaining popularity. *Here is how it works...*

VERY, VERY EFFICIENT

While you can buy indexed mutual funds, the most cost- and tax-efficient way to index today uses Exchange-Traded Funds (ETFs).

ETFs are like mutual funds, designed to mirror the performance of a market index, stock market sector or economic sector.

But rather than being purchased through a management company, ETFs trade on stock exchanges—generally the American Stock Exchange (ASE)—as do common stocks. Any broker can execute a trade for an ETF.

The first ETF was the Standard & Poor's Depositary Receipt (SPDR or, more popularly, *Spider*), created in 1993 to track the S&P 500.

Today there are 70 ETFs with assets of $88 billion. *The lineup now includes...*

•**Spiders (SPDRs).** Now Spiders track the S&P Midcap index...as well as such sectors as energy, financial services and technology.

•**Diamonds** track the Dow Jones Industrial Average.

•**Qubes** track the NASDAQ 100 Composite stocks. The name is a play on words, since the ticker symbol is QQQ.

•**Holdrs.** These Merrill Lynch ETFs track sectors such as pharmaceuticals and biotechnology and market indexes such as the Russell 2000.

•**iShares.** From Barclays Global Investors, iShares offer the largest number of ETFs, covering every major US and foreign stock market index.

●**StreetTracks,** from State Street Global Advisors, cover the Dow Jones and Morgan Stanley indexes.

MUTUAL FUNDS vs. ETFS

●**Buying and selling.** Unlike regular mutual funds, for which purchases and sales are executed at the end of the trading day, ETFs trade throughout the day.

Resources: To find price information on ETFs, go to the American Stock Exchange Web site, *www.amex.com.*

Only one mutual fund Web site, *www. wiesenberger.com,* offers performance information on ETFs, but Lipper Inc. and Morningstar Inc. plan to do so soon.

●**Minimum initial investment.** The average is $2,000. Many ETFs sell at less than $20 a share.

●**Sales and commissions.** You'll pay a brokerage commission to buy and sell ETF shares—less than $20 a trade with a discount broker. So index funds are better for small, steady investments. While no-load mutual funds carry no commission, funds that are sold by brokers carry front-end sales loads of about 5%.

●**Fees.** ETF expenses can be much less than those for regular index mutual funds. Both index funds and ETFs have far lower expenses than actively managed funds.

Example: The iShares S&P 500 has annual expenses of 0.09%, while Vanguard's S&P 500 index fund charges 0.18%.

Bonus for aggressive investors: Because ETFs trade as common stocks, you can sell them short (borrow the shares and sell them with the aim of repurchasing them at a lower price). But you can't do that with mutual funds.

TAXES MAKE THE BIG DIFFERENCE

The biggest advantage of ETFs over mutual funds is the control you gain over tax planning.

●**Funds and taxes.** All capital gains realized by a mutual fund must be paid directly to shareholders. Your fund could have a net loss in a particular year. But if it sold investments at a profit during the year, you would still incur a capital gains tax liability. And the fund manager—not you—has control over when an investment is sold.

●**ETFs and taxes.** You incur a tax liability only when you sell ETF shares at a profit—an event that you control.

Important: One selling point for index mutual funds is that they do little selling—hence, they pay out little in taxable capital gains.

But in the unlikely event that a fund is forced to liquidate holdings to meet a surge in redemptions, huge gains would be realized. There is no comparable risk with ETFs.

Added benefit: Because ETFs don't face redemptions, they needn't hold a cash reserve, which is typically 4.5% for the average fund. ETFs can be fully invested in stocks...a prudent mutual fund can't.

ETF STRATEGY

If you are investing in funds for a nonretirement account, you shouldn't sell your index funds to buy ETFs because of the tax consequences.

But consider putting *new* money in ETFs.

Here is how I would structure a diversified portfolio of ETFs...

●**US large-cap.** My benchmark would be the S&P 500. For an ETF, I would choose between the following...

●iShare S&P 500. ASE:IVV.

●Standard & Poor's Depositary Receipt. ASE:SPY.

●**US small-cap.** My benchmark would be the S&P Small-Cap 600. My ETF would be...

●iShare S&P 600. ASE:IJR.

●**Domestic value.** I like to include a value component in any portfolio. While you could buy ETF sector funds in each of the most depressed sectors, buying an entire value index diversifies your bet. *Choose between the following...*

●iShare Russell 1000 Value. ASE:IWD.

●iShare S&P 500 Value. ASE:IVE.

●**Domestic growth.** Choose between the following...

●iShare Russell 1000 Growth. ASE:IWF.

●iShare S&P 500 Growth. ASE:IVW.

●**Investing abroad.** Every portfolio needs foreign exposure. Six ETFs cover 70% to 80% of the world. *Here are my suggestions for foreign-market ETFs and percentages of foreign allocation...*

●25%/iShares MSCI Japan. ASE:EWJ.

●22%/iShares MSCI United Kingdom. ASE:EWU.

●15%/iShares MSCI Germany. ASE:EWG.

●15%/iShares MSCI France. ASE:EWQ.

●10%/iShares MSCI Australia. ASE:EWA.

●8%/iShares MSCI Switzerland. ASE:EWL.

●5%/iShares MSCI Netherlands. ASE:EWN.

Do Your Homework Before Moving Funds

Before moving funds to a tax-deferred account, make sure the prospective financial institution offers the specific type of account you are looking for. *Reason:* Not all financial institutions offer all available types of retirement accounts. If you move the funds and then find out that the new organization doesn't offer the account you want, you may be forced to accept one that doesn't meet your investment goals. And—you may have difficulty transferring again to an institution that does have the type you want.

Sidney Kess, attorney and CPA, New York City.

Biotech and FDA Approval

To choose good biotechnology stocks, find out what new drugs are in a company's research pipeline—and how close any of them are to FDA approval. About half the return in biotech stocks comes before FDA approval, the other half afterward. Look for makers of products that address big-market diseases—such as cancer, cardiovascular disease and autoimmune disorders. *Important:* Look for companies whose managers have good track records of getting drugs through the FDA. Make sure a company has substantial financial backing—or is working with a deep-pocketed partner.

Kurt von Emster, manager, Franklin Biotechnology Discovery Fund, San Mateo, CA.

How Value Investing Wizard Martin Whitman Knows When A Bargain Is a Bargain

Martin J. Whitman, chairman, Third Avenue Trust, 767 Third Ave., New York City 10017. He is an adjunct professor of finance at Columbia University School of Business and author of *Value Investing: A Balanced Approach*. Wiley.

Technology stocks have dipped so far below their highs that they seem like bargains.

But are they really? In recent months, with the economy slowing, many of these stocks have just kept sinking.

How to separate the bargain stocks from the basket cases...

●**Make sure the company is safe.** No matter how undervalued a stock is, it's no bargain unless the company is in strong financial shape.

●Examine the company's financial statements.

●Is the company earning money?

●Has the balance sheet remained solid despite setbacks?

●Is its debt-to-equity ratio low, as measured by a relative absence of liabilities?

●Does it have quality assets, such as cash or real estate?

●How strong is its cash flow?

I am partial to companies that make money without spending lots of money.

Examples: Money-management institutions, such as Legg Mason (NYSE:LM, *recent share price:* $54)...and asset-based lenders, such as CIT Group (NYSE:CIT, *recent share price:* $20.18).

• Assess liabilities. I avoid companies with uncertainty surrounding pending litigation. Tobacco stocks seem attractive, for example, but the risk factor is too great.

• Scrutinize management. It should be competent, with a history of being responsive to outside minority shareholders. This is the hardest part of corporate analysis. Look at public disclosure on compensation, perks and takeover defenses.

• Look into the company's future. Does its business model make sense? For instance, I won't bite at beaten-down telecommunications stocks, such as AT&T and WorldCom, because it is not clear how they'll replace falling revenues caused by increased competition.

• **Make sure the stock is cheap.** Review the company's financials. Determine what the value of the business would be if it were a private company or a takeover candidate by looking at prices of similar companies. Try to get it for half that figure—or less.

Example: When I found Forest City Enterprises, a developer and manager of real estate, appraisers were valuing its income-producing properties at $80 to $90 per share. I invested because the company had solid fundamentals and was selling for $17 per share.

• **Avoid playing the earnings game.** Investors' biggest mistake is to rely on a stock's price-to-earnings ratio (P/E) as a shorthand indicator of a bargain.

Reason: Negative earnings surprises are common. Best long-term values tend to be created when earnings are most depressed.

• **Have patience.** Bargain stocks are often remarkably cheap because their short-term outlooks stink. It can take years for the market to unlock the value of a beaten-down stock. But even modest appreciation will give you significant profits because you've bought the stock so low.

Example: I bought Silicon Valley Group (NASDAQ:SVGI) in 1997 when the semiconductor sector was out of favor. I expected that sooner or later, chip manufacturers were going to have to expand and reequip. *Result:* In 1998, the stock fell more than 43%. In 1999, it rose 39%...and in 2000, it shot up 61%.

Investment Opportunities And Your Taxes

Danny C. Santucci, tax attorney, owner, Santucci Publishing, 1011 Brioso Dr., Suite 111, Costa Mesa, CA 92627. He is a frequent lecturer before bar associations, CPA societies and other tax professional groups across the country, and author of more than 25 books, including the recent *Family Tax Planning.* Santucci Publishing.

The Internet is a wonderful tool for investors—revolutionary even. It's easy and exciting to invest on-line—thrilling to day trade.

But the Internet doesn't change the fact that the only true way to financial self-sufficiency is a diversified portfolio of mostly long-term holdings put together with a careful eye on the tax laws. *First planning steps...*

• **Project the after-tax returns for all your holdings.**

• **Take maximum advantage of pretax investment opportunities,** such as Keogh plans and 401(k) plans.

ASSET ALLOCATION

Before selecting individual investments, you must come up with a way to divide up your investment eggs in a way you feel comfortable with. Tying up all your assets in one type of investment is risky. *I recommend the following asset allocations for various age groups...*

Twenties—get into the savings habit: 50% liquid, 20% income, 20% growth, 10% inflation-hedging.

Thirties—you can be speculative: 20% liquid, 20% income, 50% growth, 10% inflation-hedging.

Forties—be aggressive and expand: 10% liquid, 10% income, 70% growth, 10% inflation-hedging.

Fifties—get into more conservative investments: 20% liquid, 20% income, 50% growth, 10% inflation-hedging.

Sixties—caution is critical: 30% liquid, 30% income, 30% growth, 10% inflation-hedging.

Two Web sites that will help you determine asset allocation are *www.smartmoney.com/si/tools/oneasset/* and *www.thestreet.com/tsc/assetallocation/.*

INVESTMENT CHOICES

●**Stocks have three great advantages.** *They are...*

●Highly liquid.

●Easily researched.

●And—long-term capital gains (more than a year) are taxed at a maximum rate of only 20%, just half the 39.6% maximum tax rate of ordinary income. And the longer you hold the stocks, of course, the longer you can defer paying taxes on the gains.

Among the types of stocks are cyclical, defensive, high-growth, interest-sensitive, and small companies.

A company called Hoover's operates a great Web site for screening stocks as the first step in selection at *www.stockscreener.com/.*

Among the sites offering discussion groups for investors are *www.quicken.com/forums/* and *www.stockselector.com/forum.asp.*

In addition, leading brokerage houses, both full-service and discount, have their own sites.

●**Mutual funds** offer liquidity and diversification for investors with limited amounts of money to invest, but give an investor less control over taxes, since funds by law must report dividends and capital gain distributions to shareholders annually.

In recent years index funds—those that mimic a popular index such as the S&P 500—have often outperformed managed funds, and have lower management and transaction costs. *They also offer a tax advantage:* Because holdings are seldom traded—it becomes necessary only when the index's components are changed—the annual tax bite is lessened.

When a fund's shares are sold, there will be a reportable gain or loss. Remember to include any reinvested gains or dividends in the cost basis.

A great site to begin fund selection is *www.morningstar.com/FundSelector.html/.* Another good site is *www.smartmoney.com/si/analyzer.*

●**Bonds.** Debt instruments—generally perceived as a more conservative investment than stocks—are not risk free.

● *Municipal bonds,* which are tax exempt at the federal level as well as in the issuing state in most cases, have long been popular with upper-income investors, but there have been instances of municipalities defaulting.

To determine your after-tax yield on a muni, divide the tax-free rate by one minus your tax bracket.

● *Treasuries,* which are issued by the US Government—in maturities ranging from 30 days for the shortest term bills to 10 years for the long bond—are generally perceived as the safest bonds and are exempt from state income taxes. Because of these characteristics, they also have the lowest yields—around 6% for the long bond at present.

● *Zero-coupon bonds* are sold at a deep discount to face value and pay interest only at maturity. However, interest is imputed annually making them best suited for tax-deferred accounts like IRAs and Keogh plans.

● *Corporate bonds* offer higher yields than munies or Treasuries because they have no tax advantages and greater perceived risk. The degree of risk varies greatly among issuers. Services such as Standard & Poor's rate the risk on a scale of AAA (best) to D (in default or bankruptcy).

Two useful sites: *www.publicdebt.treas.gov/* and *www.standardandpoors.com/ratings/high yield/index.htm.*

●**Tax-deferred annuities** may be attractive to people whose income precludes them from making IRA contributions and who are already making maximum contributions to qualified plans. Contributions are not tax deductible, but earnings accumulate tax deferred. They are sold by insurance companies, generally with a $5,000 minimum investment and the cost of investing is higher than the investments previously discussed because buyers must pay for the insurance wrapper as well as for the holdings in the annuity.

●**Rental real estate** can be a lot of work as an investment, and it is far less liquid than financial securities. But it does offer tax advantages—mortgage interest and depreciation are deductible. The tax laws are complex and are designed to bar upper-income taxpayers from taking advantage of what is deemed a passive investment.

●**REITs.** Real estate investment trusts, which are sold on the stock exchange, are an excellent way to invest in real estate without the hassles of direct ownership. These securities can be evaluated like stocks. Current news on realty stocks may be found at *www.inrealty. com/*, and the REIT trade association operates a site at *www.nareit.com.*

●**Life insurance** provides an excellent way to pay estate tax and, if held in a life insurance trust, can escape being subject to estate tax itself. In addition, whole-life and universal-life policies offer a tax-free cash-value buildup.

WHERE TO INVEST

Tax law plays a big role in deciding where to hold your various investments. Favorable capital gains treatment is available when long-term holdings in a regular taxable account are sold.

In contrast, money that comes out of a tax-deferred account, including IRAs, 401(k)s or pension plans, is taxed as regular income. That means there is no tax incentive to hold money long-term inside such an account. However, losses in such accounts do no good in terms of taxes, so that is a good reason not to buy high-risk investments.

Real Estate Winner's Investing Secrets

Roger Woodson, president of Expert Realty Services, Fort Fairfield, ME, a broker representing purchasers only. He has 25 years of experience as a home builder, remodeler, investor and real estate agent. He is author of *Profitable Real Estate Investing.* Dearborn.

Not everyone is inclined to invest in real estate, but the rewards can be substantial. You can start with as little as $15,000* and turn it into a major money source that will support you in retirement.

Whether you take an active role as a landlord or turn over the day-to-day management of the property to others, you can expect a return of 7% to 20% a year over the long haul.

Here is what I've learned from 25 years in the business…

●**Don't buy a single-family house for rental property.** Despite its apparent appeal —a single-family house doesn't require as much money as a larger building…and you have only one tenant to worry about—your rental income may not defray the cost of your investment. If you suddenly lose your tenant, you could be buried by the carrying costs. With a multifamily unit, some rental income is always coming in.

Safest bet for novice investors: Four-unit apartment buildings. They provide the right combination of size and manageability. Larger apartment complexes might be more profitable, but they can be difficult to monitor.

You can finance the purchase of a four-unit apartment building just as you would a house. If you're planning to occupy one of the units, you can buy it with as little as 5% down. Larger buildings require as much as 30% down.

*Assuming a 5% down payment on a $200,000 four-unit apartment building that is your primary residence, plus a $5,000 reserve for expenses.

Also, you may qualify for a residential loan rate that is one to two percentage points below the commercial loan rate. Since professional investors concentrate on larger properties, you won't face as much competition when buying a four-unit building. Four-unit buildings have been going up in value more quickly, growing by about 7% a year versus 3% for larger buildings.

Beware: Buildings made up primarily of one-bedroom apartments can be a landlord's nightmare—because of high turnover. Every time someone moves, you have to scrub the place thoroughly, usually repaint, replace carpeting and repair appliances. Also, you might not find a tenant right away.

●**Expect to hold your property for at least five years.** Few properties appreciate quickly enough to make up for real estate commissions—5% to 7% of the purchase price—and fees for appraisals, lawyers, inspections, credit checks and loan applications. Closing costs, which include all non-commission fees, are typically 3% of the purchase price.

●**Research your property the way you would a house.** It's best to buy in a neighborhood that has had slow but steady appreciation. If you buy in the hottest areas, you may have trouble recouping your investment because of excessively high prices.

Scour the real estate listings going back six months. Ask a realtor for sales data on comparable properties. If the property you want has been offered at the same price for six months, the seller is probably asking too much.

In addition to market conditions, factor in the local unemployment rate, the proximity to schools and transportation and whether the neighborhood is considered desirable.

Right now, it is a seller's market. But interest rates are moderate by historic standards.

●**Consider hiring a management company.** These firms screen potential tenants and arrange for routine maintenance on the property. It's a good way to protect yourself from unforeseen problems. *Fee:* 10% to 15% of the gross rental income.

To find a good management company, check out similar properties that appear well run, with their lawns mowed and garbage emptied. Ask tenants if they are satisfied. Call the owner, and ask for the name of the property manager.

●**Be very picky about tenants.** Bad tenants pay late or not at all...or trash the premises. And it can take six months or more to evict them.

If you're not using a management company to screen tenants, check the prospective tenants' credit and business references. If you use a management company to run your property, it can also run credit checks through the major credit bureaus.

Many landlords won't rent to people with kids or pets. But such tenants put down roots in the community and tend to stay longer than individuals or couples. If you're afraid of the wear and tear, ask for a larger-than-normal damage deposit.

●**Always have a financial reserve.** Keep enough cash in the bank to cover at the very least three—and preferably six—months of expenses.

This reserve should cover the mortgage, taxes, utilities, insurance and maintenance. Budget 15% of your annual gross income from the property to cover maintenance and repairs. You need to be in a position to fix major equipment failures quickly.

Example: Replacing a heating or air-conditioning system costs $15,000 to $20,000. If not fixed immediately, your building could be damaged and your tenants might leave.

A line of credit is also useful.

●**Don't expand too quickly.** I've never seen an investor get burned after buying his/her first building, but I've seen plenty ruined because they gobbled up multiple properties. When they had unexpected vacancies, they were unable to meet carrying costs.

Dealing with Unscrupulous Stockbrokers

If a stockbroker makes an error and refuses to admit it, talk to his/her supervisor. Ask if your phone call was taped—many firms record calls routinely. If not, and if the firm is unreasonable, ask to speak to its compliance department.

Explain the problem and how you want it resolved, and ask the compliance office to respond to you in writing within 30 days. If this does not work, contact the Securities and Exchange Commission at *www.sec.gov.*

John Heine, deputy director, SEC, Washington, DC.

A Fund's Expenses Still Matter

Some top-performing funds have high expenses—but high expenses do not bring good performance. Funds with supercharged performances are typically in sectors that do very well for a while but not so well at other times. When these funds have spectacular gains, their high expenses seem meaningless to investors.

But when performance drops, expenses become more important. Since few funds stay on top for long, paying less to fund management increases long-term return to investors.

Russel Kinnel, editor, Morningstar Fund Investor, 225 W. Wacker Dr., Chicago 60606.

Beyond Treasuries: Worry-Free Bond Investing

Marilyn Cohen, president, Envision Capital Management, a money-management firm specializing in bond investing, 1755 Wilshire Blvd., Los Angeles 90025. She is author of The Bond Bible. New York Institute of Finance.

If you like the safety of Treasury securities but don't like their relatively modest returns, federal agency bonds are a very attractive alternative.

Issued by government and quasi-governmental agencies, these securities are almost as safe as Treasuries...pay higher rates...and can be bought in denominations as small as $1,000.

There are three federal agencies that issue bonds...

●**Federal National Mortgage Association** (Fannie Mae) was founded during the Great Depression to help expand the amount of money available to mortgage lenders. Now a New York Stock Exchange–listed corporation, it is the largest source of home mortgage funds in the US. It issues a vast amount of bonds to finance its activities.

●**Federal Home Loan Mortgage Corporation** (Freddie Mac), also listed on the Big Board, helps make mortgage money available.

Note: Concerns have been raised in the media about the financial strength of Freddie Mac and Fannie Mae. I think the worries will diminish. Investors can buy Freddies and Fannies with confidence.

●**Federal Farm Credit System** makes loans to farmers, ranchers and agricultural cooperatives through seven regional farm banks.

Agency bonds don't have the same credit guarantees as Treasuries, but they are considered lower risk than corporate bonds. Normally, the spread between rates on Treasuries and agency bonds is 0.5% to 0.75%. But right now, the spread is huge—between 1% and 1.5%.

Reason: The Treasury has announced it will issue fewer bonds because the federal budget deficit has turned into a surplus. The lower supply amid continued demand has pushed Treasury bond prices up...and yields down.

With Treasuries looking pricey, agency securities are a particularly good buy. They come in maturities of one to 20 years and can be bought from brokers and big banks. Right now, the best rates are in the five- to 10-year range.

TWO CAUTIONS

● **Some agency securities are callable.** That means they can be redeemed before their maturity dates if interest rates fall. So the juicy rate you thought you had locked up for a long time may disappear after just a few years.

Ask whether a bond is callable before you buy, so you can make a more informed investment decision.

● **Interest income is not state–tax-exempt in all states**—even though it is for Treasury securities. The interest on both types of securities is subject to federal income tax.

If you are in a high tax bracket and live in a high-tax state, such as New York or Massachusetts, be sure to check the tax status of an agency bond before you buy.

The interest from government agency securities is subject to state tax, but the interest from Treasury bonds is not.

Two current noncallable favorites...

● A newly issued 10-year Freddie Mac bond yielding about 7%—more than one percentage point above a comparable Treasury bond.

● A five-year Fannie Mae bond with a yield to maturity of about 7%—almost one percentage point over a comparable Treasury.

10

Consumer Smarts

How to Win the New Electricity Game

If energy deregulation hasn't reached your community yet, it probably will soon. More than 40 states have deregulation on the books or in development. At least 70% of US households now have energy deregulation or will have to grapple with it in the next 12 to 18 months. *Yet few people understand what it means...*

DEREGULATION EFFECTS

In areas where energy is regulated, individuals have little or no choice about who supplies their electricity.

When energy is *deregulated,* consumers can shop around for the best electricity deal—much as they do for the best deals on heating oil, long-distance phone service, etc. Choices of electricity suppliers include the local supplier you've been using, spin-offs or subsidiaries of other companies and marketing companies that buy power wholesale, then sell it retail.

Of course, your power will still come from the same central grid.

Regardless of who supplies your power, your service and repairs will be provided by the same local utility and over the same wires you've always used.

If your energy provider goes out of business or can't supply enough power, your power will continue uninterrupted—most likely supplied by the local power company. You could then stay with that utility company or switch to a new provider.

MAKING THE RIGHT CHOICE

For information on what companies are licensed to sell power in your state...

● **Review advertising** from the energy companies.

● **Contact your state's public utility commission**—many states have Web sites or toll-free hot lines to handle deregulation questions.

Dan Delurey, a principal with EnergyGuide.com, an independent Web site where consumers can compare the energy choices in their regions. He has worked in the energy field for more than 20 years.

●**Go to *www.energyguide.com*,** my company's Web site, which has a state-by-state database of providers and prices.

You'll generally see more options in states that have been deregulated longer or in states where local utilities have been allowed to raise prices faster.

Examples: California, New Jersey, New York and Pennsylvania have extensive choices. Connecticut, where deregulation started in mid-2000, has fewer choices.

Compare the offers by…

●**Price per kilowatt.** This is the top consideration—but not the only one.

●**Consistency.** Some plans offer energy at a fixed rate for a set period—usually one year. Others offer variable pricing. Many consumers prefer a fixed price. The best depends on the individual's situation.

●**Environmental concerns.** Consider how the company produces its power.

●**"Bundled" utilities.** Some plans offer attractive rates if you get other energy—natural gas, heating oil, telecommunications services—through the same firm.

●**Bells and whistles.** Some energy companies use frequent-flier miles or long-distance minutes as inducements. Weigh the value of such incentives.

OTHER CONSIDERATIONS

Before making a decision, consider your state's rules, available through your state's public utility commission.

●**Can you switch back once you've made a choice?**

●**During what period?**

●**Without penalty?**

Most states make allowances for consumers who wish to return to their old suppliers, but details vary.

Deregulation is *not* an overnight change. There's usually a multiyear transition period during which there are some price controls—at least for those who remain with their current utilities.

In some states, removal of price controls starts so slowly that it makes sense to remain with one's traditional energy company for a time…*but don't get lazy*.

Once deregulation is in full swing, prices from competitive suppliers could save you 10% to 30%.

Fuel Oil Money Saver

Fuel-oil purchasing co-ops can save big bucks—for businesses and individuals. Oil suppliers won't negotiate unless you have at least 75 customers. *To get started:* Create a committee to send out a *Request for Proposal* to suppliers. *Important:* Once a supplier is chosen, have a lawyer draw up a contract for the supplier to sign…and a waiver of liability for co-op members to sign.

Daniel Barraford is a businessman in Barnstead, New Hampshire. His 1,000-member nonprofit fuel-oil purchasing group buys 2.3 million gallons of fuel oil a year, at up to a 30% discount.

Save on Duct Cleaning

Regular cleaning of heating and cooling ducts is unnecessary, says the US Environmental Protection Agency. Most dust taken into ducts adheres to walls or filters and never gets back to living areas. Cleaning ducts can actually make matters worse by knocking dust loose. Visible dust on registers doesn't mean ducts need cleaning, only that registers do.

Best: Clean ducts that are water damaged or otherwise moldy, visibly clogged with debris, or infested with insects or rodents.

Useful: The free EPA publication *Should You Have the Air Ducts in Your Home Cleaned?* is available from the Indoor Air Quality Information Clearinghouse, 800-438-4318 or *www.epa.gov/iaq*.

Nontoxic Ways To Clean Your Home... Cheaper, Too

Annie Berthold Bond, Rhinebeck, New York-based author of *Clean and Green: The Complete Guide to Nontoxic and Environmentally Safe Housekeeping* (Ceres) and *Better Basics for the Home: Simple Solutions for Less Toxic Living* (Clarkson Potter).

Save money and eliminate some chemicals from your household by making your own cleaning products:

•**Liquid cleanser** for cutting grease and cleaning countertops, baseboards and appliances: In a plastic spray bottle, combine two cups of very hot water, one teaspoon borax, half-teaspoon washing soda and half-teaspoon Murphy's Oil Soap (or similar vegetable-based detergent).

•**Antibacterial spray** for cutting boards. Fill spray bottle with one cup of water and 10 to 20 drops of essential oil of lavender. Spray on surface and leave overnight. Rinse.

•**Easy scrub** for sinks and bathtubs. Combine quarter-cup of baking soda and enough liquid soap or detergent to make a paste.

•**Floor cleaner** for wood, tile or linoleum. Put two gallons of warm water in a plastic pail, and add one-eighth cup of liquid soap or detergent and half-cup of white vinegar.

•**Oven cleaner.** Sprinkle dirty spots with water, then cover with baking soda. Rinse. Repeat, leave overnight and wipe up grime the next morning. Residue can be removed with liquid soap and water.

•**Toilet bowl cleaner.** Pour in one cup of borax, leave overnight and flush in the morning.

•**Glass cleaner.** In a spray bottle, combine half-teaspoon of liquid soap or detergent, three tablespoons of white vinegar and two cups of water.

•**Dusting and polishing wood.** Moisten a cotton cloth in a bowl containing half-teaspoon of olive oil and quarter-cup of white vinegar or lemon juice.

•**Air freshener.** Put a few slices of lemon, orange or grapefruit in a pot of water. Simmer gently for one hour to fill your house with a citrus scent.

Baking Soda: Cheap Miracle Substance

Vicki Lansky, *Family Circle* contributing editor, and author of *Baking Soda: Over 500 Fabulous, Fun and Frugal Uses You've Probably Never Thought Of.* Book Peddlers/800-255-3379.

AROUND THE HOUSE

Keep damp basements smelling fresh by hanging an old nylon stocking filled with baking soda from the ceiling.

•**Remove a child's crayon art from washable walls** by scrubbing gently with a damp sponge sprinkled with baking soda. Will also remove grease, pencil and markers.

•**Keep lawn furniture clean and fresh smelling**—especially pieces with plastic webbing—by wiping them down with a solution of baking soda and water.

•**Remove the musty smell from old books** by sprinkling baking soda between the pages.

•**Melt snow and ice from steps and walks** by sprinkling lightly with baking soda. Mix with sand for greater traction. *Benefit:* Baking soda is gentler to shoes, carpeting and outdoor plants than rock salt and deicing chemicals.

•**Loosen knotted shoelaces** by sprinkling them with baking soda and working it in.

IN THE KITCHEN

•**Rid hands of garlic and onion odors** by sprinkling baking soda on your palms... add just enough water to make a paste... "wash" hands with the paste...rinse.

•**Keep rubber gloves dry and smelling fresh** by sprinkling the insides with baking soda. *Also:* They'll slip on and off more easily.

- **Keep your microwave smelling fresh** by storing an open box of baking soda inside it. *Important:* Remove the box before using the oven.

GARDEN CARE

- **Grow sweeter tomatoes** by sprinkling the soil lightly with baking soda. *How it works:* The baking soda lowers tomato acidity. *Added benefit:* It discourages garden pests.

- **Control compost pile odors** by sprinkling liberally with baking soda.

- **Clean a birdbath without toxic cleansers** by sprinkling it with baking soda and scrubbing with a damp cloth or stiff brush. Rinse well and refill with water.

LAUNDRY

- **Clean starch buildup on your iron** by rubbing the bottom of a cool iron with a paste of baking soda and water. Clean steam holes with a cotton swab dipped first in water, then in baking soda.

- **Remove age stains from linens and clothing** by adding a half cup of baking soda to the wash water.

More from Vicki Lansky...

Surprising Uses for Bags, Paper And Plastic

There are hundreds of ways to use and reuse paper and plastic bags. *Here are some of my all-time favorites...*

- **When drilling a hole in the wall.** Tape a small bag under the spot where you're drilling to catch falling dust.

- **Remove wax drippings from table-cloths and carpeting.** Place an opened paper bag over the spot, and quickly run a *warm* iron over it. As the wax melts, it will form a greasy spot on the bag. Continue moving a clean paper area over the spot until all the wax is absorbed.

- **Emergency funnel.** Fill a plastic freezer bag with the liquid being funneled, cut one corner of the bag, insert it into the larger container and squeeze.

- **Prevent tarnishing of silverware.** Store in a plastic bag "powdered" on the inside with baking soda.

- **Keep the TV remote clean: Store it in a clear bag.** The signal will work the TV from inside the bag.

- **Ice down minor injuries.** Make a mushy freezer bag. Fill a heavy-duty bag three-quarters full of water, add a few capfuls of rubbing alcohol and put it in the freezer. The alcohol prevents the water from freezing solid, so the bag can be wrapped around the injury.

- **Keep birds and insects away from fruits and vegetables** that are still growing by slipping clear plastic bags over plants until ripe.

- **Pack each day's clothing in a separate bag** for a child who will be away for several days. No more searching through the bag each morning. Empty bags can be used to hold dirty laundry.

- **Protect hands when pumping gas** by keeping bread or newspaper bags in your car's glove compartment.

- **Store extra trash bags at the bottom of the can** so you'll always know where the next one can be found.

Very Best Buys in Power Tools

John R. Lewis, 23-year veteran of the home construction and remodeling industry in North Carolina. He is editor of the on-line magazine *Ubuild.com.*

These great tools will get the work done—and done well—and save a lot of money...

CORDLESS SCREWDRIVER/DRILL

A 12- to 14-volt drill is enough for driving screws and simple jobs. More powerful drills are heavy, expensive and better for large jobs.

My top choice: Ryobi battery drill/driver kits—the HP1441 14.4-volt drill or the HP1201

12-volt drill. Solid performance at a reasonable price. $90 and $70.*

ELECTRIC DRILL

Buy the lowest-priced, national-brand, ⅜-inch, variable-speed drill you can find for less than $75. It should give five years of fairly heavy use.

My top choice: Any of Makita's ⅜-inch variable-speed electric drills. Start at $45.

If you build furniture and use a drill often: A higher-quality drill is worthwhile. Purchase the least expensive drill that has a ball bearing shaft. DeWalt ⅜-inch variable-speed DW160K costs $110.

TABLE SAW

Essential for furniture and rip cuts—long cuts with the grain on boards. A nationally known maker's direct-drive table saw in the $150 range should last a lifetime.

My top choices: Delta model 36-545 10-inch table saw with floor stand runs $160 to $170. The Pro-tech 41061 ($145) is similar.

CIRCULAR SAW

Purchase the least expensive circular saw that has a ball bearing or roller bearing shaft. Such saws make more accurate cuts and outlast three ordinary circular saws.

Helpful: Carbide-tipped saw blades are better than standard "kerf-cut" blades.

My top choice: Makita 7¼-inch circular saws have the best balance of quality and price. Model 5007NBK is a good place to start. $245.

ROUTER

Unless you plan to make lots of furniture, stick to a standard router. Few people use a router much, but it is indispensable for certain tasks, such as fancy edge cuts for furniture.

Helpful: Purchase a router with the most powerful motor (as measured by horsepower) you can find for between $60 and $100. It rarely makes sense to pay more than this.

My top choices: Sears Craftsman routers give you a lot of power for the money, plus a wide range of models, such as 2-hp, 9-amp variable-speed router ($100)...and 1½-hp,

*Prices are manufacturers' suggested retail. Discounts may be available.

8-amp, single-speed router ($70). Also consider the Ryobi model R160K, a 1½-hp, model.

MITER SAW

While a table saw's strength is cutting with the grain of the wood, a miter saw cuts strictly across the grain—what is known as a "cross cut."

Purchase the lowest-priced 10-inch compound electric miter saw you can find. The compound feature allows you to make both angle and bevel cuts at the same time.

My top choice: Pro-Tech model 7208 compound saw for about $180.

Alternative: If you can live without a compound miter saw, save a bit by purchasing the Delta model 36-070 noncompound miter saw. It costs around $120.

RECIPROCATING SAW

A reciprocating saw can reach where other saws can't, such as flush cuts and tight spaces. Great for cutting through wood with nails and vital if you're building or remodeling a house—but not a must-have in every workshop.

My top choices: Milwaukee model 6509-21 ($250)...or any Makita model.

SABER SAW (JIGSAW)

For curved cutting and necessary for many projects—the least expensive one works fine.

My top choice: Skil's model 4445 Jigsaw is a good deal at $86. It will give a typical home owner 10 years of service.

BAND SAW

For serious woodworkers, this tool is for accurate, smooth, curved cuts and cutting thick wood. Band saws cut more smoothly and accurately than saber saws.

Downside: Band saws cost much more than saber saws—good ones run $250 to $400—and might not fit large pieces of wood. (Band saw arms generally reach only 10 to 18 inches.)

My top choice: Sears Craftsman—buy one with an arm at least 11 inches long. Starts at $220.

BELT SANDER

It is easy to economize too much on a belt sander. You can find them from big-name makers for as little as $45. But these low-end products don't do a great job for medium to heavy-duty wood sanding...and probably won't last five years.

My top choice: Porter Cable model 352. $190.

Orbital (vibrator) sanders leave scratches. I go straight from smooth belt sanding pads to hand sandpaper, rather than using an orbital sander as an interim step.

Gasoline Money Savers

Buy gas where three or four stations share an intersection—competition usually keeps prices down...Warm up the car for no more than one minute unless the weather is frigid and the windshield is coated with ice... Watch gasoline-market trends. If the trend is up, buy before the weekend...if it is down, buy after.

Geoff Sundstrom, spokesman, AAA National Office, Heathrow, FL.

The Black Belt Shopper's Guide To Unloading Unwanted Gifts

Susan Dresner is president of Ways & Means, wardrobe management and retail consulting firm, New York City. She was dubbed "The Nation's Black Belt Shopper" by *Money* magazine.

Right after the holidays, review your gift collection. Then decide what to unload. It is a terrific way to simplify your life.

STORE RETURNS

Returns are usually easy if your gifts include receipts. Trouble arises if a gift doesn't have a tag...or if you don't know where it was purchased. *With these handicaps, your two best options are...*

●**Talk to the gift giver.** Ask him/her to retrieve the receipt or at least provide more information about the purchase.

To keep him from feeling rejected, be pleasant, positive, forthright and unapologetic. Feeling guilt about returning a gift muddies the issue with embarrassment.

Example: *Thanks for the red sweater, but I already have one like it. I'd love to exchange it for another sweater. Do you have the receipt? And if not, can you tell me where you bought it? Thank you for making this so much easier.*

●**Appeal to the department manager** at the store where the gift might have been purchased...or proceed to the customer service manager. Better stores usually allow an exchange for merchandise or store credit— but for the value of the current price, which is often less than what the giver paid.

Discount chains and moderate-end department stores tend to give the most trouble. To increase your odds, be fair about what you want—and polite. Quality catalogers, such as L.L. Bean and Lands' End, take back all their merchandise.

EXCHANGE EFFICIENTLY

Before you turn in those unwanted gifts, plan an exchange strategy...

●**List the stores you need to visit.**

●**List the items you need or would like to have.**

●**Match the items from list two to the stores on list one.**

●**Phone ahead to find out each store's return policy**—the time limits, full-price exchange applied to sale items, etc. Also ask about upcoming sales—to maximize the value of your exchanges.

If returns are required within a short time after Christmas, it may be best to return items for store credit...then shop later to take advantage of sales.

Examples: I like early February for bargain-hunting—when inventory is cleared to make way for spring arrivals. Sales and special promotions are deep and wide across the retail scene.

A friend discovered that her favorite store for outdoor clothes and equipment celebrated "Membership Day," for which members of sports clubs received 20% off all inventory, including already reduced closeouts. She applied her full-credit exchange of $75 against a Gore-Tex jacket that was reduced from $140 to $70 and walked out with a super bargain and $5 to spare.

CHARITABLE CONTRIBUTIONS

In the spirit of the holidays, consider donating unwanted presents to thrift shops or for auctions run by nonprofit organizations. The value can be used as a tax deduction—if you receive a receipt.

GIFT RECYCLING

Despite your best efforts, some unwanted goods will be impossible to return or too strange to donate.

Some can be matched to friends who would appreciate them. Label by recipient's name, and give them away as thank-yous or for anniversaries and career promotions.

Have fun with those I-Don't-Know-What-to-Do-with-This gifts. Plan a "White Elephant" party, inviting friends to bring their own odd presents, playfully wrapped. Swap them in grab-bag fashion or as prizes in an outrageous gift contest.

More from Susan Dresner...

Black Belt Shopper's Favorite Catalogs

Shopping by mail is more than just a convenience—many of my favorite items are not sold in local stores.

These winning catalogs offer value-and-price-conscious products...with smart designs ...and unusual and/or high-quality materials.

Customer service is knowledgeable and friendly...and they have overstock and end-of-season bargains.

TRAVELWEAR

•**Travel Smith** specializes in wrinkle-resistant, lightweight, packable and fast-drying "miracle" fabrics in versatile styles. Outfits for travelers wanting easy-care clothing. *Fabrics to look for...*

CoolMax (wicks away moisture)...*Microfiber* (suede-like polyester)...*Supplex* (cotton-finish nylon that dries quickly)...*Tencel* (rayon-like and wrinkle-free).

Favorites: Microfiber Raincoat packs in a pouch ($199)...SPF 30—sun-blocking shirts, pants and hats ($62, $64, $25).

800-950-1600...*www.travelsmith.com*

EVERYTHING USEFUL

•**Vermont Country Store** is like a stroll back in time. Useful, hard-to-find, old-fashioned merchandise, ranging from home remedies to underwear. When was the last time you saw oilcloth tablecloths? A sweater stone to remove wool pills? A Fuller Brush dust mop? Yankee wisdom is scattered throughout the pages.

Favorites: Zout Cleaner for difficult stains ($11.50)...Swedish vegetable peeler (two for $9.90)...mildew-resistant vinyl shower curtain ($19.95).

802-362-8440.

OUTDOOR EQUIPMENT

•**Campmor** is for campers, hikers, cyclists, etc....or bargain hunters who love superior activewear, travel gear or sunglasses—all cheap. Look for "Special Purchases" highlighted throughout.

Recent specials: Jansport travel pack listed at $85 for $39.97...Serengeti sunglasses listed at $135 for $49.97.

800-226-7667...*www.campmor.com*

UNDERWEAR/ACTIVEWEAR

•**One Hanes Place** sells hosiery, pajamas, activewear, underwear (bras are a specialty)—all at 40% off list price. Items for women, men and children.

800-300-2600...*www.ohpcatalog.com*

NATURAL FIBERS

•**Garnet Hill's** products are made from cotton, wool and silk—in classic good taste, delightfully comfortable and at fair value. They range from bed, bath and home furnishings to clothes for kids, expectant mothers and women of all ages.

Favorites: Quilts that reverse to floral patterns ($125 to $300)...soft cotton knit separates from Denmark ($38 to $48).

800-622-6216...*www.garnethill.com*

LEISUREWEAR FOR MEN

●**The Territory Ahead** clothing is for the rugged male trekking across the country-side...or an urban cowboy dressing down at the office. Chic knockabouts well crafted in natural fabrics. *Note:* Its women's items don't have the same styling.

Favorites: Sueded twill pants ($55)...handwoven cotton plaid shirts ($50)...Saguaro parka in Italian brushed cotton with lining and collapsible hood ($188)...Iconoclast leather jacket ($385).

800-882-4323...*www.territoryahead.com*

PAIN RELIEF

●**FeelGood** sells products to comfort back, neck, feet and joints as well as magnetic therapy devices, exercise equipment, foot inserts and supports.

Favorites: Wraparound knee stabilizer ($39.95)...magnetic back belt ($69.95).

800-997-6789...*www.feelgoodfast.com*

NEW YORK DELICACIES

●**Zabar's** is New York's best-loved gourmet market, known for its smoked fish and meats, breads and bagels, imported cheeses and exotic foods. Plus there are great buys on kitchenware and appliances. Offers overnight shipping.

Favorites: Nova Smoked Salmon ($12/8 oz)...smoked whitefish ($10/lb)...raisin pecan bread ($6/loaf)...olive loaf ($3.50/loaf)...French Selle-sur-Cher goat cheese ($6/package)...truffle mousse pâté ($4/7 oz)...full line of Le Creuset cookware...stainless steel pasta cooker ($23.95).

800-697-6301...*www.zabars.com*

Phone Bill Checkup

Phone bills are up, even though long-distance rates are stable or declining. *Reason:* Increased charges for directory assistance, calling cards, monthly fees, surcharges and taxes. *Self-defense:* Learn to read your bill carefully at *www.nclnet.org/phonebill/index.html*. Call your long-distance carrier if you do not recognize some charges or calls. Be wary of cramming—charges for services you have not ordered—and slamming, when your long-distance service is switched without your approval. Shop around to find the most economical long-distance service. Avoid paying high prices for minimal services, such as local directory assistance—look up numbers yourself or use a Web site, such as *www. switchboard.com.*

Holly Anderson, director of communications, National Consumers League, 1701 K St. NW, Suite 1200, Washington, DC 20006.

Best Home Water Filters...They're Very Important Now

Richard P. Maas, PhD, professor of environmental studies at University of North Carolina, Asheville. He is codirector of the university's Environmental Quality Institute, a leading center for research on tap-water purity.

With regular news reports about water contamination—even in the best communities—more and more people are turning to home water filters to protect their families' health...

DETERMINE YOUR NEEDS

To choose the best filter for you, have your tap water tested.

Larger water utilities are now required to send an annual report to customers with the results of tests for about 80 different contaminants.

If you have well water—or if you don't want to wait for your water company's report—look in the *Yellow Pages* under "Water Testing" or "Laboratories—Testing." Test price depends on what contaminants you look for. The range is wide—between $17 and $800. The most likely contaminant is lead (20% of US households), which can be picked up by the household plumbing system.

Clean Water Lead Testing (828-251-6800) provides a two-sample, mail-in test (first drawn and after running water for one minute) for $17. *Warning:* Home testing kits may be unreliable.

CARAFE FILTERS

Water flows by gravity, and there's plenty of the filtering medium with which it interacts to remove lead, reduce chlorine byproducts and improve taste and smell. Inexpensive (less than $30).

Drawbacks: Slow...holds only two to three quarts...filters must be changed often, generally every 50 to 100 gallons, depending on the level of contaminants in the water.

Top carafe filter: Pur Pitcher CR-500. Half-gallon pitcher uses carbon and an active agent to improve water taste while reducing levels of lead, chlorine, copper and zinc. Safety gauge indicates when filter needs replacing. $20. *Replacement filters:* $8 each. 800-787-5463.

FAUCET-MOUNTED

Inexpensive (less than $50)...easy to install and change filters.

Drawbacks: Units are small, and water pressure forces water through the filter too quickly to thoroughly remove all impurities.

Top faucet filter: Pur Plus FM-3000. Removes microorganisms, such as giardia and cryptosporidium, as well as contaminants, including lead, chlorine and mercury. Automatic shut-off stops water flow when filter needs replacing. Filters last for 100 gallons. $30. *Replacement filters:* $15 each. 800-787-5463.

UNDER-SINK FILTER

Contains a reservoir so water has more time to pass through the filtering mechanism ...long-lasting filters.

Drawbacks: Costs $100 or more...may require a plumber for installation.

Top under-sink filter: Waterpik IF-100A. Dual-filter unit removes lead, chlorine and some pesticides—such as lindane—while improving water odor and taste. Installs easily and comes with extra-long tubing and a movable base for quick filter changing. Filters last for approximately 1,200 gallons. $159. *Replacement filters:* Lead filter/$38.59...chlorine/pesticide/taste and odor filter/$12.49. 800-525-2774.

WHOLE-HOUSE FILTER

For homes on well water and not connected to a municipal water system.

Contains sophisticated filtering material tailored to meet the home's specific needs—removes hardness...neutralizes water...removes bacteria. Filtered water is supplied to the whole house, including taps, showers and washing machine.

Drawbacks: Expensive ($1,000 to $3,000 installed plus filtering materials)...requires monthly maintenance—changing filters and/or adding filtering materials.

There is no *best* whole-house system—it depends on your water-treatment goals. Leading manufacturers include Culligan, Flek and Hauge. The company that services your well can provide guidance following a comprehensive water test. Or look in the Yellow Pages under "Water Purification & Filtration Equipment."

Energy Costs Soaring... Big Cost Cutters... Little Cost Cutters

Harvey Michaels, CEO of Energyguide.com, an on-line resource that helps consumers lower home and business electric and gas costs and includes calculators that show annual savings, Newton, MA. Mr. Michaels has spent the last 20 years in the energy field.

The high price of gasoline isn't the only energy-related concern for consumers. Natural gas prices have nearly doubled in the last year to their highest levels in more than a decade.

This winter, many homeowners could find that it costs at least 30% more to heat their homes than it did last year.

Here's what you can do to cut your energy bills in half without compromising your lifestyle...

HEATING/COOLING

●**Use a programmable thermostat** to maintain the temperature in your home.

It automatically adjusts the heat or central air-conditioning—which is much easier than trying to fine-tune it manually every night before bed or every time you leave the house.

Cost: $40 to $100 per year.

Potential savings: 20% on heating and cooling bills, which average $2,000 per year for a single-family home located in the Northeast.

Important features: Storage of at least six temperature settings a day...manual override without affecting the remainder of the daily or weekly preset program schedule...backup battery so you won't have to reprogram the timer after a power failure.

LIGHTING

•**Switch to Compact Fluorescent (CFL) bulbs.** They use 80% less energy than standard incandescent bulbs and last up to seven years.

CFLs have shaken their reputation for poor-quality light and limited fit in home fixtures. Now they're readily adaptable to any fixtures and made by reputable manufacturers.

Cost: $5 to $15 per bulb—but many local utility companies discount them or offer rebates of up to 50%.

Potential savings in energy costs: $50 per bulb over its lifetime.

•**Halogen floor lamps.** Replace with floor lamps that are made for compact fluorescents.

Cost: $30 to $50 for bulb and lamp.

Potential savings: CFLs will save you $30 per lamp in electricity annually and are far less dangerous because they generate 95% less heat.

•**Floodlights.** Replace standard floodlights in all recessed ceiling lights and outdoor fixtures with CFLs. If you have a dozen or more lights, you can save several hundred dollars a year.

APPLIANCES

•**Look for the *Energy Star* label.** Every appliance meets the minimum federal energy-efficiency standards.

Appliances that are awarded the Energy Star certification by the Environmental Protection Agency, however, use approximately 20% less energy than the minimum. Energy Star appliances are not necessarily more expensive, and they pay for themselves in energy savings within five years.

Example: Replacing an old refrigerator with an Energy Star model costs about $600. But you'll save $100 to $150 a year on electricity.

You may be able to receive rebates from your local utility company for using a variety of energy-efficient appliances.

And many stores—including Home Depot —have rebate coupons.

•**Buy a front-loading washing machine.** These models use 50% less water, require less detergent and reduce wear and tear on clothes.

While front-loading machines cost about 20% more than top-loaders, a family of four can save as much as $150 per year.

•**Turn off your computer monitor** when you step away. The monitor requires far more energy than the hard drive, and a screensaver won't help.

If you're buying a new computer system, look for a monitor with a sleep-mode feature. It automatically converts to a low-energy mode when not in use, cutting electricity usage in half.

WINDOWS/INSULATION

•**Install low-emissivity windows.** Low "e" glass is coated with a film that doesn't affect your view but provides greater insulation. Most major window manufacturers carry them now.

•**Insulate properly.** Lay down fiberglass "batts" the right way to realize greater savings.

•Attics: Lay down fiberglass between the floor joists (support beams). If existing insulation comes up to the top of the joists, add an additional layer. Purchase batts without a vapor retarder.

Do not store items on top of insulation— insulation loses effectiveness when it is packed down.

•Basements: If unheated, insulate the basement ceiling first, rather than the foundation and the walls.

Support the ceiling insulation from below by using wire mesh or chicken wire fastened to the joists under the batts.

If the basement is heated, simply insulate the foundation and the walls in addition to the ceiling—a carpet on the floor, fiberglass batts in the walls.

GENERAL

•**Choose a low-cost energy supplier.** More than half the US has deregulated electric and gas companies competing for your business. Get a list of licensed suppliers from your state public service commission. Be sure to get each supplier's *standard offer* or *price to compare.* This is the price per kilowatt-hour (therm) the utility charges.

Even easier: My Web site, Energyguide.com, provides comprehensive support for reducing energy bills by helping individuals buy more efficient products and find the best energy suppliers.

Potential savings: $100 to $300 a year for a typical home (two parents, two children).

●**Get a free energy audit from your utility company.** Some companies will inspect your home for its energy effectiveness and recommend ways to cut costs—insulating water heaters, repairing weather-stripping, etc.

Other Internet resources to easily compare and save on energy bills...

●*www.lowermybills.com* finds the best deals in nine categories of recurring bills, including energy usage, insurance, mortgages and long-distance telephone service.

●*http://hes.lbl.gov/HES/vh.html,* run by the EPA and Department of Energy, lets you compute your home energy use based on your detailed input.

●*www.ase.org,* run by Alliance to Save Energy, offers a home energy checkup. You can also order the free booklet *Power-Smart: Easy Tips to Save Money and the Planet,* online or by calling 888-878-3256.

Time to Say Yes To Satellite TV? How to Buy It Right...

Jim Scott, editor, *Satellite TV Week,* 140 S. Fortuna Blvd., Fortuna, CA 95540.

There are two kinds of home satellite systems—big dishes (C-band) and small Direct Broadcast System (DBS) antennas. Either system provides far more channels—close to 500—than cable television...*and significantly better picture and sound quality.*

Which system you buy depends on what and how you want to watch. *To decide what's right for you...*

BIG DISHES

A C-band dish (typically $7\frac{1}{2}$ to 10 feet in diameter) is for someone who selects programs in advance and stays with them. *Drawbacks...*

●**Only one channel at a time** can be seen in the *entire* household.

●**It can take several minutes to move** from satellite to satellite for signals, so channel-surfing is difficult.

●**Snow in the dish** may cause you to lose the signal temporarily.

●**Homeowners' associations** can prevent you from installing a C-band dish. Municipal codes might require a backyard location, even if reception would be better elsewhere.

Cost of a basic large-dish system: About $1,100, including installation. With a standard system, you buy programs from the providers and pay "a la carte."

Example: If all you watch is CNN and the Discovery Channel, you can buy both for just $2.50 a month.

A more sophisticated system with a digital-plus-analog receiver runs $2,500, installed. You get a lot more programming with the C-band digital receiver—about 500 viewing channels, plus thousands of music, news and other feeds, for about $12/month.

Your savings from cheaper program fees versus cable television should pay for the C-band equipment within three years.

SMALL DISHES

Minidishes—about 18 inches in diameter—collect microwave signals from one to three satellites. They sit in a fixed position on your roof or window sill. DBS is best for people who like a lot of channel choices and an easy-to-use system. Minidish owners view as cable subscribers do—they can channel-surf, and every TV in the house can be tuned to something different if a receiver is purchased for each TV.

Drawback: If you get heavy cloud cover or a downpour, you'll temporarily lose the signal.

Costs: There's a great deal of competition among minidish suppliers. Typically, either the installation or the hardware (dish, receiver, remote) is free. Either bonus is worth about $100. Hardware and programs are purchased through a single service. Packages average $240/year.

WANT NEWS? YOU LOSE!

Depending on where you live, you might not be able to get local programming—such as local news—via a satellite system. For these programs, you would still need a cable connection or a rooftop antenna. However, pending legislation may soon change this.

Bottom Line Guide to Buying a Home Generator

Gary Shipman, licensed electrical contractor and plumber. He owns and operates The Generator Store in Newbury, OH.

With America's power grid increasingly overtaxed and the continuing threat of disruptive storms, home generators are becoming more popular. *Here's what to do if you want a home generator...*

●**Determine your emergency power needs.** Most who buy a home generator want to power some—or all—of the following...

- ●Refrigerator
- ●Lights for a few rooms
- ●Furnace
- ●Water heater
- ●Air conditioner
- ●Home security system
- ●Medical equipment

Unless you have a large house with greater-than-usual heating or cooling needs, an eight-kilowatt (kW) generator should be sufficient.

Exception: If you rely on a pump to raise water from a well—or have a basement sump pump—you might need a more powerful 10-kW to 12-kW generator.

●**Pick a generator that runs on appropriate fuel.** Home generators typically use natural gas...propane ("LP gas")...gasoline ...or diesel fuel.

Primary consideration—the fuels sold in your region. If there's a local natural gas distributor, that will probably be the most economical. Propane is the second-cheapest option. If neither is readily available, choose gasoline or diesel.

Diesel is more economical, and diesel engines tend to be particularly long-lived (40 years for diesel versus 20 for gasoline), but diesel generators cost about $2,000 more than other types. The fuel tank comes with the unit. A 20-gallon tank of diesel fuel runs for 30 hours.

●**Choose a brand name.** In my experience, generators from the following companies are more reliable...

- ●*Coleman,* 800-445-1805.
- ●*Cummins,* 800-343-7357.
- ●*Kohler,* 800-544-2444.
- ●*Winco,* 800-733-2112.

To choose among them, first consider the presence of a local certified service technician. However, that won't matter if the vendor also installs and services. Otherwise, look under Generators–Electric in your local Yellow Pages...or contact the manufacturer.

Personal favorites: Coleman Power-station 8500 ($3,995)...Winco 8500 ($4,150).

●**Costs.** An 8- to 8.5-kW natural gas or propane generator should cost about $3,300 to $3,600...10-kW, $4,400...15-kW, $6,600 to $7,500. For diesel, add about $2,000 per model.

You'll also have to pay for professional installation. This isn't a job for the average handyman, since it involves electricity and fuel lines—two complex and potentially hazardous fields.

Installation cost: $600 to $1,500, depending on the distances between your generator, gas line and electrical service panel.

If your town has strict noise ordinances, there are sound-buffering systems to bring the generators well below their usual 72-decibel output.

Cost: $200.

●**Safe operation.** Properly installed, home generators are safe and easy to use. Most are located outside the house—to keep toxic fumes out of your home—and automatically shut off if problems develop. Most operate via a simple switch to change your power source over to the generator.

Important: Have your home generator professionally serviced once a year. It may be used up to 30 days consecutively before servicing.

Time-Share Buying

Buy resold time-shares to save 50% or more off original price. *But* only buy a time-share if you view it as vacation time at a premium resort at a fixed price—*not* as an investment. Time-shares almost never appreciate in value. Buyers often have trouble getting anyone to buy an unwanted time-share at even a fraction of the original price. *Time-share resource:* Time-share Users Group, *www.tug2.net,* for resale offers.

Kiplinger's Personal Finance Magazine, 1729 H St. NW, Washington, DC 20006.

Amtrak Sale

Get bargain Amtrak fares from its Web site. Every Monday, Amtrak's Rail SALE program offers fares of up to 70% off only through its Web site. Fares are available at least for a week between the two cities listed and intermediate destinations. It's possible to upgrade from coach seating on board, subject to availability. The Rail SALE Web page is at *http://reservations.amtrak.com/rs.html.*

Save with Smaller Airlines

Smaller European airlines can save you up to 40% compared with major airlines—if you are willing to accept some inconveniences. Most fly into lesser used airports and do not have baggage agreements with other airlines—so you have to pick up your own luggage after a flight and carry it to another check-in. The best way to reach most of these airlines is on-line. *Examples:* London-based AB Airlines at *www.abair lines.com*...Madrid-based Air Europa at *www. air-europa.com*...London-based Go, *www.gofly. com*...Stockholm-based Skyways, *www.sky ways.se.*

Randy Petersen, publisher, *InsideFlyer,* 1930 Frequent Flyer Point., Colorado Springs 80915.

Save Money While Calling on the Road

Keep long-distance phone costs down while traveling...

•**Use your cell phone** if your plan has reasonable charges.

•**Buy a prepaid phone card**—some have rates below 10 cents/minute.

•**Get a no-name calling card.** *Examples:* AccuLinQ (800-909-7995...*www.acculinq.com*) charges 8.9 cents/minute with no per-call surcharge and a monthly cost as low as $1—charged only for months when you use the card. Bigzoo (*www.bigzoo.com*), an Internet-based long-distance company, has rates as low as 3.9 cents/minute, with no per-call surcharge and a monthly cost as low as 75 cents. Calling cards from major phone companies have high rates and big per-call surcharges.

Neil Sachnoff, president, TeleCom Clinic, 4402 Stonehedge Rd., Edison, NJ 08820.

Buying a Reliable PC Made Simpler for You

More than ever, personal computers (PCs) are commodities, with little difference from one brand to the next. Sure, you can choose a PC with a faster or slower processor…more or less memory…or a larger or smaller hard disk.

But a high-end machine—$3,000 to $5,000 —from one vendor is much like that from another…as is a budget model—under $1,500.

Still, despite nearly 20 years of mass production, PCs continue to house the occasional bug. Too often, after you unpack your brand-new PC and try booting it up, nothing happens. To use the revealing industry term, it's *dead on arrival* (DOA).

And that's not all. Even if it's not completely unusable, one or more components may conflict with another component and cause the machine to run your most important software programs with annoying fits and starts.

And then, of course, there's the "Why me?" syndrome, where after a year or so of smooth running, the PC suddenly freezes up, shuts down or loses your files—usually when you are under intense pressure to finish an important project.

Software is often to blame, but various estimates indicate that as many as one out of four personal computers breaks each year.

GETTING IT RIGHT

Obvious lesson: The most important factor in buying a PC is *not* how fast it runs or how many megabytes of memory it has. The most important factor, by far, is reliability.

To maximize the chances of buying a reliable PC, you can start by using your past experiences and those of colleagues or friends. But you'll get a clearer picture of a system's reliability from surveys that tally the experiences of *thousands* of people.

Among the most thorough surveys of PC reliability are those by prominent computer publications. *PC World* and *PC Magazine*—the two most widely read national computer publications—often report the results of their computer-user surveys. *Consumer Reports* periodically surveys computer users as well.

CURRENT FINDINGS

Most recently, the vendor that surpassed all others in reported reliability was Dell.

PC World readers ranked Dell "Outstanding" for work and home use—the only vendor of the eight ranked to receive this designation… *PC Magazine* readers gave Dell the only A grade among the 16 desktop PC makers rated …and *Consumer Reports* readers gave Dell the top reliability score of the nine PC makers ranked in its latest published findings.

Dell was a mail-order pioneer, then an E-commerce pioneer and now has an excellent Web site at *www.dell.com.* It serves the corporate, small-business and home markets.

OTHER TOP CHOICES

Reliable as they may be, Dell's PCs aren't for everyone. Other vendors may offer a system more attractively priced or available through a more convenient channel. *Examples…*

●**IBM,** which received the second-best reliability rankings overall, has long been known for its attentive service through its worldwide system of dealers. But the company has stumbled over the years in the PC market.

After legitimizing the PC in the early 1980s, IBM, at *www.pc.ibm.com*, nearly knocked itself out of the market, a victim of proprietary designs and bureaucratic inefficiencies. Lately, it has made a substantial comeback, and today, it's a leader in many important areas, including notebook PCs, hard disks and E-business.

●**Hewlett-Packard** at *www.hp.com* is best known for its printers. But in recent years, it has developed its PC business in both quantity and quality, and now ranks third overall for PC reliability. Hewlett-Packard has become a major player in the retail market and is a good choice when shopping at a local computer, office supply or consumer electronics store.

●**Apple Macintosh (Mac).** While still a niche product, the Mac, at *www.apple.com*, has a user base that is legendary in its loyalty. Its reliability scores, though, are middle of the pack. *PC Magazine* readers, although not the most fervid of Mac fans, gave it only a C grade.

RELIABILITY FOR LESS

Locally built PCs, often called "white boxes," are a popular and frequently cost-effective choice when shopping in person rather than over the phone or Internet. Reliability here depends almost entirely on the individual store, particularly for smaller stores.

In general, though, *PC Magazine* readers gave white boxes a respectable B grade. Among the machines marketed by leading national retail chains, *PC World* readers gave Circuit City and Office Depot white boxes better reliability scores than Best Buy, CompUSA and Staples.

Bottom line: Though playing the percentages doesn't guarantee you'll have a hassle-free experience, it can stack the odds in your favor.

Buying from vendors that rank highly in reliability also sends a strong signal to the entire computer industry that it needs to pay more attention to quality control.

Reid Goldsborough, syndicated columnist, Rydall, PA, and author of *Straight Talk About the Information Superhighway.* Macmillan.

Time for an Upgrade?

Consider upgrading your computer—instead of buying a new one—if it is less than three years old. Do not spend more than $250—a good new computer can be bought for about $1,000. *Often worth upgrading:* Random-Access Memory (RAM)—$50 to $225, depending on the size of the upgrade. Most people can add RAM on their own. *Other upgrades to consider:* Improved video or sound card, $100 and up...larger hard drive, $120 and up—but you may have to pay about $80 for installation.

Robyn Bergeron, computer-industry analyst, Cahners In-Stat Group, Scottsdale, AZ.

Downloading May Be Costly

High-cost downloads may masquerade as free information or entertainment on the Web. When you click to download the program, the user agreement—if there is one—may state that you will be connected to the service through a phone number in a foreign country. But it won't tell you the cost, which

could run to hundreds of dollars depending on your long-distance plan and how long you're connected. And anyone using your computer can use services that will result in charges on your phone bill. *Self-defense:* Download only from sites you trust...read user agreements carefully...and supervise others who may use your computer.

Susan Grant, director, Internet Fraud Watch, National Consumers League, Washington, DC. *www.nclnet.org.*

Web Shopping Self-Defense

Learn if any complaints have been lodged against the vendor's Web site by visiting *www.fraudbureau.com*...learn more about safe on-line shopping by visiting *www.safeshopping.org*, an educational resource of the American Bar Association.

When you shop on-line, print a copy of the Web page you order from. If any problem with the order arises, you'll have the copy of the Web page to document the product's price, description, shipping terms, etc. *Key:* If you purchase something described in a catalog or a print advertisement, you can always refer back to the printed offer if a problem arises. But a Web page that you order from may later "disappear," leaving you no documentation to rely on.

Mary Hunt, editor, *Cheapskate Monthly,* Box 2135, Paramount, CA 90723.

Product Downsizing

Some product sizes are shrinking, even though packages are staying the same. *Example:* What used to be a one-pound coffee can has held 13 ounces in the past. Now some companies are putting 11.5 to 12 ounces in the same-sized can. *Result:* A hidden price increase. Other downsized products include cocoa, canned fish, spaghetti sauce, potato chips, soup mixes, toilet paper, pet food. *Self-defense:* Compare unit prices.

Barbara O'Neill, PhD, CFP, professor of family and consumer sciences, Rutgers University, Newton, NJ.

Prepay Is Not the Way

Don't prepay for gasoline when you rent a car at an airport. Rental car employees often urge travelers to prepay for a tank of gas when renting a car. *Reality:* Most off-airport gas stations charge less than rental car firms do. And people who prepay get no refund for gas left in the cars when they return them. *Better:* Fill up the gas tank on your own before returning the car.

Survey of 58 rental car employees at 12 airports, reported in *USA Today*, 1000 Wilson Blvd., Arlington, VA 22229.

Shopping For Diamonds

Buy a *slightly* smaller diamond to save a lot of money. The price of a diamond jumps when it reaches a true half carat or full carat. A 0.49-carat stone is priced a lot lower than a half-carat...and a 0.90-carat diamond goes for much less than a one-carat stone. Yet the difference in the size is almost imperceptible.

Fred Cuellar, founder and president, Diamond Cutters International, Houston, and author of *How to Buy a Diamond.* Casablanca.

Beware of Untrained Property Appraisers

Appraisers of personal property (such as antiques, jewelry, Oriental rugs, etc.) are unregulated and unlicensed, so anybody can call himself/herself an "appraiser."

Trap: Of all the self-described appraisers in the US, only 10% have professional training. And many of those who have professional certification are minimally trained.

Of the four largest groups that provide professional credentials to appraisers, only one, the American Society of Appraisers, requires its members to pass tests in specific areas of appraisal expertise—for example, Oriental rugs, silver, jewelry, paintings. *To find an accredited appraiser:* 800-272-8258 or *www.appraisers.org.*

Best: If you need an appraisal for a specific reason (such as estate-planning purposes), get a referral to an independent appraiser from another professional (such as an estate lawyer).

Never depend on an appraisal from a dealer who wants to buy or sell the item being appraised.

Malcolm Katt, an antique dealer and owner of Millwood Gallery, which specializes in Nippon and Pickard porcelain, Box 552, Millwood, NY 10546.

Save on Foreign Currency Exchange

Use up foreign currency overseas to avoid paying two exchange fees—one to buy it and one to exchange it for US money. Use all foreign currency—even coins, which most exchanges will not accept—toward your final hotel bill, and pay the balance with a credit card. *Important:* Save enough currency for any fares or exit taxes you will have to pay when leaving the country.

Ed Perkins, consumer advocate, American Society of Travel Agents, Alexandria, VA.

Beware of Jewelry Shows

At some jewelry shows, jewelers offer hundreds of set ("mounted") diamonds. All the diamonds on display are already in settings, so you cannot check their weight, color or clarity. And trade-in values at the shows are low. *Bottom line:* Never spend more than $2,000 on a diamond in a prefabricated setting unless the jeweler will let you see the diamond loose.

Fred Cuellar, founder and president, Diamond Cutters International, Houston, and author of *How to Buy a Diamond*. Casablanca.

Delightful, Easy Parties Don't Have to Cost A Lot

Ellen Berson, president, The Movable Feast, party planners and caterers, 284 Prospect Park W., Brooklyn, NY 11215.

Nora Feeley, president of Event by Nora, Inc., event coordinator for companies and individuals, 1407 Larimer St., Suite 206, Denver 80202.

David Ice, freelance designer and artist who specializes in private parties and charity events, 264 E. Wayzata Blvd., Wayzata, MN 55391.

Entertaining groups of 50 or more doesn't have to break the bank. *Bottom Line* asked three party planners for their suggestions on how hosts can save money... and have fun at their own parties.

FESTIVE THEMES
Ellen Berson

I always give a party a theme and employ that motif throughout—it creates a festive atmosphere...and makes it easier to plan the menu. Keep food simple by serving just one hot dish. You don't want to be running back and forth between your guests and the oven.

•**Italian supper** is inexpensive, easy to serve and appeals to a variety of tastes. Top one or more draped tables with edible centerpieces—baskets overflowing with seasonal fruits, vegetables, cheeses and breads. Use another table for salad, focaccia bread and an olive bar.

•**Summer luncheons** are a delight. Decorate your house with flats of blooming pansies or impatiens (tied with wide ribbons to hide the plastic). Use terra-cotta pots of grass and rustic wooden birdhouses as centerpieces.

Roast vegetables in advance—asparagus, colored peppers and snap peas, etc. I like to serve a roasted, boneless leg of lamb, but roast turkey is also delicious and inexpensive. Add edible flowers, such as pansies and nasturtiums, to the salad.

•**Tropical party.** Greet guests with pitchers of piña coladas or blue margaritas. For evening parties, I place punch bowls filled with floating candles and slices of citrus fruit on serving tables.

In warm weather, people love to eat Thai curries...or paella salad, with saffron rice, clams, mussels and chicken. These dishes are easy to prepare and can be served at room temperature.

Favorite moneysavers...

•*For parties with lots of children,* make platters of sandwiches cut into fun shapes with cookie cutters. Fill with fresh strawberries and cream cheese...or peanut butter and jelly.

•*To save money on liquor,* see your liquor supplier at least one month in advance and ask about distributors' specials.

Worthwhile expense: Hire people to replenish drinks and remove glasses...and to replenish food and clear plates. Otherwise, your party will get sloppy after the first half-hour and you won't be able to enjoy your guests.

BRUNCH FUN
Nora Feeley

Brunches cost less than lunches or dinners, and they can be elegant—especially in warm climates, where you can have them outside with seating at small tables.

Serve pastries, smoked salmon, omelets or quiche, fresh-baked breads and bagels, shrimp, chocolate-covered strawberries, mimosas and Bloody Marys. It's also refreshing to offer fresh-blended fruit smoothies.

To make your guests feel special...

•**Cater to nondrinkers.** I always offer nonalcoholic beer...along with little bottles of sparkling water. If a guest isn't a drinker, he/she shouldn't feel pressured to take a glass of wine.

●**Avoid long buffet tables.** People don't like lines. Instead, have stations with foods served at different spots.

SPECTACULAR SETTINGS
David Ice

Surroundings matter for a successful party.

●**Use low-cost props for dramatic results.** At one party, I wrapped gigantic balloons in fish netting and attached each to a basket filled with hydrangeas and votive candles. They looked like hot-air balloons and cost only about $15 each.

●**Set an elegant table.** Don't just put food on the table. Make it festive.

Example: Last Independence Day, I designed a beach party with driftwood as the motif. I painted driftwood (found on the beach) white with blue stripes, then used them as centerpieces with wild daisies I found. All it cost was the paint and the time.

●**Be creative.** Combine unusual accessories with a lot of sparkling silver and crystal, beautiful fabrics, sculpture, figurines, lots of candles and ribbons. Purchase items when they are on sale—after holidays—and collect an assortment at reduced prices. Always think overscale—rather than skimping.

Related Useful Sites

Tax

☐ The Digital Daily
www.irs.gov

The IRS's user-friendly site, packed with easy-to-read information on tax issues for individuals as well as businesses. Also allows you to quickly download tax forms, which means no more visits to the Post Office.

☐ The Tax Prophet
www.taxprophet.com

Useful articles on *Hot Tax Topics* for individuals. Also an up-to-date rundown of frequently asked tax questions and answers as well as an interactive service for getting answers to specific tax questions and calculating your tax liability. Includes a search engine to help you find what you are looking for.

☐ 1040.com
www.1040.com

Site includes *Tax News,* Federal and State tax forms for current and previous years, *State Dept. of Revenue Addresses* with Links. Also contains lots of General Tax Information facts and figures.

Finance

☐ Dr. Ed Yardeni's Economics Network
www.yardeni.com

Dr. Ed Yardeni, chief economist and managing director at the respected Wall Street investment banking firm Deutsche Banc Alex. Brown, offers a wealth of informative data and analysis on key US business trends, stock and bond markets and a weekly economic briefing on timely subjects.

☐ Bank-CD Rate Scanner
www.bankcd.com

A service listing the highest CD rates in the US. Allows you to find the highest rate and purchase the exact type of CD you need.

☐ Bankrate.com
www.bankrate.com

Site provides rates of 4,000 lending institutions in hundreds of cities. Whether you're looking for an auto loan, home equity loan or are interested in money market funds or IRA's, there's plenty of information to compare.

☐ Fabian.com
www.fabian.com/home.html

Accomplished and widely respected mutual fund investment adviser Doug Fabian offers a list of mutual funds to avoid at all costs, due to consistent underperformance and/or excessive expenses. The list is updated regularly.

☐ Finance and Folly
www.fool.com

The site of one of the Web's original pioneers, the Motley Fool. It's better than ever as a site with an edge. It makes all that mundane investing stuff actually fun and amusing. If you're a beginner, check out *Fool's School* and learn the basics of investing. And check out *Fool on the Hill* for interesting commentary and opinions on financial topics.

☐ INVESTools
www.investools.com

Log onto an electronic library stocked with an array of professional investment newsletters, stock reports and more. Easy to use and very informative for both experienced traders and novices.

☐ NASD Regulation
www.nasdr.com

NASDR, a subsidiary of the National Association of Securities Dealers, regulates the securities industry (generally) and NASDAQ (particularly). It accredits, and is empowered to discipline, brokers. If you have a problem with your broker, you can check here to see if the problem is a "prohibited conduct" or browse the lists for any NASDR enforcement actions against the broker or his/her parent company. If you still feel you've been subjected to improper business practices, file complaints directly to NASDR through this site. Site also carries related securities industry news, describes the disciplinary process, gives tips on avoiding problems, etc.

☐ Quote.Com
www.quote.com

All the financial market news, research sources and charts needed by both amateur and professional investors. Subscription rates vary, from $9.95 to $99.95/month, depending on how many information services you want.

☐ US Securities and Exchange Commission
www.sec.gov

The US Securities & Exchange Commission (SEC) site includes *Investor Assistance & Complaints,* articles on how to invest wisely, avoid fraud, etc. The *EDGAR Database* of corporate information provides most of SEC's electronically filed corporate forms, including 10-Ks. Clear instructions for both Web and FTP users to retrieve information. Go to *Search the EDGAR Database* to get the information. Site also offers extensive Small Business Information and a link to the *U.S. Small Business Administration* Web site.

☐ Unclaimed Assets
www.unclaimedassets.com

Find out if you're one of the millions of Americans who are owed money in uncashed checks, dormant bank accounts, abandoned stocks and bonds or unpaid insurance and retirement benefits. Browse their list of hyperlinks for general information and to learn whether there might be money waiting for you.

Consumer

☐ Consumer Information Center
www.pueblo.gsa.gov

Select from hundreds of free or very inexpensive brochures, pamphlets and reports on a wide range of useful subjects, such as health, cars, small business, money. All published by the US government.

☐ Consumer Product Safety Commission
www.cpsc.gov

The government's Consumer Product Safety Commission (CPSC) tests, analyzes and, if necessary, orders recalls of just about any product on the consumer market. Consult this site for notices of safety problems or recalls, or to get useful safety guidance on how to use various consumer products.

☐ Consumer World
www.consumerworld.org

Consumer World is a public service, noncommercial site with more than 1,700 conveniently categorized consumer resources on the Internet. Click on *Buyer's Advice* for product comparisons, reviews and pricing services for everything from books to real estate to retailers. Also find scam-prevention information, consumer protection agencies and much more.

☐ Frugal Living
http://frugalliving.miningco.com

Sign on and learn to save money in all kinds of ways. Link up to lots of sites that can help you comparison shop, whether you're looking for groceries, long-distance phone service or flea market items. It's all right here.

☐ Lowermybills.com
www.lowermybills.com

This site offers opportunities to cut basic bills such as long distance phone service...auto insurance... mortgage rates and even Internet access. Easy to use and free.

☐ ProductReviewNet
www.productreviewnet.com

Indexes and abstracts of product and service reviews from hundreds of print magazines and on-line sources. Updated daily (about 400 new reviews each week). Home page gives the option of keyword or concept searches for computers, entertainment, electronics, home life, small business, vehicles (cars, boats, vans, more) and outdoors (gear, resorts, hiking and camping, etc.). Comprehensive, flexible, easy to use.

11

Faster Grandma!

Planning Your Retirement

Valuable Opportunities— Playing Roth IRAs by The New Rules

The Roth IRA is now three years old...and clearly a success for those who have them. Wise use of a Roth IRA helps individuals build tax-free, long-term wealth.

THE BASICS

Traditional IRA: Any individual younger than 70½ with earnings of $2,000 or more can contribute up to $2,000 of *pretax* income for 2001, although active participants in qualified plans can only make fully deductible contributions for the year 2001 if Adjusted Gross Income (AGI) is below $53,000 on a joint return...or $33,000 on a single return. Earnings grow tax-free until withdrawals begin after retirement—or by age 70½, whichever comes first. Withdrawals are taxed at ordinary income rates.

Roth IRA: You can contribute the same amount to a Roth IRA, but contributions are not tax-deductible. Earnings, however, are completely tax free (not tax-deferred, as with a regular IRA). Withdrawals are never required, as they are with a regular IRA. You can begin to withdraw earnings after age 59½ without penalty if the account is owned for at least five years. You can withdraw contributions tax- and penalty-free at any time.

WHO QUALIFIES

Roth IRAs are better for lower-bracket taxpayers.

To qualify...

● **You must have earned income equal to the contribution amount.**

● **Allowable contribution starts to phase out at AGI of $95,000** and disappears completely when AGI reaches $110,000 for single

---

Ed Slott, CPA, E. Slott & Co., CPAs, 100 Merrick Rd., Rockville Centre, NY 11570. He is editor of *Ed Slott's IRA Advisor. www.irahelp.com.*

187

individuals…$150,000 and $160,000 for married couples filing jointly.

Distributions are income tax free to your Roth IRA beneficiaries, who can spread distributions over their life expectancies—possibly another 30 or more years of tax-free growth.

What to do: Your Roth IRA beneficiary should elect the life expectancy term by taking the first required distribution by December 31 of the year after you die. Otherwise, he/she will have to withdraw the proceeds over five years…and will lose a lifetime of tax-free earnings. When you leave a Roth IRA to your spouse, he can roll it over into an existing or new Roth IRA and be exempt from any required distributions.

Caution: A Roth IRA is part of your taxable estate. So when you open one, buy additional life insurance held by a trust or your beneficiaries. The insurance provides liquidity for paying estate taxes without forcing your heirs to make excessive IRA withdrawals to pay the tax.

CHANGES IN IRA CONVERSIONS

•**Converting to a Roth IRA.** When Roth IRAs were first created in 1998, you could pay the income tax owed when you converted a traditional IRA to a Roth IRA over four years.

If you are eligible and convert now, you must pay the tax in the year of the conversion. To simulate the four-year income spread, convert 25% of your traditional IRA to a Roth IRA over four years.

•**Converting from a Roth IRA.** When the market drops, you can save taxes by converting a Roth IRA to a regular IRA.

Example: You converted a $100,000 regular IRA into a Roth IRA in 2000 that shrank to $30,000 in April 2001, because the market fell. If you recharacterize the Roth account as a regular IRA, you'll remove the tax owed on the initial $100,000. You can convert the $30,000 back to a Roth IRA as a Roth conversion next year. This way, you'll regain the Roth IRA benefits.

Only one "recharacterization" from a Roth IRA to a regular IRA is permitted per year. Filing Form 8606, *Nondeductible IRAs,* removes taxes that were owed when the Roth IRA was opened. You can undo a 2001 Roth IRA until October 15, 2002, the final extended due date of your 2001 return.

More from Ed Slott…

What to Look For in an IRA

Flexibility for inherited IRAs should be a major factor when selecting an IRA provider. Look for a mutual fund company, bank, brokerage or insurance firm that allows a beneficiary to name his/her own beneficiaries after inheriting the account. This allows the IRA to be paid out to the beneficiary's beneficiary instead of being fully distributed and taxed after the first beneficiary dies.

Also important: Whether beneficiaries can draw down the account over time or must have it paid out immediately…whether an IRA with more than one beneficiary can be split into separate accounts…whether heirs can transfer the IRA to a new provider if they wish.

Also from Ed Slott…

IRA Nightmares

Errors by brokerages, mutual fund companies and other financial institutions are increasing—resulting in costly tax penalties for investors. *Reasons:* The complex tax law and high volume of customer requests. *Self-defense:* Use an IRA-savvy tax adviser to plan retirement investments and payouts. Then send your requests in writing, giving the institution plenty of time to execute them.

Protect Your IRA Beneficiaries

When you select your IRA beneficiaries, obtain acknowledged copies of the beneficiary forms you sign from the IRA trustee (bank, broker, etc.). Then save the forms with your other most important personal documents, such as your will.

Why: The forms filed with the trustee may be lost over the years that pass before you die. If that happens, your IRA won't pass as you wish. Your estate may even be deemed to be your IRA's beneficiary, causing it to be liquidated and taxed right away.

Important: An IRA may become your family's most valuable asset, if it isn't already. Be sure it will be distributed as you wish.

Jack E. Stephens, Esq., quoted in Ed Slott's IRA Advisor. *Mr. Stephens,* www.jackstephens.com, *is author of* Avoiding the Tax Traps in Your IRA. *Legal Action Publications.*

Penalty Free...IRA Early Distribution

Funds can be withdrawn from an IRA before age 59½ without penalty if taken in the form of "substantially equal" payments calculated to last over the IRA owner's lifetime.

The payments do not actually have to be made for life, but must last at least five years or until age 59½ whichever is later.

Danger: Any change in the size of the payments before the "five year or age 59½" termination date will retroactively subject all payments received before age 59½ to penalty. This rule is strictly enforced.

Example: A person sold his business and retired at age 55, then took five annual payments of $44,000 from his IRA. After taking the fifth payment, he took an extra $6,000 from the IRA to meet a financial emergency.

Conflict: The IRS said he'd changed the withdrawal schedule by taking $50,000 in the fifth year. He said he had completed the five equal payments first, and only afterward taken the extra payment. And since he was over age 59½, he was free to take as much from the IRA as he wished.

Tax Court: The individual took his first annual payment in December, and the next four payments in January of each of the following years. Then he took the $6,000 in November of the fifth year.

That was within five years of the first payment, so he had changed the distribution

schedule before five years ended. Therefore, he owed penalties on all the earlier payments he'd received.

Robert C. Arnold, 111 TC 250.

IRA Distributions Don't Have to Be Taken in Cash

If your IRA is required to make annual minimum distributions to you and has invested in stocks or other securities that you wish to continue owning, you can have it distribute the securities directly to you. *Benefit:* You end up owning the securities without paying the commissions that you'd incur if the IRA sold the securities, distributed the cash proceeds to you and you then used the proceeds to repurchase the securities.

Twila Slesnick, partner, Slesnick & Slesnick, a tax, accounting and retirement planning firm in Dublin, California, and coauthor of IRAs, 401(k)s & Other Retirement Plans: Taking Your Money Out. *Nolo.com.*

Bulletproof Your 401(k) Against a Declining Market

There is more than $5 trillion invested in retirement plans today—most of it in equity funds. So many Americans have 401(k) plans that more than 40 million people would be at risk in a serious stock market decline. *What to do if you're nervous...*

●**Don't pull money out.** Even if the investment options are limited, most plans offer alternatives that are safer than the stock market. (Under the law, retirement plans must offer at least three choices.)

●**Choose safety over yield.**

●**Come as close to a Treasury-only money market mutual fund as possible.** If your plan does not offer a pure Treasury-only money market fund, choose the safest alternative—a government-only money market fund. Barring that, pick any money market fund. They've had a strong record of safety. Next, a bond fund is almost always safer than a stock fund.

●**Fight.** If your 401(k) plan doesn't offer non-stock alternatives, get together with colleagues and petition your employer for more choices.

Martin D. Weiss is editor of *Safe Money Report*, 4176 Burns Rd., Palm Beach Gardens, FL 33410.

Hidden Costs in 401(k) Plans

Barbara Weltman, attorney practicing in Millwood, NY, and author of *The Complete Idiot's Guide to Making Money After You Retire*. Alpha Books.

Borrowing from your 401(k) account is more expensive than it sounds. It may seem inexpensive since you pay interest on the loan to yourself. But there are *hidden costs*. You forfeit all tax-favored investment returns on the borrowed funds—effectively an extra interest charge that may be very costly. And—interest you pay is not deductible, but will be taxable to you when the plan pays it back to you through future distributions. So the interest will be *double* taxed—first, because the money you earn to pay back the interest gets taxed...and then you pay tax on the interest when the plan distributes it back to you.

More from Barbara Weltman...

What to Review Before Retiring

When planning your retirement, examine the vesting schedule of your retirement benefits and other benefits such as stock options. Leaving just one or two years too early may cost you substantial wealth. If you are negotiating an early retirement package, request full vesting of your benefits. *Best:* Review your benefits with an independent expert rather than relying on explanations from

the company's benefits office. *Also:* Examine the size of the monthly retirement checks you will receive, and the terms on which they will be paid in the future.

401(k) Option Trap

Beware of 401(k) plans that offer brokerage options. These *Self-Directed Accounts* (SDAs) are on the rise. Plan participants want mutual fund choices beyond the handful picked by employers and the ability to buy individual stocks. *Trap:* Unsophisticated investors often make bad investments, squandering their hard-earned retirement dollars. *Self-defense:* Use the brokerage option only if you are very investment-savvy and willing to watch your portfolio carefully.

Robert Markman, president, Markman Capital Management, an investment advisory firm with $6.6 billion under management, 6600 France Ave. S., Minneapolis 55435.

Be Sure You Collect All the Benefits To Which You're Entitled

Judith A. Stein, an attorney and executive director of the Center for Medicare Advocacy, Inc. She is president of the National Academy of Elder Law Attorneys.

Don't let ignorance or false pride prevent you from getting all you're entitled to in the way of aid. Some of the benefits may surprise you.

Some benefits are provided on the basis of age alone...others depend on financial need.

AGE-BASED BENEFITS

These benefits are yours simply because you've reached a certain birthday. *Included...*

●**Social Security benefits.** As a general rule, provided you've worked for a certain number of years over your lifetime, you qualify for Social Security benefits starting at age 62...though the benefits are reduced at that age.

Full benefit checks don't begin until your normal retirement age—currently age 65, but it will increase to 67 over the next several years.

Spouses, former spouses and widow(er)s may be entitled to benefits based on the other spouse's (or former spouse's) earnings and may start as early as age 60.

●**Medicare.** Unless you receive Social Security disability benefits for 24 months, your Medicare coverage doesn't start until age 65, even if you elected to begin receiving Social Security benefits at age 62.

Once you turn 65 you're covered under Part A of Medicare (hospital, skilled nursing facility, home health and hospice coverage) if you worked a certain length of time.

To receive Part B of Medicare (doctors' coverage, some home health and other outpatient services), you must pay a monthly premium.

LOCAL BENEFITS

Check local papers for seniors' activities and the minimum age for participation. Also look for discounts and other help. *What you'll find...*

●**Clubs, trips and programs for seniors.** Local governments generally help seniors' groups that meet for social and recreational purposes.

Examples: Daily recreational facilities...bus trips to a wide variety of places...field programs.

●**Senior discounts.** Retailers may offer discounts to seniors of a certain age. Many places provide senior ID cards to those as young as age 50 (for example, members of American Association of Retired Persons) that can be used to cash in on discounts in the area.

●**Help with local transportation.** Cities and counties, in many places, run bus services for seniors.

BENEFITS BASED ON NEED

A number of benefits for seniors can only be obtained if there is a financial need. The eligibility requirements may change from year to year. *Included...*

●**Supplemental Security Income** (SSI) provides income to seniors.

●**Food stamps.** Monthly allotments are available for the purchase of food items. The amount depends on household size and income. *Note:* The right to food stamps is not dependent on age.

●**Meal programs.** Home-bound seniors may be entitled to receive daily meal deliveries.

●**Medicare beneficiary programs** provide assistance with premiums, deductibles and copayments.

These Medicare programs are entitled QMB, SLMB, QI-1 and QI-2—depending on the benefits provided. They are limited to those age 65 or older with financial need.

●**Medicaid pays for medical costs for those age 65 or older** who have income and assets below a certain level (which varies by state). It also provides coverage for the blind and disabled, regardless of age.

●**Prescription aid.** In some states, low-income prescription drug programs help those age 65 or older and do not have Medicaid or other insurance to cover drug costs.

●**Property tax relief** lets senior home owners reduce their property tax bill. Rules differ in each locality, but may provide relief of up to 50% of the bill for those age 65 or older with income below a certain amount.

●**Rent subsidies.** As with property tax relief, some localities provide rent assistance for those in need.

●**Home energy assistance** for both renters and home owners gives cash (or makes payments to energy suppliers) in some localities if monthly income is below a threshold amount.

No minimum age: There may not be any minimum age for eligibility for the following...

●**Emergency assistance cash** for food, rent, moving, etc., for those with income below SSI limits.

TO FIND OUT ABOUT BENEFITS

There's an elder network operating in every state that can provide information and assistance. You can tap into this network by contacting your local agency on aging or state department on aging.

Note: If you're investigating benefits for someone else, you can obtain general information without authorization. But if you need to discuss confidential information with a particular governmental agency, you may need authorization from the person you're helping.

●**Departments on Aging.** Every state has some administrative agency or subdivision for the elderly. It may go by a different name in your location—Office of Aging, Commission on Aging, Division of Senior Services, etc. Some state departments have regional offices. *This is your first contact point. This state office can provide...*

●*Information about benefits and eligibility requirements.*

●*Referral services to agencies* providing specific types of assistance.

●**Federal resources.** The Social Security Administration can provide information and help on Social Security benefits, Medicare and more. 800-772-1213 or *www.ssa.gov.*

●**The Health Care Financing Administration** (HCFA) also provides information and help with Medicare. 800-633-4227 or *www. medicare.gov.*

●**Access America for Seniors Web site** makes it easier to connect with various federal agencies. *www.seniors.gov.*

●**Administration on Aging** provides information for older Americans about opportunities and services. *www.aoa.dhhs.gov.*

●**Department of Veterans Affairs** provides information about VA programs for veterans and their families. 800-827-1000 or *www.va.gov.*

●**Private seniors organizations.** They can give you information on assistance programs. *These organizations include...*

●**American Association of Retired Persons** (AARP) at 800-424-3410 or *www.aarp.org.*

●**Gray Panthers** at 800-280-5362 or *www. graypanthers.org.*

●**Older Women's League** (OWL) at 800-825-3695 or *www.owl-national.org.*

●**The Center for Medicare Advocacy** provides assistance regarding Medicare and healthcare rights. 860-456-7790 or visit *www.medicare advocacy.org.*

●**Other organizations.** The National Academy of Elder Law Attorneys (NAELA) distributes brochures to explain various benefit programs for the elderly. 520-881-4005 or *www.naela.org.*

Social Security Alert

Start taking Social Security payouts at age 65—instead of waiting until age 70.

Most people who take the higher age-70 payout will be almost 85 before they catch up to those who start taking benefits at age 65.

You may be able to invest some benefits starting at age 65, resulting in more money than the bonus the government would give you for waiting until age 70.

Calculations are more complicated for someone considering taking early benefits at age 62—consult your financial adviser.

Avery E. Neumark, Esq., CPA, principal and director of employee benefits and executive compensation, Rosen Seymour Shapss Martin & Company, LLP, New York City.

Social Security Checkup

Check your Social Security benefit statement very carefully—errors are common and could cost you lots of money. The forms, which show your yearly contributions to Social Security, are automatically sent to taxpayers annually—about three months before your birthday. *When you receive yours:* Make sure it correctly shows all the years you worked, and compare the wage amounts subject to Social Security with those on your W-2 statements. If you find an error, follow the instructions on the form to correct it. *If you do not receive a statement:* Contact Social Security at 800-772-1213...or *www.ssa.gov.* You can request a benefits statement anytime.

Sanford J. Schlesinger, partner and head, wills and estates department, Kaye, Scholer, Fierman, Hays & Handler, LLP, New York City.

Better Retirement Loan

To retire early without tapping your retirement account and incurring a penalty for withdrawing money before age 59½, ask your stockbroker about an interest-only loan. Some stockbrokers use your house as collateral. Take out the loan for as many years as necessary to get you to the age at which you can withdraw retirement money without penalty. *Example:* If you are 55 and wish to retire now, take out the loan for five years. *Caution:* Interest is only tax-deductible on loans up to $100,000.

Ric Edelman, founder and chairman, Edelman Financial Services, Inc., *www.ricedelman.com*, Fairfax, VA, and senior contributing editor to *OnMoney.com*.

Retirement Can Be Stressful

Couples who suddenly begin spending much more time together may have disputes about how to spend both their time and their money. *Helpful:* Begin planning retirement years *before* you retire. Agree in advance how you will adjust to retirement—from spending all your time together in activities like travel…to splitting chores…to both getting part-time jobs. Review finances to project how much you will have to spend, and agree what to spend it on. Retirement will come much more easily if both of you have already agreed on how to handle both your time and your money.

Prime Times, 5910 Mineral Point Rd., Madison, WI 53705. Free with Members Prime Club dues.

Retirement Plans And Divorce

Most qualified plans, such as 401(k)s, can be divided in a divorce. But some small-employer and government plans do not have to be divided by a Qualified Domestic Relations Order (QDRO)—a court order telling the administrator of a qualified plan what percentage or dollar amount of the account is to be distributed to a nonemployee spouse under terms of a divorce settlement. *Bottom line:* Work with a knowledgeable financial planner—retirement-related issues can be complex.

Carol Ann Wilson, CFP, CDP, founder, Institute for Certified Divorce Planners, Boulder, CO.

Simple System to Help You Find the Right Retirement Community

Deborah Freundlich, copublisher of *Briefing,* a restaurant marketing newsletter from American Express, and author of *Retirement Living Communities.* Macmillan.

While you are strong and healthy, energetic and living comfortably in a community where you have good support services, friends and family, you probably give little thought to the prospect of moving to a full-service retirement community.

But—this is precisely the time to investigate possible future living arrangements. You don't want to delay the search until you are sick, injured or have lost a helpful spouse.

Look for a retirement living community (RLC) leisurely and carefully. The search can be very enjoyable.

•**Start with a paper search.** Think of it as gathering information for a vacation spot. Ask friends…and the children of people you know who have moved to such communities…and senior citizen groups in your community what places they know of *both good and bad*. Send for literature on RLCs located in areas you might find attractive.

Be open about location. Don't think only about how convenient a place is to your children or other family members. *You* will be there 100% of the time and that's what counts most.

●**Review your finances.** This will be your first opportunity to analyze the financial implications of a move to an RLC. You will have to make a substantial advance payment—in many cases more than $100,000—to qualify for most RLCs.

Be realistic about what you can afford. Above all, ask lots of questions and compare the costs of your prospective RLC with your current expenses.

CHECK THEM OUT

Visit as many RLCs as you can. Arrange short excursions or vacation travel so that you can spend some time at a prospective RLC. Call ahead in plenty of time to arrange a stay—at least one night but preferably longer—in a guest house or guest room in the community. *Check out...*

●**The food and ambience of the communal dining facilities.** Meals tend to be a focal point of your life at any such facility.

Opportunity: The dining room is the best place to meet and talk with the residents to get an idea of whether they are people you would like to spend time with.

●**Nursing and custodial services and facilities.** *Preferable:* A special wing for residents with Alzheimer's or other forms of dementia. Such people need special care and may disrupt other residents who require health care.

Extras: Be sure to get a clear—preferably written—explanation of what extra costs might be involved if one spouse needs special nursing care while the other is well enough to live independently in the RLC with minimal care.

●**Transportation.** Even if the RLC has its own golf course, swimming pool and other sports and community facilities, you will probably want the ability to travel easily to nearby shopping malls, theaters, concert halls and houses of worship. Make sure there is regular, convenient and economical van or bus service. Use it during your visit even if you have your own car.

WHAT IT COSTS

Once you narrow down your prospects, talk seriously about finances with staff members of the RLC.

Don't be pushed into a premature discussion of a contract and finances by overeager staffers during your visit. The most desirable RLCs have waiting lists. In fact, beware of those with an occupancy rate under 85%—*and* hard sell tactics. *Ask about...*

●**Advance payments.** What is refundable, partially refundable or nonrefundable.

●**Monthly charges.** And what they cover—specifically. Ask what the guarantee is that the charges will not increase—or how such increases will be determined.

●**Added charges.** Charges that might be added if you need more intensive nursing or medical services...or if you have to be moved to an affiliated hospital, rehabilitation facility or medical center.

●**All special fees.**

●**Special benevolent funds.** Should you or your spouse live well beyond any reasonable life expectancy, you could run out of money and you may need to rely on these special funds.

Once a particular RLC begins to seem like an attractive possibility, ask for a complete package of its financial statements. The RLC must make them available to you.

Be sure the statements are recent and audited by a reputable professional. Even if you feel comfortable making sense of balance sheets and profit-and-loss statements, have a CPA evaluate them. You don't want to make a substantial advance payment and then find yourself in a community that begins to skimp on services because of financial problems.

If you decide to sign a contract and get on the waiting list, you can be confident that you've done all that you can to assure yourself the best of care for the last years of your life.

To Help Your Parents Deal With Retirement Transitioning

Robert Freedman, a partner in the law firm of Freedman & Fish, LLP, 521 Fifth Ave., New York City 10175. He is a founder of National Academy of Elder Law Attorneys.

Aging parents inevitably cross a threshold—from active, vigorous middle age to retirement, when physical and financial problems are more likely. To ease that transition, parents and children should discuss critical issues—the sooner, the better...

●**Key legal documents.** Each parent should have a will...power of attorney...medical power of attorney...possibly a living trust ...a list of assets...and copies of beneficiary designation forms for retirement funds, life insurance policies and annuities.

Power of attorney documents designate someone, often a child, to make medical and financial decisions if the parent becomes incapacitated.

If parents don't want their children to see some of the documents until there is a death or some other emergency, they can be placed in a sealed envelope and left with a trusted third party.

Children's role: Ensure that key documents are up to date and accessible. Every child must know who has power of attorney and medical power of attorney. It is perfectly appropriate for children to recommend which sibling should be given this responsibility or whether it should be shared.

●**Living will or health-care declaration.** These involve such end-of-life decisions as whether measures should be used to keep a terminally ill parent alive.

Communication trap: A client with two sons had a few weeks to live. One son wanted private-duty nurses and special care to keep his father alive as long as possible. The other said, *No, Dad would rather just go in peace.* Since they had never discussed it with their father and he didn't have a living will, neither knew who was right. By the father's funeral, they were no longer speaking.

●**Living arrangements.** Children should have a say only to the extent that they will be affected by the decision. Where a parent decides to live probably won't become an issue until children are called upon to provide care. Relocation plans should factor in these concerns.

Examples: How would a child feel if parents want to move close by—even into his/her home? Or if parents want to move so far away that visits might prove a financial and physical hardship?

●**The nursing home issue.** Forcing a *no nursing home* pledge from a child is never appropriate.

Children's role: Discuss possible arrangements for later in life, when more care will likely be needed. These could include assisted living or home care—with both parents and children agreeing that a nursing home would be a last resort.

Long-term-care insurance should be purchased by people between ages 60 and 75, maybe 80. The amount of coverage needed varies depending on local cost of care. Be sure you or your parents can afford the premiums after their retirement.

●**Retirement accounts.** Tax laws about distributing IRAs and other retirement accounts after death are complex. A planning mistake could dump heavy tax liabilities on children soon after a parent's death.

Children's role: Prod parents into getting written confirmation that designation-of-beneficiary forms are on file. Also confirm that designations have been completed in line with parents' wishes—and with tax laws. Copies of these designation forms should be kept in a safe place at home and also with your attorney and accountant.

●**Grandchildren.** Given the parents' financial resources, what help do they want to provide?

Examples: The deductibility of education IRAs and other education plans varies by state. There are also college tuition programs offering tax deductions for contributions. In addition to making $10,000 annual gifts on a tax-free basis, grandparents can pay tuition and medical expenses directly.

Social Security Traps For Citizens Abroad

J. Robert Treanor, principal, William M. Mercer Inc., 462 S. Fourth Ave., Suite 1500, Louisville, KY 40202.

Social Security beneficiaries who live outside the US for 30 consecutive days or more must notify the Social Security Administration of their address, even if benefits are directly deposited in a bank.

US citizens usually will continue to receive all benefits, but restrictions may apply to noncitizens, particularly those who receive dependent or survivor benefits. *Other rules...*

●**If you receive benefits while working outside the US,** are under the full retirement age (age 65 in 2001) and your wages are not subject to US Social Security taxes—working more than 45 hours per month will cause your benefits to be withheld.

●**Many foreign countries tax US Social Security benefits.** Check the rules with the country's US embassy before going abroad.

●**Medicare generally does not cover health services received outside the US.** So if you plan to be away from the US for a substantial period, you may not want to continue Medicare Part B, due to the premium cost. However, if you return and wish to enroll in Part B, you are subject to the general enrollment period, which is January through March with entitlement effective the following July. There is a premium surcharge of 10% for each full year of nonenrollment.

12

Estate Protection

Congress Killed the Estate Tax...or Did It?

Starting in 2002 and continuing through 2010, the rules for passing on property change dramatically. But in 2011, all the new rules expire, with estate tax reverting to its 2001 status.

During this nine-year period, some individuals will no longer have their estates depleted by taxes. Others are not out of the woods entirely and still need to plan to minimize estate and gift taxes.

TAX RATES AND EXEMPTIONS

Starting in 2002, estate taxes drop in the following manner...

•**The top tax rate declines from 55% to 50%.** It continues to fall by one percentage point each year until it reaches 45% in 2007. It stays at that rate until 2010, when the federal estate tax is repealed entirely.

Caution: In 2011, the repeal expires. It remains to be seen whether Congress will act before the expiration date to make the repeal permanent.

•**The amount exempt from estate tax—** $675,000 in 2001—increases to $1 million in 2002 and 2003. It goes up to $1.5 million in 2004, $2 million in 2006, and $3.5 million in 2009.

In 2010, there is no exemption amount because there is no estate tax that year. When the old rules take effect again in 2011, the exemption amount reverts to $1 million.

Impact of these changes: Wills and trusts must be reviewed. Revisions may be necessary.

Requiring special scrutiny: Wills that contain credit shelter trusts, trusts designed to fully utilize the exemption amount in the estate of the first spouse to die.

Why: Because of the escalating exemption amount, it may no longer be desirable in an estate of less than $5 million to funnel the maximum exemption amount to the credit shelter trust.

Gideon Rothschild, Esq., CPA, partner in the law firm Moses & Singer LLP, 1301 Avenue of the Americas, New York City 10019.

Example: A couple has a combined estate of $2 million ($1 million each) and wills requiring credit shelter trusts to be funded with the "maximum federal estate tax exemption amount." If one spouse dies in 2006, when the exemption amount is $2 million, his/her entire estate would be placed in the trust. In essence, the other spouse would be disinherited.

Gift taxes: The gift tax exemption amount for lifetime transfers increases to $1 million in 2002, and, unlike the estate tax exemption, increases no further.

The gift tax is not repealed in 2010. Instead, it becomes a flat tax at the highest individual income tax rate—35%.

Wealthy individuals who have already used up their lifetime exemption amount should make additional tax-free gifts in 2002 of up to $325,000 (the difference between the $1 million exemption amount next year and the current limit of $675,000).

Gift tax exclusion: The annual gift tax exclusion of $10,000 per recipient (or $20,000 if married), and the exclusion for direct payments of tuition or medical expenses were not changed by the new law. Thus, in addition to the lifetime exemption amount, wealthy taxpayers can continue to make these tax-free gifts year-in and year-out to reduce the size of their taxable estates.

FAMILY BUSINESSES

The special additional deduction for family-owned business interests currently available—up to $675,000—is repealed for individuals dying after 2003. Business owners whose estates fall below the increasing exemption amount are not adversely impacted by this repeal. Those with substantial holdings need to consider other transfer-planning strategies to minimize taxes.

Review succession plans with tax advisers. If you don't have a succession plan, make one now.

CARRY-OVER BASIS

While the new law reduces or eliminates the estate tax burden, it potentially increases the income tax burden on heirs and can result in an overall tax increase.

Property inherited after 2009 no longer receives a stepped-up basis to its value at death. Instead, carry-over basis rules are set to apply. Heirs take over the same basis that the decedent had. This may be substantially lower than the property's current value.

When heirs sell their inherited property, they'll have to pay tax on the resulting gain—the difference between what they've realized on the sale (current value) and the decedent's original basis.

Exceptions: *Two exceptions allow stepped-up basis rules to be used...*

●**Up to $1.3 million of basis** increase can be allocated to appreciated assets passing to any heir. This dollar limit is increased by unused capital losses, net operating losses, and unused built-in losses.

●**Up to $3 million of additional basis** for appreciated assets passing to a surviving spouse.

Example: A married individual dies in 2010, leaving an estate of $5 million, $4 million of which is bequeathed to the surviving spouse. The assets have a basis of $1 million for the spouse's bequest and $500,000 for the remaining assets. The executor can allocate $3 million of basis to the assets passing to the spouse and $500,000 of basis passing to other heirs. *Note:* The stepped-up basis allocation cannot exceed the fair market value of the assets.

In the absence of contrary instructions in a will, it's up to the executor to decide which property can enjoy the stepped-up basis. It may be helpful to revise wills to include guidance to an executor on allocating the stepped-up basis amount.

PLANNING STRATEGIES

Individuals whose estates do not become tax free despite the exemption increase should continue transfer planning to ease the tax burden for their heirs.

●**The generation-skipping transfer tax** (GST) is modified by the new law. Now the exemption amount is the same as that for estate tax purposes. The same estate tax rate applies to generation-skipping transfers until repeal of estate tax. Thereafter, the same 35% rate used for gift tax applies to lifetime generation-skipping transfers. Thus, GST is still a planning issue to address.

•**Flexibility will have to be written into estate-planning documents.** Wills and trusts should consider using "but if" clauses so provisions can be tied to tax changes. *Remember:* An existing formula clause may leave too much to the credit shelter trust and nothing to the spouse.

> *Example:* A will might say that *if* the exemption amount is $1 million (and the individual dies in 2002), property passes in a certain way, *but if* the exemption amount is $2 million (and the individual dies in 2006), property is distributed in another way.

•**Trusts continue to play an important part in estate tax planning.** Dynasty trusts allowing assets to pass from one generation to another and another have not lost their appeal. Similarly, asset protection trusts should not be overlooked for the protection they can offer from creditors' claims.

•**Don't assume that life insurance** to provide estate tax liquidity is no longer needed. Don't be quick to cancel—wait and see what ultimately happens to the estate tax.

•**Valuation discounts** (such as those associated with family limited partnerships) remain an important tool for reducing estate taxes when used in conjunction with lifetime gifts.

Estate Planning For Zero Taxes

Andrew Westhem, president, The Westhem Grant Group, a retirement, estate-planning and asset-protection firm, 462 Stevens Ave., Solana Beach, CA 92075. He is author of *Getting Started in Tax-Savvy Investing.* John Wiley & Sons.

Anyone earning more than $75,000 a year is likely to accumulate a taxable estate—one worth more than $675,000.

Estate taxes can devour 55% of the net value in one generation. Pension plans and IRA rollovers can be taxed two or three times, depleting their value by as much as 80%.

Some heirs have to part with family treasures at fire sale prices to pay the tax, due within nine months after death. You can only stretch out payments if a certain percentage of the estate is an interest in a private business or real estate.

But there are ways to reduce estate taxes to zero. The Rockefellers and the Kennedys have used these perfectly legal strategies for decades. You can, too. Discuss them with your estate attorney or accountant.

LIVING TRUST

Select a trustee to manage all your assets in the event of your death or incapacitation. You can appoint yourself trustee while you are in good health—and a second trustee in case you become incapacitated or for when you die.

Tax saver: By its nature, a living trust doesn't save you money on estate taxes, but it can be used for this purpose. *Have the living trust drawn up so your estate is transferred into two other trusts after your death...*

•**"A" trust—also known as a marital trust**—allows you to pass on this money to your spouse or another beneficiary free of federal estate tax.

•**"B" trust—or bypass trust**—enables you to avoid estate tax when the second spouse dies. Typically, it has multiple beneficiaries—children, grandchildren or others. The unified credit allowance ($675,000 today, rising to $1 million by 2006) grows in the B trust and is always estate tax free, no matter how much the trust increases in value.

Your spouse has access to income and capital appreciation generated by the B trust. But since capital appreciation is completely free of estate taxes, you should use this as a growth trust and let it grow.

Many couples set up separate living trusts.

WEALTH TRUST

Many of my clients are leery of making large annual gifts to their families. They fear their children will squander the money or lose it in a divorce action.

Tax saver: Make annual gifts to an irrevocable trust. Federal law allows you and your spouse to give away $10,000 each per year per recipient. An irrevocable trust is out of reach of the beneficiaries' creditors and divorcing spouses. Upon your death, the money can stay invested without being subject to estate taxes...or distributed to beneficiaries tax free.

Even better: In certain states, a *dynasty wealth trust* can be created and subdivided into trusts for the beneficiaries of your children and grandchildren.

QUALIFIED PERSONAL RESIDENCE TRUST

In many cases, a house is an individual's largest single asset. Just leaving it to heirs can use up all of your $675,000 lifetime sheltered exemption.

Tax saver: Transfer of ownership of your home to a Qualified Personal Residence Trust (QPRT). You designate the length of the trust, at the end of which the property passes to your beneficiaries. In the meantime, you are allowed to continue living there. The IRS calculates the value of your "gift" by determining the present value of the future gift.

The IRS first determines the value of your retained interest and subtracts it from the current fair market value of your home. As a result, the gift to your children is only a fraction of your home's fair market value and uses up much less of your $675,000 lifetime exemption.

The longer a residence remains in trust, the lower the valuation of the remainder interest.

Example: A 60-year-old client owned a home valued at $500,000, which he had purchased for $100,000. He transferred the residence into a QPRT with a 20-year term. Using the 6.2% applicable federal interest rate at the time the trust was created, his retained interest in the home calculated to $422,570. The present value of the remainder interest (the gift) amounted to $77,430. And after the trust is set up, he can keep using the house as long as he pays a fair rent to the beneficiary.

Caution: Be sure to choose a trust term you are likely to outlive. If you die before the term ends, the value of the residence will be included in your estate.

CHARITABLE REMAINDER TRUST

This is a way to avoid capital gains taxes on assets that have appreciated.

How it works: A Charitable Remainder Trust (CRT) has two sets of beneficiaries...

• **You—or someone you choose**—are an income beneficiary for your lifetime. That gives you the right to receive a percentage of the trust assets.

• **Qualified charities receive the principal of the trust after your death.**

You can serve as trustee and control how assets are invested.

What comes out of the trust as income to you depends upon the payout percentage you choose and the income generated from the assets.

You must distribute to the income beneficiary (usually yourself) annually at least 5% of the net fair market value of the assets. There is no maximum—but the higher the percentage you choose, the lower the charitable income tax deduction. We like to see a maximum of 10%.

Example: A husband and wife in their early 70s who lived in California with an estate worth approximately $2 million owned an apartment building. It was fully paid for and had appreciated substantially to a value of $800,000. Although the building still produced income of $30,000 per year, my clients were tired of managing the property. They wanted to sell but learned that 35% of the proceeds would go toward the payment of federal and state capital gains taxes. Add in estate taxes after their death and their children would get only about $300,000.

Solution: The couple set up an 8% payout CRT naming themselves as cotrustees. They sold the building for $800,000, paid no capital gains tax and invested the money in a mutual fund that provided income of 8% per year. They will receive $64,000 of income per year for the rest of their lives. Based on their ages, they also get about $240,000 worth of charitable income tax deductions—30% off their current income.

FAMILY LIMITED PARTNERSHIP

Family Limited Partnerships (FLPs) are generally recommended for people with estates of $3 million or more. They enable people to give assets away but still control the assets during their lifetimes.

An FLP operates like an investment business, except ownership of the partnership units is restricted to family members. The general partners (you and your spouse) control operations and make day-to-day investment decisions. Limited partners (your beneficiaries) have an ownership interest but limited control.

Tax saver: Set up an FLP, transferring into it all stocks, bonds, mutual funds and real estate. Also transfer shares in the family business. The funding of the partnership all at once is not a taxable event.

In the initial stages, you and your spouse own all the assets. Eventually, you will divest yourself of most of your estate by giving partnership units to your children or grandchildren as gifts. You keep a 1% general partner interest initially and gift your 99% LP interest to your children or your dynasty wealth trust for your children and grandchildren when your children die. You retain control over 100% of the partnership's assets, business and cash flow.

Other advantages...

•**An FLP allows you and your spouse** to each give more than the $675,000 lifetime exemption the government allows. It is possible to gift as much as 50% more apiece. A gift of assets to a limited partner may be appraised at a lower amount due to the lack of liquidity and control of the assets.

•**You and your spouse can receive** ongoing income from the FLP because, as general partners, you're entitled to a management fee, typically 3% to 7%.

•**The lifetime sheltered exemption,** currently $675,000 per spouse, will rise to $1 million each in 2006.

Very Big Overlooked Tax Deduction

Many people who inherit IRAs overlook a potentially big tax deduction—that for "income in respect of a decedent."

Key: A bequeathed IRA may be subject to double taxation—first estate tax, then income tax when its proceeds are distributed. Combined, these two taxes may total 70% or more.

Saver: To soften the blow when inherited assets are subject to both estate and income tax in this way, those who inherit the assets can take an income tax deduction for the federal estate tax paid on the assets. And for IRAs that hold a lifetime of retirement savings, this deduction may be huge.

Example: If you inherit an IRA worth $200,000, the federal estate tax on it may be $80,000—entitling you to claim $80,000 of income tax deductions over the period during which you withdraw money from the IRA.

Trap: Many people don't take this deduction at all, simply because they don't know about it. Don't let this happen in your family. Whether you are likely to bequeath an IRA or inherit one, ask your tax adviser about the rules for "income in respect of a decedent"—and plan accordingly.

Ed Slott, CPA, E. Slott & Co., CPAs, 100 Merrick Rd., Rockville Centre, NY 11570. He is editor and publisher of *Ed Slott's IRA Advisor. www.irahelp.com.*

The Real Meaning of Wealth...to the IRS

Your wealth is determined by the cost of your assets, not their value, when seeking attorney fees from the IRS.

An estate beat the IRS in court and asked for an award of attorney fees under the Equal Access to Justice Act. This permits such awards to taxpayers with net worth under $2 million. *Key:* The act measures net worth by acquisition cost of assets.

IRS: An estate "acquires" assets at the death of an individual at their then-market price. Otherwise, Bill Gates' estate could qualify for an award because he paid so little for his Microsoft stock.

Court: Bill Gates may qualify for an award if he paid little enough for his assets. If he does, his estate will too, since it pays no more for them.

Nolan Wilkes, Jr., DC MD Fla., No. 3:97-cv-1317-J-21A; 86 AFTR2d ¶2000-5251.

Personal Asset Protection Made Very, Very Simple

Barry S. Engel, Esq., principal in Engel Reiman & Lockwood, PC, law firm, 5445 DTC Pkwy., Suite 1025, Englewood, CA 80111.

I n today's litigious world, many of us—home owners, entrepreneur and doctors—live in fear of being sued. A lifetime of savings can be drained away by an unexpected legal calamity, making the best-laid estate plan meaningless. And it's easier than ever to get sued nowadays.

Examples: A former employee sues your company, claiming you fired him/her because of age. Or a guest falls on your icy sidewalk...or drinks too much at your party and gets into a car accident afterward.

Result: If a judge or jury finds against you, you could be liable for untold dollars in damages.

Good news: There are many ways to protect yourself from this disaster. This is where the lifetime side of estate planning—asset protection planning—comes in.

How it works: Asset protection planning is based on the principle that the law allows creditors to seize only what you now own, not what you used to own—so long as any transfer of property was not made to defraud known or expected creditors.

Key: Timing. This kind of protection is like fire insurance. If you wait until you smell smoke, you can't get it. Don't begin when you've lost a lawsuit and judgment creditors are beating down your door.

All the protection plans I recommend are tax neutral—they neither add to nor save any taxes for you. The plans are also legal—they don't rely on hiding assets to be effective. For example, offshore bank accounts should be clearly disclosed to the IRS.

PROTECTION STRATEGIES

Asset protection in the US involves a trade-off among protecting your money...continuing to benefit from it...and controlling it. Unfortunately, under the US legal system, there is tension among these three goals. While some foreign countries allow you to give property away and maintain benefit and control, that's usually impossible in the US.

Starting from the easiest and least expensive plan, and proceeding up the ladder of protection, complexity and expense, the asset protection planning tools include...

● **Gifting.** A popular step is giving property away to a spouse or children to protect it from the reach of future creditors.

Examples: Give your children stock or your vacation home...or sign your boat over to your sister or brother.

Advantage: You can gift up to $10,000 per year tax free.

Disadvantage: Gifting leaves the donor with no legal control of the property. Your kids might spend the money before you need it in old age...or your brother could take the boat out so often that you never get a chance to use it.

Cost: Attorney fees in planning and implementing the gift and, possibly, gift taxes.

● **Owning property jointly.** In nature, some insects avoid extinction by tasting bad to predators. The same tactic can work with creditors. Joint property can be unappealing to creditors, since they'll have to share it with another owner, who hasn't been sued.

A creditor's easiest pickings are land, cars, planes, brokerage accounts, bank accounts and boats in the debtor's name alone. It's easy for a sheriff to grab the boat you have down at the marina if the documentation shows it's yours and no one else's.

Best: Share property with someone who has different creditors than you do. Most married couples share the same ones.

Cost: Minimal or no cost to set up a joint stock or bank account. Minor licensing fees for boat or automobile titles. To change the names on a deed, expect to pay several hundred dollars—depending on the complexity of the real estate transfer.

• **State-by-state exemptions.** The law in some states, such as Florida and Texas, puts the equity in your home outside the reach of judgment creditors. Most states shield much less—a Bible, a few pigs, a cow. Your lawyer, and probably your banker or a local sheriff, should know what's exempt in your state.

An annuity is also often exempt from creditors' attachment. Ask your insurance agent or financial planner.

• **Liability insurance**—such as homeowners' or malpractice insurance—is the next layer of protection. How much you need depends on your home, your business structure, your profession and other factors. Consult an insurance agent or financial planner.

Disadvantage: By nature, liability insurance policies are porous with exclusions and exemptions—and can be costly to enforce. And they can't protect against as broad a range of risk as do limited liability setups or a protective trust.

• **Limited liability entity.** You can create a lot of protection by conducting business as a limited liability company. Over the past 10 years, new forms have flourished—some states now offer a limited liability corporation …limited liability partnership…and limited liability limited partnership.

Cost: About $2,500 to set up.

Advantage: With these new formats, as with a traditional corporation, liability is limited to the company's own assets. But the new formats are easier to set up and maintain than a corporation.

Note: Limited liability entities can be useful even on the family investment level.

Example: A brokerage account is held in a family limited partnership between the husband and wife.

If a creditor of either or both of them gets a judgment, the creditor can't gain access to either the partnership assets or the partnership interests that are held by the husband and wife.

The creditor can only get a "charging order," which means the creditor must wait for distributions to be made from the partnership to its partners before he/she can get anything. The husband and wife can control if and when distributions are made.

In the meantime, the creditor must pay tax on the income of the partnership, whether or not he actually receives anything.

Extra benefit: The threat of phantom income may mean that the creditor won't even attempt to obtain a charging order.

How it works: A creditor with a charging order may have income from the seized partnership treated as current income to him, even if it hasn't been distributed. He would then owe taxes on funds not yet in hand.

• **"Spendthrift" trusts shield assets from almost all creditors.** You put property into trust for the benefit of someone else—and specify that it cannot be attached by creditors or pledged as collateral.

Exception: You cannot avoid child support payments with a spendthrift trust.

Alaska and Delaware recently enacted statutes that allow both residents and nonresidents to create spendthrift trusts for their own personal benefit. Trusts in these states are an option for those who are uncomfortable with an offshore plan.

Cost: About $10,000 to set up.

• **The foreign trust is the ultimate defense against creditors,** since some foreign countries allow you to retain more control over, and benefit under, assets in trust than the US does. You set one up in a country that doesn't recognize US judgments—forcing the case against you to be tried in your foreign land if the creditor wants a locally valid judgment against you. Even armed with a locally valid judgment, the creditor's chances of then forcing the trust to pay on the judgment against you is dubious at best.

Example: You create a family limited partnership, and the foreign asset protection trust is the 99% limited partner. You are the 1% general partner. This means you have control over partnership property, but the trust has 99% of the equity. The beneficiaries of the trust are typically yourself, your spouse, your children and one or more charities.

By placing the 99% equity interest in trust, you no longer own it for creditor purposes, even though you control the partnership through the 1% interest you retain.

The trust is a foreign trust—such as one created in the Cook Islands in the South Pacific or the Turks and Caicos Islands in the Caribbean—that allows you to receive benefits from the trust and also allows you to retain degrees of control over it.

In times of financial tranquility, you can administer the assets through your US-based family partnership. In an emergency, however, the foreign trustee can dismiss the US trustee and absorb the partnership assets into the foreign trust's ownership.

Then, in any subsequent collection battles, the foreign asset protection trust would cause the litigation to be brought in the foreign jurisdiction. Under such circumstances, a reasonable settlement can often be achieved quickly.

Note: Such plans are for people with net assets of seven figures or above, since they cost about $20,000 to set up...and $2,000 a year to maintain.

Protect Your Will from Challenges

Use a living trust to pass selected assets. A trust may last for years and is more difficult to challenge than a will. *Or:* Have convincing witnesses who will attest to your competency when you signed the will. Consider videotaping the signing as extra evidence. *Important:* If you think your will may be contested, you need the help of a lawyer who is an expert in the estate and trust laws of your state in order to make it contest-proof.

Barbara Weltman, Esq., Millwood, NY, author of *The Complete Idiot's Guide to Making Money After You Retire.* Alpha Books.

Common Mistake With Wills

Most people update their wills when something happens to their family—such as a birth, death or divorce. But they neglect to do so when the law that applies to them changes. *Examples:* Numerous recent changes in the federal estate tax affect basic issues such as the amount that a person can leave tax free. And...when you move your residence from one state to another, an entirely new set of state laws will govern your will. Key parts of your old will may simply become invalid. *Important:* Review your will with your attorney and estate tax adviser periodically even if your personal situation does not change.

Sidney Kess, attorney and CPA, 10 Rockefeller Plaza, Suite 909, New York City 10020. Mr Kess is coauthor of *1040 Preparation, 2000 Edition.* CCH Inc.

Important Estate Planning Strategies for Mid-Level Estates

Martin Shenkman, CPA, a New York City attorney who specializes in trusts and estates. He is author of numerous books, including *The Complete Book of Trusts* and *The Beneficiary Workbook* (both from John Wiley). His Web site, *www.laweasy.com,* offers free sample forms and documents.

Middle-income people with taxable estates should not automatically follow advice that is intended for people with multimillion dollar estates. *They need more flexibility...*

Example: Advice to reduce the taxable estate by giving annual gifts of up to $10,000 per recipient may not be appropriate for a person who may need his assets in his own lifetime.

Key estate planning strategies for midsized estates...

USE DISCLAIMERS

Instead of automatically having money taken out of the estate to fund a tax-favored "exclusion trust" on the death of the first spouse, put a disclaimer clause in the will. This allows a beneficiary to turn down a gift.

The disclaimer clause gives the surviving spouse the flexibility of having up to nine months after the death of the first spouse to determine whether—and to what extent—the exclusion trust should be funded.

The will would state that all assets are left outright to the surviving spouse—and should the surviving spouse disclaim those assets, then those disclaimed assets would be transferred to a trust for the surviving spouse.

Impact: If the estate grows more slowly than the applicable estate tax exclusion—it is to rise from $675,000 to $2 million by 2006—no funding would be necessary.

Use of a disclaimer clause could also be ideal for estates of a few million dollars, in case Congress increases the exclusion significantly.

This would simplify the estate for the surviving spouse and avoid the need to file an annual income tax return for the exclusion trust. However, the planning could be implemented, should the estate grow and Congress neither repeals the estate tax nor raises the exclusion threshold from present law.

LIFE INSURANCE

Life insurance planning may also be different for mid-level estates. Standard advice for larger estates is to form an insurance trust to get insurance out of the estate and ensure that the policy's proceeds are not taxable on the death of the second spouse.

For a mid-range estate, however, it is sometimes appropriate for the insurance to be made payable to the estate of the insured spouse.

While this would expose the insurance proceeds to claimants of the estate, for most taxpayers that is not a significant issue.

The purpose is to allow the insurance proceeds to be used to fund an applicable exclusion trust on the death of the insured spouse.

Example: If the estate is $1 million in aggregate—plus a $500,000 insurance policy...

$750,000 could be placed in the wife's name... $250,000 in the husband's name...the $500,000 insurance policy on the husband's life would be payable to his estate.

Thus, in aggregate there would be $750,000 available to fund an exclusion trust, although for the current year only $675,000 could be used.

POWERS OF ATTORNEY

Gifts: For mid-level estates, a number of changes should be made to the typical powers of attorney. Many power of attorney forms do not include the authority to make gifts, while others do so without limitation.

For mid-level estates, the authority to make gifts under a power of attorney should be limited to $10,000 per person per year, perhaps indexed for inflation.

For people who feel they have sufficient financial security to do so, additional tax-free annual gifts can be made to cover tuition and medical costs.

RETIREMENT PLANS

The provisions governing assets in a retirement plan should also be carefully reviewed. Many standard powers of attorney authorize the agent to change beneficiaries on retirement plans.

Consideration should also be given to authorizing changes in elections for payments. That may restrict the ability to change the actual persons who are to receive benefits and the proportions in which they are to receive them.

ORGANIZE ASSETS

Many people have assets spread among different firms and institutions. The cost of administering a disabled person's assets and handling probate can be greatly reduced if holdings are consolidated.

LARGER ESTATES

Sophisticated strategies: People with larger estates—$2 million to $10 million—may want to consider more sophisticated strategies, such as an aggressive gift program, gifts using family limited partnerships or limited liability companies...and qualified personal residence trusts for homes.

Dynasty trusts: People with assets of $2 million to $10 million may also want to use a domestic asset protection dynasty trust based in Delaware or Alaska, which enables them to have access to their funds, avoid creditors, and reduce taxes.

Such trusts also enable them to make gifts to move assets from the estate—often at a discounted value—and yet have access to the money should they need it.

More from Martin Shenkman...

Revocable Living Trusts

Many promoters advertise the wonders of living trusts. Indeed, such trusts offer many advantages to their creators.

But—the claims advanced for living trusts are often misleading...and sometimes just plain false. Only if you know the real benefits and drawbacks of living trusts can you construct a trust with the features that best meet your needs.

DEFINITIONS

Trusts fall into two categories...

●**Living trusts**—established while the creator (grantor) is *alive.*

●**Testamentary trusts**—those that go into effect after the grantor's death, as spelled out in a will.

Living trusts are further divided into two types...

●**Revocable trusts**—can be materially changed or even canceled altogether.

●**Irrevocable trusts**—can't be rescinded after they go into effect.

A revocable trust *must* be a living trust, i.e., set up while you're alive. However, many types of living trusts must be irrevocable, such as an insurance trust.

Simply put, a revocable trust is impermanent.

You generally can serve as trustee and beneficiary of a revocable trust you create. Therefore, you can retain control over any assets you transfer into the trust.

PRO LIVING TRUSTS

●**Incapacity protection.** For those who become ill or incompetent, a successor trustee can take over management of the trust assets. And—there will be no costly, public, time-consuming court battle for control of your finances.

This type of transfer cannot be handled as seamlessly by relying upon a power of attorney.

How it works: When you create your revocable trust and name yourself as trustee, you also select a successor trustee. You might also designate co-successors, perhaps including an institution that will assume financial responsibility.

Strategy: When the trust is created you should spell out the circumstances in which you no longer can manage your own affairs—and who will make the determination.

Example: Two doctors have to state in writing that you are incapacitated.

If this event should occur, the successor trustee can step in immediately. And, the successor or successors will have a fiduciary responsibility to protect your interests.

Example: Joe Smith's estate was to go to his two nieces. As he grew older, he no longer could care for himself. His nieces, then, could provide him with quality long-term care...or they might not, hoping to preserve Joe's assets that they would eventually inherit.

Fortunately, Joe had drawn up a revocable trust, naming a bank along with the nieces as successor trustees. The trust documents required the successors to provide the best care for Joe, and the bank made sure this instruction was carried out to Joe's comfort.

Vital: It's best to go through the formalities of transferring assets into your revocable trust so the trustee will have funds to carry out required responsibilities.

●**Probate avoidance.** Often, revocable trusts are promoted heavily as a means to circumvent the time and expense of probating a decedent's will in a local court.

Reality: In most states, probate is not burdensome or expensive. Many localities offer a simplified probate process that you may be able to use.

Many types of assets are excluded from probate anyway, whether or not you have a revocable trust.

Examples: Jointly held property passes to the surviving owner automatically. Insurance proceeds and retirement accounts (including IRAs) go to the designated beneficiary.

●**Out-of-state property.** If you own property in another state, your survivors will have to go through a separate probate for the out-of-state asset. That may mean hiring an attorney far away...or making unwanted trips.

Holding out-of-state property in a revocable trust avoids this ancillary probate as well as local probate.

Trap: Using a revocable trust to hold out-of-state property works fine for a vacation home. However, such trusts don't provide asset protection (see below), so investment property should be held in a limited liability company (LLC) or family limited partnership (FLP), for asset protection as well as ancillary probate avoidance.

●**Administrative rigor.** One of the unsung benefits of creating a revocable trust is the need to get your affairs in order. This will help you manage your affairs as you grow older and assist your heirs in handling your estate.

Example: Betty Jones created a revocable trust and began putting assets in the Betty Jones Trust. She found she had 17 mutual funds, four brokerage accounts, and two bank accounts. In re-titling her assets she consolidated them to a few accounts, making record keeping easier and reducing expenses.

DRAWBACKS

●**No tax benefits.** Despite what you might hear or read, revocable trusts are neutral from a tax point of view...

●*For income tax purposes,* trust income is taxed to you, as the grantor.

●*For estate tax purposes,* assets transferred to a revocable trust are included in your taxable estate.

Trap: Misinformation about revocable trusts can lead you to neglect necessary tax planning, especially when it comes to estate tax.

Good news: Virtually all sophisticated estate and income tax planning strategies can be used in conjunction with revocable trusts.

Example: After transferring your assets into a revocable trust you can give away trust assets to reduce your taxable estate, using the $10,000 (per recipient) annual gift tax exclusion. A recent change in tax law erased doubts about this tactic.

●**No asset protection.** Assets held in a revocable trust are just as vulnerable to your creditors as assets you hold personally.

Example: If you hold investment property in a revocable trust, a tenant whose child eats lead paint may sue you personally for damages. As mentioned earlier, a family limited partnership or limited liability company should be used for asset protection.

●**Complacency.** Merely setting up a revocable trust won't provide you with a complete estate plan. *You also should...*

●Take the time to re-title assets given to the trust.

●Have a will to cover those assets not held in the trust.

●Select suitable trustees, get their agreement to serve, and make arrangements for backup trustees.

●Work with a knowledgeable professional on tax planning.

●Explain all of these arrangements to your heirs.

SINGLE OR JOINT?

Married couples must decide whether to use a joint revocable trust or to have each spouse create his/her own trust.

Individual trusts are generally best for the following reasons...

●**Both spouses gain investment** and financial experience.

●**If one spouse dies,** the survivor may have easier access to the assets in his own trust than would be the case with a joint trust.

●**Each spouse builds an individual credit history.**

Trap: Be wary of any attorney who tells you that the cost of creating two separate trusts will be much greater. There should be only a token extra charge.

For more on revocable living trusts, including a sample document, visit *www.laweasy.com.*

Also from Martin Shenkman...

How to Ensure Lifetime Care for a Child with Special Needs

Three-pronged strategy for the best possible lifetime care of a disabled child...

●**Create a *special needs trust*** under your will to pay for things above what government programs provide. Fund the trust from your estate—rather than when you are alive—to avoid tax complications.

●**Give money to family members** with a *nonbinding* request that they use it to help the child. Their help can get around restrictions on what can be done with the special needs trust.

●**Contact charities** involved in the child's disability. Many have programs to help with lifetime-care issues.

Savings Bonds... Best Left to Charity

If you plan to make a charitable bequest through your will, consider funding it with US savings bonds that you own instead of cash.

Why: Series EE and I bonds appreciate in value rather than pay cash interest. But after their owner's death, previously untaxed appreciation in the value of both Series EE and I bonds and Series HH bonds (for which EE bonds may be exchanged on a tax-deferred basis to obtain a source of interest income) will be ordinary income taxed at top rates to the heirs who inherit the bonds.

Better: Leave cash to heirs and savings bonds to charity, instead of the reverse. Neither will owe tax on what you leave them, and you will disinherit the IRS.

IRS Letter Ruling 9845026, discussed by Sharon Goodman, Esq., American Express Tax & Business Services, Inc., in its *Not-For-Profit Watch* newsletter.

How to Ensure Your Donation Is Entirely Received

Send charitable donations directly to the charity—not to the telemarketing firm that solicits donations. That ensures your *entire* donation goes to the charity. Paid solicitors may keep as much as 90% of the money they collect for a charity. Telemarketers and the groups that hire them say high fees are justified because fund-raising companies can collect much more than charities can on their own.

Matthew Landy is vice president of National Charities Information Bureau, New York City.

How to Give Your House to Charity... Without Moving Out

William C. George is an attorney specializing in estate planning with the law firm Helm, Purcell & Wakeman, 4500 E. Thousand Oaks Blvd., Suite 101, Westlake Village, CA 91362.

You may want to make a sizable charitable donation, but not right away. What's more, there may not be assets that are obvious candidates to be given away.

If that's the case, donating your house to charity with a retained life estate may be worth considering. *Benefits...*

●**The charity receives a substantial contribution.**

●**You support a pet cause.**

●**You maintain your lifestyle.**

●**You get large tax deductions now.**

How it works: A home owner donates a house to an eligible charity, which might be a school, hospital, religious organization, etc.

At the same time, the owner reserves the lifetime right to live in the house. For a married couple, this right can span both lives.

The owner gets an immediate tax deduction even though the charity's receipt might be years away.

The amount of the deduction will depend upon several factors, especially the owner's age and the current interest rate environment.

Key: The older the donor, the greater the immediate write-off. Older donors have shorter life expectancies so the right of lifetime use is less valuable.

The less valuable the retained right to live in the house, the more valuable the interest given to charity and the greater the upfront deduction.

Example: Your 88-year-old father gives away his $400,000 house to his favorite charity but retains a life estate. He might get an immediate tax deduction of $250,000 to $275,000.

An 85-year-old would get a smaller write-off in that situation, but a 90-year-old would get a larger one.

Who pays the bills? After a gift of a life estate, little changes. The former owner (now resident) continues to pay all the bills relating to the house, including utilities, maintenance, association dues, insurance, property taxes, etc.

The resident (or younger relatives) also must keep up the value of the house until the time it actually passes to the charity.

After the resident's death, the charity can sell the house and pocket the proceeds.

One prime advantage of this tactic is that it allows a home owner to stay in a familiar house in a familiar neighborhood.

But, what if the donor decides to move out after the retained life estate transaction? Alternatively, what if the donor no longer is able to live there, because of failing health?

Technically, the house now belongs to the charitable recipient, which must preapprove any sale.

Reality: Most charities will be eager to see the house sold because an immediate cash donation will result.

Generally, the resident will share in a subsequent house sale. However, the resident's share likely will be small, in proportion to the actuarial value of the remaining life estate, which may be scant for an elderly person.

LEARNING THE LIMITS

Ideally, the charitable tax deduction will provide a meaningful economic reward to the donor.

Example: As explained, giving away a $400,000 house might result in a $250,000-plus tax deduction. Assuming an effective tax rate of 45%, the tax savings would be well over $100,000.

Trap: The Tax Code limits the amount of charitable deductions taxpayers can take each year. If the gift is an appreciated residence, the maximum charitable deduction is 30% of Adjusted Gross Income (AGI) per year.

Example: A taxpayer with $40,000 in AGI can deduct no more than $12,000 per year from the donation of appreciated property.

Excess charitable deductions can be carried forward and taken in future tax years. In the above example, with a $250,000 tax deduction and a $12,000 current deduction, the carry forward would be $238,000.

Trap: Such carry forwards are limited to five years. Altogether, the taxpayer described above would get six years of $12,000 deductions, for a total of $72,000. Most of the tax deductions will expire unused.

This situation is bound to occur when an elderly retiree with a modest AGI gives away a valuable home.

CASHING IN

In this situation, the best solution may be to donate the house to a charity that will provide a gift annuity in return.

A normal charitable gift annuity calls for the donor to give cash or securities (which might be appreciated securities) to charity. The charity, in return, pays an annuity to the donor and perhaps to other named recipients, such as the donor's spouse. Payments may be for life or for a certain number of years.

Variation: With the strategy described above, the charity receives no cash or marketable securities. Instead, the charity now owns a house it can sell at an unknown future date, at an unknown price.

Nevertheless, the charity still stands to receive a valuable asset in this transaction. If the house is desirable enough, the charity may agree to pay the donor an annuity.

Example: For a $400,000 house from an 88-year-old donor, a charity might agree to pay $2,500 per month, or $30,000 per year. Even if the donor lives another six years, until age 94, and collects $180,000 altogether, the charity then will own a house worth $400,000—a good deal.

The charity also stands to gain if the house appreciates in the interim. A house in a prime location might gain 20% in value in six years, which would mean the charity would then own a $500,000 house.

Caution: Not every charity will pay an upfront annuity in order to receive a house at some future date.

A potential donor who shops around may find a charity willing to pay a substantial annuity to the holder of a retained life estate.

Even a generous charitable gift annuity will not pay as much as a commercial annuity paid by an insurance company.

The difference between the commercial annuity payout and the charitable gift annuity rate is considered a charitable gift, resulting in a tax deduction.

Example: Instead of a $250,000 tax deduction, as described above, the donor who receives an annuity might be entitled to a $150,000 deduction. This deduction, spread over six years, may further benefit the donor by providing ongoing tax savings.

Bottom line: Working with an experienced professional, a home owner who proceeds carefully may enjoy lifelong use of a cherished house, lifetime income, tax savings and the satisfaction of a future gift to charity.

However, there won't be a house to leave to heirs. Thus, this strategy may work best for elderly home owners with no obvious heirs or those whose loved ones won't need to inherit the home in order to be financially comfortable.

Estate Trap

When Sylvia Swanson's health began to fail, she gave her nephew a general power-of-attorney to manage her affairs.

Just before she died, he made 38 gifts of $10,000 each to separate recipients, using the $10,000 gift-tax exclusion. Her estate then claimed the $380,000 had been transferred from it and so escaped estate tax.

Court: Unless state law specifically grants gift-giving authority to an agent, the power to make gifts must be *expressly stated* in a power-of-attorney—and it was not here. It was not enough that Ms. Swanson nodded when the list of gift recipients was read to her.

Thus, the gifts were ineffective and the gift property remained in the estate to be taxed.

Estate of Sylvia S. Swanson, Court of Federal Claims, No. 97-793T, 85 AFTR2d ¶2000-533.

Passing the Business to Your Kids Can Be Smooth And Simple...or It Can Be Very, Very Difficult

Irving L. Blackman, CPA, founding partner, Blackman Kallick Bartelstein, LLP, 300 S. Riverside Plaza, Chicago 60606. He is coauthor and publisher of *Transferring Your Business...When You Have Two or More Children.*

Transferring a business to the next generation is tough enough, but when more than one child is eager to manage the business, the task can be one of the most difficult for an owner to face.

There are egos and personal relationships to consider. There are also complex tax challenges and difficult business-planning choices.

Good news: The job can be made much easier by adopting a flexible plan that satisfies children who want to—and can—take part in the business...and children who don't.

And though recent changes in IRS rules make it more difficult to avoid a big tax bite, careful planning can still keep the IRS at bay. *Best options today...*

THE INSURANCE SOLUTION

Typical problem: One child is very talented at business and wants to follow in a parent's footsteps. Another has little interest in the company but still needs financial security on the same scale that his/her sibling would get by taking over the business.

One solution: Transfer the company to the child who can run it. Then make it possible for the other child to take out insurance on your life. In this way, the business-oriented child profits from running the company, and the other child inherits a similar amount from insurance when you die.

To lower tax exposure, help the nonbusiness child buy insurance through parental gifts of premiums. It may also be effective to provide insurance through a group-term plan, a tax-qualified retirement plan or other plan that results in tax savings.

Drawback: This insurance option can be expensive if there are several nonbusiness children.

THE STOCK PURCHASE SOLUTION

The principal stockholder in a closely held corporation often wants to liquidate his interest if he retires, dies or becomes disabled. To accomplish this and ensure a smooth transition of ownership, stockholders in the company must enter into a stock-purchase agreement that provides for terms of stock sales in any of these eventualities.

Failure to have this type of agreement can lead to lawsuits and disputes that often destroy the business. *Two basic types of agreements...*

●**Stock redemption agreements** in which the business entity itself will purchase the business owner's interest. In general, redemption agreements are more effective in the event of disability, and they have the advantage that corporate dollars can be used to fund the purchase price. That's usually more cost-effective for taxes than using personal funds.

●**Cross-purchase agreements,** in which the new owners will be the buyers. When three or more shareholders own unequal amounts of stock, a cross-purchase agreement can allocate control of the company in accordance with the wishes of the owner. It can also provide big tax advantages for the new owner.

Essential: Establishing—or "pegging," in tax jargon—the value of the business interest for estate tax purposes. The business interest can take the form of either stock shares or a partnership interest.

When the value is pegged, the business can't be sold for more than the price set by the stock-purchase agreement, either before or after the death of the principal stockholder. Pegging must be done with the advice of a tax adviser who specializes in this area. *Some conditions for pegging include...*

●**The value of the business interest must be fixed** by the stock-purchase agreement, or the agreement must provide a method for determining it.

●**The value of the business must be set as "fair and adequate"** at the time the agreement is made. This means that the owner cannot intentionally undervalue the business just to make it easier for his kids to buy it.

●**The agreement must restrict the owner** from selling the business during his lifetime without first offering it to his business associates or the company itself. The agreement must also determine the value of the business.

●**The agreement must require the estate of the deceased owner** to sell his interest to the surviving business associates or to the company at the value set by the agreement.

Stock-purchase agreements can ensure a smooth transition to the next generation. They also avoid conflicts with the IRS, which would otherwise make its own valuation of the business. In fact, while the IRS has never officially declared that it is bound by valuations in stock-purchase agreements, the agency has consistently recognized those valuations in court.

Variation: Combine a stock purchase with the insurance option. You can provide the business-oriented child with a life insurance benefit of, say, $500,000, which he can use to purchase the $1 million business interest from your estate.

The $500,000 is the amount that the business was valued for the purpose of death-tax assessment. Your estate would then have

$500,000 from the sale of the business to add to the nonbusiness child's inheritance.

RECAPITALIZATION

Previously, an owner could amend the corporate charter to create two classes of stock— *common* and *preferred*. He could then transfer common stock as gifts to children who wanted to be active in the business and transfer preferred stock to those who didn't.

If there is evidence that your company is about to skyrocket in value, recapitalization may be an ideal option. But in an overwhelming number of cases, new IRS rules make recapitalization a poor choice for transferring ownership or freezing assets for estate purposes.

Caution: Rules governing recapitalization are notoriously tricky. Before considering it, make sure you have retained a professional who is thoroughly familiar with recapitalization as well as with other options.

Related Useful Sites

Financial Planning

☐ Calculators on-line

www-sci.lib.uci.edu/HSG/RefCalculators.html

This site contains calculators for virtually any purpose, including figuring out car-lease payments, odds and percentages in poker, cooking measurements and personal finance data.

☐ Planning Pays Off!

www.planningpaysoff.org

This site will help you find the answer and guide you through the proper procedure for finding the right planner for your particular needs. From the International Association of Financial Planning (IAFP).

☐ Ernst & Young Personal Financial Counseling

www.ey.com/pfc

One of the country's top financial services firms offers a generous selection of useful articles, tax-saving tips and links to other useful financial planning sites.

☐ New York Times BanxQuote Banking Center

www.nytimes.com/partners/banking

This *New York Times*–sponsored site allows you to get the best rates, nationwide or by state, on car loans, home mortgages, credit cards, CDs and more. *Note:* This site requires registration.

☐ Debt Counselors of America

www.dca.org

The respected Debt Counselors of America (DCA) sponsors this very useful and well-organized site, full of advice on how to reduce, and ultimately eliminate, personal debt. Learn how to fend off collectors and consolidate debt. Chat with others who have debt problems, and find out how not to be a victim of scam artists who prey on individuals with money problems.

Investing and Finance

☐ Merrill Lynch on-line

http://askmerrill.ml.com

Get quick access to the latest analysis of equity and debt markets, from one of the largest research teams in the world.

☐ Silicon Investor

www.techstocks.com

Leads new investors and seasoned stockpickers through the maze of public companies at the cutting edge of high technology. Access stock quotes and charts. Engage in real-time on-line discussions with other investors.

☐ The Street

www.thestreet.com

Unlike the typical dry prose of most popular financial and investment publications, this on-line e-zine/ investment newsletter offers lively, somewhat irreverent, yet thoughtful comments on current investment issues. Also, discussion forums on mutual fund issues, stocks, individual companies and more. Well-written, content rich and useful to individual investors seeking hard-hitting analysis.

☐ GetSmart

www.getsmart.com

Looking for a credit card, mortgage or mutual fund? Of the many personal finance sites on the Web, this one stands out because of its usefulness to even the most financially challenged among us. It is an independent information service designed to help consumers make smart financial decisions.

☐ HomeOwners Finance Center

www.homeowners.com

Everything you need to know about the latest rates on all types of loans, refinancing, estimating closing costs and calculating mortgage payments at the tips of your fingers.

HomeFair.com
www.homefair.com

This site holds your hand through the minefield of finding a home, financing a home purchase, relocating, insuring your home. Helpful mortgage and salary calculators allow you to determine monthly payments and how much income you need to purchase a home. Well-organized with attractive graphics.

And More...

The Mortgage Manager
www.mortgagereducer.com

The Mortgage Manager not only shows how you can save huge amounts on your home mortgage, it provides the software for you to do it free! The idea: Paying off the home loan on a biweekly, instead of a monthly, basis. Download the free software to set up an electronic payment schedule between your bank account and the holder of your mortgage. For those without Windows NT or Windows 95, this site offers to fax a free, computerized mortgage savings analysis. You can even check your current loan to find any hidden overcharges.

W3C
www.w3.org

Sponsored by US and European universities, this site helps beginners learn the basics of communicating on the Web and setting up their own Web sites.

Grandparents Raising Grandchildren
www.aarp.org/confacts/programs/ grandraising.html

Did you know that 3.9 million American children live in grandparent-headed households? AARP has put together this very informative Web site which addresses the unique issues facing these families.

13

Savvy Travel

How to Get the Very Lowest Airline Fares

For travelers—especially those age 62 and over—there are many kinds of bargains to investigate before buying tickets.

SENIOR AIRFARE BREAKS

•**Coupon booklets.** Most airlines offer seniors booklets with four coupons that can save a lot of money.

Only one coupon is needed for a one-way trip between any two cities in the continental US (two coupons each way for Alaska or Hawaii). So you pay the same rate to fly 300 or 3,000 miles. There are no minimum or maximum stays required.

Typical cost: About $675 for four coupons.

While most senior coupon programs are similar, some offer better conditions or fly to more cities.

Advantages…

•**You lock in the current senior ticket price for one year.**

•**America West and USAirways** allow up to two grandchildren (ages two to 11) to travel with a senior using the same coupon booklet.

•**Coupons are refundable if not used** (but once you use one coupon, the rest become nonrefundable).

•**To have confirmed seats using senior airfare coupons** requires booking at least 14 days in advance—but immediate travel is possible on a standby basis.

•**Senior coupon flights can even earn frequent-flier miles.**

•**Coupons let you fly one way or round-trip**—there are no minimum/maximum stay limits.

Jens Jurgen, editor, *Travel Companion Exchange*, and publisher, *Senior Air Fare Report*, Box 833, Amityville, NY 11701. *www.whytravelalone.com.*

Disadvantages…

●**During special airfare promotions,** tickets could cost less than coupon prices.

●**Shorter flights could be cheaper** with an individual ticket.

●**Some Internet fares may be cheaper.**

●**Flat discount.** Except for most deeply discounted promotional fares, seniors and a companion can routinely get 10% off many domestic and international airfares.

Many foreign airlines offer 10% discounts at age 60 or 62, so always ask and compare fares.

Caution: You must tell the travel agent or airline your age and provide a photo ID at check-in to get the discount.

A companion of any age traveling with a senior can also routinely get the 10% discount.

SOUTHWEST AIRLINES SENIOR FARES

Southwest Airlines (SWA) has attractive senior fares. They are unrestricted and fully refundable, but you must be 65-plus to get SWA senior fares.

SWA flies to 29 states and has a high customer satisfaction rating.

Other airlines will usually match SWA's fares—even their senior fares—for cities where they compete so, again, check.

SWA senior fares can't be booked on-line—you must call 800-435-9792.

SENIOR TRAVELERS CLUBS

Continental Airlines has a club for seniors that offers discounts of 15% to 20% to people age 62 and older. These fares also earn frequent-flier miles. *More information: www. continental.com* or 800-441-1135.

Note: American and Delta have closed their clubs to enrollment.

United's Silver Wings Plus is open to those age 55-plus.

Caution: If you are 65-plus, other airline senior deals are better.

BARGAINS FOR ALL TRAVELERS

Regardless of age, there are travel bargains to be found…

●**Consolidators and some ethnic travel agencies** may have lower unpublished con-tract fares or discounts. But some consolidators deal only through travel agents—for instance, consolidators who deal with travel to and from India and Asia.

Fare information: No single Web site is best. You can find domestic airfares—including most senior fares—at *www.itasoftware.com.* Other airfare Web sites to try—*www.expedia. com…www.sidestep.com…*and *www.travelocity. com.* However, these sites search other airlines' Web sites and may miss fare bargains that are not available on the Internet.

Example: www.expedia.com does not include SWA fares in its searches.

More ways to save money…

●**Buy all air tickets by credit card.** Airlines and travel agents do go out of business, but if you pay by credit card, you won't lose your money.

●**Before purchasing nonrefundable tickets,** verify all fares, dates and conditions (for example, the charge for rescheduling).

●**Do not buy mileage award tickets from individuals**—they can be confiscated at the gate if detected.

●**Do not buy tickets from classified ads**—they are not transferable to another person (remember, you must show ID at the gate).

●**Do not waste time to save $10.** Your time is worth something. A better use of your time would be to research the cost of hotel rooms and car rentals where you're going. Your savings on airfare can be erased by one night in a nondiscounted hotel room. Walk-up rates are highest. Visit *www.sidestep.com* to check domestic hotel rates. Even lower hotel rates, sometimes less than $40/night for top-quality hotels, can be obtained using *www.priceline.com.*

●**The lowest fare is not always the best choice.** If you need flexibility, don't want to fly at an odd time or don't want to make an inconvenient connection, perhaps paying a few more dollars (such as for a nonstop flight) is not a bad choice.

More from Jens Jurgen...

Be Prepared with Cash

Always carry some US currency and traveler's checks—in addition to your ATM card—when you are traveling. ATMs are not reliable for cash needs overseas. Yet many travelers now rely on ATMs almost exclusively. While ATMs give favorable exchange rates, they sometimes break or run out of cash at popular locations—airports and near major tourist attractions.

Also from Jens Jurgen...

Cruise Bargains

Repositioning cruises provide unique opportunities *and* bargains. Twice a year, cruise lines reposition ships between summer and winter routes—such as from Caribbean to Alaskan or Mediterranean routes. *Special travel opportunities:* You can make a luxury transatlantic crossing to (in the spring) or from (in the late fall) Europe. Or travel all or part of the route between Alaska or Vancouver and the Caribbean—through the Panama Canal and along the Pacific coast of Mexico, the US and Canada. Bargains also exist because travel is off-season and one-way.

Finally from Jens Jurgen...

Free Pet-Sitting While You Travel

If you want to take a trip but don't know where to leave your pet, consider letting someone who is visiting your area—either on business or for a vacation—stay in your home for free in exchange for watching Fido or Felix.

Taking pets along on an airplane is hard on you and the animal, and many airlines won't even let you do it.

Trading free accommodations for pet-sitting is much cheaper than boarding your pet or paying a professional pet-sitter to feed your dog and walk it daily while you are away, and your pet—and your house—will have greater supervision.

For more information on pet-sitting: Check out the National Association of Professional Pet Sitters, 1030 15 St. NW, Washington, DC 20005 or on the Web at *www.petsitters.org* or Petsitters.com at *www.petsitters.com.*

How to Beat Traps in Airline E-Tickets

Airlines' paperless "E-tickets" cannot be lost or stolen. But there is a potential snag for travelers—different airlines' computer systems do not yet effectively share information about E-tickets.

This can prevent a traveler from being able to change to a flight on another airline if the original flight is canceled or delayed and the original airline can't offer another seat anytime soon.

Safety: If there is a possibility that you'll need to change airlines, and if your original ticket is fully refundable, get a printed E-ticket coupon or paper ticket from the airline or your travel agent to present directly to the alternative airline.

If you do not have a fully refundable fare, then you have to receive authorization from the issuing carrier to change airlines.

Also useful: If you make your own reservation, keep a printed copy of the Web page with the ticket information on it.

Neal Bibeau, president, Rosenbluth Interactive, on-line travel agency, 2401 Walnut St., Philadelphia 19103. *www.biztravel.com.*

Early Reservations Get Better Seats

Bill McGee, editor, *Consumer Reports Travel Letter*, 101 Truman Ave., Yonkers, NY 10703.

For the best airline seats, try to book as early as possible. Ask for a seat away from the galley and lavatories. Request a seat that reclines —not all do. Ask for one close to the front—many airlines book from the rear to the front. If you are flying as a couple and the plane is not full, consider booking the window and aisle seats in a three-across seat— the middle seat may stay empty—or book two aisle seats across from each other. If the only seat you can book in advance is a bad one, get to the airport several hours early and ask for reassignment—some good seats are held until departure day.

More from Bill McGee...

Don't Book Cruises On-Line

Use a travel agent, because cruise reservations are much more complicated than hotel or airline reservations. You have to choose a ship, itinerary, cabin category, shore excursions and many options. Some cruise lines do not even allow bookings to be done on-line.

Internet Travel Booking Trap

Some booking sites on the Web offer deeply discounted airfares to first-time customers to encourage them to come back—but then only provide much smaller discounts when the same customers visit later. *Best:* Seek quotes from more than one source, including a travel agent.

The Mature Traveler, Box 1543, Wildomar, CA 92595.

Carry-On Dos and Don'ts

Don't take full bottles of toiletries and cosmetics or almost-full fountain pens or aerosol cans into the cabin. Air-pressure changes can cause leaks and breakage. Be especially careful with nail-polish remover—if the bottle bursts, the chemicals are flammable and noxious. Keep bottles three-quarters full or less...consider buying a high-altitude pen if you fly often...use a pump instead of aerosol sprays.

Travel Holiday, 1633 Broadway, New York City 10019.

Rudy Maxa Tells How To Avoid Most Air-Travel Delays

Rudy Maxa, host of public radio's *Savvy Traveler* and editor of *Rudy Maxa's Traveler,* 2205 California St. NW, Washington, DC 20008. *www.rudymaxa.com.*

With the surge in air travel, aging air-traffic-control systems, runway repairs at major airports and unco-operative weather, it is a rare air traveler who hasn't experienced exasperating delays getting from here to there.

There's no way to guarantee on-time departure, but these strategies will help improve your batting average. These individual strategies are not new. *Key:* Put them all together for the best results.

●**Book the first flight out**—or at least early in the day.

Departures: According to recent Department of Transportation statistics, 94% of the flights out of Atlanta that departed between 7:00 am and 8:00 am left the gate within 15 minutes of their scheduled departure times.

But for flights that left between 7:00 pm and 8:00 pm, only 70% left on time.

The same held for arrivals: Between 7:00 am and 8:00 am, 92% arrived within 15 minutes of their scheduled arrival times. Just 62% arrived on time between 9:00 pm and 10:00 pm.

●**Fly nonstop.** The more times you land and take off on the way to your final destination, the greater the chance for delays.

Caution: Don't confuse a *direct flight* with a *nonstop flight.*

A direct flight involves one or more intermediate stops on the way to your destination and might even involve changing planes, even though the flight number doesn't change.

A nonstop flight lands only at your destination.

●Get a paper ticket. Electronic tickets may be convenient, and they can't be lost. But if your flight is delayed and your airline has to book you on another airline, a paper ticket will make the process faster and easier.

Reason: Airline computers still can't talk to each other, so electronic tickets have to be reissued in paper form at the counter for you to be transferred to another carrier.

A paper ticket needs only a stamp and a signature to get you on your way.

●Book another flight at the first sign of delay. Don't wait in a long line at the ticket counter—you may not get a seat on a desirable flight. Phone your travel agent or another airline directly to book an alternative flight.

When trying to resolve a delay: Stay calm and rational. Arrogance and outrage make things worse.

●Choose a small airport whenever possible. For Chicago, Dallas, Los Angeles and cities that have a choice of airports, the smaller airport is better. They have fewer delays than larger ones simply because they handle fewer planes.

●Mind your frequent-flier account. Make sure all your flights are reflected on your account. Try to qualify for the highest elite level—since those customers typically receive the most attention.

More from Rudy Maxa...

How to Take the Torture Out of Business Travel

Business travel has become a nightmare. Too many people are fighting for too few airline seats and hotel rooms, and heavy traffic and airline labor difficulties lead to flights that are long-delayed or cancelled.

Result: Fatigue...stress...lost time...even lost business opportunities.

Here's how to make business travel less stressful...

●Fly when other people aren't flying. Airports are mobbed on Friday evening. By noon Saturday, the business crowd is gone and airports are half empty.

Whenever possible, I stay over Friday night and take a midday Saturday flight home. With less air traffic, the flight is more likely to leave on time. Once on board, the plane is usually half empty. That means much better service and more room to stretch out.

Helpful: Fly on holidays, when most business travelers are staying home. I flew from Washington, DC, to Los Angeles on Martin Luther King Day. The flight left on time, with only 12 people aboard.

●Learn when your flight is really leaving. I'm amazed at how many people drive to the airport without first checking on the latest departure time for their flights.

By determining the status of your flight before leaving home or the office, you'll avoid wasting hours at the airport.

Caution: If you ask when your flight is scheduled to depart, you'll probably hear something like, "We're showing an on-time departure." All that means is, no matter how late the flight is likely to be, the airline hasn't actually posted a new departure time.

Instead, ask where the flight that is bringing your plane to the airport originated and when *that* flight is due to land.

Your airline may be showing an on-time departure for your flight, while showing the plane you'll be flying on is not scheduled to land for hours.

●Become an elite-class frequent flier. Once you achieve elite status, you can typically upgrade to a roomy first-class or business-class seat for the price of coach.

How it works: You must fly 25,000 to 50,000 miles a year per airline to achieve elite status. By concentrating my flying on just two airlines, I make sure I'm always Premier Executive on United and Platinum on American.

You may be able to get elite status instantly by showing an airline you already have elite status on a rival carrier.

Example: I always flew American Airlines but then got an assignment that required numerous trips from Washington's Dulles Airport to Europe—routes that American doesn't fly. I sent United a copy of my previous month's American Platinum statement. I said I would be flying to Europe frequently in the coming months and my inclination was to fly United if it granted me elite status. Within a week, United called and granted my request.

● **Take advantage of airport membership clubs.** If a flight is delayed, there's a huge difference between sitting in a crowded lounge and in a comfortable airport club. At the club, you have access to good food, clean restrooms and quiet surroundings. You can also have tickets changed without waiting in line. And you can gain access to clubs at many airports for relatively little money.

Example: I belong to both the American and United airport clubs. That lets me use the clubs of both airlines *and their partners* in airports around the world. And my American Express platinum card gives me free entry to the airport clubs of Continental, Northwest and TWA.

I also have a membership to Priority Pass, which opens the door to more than 300 airport clubs in 70 countries. *Cost:* $99/year, plus a $24 per-visit charge. *More information:* 800-352-2834 or *www.prioritypass.com.*

● **Pamper yourself when you travel.** There's nothing like a great meal to boost your morale—even when you're on a flight that will be arriving late. You won't get that great meal by eating airline food, so bring your own.

Example: I travel from Washington, DC, to Los Angeles once a month. Before flying home, I stop at my favorite deli and buy a fabulous corned beef sandwich and a piece of chocolate cake. Not particularly healthful, true, but everyone on board envies me—including the flight attendants.

When I'm in Paris, I shop gourmet food stores the morning of my flight. While other passengers are eating standard airline fare, I'm savoring pâté, salmon, cheese and French pastry.

● **Fight fatigue when you fly.** All business travel is stressful—no matter how smoothly it goes. The more you rest while aloft, the better you'll feel when you land.

Low-level jet engine noise can be very fatiguing. I tune it out with a Bose noise-canceling headset. I use the headset for listening to music or watching the movie—or just to neutralize jet noise. The headsets are now available in first class on some American Airlines flights.

You can buy them at some airport kiosks or on-line at *www.bose.com. Cost:* $300.

Helpful: A State Department official who travels constantly introduced me to Sonata, a mild prescription sleeping pill. You'll sleep for about four hours and wake up without the hangover and grogginess that most sleeping pills cause. Consult your physician.

● **Join the frequent-renter's clubs of car rental companies.** You will accrue points that are good toward discounts or other gifts and a speedier departure when you rent a car.

Examples: Becoming a member of National's Emerald Isle or Avis's Preferred program allows you to avoid stopping at a counter.

● **Get the most from your hotel stay.** Nothing is worse than arriving after a long-delayed flight and finding that the hotel has given your room away.

Self-defense: Guarantee the room with a credit card. If you are running unusually late, it never hurts to call the hotel to make sure your room is still being held for you.

Also effective: If you stay at the same hotel frequently, introduce yourself to the general manager and the concierge. Tell them you stay at their hotel on a regular basis.

Being known as a regular should get you a better room each time you visit, with occasional upgrades to a suite when one is available.

Bonus: Once you are known, the hotel staff can work small miracles for you—helping you change travel plans...getting you a table at a booked restaurant or tickets to sold-out entertainment...even making introductions to potentially valuable local business contacts in your field.

Frequent-Flier Flights Are Very Scarce

Frequent-flier reservations are almost impossible to get unless you book at least six months in advance. Work with a travel agent experienced in trips for frequent fliers. Have him/her check your primary carrier's partner airlines and less-used routings. *Worth considering:* If you see a bargain fare, buy tickets and save your miles for less heavily traveled times.

Tom Parsons, editor, *Bestfares.com,* 1301 S. Bowen Rd., Arlington, TX 76013.

To Avoid Stomach Trouble While Flying

Stay away from gum and carbonated drinks. Both increase production of gas in the digestive tract. Drink plain water or juice. Eat only well-cooked foods. Avoid ones that can produce gas, such as broccoli, cabbage, cauliflower and beans. Eat slowly and chew thoroughly. Walk around to speed digestion.

Maria T. Abreu, MD, gastroenterologist and assistant director, Inflammatory Bowel Disease Center, Cedars-Sinai Medical Center, Los Angeles.

Least Favorite Big Plane

Randy Petersen, publisher, *InsideFlyer,* 1930 Frequent-Flyer Point, Colorado Springs 80915.

MD-11. *Reasons:* Loud engines, small luggage compartments and tight cabins. While the FAA considers it safe, the MD-11 has a high accident rate versus other big planes. Your airline or travel agent can tell you which plane is scheduled for a certain flight. *Frequent-flier favorite:* Boeing 777. It looks brand-new, feels spacious and has big overhead compartments, seatback TV screens and digital sound.

More from Randy Petersen…

Getting Away from Airports… Very Frequent Flier's Inside Advice

● **Stand in a taxi line** if arriving between 9:00 am and 3:00 pm…or after 8:00 pm. Those are the least crowded times.

● **Use public transportation** when it is available and convenient.

Example: Logan Airport in Boston or any New York City area airport.

● **Use a van service.** You can book them at the airport's transportation desk. They cost less than cabs…and are more convenient.

● **If the airport has a hotel on the premises,** take a courtesy van or walk and get a cab from the hotel.

● **Fly to a less-used airport.**

Examples: Midway, not O'Hare, in Chicago…Colorado Springs instead of Denver. *Bonus:* Flights to these airports often cost less.

● **Walk to the departure area**—instead of waiting for a cab at the arrivals area—and take a cab from someone who is arriving for a flight. *Caution:* Not all airports allow this.

Also from Randy Petersen…

Free Travel for Your Troubles

Airlines are offering more vouchers for complaints. *Reason:* The number of complaints has soared in the past year. Write a forthright letter seeking specific compensation. Explain what the problem was, and ask for something reasonable for your trouble.

Flying Makes Most People Sick

Diana Fairechild, a retired international flight attendant, is founder of The Fair Air Coalition, a nonprofit airline passenger advocacy group based in Anahola, Hawaii. She runs the "Healthy Flying" Web site. *www.flyana.com.* Ms. Fairechild is author of four books, including *Jet Smarter: The Air Traveler's Rx.* Flyana Rhyme.

More than 90% of frequent fliers suffer from physical and mental ailments associated with air travel, according to surveys I have conducted on my Web site. The problems include fatigue, digestive problems and temporary memory loss.

Having flown 10 million miles, I know it is possible to lessen the symptoms caused by jet lag and jet cabin conditions. Here are the main factors that contribute to flying-related ailments...and the simple steps to help you remain healthy after landing...

RECYCLED AIR

About half of the air in jet cabins is recycled—pumping more fresh air into the cabin is a cost airlines want to avoid. The feelings of not being able to breathe deeply, clammy skin or trouble concentrating all indicate that you may not be getting enough oxygen.

Self-defense: Write a note to the pilot asking him/her to provide more fresh air and less recycled air. Politely ask the flight attendant to deliver the note—you don't want him to think you are a hijacker.

If you don't feel better within 15 minutes, ask the attendant to bring you—free of charge—a portable oxygen bottle. Oxygen is one of the most important remedies for jet lag. Taking a long walk outdoors after landing is also helpful.

CONTAGIOUS DISEASES

The most critical danger of recycled airplane air is contagious diseases—colds, flu, tuberculosis, etc.—transmitted from infected passengers.

Of course, the first line of defense is to change seats if you are sitting near an obviously ill passenger, but this is not possible on full planes.

When I fly, I cover my nose and mouth with a cotton handkerchief. While some people may say this looks a bit silly, the handkerchief helps block the spread of germs.

DEHYDRATION

The airplane cabin is dryer than any of the world's deserts. Dehydration can affect digestion, stamina, memory and more.

Self-defense: Avoid all caffeinated beverages, which are dehydrating. Drink a lot of water.

Good rule of thumb—drink at least twice as much water as you normally do. Don't wait until you feel thirsty to drink. By then, you are already showing signs of dehydration. It is safer to drink *bottled* water, rather than airplane water from a pitcher.

If you choose to keep a cotton handkerchief over your nose, moisten it to provide humidity for your lungs.

HIGH ALTITUDE

The interior altitude on most transcontinental and transoceanic flights is roughly equivalent to standing on an 8,000-foot mountaintop.

Passengers with poor circulation or heart disease can suffer life-threatening blood clots—especially if they sit with their legs crossed. And when feet swell, tight shoes can damage the capillaries in feet and cause blood clots. It can take weeks for swelling to go down. *Self-defense...*

• **Wear loose-fitting clothing.** I also wear shoes that are one-half size too big. Then, on the ground, I use cushioned inserts to make them fit my feet properly. I remove the inserts when I'm in the air.

• **Elevate your feet whenever possible.** In the airport lounge, rest your feet on top of your carry-on bag.

• **Exercise on the plane.** Walk the aisle when it is not blocked by carts. Practice little movements at your seat, such as rotating your ankles and contracting and releasing your buttock muscles.

INAPPROPRIATE ATTIRE

When choosing what to wear during your flight, consider whether any item will hinder you in an in-flight emergency.

In the event of an onboard fire, synthetics might ignite. If you have to slide down one of the emergency escape chutes, synthetics—especially pantyhose—can cause raspberry "burns" on legs and fannies.

Wear flat, comfortable shoes so you won't end up on the tarmac shoeless. Shoes with sharp points or high heels can puncture a slide. If you have to evacuate the plane, you will be required to remove them.

Also helpful: Dress in layers. There will likely be a climate difference between your departure and arrival locations. There will also be a variety of temperatures inside the aircraft. Layers enable you to stay comfortable.

STRESS

Flying, even at its best, is stressful. Passengers miss sleep...skip meals or overeat unhealthful foods...lug unwieldy bags...and sit in crowded cabins. Do whatever it takes to relax on your travel day. *Steps I take to cut down on stress...*

•**Pack light**—so you can carry everything onboard instead of worrying whether your checked luggage will make it to your destination.

•**Arrive at the airport with plenty of time to spare.** Security checks are less hassle when you're not in a hurry.

•**Smile**—it will speed up the process at every step because personnel will be more eager to assist you.

•**Power walk in airport corridors.** Then do some stretches in the lounge before boarding.

•**Stretch again before going to sleep.** This will help your body recover more quickly from air travel.

•**Keep a positive mental attitude.** Positive thinking keeps you mentally clear and emotionally balanced. It also boosts your immune system.

No Extra Baggage

Travel without luggage by shipping suitcases and equipment—particularly golf clubs or skis—directly to your destination. UPS (800-742-5877) and Federal Express (800-463-3339) both handle such shipments. So does Virtual Bellhop, a service of Travelite (877-235-5467). Costs vary widely—but can be high. Expect to spend as much as the cost of an additional airline ticket. Check with your destination hotel to be sure it is set up to receive and hold your luggage for you. Call each shipping company for rates, insurance coverage and delivery schedules.

Betsy Wade, travel columnist, The New York Times.

Born to Shop Duty-Free

Antiques can be brought through US Customs *duty free* from abroad. By US Customs definition, an antique is any object more than 100 years old.

Best: Whenever possible, bring the items you acquire with you when you return through customs rather than ship them separately. Have documentation of age.

Your presence will expedite their passage through customs...save time and money...and assure that delicate or breakable items are handled properly.

It can be well worth it to pay excess baggage charges to have items accompany you.

Cathy Roe, US Customs import specialist, 11099 S. La Cienega Blvd., Los Angeles 90045.

Travelers, Beware

Theft is still rising...in the US and abroad—especially in airports but elsewhere, too. *Old—but still very effective—scam:* Two thieves ride in front of and behind a victim on an escalator or moving walkway. The first pretends to stumble. As the victim turns to help him/her, the second thief knocks into the victim and steals a wallet or purse. *Worth repeating:* Stay alert. Wear a fanny pack or money belt—under a jacket or sweater. Do not advertise yourself as a tourist by wearing a baseball cap or a T-shirt with a logo. Carry guidebooks and maps inside a local shopping bag, and read them within the pages of a local newspaper.

Nancy Dunnan, managing editor, *Travel Smart*, 40 Beechdale Rd., Dobbs Ferry, New York 10522.

Surprise Hotel Fees

Hidden charges are mounting at US hotels. *Unwelcome surprises:* Fees for amenities or services most people expect to be free— charges for incoming faxes…early-departure …"free" local calls that turn into toll calls after a certain time…parking in hotel garages. *Self-defense:* When making a reservation, ask about extra charges—and ask again at check-in. Read paperwork before signing. Fees can sometimes be waived or your room upgraded in exchange. Review your bill carefully at checkout. *Also:* Do not assume anything is free. Wine, bottled water and other items in the room are probably *not* complimentary.

Bjorn Hanson, PhD, global hospitality and leisure consultant, PricewaterhouseCoopers, New York.

Sunday Freebies in Paris

More than two dozen museums and monuments have free admission every Sunday, including the Louvre, d'Orsay and Rodin museums. Versailles is free as well. Notre Dame is not only free but has free' guided tours.

Travel & Leisure, 1120 Avenue of the Americas, New York 10036.

Secrets of Very Safe International Travel

William McCarthy, PhD, president, Threat Research, Inc., 7600 Admiral Dr., Alexandria, VA 22308.

Benjamin Weiner, director, Probe International Inc., Stamford, CT.

Mark Hall, principal, Air Security International, an intelligence and security company, Houston. Its Web site, *www.airsecurity.com*, provides daily updates on problem areas of the world.

The threat to Americans in the Middle East—and elsewhere in the world—is real. Three top security experts give their advice on how to stay safe despite increasing hostility dangers.

AVOID HOT SPOTS
William McCarthy, PhD

Ordinary defensive measures are not enough right now. Even if you do not look like a tourist, your speech or behavior will identify you as someone who does not belong.

A determined terrorist will find a target for his/her terror. The *only* way to be sure you are not the target is to stay away.

Americans should not travel to world hot spots at this time. If a crucial business meeting must be held, arrange a real-time teleconference. If the meeting must be in person, pick a safe place for it where you won't look so obviously different and you can move about in anonymity. *Examples:* Quiet places in Europe and Australia.

USE CAUTION EVERYWHERE
Benjamin Weiner

Terrorism can occur anywhere—not just in world trouble spots.

Even immigrants to the US—who hoped to leave the conflicts of their homelands behind —may bring them. The same is true in other Western nations.

I don't think it is necessary to stop traveling—that closes down your life or business. *But…*

•**Join airline clubs** to avoid crowded airport waiting areas.

•**Take only carry-on luggage** if possible. If you must check your baggage, do not linger in the claim area once you retrieve your items.

•**Dress and act inconspicuously**…and rent ordinary cars.

•**Be aware of—and understand—the local circumstances.** The Middle East is not the only trouble spot. Areas such as Kashmir and Sri Lanka can erupt in violence as well. In India, some Christians and Muslims have been killed in conflicts with Hindus.

•**Pay close attention** to religious customs.

Example: In Islamic countries, stay off the street after 3 pm on Fridays. Prayers end in mosques at that hour, and Friday is preaching day, which may include emotional attacks on perceived enemies.

•**Learn what events** can be expected to provoke violence.

Example: The Muslim mourning period varies, but it can last 40 days. So 40 days after Palestinian deaths in the Middle East, violent acts of revenge may erupt. If anyone dies in those subsequent acts, the process could be repeated 40 days later.

Bottom line: The number of people killed or harmed by terrorist violence is statistically low. But you don't want to become a statistic. So before traveling, study the areas you are visiting…understand possible flashpoints…and find ways to be as inconspicuous as possible.

PLAN AHEAD
Mark Hall

If you feel that you must travel during this threatening time, here are important precautions to take…

•**Do not wear clothing that would identify you as from the US**—avoid designer and company logos…American flags…college names…etc.

•**Do not strike up conversations with strangers** or accept drinks or cigarettes from them.

•**Don't wear flashy jewelry** and other signs of wealth.

•**Set your watch to local time.**

•**If a demonstration starts, don't be curious about it**—head in the other direction.

For regional information: The US State Department provides warnings about security worldwide, 202-647-5226…*http://travel.state.gov/travel_warnings.html.*

Contacting other nations' embassies directly may not provide much information. For political reasons, they minimize problems.

Off-Peak Travel Bargains

Find out the best off-season weather so you can avoid tourist season and still have a pleasant trip. *Best bargain months:* Australia—April, May and November, and in some areas, June through August, too…Austria—spring and fall for good ski bargains, winter for good prices in Vienna…most of Europe—mid-fall and mid-spring…Caribbean islands—June through mid-December…Fiji—April through August…Hawaii—mid-September through mid-December and post-Easter through mid-June.

Consumers Digest, 8001 N. Lincoln Ave., Skokie, IL 60077.

Dr. Toy's Great Games For Travel

Stevanne Auerbach, PhD, consultant on child development, toys and play and author of *Dr. Toy's Guide (www.drtoy.com)…Toys for a Lifetime* (Rizzoli/FAO Schwarz)…and *Dr. Toy's Smart Play* (St. Martin's).

While travel can be enriching, it can also be tedious—and not just for children.

Suggestion: Before a trip, assemble a fun pack filled with favorite books and magazines, a tape player and earphones, assorted tapes, notebooks and pens.

To help the miles whiz by, and to reach your destination in good spirits, consider these games—all are appropriate for ages eight to adult...

GAMES FOR ONE

• **Port to Port...Rush Hour...and Stormy Seas.** Handheld logic puzzles that all follow similar rules. Rearrange pieces to create an exit path for a key vehicle or boat. Each game includes 40 challenges, from beginner to expert. Additional challenge cards available for *Rush Hour.* Binary Arts, 888-789-9538. $10 to $16.*

• **Rubik's Cube.** New version of the old favorite includes a booklet of hints. Fun way to practice problem-solving. Hasbro Games, 800-752-9755. $9.99.

• **Yahtzee.** Electronic handheld version of the popular game. Automatic sound effects and victory tune add to the fun. Hasbro Games, 800-752-9755. $7.99.

GAMES FOR TWO OR MORE

• **Battleship.** Smaller version of the classic game. Players move pegs to set up fleets,

*Prices are manufacturers' suggested retail. Discounts may be available.

mark hits and sink opponent's fleet. Hasbro Games, 800-752-9755. $17.

• **Diversity Works.** *Trivial Pursuit*–style card game challenges knowledge of different cultures. Players work together to answer questions and win by spelling "diversity." Cultural Concepts, 800-497-8221...*www. cultural-concepts.com.* $18.

• **Monopoly card games.** In *Feed the Meter,* move and make sure you return before the meter expires. *Leaky Pipe* challenges players to reconnect pipes. Hasbro Games, 800-752-9755. $16.

• **Quick Chess.** Beginner's set teaches chess moves by introducing one piece at a time. Amerigames International, 800-344-4241. $9.99.

14

Enjoying Your Leisure Time

Welcome to the New World of Digital Imaging

Digital imaging now offers a practical and increasingly affordable complement to film photography.

With a digital camera you can take a picture, view it immediately, share it on the Web—or make a print. A scanner lets you convert favorite photos into image files that you can retouch and restore on your computer and distribute on-line…or as prints.

Most photo centers can now upload pictures captured on film to the Internet, as well.

While film still offers the most economical solution for quality prints, digital imaging's advantage and appeal is as an extension of your computer system for visual communications.

HOW IT WORKS

A digital image begins as a file of information. That file is the digital equivalent of a negative, but you can work with it in ways never practical with film: Revise it, enhance it, archive it to disk or transmit it over the Internet. *Some basics…*

●**Resolution.** The quality of a digital image is defined by its *resolution,* expressed in pixels—the more pixels the better.

Most digital cameras offer several resolution modes, from standard to super fine. Typically, the higher the resolution, the higher the quality of the image. Resolution determines the size of the image file.

●**Image capture.** This is accomplished with a CCD (Charged Coupled Device) or CMOS (Complementary Metal Oxide Semiconductor) image chip. CMOS is better for dim lighting situations, but CCD is said to deliver cleaner images generally.

Pictures are stored in microchips or PC cards as a kind of "digital film." These are

Bill Schiffner, editor in chief of the imaging industry publication *Photographic Processing* and a contributor to *Digital Photographer* magazine and *JetPrintPhoto.com.* Mr. Schiffner has been covering the photo industry for more than 15 years.

removable memory cards, such as Compact-Flash, MiniatureCard or SmartMedia. With removable storage cards you can take unlimited pictures by just replacing the storage cards.

● **Printing.** Producing a quality print from a digital image at home requires buying inks and paper. Even then, the results may not be what you'd expect from film. However, you can also have them printed at a photo lab, as well as share them on-line.

WHAT YOU'LL NEED

● **Imaging system.** The computer is the core of any digital-imaging system. Know your system specs when you shop for a camera. Suppliers publish the minimum requirements in computer RAM, processor speed and hard drive needed to support their cameras or scanners.

● **Cameras.** Digital cameras start in the $200 range and climb to more than $1,000. Available from traditional suppliers of photographic, computer and electronics equipment, they are best purchased in stores specializing in these products where experts are available to advise you.

If you merely want to share photos on-line, an entry-level camera will prove adequate. These are the digital equivalent of a point-and-shoot 35mm camera and offer basic features. *Good beginner models include...*

● **Canon PowerShot A50.** Very compact... 2.5x zoom lens...optical viewfinder...two-inch LCD. Uses CompactFlash cards. 800-652-2666. *Price:* $299.*

● **Kodak DC240I.** Five colors available (to match the iMac personal computer)...3x optical and 2x digital zoom lens...close-up focus to 10 inches...1.3 megapixel CCD sensor... images are detailed enough for larger-than-standard prints. 800-235-6325. *Price:* $549.

To print your images at home, you'll need a digital camera that offers at least a million pixels. The latest models go up to 3.5 million pixels. They cost $500 and up. Features include a zoom lens, larger LCD screens, several flash and shooting modes. *The best in this price range...*

*Prices are manufacturer's suggested retail. Discounts may be available.

● **Fujifilm FinePix 1400 ZOOM.** Has 1.3 megapixel CCD sensor...fixed focal length lens...3x optical zoom lens...manual exposure options. Uses SmartMedia cards. 800-800-3854. *Price:* $399.

● **Kodak DC280.** Two mega-pixel resolution...power flash...uses 8 MB CF card. Uses CompactFlash cards. *Price:* $599.

● **Olympus C-2020 Z.** Very high image quality...3x optical zoom lens...2.1 megapixel resolution...multiple exposure controls. Uses SmartMedia cards. 800-622-6372. *Price:* $699.

● **Casio QV-2000UX.** High-tech design...3x zoom lens...optical viewfinder...two mega-pixel resolution...fast USB interface for quick downloads. Uses CompactFlash cards or IBM Microdrive. 800-836-8580. *Price:* $799.

● **Fujifilm FinePix 4700 ZOOM.** Has .58-inch Super CCD....4.3 megapixel resolution... 80-second AVI video playback feature with sound. *Price:* $799.

● **Nikon CoolPix 950.** Sleek metal body... 3x optical zoom lens...2.1 megapixel resolution...burst shooting mode...power flash. Uses CompactFlash cards. 800-526-4566. *Price:* $899.

● **Scanners.** A scanner offers a less-expensive entry into digital imaging. Basic flatbed scanners, adequate for home users, sell for $100 or less. These "read" your photos, reflective art or text documents and convert them into a digital file within seconds.

Many people find the scanner the ideal way to copy treasured family photos, preserve them on disk and share them with family and friends. With the right paper, some photo realistic printers can give the images from your digital camera or your scanner the look and feel of prints from regular 35mm film.

● **Digital services.** Want to experiment with digital imaging without buying new equipment? Inquire at local photofinishing centers about what digital services they offer. Most now "digitize" film as part of basic services.

Along with prints, you can copy photos to CD-ROM or upload to the Internet to a photo-sharing site such as *www.photoprint.com* or *www.zing.com*—where they can be shared by family and friends.

You'll also find more of these centers equipped with digital minilabs and self-serve kiosks. These minilabs combine traditional print and digital services, regardless of what camera you use. With the kiosks, you step up, insert your digital "film," place your order and it's ready in minutes.

TAKING IMAGES ON-LINE

There are two ways to share your images on-line…

●**E-mail.** Compose a message, attach an image file and send. All the recipient needs to do is click on the message and view the image. Or, you can upload images to your Web page or a commercial Internet site for viewing.

●**Upload to the Internet.** You can also have your photofinisher digitize and upload your pictures to the Internet. Once there, the images are assigned a URL, which you and others can use to view the pictures.

Senior Softball World Series

For people over 50, series includes teams for age groups up to 80-plus. Women and men play on separate teams. Last year's play-offs involved 139 teams from 40 states. *More information:* National Association of Senior Citizens Softball (NASCS), 810-792-2110.

Ken Maas, president and founder, NASCS, Box 1085, Mt. Clemens, MI 48046.

Free, Healthful Outdoor Vacation

Volunteer to maintain forest hiking trails and you can get a free one- or two-week vacation, except for a $75 registration fee and the cost of transportation to the trail site. The American Hiking Society offers more than 70 of these work projects, which include three meals a day. *More information:* 301-565-6704 or *www.americanhiking.org.*

Antiques Can Lose Their Value

Beware of cleaning or repairing potentially valuable antiques. Cleaning or repairing antiques to make them look or work better can destroy much of their value. This is a very common and costly mistake. *Example:* "Improving" the old finish on a piece of 18th-century furniture could reduce its value by 80%. *Safety:* Before "fixing" a family heirloom that might have collector's value, have it appraised by an expert. And before buying an antique, ask what repairs the seller has performed on it. Have the repairs noted on a receipt if you make a purchase.

Leigh Keno, antique dealer, NY, appears frequently on the *Antiques Roadshow* and is coauthor of *Hidden Treasures: Searching for Masterpieces of American Furniture.* Warner.

What's Hot…What's Not At Flea Markets Now

Ralph and Terry Kovel, Cleveland-based experts on collectibles. Their TV show, *Flea Market Finds with the Kovels,* airs on Home & Garden Television (HGTV). They are authors of many books on collecting, including *Kovel's Antiques & Collectibles Price List 2001.* Three Rivers.

Flea markets and antiquing have soared in popularity as more people realize the money-making potential in their attics …and enjoy finding bargains on eclectic home furnishings.

Every year, Ralph and Terry Kovel criss-cross the country visiting dozens of major flea markets. *Their report from the front lines...*

CRAFTS & COLLECTIBLES

● **Lithographed tin banks from the 1940s through the 1970s.** Those shaped like children's books, globes and houses are very popular.

Price: $30 to $100. Registering banks—which have a coin-counting mechanism—can be worth several hundred dollars.

Collector's edge: Look for banks made by J. Chien & Co, a well-known East Coast toymaker that produced 65 different designs from 1903 to 1977. An Uncle Wiggily Chien rabbit bank recently sold for $440. A "Save for War Bonds and Stamps" Chien bank shaped like a bullet shell sold for about $600.

● **Flower/plant prints from the US Patent Office.** This is our favorite undervalued find. In the early 1930s, the US government began issuing patents on new varieties of flowers and plants. These official photographs and chromolithographs of patented roses, geraniums, etc. are showing up at flea markets for just $10 to $20 a print. They'll be worth much more when people realize what they are.

● **Czechoslovakian pottery from the first half of the 20th century.** The most popular of old Czechoslovakian pottery has either brightly colored flower designs or airbrushed designs.

Price: $50 and up.

Collector's edge: Don't be fooled by new reproductions. Look inside pitchers and cups where the handle joins the body. New pottery looks smooth. Older stuff is slightly dented.

HOME FURNISHINGS

● **Reproduction Colonial American furniture from the 1930s.** Copies—yes, copies—of famous makers such as Chippendale, Hepplewhite and Sheraton have modern touches, such as patterned veneer tops. You can get especially good bargains on dining room sets and coffee tables.

Example: A dining room table with six chairs goes for between $500 and $1,000.

● **Navajo wool rugs.** Made between 1920 and 1970, many from Navajo reservations in Arizona and New Mexico.

Price: $800 to $3,000.

Look for: Rugs made from homespun, vegetable-dyed wool rather than slicker commercial yarn...intricate and centered pattern...undamaged corners...no bleeding of colors.

POLITICAL MEMORABILIA

● **Protest/political bumper stickers, posters and buttons.** Anti–Vietnam War items start at $5 and go up to several hundred dollars. Be careful—fake war memorabilia are common.

Collector's edge: White-painted buttons weren't used until after 1972...buttons with yellowish or pinkish rust may be knockoffs that were "aged" to look valuable. Natural rust is reddish-brown.

● **WWI- and WWII-era satin pillows featuring military camps or ships.** Sought by decorators on both coasts for use in vacation homes.

Price: $25 and up. A pillowcase featuring a WWI navy ship sold recently for $145.

SILVERWARE

● **Victorian-era serving pieces.** Created between 1850 and 1900, these usually have a very ornate and eclectic look. Sterling silver from Gorham or Tiffany is quite expensive. Silver-plated pieces, such as asparagus servers or soup ladles, go for a reasonable $50 to $100 per piece. The gaudier and more elaborate the design, the better.

TOYS

● **1960s dolls.** Most popular include Chatty Cathy/$150 to $250...Nancy Ann Storybook/$100 to $200...Toni dolls with a "permanent wave" kit/$250 to $300.

Collector's edge: A doll in its original box would be worth twice as much.

● **Wind-up toys.** Disney character memorabilia always fetch good prices. German- or Japanese-made tin windups from the 1950s and 1960s are especially in demand.

Price: $300 and up. For example, a six-inch Mickey Mouse playing a xylophone recently sold for $385.

ELECTRONICS

• **1960s transistor radios.** American models from General Electric, Philco and Zenith go for between $30 and $125. Japanese-made radios from Hitachi and Sony sell for up to $600.

GENERAL TRENDS

Use these flea market trends to your advantage when buying collectibles...

• **Trading over the Internet has flooded the market with certain items,** greatly cooling off the prices that you can get.

Most affected: Antique and rare books... World's Fair handkerchiefs, tablecloths and other textiles and pennants...souvenir spoons from the 1950s and 1960s.

• **Mix-and-match sets were huge in the 1950s and are back now.** Using unmatched cups, saucers and plates from different periods, you can put together place settings for $10 a set. You can do the same with chairs around your kitchen table.

• **Pink is the hottest decorating color of 2001,** replacing light green. Favorite flower of 2001 is the pansy. Collectors are filling their kitchens with pansy-decorated accessories.

• **Oversized furniture is in.** New homes tend to have large rooms and high ceilings. Decorators are combing flea markets for large pieces—tall beds, armoires and grandfather clocks.

EVALUATING YOUR STUFF

If you think you've uncovered a hidden treasure, the following auction houses will appraise it free. Print an estimate-request form off the Web site, and mail it along with several photographs. *Allow at least four weeks for a response...*

• **Butterfields Appraisals,** 415-861-7500... *www.butterfields.com.*

• **Sotheby's Appraisal Department,** 212-606-7000...*www.sothebys.com.*

Bottom Line Guide to Getting Started in Golf

Joel Zuckerman, golf writer and single-digit handicapper, based in Savannah, GA.

Three million Americans take up golf each year...and an equal number give it up. If you're eager to start, it's best to begin simply in order to avoid frustration.

EQUIPMENT

The basics—an inexpensive starter set of four clubs, including a single wood, middle iron, short iron and putter. *Cost:* $20 to $50 per club.

This is all you need for at least the first few months. Any knowledgeable salesperson can help pick the right-sized clubs. Buying used clubs at driving ranges, pro shops or used sporting-goods stores makes starting even less expensive. Having fewer clubs minimizes confusion. Beginners can concentrate on the fundamentals of the swing, not on minuscule differences among the 14 clubs in a full set.

ATTIRE

Most players use gloves and golf shoes, but neither is required. *Clothing:* Basic slacks, Bermuda shorts or khakis...collared shirts...a hat. No cutoffs, tank tops or T-shirts.

You will need a bag for clubs, balls, tees and a bottle of water.

LOGISTICS

Golf is a walking game, but these days many players rent carts. If your golf bag is too heavy, try a pull cart with wheels.

Costs to play: From $10 for nine holes at a municipal course to $350 per round at the prestigious Pebble Beach resort. Figure $50 to $60 on average, plus about $10 to $20 per person for a cart.

LEARNING THE GAME

Bookstores and magazine stands overflow with golf-instruction tools.

Some favorites: Ben Hogan's Five Lessons (Simon & Schuster)...*Learn Golf in a Weekend* by Peter Ballingall (Knopf).

But books and tapes are no substitute for direct feedback. Without an instructor's trained eye, it's impossible to know whether your grip, stance, alignment or swing changes are effective.

Best way to start: Private lessons several times a month. As you improve, once a month. After a year or so, get an occasional tune-up.

Lessons are offered at private and public golf courses and most driving ranges. *Best:* A certified PGA teaching professional.

Cost: $20 per hour to more than $500 per hour for a "big name" instructor.

Golf schools and camps are popular, but it's difficult to assimilate the torrent of information provided in a typical three- to five-day course.

Cost: Depending on the school's amenities and the celebrity quotient of the instructors, fees can range from $40 for a short clinic to $3,000 per week at a posh resort.

Golf school is best for players who have some experience, although almost any resort has teaching facilities, a driving range and at least one course that won't be too taxing.

PRACTICE EFFICIENTLY

For all players, but especially beginners, short-game practice is essential. Most shots in golf come from within 100 yards.

A great new book on how to practice at the range is *Range Rats* by Roger Maltbie (Woodford).

Maintain contact with someone who knows your game and swing...and who can catch and correct bad habits before they become ingrained.

It's best to play with someone a bit better than yourself, preferably someone with patience. But lots of people fall in love with the game just playing on their own.

Simple Rule for Better Gardening

Do not be predictable. *Example:* Vary plant heights. Gardens with single-height plants look monotonous.

Jeff Cox, gardening columnist and television host, Kenwood, CA, and author of *Perennial All-Stars: The 150 Best Perennials for Great-Looking, Trouble-Free Gardens.* Rodale Press.

Best and Worst Casino Bets

John Grochowski, Chicago–based author of four books on gaming, including *The Casino Answer Book: How to Overcome the House Advantage When You Play Blackjack, Video Poker & Roulette.* Bonus.

Some bets in a casino offer players a decent chance to win. Others are skewed in favor of the house.

The difference between good and bad bets can be enormous. If you play perfect basic strategy in blackjack, for example, you can narrow the house edge to 0.5%. But if you make the worst bet, you give the house a scary 22.2% advantage.

In some cases, particularly in video poker, the best bets can be counterintuitive. So it's important to follow your strategy rather than your gut instincts.

Here are the best bets—and the bets to avoid—to maximize your prospects of winning and your fun...

BACCARAT

Appearances not withstanding, this is a very simple game.

Best bet: Bet with the banker, which gives the house a 1.17% edge. If you bet with the player, the house has a 1.36% advantage.

Worst bet: Betting on a tie. While this bet pays 8-to-1, the house has a 14.4% edge on this wager.

BLACKJACK

The only way to improve on perfect basic strategy is to count cards. And even that is no guarantee because few players have sufficient bankroll to increase bets in favorable situations and the casino can reshuffle at any time. After that, the best way to increase your chances of winning is to bet aggressively when appropriate.

Best bets: Take every opportunity to double down and split pairs when odds are in your favor—even if you're on a losing streak.

Double down when you have…

- **11,** unless the dealer has an Ace
- **10,** unless the dealer has an Ace or 10
- **9** and the dealer has 3, 4, 5 or 6
- **Ace and 2 or Ace and 3** and the dealer has 5 or 6
- **Ace and 4 or Ace and 5** and the dealer has 4, 5 or 6
- **Ace and 6 or Ace and 7** and the dealer has 3, 4, 5 or 6.

And—always split Aces and 8s…never split 5s or 10s.

Worst bet: Taking insurance. The dealer offers insurance when his/her face card is an Ace. You put up half of your original bet and are paid 2-to-1 if the dealer has blackjack. This would be fair if the dealer's chances of getting blackjack were 33.3%. But they're only 31%, so this is a bad wager.

CRAPS

If you know what you're doing, craps offers good odds by casino standards.

Best bets: *Pass* and *Don't Pass*. These give the house an edge of 1.41% and 1.4%, respectively. This is a bet on a sequence of rolls.

If you make a *Pass* bet and the shooter rolls a 7 or 11, you win.

If he rolls a 2, 3 or 12, you lose. If he rolls anything else, that number becomes his point and you are betting that he will roll the point again before he rolls a 7. The *Don't Pass* bet is exactly the opposite, except it is a "push" if the shooter rolls a 12.

The best thing about these bets is they enable you to take advantage of "free odds." If the shooter's first roll is a 4, 5, 6, 8, 9 or 10, you can back up your bet with an additional wager that is paid at true odds instead of even money. How much that free odds wager can be depends on house rules. The more odds allowed, the better for the player.

If odds of 10 times your original wager are allowed, your bet of, say, $5 would still give a slight advantage to the house, but the rest of your bet—perhaps as much as $50—would give the house no edge at all.

To increase this benefit, lower your original bet. That lowers your exposure to the house's edge. Then take maximum advantage of free odds whenever you can.

Worst bet: Betting the next roll will be a 7. This gives the house a 16.67% edge.

ROULETTE

As in video poker, the equipment matters. Whenever possible, play a wheel that has only a 0, and not both 0 and 00, to reduce the house advantage from 5.26% to 2.7%. "0"-only wheels are common in Europe, but they are almost nonexistent in the US—although you can find them at the Paris and Monte Carlo hotels in Las Vegas.

Best bet: On a standard American wheel, there is no best bet. Betting black or red, odd or even, is no better than putting every bet on a single number.

If you want to play a long time, stick to the bets with low odds, such as black or red. If you want to increase your chances of walking away a big winner, bet individual numbers.

Worst bet: The five-number bet. This raises the house edge to 7.89%.

VIDEO POKER

Whenever possible, in the basic *Jacks or Better* game, play the 9–6 version (which pays 9-to-1 for a full house and 6-to-1 for a flush)…rather than the 6–5 version (which pays 6-to-1 for a full house and 5-to-1 for a flush).

The 9–6 machines are common in Las Vegas and can be found in New Jersey, Mississippi, Missouri and Illinois. If you play 500 hands an hour for $1 a piece, your expected loss in a 9–6 game is $12.50 per hour. In a 6–5 game, your expected losses rise to $125 per hour.

Best bet: A royal flush hardly ever occurs in a regular poker game, but it is a significant factor in video poker. This leads to some strategies you would never employ in real poker.

Example: If you have four to a royal flush, discard your fifth card even if the discard gave you a straight or a flush.

To win more: Play the maximum number of coins at a low-priced machine, rather than the minimum number of coins at a higher-priced machine.

Reason: You'll receive a higher payout—800-to-1 instead of 250-to-1—for a royal flush.

Worst bet: Other than drawing to an inside straight,* the biggest mistake people make is underestimating the value of a small pair. Many players—knowing that they need at least a pair of Jacks to have a winning hand—will discard a small pair to retain a single high card. This is a mistake. Keep the pair. Even if you hold four to a straight and a low pair, keep the pair and draw three cards, hoping to draw two pair, three of a kind, a full house or even four of a kind. If you have a small pair and four to a flush, draw for the flush.

*An inside draw limits the number of cards that can complete a straight because the card needed is "inside," or between two other cards.

Casino Gambling Self-Defense

Play only games that you have a fair chance of winning—blackjack, video poker and craps.

Winning blackjack tip: Play better by taking a card if you have 13, 14, 15 or 16 and no ace...and the dealer shows a 7 or higher. *Exception:* If you are dealt two 8s for 16, the best strategy is to split cards for better hands.

Winning slots tip: Play slots near cashiers or change booths—they usually have higher payouts. Search out a single payline, two-coin maximum with a "double" payout feature—these basic slots stretch your gambling bankroll. If you win big, ask for a check to avoid wasting your cash—and as protection against robbery. If you choose to drink while gambling, eat carbohydrates so the alcohol is absorbed more slowly.

Gayle Mitchell, president, Casino Players Workshop & Seminars, Phoenix.

15

Car Smarts

Sneaky...and Illegal Car-Leasing Traps—Proven Ways to Avoid Them

There are many virtues for consumers to leasing a car, but dealers push leasing for one main reason—it is often more profitable for them than selling cars outright.

Despite major investigations and new disclosure requirements for lease contracts, it is easy to mislead consumers about the costs of leasing versus buying. Common traps...

BOGUS LEASE RATES

Leasing companies and dealers are not required to disclose the effective *Annual Percentage Rate* (APR) on a car loan, which is now 8% to 9%.

Instead, a car dealer may disclose only the *lease factor*—also called the *lease rate* or *money factor*—which is a much lower number. It is used to calculate the interest portion of the monthly lease payment. Multiply the lease factor by 24 to figure out the real interest rate.

Example: A lease factor of five is 0.005. So the actual interest rate is 0.005 x 24, or 12%.

A salesperson might inflate quotes on monthly payments on a purchase to make a lease look better. Or he/she might draw up a lease using an inflated cap cost—the car price used to calculate the monthly payments. This is higher than the actual price you would pay to buy the car outright. A higher cap cost is sometimes explained away by saying that it includes finance charges—but in reality it doesn't.

Self-defense: Don't sign a contract on the spot. Take it home, and do the math with a knowledgeable friend.

Mark Eskeldson, consumer advocate and auto expert based in Fair Oaks, CA. His Web site, *www.CarInfo.com*, provides useful information on a wide variety of automotive topics. He is author of *Leasing Lessons for Smart Shoppers* and *What Car Dealers Don't Want You to Know*. Technews Publishing.

LEASE-TO-OWN TRAP

If a dealer claims that leasing can save you money even if you ultimately want to own the car, check the residual value—the *option-to-purchase* price in the lease contract.

Dealers often greatly inflate residual value to lower monthly payments, but at the end of the lease you usually end up paying more than what the car is actually worth.

When your lease is ending, check residual numbers in the *Automotive Lease Guide*. It is available in most libraries. Check used-car values in car-buying guides, such as National Auto Dealers Association price guides. Your residual value should be no higher than the wholesale or trade-in price. *Useful resources...*

• ***www.carinfo.com*** (click on Leasing Secrets Part II) to learn how to calculate lease payments.

• ***Expert Lease Pro*** from Chart Software (*http://www.autoleasingsoftware.com*) analyzes auto leases for you. *Cost:* $69.95.

THE CALL-BACK TRAP

A few weeks after leasing, a customer may get a call from the dealer, asking for more money or saying he needs to sign a new lease because of a mistake in the contract or an unacceptable credit rating. The customer is told to sign a corrected copy, which might cost "just a few dollars extra" per month.

What to do: You are under no legal obligation to accept a new contract. Respond that you will not sign or pay anything without consulting your attorney, and ask the dealer to put his request in writing. In most cases, a dealer cannot legally rescind the contract or repossess your vehicle as long as you make your payments on time.

SELF-DEFENSE

If your dealer engages in any of these deceptive and illegal sales practices, contact your state's board that licenses auto dealers. That is usually the Department of Motor Vehicles.

Editor's note: The Federal Reserve Board, state regulators, consumer groups and the National Automobile Dealers Association have put together a Web resource on car leasing, *www.bog.frb.Fed.US/pubs/leasing*.

You can also send for the free booklet *Keys to Vehicle Leasing* from the Division of Consumer and Community Affairs, Mail Stop 800, Federal Reserve Board, Washington, DC 20551.

Trade-Ins May Be Better

Trading in a car may be a better deal than selling it yourself. The traditional advice is to sell on your own to make more money than a dealer would allow as a trade-in. But this advice ignores sales taxes—which can add a lot to the cost of a new car. When you trade in, you are generally required to pay the sales tax on the difference between the price of the new car and the trade-in value of your old one. That tax saving can be significant—perhaps matching the extra amount you would get by selling privately. Local sales tax varies—check your state's rules.

Randy Bruce Blaustein, senior tax partner, Blaustein, Greenberg & Co., 155 E. 31 St., New York City 10016.

Best Time to Car Shop

During nasty weather, when there are few customers. Showrooms will be empty and salespeople will be looking to make deals. *Other good times:* Tuesday, Wednesday or Thursday, particularly toward the end of the month. Avoid weekends. *Also helpful:* Shop against the season—buy a convertible in winter...a four-wheel-drive vehicle in summer.

W. James Bragg, founder, Fighting Chance, an information service for new-car shoppers. www.fighting chance.com.

Smart Car Leasing

Make money by getting out of your car lease *early*—when you have six months or less to go. *Reason:* When a lease ends, a number of terms and conditions come into play. You can be penalized for being over mileage limits...not having matching tires...or window glass that is not in perfect shape. *Best:* Six months before your lease is up, market the car on your own. When you have a buyer, transfer ownership through the leasing company. Most leasing companies will let you do this penalty free close to the end of the lease. And the leasing company will often let you transfer the car for less than the market value—you will be able to sell the car for more...and pocket the rest.

Ashly Knapp, CEO of AutoAdvisor.com, independent car buying and leasing firm in Seattle.

More from Ashly Knapp...

Photograph Your Car at the End of the Lease

Worrisome: Leasing companies can bill for damages up to one month after a car is turned in...and unscrupulous ones may try to pin you with damage incurred by someone else. *Best:* Park the car in front of the dealership, and take pictures of the front, back and sides of the vehicle...the interior...and the odometer, so there is no denying that the car was in good condition the day you turned it in. *Helpful:* Use a camera that puts the date on photos.

And more from Ashly Knapp...

Bargain-Hunting Car Buyers

Forget what you have heard—you cannot buy a car directly from the factory over the Internet. Automakers are currently developing systems that make it possible to *order* a car to your specifications, but the purchase will still have to be negotiated and concluded

through a dealer. *True on-line bargains—for a limited time:* Brokers such as *www.carsdirect.com* or *www.carorder.com*. To build a dealer network and attract customers, these brokers are subsidizing the dealers so they can offer bargain prices...but they cannot afford to keep doing this much longer.

Much Shrewder Car Buying

No matter what car price you have negotiated, a salesperson typically will make at least three more attempts to raise the price.

He/she will tell you that the manager won't approve the deal—but in reality he won't talk with the manager until he has tried to bump up the price several times. *Self-defense...*

- **Before shopping,** use the Internet to find the "true" best price for the car you are considering at Web sites such as *www.carsdirect.com* and *www.kelleybluebook.com*.

- **Use prices from one dealer** (or the Internet) to work against the others. This improves your chances of getting the best deal.

- **Not happy?** Leave your number and walk out. Many salespeople will call within 24 hours to match the price quoted by the competition.

David Solomon, president, Nutz & Boltz, automotive information membership organization, Butler, MD. *www.motorminute.com.*

More from David Solomon...

Bottom Line Guide to the Very Best Tires

The recent recall of millions of Firestone tires reminds us just how important tires really are.*

When buying new tires, the first step is deciding what means the most to you.

If you want a comfortable ride, you're not going to get the very best performance. High

*It is safest to buy from a reputable tire dealer that will send recall notices to customers. Ask before purchase.

237

performance may provide inferior poor-weather traction.

Top tires in the basic categories...

TOURING TIRES

Touring tires provide the smoothest ride for driving mostly on paved roads during good weather.

●*All-around favorite:* **Cooper Lifeliner Classic II.** Standard and extra load (for cars that carry extra weight or a trailer). Free replacement for manufacturer's defects. 70,000-mile warranty. *Starting at $39.95.***

●*Sport-utility vehicles (SUVs):* **Cooper HT Discoverer.** Conservative, all-season tread makes this tire appropriate for virtually any road condition, particularly rain. Quiet, comfortable ride. 60,000-mile warranty. *Starting at $59.95.*

●*Minivans:* **Goodyear Regatta 2.** An all-purpose tire with a 75,000-mile warranty. *Starting at $45.*

PERFORMANCE TIRES

Designed mainly for sports car drivers who want agile handling.

Beware: Performance tires often handle poorly in bad weather. Their stiff sidewalls mean a bumpy ride, and they typically have below-average tread life and fuel efficiency.

●*All-around favorite:* **Goodyear Eagle HP Ultra Plus.** Excellent high-speed tire. No warranty, but Goodyear projects a 30,000-mile life. *Starting at $76.*

●*European cars:* **Pirelli P-6000 Sport Veloce.** Offers best combination of ride and high-speed handling for European cars (with a speed rating of up to 140 mph). Comes with a 40,000- or 50,000-mile warranty, depending on the tire. *Starting at $65.*

●*SUVs:* **Pirelli Scorpion.** Provides sportier on-road handling than other SUV tires. 50,000-mile warranty. *Starting at $100.*

POOR-WEATHER TIRES

For those who frequently drive in poor weather or anyone concerned enough about

**Prices vary according to tire size. Prices listed are manufacturers' suggested retail prices. Discounts are usually available.

poor-weather driving that he/she is willing to sacrifice some fuel efficiency or riding comfort. *Top pick...*

●**Goodyear Aquatred-3.** The government rates tire traction from A (best) to C (worst). This tire received top marks, with a unique AA rating. 80,000-mile warranty. *Starting at $50.*

OFF-ROAD DRIVING

Worthwhile for SUV, truck and other four-wheel-drive (4WD) owners who take their vehicles off-road. *Top picks...*

●**Goodyear Wrangler ATS.** For SUVs. Excellent traction on and off road. No warranty. *Starting at $117.*

●**Goodyear Wrangler MTR.** For all off-road 4WDs and SUVs. Puncture-resistant sidewall. No warranty. *Starting at $140.*

SELF-SEALING/RUN-FLAT TIRES

Within two years, all tires will be offered in run-flat versions. These cost about twice as much as conventional tires. A sensor must be installed in each rim and an indicator on the dash.

The technology is so new that I wouldn't recommend these tires yet unless they come with your new car.

Exceptions: Run-flat tires might make sense now for cars with no room for a spare...for people who travel outside of populated areas and don't want to change a flat tire themselves...for people who are willing to pay a premium for absolute safety.

More from David Solomon...

Flat-Tire Self-Defense

Practice changing a tire *before* you have to do the real thing. Make sure you can remove the lug nuts that secure the wheel. Some cars have locking lug nuts as an anti-theft feature—be sure you know where to find the key. Make sure your spare tire is properly inflated—miniaturized ones require high inflation pressures and can only handle slow speeds. *To lengthen tire life:* Check inflation regularly. Have tires rotated and balanced periodically.

Also from David Solomon...

Improve Your Car's Fuel Economy —Big-Time

Use synthetic motor and transmission oil. Synthetic lubes offer extended drain intervals, less wear and better lubrication. *Best:* Red Line Synthetic Oil, 800-624-7958.

•**Install Jacobs Ignition Wires.** They produce better spark, faster starts and increased combustion efficiency. Jacobs Electronics, 800-627-8800.

•**Install Bosch Platinum +4 spark plugs** (if available for your engine size) for better ignition performance, especially while accelerating and during cold warm-up. Bosch, 800-867-7584.

•**Clean leaves and road debris** from the air conditioner condenser to improve its efficiency.

•**Change the air filter** every 30,000 miles.

•**Change the thermostat** every five years or 60,000 miles. As the thermostat ages, it won't close properly, resulting in longer warm-up times, overly rich fuel mixtures and high emissions.

•**Remove extra weight** from your trunk.

•**Inflate tires** to the upper end of the manufacturer's suggested inflation range.

•**Get a major tune-up every 60,000 miles** —even if the owner's manual says 100,000 miles.

•**Install an Optima Spiral-Cell Battery** (if available for your car) for quicker starting. It also uses less horsepower to recharge after starting for much more efficient running. Optima Batteries, 800-292-4359.

And from David Solomon...

Diesel Days?

Diesel cars are making a comeback because of new US rules reducing sulfur in diesel fuel. The rules require that sulfur content drop to 15 parts per million by 2006...down from the current average of 500 parts per million. Cleaner diesel fuel should make diesel engines more efficient, less smelly—and more attractive to US car buyers. *Downside:* Diesel fuel prices are expected to rise in the future—but over its lifetime, a diesel car is still cheaper to own and operate.

Finally from David Solomon...

Donate That Unwanted Car

To get rid of an old car that nobody wants to buy: Give it to one of the many charities that solicit used-car donations. Approximate the car's value (based on mileage and condition) on the receipt, which you can use to justify a tax deduction.

•**Donate it to a technical or vocational school,** which can use it for training purposes and will also let you write it off.

•**See which local auto salvage places will pay the most for it.**

•**Sell it for parts on Internet auction sites.**

Super-Safe Winter Driving

Michael J. Scippa, executive director, Citizens for Reliable and Safe Highways (CRASH), Tiburon, CA.

Always wear a seat belt (about one-third of adults *don't*). Make certain children are safely buckled in *before* you start to drive.

•**Slow down.** It takes four to 10 times as long to stop on ice as on dry pavement.

•**Look far enough down the road** so that you can see tricky situations developing. *Also:* Check your rear- and sideview mirrors frequently for problems approaching from behind.

•**Don't drive when road conditions are poor.** Wait for things to improve.

•**Never drive when fatigued** or under the influence of alcohol or drugs.

•**Keep headlights on**—even in daylight— to make yourself more visible to other motorists.

• **Do not rely on four-wheel drive and antilock brakes.** They are no substitute for slow, careful driving.

• **Keep the inside of the car cool.** You will stay more alert—and windows will stay clearer.

• **In a skid, ease off the accelerator** and steer where you want to go. Avoid using the brakes.

• **Keep jumper cables,** a flashlight and a first-aid kit in your vehicle.

Avoid a Tire Blowout

Keep tires inflated to *exact pressure* recommended by the manufacturer. Check pressure once a month, when tires are cool. *Also:* Look for uneven wear. Place a penny in the tread with Lincoln's head down. When his entire head shows, replace the tire. *Beware:* If you hear thumping while driving, treads are worn. *If you have a blowout:* Lift your foot off the accelerator, and steer to the shoulder. Avoid braking.

Donna Wagner is president of Car Care Council in Port Clinton, OH.

Use Your Car-Safety Features Safely

For the most air bag protection, angle the steering column so the wheel directly faces your chest and abdomen…and adjust your seat to keep at least 10 inches between you and the wheel.

• **Extend your headrest** so it supports the upper part of your head and restricts neck movement backward.

• **If your car has an automatic shoulder belt** and manual seat belt, always use both—people using only the shoulder belt suffer many more chest and abdominal injuries in crashes.

• **Stay focused on driving.** Pull off the road to make phone calls, change CDs, etc.

Tim Hurd, spokesperson, US National Highway Traffic Safety Administration, 407 Seventh St. SW, Washington, DC 20590.

Wisest Way to Jump-Start Your Car

To avoid a mistake that could lead to your car battery blowing up—follow these steps…

• **Inspect the battery.** If the casing is cracked, bulging or showing signs of leakage, don't try to jump-start the car. Instead, have it towed.

• **Attach jumper cables** after making sure that the ignitions of both cars are turned off. Connect one positive terminal to the good car, the other to the dead car, using the same-color cables. Then attach one end of the other cable to the negative terminal of the good car's battery—and the other end to the dead car's engine block.

• **Start the engine of the good car.** Wait about 10 minutes, turn off the engine and then try to start the dead car. Let it idle for three to five minutes, until it can run on its own. Then turn off the revived car. If it does not catch immediately, wait a minute before trying again.

• **Disconnect both ends of the negative cable**—starting with the revived car—and then the positive one. Start the revived car and run it for at least one-half hour to recharge the battery.

Self-defense: If your car battery were to blow up, dangerous acid could fly up in your face. Always wear safety glasses when jump-starting a car. And—after a problem with your battery, have your mechanic check it out.

Dennis Spano, manager, Sears Auto Center, Paramus, NJ.

Car Safety for Kids

Kids should ride in car booster seats until they weigh at least 80 pounds—usually around age nine? Children who are shorter than four-foot-nine and who weigh less than 80 pounds cannot safely use adult seat belts. The belts do not fit properly, which can result in injuries to a child's head, internal organs and spinal cord in a crash.

Dennis Durbin, MD, pediatric emergency doctor, Children's Hospital of Philadelphia.

Side Air Bags Are Lifesavers

Only 12% of cars have them—but in a recent safety ranking, more than two-thirds of the 30 safest vehicles had side air bags. Expect to pay $250 to $400 for side air bags when they are offered as an option. On some luxury models, they are standard equipment.

Study of the safest autos, minivans and sport-utility vehicles by *The Wall Street Journal*.

The Best Air Bags

Safest car air bags feature a two- stage design. They deploy with low force in low-speed crashes…and with more force in high-speed accidents. Many luxury sedans—as well as Ford Taurus and Honda Accord—have two-stage air bags. *Also:* If you are buying a used car and are concerned about air bags, look for a 1998 or newer model. Many air bags were redesigned for greater safety in the 1998 model year, when automakers were permitted to reduce the power of air bags by 20% to 35%.

Noble Bowie, director, Office of Planning and Consumer Programs, National Highway Traffic Safety Administration, Washington, DC.

Proper Mirror Adjusting

Properly adjusted side mirrors help you see on the sides of your car—*not behind you*. Adjust each mirror so you can just see the back corner of your car when leaning slightly toward the mirror.

Mark Lee Edwards, PhD, managing director, traffic safety department, American Automobile Association, Heathrow, FL.

Get Rid of that Smelly Car

To reduce the rotten-egg odor common in and near newer cars that have three-way catalytic converters, try different brands of gasoline—some may contain less sulfur. Use an emissions-control-system cleaner, available at service stations and auto parts stores. Avoid full-throttle acceleration—that increases unburned gasoline, intensifying the odor. Be sure your ignition timing is set properly. *If these ideas fail:* Ask a mechanic about recalibrating the engine computer or changing the air/fuel mixture.

Bob Sikorsky, author of *Drive It Forever* (ATG Media) and syndicated automotive columnist.

They're Big, but Are They Safe?

Don't get taken in by the perceived safety of a sport-utility vehicle (SUV). SUV drivers tend to take bigger risks than other motorists. It's easy to overestimate an SUV's maneuverability. *Biggest danger:* An SUV's high center of gravity can cause it to flip over during sharp turns. *Braking:* Because of the extra weight, most SUVs take longer to slow, especially during turns. *Winter driving:* SUVs do well pushing through snow—but can lose their grip when they are cornering on wet or icy pavement as easily as cars can. *Helpful:* Consider a hands-on class at a driving school.

Anthony Ricci, president of Advanced Driving & Security, Inc., North Kingstown, RI.

Better Cruise Control

Adaptive cruise control keeps your car a set distance away from the vehicle you're following. The systems—available as an option on top Mercedes models and included in the ultraluxury package of Lexus models—use radar or laser units to send signals that are reflected back from the vehicle in front of you. If you are too close, your car slows automatically. Warning lights and audible signals alert drivers when they must take over from the automatic systems. *Cost:* Mercedes, about $2,800...Lexus, about $12,500 for the ultraluxury package.

Stephan Wilkinson, automotive editor who has test-driven and reviewed cars independently for more than 20 years.

16

Home and Family

Stop Throwing Dollars Down the Drain... Up the Chimney... Big Home Money Wasters

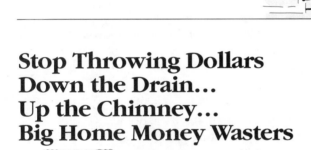

Some homeowners spend money needlessly when it comes to taking care of their homes. *The most common home-maintenance money wasters...*

HIGH-END PAINT

Repainting is one of the most common home-maintenance jobs. And since time and labor—not the paint itself—are the major expenses, many consumers select high-end paints.

Overspending on paint does not necessarily improve the quality or life of a paint job.

An expensive paint might spatter or drip less—but for most of us, that's not enough to justify paying as much as $40 a gallon, rather than $20 or less.

I'm a big fan of store brands, such as Ace Hardware's. I would certainly think twice before buying any paint selling for more than $20 a gallon.

When repainting the exterior: Certain mistakes mean the whole job will have to be redone. *Biggest problems...*

●**Scraping off loose paint,** then failing to coat exposed wood with oil-based primer before repainting.

●**Painting when the temperature is below 50°F.**

DECK REPLACEMENT

I get many calls from homeowners who want to replace decks that are showing their age. At a typical price of $10 to $12 per square foot, installing a new deck can easily cost $1,500 to $3,500. To make an older deck

---

Bill Keith, owner of Tri-Star Remodeling in St. John, IN, and a 16-year contracting veteran. Mr. Keith is host of the cable-TV program *The Home Tips Show*, broadcast in the upper Midwest. He has a free remodeling answer service through *www.billkeith.com.*

look great for another 10 years or more, pull out the nails on the flooring and turn over the boards. The wood's underside is rarely as weathered as the top. Have it pressure-washed, sanded and water-treated.

Since nails pull out of wood over time, consider replacing them with deck screws. This is easy with a cordless drill. *Best screws:* Square-drive deck screws one inch longer than the thickness of the deck board.

NEW FIXTURES

Repairing or reconditioning bathroom and kitchen fixtures is far cheaper than simply replacing them.

Example I: Cast-iron tubs eventually chip or fade—or simply no longer match a redesigned bathroom. Most homeowners replace them with modern fiberglass tubs.

A cast-iron tub was most likely installed before the wallboards went in—so walls must be torn apart to remove it. The new tub might cost $300—but the cost of removing the old one and installing the new one could easily tack another $1,500 onto the bill.

Better: Recoat a cast-iron tub through a process called *refinishing.* Your local plumbing store should be able to recommend someone to do this for you. *Cost:* About $300.

Example II: Leaky faucets are among the most common kitchen and bathroom problems. A new faucet might solve the problem—but it's likely to cost more than $100, and it may not match the room and the original unit.

Better: Take the leaky valve cartridge to a local plumbing store. Chances are a 59-cent washer will do the job. If not, the plumbing store should be able to replace the whole valve for $8 to $12.

Refurbishing also can be better for kitchens. It costs $8,000 to $30,000 to redo a typical kitchen. But you can refinish cabinets and replace the countertop and the sink for less than $5,000.

If you have solid wood kitchen cabinets, refinishing might be the only way to avoid taking a step down in craftsmanship. Few modern companies make solid wood cabinets. Check with a local hardware store or a trusted contractor for cabinet-resurfacing recommendations.

RELYING ON WARRANTIES

Warranties are only as good as the companies behind them.

I'm embarrassed to say that this is a mistake I made a number of years back. I was replacing the thermalpane windows on the second floor of my house, and I decided to use a lesser-known brand. I felt safe because the windows came with a long-term warranty.

Seven years later, the windows began fogging up—the most common form of failure with thermalpane windows. When I tried to use my warranty, I found the company was out of business.

Stick with well-known companies. Most established companies have 10-year warranties and supplies to service older windows at a fraction of the cost to replace them.

Roof shingles are another place where people pay extra for long warranties of questionable value. Most roof shingles come with a 25-year warranty. But you can pay up to double to get shingles with a 40-year warranty. Unfortunately, in most climates, you are unlikely to get more than 25 years on any asphalt or fiberglass shingle.

OVERCLEANING

Some people take their desire for cleanliness too far and damage their homes. Overcleaning leads to premature aging of components.

Example I: Overscrubbing sinks and tubs with abrasive cleansers is a sure way to wear off the finish.

Better: Head to a plumbing store—or a well-stocked home-improvement store—for a bathroom-fixture coating such as Gel Gloss. This provides a protective coating for both fiberglass and ceramics that lasts six to eight weeks. Water spots can be easily removed with a soft cloth.

Example II: Overcleaning carpets. Steam cleaning more than twice a year damages the carpet. If that doesn't provide enough cleaning for you, consider putting inexpensive throw rugs over high-traffic areas.

Also: When replacing carpeting, few homeowners pay attention to the padding underneath. But a poor-quality pad can contribute as much to reducing the life of the carpet as the quality of the carpet itself. I recommend a minimum of six pounds rebound padding—eight pounds is better and should add only $75 to $150 to any job.

HIGH ENERGY BILLS

Everyone complains about high heating bills, yet few homeowners take the simple home-maintenance steps necessary to reduce them.

Mistake I: Not putting in enough attic insulation. More heat is lost through inadequate roof insulation than through any other part of the home. Adding attic insulation is an inexpensive and easy job. A professional can blow insulation into ceiling areas for $250 to $750.

Important: Without proper venting, you could get ice damming or attic moisture leading to wood rot. Hardware stores sell Styrofoam baffles that can be slid down into the eaves near where the roof meets the attic floor to ensure the necessary air flow.

Mistake II: Using a furnace made before 1980. Old furnaces were only 67% efficient at best—one-third of the fuel they burned was wasted. Modern furnaces are 90% efficient. A new furnace costs $1,500 to $5,000—but with current energy prices, it is money well spent.

Power Outage Remedy

Gasoline-powered home generator is a smart buy if your home is prone to lengthy power outages. A 5,000-watt generator—available at home centers—should keep the refrigerator, heat, lights and even television running until power is restored. *Cost:* $1,800 to $2,700. *Favorite brand:* Honda. An electrician will install a manual transfer switch, which changes over power from your usual electric service to the generator. *Cost:* $90 to $150. *Precautions:* Start the generator once a month to exercise the motor. Keep some gasoline on hand—in a metal or plastic can outside or in a shed. Refill it every three months—gasoline is only good for about 90 days.

Allen Gallant, master electrician, *This Old House* magazine, and owner of Gallant Electric, 100 Villa St., Waltham, MA 02453.

Better Curb Appeal

Improve your home's curbside appeal—and you'll increase its value by 10%. For the front of the house, choose flowering trees and shrubs that bloom in the spring, produce fruits and berries in the summer and have attractive foliage in the fall. *All-time favorites:* Aromatic sumac, bayberry, firethorn, hawthorn, American cranberry bush.

Allan Swenson, Kennebunk, Maine, author of more than 50 books on plants and gardening, including *Fruit Trees for the Home Gardener.* Lyons.

Home Sellers, Beware

People posing as buyers are committing a number of assaults and other crimes. *To reduce risk while showing your home...*

- **Ask to see a photo ID**—to make sure the potential buyer is who he/she says he is.
- **Keep all lights on**...and drapes and shades open during a showing.
- **Have someone else in the house with you.**
- **Carry a cell phone** with quick-speed dialing to 911.

And: Trust your intuition. If someone makes you uncomfortable, have an excuse available—for example, a last-minute appointment—to end a showing quickly.

Jim LaValley, personal safety instructor and real estate broker in upstate New York.

Mortgage Opportunities

No-money-down mortgages are being offered by some lenders at rates one-half to one percentage point above rates on conventional mortgages. *Reason:* Lenders are facing more competition in a dwindling refinancing market. Zero-down mortgages usually require borrowers to have higher incomes and better credit ratings than people seeking mortgages with a down payment. *Some major lenders offering zero-down mortgages:* Bank of America, 888-391-7538...Countrywide Home Loans, 800-669-6659...GMAC Mortgage, 800-638-4622...Wells Fargo Home Mortgage Inc., 800-234-1625.

Keith Gumbinger, vice president, HSH Associates, mortgage research firm, Butler, NJ.

Very Wise Kitchen Renovations Look Luxurious for a Whole Lot Less

John Rusk, president of Rusk Renovations in New York City. He has been doing home renovations for 15 years. He is author of *On Time and on Budget: A Home Renovation Survival Guide.* Main Street.

Renovating your kitchen is one of the best ways to increase your enjoyment of your home. It is also the best way to increase the value of your home. But remodeling is expensive—$20,000 and up... and up.

The secret of a cost-efficient renovation is knowing where to be thrifty and where to go all out...

● **Consider how long you plan to stay in your home.** If you plan to live there for at least 10 years, renovate according to your personal taste.

If you might move within 10 years, it is safer to go for a classic look. If you are not sure whether people will like a style in a few years, don't use it.

● **Consider safety.** Too often, people ignore the kitchen's underlying infrastructure.

Your first dollars should go toward replacing old pipes and wiring. Plumbing or electrical problems that surface after your renovation could force a costly "renovation of the renovation."

If you have an older house or suspect that there is a problem, have a house inspector or an engineer assess the electrical, plumbing and heating systems before you start remodeling.

● **Consult a design professional.** Use a kitchen planner—at $50 to $200 per hour—to avoid costly mistakes.

If you are only doing your kitchen: Consult a kitchen planner in lieu of an architect. A consultation should take between two and five hours.

If your renovation is more extensive than just the kitchen: Use a kitchen planner in addition to an architect. *Resources...*

● Ikea and Home Depot offer free planning services to their customers, but local kitchen stores often have more experienced professionals.

● National Kitchen & Bath Association (877-652-2776...*www.nkba.org/consumer/find-apro.asp*) can recommend certified designers in your area.

● **Splurge on "jewelry"...pinch pennies on big-ticket items.** To give your kitchen a high-end look, go all out on the things you see and touch every day. Stylish cabinet knobs or faucets go a long way toward improving the look, yet they cost little more than plain knobs or faucets. *Resources...*

● For interesting and affordable hardware, try Restoration Hardware (888-243-9720... *www.restorationhardware.com*).

● For fixtures, try The Renovator's Supply (800-659-2211)...or Waterworks (800-899-6757).

● **Reface cabinetry.** Unless they're in bad condition, don't replace old cabinets. Reface them by changing the doors and hardware. *Savings:* One-half to two-thirds the cost of replacing the entire cabinet.

● **Buy midrange major appliances.** The difference between medium- and high-end ovens and refrigerators can be thousands of dollars—with only a marginal improvement in quality and looks.

Check out the GE Profile Series—beautiful and functional but not outrageously expensive.

Exception: A high-end dishwasher can make a difference in day-in and day-out performance. Try Miele (800-843-7231) or Bosch (800-944-2904).

●**Change the colors instead of the architecture.** If you are on a tight budget, make paint your renovation tool of choice. A set of high-fashion Ralph Lauren colors may give your kitchen the lift you want—for less than $2,000.

●**Make your kitchen appear larger without moving walls.** Tearing down old walls and building new ones is very expensive. Instead, consider adding a skylight. It adds natural light and raises a portion of the ceiling, visually expanding the space...and it can cost as little as $1,400 to $4,000.

Lower-cost alternative: A "sunpipe," a tube inserted through a hole drilled into your roof. Prices vary depending on size. *Average cost:* $300 to $500. 800-844-4786...*www.sun pipe.com.*

Bright wall colors, light-colored cabinets, open shelves and glass cabinet doors also make a small kitchen look spacious.

MORE WAYS TO SAVE

●**Countertops** can easily cost $10,000.

For high-end renovations: Granite still remains the hardest and most scratch-and-stain resistant material. Corian, DuPont's synthetic countertop material, is more popular—but it is often as expensive as granite, depending on your area of the country.

For tight budgets: Formica is inexpensive and durable. Give it a high-end look by edging it in oak, maple or cherry. The edging will also protect the Formica from chipping. *Cost:* About $10 to $20/foot.

For a cool, "retro" look: Edge Formica counters with aluminum, just as in diners of the 1950s. Available from Meyer Decorative Surfaces (800-696-8502). *Cost:* $10 to $20/foot.

●**Lighting.** Every kitchen benefits from under-cabinet lights. Inexpensive ministrip fluorescent or quartz halogen lights make a big difference. They're easy to install yourself. But make sure your cabinets have trim at the bottom to hide these fixtures.

The right ceiling fixture will do more to define the look of your kitchen than anything else. For great reproduction fixtures, try Rejuvenation Lamp and Fixture Co. (888-343-8548).

●**Flooring.** Wood is one of the least practical choices. Over time, moisture will cause the finish to wear. It especially doesn't hold up well in wet, high-traffic areas, such as in front of a sink. If you insist on wood, be sure it is well-coated with polyurethane.

Good alternatives: Vinyl or ceramic tile are durable and attractive.

For something that is easy on the eyes and feet, try laminated cork. It is resistant to moisture damage and decay, and it wears well. Wicanders Cork flooring (800-828-2675) makes both cork-vinyl composite floor tile and natural cork tile.

●**Backsplashes.** A countertop should have a four-inch backsplash covering the wall, but it's a good idea—and good-looking—to add a full-height tile backsplash, at least behind the stove. It simplifies cleanup. Translucent glass tile backsplashes are popular now. *Cost:* As low as $10/square foot...but can exceed $70/square foot.

For a professional-looking kitchen, install cut-to-size stainless steel backsplashes, which are durable and inexpensive.

To Get Rid Of Roaches

Eliminate their drinking sources—they can only survive three weeks without water. Plug leaks, insulate sweaty pipes, empty bottles and don't leave dishes in the sink. Sprinkle boric acid powder where roaches like to frequent—in the kitchen and bathrooms. When they eat it, they die.

David George Gordon, author of *The Compleat Cockroach*. Ten Speed Press.

Kidspeak 101: Better Communications With Your Children... Much Better

Paul Coleman, PsyD, psychologist and family therapist in private practice in Wappingers Falls, New York...and father of three. He is author of five books, most recently, *How to Say It to Your Kids: The Right Words to Solve Problems, Soothe Feelings, & Teach Values*. Prentice Hall.

The way that parents talk to their children can either foster closeness or turn them away. It's all in how it is done.

There are six communication styles, which I group under the mnemonic **TENDER**—*Teach, Empathize, Negotiate, Dos & Don'ts, Encourage and Report*.

Parents use all of these styles, but frequently rely on only one or two.

It's best to vary your style according to the situation. Just as cross-training—exercising various muscle groups—builds a stronger body, varying conversational styles strengthens parent–child relationships.

TEACHING

Teaching can be a warm, meaningful experience. But if it degenerates into lectures and nagging, the message gets lost.

Best times for teaching: When kids calmly ask questions...aren't anxious or preoccupied...and you are unlikely to be critical.

Watch your tone—a harsh, exasperated voice will add to a child's stress and discourage discussion. *You might begin with phrases such as...*

Let me explain...

Watch how I do it and then you try...

Interesting choice—why did you pick that answer?

EMPATHIZING

Empathy is important when children are feeling strong emotions.

It is easier for children to express concerns to someone who listens and accurately reflects their feelings, rather than someone who dismisses them.

Example: Your daughter comes home upset because her best friend dumped her to join a more popular crowd. You might be tempted to say, *Don't worry, she wasn't much of a friend anyway. You'll make new friends.* But that isn't empathy.

An empathic response mirrors her feelings. You might reply, It must hurt to have her reject you...or You're feeling pretty sad about losing her friendship.

Best time for empathy: When a child is emotional and unlikely to listen to reason. If your child is sensitive by nature or if you are unsure about what's bothering him/her, empathizing is a valuable way to open a conversation.

NEGOTIATING

Negotiating is an important social skill as kids mature. Use negotiating prudently—not out of desperation and not in the form of bribery.

Some things are nonnegotiable—bedtime, curfews, finishing homework, playing fairly, etc. You are the parent and you set the standards. Stick to them.

As kids ask for more privileges, such as buying their own clothes or staying out later, begin negotiations by discussing the responsibilities that go along with those freedoms. Listen to their requests...ask for their reasoning ...then negotiate an agreement.

Examples of negotiation-style statements...

Before we leave for the movies, I want you to pick up your things. Which room would you like to start with?

Before we get into what you want, I need these things to happen...

Best times for negotiating: When you want your child to take on more responsibility...to learn to compromise...or to understand the consequences of keeping or breaking his agreements.

DOS AND DON'TS

Dos and don'ts are nonnegotiable rules and commands. State them briefly in a friendly or neutral tone—and no more.

If you follow your statements with a rationale, you invite your child to try outwitting you or bending the rules. And don't plead, as in *I reeeaaaallllly would like you to....*

With young children, rules can be stated in the teaching style.

Example: No eating food in the living room because....

However, if you explain every rule as children get older, you invite unnecessary discussion, as in *But I promise I won't spill my juice on the new sofa...*

If your child tries to argue, reply calmly but firmly. *Example...*

Child: But my friends stay out later...

Parent: Your friends don't set curfews in our family.

Sometimes enforcing a rule is best done by linking it with an empathic or negotiating statement.

Examples: I know you don't agree, but the rule is...or You can ride your bike to the store, but only if you wear a helmet.

Best times for dos and don'ts: When you have your child's full attention...when he is causing or risking harm...when you are clear about what you want...when you are capable of enforcing the rules.

ENCOURAGING

Encouraging includes praise of positive actions and efforts...as well as reassurance.

Too many parents are quick to criticize poor behavior but slow to praise good behavior. Criticizing is not helpful without explaining a desirable alternative.

Instead of criticizing, guide and reinforce good behavior with statements such as...

That was thoughtful of you to share your snack with your friends...

I know that science project wasn't easy, but I'm proud of you for working so hard to finish it...

Great job! I really liked it when you....

Then mention a specific detail to show that you noticed and appreciated the result.

Best time for encouragement: As soon as possible when you observe self-control, considerate behavior or a good effort. Use common sense, however. If you lay it on too thick, your encouragement will seem insincere.

REPORTING

Reporting refers to statements of fact. It is normal conversation. Parents often underuse this conversational style because they're too focused on instructing, disciplining or criticizing.

Best times for reporting: Talking about your day at dinner...mentioning what you would like to do next weekend...stating your appreciation, such as *I really like it when you're on the phone only 15 minutes.*

Reporting invites conversation with questions, like *How was school?* or *What did you learn at your swimming lesson?*

It also involves stating your opinion (*I like going to the beach...*) or expressing your feelings (*I was so annoyed at work today when...*).

Don't misuse reporting when you mean something else. For example, don't report that you dislike a certain behavior when you really mean, *Stop doing that.*

Better Disciplining For Children

Don't use read-aloud time to reward children for washing up...or as punishment for bad behavior. If you connect books with behavior, children will see reading as a weapon. *Also:* Avoid turning off the TV for reading. Children will blame reading for their loss of TV time. *Better:* Limit the amount of time a child can spend watching TV. If TV limits are new in your house, wait a week before books become one of the suggested non-TV activities. This way, books are associated with fun, not with deprivation.

Jim Trelease, education consultant, Springfield, MA, and author of *The Read-Aloud Handbook*. Penguin USA.

Weigh Your Child's Backpack

If it weighs more than 20% of his/her body weight, he is at risk for back and muscle strain. *Helpful:* Have your child weed out unnecessary items every week...leave items such as gym clothes in school if possible... store things in his school locker instead of carrying the backpack during the day. *Also:* Shoulder straps over each arm should be tightened so the pack is flush against his back. *And:* A wheeled pack can be helpful for kids who must carry heavy loads.

Charlotte Alexander, MD, orthopedist, Houston Orthopedic Sports Medicine Associates.

Danger Year for Kids And Drugs

Sixth grade is a dangerous time for kids and substance abuse. Four times as many sixth-graders as fourth-graders report smoking cigarettes or marijuana...twice as many say they drink beer. The actual percentages are small —but there is clearly increased substance abuse by the time children reach sixth grade. *One possible reason:* Incorrect perception of peers. Fourteen percent of sixth-graders say they think their friends smoke marijuana—but only 4% say they actually do.

Jay DeWispelaere, executive director, Pride, an organization that educates schools and parents on drug abuse, Newaygo, MI.

Antibiotic Trap

Babies given antibiotics during their first year of life are almost twice as likely to develop allergies later in life—if at least one parent also has hay fever. This recent finding supports the theory that infectious disease plays a key role in "toughening" a child's immune system so that it's better able to ward off serious illness later on. *Implication:* Some conditions warrant antibiotics, but their use should be restricted, whenever possible, in early childhood.

Jos Droste, MD, epidemiologist, University of Antwerp, Antwerp, Belgium. His study of 1,206 children seven to eight years of age was presented at a recent meeting of the European Respiratory Society.

Weather Outside Is Frightful...What to Do With the Kids

Volleyball. Use balloons instead of balls. Separate the sides with a rope stretched across the floor.

●**Miniature golf.** For clubs, attach a stiff sponge to a yardstick with masking tape. *For obstacles*—use building blocks...ramps or "tents" made from cardboard...shoe boxes with ends cut out.

●**Races.** Have kids rush to the finish with balloons between their knees...or tennis balls balanced in soup spoons...or shoe boxes on their feet.

●**Crazy catch.** Paper cups for mitts and crushed aluminum foil for the ball.

●**Magazine scavenger hunt.** Look for specific pictures—smiling child, new car, sports player, purple object, etc.—in old magazines. Pictures can be cut out to make a collage.

●**Chez Kids restaurant.** Kids choose the name...make a sign...plan the menu...invent names for the dishes...set the table...take the orders...help with food preparation and serving.

●**"Tell-it-like-it-is" videos.** Have kids videotape a day in the life of your family—waking up, shaving, playing with pets, getting ready for bed, etc.

Linda Hetzer, mother of two and New York–based author of *Rainy Days & Saturdays* (Workman) and *50 Fabulous Parties for Kids* (Crown).

For a Much Better Present and Future with Your Teenager

Lawrence Bauman, PhD, clinical psychologist in New York City and father of two. He is author of *The Ten Most Troublesome Teenage Problems and How to Solve Them*. Citadel.

When children are young, it is easy for parents to find activities to entertain them. But as they grow older, it becomes more challenging.

Once they hit their teens, you may think it is impossible to come up with activities kids will enjoy doing with you. *But try these...*

●**Rent a video.** Let your teen choose the movie...get some snack foods...and sprawl out for two hours of fun and no-brainer activity.

●**Invite your teen to a movie.** Let him/her choose which one he wants to see. Talk about the movie on your drive home. Once again, sharing and communicating are the keys. The movie is merely the medium.

●**Cook a meal together.** Let your teen choose the menu...and don't worry about nutrition. Working in close quarters and dividing up the cooking chores provides an opportunity for small talk, which establishes teamwork and trust.

●**Go out for coffee or hot chocolate.** Stepping out to the local café—especially on a cloudy Sunday afternoon—is a great way to break up a dreary day. This promotes small talk, which often leads to discussion of weightier issues.

●**Do your chores together.** You don't have to call it work. Washing the car or running errands provides time to talk. Use the opportunity to tell your teen something that you like about him. Everyone needs to hear compliments.

●**Go shopping.** This activity is not limited to mothers and daughters. My son and I like to go shopping for jazz CDs.

●**Exercise together.** It should be an activity that you both enjoy. Teens like to show off what they've learned. In my family, we're big tennis players. My son always likes to impress me with his slice serve...and my daughter is proud of her passing forehand.

●**See a play.** Most kids prefer musicals with a beat and great singing or dancing. When our daughter was 15, we took her to see the musical *Rent*. She sang along to the sound track for almost a year before moving on to other recordings.

●**Travel.** Going away for a few days affords parent and teen an opportunity to share time in a new environment...get needed rest and relaxation...eat at different restaurants.

●**Make the most of drive time.** Find an oldies radio station and sing along together—hum when the lyrics escape you—or bring along your favorite cassettes or music CDs. This is a great way to put a positive spin on idle time.

Subtle Signs of Newborn Health Problems

Call a doctor immediately if your infant exhibits any of these symptoms...

●**Poor appetite** or difficulty sucking.

●**Lethargy** or difficulty being awakened.

●**Weak, mousy cry,** high-pitched whimpering or excessive irritability.

●**Pain** or tenderness in any area.

●**No urination** for eight to 12 hours.

●**Sunken eyes** or doughy skin that doesn't return to normal when pressed.

●**Any elevation of temperature** in a baby six months or younger.

SIGNS OF A VISION PROBLEM

●**Gazes at something intently** but only one eye seems aimed at the object.

●**Squints or tilts his/her head** to one side when examining something.

●**Doesn't appear to see** or react to a family member at a distance.

●**Has one eye wandering** or crossed eyes.

SIGNS OF A HEARING PROBLEM

Have your child evaluated by a specialist if in the first six months he…

●**Does not react to unexpected loud noises.**

●**Does not freely imitate sound.**

●**Does not turn his head in the direction of a voice.**

Bethany Kandel is mother of two young children and author of *The Expert Parent: Everything You Need to Know from All the Experts in the Know*. Pocket.

Teach Your Children To Think for Themselves… And Solve Their Own Problems

Myrna B. Shure, PhD, developmental psychologist and professor of psychology at MCP Hahnemann University in Philadelphia. She is author of *Raising a Thinking Child* (Pocket) and *Raising a Thinking Preteen* (Holt).

When it comes to disciplining their kids, most parents resort to power, suggesting or explaining. These methods are *ineffective*.

●**Power** means yelling, spanking, commanding or otherwise trying to impose your will on your children. All parents yell at their kids sometimes. But if power is the main disciplinary technique, kids get angry and frustrated…and that can lead to even more behavior problems.

●**Suggesting** is a more positive approach —although it is still inadequate. Instead of telling kids what *not* to do, the parent tells them what they *should* do.

Example: You should *ask your brother for what you want—instead of grabbing it from him.*

●**Explaining** takes suggesting one step further—the parent tells the child *why* he/she should be doing things differently.

Example: If you grab, you might break the toy…or Kids won't want to be friends with you.

Though more constructive than the power approach, both suggesting and explaining treat the child as passive. The parent does all the talking and thinking. The child tunes out—he has heard all this before.

PROBLEM-SOLVING

A more effective approach is *problem-solving*—coaching your child to analyze his behavior and its consequences. Then he can devise his own alternatives. By age four, most children have the reasoning ability to benefit from this process.

Children who solve their own problems are less aggressive, better able to cope with frustration and more empathetic. They do better in school and are more resourceful. They can stand up to peer pressure.

Problem-solving is a dialogue—not a monologue. To do it, resist the urge to tell the child what's wrong or how to improve.

ASK QUESTIONS

●**What happened?** You may have to ask this question several times to get the full story.

●**How do you think he felt when you…?**

●**How did you feel when he…?**

●**Can you think of a different way to solve this problem?**

Example: A mother saw her five-year-old, Mike, fighting with his friend Joey.

Mother: What happened?

Mike: Joey took my truck.

Mother: What happened when he took your truck?

Mike: I grabbed it back.

Mother: What happened then?

Mike: Joey hit me.

Mother: How do you think Joey felt when you grabbed the truck?

Mike: Mad.

Mother: How did you feel when Joey hit you?

Mike: Mad.

Mother: *What can you do so you both won't be mad and Joey won't hit you?*

Mike(*after thinking a few seconds*): *I could let him play with my race cars.*

Mother: *Good thinking.*

Problem-solving works because it gets children to reflect on what they're doing—and the impact their actions have on themselves and others. It helps children understand other points of view. It also works because the parent listens instead of lectures. The child is made to feel that his point of view matters—and he doesn't have to make a scene to get it across.

BE PERSISTENT

If your child doesn't cooperate at first, be persistent. *Example...*

He may say, *I don't know how Joey feels...* or *I don't care.*

Then you could say, *What might happen if you keep blaming things on Joey?...Can you think of a different way to solve this problem?*

If he simply whines, say, *Can you think of a different way to tell me how you feel?*

Resist offering solutions. If he can't think of any, say, *I know that if you think really hard, you can think of something other than grabbing the toy.*

You may feel that you lack the time to ask all these questions every time your child acts up. But problem-solving actually takes *less* time—and involves much less stress—than lecturing or arguing with your child.

After you've used this technique a while, you'll be able to skip right to the fourth question—*Can you think of a different way to... (solve this problem/tell your friend what you want/tell me how you feel)?*

OLDER CHILDREN

For children ages eight and older (including teenagers), problem-solving can help them deal not just with behavior problems, but also with hurt feelings, fear and disappointment.

Helpful: Add the question, *Why do you think he did that?* Kids this age are old enough to think about complex motives.

Example: Twelve-year-old Cara was hurt because her friend, Suzanne, passed on a secret she had told her. Coached by her mother, Cara guessed her friend might have given away her secret to feel important—or to make a new friend. Cara's mother asked Cara what she could do or say so Suzanne wouldn't do that anymore.

Cara decided to tell Suzanne she was hurt—and that they couldn't be friends if Suzanne continued to be untrustworthy. Suzanne promised to be more careful, and the girls mended their friendship.

If Cara's mother had simply told her to talk with her friend, Cara and Suzanne might well have ended the friendship.

TEACHING KIDS TO PLAN

Most children ages eight and older are also able to learn *sequential planning.* This form of problem-solving helps kids set goals and overcome obstacles. It is useful for a variety of challenges, from homework assignments to making new friends.

What to do: Ask your child to think about the steps involved in reaching a particular goal.

- **What should he do first? And next?**
- **How long is each step likely to take?**
- **What problems might arise?**
- **And how might he handle those problems?**

To help your child finish his homework, ask questions such as...

- **Which subject do you want to start with?**
- **Will you do math before or after soccer practice?**
- **What will you do if a friend calls** while you are working on your English assignment and wants to talk?

This works better than saying, *You're not turning on that TV until you have finished your homework.* A child is more likely to adhere to his own plan than to a plan that has been imposed upon him.

Make Love, Not War... Secrets of Much Happier Marriage Magic for Troubled Relationships

Ellen Wachtel, PhD, JD, psychologist and marital therapist in private practice in New York City. She is author of *We Love Each Other, But....* St. Martin's.

Couples who are dissatisfied with their marriages don't have to resign themselves to lifelong misery...or get divorced. Often, simple changes can turn around even the most troubled marriage.

Insight: Recognize that things you have been doing haven't been working.

Change: Stop doing the wrong things... and start doing what creates good feelings.

This sounds simple—and it is. But many couples keep nagging, criticizing, shouting—even while recognizing that those behaviors only make things worse.

It takes only one person to break the vicious cycle of hurt. *Strategies to improve any marriage...*

REMEMBER THE GOOD TIMES

To stay motivated through tough times, think back to your courtship. What first attracted you to your spouse?

Now—look to see those qualities in your spouse. The more you pay attention to glimmers of positive feelings, the more positive feelings you will have.

COMPLIMENT GENEROUSLY

We feel closest to people who make us feel good about ourselves. If you say and do things that build up your partner—and avoid things that make him/her feel worse—your relationship will improve.

Of course, when your marriage is stressed, complimenting your spouse may be the *last* thing you feel like doing. It's much easier to think of all the things he is doing wrong.

Remember: People *don't* change because they're criticized. They change when warmth and goodwill motivate them to please their spouse...or to make their spouses happier.

Train yourself to notice the things you admire about your spouse—no matter how small. Then tell your spouse.

If this still seems difficult, think about how parents behave. They may be frustrated or disappointed with their kids—but they still find ways to acknowledge their good qualities. Adults need this as much as children.

Don't fake admiration. Compliment your spouse on things you admire.

Examples: I was really impressed with the way you negotiated our lease...That was a delicious meal—you're a great cook.

WARM YOUR PARTNER'S HEART

Early in your relationship, you probably made a point of learning what actions made your partner feel cared for—and you did them. When a marriage is under stress, spouses stop making these loving gestures... and resentment grows.

Look for opportunities to do special things for your partner.

Examples: Make your spouse a morning cup of tea...offer to watch the kids so your spouse can spend an evening with friends.

PRAISE SMALL CHANGES

Your partner may take a while to notice that you're acting differently—and even longer to respond with loving gestures of his own.

Be patient. Try to notice any small steps in the right direction. Praising these improvements will encourage your spouse to continue making them.

Example: A wife was upset that her husband was always late for dinner. As she made changes to make the relationship more affectionate, he continued to come home late—but started calling to tell her. She thanked him when he called ahead, resisting the urge to add, "I wish you would come home on time." Within a few weeks, he began to arrive at dinnertime.

DON'T PUT OFF SEX

Many couples avoid sex when they are having marriage problems because they feel emotionally distant. Yet sex can help couples feel closer.

If you're not in the mood, make love anyway. Don't think of it as something you are doing for the marriage…but as something that will make *you* feel good.

POSITIVE ANGER

All this talk about positive communication doesn't mean that you should bury what bothers you. But express complaints in a constructive way.

● **Raise your complaint when you are not feeling angry about it.** This will help you keep your tone calm—and prevent a nasty fight.

● **Start with something positive.** Your partner is more likely to listen if you acknowledge what he is doing right.

● **Keep it short.** Don't say more than a sentence or two before giving your partner a chance to respond. If you spend a lot of time detailing your point of view, your partner is likely to feel that you are lecturing—and will stop listening.

● **Don't use past hurts to illustrate your gripe.** Your spouse will feel that he can never stop paying for what went wrong in the past. Keep examples current.

● **Avoid your partner's alarm buttons.** Words like "abusive" are overused—and offensive. So are psychological interpretations such as, *You're overreacting because your mother is so controlling.*

● **Listen nondefensively.** Instead of rebutting what your partner says, search for some small part with which you agree.

Example: Your partner says, *The minute you walk in the house, you're grumpy. All you do is criticize me.*

Ineffective response: That's not true. Two days ago, I sat down and had a drink with you. Don't you remember?

Better: I do feel tense when I come home.

Nondefensive listening stops an argument quickly…so you can work on a solution together.

Keeping Love Alive… Creative Ideas

Michael Webb, syndicated columnist in Cary, NC, and author of *The RoMANtic's Guide: Hundreds of Creative Tips for a Lifetime of Love.* Hyperion. *www.TheRomantic.com.*

Romance shouldn't be reserved for special occasions, holidays or just to get out of the doghouse.

Romance has little to do with jewelry, chocolates, roses and expensive dinners. It is a combination of all the little—and big—things you do to tell your partner "I love you." *Suggestions for keeping romance alive year-round…*

● **Kiss a Spot-of-the-Week.** Each weekend, I designate a place on my wife's body to kiss. It might be her right eyebrow, left ear or elsewhere. I kiss that place repeatedly the following week.

● **Keep dating each other—even if you're married.** This advice rarely gets followed. Plan at least one date each week. Be creative—they don't all have to be dinner dates. My wife and I have been on dates to museums, to the zoo, on a train and even to bookstores. We've also enjoyed the Quarter Date, in which we spend $10 in quarters on arcade games (only two-player games), kiddie rides, tourist binoculars, gumball machines.

● **Celebrate your *monthly* anniversary.** Don't wait a whole year to do something special. For our 75th (monthly) wedding anniversary, I created a coloring book for my wife. Using a black marker, I doodled pictures of our memorable experiences and had them bound. Periodically we take out the book—and a pack of crayons—and relive the memories.

● **Surprise your sweetie…**

● Tie a nonbreakable gift to a three-foot string. Attach it, with some streamers and balloons, to the handle of an automatic garage door. When your honey comes home, the gift will rise to greet him/her.

• Hide confetti or flower petals atop a ceiling fan.

• Pack lunch for your spouse. Spice it up by carving a heart on an apple or a pear...include love notes, a favorite comic strip or Hershey kisses.

• Buy glow-in-the-dark stars from a toy store, and arrange a loving message on the ceiling above your bed before leaving on a business trip.

How Not to Disagree With Your Spouse

Nancy Samalin, founder and director of Parent Guidance Workshops, New York. *www.samalin.com*. She is author of several parenting books, including the best-seller *Loving Your Child Is Not Enough: Positive Discipline That Works*. Penguin.

A united parenting front sounds like a great goal, but it's unrealistic. It is normal for parents to disagree about discipline. Mom and Dad aren't joined at the hip. Each has an individual temperament, preferences and priorities.

Key: Strive for common ground and compromise, not a false united front.

RECOGNIZE YOUR DIFFERENCES

Each of you was raised differently. One of you may have been brought up in a laid-back family with few rules, while the other may have had drill sergeants for parents.

Whether we duplicate or reject our own parents' disciplinary methods, our childhood experiences have an enormous influence on how we raise our own kids. Our parents were our first and most powerful teachers.

• **Evaluate your individual parenting styles.** Is one of you authoritarian and the other permissive? Does one have strong beliefs about healthful eating, while the other loves junk food? What issues or behaviors bother each of you?

Examples: Dawdling at bedtime...picky eating habits...messy rooms...back talk...broken curfews...homework excuses...bickering with siblings.

Helpful: Agree that whichever parent holds the stronger opinion about a particular issue will handle it without interference from his/her spouse.

Example: Next time Sally refuses to clean her room, it's Mom's job to dish out a consequence—because that's Mom's area of concern. Dad doesn't have to step in since it doesn't bother him.

• **Agree to disagree—but in private.** If you disapprove of the way your spouse handles a problem, bite your tongue. Don't contradict or undermine your partner in front of your child. In private, you might say something like...

I know Billy's behavior is irritating, but I wonder whether there's another, more effective approach. Any suggestions?

TEAM-PARENTING STRATEGIES

• **Have a plan.** You know from experience how your kids are likely to behave—or misbehave—in certain situations. For example, when they're watching a TV show, they'll often whine and beg to stay up for the next program—even if it runs beyond bedtime.

Talk with your spouse about these predictable problems and formulate a strategy *in advance* for handling them. Being prepared is far more effective—and less stressful—than reacting when you're caught off guard.

• **Don't get trapped in the *divide-and-conquer* game**—also known as "If Mom says *no*, go ask Dad." Establish consequences if children violate this rule...and enforce them.

• **Stay out of the middle,** even if your child pleads with you to intervene in a conflict he has with your spouse. *Simply say...*

That's between you and Mom. The two of you need to work this out. Talk to her about it.

This strategy is critical in blended families, which present even more opportunities for the divide-and-conquer game.

• **Buy some time.** When your child asks for something you believe will create conflict between you and your spouse, discuss it between yourselves first—*Dad and I will talk this over privately and then get back to you.*

• **When you argue, remain civil.** It's inevitable that parents sometimes disagree in front of the kids. *Strategies...*

●**Avoid name-calling and sarcasm, easy traps to fall into.** Cut short your argument and revisit the problem later. Don't attack or place blame. Instead of…

You always let him get away with murder …or You never back me up…

state how you feel…

I get angry when the kids see me as the Bad Guy and you as the Fun Parent…or I need your support when they're hassling me.

●**Don't "futurize"** by criticizing your spouse's approach as though it will inevitably lead to a negative outcome…

If you let him get away with that now, he'll become a spoiled brat.

Deal with the problem at hand, rather than blow it out of proportion.

●**Reassure children that it's not their fault when you and your partner argue.** If they've witnessed an argument, let them know you've resolved it. Show them that parents can have disputes and still care about each other.

Create Your Own Family Web Site

A family Web site can keep family members all over the world in touch—no matter where they might live or travel.

The Web site can present pictures, videos, sound messages, news, a family bulletin board, kids' pages and a private E-mail service for family members.

You can host your own site through a commercial Internet service provider, or set up a site through one of several family Web site hosting services.

Advantage: Family-site hosting services provide…

●**Special features** designed just for family Web sites.

●**Tools** that make it easy to manage a Web site even if you have no computing expertise.

●**Security systems** that limit access to a family site to family members and approved friends. Recommended hosting services…

  ●*eCircles.com*
  ●*FamilyPoint.com*
  ●*Homestead.com*
  ●*MyFamily.com*
  ●*SuperFamily.com*

Visit each service's own Web site to compare features and prices.

Frederick G. Levine, features editor, Family Fun, 114 Fifth Ave., New York City 10011.

How to Enjoy The Birth of a New Grandchild

Arthur Kornhaber, MD, psychiatrist and president, Foundation for Grandparenting, 108 Farnham Rd., Ojai, CA 93023. Dr. Kornhaber is author of Grandparent Power: How to Strengthen the Vital Connection Among Grandparents, Parents, and Children. Crown.

To fully experience the special event, plan to be there for the delivery. If that's not possible, make a trip to see the infant— and the *parents*, of course—as soon as you can.

Why is it so important? Because a grandchild's birth brings the family together. With you on the scene to welcome the baby, the occasion becomes a family celebration. *Special reasons for doing special things…*

●**You can be the family reporter,** recording the birth and accompanying celebration with a camera or a video camera.

●**Your presence can be a great help to the parents.** Chances are the new parents will have their hands very, very full.

●**The new baby's siblings** will need the kind of attention and support that loving grandparents can provide so well.

A new birth in the family is an important enough event for you or your spouse to take time off work to attend. When you look back on it, a few days of missed work will seem inconsequential by comparison.

PLAN AHEAD

● **Discuss the visit with the parents-to-be** so you'll be able to comply with their wishes.

● **If travel will be necessary,** schedule your vacation for the time of the expected birth—but keep a bag packed, in case your grandchild makes an early arrival.

● **Coordinate your plans with those of the other grandparents** to avoid any conflicts.

● **Find out the hospital rules from the doctor** who'll be performing the delivery. Sometimes grandparents (even grandfathers) are allowed in the delivery room, perhaps in the background to respect the mother's privacy.

CLOSE ENCOUNTERS

You don't have to be looking over the doctor's shoulder when the baby comes. Indeed, hospital policy or the new parents' wishes may prohibit such an intimate presence. *Exception:* Grandmothers may be allowed in the delivery room, especially if it's their own daughter who's giving birth.

One grandmother who was fortunate enough to help her daughter in the delivery room put it this way: "Helping my daughter give birth was truly an incredible experience. She had a beautiful, unmedicated birth…love and her family surrounded her."

The moment of truth: My own experience delivering babies has shown me that the emotion flowing between new mother and new grandmother at the moment of birth is especially powerful, a time both will cherish forever.

If you can't witness the birth, you can be in the waiting room. Then you can hold the newborn, and present your new grandchild with his/her first teddy bear.

Key: Not only should you be there to welcome the new baby, you should thank the new parents for the incredible gift of a grandchild.

Sometimes, the new parents won't want anyone—even grandparents—in the hospital at all. The thought of relatives sitting impatiently in the waiting room may add to the expectant mother's stress. If that's the case, let the parents-to-be decide how to keep you posted.

SAFE AT HOME

Today, hospitals don't encourage long maternity stays. In most cases, Mom and Baby will be home within a day or two. That's when Grandma and Grandpa are *really needed.*

The new parents may not have provided anything to eat for their return home. If that's the case, why not bring in something special for the happy couple, so they'll have meals for several days?

Grandparents can help in countless ways, from basic housekeeping to making sure that older grandchildren get to and from school and play dates, etc. If there's no live-in housekeeper, one grandparent may actually move in for a while to ease the burden.

Just keeping your eyes open may provide some insights as to how you can help. "I noticed how gingerly my daughter-in-law eased herself into the maple rocker she sat in to nurse my grandson," one grandmother wrote. "I brought her a doughnut pillow and she said it was the best present she received, aside from the baby himself."

Most important: Be sensitive to the wishes and comfort level of the new parents, yet make it clear that you want to provide meaningful support.

In particular, first-time parents may not know what they will need until that need actually arises. Exercise resourcefulness, creativity and good judgment in suggestions you offer.

If you do so, your presence can add immeasurably to this memorable event. The happiness, fulfillment and spiritual joy that every baby brings reach far beyond the new parents to resonate within the hearts of all family members—and that goes double for grandparents!

How to Survive Family Gatherings

Sylvia Bigelsen, EdS, author of *The Ties That Bind: A Survival Guide to In-Law Relationships.* Element. She has been a family therapist for the past 25 years in Morristown, NJ.

W hen family relationships are working well, they bring joy to your life and to those you love.

Parents want their children to be part of their lives. Brothers and sisters want to be friends. In-laws want to get along.

But when these relationships are strained and problematic, the results are often untold heartbreak and pain.

I have found that difficult family relationships play a major role in driving many couples into therapy...and contribute substantially to today's high divorce rate.

COPING STRATEGIES

Here are steps you can take to deal with difficult family members.

If the problems don't improve, focus on preserving your relationship with your spouse and protecting your children.

And—gently pull back and spend less time with the troublesome relative. You don't have to explain your reasons.

●**Confront problems in private.** If you speak to a relative about a problem when others are present, he/she will become defensive.

When the two of you are alone, talk about how you feel, rather than asking the other person to change.

Example: If your father makes insensitive comments, say—*It really hurts me to hear you say things like that. I especially don't like it in front of the children.*

●**Be prepared to make unpopular decisions.** You can't set limits or make decisions about your life without ever hurting someone's feelings. Be gentle but firm as you state those limits—whether that means decreasing the time you spend with annoying relatives or deciding not to discuss certain topics with your parents.

●**Be willing to compromise.** Having it all your way isn't how families work. Compromising on certain issues is the only road to long-term happiness.

Example: If your wife likes to go to her parents' house for Sunday brunch but you don't enjoy their company, you could agree to alternate activities each week.

●**Keep your sense of humor.** One patient's mother-in-law polished her son's—my patient's husband's—shoes during her frequent visits,

implying that her daughter-in-law's "work" wasn't getting done.

My patient simply laughed it off. She even moved all the shoes to be more accessible when her mother-in-law visited.

SIBLINGS

Establishing good relationships with siblings can be difficult because we compete with one another for our parents' attention. *Helpful...*

●**Be honest and open.** You may have an overbearing, obnoxious sister you don't like ...but you also love your parents and want to spend time together as a family.

Talk to your sister about how you feel, but don't attack her. *Use phrases such as...*

> *My feelings were hurt when you...*
> *I guess I misunderstood when you...*

●**Bite your tongue.** If talking fails but you want to keep peace in your family, keep your frustrations to yourself. Limit your time with the offending sibling to important family events. If you have to vent, save it for a sympathetic friend.

PARENTS

Many family squabbles develop once grandchildren are born. That's when parents who weren't intrusive earlier in your adult life may try to become more involved.

Although grandparents and grandchildren share a special bond, there are boundaries that grandparents should not cross—especially if their involvement undermines your parenting.

●**Establish guidelines** for how much time you want your children to spend with their grandparents.

●**Don't take advantage of grandparents.** They are not your built-in baby-sitters. They are adults with interests and lives of their own. Don't be disappointed if they don't jump at every opportunity to spend an evening with your child.

●**Let grandparents spoil your children**—a little. A moderate amount of spoiling is fine, especially for holidays or special occasions. But—you can choose the areas in which children may be indulged.

Example: No junk food, but new toys or books are okay.

● **Use kindness.** If grandparents become intrusive, explain that you need more time alone as a family. Together, establish specific times when grandparents can be with you. Stick to your guns even if grandparents seem hurt.

PROTECT YOUR MARRIAGE

If your marriage is strained by bother- some family members, it may be *your relationship* that's the problem—not the relatives. *Look at yourselves as a couple...*

● **Identify the issues each of you brings to your relationship.** Is the husband too dependent on his parents? Is the wife jealous of the closeness between her husband and his parents?

Discuss how the problems make you feel—and don't make hurtful statements.

Example: Rather than saying, *I hate your mother...*, say, *I feel uncomfortable and degraded when your mother starts cleaning the kitchen.*

● **Establish rules for dealing with problem family members.** If husband and wife agree to support each other, family members will have little choice but to abide by that couple's decisions.

Present a united front and stick to the limits and boundaries you set. Decide issues like...

● How much time you want to give to in-laws.

● How much you want to tell them about your personal and financial life.

● How you'll distribute time between families at holidays.

● How much help you'll accept from each set of parents.

● **Take responsibility for your own family.** In-laws often don't get along. Accept that you'll each spend some independent time with your own family. Don't hold this against your partner.

● **Don't criticize your partner's family.** Think twice before you tell your spouse that his brother is a jerk or his mother is stupid. Most of us defend our relatives, even when we know the criticism is valid.

Focus instead on what you want and how you would like to be treated.

17

The Winning Edge

Optimists Live Better Lives than Pessimists— The Secrets of Happiness...

To pessimists, the "movie of life" is a documentary that has an unchangeable script.

Optimists grab the story line and become directors. They edit, refocus and add color to concoct a brighter, happier picture. This hopeful, in-control attitude shields them from outside influences...and inner emotional turmoil.

The good news for pessimists is that they can train themselves to think optimistically.

STEPS TO HAPPINESS

•**Fake it—even if you don't feel like it.** Acting happy—even when you are not— makes you *feel* happier.

Try smiling to improve your mood. Sitting up straight will make you feel more alert.

Consciously relaxing your muscles helps alleviate anxiety. Suppressing a frown or grimace can make an unpleasant emotion—or experience—less painful.

•**Adjust your explanatory style.** With a half-empty viewpoint, the individual assumes blame for all failures. Every mistake provokes anxiety. Any success seems like a fluke.

From the half-full perspective, difficulties are ascribed not to personal shortcomings but to transient conditions—a computer glitch...a boss in a bad mood...and having an off day. Accomplishments are the well-deserved rewards for talent and hard work.

Optimist's advantage: *Externalizing* causes of temporary setbacks protects you from feelings of defeat. You know there will be bad days—but they're not the story of your life. Having that conviction helps you

Susan C. Vaughan, MD, assistant professor of psychiatry and psychoanalysis at Columbia University College of Physicians and Surgeons, New York City. She is author of *Half Empty, Half Full: Understanding Psychological Roots of Optimism.* Harcourt.

261

make the best of difficult situations without "catastrophizing."

●**Practice *downward* comparison.** Comparing ourselves with others who have more may trigger a sense of deprivation. But a contrast with those who are less well off makes us feel fortunate.

Example: In the film *My Life as a Dog*, the main character, a young boy, endures painful times by assuring himself he's doing better than Laika, the Russian space dog lost in the cosmos.

●**Avoid negative influences.** Willing or not, we pick up other people's vibes. Beyond dodging pessimists and the evening news, you may want to avoid unnecessary and mood-deflating confrontations.

Be wary of emotional signals from your environment as well. Experimental subjects forced to listen to grunge rock showed significant increases in negative emotions and reductions in positive ones, a recent study found.

●**Take a time-out.** Particularly when details threaten to overwhelm you, distract yourself. Try a quick walk—or do some stretches. Or lock your office door and dance—music adds enjoyment to movement. Savor life's small pleasures—from a few minutes with your eyes closed, to a cup of espresso.

If real-world mood lifters are unavailable, mine your memory. Mentally relishing a delicious meal or inspiring view—the more vividly, the better—nudges you toward a rosier outlook.

Caution: Gloomy images produce a downward mood shift, so resist ruminating on negative experiences.

●**Rewrite the script.** When life provides a less-than-happy ending, do a mental rewrite —where you make the brilliant remark or win the contract.

Like the positive explanatory style, this strategy keeps you from getting trapped by feelings of defeat. And visualizing yourself succeeding encourages you to duplicate your performance in reality.

●**Learn your own triggers.** By observing the flow of thoughts and sensations that accompany emotional shifts, you'll eventually be able to pinpoint when an unpleasant thought threatens your mood or an agreeable one improves it. Then you can actively block the negative while encouraging the positive.

Nine Ways to Get Yourself Out of a Bad Mood

Sandra A. Crowe, president of Pivotal Point Training and Consulting, Inc., Rockville, MD, which teaches relationship techniques. *www.pivpoint.com.* She is author of *Since Strangling Isn't an Option: Dealing with Difficult People.* Perigee.

Bad moods magnify trivial annoyances and dampen enjoyment. *Once you get to the root of the problem, use these quick-fix tactics to restore emotional equilibrium...*

●**Eat some chocolate.** It prompts the release of *serotonin,* the brain's natural chemical upper. Eat slowly, savoring the sweetness and texture. Limit yourself to two pieces—a chocolate binge will only make you feel worse later.

●**Play with a toy.** Something as simple as a yo-yo or windup toy can distract your mind and relax your body.

●**Get active.** A quick walk also prompts the release of endorphins and provides a change of scenery to distract you from problems.

●**Shift the focus away from your bad mood** by doing something for others—send a funny card to a friend...do volunteer work.

●**Listen to music.** Familiar songs evoke pleasant memories and good feelings. If singing along helps, then belt it out.

●**Contact someone who makes you feel good.** Simply ask that person to help you cheer up or bask in the glow of his/her positive outlook. Just being around a child, for instance, may awaken your own natural joy and enable you to regain your perspective.

In case you can't reach anyone, keep a photo of a loved one nearby.

Important: Avoid people who bring you down.

• **Give yourself a break.** Choose a task to postpone or delegate...cancel your dinner plans so you can enjoy a restful evening.

Helpful: Carve out 15 minutes to recharge. Meditate...take a catnap...or just close your eyes and visualize comforting, enjoyable experiences.

• **Get a massage.** Beyond easing muscle aches, a massage makes you feel indulged. When stuck at your desk, gently massage your own neck, shoulders—even your feet.

• **Play with your pet.** It has a soothing effect on heartbeat, blood pressure and respiration rate.

To Boost Performance Under Pressure...

Robert Nideffer, PhD, chief executive officer of Enhanced Performance Systems, a consulting company specializing in improving performance under pressure, 1010 University Ave., Suite 265, San Diego 92103. *www. enhanced-performance.com.*

The ability to perform well under pressure is crucial to career success—so crucial that General Motors, Lucent Technologies and other corporations use the test I developed to predict how potential hires will do under difficult circumstances.*

Follow these steps to stop stress from sabotaging your life and career...

TAKE A STRESS TEST

Stress is a constant today. Rapid technological change and globalization are making jobs increasingly complex.

We can't escape workplace stress, but we can identify episodes when it has gotten the better of us. *Stress overload often leads to one of these mistakes...*

*The Attentional and Interpersonal Style (TAIS) inventory test comprises 144 questions and is widely used to enhance performance in business, sports and military settings. It is an invaluable tool for selection and screening in high-stress environments. Results should be analyzed by a TAIS-certified consultant.

• **Overthinking.** You and your team are paralyzed by information overload. When trying to balance divergent views, you give directions that are too confusing or complex to be carried out.

Most susceptible: Managers and executives. They are trained to sift through information carefully before acting. Under pressure, endless demands for information can become a substitute for taking action.

• **Overfocused.** You become less flexible as a project goes on. You cling to your initial plan long after its flaws have been discovered. You fail to consider alternatives.

Most susceptible: Engineers and financiers. When pressured, their attention to detail can turn into rigidity.

• **Overreactive.** Instead of planning ahead, you count on being able to pick up enough cues to wing it through meetings and negotiations. You stop championing your own ideas and start echoing those of others.

Most susceptible: Sales and marketing professionals. They are trained to compromise and be agreeable. Under pressure, the need to give all choices a fair hearing deteriorates into an inability to make any firm decisions.

PRESSURE TRIGGERS

Review your work history to find instances where pressure caused you to make serious mistakes. *Most likely culprits...*

• **Deadlines.** You are under enormous pressure to make a decision *now*. You're afraid that if you relax even for a moment, a big deal or sale will be lost.

• **High-impact decisions.** Much is riding on the outcome. If you mess up, you fear the impact could be financially or professionally devastating.

• **Loss of operating control.** You have responsibility for a project's success but not the necessary decision-making authority.

PLAN FOR PRESSURE

Once you identify your pressure triggers, you can better prepare for the next time you are thrown into a stressful situation.

Danger: Stress is cumulative. The longer a meeting or a negotiation, the greater the risk of stress-overload mistakes.

When the pressure gets intense, request a time-out. Take a 10-minute "fresh air" break ...or make an excuse to escape to your office to cool off.

Stay away until the "do-it-immediately" panic has passed—and you again are in control of your emotions.

How to use the time-out...

If you are overanalytical: Use the time-out to refocus on the key issues of the project or negotiation. Remember to address points that the other side has made.

If you're inflexible: Force yourself to listen to the rest of your team to see if there are alternative approaches—beyond the plan you are pushing—for wrapping things up.

If you're overreactive: You've been bombarded by people's suggestions. Review your own goals.

Lessons in Laughter From the Great Student of Laughter

Robert R. Provine, PhD, professor of psychology at University of Maryland, Baltimore County, and author of *Laughter: A Scientific Investigation.* Viking.

Having written *Laughter: A Scientific Investigation*, I am often asked to tout the miraculous effects of laughing—such as that it can cure colds...boost the immune system...and stimulate creativity.

I hate to douse the media's enthusiasm, but there is little scientific evidence that laughter offers great health—or even psychological—benefits.

That said, I suggest that life *with* laughter certainly beats life *without* it. We don't need scientists to tell us laughter makes us feel happy. Besides, it's free and has no negative side effects. It certainly can't hurt.

RELATIONSHIPS AND LAUGHTER

The real benefits of laughter stem in large part from the circumstances in which you laugh. Spending time with friends and family promotes happiness as well as laughter. It's hard to distinguish the effects of laughter from the playful situations that produced it.

Researchers have tried to prove that laughter results from detecting incongruities or responding to humorous stimuli. I think that it's really about communication—you seldom laugh when alone. Laughter is also about intimacy. The better you know someone, the more you have to laugh about.

Successful comedians must both have good material and establish a relationship with the audience. That explains why so many comedians set up jokes by saying something like, *Have you ever been to the airport and the guy behind you says....* The comedian tries to create common ground.

Laughter is unconsciously controlled—try laughing on command. Thus, laughter provides uncensored and unappreciated insights into organizations, relationships and the retail enterprise.

LAUGHTER ADVANTAGE

Laughter can be an effective coping mechanism against short-term stress, as in laughing off workplace hassles, but it can have risks.

Warning: Joking about a serious situation can be counterproductive. You don't want to laugh off risky behavior, such as smoking or reckless driving.

Another use of laughter: Pain relief. Studies have found laughing comparable to progressive relaxation and minor analgesics in reducing stress and pain.

INVITING HUMOR

Here are my guidelines for inviting laughter into your life...

●**Be social.** When you build friendships, you're building laughter. The best way to start yourself laughing is to find someone to laugh with.

Television is only a last resort. And pets, though good for company, fall way short in stimulating laughter.

●**Seek out groups.** The old adage *The more the merrier* is true. A large crowd laughs more than a small one.

●**Follow the sound of laughter.** Laughter is contagious, so put yourself in situations where you'll catch it.

Say you're at a party and see a group of people laughing. Join that group. Whatever is going on there is likely to elicit laughter and humor in you.

●**Lower your laughter threshold.** We tend to do this automatically in certain situations. If you are with someone who once made you laugh, you expect to repeat the experience. Once you're primed for laughter, even mild humor may seem hysterical.

We don't walk into an annual performance review with the boss in the same spirit.

●**Keep funny things around**—photographs, joke books, movies you've enjoyed, etc....or something that connects you to another person even in his/her absence, such as a funny card he has sent you. Such items can be potent pick-me-ups, so make them readily available for when you need them most.

●**Think beyond your own laughter.** A sense of humor, a trait admired by everyone, refers not to your yuks and titters, but to your ability to give the gift of laughter. Laughter is a gift that is always returned with interest.

Let Colors Affect Your Mood

Watery blues and fresh greens can help you relax after a tiring day. Warm tones, such as reds, oranges and yellows, can help get you up and going. Use different colors in different parts of your home, to help create the moods you want. *Examples:* Cool colors where you want to relax, such as a bedroom...warm ones where you want a feeling of high energy, such as the kitchen.

Frank M. Don, whose writings and studies on color are included in *The Faber Birren Book Collection on Color*, Yale University Art and Architecture Library, New Haven, CT, and the Royal College of Art, London. Mr. Don is author of *Color Your World.* Inner Traditions.

The Simple Secrets of Power and Influence

John Hook, DPA, business consultant and professor of management at Mount St. Mary's College, Emmitsburg, MD. He is author of *The Agile Manager's Guide to Influencing People.* Velocity.

There are two ways leaders motivate people to do what they want—*power* and *influence.*

People may give us our way—out of fear or respect—because of our power. But they might not agree with us.

The goal of influence is to motivate others to want what we want. Influence is the most desirable way to effect lasting change because it produces commitment, not just compliance. Even when influence fails, it builds goodwill.

Steps to influence and make friends...

●**Present the facts.** You won't get far unless you explain the arguments supporting your view. This includes doing the necessary cost-benefit analyses.

●**Appeal to emotions.** If logic fails, present a vision of your plan that appeals to the emotions and values of others.

Example: "If we meet this goal, our team's reputation—and regard for your personal expertise—will grow."

This type of argument creates excitement and motivation.

●**Make it *his/her* idea.** Draw the other person into a dialogue at the end of which he wants what you want because he helped devise the plan.

Beware: You might not get exactly what you want because you must accommodate the other person. Sometimes stating your views first will move that person toward your direction.

TACKLING CONFLICT

All leaders run into conflict. The easiest solution is to accommodate the other person's desires if possible. That usually makes him more cooperative.

Helpful: When tensions run high, break off negotiations temporarily. Don't let anyone walk out of the room a loser.

Differences of opinion are a source of creativity. With good people, you want those differences to bubble up freely.

How to Negotiate Without Giving In

Roger Fisher, Esq., director, Harvard Negotiation Project, Harvard Law School, Cambridge, MA. He is coauthor of the classic *Getting to Yes: Negotiating Agreement Without Giving In*. Penguin Books.

Everyone negotiates. You negotiate with your spouse about where to go for dinner or what movie to see, with your boss about salary.

Yet standard negotiation strategies often leave people dissatisfied, worn out and alienated. A better way to deal with differences is called "principled negotiation." *How it works…*

● **Listen actively.** Frequently, negotiators talk, but not to each other. Instead, they talk merely to impress third parties or their own constituency.

Example: Following World War II, negotiations over the city of Trieste involving large delegations from Yugoslavia, Britain and the US stalled until representatives abandoned their large delegations and began meeting alone and informally in a private house.

Remedy: Listen actively and acknowledge what is said.

Helpful: Pay careful attention and interrupt occasionally to say, "Did I understand correctly that you were saying that…" This tells the other side you're not just killing time.

● **Speak to be understood.** You or your opponent may not be hearing what the other is saying. Perhaps you forget to listen because you're so busy thinking about what he/she is going to say next or preparing your response.

Remedy: Treat your opponent as a fellow judge with whom you're attempting to work out a joint position. Instead of placing blame, engaging in name-calling or raising your voice, try to move forward as a team challenged with a joint problem.

● **Reconcile interests, not positions.** Your position is something you decided upon. Your interests are what caused you to decide. Interests motivate people—they are the silent movers behind the hubbub of positions. To determine interests, ask what it is that you really care about, hope for, need, want and fear. Consider your opponent's interests, too.

Example: Prior to 1978, Egypt and Israel's positions concerning the Sinai Peninsula seemed intractable. Israel insisted on retaining some of the land to ensure its security, yet Egypt wanted it all and wouldn't compromise an inch. At Camp David, Israel agreed to a plan that would cede complete sovereignty to Egypt, yet agreed that a large portion of the area was to be demilitarized. The Egyptian flag would fly over the peninsula, but Egyptian tanks would be nowhere near Israel. Looking to their interests—instead of their positions—made a solution possible.

● **Don't let "people problems" get in the way.** People problems cannot be swept under the rug, so instead you must build a working relationship independent of agreement or disagreement. A good working relationship is one that can cope with differences.

Helpful: Disentangle substantive issues (terms, conditions, prices, dates, etc.) from relationship issues (personal annoyances and frustrations, ease of communication, trust and reliability, degree of mutual understanding, etc.). Distinguish how you treat your opponents from how they treat you. There's no need to "teach them a lesson." Always deal rationally with irrational behavior.

● **Invent options for mutual gain.** Often, there seems to be no way to split the pie that leaves both parties satisfied.

Remedy: Expand the pie before dividing it.

Helpful: Without either side making a demand, commitment or concession, hold a brainstorming session to develop new possibilities for reconciling your differing interests. The key ground rule during these sessions is not to criticize or otherwise evaluate these proposals. Allowing ideas to flow unimpeded may help percolate more ideas.

● **Insist on using objective criteria.** Whenever possible, commit yourself to reaching a solution based on principle, not pressure.

Possible objective criteria include precedent, market value, etc.

Example: You're building a house and the contractor suggests a reinforced concrete foundation that's two feet deep. You think five feet is closer to the usual depth for your type of house. Instead of agreeing because the contractor made concessions on other matters, you should instead insist the issue be decided based on objective safety standards. How deep are the foundations of other buildings in the area? What is the earthquake risk? What do local building codes require?

• **Develop your best alternative** to a negotiated agreement. This is the standard against which any proposal must be measured. It will protect you both from accepting terms that are too unfavorable and rejecting those in your best interest to accept.

Example: In selling your house, instead of setting a minimum price you'll accept, determine what you'll do if it's not sold by a certain date. Will you keep it on the market indefinitely, rent it, let someone live in it rent free? Which of these alternatives is the most attractive? And is it a better option than the best offer you've received on the house?

• **Reaching closure.** There's not one best process for moving from inventing options to making commitments, but here are some general principles worth considering...

• Think about closure from the beginning. This will help you figure out what issues need to be dealt with and what it might take to resolve them.

• Consider crafting a framework agreement. This is a draft document with blank spaces for each term to be resolved by negotiation. Working from such a framework will help ensure that important issues are not overlooked during negotiation.

• Move toward commitment gradually. Be prepared to move through the list of issues several times, going back and forth between specific issues and looking at the total package.

• Be persistent in pursuing your interests, but flexible in pursuing any particular solution.

Example: When a proposal is challenged, don't defend the proposal. Rather, explain again your underlying interests. Ask the other side to suggest a better way to meet those interests, as well as its own.

• **Make an offer.** Once an issue or group of issues is well explored, be prepared to make an offer.

Example: "I'll agree to a June 30 closing if the down payment isn't more than $50,000." Such an offer shouldn't come as a surprise to the other party, nor should it be presented as a "take it or leave it" offer. But neither should it be seen as an opening position. Instead it should be something that makes sense for both sides—something that satisfies the interests of both sides.

• **Be generous at the end.** Consider giving the other side something you know to be of value to them that's still consistent with the basic logic of your proposal. Be clear that this is your final gesture, so you don't raise expectations of further concessions.

Reason: You want the other side to leave the table feeling satisfied and fairly treated. This can pay off handsomely in the implementation of the agreement and in future negotiations.

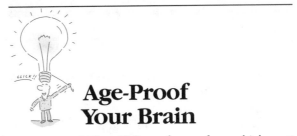

Age-Proof Your Brain

Lawrence C. Katz, PhD, professor of neurobiology at Duke University Medical Center and an investigator at the Howard Hughes Medical Institute, both in Durham, NC. He is coauthor of *Keep Your Brain Alive: 83 Neurobic Exercises* (Workman) and has published more than 50 scientific articles on brain development and function.

Doctors used to think that brain development occurred only during youth and that as we age, our brain cells (neurons) inevitably die off.

But recent research confirms that humans can add new neurons throughout life. This means we can continue learning new ideas and mastering new skills.

Each neuron has branch-like appendages called *dendrites* that extend in different directions. Whenever the brain is stimulated by an experience—even in old age—new dendrites form.

Neurons communicate with each other via electrochemical impulses sent through dendrites. More dendrites mean greater brain power. As we age, some dendrites naturally wither and die. The more we have left, the better our cognitive abilities remain.

Key: Building as many dendrites as possible. Here are eight ways to stimulate dendrite growth and keep energizing your brain…

●**Switch hands.** Most of us rely on a dominant hand for daily activities. Switch to your nondominant hand. Research has shown that this type of exercise can substantially increase the number of circuits in the cerebral cortex.

If you brush your teeth with your right hand, use your left for a few weeks.

Switch to your nondominant hand as frequently as possible—when eating…styling your hair…writing…painting.

●**"Lose" a sense.** An abundance of new neural pathways form when you exercise your senses in ways you normally don't. It's well known, for example, that blind people end up developing other senses to a much higher level than those who have their sight.

Brain-imaging experiments involving blind braille readers show that extensive practice using the fingers to make fine distinctions between objects or textures causes "rewiring" of the brain.

Most of us rely on sight above all. Substitute the sense of touch for daily tasks and activities, as blind people must.

●Learn to distinguish different keys by touch.

●Get dressed without looking…then try it with one hand.

●Close your eyes and explore a familiar room, such as your bedroom, with your hands.

Then "lose" other senses…

●Turn off the sound on the TV, and try to follow the plot.

●See if you can tell what's for dinner by the aromas you smell.

●Taste foods while holding your nose. This forces you to use different neural pathways to experience the food.

●**Use *all* your senses.** Something as simple as grocery shopping can stimulate the brain if you consciously use all your senses.

Smell the tomatoes…thump the melons… feel the plums…taste food samples offered. Buy foods for a theme meal—say a meal made up of only red foods.

The same can be done on a grander scale outdoors. Whether you're fishing, hiking or just taking a stroll…

●Feel changes in wind direction on your face and arms.

●Smell the air…and try to identify natural odors. Extensive research shows that linking places or things to the olfactory sense (smell) enhances memory.

●Listen intently to water splashing or a bird's song.

●**Be adventurous.** The less familiar an activity is to you, the more it stimulates your brain. Try things you've wanted to do, even if they initially feel uncomfortable.

Brain-imaging studies show that new experiences activate large areas of the cerebral cortex, indicating brain stimulation.

●Sign up for an acting camp.

●Travel by train across the US or by ship across the ocean.

●Vacation on a dude ranch.

●**Make small changes.** Even minor changes in your routine activate the cortex and hippocampus (a part of the brain crucial for memory formation) to create new neural pathways.

●If you always watch TV from the same chair, switch.

●Dine in a different room.

●Reorganize your desk.

●Rearrange furniture.

●Take a different route to work or the gym.

Or simply do the same things—but *in a different order*. Eat breakfast for dinner and dinner for breakfast…or shower after drinking your coffee instead of before. Travel around the grocery store in the opposite direction.

●**Take up a challenging hobby.** Devote yourself to a new pastime that calls for complex skills. Artistic pursuits, for example, activate nonverbal and emotional centers in the cortex.

- Learn a musical instrument.
- Study a foreign language.
- Take up a sport, such as tennis or golf, that requires mastering multiple techniques.
- Take up photography.
- **Go low-tech.** Although technology has made our lives easier, it also has removed us from many experiences.

    Example: Television, movies and the Internet may be entertaining, but they often pacify rather than actively engage the mind.

    Take technology breaks. Do things the way people did them decades ago.

- Bake bread or make spaghetti sauce from scratch.
- Run or walk outdoors, instead of on a treadmill.
- Go camping. Bring a sleeping bag, tent, simple food and a small gas stove. Leave the radio home.
- **Become more social.** Interacting with other people is the best single brain exercise. It brings all the senses into play, forces you to think quickly and hones your speaking skills.

    Social contact is also important for psychological health. People with good social networks have fewer physical and psychological problems as they age than those who are socially deprived. Seek out social interactions of every sort.

- Go to the bank teller instead of the automatic teller machine.
- Make small talk with the supermarket clerk.
- Telephone friends daily.

    Also strive for more ambitious interactions. Arrange social gatherings that involve a variety of brain-boosting strategies.

- Join a book club.
- Hold a wine-tasting party to learn about tastes and bouquets of different vintages.
- Organize a potluck picnic in a nature preserve.
- Set up a musical jam session or an informal chorus group.
- Arrange a weekly game night for poker, bridge or Monopoly—anything that involves complex thought and social contact.

Dr. Tom Crook's Six-Step Program to Keep Your Mind Very...Very... Very...Sharp!

Thomas Crook III, PhD, a clinical psychologist, memory researcher and president of Psychologix, Inc., in Annapolis, MD. He is author of more than 200 scientific publications and coauthor of *The Memory Cure—The Safe, Scientifically Proven Breakthrough That Can Slow, Halt, or Even Reverse Age-Related Memory Loss.* Pocket Books.

The decline in our ability to quickly recall names, dates and other memorized facts is known as Age-Associated Memory Impairment (AAMI). It is due to chemical changes in the brain cells as well as a general shrinkage of brain mass—a phenomenon that occurs in everybody, starting at about age 40.

That's the bad news. The good news is that, unlike Alzheimer's Disease (which strikes a relatively small percentage of people and is largely untreatable in its later stages), AAMI can be minimized and/or delayed indefinitely. How? Through a mix of mental and physical exercises combined with daily supplements of a remarkable compound called *phosphatidylserine*—more commonly referred to as PS.

WHAT IS PS?

Derived from soy, phosphatidylserine is the only medication that's been proven to reverse age-related memory loss in clinical studies. Best of all, this compound—which has been used for years in Europe —is now available as a food supplement in the US and can be purchased over the counter.

How it works: PS is a phospholipid—a natural fat that is present in every cell membrane of the body. PS occurs in much higher concentrations in brain cells than elsewhere, and it is essential for memory and other higher brain functions.

When consumed as a dietary supplement, PS will act within minutes to literally bathe and rejuvenate brain cells—increasing the activity of receptors on the cell surface and stimulating the production and release of various neurotransmitters, including acetylcholine, norepinephrine, serotonin and dopamine.

While small amounts of PS are found in rice, fish, soy and green leafy vegetables, these sources can't provide enough PS to "jump-start" aging brain cells. That's why supplements of PS are recommended as the first and most important step in preventing or minimizing AAMI.

Note: There is some evidence that PS supplements can produce marginal improvements in people with early-stage Alzheimer's disease.

GETTING ON THE PROGRAM

●**Take a daily supplement of PS.** The recommended dosage of PS supplements will vary according to age and degree of memory impairment. For people in their 40s or 50s who have not yet experienced significant memory loss, 100 mg a day is enough to stave off AAMI.

For people who have already experienced notable memory impairment, a dose of 200 mg to 300 mg a day is recommended for 30 days —taken in separate doses of 100 mg each, two or three times a day. This higher dose will allow the PS to saturate cell membranes.

After 30 days, many can maintain the memory-enhancing effect by switching to 100 mg a day. People with severe AAMI, however, may wish to continue taking the 200 mg to 300 mg daily dosage.

Where to buy: You can buy PS in a pill or gel capsule at some pharmacies or most health food stores. *Cost:* About $30 per month.

Be sure it is soy-derived PS (phosphatidylserine) and that it carries the name of a well-known manufacturer or has the Lucas Meyer logo on the bottle. (Lucas Meyer is the major supplier of commercially available PS and it guarantees the quality of its PS products.)

PS is also available in chewing gum form, under the name of Brain Gum. (*Cost:* $59.95 plus $5.95 shipping and handling for 144 pieces—about a one-month supply for the higher dosage or a three-month supply for

maintenance. Call 888-472-6678 or *www. braingum.com*.)

●**Exercise your mind.** By challenging your brain, you can make new neuronal connections at any age. *Suggested exercises for maximizing your memory...*

●*Make a conscious effort* to memorize one list of items each day.

●*Do word games,* mind teasers or puzzles on a regular basis.

Examples: Learn a new word every day...put together a jigsaw puzzle...read a poem and mentally illustrate each line...or write your full name on a piece of paper, then make up a sentence or two, using words that begin with each letter of your name (for Tom Crook, I might write "The old man calls regularly only on Kate").

●*Try associating items you need to remember* with humorous images or bright colors. "Linking" two items together can help.

Example: If Belinda needs to buy cat food and then stop by the dry cleaners to pick up a coat, she might imagine her cat sitting on her coat and getting hairs on it.

●*Before you watch your favorite television show, make a list of a dozen questions* that will test your memory. After the show is over, see how well you can answer your list of questions.

Examples: What are the names of the characters in the show? How many locations were shown?

●*Build a "memory bank"* by keeping a daily journal and saving postcards, mementos, etc. Review your "deposits" regularly.

●**Look after your health.** Age-related memory loss is hastened by poor diet and other health problems. *To protect your memory...*

●*Moderate your drinking.* Consuming more than a couple of drinks a day is believed to hasten the brain's aging.

●*Don't smoke.* Smoking reduces the brain's oxygen supply by lowering the oxygen-carrying ability of red blood cells and reducing overall cerebral blood flow.

●*Prevent the deterioration of brain cells caused by free radicals* by taking daily supplements of the antioxidants vitamin E and vitamin C. It's important that vitamin E be derived from soy rather than synthetic sources. Dosage should be about 400 IU per day. The average multivitamin contains sufficient vitamin C. A recently published 22-year study showed that high blood levels of antioxidants in people 65 or older are associated with better memory.

●*Eat a healthful diet,* low in saturated fats and high in carbohydrates, including plenty of fruits and vegetables. In addition, eat fish two or three times a week for the omega-3 fatty acids it contains—or take at least 250 mg of fish-oil capsules daily, along with a meal.

Take a daily multivitamin, including the full complex of B vitamins.

●**Change how you handle stress.** If you're worried by stress, the negative emotions involved will interfere with your ability to learn and remember. *Instead, make a conscious decision to manage stress…*

●*Deep breathing.* Resolve to take a few minutes to breathe deeply whenever worry sets in.

●*Relax.* Develop a favorite way of relaxing when you feel stressed out. This might be yoga, stretching, listening to music, walking outdoors, meditation or visualizing yourself in a relaxing setting.

●*Sleep.* Be sure to get sufficient sleep, since chronic sleep deprivation actually impairs the brain's ability to revise and store memory, which happens while you sleep.

●**Get regular aerobic exercise.** Going for a walk, swim or bike ride for 45 minutes, four times a week, boosts more than just your physical health. Studies have shown that exercise enhances all mental functions, including memory, and decreases stress and depression—both of which interfere with memory in various ways.

●**Keep a positive attitude.** If you believe you can improve your memory, you can.

One recent study found that people's attitudes about the impact of aging on their intellect correlated directly with how frequently (or infrequently) they forgot key pieces of information.

As you follow the other steps outlined above, repeat to yourself, "*I believe I can remember better than before.*" Like the little engine that could, you'll find that by refusing to accept a lower level of cognitive functioning, you'll automatically increase your ability to remember.

Useful Lessons From the Wisdom In Your Dreams

Tony Schwartz, New York–based journalist and author of *What Really Matters: Searching for Wisdom in America.* Bantam. He and his wife, Deborah Pines, a psychotherapist, have run dream-analysis groups for 10 years.

Although dreams often seem nonsensical, close examination can yield self-knowledge and practical guidance for everyday living.

Interpreting dreams is usually a challenge. They so often deal with thorny issues that we avoid thinking about when we're awake. And most dream-analysis systems impose rigid symbolism and meanings that don't fit everyone.

The dream-analysis method I use involves freely exploring a dream with others but accepting only the insights that strike a personal chord.

My dreamwork programs normally contain eight to 10 people, but the system also works with just two or three.

PRESENT THE DREAM

To allow for wide-ranging speculation, the dreamer first tells the "straight story." He/she should write out and distribute clear details of the setting, sequence of events and images, including only those observations, thoughts or feelings in the dream. The dreamer should not try to interpret or add commentary.

Many people can recall entire sequences, but even small fragments yield information.

Example: One group participant could remember only "a pastel color." From this snippet came a revelation that his commitment to his work was pale and half-hearted. This led to a major career change.

OFFER OPINIONS

Having someone else discern a message in your dream may feel invasive. Therefore, each participant should preface his interpretation with, *If this were my dream, it might mean…*Input can center on the whole dream or on just one or two images.

Important: The dreamer, of course, need not accept any idea unless it rings true for him.

FIND MEANING

Using any of the group interpretations, as well as personal associations and concerns, the dreamer begins to formulate his own meaning. At this point, any of what I call *day residue* is also shared—say, a disagreement with a spouse or a dramatic television program that could have prompted the dream.

Working with this additional knowledge, the group reexamines the dream. Again—*If it were my dream* should preface each comment.

SUM UP

The goal in this stage is to apply the dream to life and personal issues.

Dream decoded: A woman who felt guilty about spending a week away from her young daughter dreamed that a harsh older woman was criticizing her neglect. Later in the dream, the daughter climbed into her mother's lap to chat about her adventures. In summing up, the mother realized that on an unconscious level, she did not believe her daughter had been hurt.

TO REMEMBER YOUR DREAMS

To analyze dreams, you must remember them. *Helpful…*

●**Intend to remember.** As you fall asleep, say, I want to remember a dream. This nudges your subconscious to oblige. You can also try to prompt a dream to elicit guidance in a certain area.

How: As you fall asleep, pose a short, specific question, either in writing or out loud. Then interpret the resulting dream in light of what you asked yourself.

●**Maintain a dream journal.** Keep it on your nightstand, and put the date at the top of a page each night. If you awaken after dreaming, outline the images. If this writing keeps you from falling back to sleep, mentally recount the dream so it is more easily recalled in the morning.

●**Awaken slowly.** Jumping out of bed can shatter dream memories. Lie quietly, eyes closed, to see what comes back to you. Write whatever you remember.

Best Ways to Say "I'm Sorry"

A heartfelt note can help you apologize to someone who was once important in your life…

●**Write and rewrite your letter** until you could feel good about it in 20 years.

●**Take full responsibility for your mistakes.** Use the words *I'm sorry* or *I apologize.*

●**Before sending the letter**—spend several days thinking about the letter and how you would feel receiving it.

●**Consider sending it at a meaningful time for the person,** such as a birthday.

●**Give your current address**—but do not expect a response.

●**Do not be upset if you get an angry letter back.** The other person may not have come to terms with what you did.

Jan B. King, president, The King Group, a human resources and business management company, El Segundo, CA. www.janbking.com.

Loneliness Threatens Your Health

Mary Ellen Copeland, a teacher, writer and lecturer in Dummerston, Vermont. She has extensively studied how people beat loneliness and other mental health issues. She is author of The Loneliness Workbook and The Depression Workbook. Both from New Harbinger.

L oneliness isn't just emotionally painful. *People who are cut off from others—and who feel sad about being alone—are at higher risk for…*

•**Heart disease.** A National Institute of Mental Health study found that individuals who suffer from depression—a common response to loneliness—are four times more likely to develop heart disease than those who are not depressed.

•**Cancer.** A study conducted at Johns Hopkins School of Medicine found that students who eventually developed cancer were more likely to have suffered from loneliness.

•**Weakened immunity.** An Ohio State University study found that a network of close friends helps prevent stress-related declines in the immune system.

To avoid loneliness, most of us need at least five close friends. These are the people we keep in touch with regularly...have fun with...ask for help when we need it...and who rely on us for help, too.

If you don't have enough friends—or feel dissatisfied with those you do have—you may be missing opportunities to meet new people or behaving in ways that prevent meaningful friendships from developing.

To change such patterns, follow these simple steps...

•**Overcome your fear of being alone.** People who hate spending time alone often come across as desperate. That makes them less attractive as potential friends.

Helpful: Create a list of things you love to do—by yourself. Include activities you enjoyed as a child but haven't done for years—sketching...shooting hoops...building models...playing the piano...fishing...window-shopping.

Resume these activities. You'll start to think of time alone as a gift...and become more interesting to others.

•**Consider your strengths.** The better you feel about yourself, the easier it will be to build friendships.

Think about the assets you bring to a friendship—good listener, supportive, like to laugh, etc. Write them down to help you remember them.

Then write down the qualities you would like to develop to make yourself a better friend. Consider steps you could take to develop these qualities.

•**Strengthen relationships with the people you already know.** You may have friends you haven't been in touch with for a long time. Call them.

Don't wait for an excuse or worry about coming up with a fancy speech. Simply say, "I'd like to renew our friendship" or "I don't want to go another year without being in touch."

If you don't know how to get in touch with an old friend, check *www.bigyellow.com* and select "People Pages" to locate an address and phone number.

If the person you're looking for is an old classmate, contact your alma mater's alumni relations office or search the database at *www.classmates.com.*

•**Meet new people.** Community events, where you see the same faces again and again, are the best places to make friends.

Examples: Adult-education classes...hiking clubs...community theater groups...gyms and amateur sports teams...religious organizations...interest groups (book clubs, bird-watchers, etc.).

To learn about such groups, look at bulletin boards, newspaper listings and college-extension catalogs. Check *www.realcities .com* for a list of local activities.

Another option: Support groups. You don't need to be recovering from illness or emotional issues. There are men's groups, women's groups—even loneliness groups.

To find them, check newspaper listings or call community health agencies and hospital social work departments.

Helpful: Make a list of events and groups you would enjoy. Attend at least one per week. Ask other attendees about the organization, how long they've been coming, their opinions about that evening's discussion, etc. Go four times before deciding whether the group or activity is a good fit.

Volunteering is another option. Working with other people on a shared cause builds bonds.

To find volunteer opportunities in your community, visit *www.volunteermatch.org.*

•**Turn acquaintances into friends.** Some friendships develop casually and naturally. But often, you must take the initiative.

If you have something in common with someone, suggest that you get together for coffee…talk during a break or intermission…or offer him/her a ride home from an activity.

Make the first move. You won't become less lonely without taking a few risks. The more you do it, the easier it will be.

●**Improve your communication skills.** We don't often recognize how we make it difficult for people to get to know us well. *Watch out for…*

●*Interrupting*—jumping in before the other person has finished talking.

●*Self-centered listening*—planning your reply while the other person is still talking.

●*Giving unsolicited advice*—telling the other person what to do.

●*Being vague*—dropping hints and expecting others to decipher them.

Ask yourself, "What do I want from this communication?"

Examples: "I need a ride to the doctor"…"I get upset when you're late"…"I need to get eight hours of sleep tonight."

●**Continue making new friends.** Circumstances change, and even close friends may not always be able to support you.

To avoid becoming too dependent on one or two friends, keep seeking out new acquaintances.

How to Make New Friends

Learn to read body language. *You'll have a better idea of what someone is really telling you…*

●**When someone smiles, look at his/her face**—real smiles crinkle the eyes.

●**A tilted head and wide-open eyes** suggest a willingness to listen.

●**Someone who is biting his lips** may feel he is being criticized.

●**People cross their legs** when they feel defensive and cross their arms when they want to be convinced.

●**Leaning back shows friendliness**—or feeling in control.

Helpful when meeting someone new: Establish rapport by mirroring some of his signals, such as leaning forward or smiling. Or use the same body positions.

Jo-Ellan Dimitrius, PhD, is a jury consultant and coauthor of *Reading People: How to Understand People and Predict Their Behavior—Anytime, Anyplace.* Ballantine.

How to Help Heal Yourself

Rachael Freed, MSW, founder of Minneapolis-based Heartmates, Inc., which provides resources for heart patients and their families.

After a heart attack, life changes forever. We mourn our old innocent ways…and our lost certainties. And—we face changes in lifestyle, financial security, retirement and our spouses' physical capabilities.

Learning to live with uncertainty is one of the greatest challenges for the partner of a person with heart disease.

Over the years, you have developed an idea of security. Now the rules have changed.

Important: Give yourself permission to break with family protocol and do whatever it takes to get all of you through. The task of a cardiac couple is to develop a "new normal" that incorporates heart disease.

The upside: A brush with mortality can reorder a couple's priorities for the better.

You don't have the power to eradicate your spouse's heart disease or to eliminate its effects on your life. Your goal is to be prepared to support his/her recovery—*and yours*.

Years after a cardiac event, people expect the heartmate to be a constant cheerleader.

My experience: During the crisis period, friends asked only about the patient. When the emergency was over, they were too uncomfortable to rally around. But I needed help—a lot of help.

GRIEF AND LOSS

After my husband's heart attack, I was coping, but I felt overwhelmed by strong feelings that took months to define. It was the grief that accompanies loss.

Since my husband was alive, how could I be feeling grief and loss? Because our life together had changed forever.

During an early presentation I made to spouses of heart attack survivors, I said, *"You are feeling grief."* Their tears and thanks convinced me that I was on the right track.

YOU'RE A TOP PRIORITY, TOO

The most important person in a heart patient's recovery is not the doctor, but the spouse. To maintain your role as a positive caretaker, you must pay attention to your own recovery.

Example: Airplane travelers are instructed to put their own oxygen masks on before helping someone else.

Taking care of yourself helps you come to terms with a life-changing crisis. *Steps to take…*

●**Make a list.** It should contain actions that would nourish your body, feelings, mind and spirit. Write one on your calendar every day—and do it.

Examples: Listen to music…sit in a chapel…take a walk.

●**Gather information.** Learn how diet, exercise and stress affect heart patients.

●**Confide in someone.** To reduce your sense of isolation, share your concerns with a nonjudgmental sibling, close friend or neighbor.

Many people find great relief by communicating with others in similar situations. *Good resource:* The Heartmates Web site at *www. heartmates.com.*

TAKE YOUR TIME

The nagging fear of another attack always churns below the surface. The fear never disappears entirely, but you'll begin to believe that your mate won't collapse every time he coughs.

Healing is a process, not an event. It takes at least a year, often two, to recover from a spouse's heart attack or cardiac event. No one but you can know the limits of your grieving period.

EMBRACE YOUR HEALING ROLE

Take these steps to reinforce family bonds and your vitality as a couple…

●**Involve the whole family.** The patient and family members may experience different realities. Learn what your family is feeling. At weekly problem-solving meetings, ask each person to describe his greatest concerns. Then discuss them.

Example: If your children are grown and living elsewhere, performing this exercise even once during a visit can break the tension and be extremely helpful.

●**Fight your guilt and fear of stressing the patient.** Use caution in all things, but be aware that the patient won't die if you accidentally sprinkle a little salt on his food…use a noisy vacuum cleaner…take some time for yourself…or cry.

●**Repair the heartmate connection.** Fear of communicating is common after the hospital stay has threatened the marriage bond.

The trauma pulls some cardiac couples apart, intensifying existing conflicts. For others, the crisis provides an opportunity for enriching the relationship.

Honest confrontation of the changes in your relationship is a step toward deepening the marriage connection. *Avoid these traps…*

●**Concealing your concerns** from the patient.

●**Thinking you can reduce stress** by withholding your anger and other negative feelings.

●**Assuming you must always agree** with the patient.

●**Disregarding your own emotional needs.**

●**Letting TV preempt precious time** to communicate with each other.

SEX: THE UNASKED QUESTION

At my group presentations, people almost never ask about sex. Privately, they are distraught by the silence, isolation and lack of information about impotence.

These misconceptions contribute to spouses' fear and apprehension…

***Myth:* Sexual activity is hazardous for heart patients.**

Reality: For most, not so. The amount of energy expended during sex is roughly equivalent to climbing two flights of stairs. A patient who can do the latter can probably do the former safely.

***Myth:* Heart disease decreases sexual drive and impairs sexual functioning.**

Reality: Fatigue, depression and medications for angina, high blood pressure or palpitations can cause impotence. Fatigue and depression can be treated. If medications are the problem, the doctor may be able to prescribe a different one.

***Myth:* Heart disease signifies the end of normal sexual activity.**

Reality: After a few weeks of recuperation, the overwhelming majority of cardiac couples can resume their sexual relationship…and mend their bond through affection and physical intimacy.

Elaine St. James Tells All About Living the Simple Life

Elaine St. James, lecturer located in Santa Barbara, California, and author of several best-selling books, including *Living the Simple Life.* Hyperion.

We all have so many possessions now, so many places to go and so many things to do that we wear ourselves out just trying to keep things straight. Not surprisingly, the desire to simplify life has become very important in recent years.

COMPLICATIONS TODAY

Three forces make life more complicated than it has to be…

●**Consumerism.** Modern society is shaped by a powerful consumerist drive that makes us want more and more objects that we don't really need. We work harder to afford them and take up precious time acquiring and using them while they are still novel. Then, it's hard for us to get rid of them even after we have tired of them.

●**Lack of boundaries.** We find it easier to say "yes" when offered new objects, experiences and places. And, even when we really want to say "no," we often say "yes" when others ask for the use of some of our limited resource of time.

●**Distractions.** Keeping our lives complicated gives us an excuse to avoid serious thinking about our real needs and desires, which might involve uncomfortable changes.

SIMPLE WAYS TO SIMPLIFY

It is compelling to simplify your life drastically overnight, but you can succeed surprisingly quickly by taking one small step at a time.

Set aside some time—a few hours to a few days—to think about your true priorities.

To find time to think: Get up an hour earlier…stay in the office an hour after work…stop watching TV…limit social phone calls …don't go shopping except for food.

Find a distraction-free environment and write out the answers to a few simple questions…

●**What parts of my life are complicating it right now**—and how can I simplify them?

●**What are the most important things in my life?**

●**What can I stop doing so I can focus on my priorities?**

One of your toughest tasks may be forcing yourself to pay attention to your answers. You may be hearing things you don't want to hear. Your inner voice may be telling you that what you need to do is quit your job or find a new career or move on from a relationship that isn't working.

Remember, often we keep our lives complicated so we won't have to listen to our inner voice telling us what we need to do to make our lives work better.

GETTING RID OF STUFF

Your house is probably full of all sorts of things that you don't need now—if, in fact, you ever did. One incentive to get rid of the clutter is to realize that if you don't, your children will eventually be left with the task. *How to get started…*

●**Linen closet.** Throw out all the worn-out bed sheets. Give away towels that don't match your current decor…as well as any table linens you never use. Many people would be happy to have them.

●**Kitchen.** Clear the shelves of all the pots, pans, appliances and gadgets you have not touched in years.

●**Closets.** Sell or give away whatever you don't care about. It's OK to keep items you are sentimentally attached to—but if they take up a lot of space, consider just photographing them and keeping the pictures to preserve their memory.

●*Hint #1:* Imagine all your possessions had been destroyed in a fire. Keep only things you would feel you absolutely had to replace.

●*Hint #2:* Ask a friend to go through your things with you and help you decide what to get rid of.

KEEPING THINGS SIMPLE

To keep from rebuilding the clutter you have just eliminated, follow two rules…

●*Rule #1:* Keep a 30-day list. If you are in a store and feel a powerful urge to buy something, write it down on your list together with the date. Decide 30 days later if you still want the object.

●*Rule #2:* Every time you buy something new, get rid of one thing you already own. *Better still:* Get rid of two things.

SIMPLIFY YOUR TIME

Some simple ways to accomplish routine tasks…

●**Household chores.** Schedule particular tasks on fixed days each week.

●**Meal preparation.** Make a weekly menu plan with a standard meal for each day of the week. This simplifies meal planning, grocery shopping and cooking.

●**Bill paying.** Most companies that send regular monthly bills are happy to arrange an automatic payment schedule with your bank. You only have to fill out a form once—and remember to keep enough money in the bank.

How to Say *No* Without Feeling Guilty

Patti Breitman and Connie Hatch, coauthors of How to Say NO Without Feeling Guilty, and Say YES to More Time, More Joy, and What Matters Most to You. Broadway. Ms. Breitman is a literary agent in Marin County, CA. Ms. Hatch is a freelance writer in New York City.

There is a rampant myth in our culture that to be considered nice, you have to say *yes* all the time.

Women are particularly afflicted with the need to say yes because they are traditionally raised to believe their job is to make others happy.

Problem: When we keep saying *yes*, resentment and anger build.

All of us need time to pursue happiness. Learning to say *no* helps you reclaim that time.

BETTER NAY SAYING

To use no with skill and sensitivity—and without guilt…

●**Start small.** Practice saying *no* in non-threatening encounters, where little is at stake and success is almost assured.

Examples: Tell your best friend you don't want to go to her favorite restaurant…then suggest another. Tell your son he can't have more ice cream before bedtime.

●**Keep it simple.** The most effective nos are the least complicated. The more details you supply, the more likely the other person will try to change your mind.

●**Buy time when responding to requests.** It relieves pressure when you're not sure how to say *no* diplomatically…or simply need more time to make a decision.

Useful responses: I'll check my calendar and get back to you…Let me ask my husband/wife/partner if we're free that day.

●**Pretend you're confident**—even if saying no makes you uncomfortable. Before you know it, you *will* feel more confident and won't have to pretend.

●**Remain generous.** Saying *no* without guilt is much easier when it is done in the context of generosity. This means being helpful and available to family, friends and coworkers whenever you can—as long as it doesn't cause you significant stress or inconvenience.

NO AT WORK

Men have almost as much trouble as women saying *no* in the workplace. To leave at a reasonable hour, use some version of the statement, *I have plans*. No elaborate explanation is necessary.

If you supply too many details, your manager may feel your "excuse" isn't good enough.

NO TO KIDS

For some parents, saying *no* to their kids is hardest of all. Yet setting limits—often by saying *no*—contributes to kids' emotional security. *Keys with kids...*

●**Always keep your explanations age-appropriate.**

●**Give only one reason.** The more you talk, the less you'll be heard. Don't hesitate to end the discussion with a classic line like, *Because that's the rule*.

NO TO BORROWERS-TO-BE

Say *no* to requests for money in simple language, without offering a reason—*I wish I could, but I can't*. With luck, the person will stop there. If not, invoke a "policy"—*I have a strict policy about not lending money to friends*. This will make your no sound less personal.

UNDERSTAND YES

You will feel most confident saying no if you have a strong vision of what you want to say yes to. Why are you saying *no* to a particular request? What obligation or priority are you trying to make room for?

Once you stop investing the better part of yourself doing things you don't want to do with people you don't want to see, you can focus your actions on your core beliefs, priorities and passions.

Related Useful Sites

Cars

☐ Auto Trader Online

www.traderonline.com/auto

Buy or sell a used car, a new car, a truck, an RV or a motorcycle. Link to auto magazine Web sites, find the high, low and average price of any car in Auto Trader's database, find a dealer near you, link to manufacturers' sites and more.

☐ AutoSite

www.autosite.com

Not only does this site allow you to create your own sticker price for cars you're interested in, it offers a massive amount of easy-to-access information about car safety, maintenance, leasing, financing and more. It also contains helpful used-car buying advice.

☐ Car and Driver

www.caranddriver.com

Useful site for both car buyers and car owners. Shopping for a car? In *Car and Driver* magazine's Buying Guide, you can browse by manufacturer, vehicle type (convertibles, luxury cars, pickup trucks, etc.) or winners of the magazine's best-vehicle awards. Conduct a search by entering combinations from each vehicle category.

☐ CarTalk

www.cartalk.com

A useful automotive site that's also fun! If you're a fan of National Public Radio's Click and Clack (Tom and Ray Magliozzi), you'll visit this site often. Site offers four years' worth of their syndicated newspaper columns. *Got a Car?* is the most useful part of the site, with vehicle and mechanic databases, user surveys, car talk reports, test drive notebooks and much more.

☐ Nutz & Boltz

www.nutzandboltz.com

A free on-line automobile club with lots of useful tips for car care in general and for your car in particular. Updated weekly. Site includes information on secret warranties by make, model and year.

Home

☐ Home and GardenTV

www.hgtv.com

This site is brought to you by the producers of *Home & Garden Television* and is chock full of great ideas and tips. Click on building and remodeling, crafts & collectibles, gardening & landscaping and share your ideas or get new ones.

☐ Adventures in Gardening

www.gardenguy.com

This site boasts some of the most current information the Web has to offer on plants, gardening and techniques to help your garden flourish. There are reviews of the latest books on the subject. You can pose questions and receive expert answers. Check out links to other great gardening sites, and view photos of some of the world's most splendid gardens.

☐ HomeDelivery.com

www.homedelivery.com

Need to find the closest drycleaner, hairdresser, pet shop, video store? This site offers one-stop shopping at local retailers as well as global catalog merchants. You just enter your zip code and select from a large list of categories. You'll get a list of conveniently located shops. Or you can select from the "anywhere" category to get mail-order services.

☐ HomeWorkingMom.com

www.homeworkingmom.com

This site provides ideas, encouragement and support to mothers who work at home. Lots of useful advice on how to balance career and family. Learn how to have happy kids while you work. Check out the best home business opportunities, meet a mentor and check out the site's daily success strategy.

☐ The Internet Movie Database

http://us.imdb.com

More than 150,000 movies, from silents to latest releases, even movies still in production. Information includes plot summaries, critics' reviews, ratings, year of release, running times, trivia and much more.

□ The Kitchen Link
www.kitchenlink.com

An amazing collection of recipes and other food information as well as links to almost 10,000 food and cooking sites on the Web. Click on *Recipe Clippings* and dive into the Kitchen Link's archives. There's also a free newsletter, message boards and more.

□ Almanac.com
www.almanac.com

Here's the Web's version of *The Old Farmer's Almanac,* first published in 1792. Of course, there are long-range weather forecasts, but that's not all. Find out what time the sun or moon will rise and set on any given day, check out the Question of the Day (or ask one) and enjoy the editor's favorite puzzles and games.

Travel

□ Bureau of Consular Affairs
http://travel.state.gov

Visit this site before you travel abroad. Check on *Travel Warnings* (by country), *Passport Services and Information, Visa Services, Judicial Assistance, International Adoption & International Parental Child Abduction, Travel Publications,* even the *State Department* home page. Site also has useful links to embassy and consular Web sites worldwide.

□ BaseCamp
www.bpbasecamp.com

From the publishers of *Backpacker Magazine,* this site has great tips for tackling the great outdoors. Click on *GearFinder* and choose the gear that's just right for you. Learn how to use a map and compass, check on what the weather's going to be in your neck of the woods, and check out the women's page.

□ Hotels & Travel on the Net
www.hotelstravel.com

Search hundreds of listings by state, gender, country, religion, session length or name. Browse categories, including overnight camp, day camp. Try specialty camps, categorized by academics, arts, sports and/or special needs. Listings for family camps, tour and adventure. Also includes a home page hot button for *Grown-up Camps,* which links to a comparable Web site for adults.

□ QuickAID
www.quickaid.com

Unusually comprehensive site. Get detailed information on any major airport (hotels, airlines, ground transportation, even a map of the terminals).

□ Roadside America
www.roadsideamerica.com

Looking for offbeat attractions when you're on the road? Check out this fun and colorful site. Learn where you can find premium quality strawberries and the world's largest olives at *Salads of the Gods.* Click on *The Vortex* and find places to visit that you never knew existed.

□ Small Ship Cruises
www.smallshipcruises.com

Looking for a cruise with a five-passenger maximum? This is the only site on the Web that lists all small ship cruise lines (five to 500 passengers). You can search by cruise line or destination. There are weekly updates with deals and discounts and you can book your trip right on-line.

□ Travel Health Information Service
www.travelhealth.com

An excellent, comprehensive site for world travelers. There's loads of information on everything, including food and water safety precautions, immunization information, specific risks in the country you are visiting, CDC information about the region you're headed for. You can even apply for a passport.

□ TravelWeb
www.travelweb.com

Fast, graphically appealing Web site. Make hotel reservations by searching hotel database by city, state or province, country or region. Or search by property name, hotel chain, type of hotel and/or room rates, even amenities. Browse hotel choices (lodging chains/independent hotels). For flight availability and airline reservations, go to *Flight Search.*

18

Business and Career

Stay a Step Ahead of The Business Slowdown... Cut Costs and Boost Revenue...Now

Regardless of how long it takes the economy to bounce back from its dotcom-based malaise, one thing is clear—now is the time to cut costs and boost revenue.

Caution: Reacting to a downturn by immediately laying off employees often backfires. You may inadvertently hurt a critical part of the business, such as product quality...productivity...or customer service.

PAINLESS COST-CUTTING

Before downsizing your payroll, consider these simple, but highly effective, ways of weathering an economic downturn...

●**Collaborate on purchasing needs.** By joining other small businesses to purchase collectively as a group, you can save on more products and services than most companies realize.

Examples: Long-distance phone service, printing and copying, classified advertising, overnight deliveries.

Talk with other business owners, and approach vendors from whom you would like to buy. Speak with several vendors in each product area. Then negotiate by telling each that you're talking with several suppliers.

Some may ask for guaranteed minimum orders, but most won't. Today, more and more vendors are eager to deal with consortiums of small companies because it's more efficient than dealing with individual companies. And vendors pass part of their savings on to the customers.

Many vendors like to deal with buyer groups so much that they'll arrange to bill

Perry J. Ludy, president of LUDYCO International, management consultants,1440 Whalley Ave., New Haven, CT 06515. *www.ludyco.com.* He is author of *Profit Building: Cutting Costs Without Cutting People.* Berrett-Koehler.

each member company individually even though they purchase collectively.

•**Boost sales to existing customers.** By selling customers two or three products when they originally ask for one, many businesses can quickly increase profits. To find out which products are effective for add-on sales, ask customers about their buying patterns.

Example: A few decades ago, stationery stores discovered that customers often wanted copying services. Today, stationers routinely offer this service.

Also look at competitors who might already be offering add-ons, and talk with your vendors, who may be supplying competitors with products that they sell as add-ons.

•**Deposit payroll checks directly.** The cost of printed checks, plus the management time to process them, is often greater than bank fees for direct deposits. Compare the two and opt for the less expensive means of paying employees. The more payroll checks you write, the greater the savings on direct deposit.

•**Analyze utility costs.** Hire a consultant to analyze your utility bills—especially if your company owns its own building or work space. Savings typically outweigh the price of a consultant. Look for consultants in the Yellow Pages or through business groups, such as your area Chamber of Commerce.

•**Trim insurance costs.** Most companies automatically renew insurance policies without reviewing them. You can save by eliminating unnecessary coverage.

General rule: Make sure you're fully covered on items that are critical to the business. Then take a hard look at everything else.

•**Cut travel costs.** Instead of reimbursing employees for expensive meals and hotels, pay them an adequate per diem travel allowance.

Example: If the daily cost of hotels and meals has averaged $150, cut it by 20%. Give traveling employees a per-diem allowance of $120.

There might be some opposition at first, but employees will soon realize the advantage of traveling more economically and pocketing the difference between travel expenditures and the per diem allowance.

•**Work harder to keep customers.** Large companies spend huge amounts of money to keep their customers. *But there are many* inexpensive *ways of doing it that are often overlooked…*

•Stay in close touch with your customers. Keep records of what they buy. Then write or phone them when you think they would be interested in a new service or product you can offer.

•Use after-sale service to solidify the relationship. Don't wait until customers contact you. Instead, contact them to ask how they like your product and respond immediately when a problem occurs.

•Take advantage of after-sale service to recommend other products and pave the way for future sales.

•Ask customers to recommend others who might be interested in your products or service.

•**Market your customer data.** Even if you have a customer list of only 1,000 names, marketing firms or mailing list companies may still want to rent it so they can combine it with lists from other small businesses.

Possible income: Up to $150 per 1,000 names each time the list is rented. Also, one list can turn into two when you include E-mail information.

Or consider renting your customer list to a noncompeting business…or swapping lists with other businesses.

Example: A public relations consultant could benefit from swapping lists with a printing firm.

•**Reduce turnover.** The most effective way to retain valued employees is to get them directly involved in company operations and strategy. Unfortunately, that's all too easy to forget, especially in the midst of worries about a slowdown.

Solution: Instead of trying to change your company's culture overnight, begin taking small steps to involve employees…

•Regularly ask your people for advice, and follow through whenever possible. Solicit suggestions for saving time and resources and for making the company more competitive.

•Reward employees who contribute winning ideas.

•Hire managers who, in addition to being skilled professionals, also demonstrate good "people skills."

•Hold periodic social events.

•Reward managers for boosting morale and getting workers involved.

•**Take advantage of government employment incentives.** A variety of state and federal programs offer tax benefits to companies that hire and train workers. For more information, contact your state agency that deals with employment matters.

In some instances, tax benefits compensate businesses for all of a new employee's salary during the training period.

Employee Severance Basics

Document every new hire's performance from the time he/she starts—in case termination becomes necessary.

Important: Offer frequent feedback to employees, so they know if they are performing poorly and know what they must do to keep their jobs. If repeated warnings don't work, tell an employee on Friday to take Monday off to make a career decision—accept termination or agree to substantial improvements. If he opts to keep his job, set clear goals—with deadlines.

John Cowan, editor, *Positive Leadership*, 316 N. Michigan Ave., Chicago 60601.

ADA Trap Removed

It is not always lawful to ask employees about their health. Because the Americans with Disabilities Act (ADA) bans questions that might lead employees to reveal a disability, many supervisors have been afraid to raise any health-related subject.

Now the Equal Employment Opportunity Commission has created guidelines of permissible questions that do not violate ADA rules.

Examples: Asking an employee how he/she feels today...asking a worker who has lost a loved one how he's coping...asking someone who is sneezing if he has allergies.

Peter M. Panken, Esq., leading management-side expert on labor and employment law and partner with Epstein Becker & Green PC, 250 Park Ave., New York City 10177.

Easy...Important... Formula to Avoid Losing Key People

Sharon Jordan-Evans, president, Jordan Evans Group, a leadership consulting firm, Cambria, CA, and coauthor of *Love 'Em or Lose 'Em: Getting Good People to Stay.* Berrett-Koehler.

If you think there's nothing you can do to keep talented employees motivated, productive and working for you in today's tight labor market...think again.

Take the time now to cultivate relationships with your employees, and you'll be less likely to spend time and money recruiting their replacements later.

We surveyed employees and discovered that an open, honest, mutually respectful relationship with the boss is one of the key factors influencing their decision to stay with their current companies.

SERIOUS WORK

Good relationships don't just *happen*... they are initiated and nurtured by bosses who realize that it costs far more to replace top performers—70% to 200% of an employee's annual salary—than to keep them on the payroll.

This does not include the "hidden" costs sustained as a result of disrupted work flow... lost sales...unhappy customers...and perhaps even low morale company-wide.

How do you keep an excellent employee working for you when he/she has one eye on the classifieds and the other on the heap of offers coming in from recruiters? *While some people will be impossible to keep no matter what, you can drastically reduce turnover of valued employees by following these relationship-building steps...*

●**Build trust** by listening to and talking informally with every employee—one-on-one. You don't have to be best friends with your subordinates to show that you support, consider and respect them as individuals who have lives outside of the company.

Your heartfelt interest will make them feel recognized and valued.

Example: One manager let his receptionist have a few hours off in the middle of the day to see her daughter sing *The Star Spangled Banner* at a pep rally. Afterward, the manager not only asked how the performance went...he noticed the videotape in the employee's hand and asked her if she would share it with him and her coworkers. "It was such a small thing, but it meant so much to me," she said.

●**Regularly ask key employees** how they feel about their jobs...what their goals are ...and what employment-related issues matter most to them. *Sit down with each of your employees at least every quarter, and ask several or all of the following questions...*

●Are you challenged in your day-to-day work?

●Is the training you need available to you?

●Do you receive regular, candid feedback?

●What is difficult or unproductive about working here?

●Is there anything about your job that you are struggling with all the time?

●What would lure you away from our company?

●If you were tempted by a job offer outside of this company, would you tell me about it before you accepted it?

USING THE INFORMATION

You may learn that equipment needs upgrading...training hasn't been provided...or some teammates aren't doing their share of the work.

By fixing these problems, you demonstrate the degree to which you value each person who works for you.

Beyond day-to-day problems, what you'll learn through open and honest discussions with employees is that there is far more to job satisfaction than money. *Here are the top three reasons our survey respondents gave for staying with their current employers and what you can do about them...*

●**Career growth, learning and development.** Keep employees growing by helping them consider and achieve multiple career goals.

Meet with each employee quarterly or annually to discuss what they like and don't like about their work and to brainstorm ways to improve their jobs.

Even the smallest company can find creative ways to redefine an employee's job to make it more interesting. *Examples...*

●Moving an employee laterally in the organization gives him a new job without changing his salary or level of responsibility.

●A detailed exploration of the existing job analyzes what duties could be added or changed to better suit the employee.

●Enrichment helps an employee grow in place through training.

●Realignment involves moving an employee down in the organization to slow or redirect his career—if he needs time for personal obligations.

●A vertical move involves promoting the employee to a position of increased responsibility.

When an employee admits—because you asked—to being bored by his work, find ways to make his job more stimulating. *Examples...*

●Put employees in touch with clients. Visiting a client's office to help troubleshoot a problem or provide personal service can be exciting.

●Rotate assignments. Suggest that employees swap certain duties on a regular basis, and let them work out a schedule for doing so. They'll feel empowered and newly challenged as a result.

●Nurture creativity. Ask for—even insist on—employees' ideas for solving business problems...coming up with new products/services...addressing ongoing workplace challenges...increasing production...improving customer service, etc. Acknowledge ideas and reward participation.

•*Meaningful work.* Making a contribution to your company's growth and success is important to almost all employees. Make sure that your employees understand your business, its industry, your plans for growth and how their jobs fit into the big picture. Help them understand your company and the way their jobs contribute to overall success.

Bottom line: The better you know your employees and the more willing you are to find creative ways to keep them happy and productive, the more likely they'll be to ignore outside job offers and choose—over and over—to work for you.

Benefits Employees Value Most

1. Health insurance.
2. Retirement plan.
3. Employer match to retirement plan contributions.
4. Paid vacation and holidays.
5. Paid sick leave.
6. Ability to select among benefits.
7. Retirement health plan.
8. Prescription drug coverage.
9. Preventive health coverage.
10. Life insurance.

Survey conducted by Aon Consulting's Loyalty Institute, the research arm of Aon, an international human resources firm, 123 N. Wacker Dr., 11th Fl., Chicago 60606.

Job Earnings on the Web

Top on-line salary sites for information on current pay scales: *www.salary.com* is easy to use and covers more than 1,100 job titles...America's Career InfoNet, *www.acinet. org*, offers career advice and job-market outlook...US Bureau of Labor Statistics, *www. bls.gov*, is text-heavy but can help you plan a career path...Economic Research Institute, *www.erieri.com/doltrends*, offers detailed job listings—but gives salary averages, not ranges ...Korn/Ferry International, *www.futurestep. com*, gives individual earnings profiles after you fill out a questionnaire.

Jacqueline Whitmore, founder and executive director, Protocol School of Palm Beach, FL.

Essentials of Preventing Inventory Rip-Offs

Barry Brandman, president, Danbee Investigations, a firm that provides professional investigative and consulting services to help companies prevent and investigate white- and blue-collar crimes, 1 Godwin Ave., Midland Park, NJ 07432.

Inventory theft affects companies of all sizes—in a big way. A corporate giant's "minor" loss, though, may be enough to put a small company out of business.

Unfortunately, many business owners believe their operations are immune to inventory theft or think it's a problem that only affects other companies. Because they know and care for their employees—many of whom are considered loyal—these employers fail to implement safety and security measures until after a loss or two has occurred. At that point, it may be too late to save the business from serious financial harm.

PREVENTIVE MEASURES

Preventing theft of inventory assets is far less expensive and easier to achieve than investigating and prosecuting criminals after the fact.

Here are the key steps to take to protect your inventory from rip-offs of all kinds...

•**Conduct thorough background checks before hiring an applicant.** A startling number of criminals and substance abusers are hired simply because business owners fail to call former employers to ask if an applicant is "eligible for rehire"…or they fail to notice significant time gaps on résumés, which can be suggestive of jail time.

Caution: Don't fall prey to a tight labor market. When you hire too hastily, relaxing your standards "just to fill the position," you may trade a bad problem (having no employee) for a worse one (hiring a criminal or a substance-abusing employee).

Solution: *Always* call an applicant's references. And—if the position that is being filled involves exposure to sensitive information or large sums of money/inventory—consider hiring an investigations firm to conduct a thorough background check for you. In addition to combing through courthouse files looking for criminal convictions, today's best investigative firms use sophisticated databases to research people's backgrounds. We find deliberate falsifications or omissions on about 20% of the applications we process.

●**Do a "theft vulnerability assessment" at your company.** How easy is it for employees, vendors and customers to walk away with your inventory?

Key issues to consider…

●Are package inspections regularly performed to prevent employees from pilfering inventory?

●Do you regularly conduct unannounced loss-prevention audits on checkers responsible for inbound and outbound inventory to determine whether they're negligent or dishonest?

●When trash is removed from your distribution center, is it always inspected by a manager to ensure that good product isn't being concealed inside bags or discarded boxes?

●Do your ongoing loss-prevention safeguards consist of more than an alarm system, closed-circuit television and/or uniformed guards? (All of those can be easily circumvented by devious thieves.)

●**Give employees a risk-free,** anonymous way to report theft. Put into place a safe "whistle-blower" system that employees can use anonymously and without risk—to let you know about on-the-job theft, fraud,

embezzlement, drug abuse and other illegal activities.

Example: We offer clients a toll-free hotline that employees can call to report suspicious activity they've observed or heard about. The cost of this service is only about $2,000 annually per location. That expense is often covered with prevention of a single theft, drug-related accident or act of workplace violence.

●**Give managers and frontline supervisors** thorough targeted training to recognize "red flags" of dishonesty. Serious problems can be averted if supervisors are taught to recognize the early warning signs of dishonesty, collusion and substance abuse.

Common examples: Absence of competitive vendors bidding for jobs…an employee who refuses to take a vacation…overly friendly relationships between warehouse personnel and truck drivers, or customer complaints concerning incomplete shipments—or no shipments at all.

IF YOU ARE HIT

If you do suffer a loss and you're not sure what to do about it, follow these steps…

●**Think of theft *first*.** It's tempting to look for possible reasons inventory might be missing rather than considering the likelihood of employee-related theft. However, the truth is employees and long-time employers' and customers' vendors can and do steal inventory right out from under employers' noses.

Example: A Midwestern small-business owner lost $50,000 worth of inventory and started exploring all of the ways that it might have happened—except for theft. He figured "there's no way anyone could be taking inventory without being seen." When the possibility of theft was finally explored, however, it was discovered that long-time employees were giving away extra product to certain customers coming through the "cash and carry" business department. Customers would pay for $200 worth of product and receive $800 worth. Seen from a distance, this criminal operation looked like business as usual.

But by investigating every possible cause of shortage *except* theft, the owner lost the important advantage of surprise. Thieves usually either stop stealing or perfect their technique if they suspect someone is looking into the loss.

●**Proceed calmly, quietly and covertly.** *Helpful...*a professional, business-oriented private investigations company. Share your suspicions with them. Don't try to conduct an investigation into the matter yourself. You may uncover evidence and be unable to use it due to a technical bungling of the law. Or —even worse, you might find yourself in a dangerous situation. *To choose a good firm...*

●Look for a firm that specializes in business issues, not matrimonial ones or providers of guard service.

●If you haven't heard of, or read about, firms you're considering, meet with them at their headquarters to make sure they're professional, experienced and clear about how to proceed with your case.

●Request at least six reputable corporate client references from the firms you're considering, and don't take "no" for an answer. If a firm claims it can't provide references because of "client confidentiality," be suspicious. Most firms that don't have references use this as an excuse.

●**Limit the number of people you tell about an investigation.** It's tempting to confide in long-term employees and senior managers—or even to call a company-wide meeting to share your suspicions and request information.

Again, resist the temptation. It's possible that one or more of the people responsible for the theft may end up sitting in the room with you.

Better: Operate strictly on a need-to-know basis. Confidentiality is essential for a successful investigation.

●**Watch your body language and behavior.** Don't compromise the investigation by acting differently toward people you suspect might be involved in a theft. Perpetrators pick up on changes in attitude, tone and behavior very quickly, and may suddenly resign or become much more careful—and harder to catch—when stealing inventory.

Best Ways To Boost Collections

Carol Frischer, collections consultant, Parks Palmer Business Services, Inc., CPA business management firm, Los Angeles, and author of *Collections Made Easy: Fast, Efficient, Proven Techniques to Get Cash from Your Customers*. Career Press.

When making business-to-business collection calls, you can expect debtors to have well-prepared excuses...you aren't the only one calling them.

To get past excuses and get paid, be prepared for every excuse you might hear.

Effective: Be polite and assume that the excuse the debtor gives is valid. Don't threaten. Instead, take constructive steps to remove the excuse. *Examples...*

●**We never received a bill.** Immediately send another bill by fax, E-mail or certified mail. Get a promise of prompt payment when the bill is received.

●**The check is in the mail.** Ask when it was sent and verify that it was sent to the correct address. After 10 days, if the check hasn't arrived, ask the debtor to stop payment on it and send another by Express Mail with you paying the express charge.

●**The computer prints checks at the end of the month.** Ask when checks are printed and when they must be submitted to be paid in each cycle. Time future invoices accordingly. Call during each cycle to assure that you are being paid.

●**The computer is down.** Ask a series of questions such as: *Why can't you write a check manually?...When will the computer be up?...What's being done to fix it?...How can you operate without it for so long?...How are other tasks accomplished without it?* The debtor will have to make so many excuses that often writing a check will be the easier option.

●**We're expecting a big check soon and will be able to pay you in full.** Say you'll be happy to accept partial payment now, and they'll be better off by reducing late charges and protecting their credit record.

How to Get the Most Mileage from Limited Cash

Randy Bruce Blaustein, Esq., senior tax partner, R.B. Blaustein & Co., 155 E. 31 St., New York City 10016. Mr. Blaustein is author of *How to Do Business with the IRS.* Prentice Hall.

Some small businesses are lucky enough to generate so much cash that meeting payroll and paying the bills is rarely if ever a major concern. But most small companies aren't so lucky. They are forced to make every dollar of revenue work as hard as possible—to keep the business going month to month.

For those companies it is especially worthwhile to follow the time-honored tactics for getting the most bang for every buck…

NEGOTIATE, NEGOTIATE, NEGOTIATE

You can conserve a lot of cash by learning to negotiate aggressively with vendors. Use more than one supplier so you will have more flexibility. And—build a relationship with each one so that they will gradually extend you more and more credit.

Examples: In the beginning, a vendor might require you to pay COD. But you should quickly advance to asking for 30-day, then 60-day credit. Next, you can try to negotiate a discount for paying promptly. Never hesitate to ask a vendor to whom you may owe, say, $250, if he/she will settle for $200 right now.

Most are only too happy to get the cash in hand—and your savings add up over time.

General rule: Pay your bills slowly, short of incurring penalties, *and collect what's owed to you quickly.*

Every small business must aggressively monitor accounts receivable. Earn a reputation for paying attention to these matters. Send bills out promptly. Follow up as necessary. Here again, however, it's important to be flexible and ready to negotiate.

Example: A customer owes you $1,000 but there is little likelihood that he's willing—or able—to write a check in that amount. Suggest that he pay you $100 a week. It's always better to get a little on a regular basis than to write off the whole debt. If the situation deteriorates to the point that you must turn it over to a bill collector, you've lost the customer and you still may not get paid in full…and you will owe something to the collection agency.

LEASING VERSUS BUYING

Another highly effective way to conserve cash is to lease equipment instead of buy it. You will pay a slightly higher interest rate than if you borrowed from a bank, but you avoid all the irritation of dealing with the bank.

In some cases, you may want to lease with an option to buy. Otherwise, simply lease for a finite term and recognize that you are getting use of the equipment without tying up any of the company's capital.

The same concept applies to employees. It's far less expensive to hire independent contractors as you need them than to add people to the payroll who may become extra baggage later on.

Each full-time employee comes with a costly obligation to pay payroll taxes and fringe benefits from day one forward.

There are also an increasingly onerous number of federal, state and local regulations that apply to permanent employees. Compliance can be extremely costly.

DON'T OVERPAY TAXES

Be sure to recalculate the company's income tax projections on a regular basis so that you don't give Uncle Sam an interest-free loan. Pay the minimum amount necessary to avoid penalties, but no more.

Example: If the company paid taxes of $1,000 last year but will owe $20,000 for this year, don't pay quarterly estimated taxes of $5,000. The law generally requires you to pay estimated taxes of up to 100% of last year's tax bill. You can hold off paying the additional $19,000 until the taxes are actually due.

INVEST IDLE CASH

Never let idle cash sit around without earning something. Obviously, investing in high-risk securities is not a prudent way to manage the company's spare cash. But—by buying 30-day Treasury bills or CDs or shares in money market funds you can put the cash to work without having to worry about market fluctuations.

Most small companies don't have enough funds to justify sophisticated bank sweep accounts, but be sure to look into possible connections that would enable you to switch funds from savings accounts to checking accounts within the same bank.

In addition, while small companies lack the clout of bigger operations, it still may be possible to persuade your banker to waive certain fees on your various accounts. If competition is especially intense among local banks, for example, you may be able to get free checking or reduce payroll account fees—just for the asking.

This is especially true during times of slowing economic growth. Banks competing for shrinking amounts of available business will often be more generous than usual to beat out their rivals.

Adding to Profits... Insurance Savings

In addition to the active steps for building your company, there are also cost-saving steps you may be overlooking. One of the most commonly ignored cost savers is cheaper insurance.

Have your insurance agent review every policy—pointing out where you might save money. Invite competitive agents to review your coverage and offer quotes. Consider a change if the newcomer has money-saving suggestions that your old agent never mentioned.

Example: One client's deductible on its vehicles was $250. Just raising the deductible to $1,000 slashed its insurance costs by up to 30%!

Health-Care Costs: How to Beat the Latest Increases

Alan Mittermaier, president, HealthMetrix Research, Inc., a provider of information on managed-care health plans, 3070 Riverside Dr., Columbus, OH 43221.

Health-care costs are likely to keep increasing by up to 12% a year for at least the next few years.

Reasons: Big increases in prescription drug prices plus higher rates from doctors, hospitals and HMOs to compensate for a drop in Medicare payments.

Good news: With careful planning, your business may be able to beat the increase—completely.

OPTIONS TO CONSIDER NOW

●**Self-insurance.** Self-insuring is not as risky as it may sound because insurance companies still play a role in limiting a company's exposure.

How it works: Your business contracts with an insurance company to administer health benefits to employees. The insurance carrier shops for the best prices and pays employee medical bills. Your company then reimburses the insurance company, usually on a monthly or quarterly basis.

Insurance companies have several ways of charging for their services, which typically run $14 to $18 per month per employee.

To avoid the possibility of having to pay extraordinarily large medical bills—for an organ transplant, for instance—the insurance company offers stop-loss coverage, which obligates the insurer to pay all bills above a certain level, typically $100,000 to $200,000 a year per employer.

Cost: About $30 to $50 annually per employee.

Advantages of self-insuring...

●**The combined cost of medical bills and stop-loss coverage** is usually cheaper than the price of a regular managed-care plan, especially for businesses with healthy

289

workforces that are located in areas with comparatively low health-care costs.

● **Companies that self-insure are generally exempt** from federal and state laws that require employers to offer specific health benefits. However, since these laws can be tricky, consult an attorney for advice on setting up a self-insurance plan.

Disadvantages of self-insuring…

● **Many insurance carriers won't provide** self-insurance to businesses with fewer than 50 employees.

● **In most plans,** employee choices are limited because the insurance company selects the health-care providers.

● **Self-insurance can cost more** than other plans for companies that have a high percentage of smokers or other workers that are prone to illness. Plans can also cost more for businesses that are located in areas where medical costs are high.

Helpful: If you do decide on self-insurance, it is almost always most cost-effective to start a company wellness program to educate workers on ways to stay healthy and to provide other health incentives, such as health-club memberships.

● **Shop smart.** A business may cut premiums by more than 10% just by shopping nationwide for health insurance carriers. Thanks to the Internet, nationwide shopping is easier today. *Useful Web sites…*

● *www.quotesmith.com* helps businesses search for carriers and compare premiums online.

● *www.insure.com* provides a broad range of insurance information for businesses and individuals.

The Internet can help cut costs by giving you easy access to insurance carriers—both large and small and located across the country—that you wouldn't hear about locally.

Insurance carriers can cut costs by providing coverage and premium information on the Web. The fact that Web sites invite cost comparison is forcing premium rates down among some carriers.

Essential: When dealing with any insurance or health-care companies, especially one with which you're unfamiliar, do a background check by contacting the state insurance department in its home state as well as in the state where your business is located.

Log on to the National Association of Insurance Commissioners Web site, *www.naic.org*, which acts as a clearinghouse for information on insurance companies.

Do not contract with an insurance carrier or health-care provider for longer than two years. You'll be locked in for a period when rates will likely continue rising but will preserve your options after that.

● **Buy group coverage.** A wide variety of organizations, including many chambers of commerce and industry associations, offer group health plans.

Advantage: Premiums are typically 10% to 15% less than the cost of a health benefit plan that a small business can negotiate on its own or with a major insurance company or health-care provider.

To find a group plan, contact your company's trade or professional association, local business groups and other small businesses in your area.

Helpful: The National Federation of Independent Business, which supplies information on health-care plans for small companies (53 Century Blvd., Nashville 37214. 800-634-2669. *www.nfib.com*).

● **Lease employees.** This increasingly popular practice can cut costs because the leasing company pays certain costs, which are indirectly passed on to its clients.

How it works: Leased employees technically work for the leasing company, which handles paperwork, payroll and benefits—but workers are under your authority and supervision.

Employee-leasing companies can often hold down benefits costs by buying group insurance or joining purchasing consortiums.

You may save as much by leasing employees as you would by buying group coverage itself—10% to 15%.

Most human-resource consultants offer advice on employee leasing.

COBRA Trap

According to regulations, COBRA eligibility begins on the day an employee is initially covered by a company health plan.

If your company has a probationary period that requires new employees to be covered by the company's health care plan for, say, 90 days, before COBRA can apply, a court may not uphold that policy.

Example: A company that requires employees to be covered by its health-care plan for 90 days before COBRA can apply may be forced to provide COBRA coverage if an employee quits after, say, 65 days.

Scott Bellin, benefits specialist, Thesco Benefits LLC, 320 W. 57 St., New York City 10019.

Make Learning Pay

Motivate employees to attend after-hours training sessions by offering creative awards to attendees.

Example: One company has monthly sessions that include a drawing of the names of all participants. The winner gets $50. Every employee who attends all of the meetings throughout the year is entered into an annual drawing. The winner of that drawing gets $1,000 in travel credit.

Bob Nelson, editor in chief, *Rewarding Employees*, 11848 Bernardo Plaza Ct., San Diego 92128.

Very Important 401(k) Responsibility

When an investment option provided to employees through a 401(k) plan seriously underperforms relative to market standards, the plan's managers have a fiduciary responsibility to remove and replace the option.

This requirement is imposed by law. Failing to meet it may result in legal liability.

Danger: Small- and midsized companies often fail to effectively monitor the performance of the investment options in their 401(k) plans. If employee benefits are consequently reduced, a lawsuit by plan participants or action by the Department of Labor could result.

Solution: Set up an investment option monitoring program to head off such problems. Consult your attorney for details.

C. Frederick Reish, Esq., and Bruce L. Ashton, Esq., partners, Reish & Luftman, Los Angeles, writing in *401(k) Advisor*, 1185 Avenue of the Americas, New York City 10036.

Debt: When to Take It On...When Not to... Where to Borrow

Edward Mendlowitz, CPA, partner, Mendlowitz Weitsen, LLP, CPAs,Two Pennsylvania Plaza, Suite 1500, New York City 10121.

Borrowing money to run your business is something you should do only if your cash reserves are too small to operate efficiently or to expand. Otherwise— why pay interest if you don't have to?

Most businesses, however, find themselves in need of additional cash at some point. So borrowing will probably become a necessity for most companies.

Crucial questions: When to borrow... how much to borrow...what terms to accept.

WHEN TO BORROW...

The best reason to take on debt is to increase your business—by expanding your product line...enlarging your facilities or premises...adding a salesperson...developing an Internet strategy...opening up a new territory...acquiring another company.

...AND WHEN NOT TO

Too many companies make the mistake of borrowing just to maintain the status quo without having a growth strategy in mind.

This usually happens when the owner is too comfortable in the business and has no strong desire to increase sales...or when the business is not doing very well.

Problem: If you're paying, say, 10% interest ...and the business is growing at only 3% a year ...and inflation is running at 3%, you may eventually have trouble making the loan payments.

Example: You borrow $100,000 to buy a business with $100,000 in annual sales. If the interest rate is 10%, but the business grows at only 3%, the extra 7% must come out of the profits. Eventually, there might not be enough income to make the loan payment.

SHORT-TERM WORKING CAPITAL

In addition to financing growth, another sensible reason to borrow is to fill in the peaks and valleys of cash flow. Most businesses are seasonal to some extent. There are periods when inventories or accounts receivable may build up.

To tide you over until sales return to normal, consider getting a short-term working capital loan from a bank. This is typically the cheapest way to borrow—often for as little as one-half point less than the bank's prime rate (currently 9.5%).

Caution: You should do this kind of borrowing only if you are sure you'll be able to "clean it up"—pay it back in full—within a year.

If you don't think you could pay the bank back within 12 months, you need a different type of loan. Once the short-term loan is no longer short-term, the interest rate jumps.

TERM LOANS

A term loan—one with a life span of three to five years—can be used for working capital or buying equipment that will be used to expand your business during that time period.

As mentioned previously, you should use these types of loans only when you have a growth strategy in mind. Banks want to see growth ahead so they know you will be able to pay them back. The payback is done monthly. Interest rates can range up to five points above the bank's prime rate—around 14.5% today.

REVOLVING LOANS

Also called a line of credit, the revolving loan is used for continuous financing of working capital, accounts receivable, inventories, etc. Advances are made as needed and interest is paid on a schedule set by the bank.

As long as the company maintains its level of business or grows and interest payments are made on time, there is no required payback of the principal.

Danger 1: If there is a sudden economic downturn and the value of your collateral decreases or you can't make the required payments, the bank may cut off new financing, causing you to suffer a cash squeeze.

Danger 2: If the business experiences a growth spurt, your needs may exceed your established credit line.

Self-defense: These revolving arrangements need continuous maintenance, oversight and review by you, your accountant and the bank.

OTHER SHORT-TERM DEBT SOURCES

Onerous as their terms may seem, bank loans are almost always preferable to venture-capital financing.

Reasons: Venture capitalists not only charge much higher interest rates, they also insist on an equity position in your company—often quite a large one. And—they want an exit strategy so that they can cash in big after, say, five years.

If you make a deal with venture capitalists, you must stick to it—whether or not it suits you when that time comes.

Finance companies and factoring organizations are alternative sources of operating capital. These institutions are usually more expensive than banks because companies only go to them after they have been turned down by banks.

They, too, want collateral and have requirements and restrictions. However, as an advantage, they also offer credit insurance against the danger of default by your customers.

LONG-TERM LOANS

Long-term loans, such as mortgages, are certainly the most desirable for financing buildings, real estate and some equipment. They are structured differently than short-term loans and can cost less—currently around 7% to 9%.

When possible, negotiate for a guaranteed rate instead of a floating rate, which may be used as a teaser.

Most commercial mortgages today are paid down on a monthly schedule as if they were for 15 or 30 years, with a large balance (balloon) due at the end of a short period—around seven to 10 years. At that point, you must refinance the loan either at the same bank or another one.

Opportunity: Right now, big finance companies, such as General Electric Credit Corp. and Merrill Lynch, are aggressively entering the commercial loan market. Once they have targeted a market, they want to achieve critical mass quickly, so they often will underprice the local banks. Consider them as possible sources of long-term financing. Your accountant can advise you.

Important: Shop around. Get at least two bids on your loan needs.

THE CREDIT CARD OPTION

Some business advisers strongly discourage using credit cards to finance businesses. I think that's overly simplistic advice.

Example: If your business hits a slow spell and you don't have enough money in the bank to make your next payroll, getting a cash advance on your credit card may be an easy, prudent way out. If you're confident that business will pick up in a month or two and your cash reserves will grow enough to pay off the advance, you lose nothing.

Of course, if you choose credit card debt and the business doesn't bounce back, the 15% to 20% annual interest on the outstanding balance is an excessive cost, no matter how well your business eventually does.

OTHER OPTIONS

If appropriate, industrial development bonds —issued by banks or finance companies—are less expensive long-term financing alternatives because they're tax-free to the lender.

Also, check out the Small Business Administration, which guarantees loans to small business either directly or through specialized finance companies.

For help in financing exports, try the Export-Import Bank.

Costly New Credit Card Trap to Avoid

The problem: Customers are disputing suspect adult Web site charges in record numbers. Card merchants are hit with huge numbers of "charge-backs." Card companies are now penalizing companies with too many charge-backs as a percentage of total transactions.

Trap: A small business needs only a few illegitimate card charges to hit the new charge-back limits and incur big penalties.

Self-defense: Tight control over charges. Post your phone number prominently on credit card bills. Be especially wary of card orders via the Internet from unknown foreign buyers.

Bob Aguirre, Cardservice International, a major credit card processing firm in Agoura Hills, CA.

Big Cash Flow Advantages

Jack Schacht, president, Illinois Trade Association, an independent retail barter company, Niles, Illinois, and John Kramer, president, ICON International Inc., a specialty finance company that engages in corporate barter, Stamford, CT.

Too much inventory is one of the costliest things for any business, especially for those that operate within a tight cash flow.

Solution: Use *barter* to turn your excess goods and services into promotional and purchasing power.

Bartering is a simple procedure—exchanging goods and services without using cash. Businesses can get what they need—without dipping into cash reserves.

You can barter on your own if you have a network of business owners who have what you want and want what you have. But—you'll probably get more benefits from bartering if you join a trade exchange.

HOW IT WORKS

Trade exchanges are for-profit companies that facilitate bartering between businesses. In exchange for your goods or services, they issue trade credits.

You can use these credits to "buy" the goods and services you need from other exchange members. The trade exchange handles all of the paperwork and issues you a receipt for tax purposes—trade transactions are considered the same as cash by the IRS.

Exchanges typically charge a membership fee and a commission between 8% and 15%—either for the "buyer," the "seller" or split between the two.

SAVING CASH...AND MORE

The most obvious reason to barter is to conserve cash. *But an exchange membership has other positives...*

●**Wide-reaching,** low-effort marketing. Exchanges advertise their members to one another through directories, newsletters, telemarketing programs and more. This gives members many more potential customers for excess products or services than they might have found on their own.

●**Access to new markets.** Through a trade exchange, your business will attract customers who live and work outside of your normal market area.

Example: A cash-paying customer typically travels a mile or two away from home or work when he/she wants to dine out. A bartering customer, on the other hand, will travel four or five miles to a restaurant where he can use trade credits instead of cash.

Trade exchange members often refer their cash-paying customers and friends to other members. This means that barter can actually boost your business's cash flow by expanding your paying customer base.

●**Stretching dollars.** When you barter, you often earn top dollar for your surplus inventory or services. So—products and services you acquire actually cost you less than they would if you paid cash for them.

Example: A photographer who needed $1,000 worth of printing services purchased it with $1,000 in trade credits. Because she operates at a 50% gross profit margin, she basically purchased $1,000 worth of services at a cash cost of $500.

WILL IT WORK FOR YOU?

If you operate at a low profit margin...have all the business you want or need...sell a product or service whose price fluctuates...or sell something few people desire, then you may not benefit from barter.

If you don't fall into any of these categories, consider joining the 400,000-plus companies—most of them small businesses—that are now benefiting from bartering through commercial exchanges. *To get started...*

●**Locate a local trade exchange.** Look in the *Yellow Pages* under "Barter and Trade Exchange."

Also, search the membership lists of the National Association of Trade Exchanges (*www.nate.org*) and the International Reciprocal Trade Association (*www.irta.net*).

●**Evaluate the exchange companies you find.** Start by asking each company how many clients it currently has trading and how many are on standby or reserve—meaning the exchange will not take any more goods or services from them until they spend the trade dollars they have.

These numbers will give you a sense of how successful each exchange's members are at trading goods and services.

Next, look at the exchange's membership lists to determine if they offer products and services you can use and are close enough geographically. Study the lists to determine how many of your competitors are already members. Too much competition could limit the amount of trade business you get.

Then ask for a list of member names and phone numbers. Call the references you get to find out how often other members use the exchange's services...how satisfied they are ...if they plan to renew their membership, etc.

Check each exchange's barter prices against comparable cash prices to determine whether the products and services are priced fairly and competitively.

Compare barter contracts from the exchanges you are interested in—to make sure you will get the best deal.

GETTING MAXIMUM BENEFIT

After you have joined a trade exchange, participate actively in it and continuously try to spend trade dollars instead of cash. *Boost your chances for long-term success with…*

•**Patience.** Trades don't always happen quickly.

•**Flexibility.** Your dream computer might have a one-GHz processor, 256 MB of RAM and a 20-GB hard drive. But you may have to settle for a less state-of-the-art model.

•**Persistence.** Successful trades don't magically happen, even when you use a trade exchange. You have to work hard within the system to get it to work for you.

Easy Way to Sell to The Government

Selling to the US government does not always involve bureaucratic contracting. The government buys all the same kinds of products and services that private businesses do—and contracts aren't needed for purchases under $2,500.

Key: More than 500,000 federal employees have "SmartPay" credit cards for business purchases. They make more than $13 billion in purchases annually.

Opportunity: A recent study found the Web has become the number-one tool for federal buyers seeking information about products and services—surpassing peer recommendation.

To develop government employees as customers, display the SmartPay logo on your Web site. It is available from the Federal Supply Service Web site at *www.fss.gsa.gov/services/gsasmartpay/business.cfm,* along with additional information for business about the SmartPay program.

Helpful: Extensive information about selling to the government is available through the Selling to the Government link at the home page of the General Services Administration, *www.gsa.gov.*

Mark Amtower, partner, Amtower & Co. Federal Direct Marketing, consultants specializing in marketing to the Federal government, 13491 Allnutt Ln., Highland, MD 20777. *www.federaldirect.net.*

Success Secrets for Sales Reps

Keep sales GOALS in sight…*Gather* information, both on the big picture and on the specifics of each prospect.

Organize and prioritize data to be sure you are taking the right steps to get where you want.

Act. Never stop making calls, following up or sending your customers articles of interest.

Look to the past and the future. Learn from past mistakes…and keep an eye on how you want your career to grow.

Set new goals regularly, reaching higher every time.

Barry Farber, sales and motivational speaker, 66 E. Sherbrook Pkwy., Livingston, NJ 07039. *www.barryfarber.com.*

Safe and Secure Ways to Use On-Line Auctions In Your Business

Paul Hartunian, PhD, a marketing consultant to small businesses, 155 Bellevue Ave., Upper Montclair, NJ 07043. He is author of the multimedia kit *How to Get One Million Dollars Worth of Publicity Free* (Clifford Publishing) and editor of *Million Dollar Publicity Newsletter.*

Businesses that don't use such on-line auction sites as eBay, uBid or Amazon.com to buy goods and services or to sell off surplus are robbing themselves of substantial profits.

Buy at on-line auctions for 30% to 70% less than you would pay at a brick-and-mortar store. On the flip side, excess inventory that might bring five cents on the dollar from a jobber or closeout specialist can fetch 50 to 60 cents on the dollar at an on-line auction. Here's how you can use on-line auctions shrewdly—to avoid getting stung when you buy and to get the most when you sell.

WHAT'S AVAILABLE

Mention on-line auctions to most people and the knee-jerk response is Beanie Babies and Barbie Dolls. You can buy those items at eBay and other auction sites, but you can also buy almost everything the business needs— from office supplies to vehicles to very specialized machinery. *Examples...*

●**I use lots of padded envelopes in my business,** which cost $1 each at the stationery store. I buy brand-new, top-quality envelopes at auctions for 20 cents to 30 cents each.

●**I recently bought a Pitney Bowes sealer-stamper** in excellent condition at an on-line auction for $70. The original price was $2,300.

●**I have bought two fully functioning Internet businesses at eBay** for about two cents on the dollar. They sold for far less than they were worth because the seller had no idea how to get a better price.

HOW TO FIND WHAT YOU NEED

New auction sites appear almost daily, but the starting point for nearly anything still is the industry pioneer—eBay. There's so much more available at eBay than at other sites, it's almost always the first place you want to look. Another site might offer five items. At eBay, you'll get to choose among 200 items. Similarly, when you're selling at on-line auction, you'll get far more bids at eBay than anywhere else on the Internet.

Exceptions: Some auction Web sites other than eBay are better when it comes to specialized items or services, such as...

●**Computer gear.** I find the auction sites at both Yahoo! and Amazon.com better than eBay for anything related to computers.

●**Inventory closeouts.** TradeOut.com is excellent for finding inventory that other businesses are selling—or for selling inventory your business can't use.

●**Buying and selling businesses.** If you're looking to add new businesses or to sell the business you're in, check out *BizBuySell.com* and *Sell-a-Biz.com.* Both sites define buying and selling businesses loosely. Both will often feature bargains on excess inventory and used machinery.

GETTING STARTED

To buy from an auction site, start by doing a Web search to find auction sites that specialize in what you're looking for. My favorite search engine is AskJeeves.com. It lets you search in the form of a question, such as, "Where can I buy a used printing press?"

Once you've arrived at an auction site that seems to have what you need, familiarize yourself with the auction site's steps for placing bids.

AVOIDING RIP-OFFS

Next—*before* you enter a bid, you'll need to start the critical process of ensuring that the seller is legitimate. Many auction sites— including eBay—have gotten bad publicity as a result of con artists or just plain dishonest people selling bogus merchandise to innocent bidders. *It's easy to avoid being a victim.*

Start by finding out exactly whom you're buying from. Many auction Web sites, including eBay, offer feedback about sellers. What you are looking for are dozens—even hundreds—of positive mentions.

I have 580 positive mentions at eBay. Be wary if the seller has positive feedback from only two or three people.

*Next step...*contact the seller. Most auction sites have a feature that says, "Ask the seller questions." Ask as many questions as it takes to convince you the seller is legitimate and the item is what you expect it to be. If the seller won't answer, or fudges his/her answers, walk away.

Often the seller will respond with a telephone number as well as an invitation to call and discuss the sale. When I'm shopping, sometimes I will call the seller...and sometimes I won't.

The fact that a seller gives you his phone number usually gives you enough confidence to bid.

If a seller won't provide a phone number, an E-mail address is just as good.

MAXIMUM SAFETY

Your real protection when you buy is making use of an escrow service. eBay has one and so do many other auction sites.

Example: If your bid wins, you send your money to the escrow service—which is independent of the auction site. Only when you get the item and decide it's OK, do you tell the escrow service to release the money to the seller.

Using the escrow service lets you look over the item, test it—even have it appraised—before the seller is paid.

BIDDING STRATEGIES

The difference between bidding smart and bidding dumb at on-line auctions can amount to hundreds of dollars.

Items are listed for auction for set periods of time—usually from three to 14 days. A big mistake is to start bidding when the item is first listed. Other people respond with a counterbid. That kicks off a bidding war and the price can go out of control.

Shrewder: Watch from the sidelines until the last 10 or 15 minutes of the auction. Then bid. If the auction is for seven days, and you show no interest for six days, 23 hours and 50 minutes, your bid will surprise everyone. You'll get what you want for less than you might have expected, because you haven't helped to fuel the price escalation.

THE SECRETS OF SELLING ON-LINE

Anything the business doesn't need—from old computers to last year's stock—can be turned into cash by selling it on-line.

Challenge: Many sellers get only a fraction of what they could, because they don't know how to generate active bidding.

When you put something up for auction, you get to describe the item as fully as you want. Don't make the mistake of writing a one-sentence description and letting it go at that. Since there's nothing to grab the attention of bidders, you'll just kill your chance of getting real money for what you're selling. *Much better...*

●**Make it look good.** You can use such tools as Netscape *Composer* to create an auction page for your merchandise or service that looks very professional. Or pay around $200 to have a professional Web designer do it for you.

●**Write a headline that sells.** Don't just say "Laptop Computer" in your headline. Be specific about what you have and the condition it is in. Tell bidders that you're selling a "Compaq Presario 300 MHz laptop in mint condition."

●**Add a picture.** Using a photo to illustrate what you're selling will increase the price you get by 20% to 30%.

●**Limit the bidding time.** Give buyers just enough time to bid on the item—and no more. eBay has a pull-down list that lets you list the item for auction for three, seven, 10 and 14 days. I find that 14 days is much too long, and seven days is usually just right for business-to-business auctions.

●**List a minimum bid that you'll accept.** If it's a low-ticket item you will sell, you can open the bidding at $1 and see how high buyers are willing to go.

If it's capital equipment, in which you have an investment, set the price you hope to get as your minimum. If you've created the right auction page for the item, you'll probably get that minimum price—if not more.

Web Shopping Incentive

Attract first-time E-shoppers by assuring them that ordering on-line is convenient, easy, reliable and secure. Many consumers are reluctant to shop on-line because they are not sure when they will receive their orders. They are used to shopping at brick-and-mortar stores, where they take the items with them. To turn them into buyers, you might create a highly visible home-page graphic stating how quickly items will be shipped. *Example:* "Orders placed Monday to Friday by 5 p.m. Eastern time will be shipped the same day."

Alan Field, editor, *Internet Marketing Report*, 370 Technology Dr., Malvern, PA 19355.

Key to Internet Marketing

The essential element of marketing through a company Web site is collecting E-mail addresses from visitors. If the company fails to do this, then no matter how good its Web site may be, it can only hope visitors will return. *Contrast:* Collecting E-mail addresses enables the company to initiate interactions with customers to drive traffic to the Web site. *Strategy:* The best way to collect E-mail addresses varies, depending on the business. The company may need to offer something in return, such as a premium or an electronic newsletter, and should test different approaches.

George Colombo, president, Influence Technologies, Inc., conductor of workshops and seminars for sales professionals, Winter Springs, FL, and author of *Capturing Customers.com.* Career Press.

Advantage of "Trade Secrets"

A business innovation may be best protected as a trade secret even if it can be patented.

Reason: Patent protection lasts only a limited number of years, while a trade secret can be kept forever. And the ideas behind patented innovations must be disclosed to the public, while a trade secret is truly secret.

Drawback: Others can use your secret idea if they discover it—such as through reverse engineering. Consult a lawyer for details.

Maxine L. Retsky, Esq., partner, Piper Marbury Rudnick & Wolfe, 203 N. La Salle St., Suite 1800, Chicago 60601.

Mandatory Overtime Is Legal

Make it clear during the hiring process that overtime can and will be required from time to time. Include a policy in the employee handbook showing when overtime will be required and documenting reasons employees can refuse it—such as illness. Have each employee sign a statement saying he/she understands the policy. When you know overtime will be needed, give employees advance notice—and ask for volunteers before making overtime mandatory.

Patrick DiDomenico, editor, *Research Recommendations*, 1750 Old Meadow Rd., Suite 302, McLean, VA 22102.

Dangerous Tax Traps in Choosing and Switching Business Entities

Stu Kessler, CPA, and Paul Dailey, CPA, managing directors, American Express Tax and Business Services, 1185 Avenue of the Americas, New York City 10036. Mr. Kessler is past chair of the American Institute of Certified Public Accountants, while Mr. Dailey cochairs the Small Business Conference of the Foundation for Accounting Education.

When you own a small business, selection of the legal form (entity) in which you operate can be crucial for tax and other reasons. You need to choose carefully up front because a later change may be fraught with problems.

CHOICES

Main types of business entities...

●**Sole proprietorship.** This is the simplest form of business. You pay tax on the income you receive, minus expenses, on Schedule C (or C-EZ) of your personal tax return.

Advantage: Legal and accounting fees usually are lower for a sole proprietorship than for other types of entities while overall administration tends to be less expensive.

●**Partnership or joint venture.** These entities provide a great deal of flexibility. Taxable income may be allocated among the partners, for instance.

Advantage: For sole proprietors and partners, losses from a bona fide business may be deducted from other income. To deduct losses, you must have sufficient basis in the enterprise and you must comply with the limits on passive activity losses.

Drawback: Neither proprietors nor partners in traditional partnerships enjoy limited liability. Your personal assets may be exposed to claims arising from the business.

●**C corporation.** This is the regular corporate structure, which provides limited liability to shareholders.

Example: A customer trips on a loose carpet in your place of business and suffers an injury. Damages may be collected from corporate assets but your personal assets likely will be protected.

Advantages: Fringe benefits, especially health insurance, may be fully deductible for a C corporation but not for other entities.

Drawback: With a C corporation, double taxation is a burden. Corporate income will be taxed and so will profits distributed as dividends to shareholders.

The corporate income tax may be minimized or avoided by distributing virtually all corporate income and compensation to employees, providing that such compensation is reasonable.

Trap: If a company needs to retain capital for business purposes, double taxation will be triggered when profits are distributed.

●**S corporation.** If certain criteria are met, corporations can elect to be taxed as S corporations.

Advantage 1: S corporations provide limited liability to shareholders, yet they're usually exempt from the corporate income tax, so double taxation is not a threat.

Advantage 2: An S corporation election provides relief from certain corporation tax traps, such as unreasonable compensation, excess accumulated earnings, and the corporate Alternative Minimum Tax.

●**Limited liability company (LLC).** This entity provides the limited liability of a corporation along with the tax treatment of a partnership, so double taxation is avoided.

Advantage: Operating losses may be passed through to LLC owners, according to agreed-upon terms, so special allocations are possible.

An LLC may have foreign owners while an S corporation can't.

●**Limited liability partnership (LLP).** This entity, similar to an LLC, is increasingly adopted by professional partnerships such as law and accounting firms.

●**Limited partnership.** A partnership consisting of passive investors (limited partners) and the venture's operator (the general partner). Limited partners enjoy limited liability while the general partner has liability for claims against the limited partnership.

TRADING PLACES

Suppose you're already in business and you'd like to change to another entity. *Some moves are easier than others, tax-wise…*

●**Switching from proprietorship** or partnership to corporation. Generally, there are no tax problems with such a move, which may come in handy if you want limited liability.

●**From C corporation to S corporation.** The formalities here are simple. As long as a corporation meets a few relatively simple tests (one class of stock, for example, and no more than 75 shareholders), it can elect S corporation status.

BIG TROUBLE

C corporations electing to become S corporations have to cope with the built-in gains (BIG) tax. In essence, at the time of conversion a "snapshot" must be taken, comparing fair market value with book value of assets owned by the company. If those assets are sold within 10 years, the corporation will owe tax on the difference.

Example: Years ago, your company purchased a warehouse for $1 million and depreciated the property down to zero. For the year 2000, when your company elects S corporation status, the warehouse is valued at $1.2 million at the time of conversion. If your company sells the warehouse before December 31, 2009, for $1.5 million, then $1.2 million is subject to BIG tax.

Outcome: If your company sells the warehouse before April 2010, a $1.2 million taxable gain will be triggered. The company's shareholders will owe tax, too, although the taxable income can be reduced by the corporate tax paid.

You can avoid the BIG tax by not selling the property within 10 years. You can lease an unwanted warehouse to another user, if that's feasible.

The amount of gain subject to the BIG tax can't exceed the S corporation's taxable income for the year of the sale. However, taxable income subsequent to the year of sale yet within the 10-year period could trigger the gain.

Example: When you sell the warehouse in 2010, your S corporation has taxable income of only $300,000. Thus, the taxable gain triggered by the sale will be $300,000, not $1.2 million.

As long as compensation is reasonable, your S corporation can pay out all of its income to shareholder-employees. As long as the S corporation reports no net income, the BIG tax won't apply.

LIVING WITHIN THE LIMITS

● **LLC to corporation.** In general, this will be a tax-free conversion, similar to going from a proprietorship or partnership to a corporation.

● **Corporation to partnership-type entity.** If a corporation (C or S) switches to an LLC, a partnership, or a limited partnership, tax complications are likely to arise.

Trap: Under the Tax Code there will be a "deemed liquidation" of the corporation. Taxes on unrealized appreciation will be due.

Example: Your corporation owns a warehouse with zero basis and a $1.2 million fair market value. At the time of conversion to an LLC, a $1.2 million tax will be triggered, even if the company continues to use the warehouse.

All of the corporation's appreciated assets will be subject to the same tax treatment.

This situation is bad enough when an S corporation shifts to an LLC. When a C corporation converts, there will be a double tax bill, corporate and personal.

Caution: If possible, don't convert your corporation to a partnership or LLC. Instead, keep your corporation in place and start a new partnership or LLC.

Try to wind down the existing corporate business and shift operations to the new entity.

Example: Your new LLC can lease the warehouse from your corporation. As long as the corporation is a going concern there won't be a deemed liquidation to trigger taxes.

Alternatively, your corporation might sign a management agreement with your new LLC, effectively rendering income from the corporation to the LLC, if that's your desire.

STATE'S RIGHTS

The above information is necessarily general. Laws of the individual states may have a great impact on the taxation of all business entities, so work with a knowledgeable local attorney before making any decision.

19

Education Smarts

You Don't Need Top Grades to Win Big College Scholarships

The average cost of attending a top university today is more than $120,000 for four years—and that figure is increasing. College financial aid departments can help...but this help can be limited. Many families are forced into assuming enormous student loan burdens.

Merit-based programs, which award college money that doesn't have to be paid back, are an alternative. Thanks to scholarships, I attended Harvard virtually for free.

These scholarships are available to high school, college, graduate and returning students as well as to children under age 14. And you don't need top grades to win these awards.

Since graduating, I have interviewed many other scholarship winners for my book. *Here are some of our best secrets...*

GETTING STARTED

● **Go on-line.** The Internet is a great place to start the scholarship hunt. More than a dozen sites help students identify appropriate scholarship programs. No one site is comprehensive—so try all of them. Links to all of these sites can be found at *www.winscholarships.com*.

If a site's search capabilities are limited—for example, it allows a maximum of three extracurricular activities per search and you have five activities—log on to the Web site a second time (using a different name if necessary) and enter your other activities to be sure you haven't missed any opportunities.

Search your area of interest in different ways. A scholarship for students who are interested in studying biology might not be cross-listed under science.

Harvard graduate Benjamin Kaplan, who earned nearly $90,000 in scholarships and saved one year through Advanced Placement credits. He is author of *How to Go to College Almost for Free*, which was published by his own company, *WaggleDancer.com*, Gleneden Beach, OR.

301

● **Start early…and stick with it.** The scholarship hunt is not solely for high school seniors. If I had it to do over again, I would start my scholarship hunt in seventh or eighth grade and continue through college.

Different programs are aimed at different age brackets. Scholarships awarded to younger students are either held for them until they enter college or are given as outright cash. *An early start…*

●Increases the number of potential scholarships available to you because the applicant pool is often smaller.

●Allows you to position and prepare yourself for later opportunities.

●Gives you a chance to perfect your application skills.

●Think local. Large national scholarships get attention, but local scholarships are well worth seeking out. Although prizes are often smaller, the competition is lighter—so you have better odds.

Call or drop by local clubs and organizations to ask if they offer any scholarships.

Possibilities: American Legion Posts, Elks Clubs, Key Clubs, Kiwanis Clubs, Knights of Columbus, Lions Club, VFW, YMCA/YWCA, 4-H Clubs.

Also look into local unions, small local banks, savings and loan institutions, credit unions and parents' employers and unions. Scholarships often are available even to those who don't belong to particular clubs or who don't have accounts at specific banks.

● **Target scholarships tailored to your strengths.** Some scholarships are academically focused, but others don't require you to submit grades or test scores.

Scholarships may be awarded based on success at a single task, such as drawing a picture or delivering a speech…or according to criteria such as community service, obstacles overcome or character.

If you have a specific career goal or hobby, contact organizations in these areas and ask if they offer any scholarships.

Useful resource: The Encyclopedia of Associations, which can be found at most libraries.

Example: I know someone who wanted to be a pilot and heard about a scholarship for aspiring pilots. He didn't apply, thinking his academic record was too weak to win. Later he found out that no one had applied that year. Had he entered, he would have won.

● **Take advantage of Advanced Placement (AP)** high school credits. I placed out of one full year of college by using these…and I also saved a lot of money.

My high school didn't offer AP classes in psychology, so I got the books and studied on my own. There is no rule that says you have to take a class in order to take an AP test.

Start racking up AP credits early in high school so you won't have to work too rigorously as a senior.

WINNING APPLICATIONS

Here is a brief sampling of what I have culled from lengthy conversations with dozens of scholarship winners…

● **Paint a portrait.** Scholarship judges award money to people, not résumés. Focus on who you are, not just what you've done.

Example: In each component of my college application—essay, activity list, etc.—I highlighted my passion for writing, my future goals as a writer and how writers could truly make a difference in the world.

● **Don't make excuses for blemishes on your transcript.** Instead, treat them as obstacles that you have overcome. One scholarship winner, who had gangs and drugs in his past, described what he had learned from these experiences and how he was trying to turn his life around.

Many applications require a short essay. *Strategies…*

●Make it personal. Don't submit an essay that anyone could have written. Include plenty of unique experiences, perspectives and details.

●Keep it snappy. Concise, interesting essays will be noticed.

●Recycle essays from class work and other applications whenever possible.

SOME INTERESTING SCHOLARSHIPS

● **Think Quest Internet Challenge** (914-273-1700…*www.thinkquest.org*). Students ages 12 to 19 work in teams to design a Web site.

Prizes are big—up to $25,000 per team member. If you don't have Internet skills, team up with someone who does—you can write the content for the site.

●**Prudential Spirit of Community Awards** (800-843-7625...*www.prudential. com/community/spirit*). Rewards students ages 11 to 19 who have started volunteer community service programs in their region. Scholarships range from $1,000 to $5,000.

●**The Scholastic Art & Writing Awards** (212-343-6493...*http://scholastic.com/artand writing*). More than 1,000 prizes awarded in a wide range of art and writing categories. Prizes start at $100 and can climb as high as $20,000.

 # More Financial Aid for College

Kalman Chany, president, Campus Consultants, Inc., 1202 Lexington Ave., New York City.

Ask for more college aid if your financial situation changes suddenly. Aid is usually based on the family income one year earlier. But a job loss or a major illness can change your financial status dramatically. Contact the college's financial-aid office immediately to ask for additional help. *Also:* Look into loans and scholarships for which you might qualify, given your altered financial status.

More from Kalman Chany...

Financial Aid Concerns

If your child wins an outside award from a fraternal association, union or private foundation, many schools reduce your aid package by the amount of the scholarship. Try to convince the school to reduce the loan and work-study portions of the package rather than grant money dollar for dollar.

Biggest Bargains in Higher Education

The four US military academies—West Point (Army), Annapolis (Navy), Air Force Academy and Coast Guard Academy—offer students a free top-quality academic education, plus free room and board and uniform allowance...and pay a monthly allowance. Cadets can major in fields such as foreign languages or political science as well as engineering. Graduates are sought for high-paying, fast-track business leadership positions after their required military service. *Drawbacks:* Cadets are subject to strict military discipline, from prescribed early rising to lights out. And graduates must serve in the military for five to six years. Admission requires passing three hurdles—an application process similar to that at other top-notch schools...a rigorous physical exam...a nomination letter from your congressional representative.

Ed Custard, certified educational planner and senior vice president for educational services, PureAdvice, Inc., New York. *www.pureadvice.com*.

Murray Baker Makes A College Education Affordable

Murray Baker, author of *The Debt-Free Graduate: How to Survive College Without Going Broke*. Career Press. He operates *DebtFreeGrad.com*, a free resource about college financing options for students and parents, and is the former coordinator of first-year programs at The University of Western Ontario, London, Ontario, Canada.

With college costs so high, even relatively well-off parents can have trouble paying for their children's educations.

Here are ways to help without pulling out your checkbook...

START AT A STATE SCHOOL

To get a degree from a particular school, it is generally only necessary to spend the final two years there. Postpone private college until then and save thousands.

Example: Tuition for state college averages $3,356 for in-state students. Private school tuition averages $15,380...and runs up to twice that amount at many colleges.

APPLY FOR FEDERAL GRANTS

Everyone should fill out a Free Application for Federal Student Aid (FAFSA) for Federal Pell Grant money *(www.fafsa.ed.gov...800-433-3243)*. *To boost your chances...*

●**Put college savings in your name**—not the child's name.

●**If either parent or another child is thinking about going back to school**—even part-time—consider doing it at the same time. The formula for determining aid is based in part on the number of family members attending college.

●**If you're divorced,** the parent with lower income and fewer assets should be named the custodial parent. Assets of the other parent will not be considered.

●**Pay off any other debts you might have** and prepay your home mortgage to reduce your available assets.

APPLY FOR SCHOLARSHIPS

There's plenty of money out there—and not just for top students.

●**Check with social organizations,** employers, unions, religious groups and other groups to which you belong—to see if they offer scholarships.

Scholarships that are sponsored by local organizations tend to be poorly advertised. Competition is therefore usually less intense than for national awards. Most awards target students that fit a certain profile. It is best to research scholarship opportunities during freshman year of high school.

Example: An organization's scholarship might require winners to start programs to better their communities. Senior year is too late to undertake such projects.

Web resources for scholarship information: *www.fastweb.com* and *www.college quest.com.*

●**Continue the search after your child is in college.** Plenty of scholarships are available for those already in college...and the competition then tends to be less fierce.

LIVE OFF CAMPUS

Consider allowing your child to live off campus, at least after freshman year. As a rule, on-campus food and housing are more expensive. Your children can save even more money by living with roommates rather than living alone.

WORK PART-TIME

Suggest that your child head to campus a day or two early so he/she can land a job before other students arrive.

Helpful: Campus jobs might pay less than jobs in the local community, but they are generally more interesting. *Other pluses:* Understanding bosses and no commute.

CHOOSE THE RIGHT LOANS

If loans are unavoidable, be sure to choose the right ones.

Best: Perkins loans and subsidized Stafford loans offer low interest rates, currently 5% and a maximum of 8.5%, respectively. Repayment doesn't begin until after graduation.

Worst: Financing college with plastic. In recent years, credit card companies have been targeting college students.

HELP FOR PARENTS

If you help your child with the costs of college even a little, education-related tax breaks are available...

●**Hope Scholarship.** You can deduct up to $1,500 a year, but only during a student's first two years in college.

●**Lifetime Learning Tax Credit.** A maximum deduction of only $1,000 a year, but not limited to the first two years.

Most parents get the Hope Scholarship the first two years...and the Lifetime Learning the second two. You cannot use both in one year.

Here's How You Can Help Your Children Choose the Right Colleges for Them

Arthur Mullaney, former director of guidance to college admissions for several school systems in Massachusetts. He is publisher of the newsletter *College Impressions,* about choosing colleges, Box 665, 4 Glendale Way, Canton, MA 02021.

Colleges and universities have gotten very savvy about marketing themselves. Here are my secrets to cut through the hype so your child can make the best choice...

BEFORE YOU VISIT SCHOOLS

• **Have your child put together his/her résumé.** This will focus on his qualifications and what he really wants. He should include work and academic histories, College Board scores, distinctions and five solid interests.

• **Choose the type of setting he wants—** rural, suburb or urban.

• **Choose the type of learning environment that is best for him.** A large university? A small college?

YOUR FIRST VISIT

Tour and interview with at least six schools. To get the most from these preliminary school visits...

• **Go during the summer of your child's junior year.** Admissions people won't be rushed...you'll still get a feel for the campus...and your child won't miss any school.

• **Read the letters to the editor in the college newspaper**—where you'll find out about the real issues on campus.

• **Study the information boards to get a sense of the social life.** Graffiti provide excellent insight into the quality of students' minds.

• **Stand in front of the college admissions office,** and ask where it is. This is how I find out about a school's spirit. Are students' responses cold and sarcastic? Do they give directions pleasantly—even walk you in?

• **Be aware of what tour guides may not show you...**

• Check out the computer terminals and multimedia room in the main library.

• How is security? Are there 24-hour security escorts? Can you walk into a dorm unannounced? Ask for crime statistics.

• Explore the areas just off-campus. What do the local residents say about the school and its students?

• *Parents:* **Take a separate tour,** and sit in on different classes than your child. This gives your child more freedom to form his own impressions.

• **Ask questions that require real answers** —not just *yes* or *no. Particularly useful...*

• If you could change three things about the college, what would they be?

• What three things would you fight not to change?

• If you could do it all over again, would you choose this college? Why or why not?

• How accessible are professors?

• Do students evaluate faculty performance ...and are those evaluations published?

• **Keep notes about each campus.** Also take pictures, or ask for a free view book from the admissions offices. To help you rate each school in different categories, print out the checklist at *www.collegeboard.org/collapps/html/checklst.html.*

YOUR SECOND VISIT

Your child should stay overnight in the dorms at his top two or three schools.

Important: Have him meet with a professor in the department in which he is most interested. That professor may very well become an advocate.

Example: A student I counseled did not have the best grades but was a talented singer. When she visited Harvard, she set up an informational interview with a music professor. He was so impressed when he heard her sing that he personally lobbied for her acceptance...and she got in.

USEFUL RESOURCES

• ***Links to college sites:*** *www.campustours. com.*

- ***Virtual tours on-line:*** *www.collegeview. com/home/index.html.*
- ***College Admissions: A Crash Course for Panicked Parents*** (IDG Books).
- ***College Admissions Data Handbook*** (Wintergreen/Orchard House).

College Admissions: The Big Myths Debunked

M_yth:_ **The well-rounded student is the most desirable.**

Reality: Colleges like students who have focused on one or two areas and developed excellence and leadership in them.

Myth: **The admissions essay matters only in close decisions.**

Reality: It almost always counts heavily. It is read very carefully at small schools and almost as carefully at medium-sized and large ones. Only the biggest universities focus more on numbers than on essays.

Myth: **The student should not seem too eager to attend, except when applying for early decision.**

Reality: Colleges want enthusiastic students. They favor applicants who make it clear that they want to attend—and explain why.

Myth: **If you know the right person, you can get in easily.**

Reality: This works in perhaps 1% of cases —if you know someone who has made enormous donations. Otherwise, acceptances are based on merit.

Schools do value legacies, however. Sons and daughters of graduates are often in a separate "legacy" pool, which may double their chances.

Frank Leana, PhD, educational counselor in New York City.

College Starts In High School

Pay less for college by earning as many credits as possible through advanced-placement high school courses. Or get transferable credits from less-costly institutions. *Other ways to cut college costs:* Take courses during the off-season or at night, when they often cost less…consider a college with a three-year liberal arts degree.

Marshall Glickman, former Wall Street stockbroker turned environmental activist, South Newfane, VT, and author of The Mindful Money Guide. *Ballantine Wellspring.*

Advice from Yale's Margit Dahl on Writing A Winning College Entrance Essay

Margit Dahl, director of undergraduate admissions, Yale University, New Haven, CT. The university receives 13,000 first-year applications each year to fill 1,350 spots.

When students apply to college, their grades, extracurricular records and recommendations are clear.

The application essay, however, is *the* opportunity for students to present themselves most effectively.

When admissions officers read essays, they search for evidence of curiosity, strong moral character and the capacity to commit to meaningful endeavors.

To write the best essay possible…

- **Don't be shy…be personal.** Applicants sometimes make the mistake of writing from the third-person point of view. That may work for term papers…but for a winning college essay, first person usually works better.

Admissions officers want to get a sense of your unique voice and distinctive qualities. Write from your soul.

Warning: Admissions officers often assume that essays with lofty prose were written with the liberal use of a thesaurus and too-close adult supervision.

● **Narrow your focus.** If you took a trip to Germany, find a way to vividly integrate your personality into the experience. If you can't, you're better off penning a piece on something closer to home.

If you spent the summer working at a fast-food restaurant, did flipping burgers make you appreciate the value of an education? Were your coworkers interesting? Did those people influence your outlook on the world?

Your answers could be the basis of a compelling essay.

● **Be unusual.** Discovering something extraordinary about an ordinary experience is strong fodder for an essay.

Example: One great essay sent to Yale was about a trip to a family farm. From a perch atop a barn, the writer reminisced about how the environment around the farm was changing. In the process, she communicated a mature level of insight about economic and environmental change...and the importance of personal roots. She wrote with feeling, authority and vivid detail.

● **Convey your curiosity.** Another favorite essay came from an applicant who seemed destined to become a scientist. He wrote about his adolescent experiences conducting experiments in his basement.

The applicant's natural sense of humor shone throughout the essay. And it was clear that even if this aspiring scientist unexpectedly discovered in his sophomore year that music was really his future, he would approach Beethoven with the same intensity that drove him to dismantle old toasters.

● **Consider your audience.** The reader probably has been through a heavy pile of essays, with a fat stack beneath yours. Write in a way that holds the reader's interest. Make yourself come alive on paper.

Better College-Application Essays

Advise high school students to write in a distinctive, personal voice. They should reveal their personalities, not rely on quotations from others—applicants may think quotes are impressive, but admissions committees do not. Avoid national or global issues—young people do not have the experience to offer impressive insights on these affairs. Instead, they should focus on narrative—not description—explaining a life-changing event they experienced without dressing up the essay with lots of adjectives and adverbs.

Frank Leana, PhD, educational counselor specializing in secondary school and college, New York City, and author of The Best Private High Schools. *Princeton Review.*

Four-Step System For Much Higher Grades

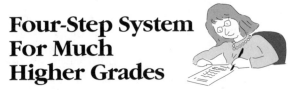

L. Stewart Barbera, Jr., LSW, a guidance counselor at St. Joseph's Preparatory School in Philadelphia.

Students want to succeed academically—but most could use guidance about how to do it.

Several factors help students work to their potential...

● **Supportive parents** who promote the value of education.

● **Effective study skills.**

● **Realizing children are the architects of their own success** and that learning is proactive, not passive.

I use the following program with my students. Parents can use it to help their children take responsibility for their success and become better students.

ESTABLISH A GOAL

Have your child choose a subject in which he/she most wants to improve. After he gets better in one course, he can use what he learned in others.

Help your child choose a specific goal for a particular subject. The goal must be attainable—but it must also force the student to stretch himself.

Example: Saying he wants to do well in science. This goal is too vague.

Better: I want to earn a B+ average in science for the first marking period. This goal is reasonable, concrete and measurable.

DEVELOP A STRATEGIC PLAN

Brainstorm strategies with your child for reaching the goal. Encourage imaginative thinking—the best ideas often come at the end of the brainstorming session. Ask him to choose the five best strategies from the list. Since strategies are the pathways to achieving goals, these, too, need to be realistic and attainable...and stated in a way that is concrete and measurable. *Examples...*

The strategy *I will try harder in science class* needs to be refined.

Better: I will ask at least two questions in each class.

If he comments that he would study more, it would be better to specify, I will spend 30 minutes each school night studying science.

TAKE ACTION

Have your child write down a checklist of the five strategies. Review these strategies, and talk about how each one relates to achieving the goal. Your child should look over the checklist every school day, and mark off each step as it is completed.

CONTINUOUS IMPROVEMENT

Meet with your child for 15 minutes each week to see how the plan is progressing. Sunday evenings are ideal. Your role is that of an academic coach—listen carefully...stay supportive and positive. Ask him to think about which strategies are working.

As your child weeds out the unhelpful activities, have him experiment with new strategies for meeting the goal.

Investing this time with your child shows him how important he is to you...and how much you are committed to his success.

You also help him learn critical lifelong skills—self-reflection and continuous improvement.

Beware of Senior Slump

Colleges are looking more closely at how high school seniors perform *after* they are accepted early in senior year. Students who drop tough courses or whose grades show significant declines after acceptance may have their admissions revoked. Colleges have always had the right to do this, but revocation was rare in the past. Now, with increasingly competitive admissions, colleges are tough on high school seniors who slack off.

Larry Griffith, admissions director, University of Delaware, Newark, quoted in College Spotlight, *Box 190, Garrett Park, MD 20896.*

20

Self-Defense

How to Jump from A Runaway Car and Other Super Survival Strategies for Life's Trickiest Situations

You never know what danger is lurking around the corner…hovering above…or swimming beneath the surface. But when confronted with unexpected, potentially dangerous circumstances, you'll want to know what to do.

RUNAWAY CAR

Apply the emergency brake, if possible, to slow the car. Open the door. Aim for an angle that will take you out of the path of your car. Look for a soft landing site, such as grass or brush—anything but pavement. Tuck in your head, arms and legs. Roll when you hit the ground.

SINKING CAR

Open the window as soon as you hit the water. This allows water to enter the car and equalize the pressure between the inside and outside, making it easier to open the door or escape through the window.

If the power windows don't work, break the glass with a heavy object, such as a steering wheel lock, and get out.

If you can't open or break the window: Wait until the car fills to the point where the water reaches your head. Take a deep breath and hold it. By then, the pressure inside and outside the car should be equalized, so you can open the door and swim to the surface. *Precaution:* Drive with

---

Joshua Piven and David Borgenicht are Philadelphia–based writers and coauthors of *The Worst-Case Scenario Survival Handbook*, based on interviews with dozens of experts. Chronicle. *www. worstcasescenarios.com.*

the windows slightly open whenever you are near water or ice.

LEG FRACTURE

Most leg injuries are only sprains, but the treatment is the same.

To stop bleeding, apply direct pressure to the wound using bandages or clean clothes. If the skin is broken but there is no bleeding, do not touch or put anything on the wound.

Do not move the injured leg. Make a splint from two stiff objects of the same length—wood, plastic or folded cardboard. Put the splints on either side of the injured area, and tie them together with rope, belts or adhesive tape. Do not tie too tight, which could cut off blood circulation.

If help can't come to you, make sure the leg is immobilized before moving.

Best: The injured person should remain on his/her back until help arrives.

EARTHQUAKE

If you are indoors: Stay there. Get under a desk or table. Stay away from windows, a fireplace, furniture and appliances. Kitchens are very dangerous.

If you are outside: Get out in the open, away from anything that might fall—power lines, a chimney, etc.

If you are driving: Stop—but not on or under a bridge...under an overpass...or near a tree or light posts. Stay inside your car.

ADRIFT AT SEA

Stay aboard your boat as long as possible before you get into a life raft. Your best chance of survival is on a boat, even a disabled one.

Put on dry clothes, and stay out of the water. Protect yourself from the sun.

If you must get on a life raft, take whatever you can. Drinking water is most important. You can last longer without food than you can without water. Canned foods are often packed in water, so bring those and a can opener.

Life rafts often include survival kits that have fishing hooks. If you are adrift for several weeks, seaweed will form on the underside of the raft and fish will swim in the shade under you. You can catch the fish and eat the raw flesh.

If you see a plane or a boat nearby, signal with a VHF radio, flare or mirror.

AVALANCHE

Stay on top of the snow by using a free-style swimming motion.

If you are partially buried: Dig your way out with your hands and/or by kicking the snow. Poke your ski pole through the snow in several directions until you see or feel open air. Then dig in that direction.

If you are completely buried: Dig a small hole and spit in it. The saliva should fall down, giving you an idea of which way is up. Dig up as fast as possible.

TAKE A PUNCH

For a blow to the body: Tighten your stomach muscles and shift slightly so that the blow hits your side. While the blow might crack a rib, it will be less likely to damage your internal organs.

For a blow to the head: Move in toward the blow. Getting punched while moving backward will result in your head taking the punch at full force. A punch to the face can cause head whipping, in which the brain moves suddenly inside the skull, and may result in severe injury or death.

Tighten your neck muscles, and clench your jaw to avoid scraping upper and lower palates and damaging your teeth.

LETTER BOMB

Check an unexpectedly bulky letter or parcel for lumps, bulges or protrusions—but don't apply pressure. Also consider calling the police if you notice these suspicious signs...

● **A package wrapped in string.**

● **Handwritten address from a company.** Check to see if the company exists and if it sent the package.

● **Excess postage on a small package**— this indicates it was not weighed by the post office or a company's mailroom scale.

● **Leaks,** oil stains, wires or excessive tape.

● **Missing return address**...or a return address that doesn't make sense.

Half a Seat Belt May Be Worse than None

In recent findings, drivers and front-seat passengers who wore a shoulder belt without a lap belt were at greater risk of dying in a crash than those who wore no belt. Skipping the lap belt transfers the full force of the crash to the shoulder belt, which increases risk for chest injuries sevenfold and abdominal injuries threefold. *Problem:* There are still 10 million cars with an automatic shoulder belt but only a manual lap belt. *Bottom line:* Always use both belts.

Frederick R. Rivara, MD, MPH, professor of pediatrics and epidemiology, University of Washington School of Medicine, Seattle.

Road Rage Self-Defense

Allow plenty of time to get where you are going—50% more than the optimum time. Focus on something to make the extra time seem worthwhile—music, recorded books, etc. Accept the fact that traffic inconveniences are inevitable and some drivers will behave badly. Do not take their actions personally or try to get even.

Jerry L. Deffenbacher, PhD, professor of psychology, Colorado State University, Fort Collins.

Hidden Hazards Around Your House

Stephen Elder, a general contractor with 16 years of experience as a private home inspector, Pittsboro, NC. He is a member of American Society of Home Inspectors. www.ashi.com.

Many of the common household hazards are overlooked. *Dangerous problems too many of us live with—and what to do to fix them...*

KITCHEN

• **Vent the gas stove exhaust fan *outside*.** The fan eliminates dangerous gas fumes and excess humidity, reducing allergies and growth of mold.

• **Secure the stove.** New stoves come with anti-tipping brackets—so if a child opens and climbs on the oven door, the stove won't tip. Do-it-yourselfers—and professional installers—often don't install these brackets. If they are missing, install them. You can also buy these brackets for your current stove.

CLOSETS

• **Use low-wattage lightbulbs**—no more than 15 watts—so that stored items won't heat up and cause a fire if a closet light is left on.

Even better: Use compact fluorescent bulbs, which don't produce as much heat and last longer than ordinary bulbs.

DOORS

• **Make sure you can open doors if they're locked accidentally**—especially if you have children. This is very important in children's bedrooms, but it could happen in any room with a lock.

Even better: Install nonlocking doorknobs on children's bedroom doors.

• **Hallway doors should always open over a landing**—never over stairs. People remodeling their homes sometimes forget to put in a landing. Then the first step is a hazard.

STAIRWAYS

• **Install a handrail wherever you have more than two steps.** It should be firmly attached at an average height of 36 inches (building codes vary).

• **All steps should be the same height.** Old stairs sag—a tripping hazard. Repair or replace when necessary.

GARAGE

• **Automatic door openers** should have electric eyes and automatic safety-reverse features so they open if a small child or pet tries to slip under a closing door. Use the most sensitive setting. Replace an opener without these features.

Important: Place electric eyes within five inches of the pavement.

● **If you have a water heater in your garage,** bolt a wheel stop to the floor so you don't accidentally drive your car into the heater.

ELECTRICAL SYSTEM

● **Install Ground Fault Circuit Interrupters (GFCIs)** any place where water and electricity might meet. They switch off the electricity flow if, for example, a charging electric razor falls into a sink full of water.

Codes now require GFCIs in the bathroom, kitchen, garage and outside receptacles. Homes built before 1978 may not have GFCIs.

Important: Press the "test" buttons once a month to make sure GFCIs are still working. If the "reset" button doesn't pop up, the GFCI should be replaced.

● **Have an electrician add circuits if necessary.** People tend to convert spare bedrooms into home offices. But an office full of equipment can overload the wiring.

Gas Grill Warning

If a gas grill does not light in five seconds, shut off the gas and leave the lid open for five minutes. *Reason:* Propane is heavier than air and accumulates at the bottom of the grill. People injured in grill explosions are usually hurt because they keep trying to light the grill while gas builds up in it.

Ian Cummings, MD, PhD, emergency physician, Day Kimball Hospital, Putnam, CT.

Save Your Life with Brighter Lights

Karen Jacobs, EdD, clinical associate professor of occupational therapy at Boston University and president of the American Occupational Therapy Association (AOTA) in Bethesda, MD. She is the editor of Ergonomics for Therapists. *Butterworth-Heinemann Medical.*

Accidents—often caused by diminished balance, vision and/or muscle strength —are the sixth leading cause of death in people over age 65. Most accidents involve falls at home.

Beyond the physical risks involved in falling—hip fracture, joint damage, head and face injuries—there are psychological costs. Up to 25% of people who sustain a serious fall curtail activity for fear of falling again.

Good news: Most falls can be prevented via planning and a little help from technology...

● **High-wattage bulbs.** As we get older, we may have trouble seeing in dim light. Use bulbs 75 watts or brighter. *Best:* Soft-white bulbs—they reduce glare and confusing shadows.

● **Timed lighting.** Falls often occur at night or in early morning. For $5, you can buy a timer that automatically turns on lamps at night.

Another option: Lighting fixtures with photoelectric sensors that switch on when it gets dark. *Cost:* Less than $20.

● **Remote-control lighting.** With a hand-held electronic device—from anywhere in the house—you can turn on lights or appliances in any room. Units such as X-10 Pro and Lite-Touch may cost $1,000 or more and require an electrician to install.

Extra precautions: Keep flashlights in the bathroom, kitchen and other strategic locations. Consider nightlights to illuminate hallways, bathrooms, etc.

● **Fluorescent tape.** Impaired vision makes it hard to distinguish where one stair ends and the next begins. Put glow-in-the-dark fluorescent tape—available in hardware stores— on each step. This thin tape sticks well even on carpeted stairs—which are advisable for older people.

If stairs aren't carpeted: Paint alternating steps in different bright colors, such as red and yellow. The appearance won't please everyone, but it enhances safety.

For extra protection: Leave on a light at the top and bottom of the staircase.

● **Support poles.** These floor-to-ceiling metal rods can be gripped with one hand when you're getting out of bed or rising from a low chair.

Some older people experience postural hypotension—dizziness that's caused by a sudden drop in blood pressure when getting up.

Safety poles offer something solid to hold onto until you regain equilibrium. You don't need tools to install them—they require only minor installation. More versatile than grab rails (which are affixed to walls), they weigh only about 15 pounds and are easily positioned anywhere. They can support up to 275 pounds. *Cost:* About $150.

•Bathroom grab rails. Install them next to the toilet and shower. Most falls occur in the bathroom—the result of postural hypotension associated with standing up from the tub or toilet. Grab rails help keep you upright if you start to fall.

If you're handy, install the rails with a drill, wall anchors and long mounting screws. Call a contractor if you're not sure you'll put them in firmly.

•Nonslip rubber mats. Place them in the tub or shower and in other rooms where floors get wet—kitchen, laundry room, etc.

•Tub/shower seats. Sitting is safer than standing in a slick, soapy tub. Plus, it's easier to sit on a seat than it is to lower yourself all the way into the bath.

If you use a tub seat, install a handheld showerhead so that you can direct the water flow.

Some handheld showerheads are connected to a rubber hose that fits over the faucet. These cost only a few dollars but often come loose. The best models—up to three times the price—attach to the water pipes and should be installed by a plumber.

•Personal alarms. Battery-powered units, such as Life-Link Transmitters and MediEquip Personal Alarms, can be worn on the wrist or around the neck. If you fall and can't get up, pressing a button on the alarm dials preset telephone numbers. Program the unit to dial a friend, relative or 911.

Personal alarms are invaluable for people who live alone. Lying on the floor for a sustained period after a fall increases risk of excessive bleeding if you've suffered serious

cuts or abrasions...and risk of kidney failure from dehydration. *Cost:* About $150.

Option: A portable phone. Buy a "holster" at a hardware or department store, so you can keep the phone with you. *Best:* A phone with a memory. It allows you to dial 911 by pressing one button.

•French-style door levers. They're easier to grip than doorknobs...and less likely to make you lose balance opening doors.

•Wheeled utility carts. The kitchen is a high-risk area. You move from place to place preparing food...carrying pots or other heavy objects...and it's easy to lose your balance, especially in an unseen wet spot on the floor.

Utility carts have built-in trays or baskets to hold food and cooking utensils. Put everything you need on the cart, then roll it to your food-preparation or dining area. *Cost:* Less than $50.

Important: Keep often-used kitchen items, such as soup cans, cereal boxes and mixing bowls, in easy-to-reach places. Standing on stepstools or reaching on tiptoe increases risk of falling.

•Nonslip rug backing. Rolls of inexpensive nonslip material are available in hardware stores. Cut to match the size of throw rugs, and the sticky surface keeps rugs from "skating."

OTHER PREVENTIVE MEASURES

Route electrical cords and phone lines behind furniture to prevent tripping...move end tables so that they don't extend into walking areas...and remove elevated doorway thresholds. Pick up books, newspapers, toys or anything else on the floor daily.

RESOURCES

Home-safety-device retailers are in every city. You can also use the Internet to find out more about assistive tools and devices...and to purchase products.

•Abledata, at *www.abledata.com*, lists more than 25,000 assistive and home-safety devices and where to get them.

•Timers and electronic sensors are sold at Radio Shack and other electronics supply stores, as well as building supply stores, such as Home Depot. Order the remote-control lighting unit X-10 Pro at *www.x10pro.com*.

• **Support poles and grab rails** are available at building supply stores such as Home Depot. You can also order them from the manufacturer or at *www.sunrisemedical.com*.

• **Tub/shower seats** are available at pharmacies and medical supply stores.

• **Hardware stores** carry handheld showering devices.

• **Home medical suppliers** and electronics stores sell personal alarms.

Latex Trap

People who are allergic to latex should be careful when eating out. Many restaurant workers wear latex gloves, which often come in contact with food. *Self-defense:* Ask if restaurant workers wear the gloves. Always carry a prescription antihistamine—and, if you have had a severe reaction, an epinephrine injector. Those allergic to latex should also avoid latex condoms.

William Franklin, MD, clinical associate professor of medicine, Harvard Medical School, Boston.

Antibacterial Know-How

Antibacterial products do not kill all germs—they only kill the weakest ones. The surviving organisms are stronger. As they multiply, bacteria can evolve that are resistant to antibacterial products and antibiotics, resulting in diseases that are harder to fight. *Self-defense:* Develop hygienic habits, but do not become fanatical about germs. *Examples:* Rinse fruits and vegetables under running water…wash hands with soap and water after using the toilet and before preparing or eating food…to sanitize surfaces, use a solution of bleach, denatured alcohol or hydrogen peroxide—not

antibacterial products. Reserve antibacterials for sick and vulnerable patients, not for use in a healthy household.

Stuart B. Levy, MD, director, Center for Adaptation Genetics and Drug Resistance, Tufts University, Boston.

Web Food Safety

Food bought on-line may have much higher microbiological counts than store-bought food…it may not look like what is shown on Web sites…and it may be unappealing when it arrives. *Bottom line:* Do not expect exceptional value. Food may be insulated in its package, but not refrigerated during transit—carriers such as FedEx and UPS are not equipped for this. *Self-defense:* Follow the same safe-handling guidelines for food purchased on the Web as you would for store-bought food. Check it when it arrives—frozen and refrigerated foods should be cold. Smell it to check for freshness—if in doubt, throw it out or return it to the vendor. Understand a site's return policies in case a shipment is bad. Wash everything, and cook items well.

Aaron Brody, PhD, adjunct professor and food technologist, University of Georgia, Athens.

Lightning Is an Even Bigger Risk Now

More homes than ever now have electronic equipment that is sensitive to lightning. So if lightning does strike a home, the damage is likely to be greater, although the *frequency* of lightning damage has not changed. *Self-defense:* Install quality surge suppressors on individual pieces of electronic equipment in your home. Standard whole-house protection and lightning rods are designed to prevent fire—but not to protect individual items.

Richard Kithil, CEO and founder, National Lightning Safety Institute, Louisville, CO. *www.lightningsafety.com*.

Hotel Cribs Are Safety Hazards

In one recent inspection, 82% of the cribs had at least one safety hazard. *Self-defense:* Ask the hotel if cribs are routinely inspected and if the staff makes sure the cribs have not been recalled. Check a crib very carefully before using it. *Helpful:* A crib safety check-list, available at *www.safekids.org.*

Sally Lee, editor, *Parents,* 375 Lexington Ave., New York City 10017.

Better Hotel Security

When you go out and must leave valuables in a hotel room, ask the head of security to engage the deadlock bolt to the room *from the outside.* No one will be able to enter the room—including you—without the assistance of security personnel. Not all hotels offer the service…but if yours does, it is likely to be more secure than leaving your possessions with hotel personnel or in a conventionally locked room.

Jens Jurgen, editor, *Travel Companion Exchange,* Box 833, Amityville, NY 11701. *www.whytravelalone.com.*

Scam Avoidance Secrets

Sheila Adkins, public affairs manager, Council of Better Business Bureaus, 4200 Wilson Blvd., Suite 800, Arlington, VA 22203. *www.bbb.org.*

Prosperity always brings a rise in scams against business—since fatter profits make for richer pickings for crooks. Unfortunately, small businesses tend to be most vulnerable to scams, since relatively few have the specialized employee functions that can safeguard against fraud.

Scams against business now often involve the Internet. They're mostly the same old swindles, repackaged for delivery on-line. But they're harder to defend against because the Internet makes it so easy for the swindler to pretend to be someone or something he/she isn't.

Here are the scams most often directed against small business today—and how to defend against them…

•**The phony invoice.** The bill—more and more often delivered by E-mail—demands payment for a product or service. It may say "second notice" or "final warning" or "don't force us to turn this over to a collection agency." The company billing you sounds legitimate. Its Web site, when you look it up, looks impressive. You don't recall making the purchase, but you don't want a collection agency hounding the business, so you pay the bill.

Trap: **You never made the purchase,** and the company sending the bill doesn't exist. That impressive Web site is just a sham. You've thrown away good money—and fallen for a new twist on one of the oldest scams in the book.

Self-defense: Never pay for anything which you have no record of having ordered—no matter how intimidating the invoice or how legitimate the biller's Web site looks. You don't even have to pay for merchandise that shows up in your mail room but which was never ordered—another variation on the same scam. The law allows you to treat unordered merchandise as a gift.

Keep a record of all purchases. Preferably —have one employee responsible for doing all your buying. Check every invoice against your purchase orders to make sure you really owe the money. When in doubt, insist that the biller produce documentation that you actually placed the order.

•**Phony directory.** Crooks have been billing businesses for placement in phony directories for years. The current version of that scam is that the directory is on-line, and your listing will supposedly guide people to your business Web site. For the $100 or $200 the directory service is charging, that seems like a good deal.

***Trap:* There is no on-line directory.** Your money vanishes into the crook's pocket, without a trace.

Self-defense: Check out every company you do business with for the first time—no matter what promises are being made to you. Get a name, phone number and physical address for the directory company. Insist on seeing the directory in operation before paying a penny. A legitimate company will provide this information, while a crook will usually just end his dealings with you.

●**"Free" Web site.** You're thinking of putting up a Web site to boost your business. You receive an E-mail from someone who is offering to create one for you for free. You're being offered such a great deal because your site will serve to advertise the Web site designer's skills to other potential clients.

***Trap:* Your site, if it ever gets created, is so poorly designed that you'd rather no one else see it.** Worse, you get billed for all sorts of costly extras you never heard about before.

Self-defense: Get a name, phone number and physical address for the company making the "too good to be true" offer. Insist on a formal contract, with everything—including possible extra costs—set down in writing. Most important, never deal with any vendor who can't provide references of satisfied customers. And—if you do get references, check them out.

●**Internet cramming.** This is a variant of the well-known scam called telephone cramming—in which you contract for some service at a set price, then find your phone bill crammed with all sorts of additional charges. In Internet cramming, the service you contract for is Web site hosting at a very favorable price.

***Trap:* As with telephone cramming, your hosting bill is crammed with all sorts of extra charges you didn't authorize.** We're seeing a great many small businesses victimized by Internet cramming, because so many of these businesses got off to a late start and need a Web presence in a hurry.

Self-defense: Carefully review your Web hosting bill as soon as it comes in, looking for charges for services you haven't ordered or authorized. Best approach, again, is to assign all purchasing to one employee, who then reviews all bills that come in. If you do sign up with someone to do Web hosting, get everything in writing before the work begins.

●**Paper piracy.** This is another age-old scam, reconfigured for the Internet. Traditionally, the scam was pulled off by telemarketers who promised the company unbeatably low prices on such frequently needed supplies as copier paper, toner, print cartridges, pens and pencils. Often, you're promised that your first order will be free—to help the company "break into the business." Today's variant is for the pitch to arrive by E-mail or to be made on a very slick, very legitimate-looking Web site.

***Trap:* The supplies—if you get them at all—are shoddy.** Not only is your first shipment not free, you are billed at prices that are sky-high for what you receive. Sometimes your business's first contact with the crook is a phone call or E-mail by someone who "just wants to confirm your order" or "just wants to make sure we have your correct address." In a worst case, the employee who fielded the call is named on the invoice as the person placing the order. Blame for being scammed then falls on this employee.

Self-defense: Create a centralized purchasing system, with only one person authorized to buy for the business. Educate employees that all pitches from vendors must go to this one person. Make it business policy never to buy from unknown vendors and that all solicitations for your business must be made in writing.

●**Advance-fee loan scams.** Small businesses often need cash to expand or launch new lines or upgrade facilities. The advance-fee loan broker promises to find money for the business, no matter what your credit situation is. The only snag is that you must pay an up-front "fee"—which can run into the thousands of dollars—to get the loan approved.

Pitches from advance-fee loan brokers used to come by mail. Now, many of them have very impressive Web sites.

***Trap:* You pay the fee—only to be told your loan application was turned down.** Or, once you have paid the fee, you may never hear from the loan broker at all.

Self-defense: Thoroughly check out the loan broker before doing anything else. Get a physical location, and check the broker out with the local Better Business Bureau. If the broker claims to be licensed, insist on knowing where. Check out that claim as well. And remember, you never have to pay any fee on a loan until you know whether you have been approved or not.

●**Charity scams.** A seemingly legitimate charity solicits the business for a tax-deductible contribution. The pitch used to be made by mail or telephone. Now, it increasingly comes in by E-mail.

***Trap:* The "charity" is phony.** Instead of doing good, your money winds up in some crook's pocket.

Self-defense: Insist on having the solicitation made to you by mail. Ask the charity to send you its financial statement—showing how much it raises and how the money is spent. A legitimate charity will be glad to oblige you. A crook has nothing on paper to show you.

How Not to Be a Victim of Fast-Growing Credit Card Fraud

Bob Aguirre, manager of the Special Investigations Unit of Cardservice International, an independent sales organization in the electronic transaction processing industry, 26775 Malibu Hills Rd., Agoura Hills, CA 91301.

As ubiquitous as credit cards are, I keep seeing sloppy credit card practices that could—and often do—cost businesses money and create other bothersome problems.

The Internet compounds the problem for merchants, since the true identity of on-line charge customers is so hard to establish.

Result: An epidemic of credit card fraud.

Easy solution: Commonsense defensive procedures. Even if you make an effort to guard against fraud, the issuing bank will normally pursue its charge-back rights if the transaction is disputed by the cardholder. That is the issuing bank's responsibility to its customer. Therefore, it is in the merchant's best interest to follow the best practices to avoid disputed charges. *Steps to take...*

●**Set up detailed systems for processing card transactions *after* sales are made.** You're in business to make sales. Once the sale is complete, the normal tendency is to move to the next customer and let someone junior handle the credit card charge on the concluded sale.

Problem: Not training employees to process card transactions properly can be a huge mistake. *What can go wrong...*

●Because of an employee oversight, the card might never be swiped through the point-of-sale terminal.

●The credit card receipt goes unsigned.

●No effort is made to establish that the person signing the receipt is the legitimate cardholder.

Lesson: A sale isn't completed until the charge appears on the cardholder's bill and is accepted. If the cardholder disputes the charge —because the receipt was never signed or the charge was fraudulent—and you can't demonstrate due diligence, the issuing bank is likely to throw the charge back to you.

That effectively cancels the sale. Worse, it marks your business as a high-risk customer for the bank that issued the card.

That's especially unfavorable for small markets, which generate little profit for card companies. The more a low-volume merchant gums up the works with charge-backs, the likelier the issuing bank is to get tough.

Result: Besides the lost sale, unsubstantiated charge-backs could cost you the ability to process card transactions for several days while the charge-back is being investigated. Repeated charge-backs could lead to termination of your access to credit card processing. Few businesses today could survive without credit card access.

●**Make fraud detection your business.** Retailers put so much reliance on the systems that service their credit card accounts, that they tend to forget about common sense and normal skepticism.

Example: Many business owners assume everything is "A-OK" once the system gives them an authorization code for a transaction. That's not what the authorization code is intended to do. Authorization only establishes that the card account has enough credit to accommodate the price of the transaction and that the issuing bank has not received any notification that the account should be blocked for some reason.

It doesn't mean that the individual giving you the card is the person to whom the card was issued.

●**Check the card user's identity carefully.** Due diligence includes a serious attempt to confirm the identity of the card user. If you have some question about the legitimacy of the person, ask for some other identification for comparison.

Ask for another credit card in the same name as well as a driver's license if the customer is new to your business.

●**Examine the card.** It takes approximately a half second to check out a credit card. Does it look legitimate? There are some counterfeit credit cards that are truly excellent. But most counterfeit cards are such low-grade work you won't have much trouble spotting them.

Checking the card to make sure it is signed sounds obvious. Yet I keep finding merchants who never look to see if the card is signed… or that the name on the front matches the signature on the back…or that the signature on the transaction receipt matches the signature on the card.

●**Don't take everything the customer says at face value.** I see this all the time. The customer makes a substantial purchase and tries to pay for it with a credit card in someone else's name.

There is always a logical explanation—"It's my girlfriend's card and she said I could use it," or "My aunt sent me out to buy a gift for my mom."

Fact: Issuing banks do not allow you to accept a credit card from anyone but the cardholder—even if the person presenting the card claims to have permission to use it. If you accept a charge from someone else and it is challenged by the cardholder, the issuing bank will charge it back to you.

Not accepting that "third-party" card may cost you a sale. But accepting it could cost you the sale anyway—if the charge is challenged. And you get a black mark at the issuing bank.

●**Screen for patterns of fraud.** Credit card fraud can look like every retailer's dream come true—a customer who "buys out" the store. Because it's the best day the merchant has had all month, approval of the credit card charge becomes a mere detail. A month later, the person whose card was used in the fraud disputes the charge.

Self-defense: When a customer makes an unusually large purchase, you should automatically become suspicious. It should prompt you to do more—not less—verification work before approving the charge. *Other suspicious patterns…*

●Legitimate buyers pick their sizes and colors carefully. Crooks buy indiscriminately—regardless of size or color—because all they want is merchandise they can quickly fence.

●If you ask why someone has bought five of the same model laptop computer, you'll be told the purchase is for a business. Common sense should tell you that anyone legitimately buying five computers for a business would try to negotiate a volume discount.

●**Don't underestimate the potential for fraud in Internet sales.** The risk of fraudulent credit card charges is even greater on-line than it is face to face. Yet Internet selling is so new and most merchants still do so little business on-line, that due diligence tends to get glossed over.

Businesses at greatest risk are those selling products that thieves will find easy to sell—such as consumer electronics and computers.

Self-defense: Since you can't pinpoint exactly who your on-line customer is, look for things that don't add up. Is the credit card from a bank in the region of the country from which the order is being placed? If the card was issued in the US and the order is coming from a European country, ask the customer why. If you get a flimsy answer, consider turning down the order.

Watch for multiple charges from cards issued by one bank. The first six digits of the card number identify the bank. Why would a large number of your Internet customers all have cards from the same bank? If the customers can't provide a convincing reason for all using the same bank, walk away from the sale. It probably means that a thief has manufactured a slew of counterfeit cards that are all going into circulation at the same time.

New Telephone Cramming Threat

Cramming occurs when a phone service provider adds charges to your bill for services or products you never used or requested. But—a new type of cramming that now affects businesses involves unauthorized charges for Web design or Internet services. Dozens of state attorneys general are investigating cramming. But the first line of defense is your accounting department. Have all phone bills carefully reviewed as soon as they arrive. Immediately call the phone company if you find any unordered services, and refuse to accept the charges.

Neil S. Sachnoff, president, TeleCom Clinic, telecommunications consultants, 4402 Stonehedge Rd., Edison, NJ 08820.

E-Mail Scams

Be wary of E-mail solicitations with questionable claims—about earnings or curative properties. *Other red flags:* Solicitations —with no return E-mail address or phone number—that ask you to send money to a post office box. *Self-defense:* Do not reply—

not even to ask to be taken off the mailing list. Send the E-mail to *uce@ftc.gov,* a Federal Trade Commission site that collects solicitations for investigation.

Eric A. Wenger, chair of Internet Coordinating Committee, Federal Trade Commission, Washington, DC.

Guarding Against Potential Cell Phone Dangers

Timothy McCall, MD, is a New York City internist and the author of Examining Your Doctor: A Patient's Guide to Avoiding Harmful Medical Care. *Citadel Press.*

Recently, I became one of the 100 million Americans who carry a cell phone. I had resisted for a long time—primarily because I don't like to be accessible at all times. But I finally gave in.

Like many of you, I've been following the ongoing debate about cell phone safety. Some scientists argue that the phones can cause everything from memory problems to brain cancer—and some preliminary findings do seem to support this view. Other scientists say there is no danger.

The central issue is whether microwave radiation given off by the phones affects the brain. Studies involving rats suggest that long-term memory can be affected by cell phone use. And a new study from Sweden found that—among brain tumor patients who used a cell phone—tumors tended to develop near where the cell phone was habitually held.

Since cell phones have only recently come into widespread use—and since cancer can take decades to turn up—it will be years till we can sort out this controversy. *In the meantime, here's what I suggest to stay on the safe side:*

•**Use cell phones wisely and sparingly.** Cell phones can be lifesavers in an emergency, and they're an invaluable convenience when a conventional telephone is not handy. It's prudent to use a land line whenever and wherever possible—especially for conversations that last more than a few minutes. Of course, conventional phones usually cost less to use and offer better sound quality.

●**Choose the model carefully.** Studies suggest that digital phones give off less radiation than do older analog models.

Another important feature to look for is a built-in speakerphone. That lets you put more distance between your head and the cell phone antenna—the source of the radiation. The greater this distance, the lower the potential risk.

I often switch my cell phone to the speakerphone and put it on the desk in front of me—especially when the other person is doing most of the talking.

●**Forget about "radiation blockers."** Several devices now on the market are said to reduce radiation from cell phones. But recent tests cast doubt on their effectiveness. And some recent research suggests that headsets—sometimes touted as a way to reduce radiation exposure—can act as antennas, actually increasing the dose to your brain.

●**If you have a pacemaker, watch out.** Cell phone radiation can interfere with pacemaker signals, so it's best to keep the cell phone as far as possible from the pacemaker. Use the phone on the opposite side of the body from the pacemaker, and don't keep the phone in a breast pocket.

●**Take extra care with children.** If cell phones do turn out to affect brain tissue, kids could pay the highest price. Their skulls are thinner, their neurological systems are still developing and they are more sensitive to the effects of radiation. I believe it's prudent to limit kids' use to emergency situations.

●**Limit cell phone use in cars.** Unless the phone is connected to a roof-mounted antenna, using a cell phone inside a car exposes your brain to more radiation.

But the biggest risk faced by motorists who use cell phones is distraction. Talking on a phone while driving is just as dangerous as driving drunk, according to a recent *New England Journal of Medicine* study. If you must use your phone while driving, dial only

when you're stopped—or have a passenger dial for you.

How Not to Be a Victim Of Identity Theft

Betsy Broder, assistant director, FTC Bureau of Consumer Protection, 600 Pennsylvania Ave. NW, Washington, DC 20580.

Y ou may not be aware that someone is committing fraud or theft using your good name—until you are inexplicably turned down for a mortgage or are harassed by a collection agency. *To minimize your risk...*

●**Don't give anyone your Social Security number,** credit card number or any other personal identification number without knowing exactly how it will be used and whether it will be shared with anyone else.

●**Keep track of your credit card bills and billing cycles.** Missing bills could mean that someone has changed your account's billing address—and taken your account.

●**Don't let mail—both outgoing and incoming—linger in your mailbox** or anyplace else where it can be picked up by strangers.

●**Create passwords for all your accounts**—bank, credit card, telephone. Passwords should not use easily available information (birth date, phone number, etc.).

●**Don't carry more identifying information or credit cards than you actually need to use.**

●**Don't carry your Social Security card with you**—keep it in a secure place.

●**Never give out personal information over the phone,** through the mail or over the Internet unless you have initiated the contact—and know who you're dealing with.

●**Tear up or shred anything bearing personal information**—charge receipts, credit applications, insurance forms, bank checks and statements, expired charge cards, unsolicited credit offers—before discarding it.

●**At home, keep personal information where it cannot be found by strangers—** particularly if you have hired help or service contractors working in your home.

●**At work, confirm that only appropriate personnel have access to your personal information**—and that it is securely stored.

●**Every year, check the accuracy of your credit report** by getting a copy from the three major credit reporting agencies…

●Equifax Information Services, 800-997-2493 or *www.equifax.com.*

●Experian, 888-397-3742 or *www.experian.com.*

●Trans Union LLC, 800-916-8800 or *www.transunion.com.*

By law, you should not be charged more than $8.50 per copy for your credit report.

To report identity theft, and to find out how to repair the damage if you've been a victim, call the Federal Trade Commission toll free at 877-IDTHEFT (877-438-4338) or enter your complaint via the on-line complaint form located at *www.consumer.gov/idtheft/index.html.* Also request a free copy of the FTC's booklet *When Bad Things Happen in Your Good Name.*

Computer Theft Deterrence

Thieves are most likely to go after anything small and portable. So notebook computers and handheld devices, such as personal digital assistants, are likely targets.

Be sure to record serial numbers of all equipment and give each unit an etched identifying mark upon receipt.

Purchase locking devices for your equipment—they cost only about $30 and are effective as long as employees use them. Locks for hard drives and disk drives are also available.

Be sure to lock equipment every time you leave your work area or office.

Janet Dulsky, director of security, Kensington Technology Group, locking-device manufacturer, San Mateo, CA, quoted in *Investor's Business Daily,* 12655 Beatrice St., Los Angeles 90066.

Computer Virus Self-Defense

Dana Blankenhorn, computer and Internet consultant, a-clue.com, Atlanta.

Be especially careful when using Microsoft Web or E-mail programs. Microsoft gives its software access to much of the Windows operating system. So a virus that gets into one program can rapidly spread to others. *Self-defense:* Install antivirus software and update it frequently…back up important files regularly…and do not open any E-mail attachment that you are not sure is legitimate.

More from Dana Blankenhorn…

Internet Copyright Infringement News

Normally, anything on a Web site can easily be downloaded and copied—and then altered and/or duplicated. *To protect your site against unauthorized copying:* CopySafe can protect images, text and Web page backgrounds from copying by site visitors. *More information: www.artistscope.com.* Digimarc Corp.'s "watermark" technology places an invisible, permanent identification mark in images. A "watermark reader" allows you to read a digital watermark. *More information: www.digimarc.com.*

Protecting Your Computer

Get the right surge suppressor to protect your electronic equipment. Discount-store models may not do the job. Find a unit that guards power *and* phone lines…offers a warranty covering the value of your equipment…and can handle the large plug-in units found on many peripherals (Zip drives, external modems, printers, etc.). *Cost:* About $30. *Alternative:* An Uninterruptible Power Supply (UPS) offers surge protection plus about 10 minutes of backup power—enough time for you to save open documents and shut down your system safely. *Cost:* $100 and up.

Mark J. Estren, PhD, technology columnist and consultant, McLean, VA.

Caring for Your Laptop

Never leave your laptop in a hot—or cold—car. Extreme temperatures can ruin it. If it does become overheated or too cold, bring it inside as soon as possible. Give it several hours to come to room temperature before you try to open or use it. *Another surprising danger to laptops:* Car audio speakers. Speaker coils generate magnetic fields that can destroy data. Place a laptop well away from speakers. And back up data on your laptop regularly.

Scott Gaidano, cofounder, DriveSavers, data-recovery specialists, Novato, CA. *www.drivers.com.*

Choose Your Passwords Even More Carefully

A recent security test at Stanford University found that a simple password-cracking program could deduce one-fifth of all university account passwords. *Helpful:* Choose longer passwords…mix letters, numbers and special characters…use different passwords for different applications…change passwords at least every six months. *Avoid:* Your name…mother's maiden name…birthday… Social Security number. *Critical:* If you sus-

pect someone is trying to determine your password, report it to relevant authorities.

John Featherman, president, featherman.com, consumer privacy consultants, Philadelphia.

Practical Privacy Secrets from Former FBI Insider

Kevin McKeown, security expert, Box 7228, Washington, DC 20044. He has worked on cases with the FBI and US Customs and for private clients. He is author of *Your Secrets Are My Business.* Plume.

If someone really wants to dig up personal information about you, he/she probably can. But there are steps you can take to protect your most private information—and to limit the damage if someone sets out to learn your secrets and do you harm…

YOUR CAR

Anyone who sees your car has an important piece of information about you—your license plate number. A cop, ex-cop or auto insurance company employee can "run" any plate in minutes.

If that fails, almost any private investigator can get the license information for less than $50. That alone is enough to find out your name and address. *This can be a real concern…*

Example: If your car is parked in airport long-term parking or you are traveling out of state, it is a good bet that your home is vacant.

You can't hide your license plate, but there are ways to reduce the risk…

●**Use a post office box or business address for Department of Motor Vehicles (DMV) records,** rather than your street address. *Note:* This strategy is not possible in all states.

●**Avoid providing other hints about yourself.**

Examples: Bumper stickers proclaiming affiliations to specific groups or schools…parking stickers listing specific organizations. Remove these pieces of information, which can be used to track your whereabouts.

●**Never leave anything with your address visible.**

●**When selling your car yourself,** don't provide a phone number that can be traced back to the car or its occupants—a favorite for auto thieves and stalkers. Use a voice-mail service or a beeper number so that you can call back the potential buyer.

DISCARDED PAPER

Few paper shredders are as helpful as people think.

The typical "spaghetti" shredders produce long strips of paper that can be reconstructed without much trouble. Shredded papers actually attract special attention from anyone picking through your trash.

The proper solution depends on how sensitive your material is. If you have no particular reason to believe that someone would pick through your trash but still want more security, a traditional paper shredder may be fine.

A cross-cut, or "confetti," shredder does a significantly better job of destroying documents. But it, too, is less than perfect.

Reason: Technology now exists that can make your shredder fax a copy of the document to an unknown location just before it is destroyed.

The government has been "modifying" targets' fax machines with cell-phone fax technology for about a year (with court orders, of course). So, you know private operatives are using it as well.

More effective solutions…

●**Rip up or shred the most sensitive materials**…and flush small amounts down your toilet.

●**Soak all your papers in a bucket containing water and bleach** (10:1 ratio) before disposing of them. The government has been using this technique for years.

SOCIAL SECURITY NUMBER

While it is important to protect your Social Security number, it is already in many databases around the country. So if someone really wants the number, he can get it.

Solution: Every year, check your Social Security Earnings Statement (*www.ssa.gov*) and your credit reports for errors.

In some states, citizens can access their own credit reports for free. Otherwise, modest fees apply. *Contact the credit rating agencies for details…*

●**Equifax** (800-685-1111…see their web site at *www.equifax.com*).

●**Experian** (888-397-3742…see their web site at *www.experian.com*).

●**TransUnion** (800-916-8800…see their web site at *www.transunion.com*).

Such caution is a good policy even if you aren't concerned about security.

Example: A friend found that the records of someone who shared his name had been intermingled with his own. The other man's credit problems delayed the closing on my friend's house by two months.

TRAVEL CAREFULLY

When you travel, you, your home and your office are at risk. Someone can learn your plans by calling airlines and posing as a travel agent. *To reduce risk…*

●**Put passwords on frequent-flier accounts.** Few people do this.

●**Be careful when revealing your identity at airports or hotels.** Never do so to anyone who is not an employee.

When you must show ID, make sure no one is looking over your shoulder. Once on an assignment, I learned someone's name and address by asking if he would break a $10 bill. When he opened his wallet, his driver's license was visible.

●**Suitcases and briefcases should not have visible identification.** Name tags should have covers. Write "see other side" on the exposed side of an uncovered label so your identification is not easily seen. Consider listing your name and telephone number only.

●**When abroad on business, be very careful**—even when speaking over the phone. Phone taps are common outside the US. Virtually all other countries encourage industrial espionage in order to help their own economies.

SECURE YOUR MAIL

A tremendous amount of private information is sent to us through the mail. That's why a locked mailbox or door slot is preferable to an easily opened mailbox. A post office box is best.

For businesses: If rivals would benefit from a look at your mail (even return addresses), review your mailing procedures. In many offices, the mail is easily observed after-hours and on weekends.

BE CAREFUL ON THE PHONE

As most people know, cell-phone conversations can be intercepted quite easily. Today's digital phones are more secure than analog cell phones, but the "bad guys" will find a way to listen in on even the highest security cell-phone conversations before long.

Speak in general terms. Don't use specifics.

Few people consider the lack of security on calls made from land-line phones. Phone records are not legally protected. So while it might be difficult to find out what you've been talking about, it is possible to find out to *whom* you've been speaking.

The most secure way to make a sensitive phone call is to purchase a prepaid phone card. Use it to make calls from a pay phone.

Businesspeople: If you believe someone might attempt to get your phone records, call a few firms you have nothing to do with and chat for a few minutes. This tactic makes it much harder for anyone checking your calls to learn anything useful.

Note: Your phone bill will only show completed long-distance calls—but this does *not* include 800 numbers since they are free. Technically, you're placing your long-distance call through another phone line (the 800 provider, etc.).

Workplace Ailments

Respiratory problems are common among workers who handle carbonless copy paper. Nasal irritation is increased among workers who photocopy often. And—no surprise here—heavy computer work causes eyestrain. *Self-defense:* Rotate office tasks...

improve ventilation of your work space...take regular breaks...and avoid uninterrupted staring at the computer screen.

Maritta S. Jaakkola, MD, DSc, consultant in pulmonary medicine, Finnish Institute of Occupational Health, Helsinki.

Mail Theft Self-Defense

Inspector Molly McMinn, criminal investigative arm, US Postal Inspection Service, Washington, DC.

Postal theft is on the increase in the United States—and much more is at stake than just your mail...

●**Criminals who have obtained your Social Security number** or other personal information can establish and use credit in your name.

●**Crooks who find out your checking account number** can print phony checks.

●**An intercepted check can be *washed*,** leaving the signature but making it payable to a different person for a greater amount.

HOW TO PROTECT YOURSELF

●**Do not use an unsecured mailbox,** such as an outbox at a hotel.

●**Incoming mail should go into a front-door slot or a locked mailbox.**

●**Hand outgoing mail to a letter carrier...**use collection boxes...or bring it to the post office.

●**Know when you should be receiving** bank/brokerage statements, blank checks and other valuable mail. Contact the sender if your mail is delayed.

●**Check your credit rating** at least once a year by calling one of the big three credit bureaus—Equifax (800-997-2493)...Experian (888-397-3742)...Trans Union LLC (800-916-8800).

●**Don't write your Social Security number** or other personal information, such as your driver's license number or account number, on checks.

• **Protect yourself from *dumpster divers*** by shredding all preapproved credit card and loan offers, discarded bills, etc.

• **When it is an option, consider paying bills electronically**—through your financial institution...US Postal Service, *www.usps.com* ...the on-line giant Quicken, *www.quicken.com.*

Dangers Where You Least Expect Them...

Melinda Muse, a health journalist and author of *I'm Afraid, You're Afraid: 448 Things to Fear and Why.* Hyperion. She lives on the coast of Maine.

As a health journalist, I read and write a lot about medical advances. One big lesson I've learned is that life today is no longer survival of the fittest—but of the wariest.

Here are some surprisingly dangerous places, things and situations...

• **Firing someone.** Workplace stress increases the risk of heart disease. Researchers asked 800 cardiac patients about their workweek just prior to their heart attacks and discovered that being laid off, quitting a job or being promoted slightly raises the probability of a heart attack—but that having to fire someone *doubles* the risk.

• **Personal computers and the Internet.** The Web is a virtual downer. People who spend even just a few hours a week on-line are more depressed and feel more isolated than those who log on less frequently.

Hunching over your computer for hours isn't good for your physical health, either. After observing elementary school students slumped at computer workstations, Cornell University researchers concluded that at least 40% were at risk for serious repetitive stress injuries.

• **Frequent flying.** Hazards of flying include luggage carts, which have those elastic tethers with metal hooks on each end. They

have snapped back into eyes, causing dislocated lenses, internal bleeding, retinal detachment and temporary loss of sight.

Think twice before grabbing that aisle seat. Every year, some 4,500 passengers are hit by items falling from overstuffed luggage bins. Briefcases are the most common missiles in the carry-on arsenal, but it also includes laptops, golf clubs and heavy backpacks.

• **Long flights.** An estimated 350 passengers die in-flight in the US every year, with heart attacks the leading cause. Sitting for four hours or more in arid cabins risks dehydration and reduces circulation in the legs by half, which could cause blood clots. If a piece of the clot breaks off and makes its way to the lungs, it can be deadly.

What to do: During long flights, walk the aisles often...and drink plenty of bottled water (unbottled airline water can carry additional health risks).

• **Hotel rooms.** Check out your room before you check in. Blood, semen and other bodily fluids have been found on purportedly "clean" sheets, blankets and bedspreads.

According to Johns Hopkins School of Public Health, it is possible to contract hepatitis from soiled bed linens, as well as to pick up body lice, which burrow in mattresses and covers.

What to do: Never lie on a hotel bedspread—strip it off. Check sheets for freshness. And don't pad around barefoot, since bathroom floors may host athlete's foot fungi.

• **Yardwork.** Need good reasons not to spend hours grooming your lawn?

Americans scatter 70 million pounds of pesticides on their yards every year. Your hands are most likely to be exposed, but your forehead, abdomen and crotch absorb pesticides faster than other body parts.

Research at Memorial Sloan-Kettering Cancer Center in New York suggests that sunscreen, while preventing sunburn, gives people a false sense of security, making them feel they can indulge in more sun time. One million Americans are diagnosed with skin cancer every year. Protect yourself by covering up.

●**Garage sales.** These hagglers' havens are notorious for unloading unsafe products, including bunk beds that can strangle…cribs that can suffocate…dangerous baby carriages…collapsing playpens…beanbag chairs stuffed with foam pellets that have choked children.

●**Money.** Coins and greenbacks are cruddy with germ colonies, including fecal bacteria…Staphylococcus, which causes food poisoning…and acne-causing Propionibacterium. It seems the smaller the denomination, the more dangerous.

A test of $20 bills uncovered money's other dirty secret—cash is contaminated by cocaine. *The Journal of Forensic Sciences* says, "…most Americans handle small amounts of cocaine every day…on dollar bills." Follow Mom's advice about keeping your hands out of your mouth.

●**Gemstones.** Radiation is sometimes used to deepen the color of gemstones, which greatly enhances their value. Although "nuked" gems should be kept in lead casings for several years while their radiation levels taper off, unscrupulous traders have released to the market "hot" cat's-eye gemstones, some registering 51 times the US radiation limits. Experts estimate that thousands of radioactive stones are in circulation in the US, Europe and Asia.

●**Mondays…Fridays…and Saturdays.**

●Monday is the day of the week when the majority of suicides occur, says the American Association of Suicidology. It is also the day when the most heart attacks occur.

●Fridays produce more car accidents than any other day of the week.

●Saturdays produce the greatest number of fatal motor vehicle crashes. Most occur between 4 p.m. and 4 a.m.

●**Casinos.** The odds are lousy. Only 150 of 736 high rollers who suffered a heart attack in Las Vegas casinos lived to place another wager, according to a recent study. Paramedics must maneuver through throngs in the mammoth gaming halls, wasting valuable life-saving time. Hedging their bets, many casinos have installed defibrillators.

●**Kissing your dog.** Each year, more than one million Americans get parasites, such as roundworms, hookworms and pinworms, from kissing their canine pals. Since parasitic infections are difficult to diagnose in humans, people often never discover the causes of their headaches, liver ailments or sinus infections. Teach Rover to shake.

Although in my book I chronicled 448 things to fear, I urge everyone to not let their fears overwhelm them. After all, optimism is a tonic for a longer, healthier and—dare we hope—safer life.

21

Very, Very Personal

Jump-Start Your Sex Life...*Naturally*

Well before *sildenafil* (Viagra), people relied on aphrodisiacs to increase sexual desire...boost stamina...improve performance...and increase pleasure.

Many of these compounds owe their reputation to folklore, but several herbs and dietary supplements have proven sex-enhancing effects.

Good news: Products that improve sex naturally may be less likely to cause serious side effects than prescription drugs. Many strengthen the cardiovascular system and help regulate hormone production. That's as important for good sex as having an erection or being sufficiently lubricated.

Unlike sildenafil, sex-enhancing herbs and supplements aren't taken just an hour or so before sex. They're taken daily until there's a noticeable improvement in sexual performance.

At that point, some people take a pause to see if the herbs and supplements are no longer necessary. Others continue taking the preparations indefinitely.

Important: Use herbs and supplements only under medical supervision. That way you'll be sure to get the product and dosage that's right for you.

Caution: Fresh or dried herbs differ greatly in potency from batch to batch. Use capsules or tinctures, instead. They've been standardized to contain the proper amounts of active ingredients.

For better sex, try one of the following natural enhancers. Select the one that best suits your needs. Give each preparation a few months to work. If you see no effect, try another.

Chris D. Meletis, ND, dean of clinical affairs and chief medical officer of the National College of Naturopathic Medicine in Portland, Oregon. He is author of *Better Sex Naturally*. Harper Resource.

GINKGO BILOBA

Ginkgo contains a variety of compounds that relax blood vessels and increase circulation to the brain and pelvic area.

For women, increased blood flow improves vaginal lubrication and sexual responsiveness.

For men, adequate blood flow is essential to achieve and sustain erections.

Typical dosage: *Capsules:* 40 mg to 60 mg of 24% standardized powdered extract three to four times daily. *Tincture:* 30 drops three to four times daily.

Side effects: Ginkgo may cause dizziness, headache or heart palpitations.

Caution: Ginkgo is a blood thinner and can increase the blood-thinning effects of aspirin and *warfarin* (Coumadin). Check with your physician before using ginkgo if you're taking either medication.

MUIRA PUAMA

Also known as "potency wood," this herb contains sterols and other compounds that boost levels of testosterone, a hormone that plays a critical role in sexual desire in women as well as men.

Muira puama also contains volatile oils, including camphor and beta-carophyllene. They're thought to restore sex drive by stimulating nerves in the brain's pleasure center.

Typical dosage: 250 mg three times daily in capsule form.

Side effect: Muira puama may lower blood pressure by as much as 10%. Check with your doctor before using this herb if you have low blood pressure (hypotension).

GINSENG

This herb is an "adaptogen," meaning it helps the body compensate for extended periods of stress. Stress can cause sexual desire and performance to plummet.

Compounds in ginseng root stimulate the adrenal glands to release substances that lower the levels of adrenaline and other stress hormones.

These compounds also improve blood flow to the penis, help tissues use oxygen more efficiently and boost production of testosterone in men and progesterone in women.

Typical dosage: *Capsules:* 10 mg to 50 mg one to three times daily. *Tincture:* 30 to 60 drops daily.

Side effect: Ginseng may cause diarrhea …high blood pressure…sleeplessness.

ASHWAGANDA

A member of the pepper family, this herb contains *withanolides*, substances that increase the activity of testosterone and progesterone. Ashwaganda also relieves stress and anxiety.

Typical dosage: *Capsules:* 1,000 mg once or twice daily. *Tincture:* 60 to 90 drops two or three times daily.

Side effects: Because ashwaganda has antianxiety properties, it should not be used by anyone taking medications to treat anxiety and/or depression. The herb could intensify the drugs' actions as well as their side effects. Ashwaganda may also trigger miscarriages.

ARGININE

Taken in supplement form, this amino acid has been shown to relax smooth muscle contractions. This boosts arterial dilation, bringing more blood to the pelvic area.

The body uses arginine to produce nitric oxide, a chemical needed to achieve erections. (Sildenafil works in part by making nitric oxide more readily available in the body.)

Typical dosage: 1,000 mg to 2,000 mg twice daily in capsule form. Take capsules between meals, since many foods contain lysine, an amino acid that counteracts arginine's effects.

Side effect: Don't take this herb if you get cold sores caused by the herpes simplex virus. Arginine stimulates viral replication.

FOR MEN ONLY

The herb *yohimbe* is approved by the FDA for treating impotence and low sex drive.

Yohimbe contains a compound called *yohimbine*, which helps dilate blood vessels in the penis. Most men who take yohimbe experience an increase in sexual desire within an hour.

Typical dosage: 15 mg to 25 mg daily in capsule form. Divide into several doses throughout the day to minimize side effects.

Take smaller amounts at first—for example, 5 mg or 10 mg a day—then gradually increase the amount over several weeks.

Side effects: Elevated blood pressure, nausea, racing heart and anxiety. Use yohimbe only under medical supervision.

FOR WOMEN ONLY

The herb *dong quai* contains plant sterols that help correct estrogen deficiencies.

Studies suggest that dong quai can increase sexual desire as well as the intensity of orgasms.

Typical dosage: Capsules: 1,000 mg three to four times daily. *Tincture:* 45 to 60 drops two or three times daily.

Caution: Pregnant and lactating women should not use dong quai. The herb also increases sensitivity to sunlight.

Seniors And Sex

To improve your sex life as you grow older—take your time. Stick to easy positions, and try alternating occasions—each of you is touched one day and does the touching the next. *For men only:* Thinking about sex or looking at sexy pictures may no longer be enough to arouse you. But touching yourself—or having your partner touch you—usually works.

Ruth Westheimer, PhD, authority on human sexuality and intimacy, writing in *Are You Old Enough to Read This Book? Reflections on Midlife.* Reader's Digest Association, a collection of writings from prominent individuals over age 50.

Viagra and Conception

Viagra, the popular impotence drug, may enable infertile women to conceive. *Recent study:* Four infertile women used a vaginal suppository containing *sildenafil* (Viagra) four times a day for one week. Three

were then successfully impregnated through in-vitro fertilization. Sildenafil increases blood flow to the uterine lining, making it thicker and more receptive to embryos.

Geoffrey Sher, MD, executive director, Sher Institute for Reproductive Medicine, Las Vegas, NV.

Penile Enlargement Surgery Can Be Very Dangerous

It can lead to erectile dysfunction, scarring, infection and numbness or irritation...and does not produce good cosmetic results. *How it's done:* The penis is lengthened by surgically detaching the ligaments that attach it to the pelvis...girth is added by injecting fat or wrapping grafts of fat around the penis. The Society for the Study of Impotence has issued a statement against penile enlargement. Urologists do not commonly perform it.

Arthur L. Burnett, MD, associate professor of urology, Johns Hopkins Hospital, Baltimore.

Condoms Come in Different Sizes

Average-sized condoms fit about 80% of men. *For the other 20%:* Some brands, such as Beyond7 and Exotica, fit more snugly...others, such as Bareback and Trojan Magnum, are larger than average. Latex condoms are the overwhelming choice for contraception and disease prevention. But some men prefer polyurethane condoms, which may conduct heat better and are much thinner than latex models. *Caution:* Polyurethane condoms break or slip off 8.5% of the time, compared with only 1.6% of the time for latex condoms.

Ron Frezieres, MSPh, director of research, California Family Health Council, 3600 Wilshire Blvd., Suite 600, Los Angeles 90010.

Women's Sexual Desire May Grow Stronger Following Hysterectomy

That was the surprising conclusion of a study of 1,000 women by the University of Maryland School of Medicine. Researchers discovered that after surgery, 15% more of the women desired sex at least once a week, 12% more made love at least five times a month and 9% more experienced orgasms. Only 5% felt the quality of their sex life had deteriorated.

Kristen H. Kjerulff, PhD, associate professor of epidemiology, University of Maryland School of Medicine, Baltimore.

Sex *Is* Possible after Prostate Removal

After radical prostate surgery, a man has a 2% or less chance of retaining normal sexual function. In a study of 12 patients, nerve-grafting—in which a small nerve from the foot is implanted in the penis—made it possible for four of the men to have unaided intercourse and four others to have sex by using Viagra. It takes six to eight months after the grafting to notice any results. *Major cancer centers that currently perform the procedure:* Baylor College of Medicine, Houston …Memorial Sloan Kettering Cancer Center, New York City…M.D. Anderson Cancer Center, Houston…University of Tennesee, Knoxville.

Edward Kim, MD, associate professor of urology, University of Tennessee Medical Center, Knoxville.

Prostate Pain Relief

Prostate pain can often be eased with supplements of *quercetin*, a potent antioxi-dant found in red wine, onions and green tea. In a recent study, 500 mg twice a day relieved pain in two out of three prostatitis sufferers. *Theory:* Quercetin boosts levels of painkilling endorphins in the prostate. Quercetin supplements are sold in health food stores. Choose *Prosta-Q* or another brand that also contains *bromelain* and *papain*. These enzymes increase absorption of quercetin.

Daniel A. Shoskes, MD, director of renal transplantation, Cleveland Clinic, Ft. Lauderdale, FL. His study of 47 prostatitis sufferers was published in *Urology,* 9105 Franklin Sq. Dr., Baltimore 21237.

New Reason to Practice Safe Sex

Incidence of gonorrhea is on the rise—and the disease is increasingly resistant to antibiotics. In Hawaii last year, nearly 10% of evaluated gonorrhea cases were resistant to treatment with *ciprofloxacin* (Cipro). In Kansas City, Missouri, a group of gonorrhea cases had shown increased resistance to *azithromycin* (Zithromax). *Troubling:* More than 360,000 cases of gonorrhea were reported in 1999 in the US—but only 327,000 cases two years earlier.

Robert E. Johnson, MD, medical epidemiologist, Centers for Disease Control and Prevention, Atlanta.

Birth Control Pill Users, Beware

St. John's wort may reduce the effectiveness of oral contraceptives. Other dietary supplements may be dangerous as well. Many common drugs reduce the effectiveness of birth control pills, too. *Examples:* A number of antibiotics, including erythromycin and penicillin…Dilantin and other antiepileptic drugs. *Self-defense:* Ask your doctor if you need to use an additional form of birth control when taking medications or dietary supplements.

Stephen Piscitelli, PharmD, is coordinator of clinical pharmacokinetics research laboratory, Clinical Center, National Institutes of Health, Bethesda, Maryland. He recently led a study of the effect of St. John's wort on drug metabolism.

Managing Menopause Without Drugs

Toni M. Cutson, MD, associate professor of community and family medicine and associate professor of medicine, both at Duke University Medical Center in Durham, NC. She is coauthor of "Managing Menopause," a report in *American Family Physician*.

Hot flashes, mood swings, vaginal dryness, sleep disturbances and other annoying symptoms affect about 75% of menopausal women.

Even more troublesome is the increased risk for heart disease and osteoporosis associated with menopause.

To help control these common problems, doctors often prescribe hormone-replacement therapy (HRT). HRT may also protect against stroke and Alzheimer's disease.

Hormone therapy can cause side effects, including breast tenderness, bloating and headaches. It has also been linked to a slightly higher risk for breast cancer, especially in women with a family history of the disease.

To avoid the possible drawbacks of HRT, many women treat their symptoms with a variety of nondrug alternatives—eating a low-fat, high-fiber diet...exercising regularly...and quitting smoking.

These are a good start. But there are additional ways to relieve the symptoms. *Whether she takes hormones or not, a woman can benefit from these eight commonly overlooked strategies...*

• **Eat at least eight servings of fruits and vegetables each day.** These high-fiber, low-fat foods are typically rich in folic acid and other B vitamins, which reduce the risk for heart disease by helping to prevent arterial blood clots.

One serving equals one piece of fruit, one-half cup of cooked vegetables or one cup of raw vegetables.

Other osteoporosis-fighting foods: Calcium-rich products, such as dairy products (milk and yogurt) and fortified orange juice.

• **Eat whole soy foods.** They contain *isoflavones*, estrogen-like compounds that reduce hot flashes, bone loss and LDL (bad) cholesterol. Sources include soy nuts, soy milk and tofu.

Caution: Avoid nutritional supplements and powders that claim to have the same active ingredients as soy foods. These products may contain unknown chemicals that could be harmful.

Worse, they may contain *excessive* levels of isoflavones, which increase breast cancer risk. Limit your soy intake to about 60 grams of isoflavones a day.

• **Take a daily multivitamin.** Choose a name brand, such as One-a-Day or Centrum, to get the recommended requirements for most vitamins and minerals. Do *not* take individual vitamin megadoses, however. They can be harmful.

Too much vitamin A, for example, can damage the eyes and skin. Megadoses of vitamin D can cause excess calcium in the bloodstream.

To prevent liver damage, avoid pills that provide more than 18 mg of iron. Because menopausal women no longer lose iron through menstruation, iron supplements make sense only if you've been diagnosed with an iron deficiency.

• **Take a calcium supplement.** A daily 1,500-mg dose helps prevent osteoporosis.

Calcium carbonate found in Tums is cheap and readily absorbed. Each Tums tablet provides 200 mg of calcium. For higher doses, try Tums E-X with 300 mg or Tums 500 with 500 mg.

• **Try proven herbal remedies.** Some menopausal women now take chasteberry to prevent hot flashes. But little research exists to support its effectiveness.

Similarly, avoid dong quai and licorice root. Dong quai can cause excessive blood thinning. Licorice root may precipitate headaches or high blood pressure.

Better: Black cohosh. This herb suppresses *luteinizing hormone* (LH), which triggers hot flashes. Some women claim it also improves their sex drive and eases night sweats and sleep disturbances.

Black cohosh is sold as Remifemin at health food stores.

●**Limit alcohol consumption.** Have no more than three glasses of wine—or three ounces of hard liquor—a week. Drinking wine in moderation may be beneficial to the heart, but too much alcohol exacerbates hot flashes.

●**Relax.** Many menopausal women blame hormone fluctuations for mood and memory problems. But psychological stress is often the real cause. While they're going through menopause, they may also be caring for elderly parents, sending children off to college or dealing with job stress.

To combat stress: Seek help for difficult situations. Turn down extra projects at work...ask siblings to help care for an elderly parent...or find a day program that caters to the social needs of seniors.

Get plenty of sleep and give yourself 30 minutes of quiet time each day. If your schedule doesn't permit it, five minutes is better than nothing.

●**Rethink your sex life.** The physical and psychological aspects of menopause often put a damper on a woman's sex life. But abstinence is not the answer.

Frequent sexual activity decreases vaginal dryness, improves sleep, reduces stress and helps alleviate moodiness.

Bonus: Regular sex also increases your libido.

Impotence Predicts Heart Disease

Twenty-five percent of men who see doctors for impotence caused by vascular problems have a heart attack or stroke within five years of the start of impotence. *Reason:* Sexual impotence is often caused by the same problems that cause heart trouble, including diabetes, smoking, high blood pressure and high cholesterol levels.

Kenneth Goldberg, MD, director, Male Health Center, Lewisville, TX.

Love Handles And Impotence

Love handles often go hand in hand with impotence. *Recent finding:* Men with a 42-inch waist were twice as likely to be impotent as were men with a 31-inch waist. *Theory:* In overweight men, inability to achieve or maintain erection is an early sign of heart disease—which is often associated with impotence. *Best advice:* Shape up. Inactive men are 40% more likely to experience impotence than those who exercise.

Eric Rimm, ScD, assistant professor of epidemiology and nutrition, Harvard School of Public Health, Boston.

Another Impotence Treatment

Impotence that cannot be controlled with *sildenafil* (Viagra) may be treatable with a drug that acts on the brain—*apomorphine* (Uprima). *Recent finding:* A rapidly absorbed apomorphine pill placed under the tongue enhanced ability to achieve erections in 44% of impotent men. *Bonus:* Apomorphine takes effect within 20 minutes. Sildenafil typically takes about an hour. Apomorphine could be approved for use as an impotence treatment as early as next year.

Eugene Dula, MD, medical director, West Coast Clinical Research, Van Nuys, CA.

Exercise Boosts Sex Life

Couples who exercise together report better relationships on many levels, including sex. *Reasons:* People who work out feel better about their bodies...working out releases brain chemicals that make women and men feel energetic and happy...and working out together makes them feel better about being with each other.

Lonnie Barbach, PhD, assistant clinical professor of medical psychology, University of California Medical School, San Francisco, and author of *Turn Ons.* Plume. *www.sex-centre.com.*

Risky Fertility Treatment

Hormone injections that stimulate ovaries to release eggs increase the risk of pregnancies with three or more fetuses. *Special problem:* Such pregnancies are more likely to produce babies with cerebral palsy, blindness and other problems. *Much safer:* In vitro fertilization (IVF). It allows better control of fertility treatments and has a higher likelihood of success—40%, compared with 15% for hormone injections. *IVF costs more:* About $7,800, nearly three times the cost of injections, but it significantly increases your chance of getting pregnant.

Norbert Gleicher, MD, president, Center for Human Reproduction, New York City, and leader of a study comparing IVF with injectable hormones.

Menopause Alert

Natural remedies for menopause symptoms present new challenges.

Conventional hormone replacement therapy uses powerful drugs that combat osteoporosis and relieve unpleasant symptoms of menopause but increase the risk of blood clots and breast cancer.

Many women are instead choosing to take herbal supplements containing phytoestrogens—plant chemicals with properties similar to estrogens. The plant-derived chemicals are less potent than hormone replacements, but are often taken in much greater volume.

While people have been safely eating soy foods for a long time, there is no similar history of people consuming isolated and concentrated components from soy in large amounts. There are no long-term studies that indicate this is safe to do—particularly for women who have or who are at risk for breast cancer.

Fredi Kronenberg, PhD, is associate professor of clinical physiology, and director of the Rosenthal Center for Complementary and Alternative Medicine at Columbia University College of Physicians & Surgeons in New York City.

 # Better Relationships

Sleeping in separate beds can help a relationship. *Reasons for sleeping separately:* Snoring, kicking or flailing during sleep...or conflicting work or sleep schedules that cause one person to be awakened when the other goes to sleep or gets up. *Key:* The objective is to have the best relationship possible when awake. If sleeping separately improves the daytime relationship, it is the thing to do.

John Gray, PhD, certified family therapist and author of *Men Are from Mars, Women Are from Venus.* HarperCollins.

HRT & Mammograms

Hormone replacement therapy (HRT) can raise the risk for false mammogram readings.

Recent finding: Mammograms detected only 64% of breast cancers in women 50 to 69 years of age who were on HRT. The test detected 80% of cancers in women of that age who were not on HRT.

Theory: HRT increases the density of breast tissue, making it more difficult to detect signs of cancer.

Important: Despite these findings, mammograms remain the most effective way to screen for breast cancer.

Anne M. Kavanagh, PhD, senior research fellow, Australian Research Centre for Sex, Health and Society, La Trobe University, Melbourne. Her two-year study of 103,770 women was published in *The Lancet*, 42 Bedford Square, London WC1B 3SL.

Arthritis in Young Adults

Arthritis in sexually active adults—especially those under age 30—may be caused by gonorrhea. Disseminated gonorrhea—an infection that spreads throughout the body—occurs in up to 3% of all cases of gonorrhea. It can cause septic arthritis, a serious bacterial infection of the joint. *Chief symptom:* An arthritic joint that feels hot and swollen. While gonorrhea is easily cured, untreated infection will eventually destroy the joint.

Diane Birnbaumer, MD, associate professor of medicine, University of California, Los Angeles, School of Medicine. She spoke at a recent conference on primary-care emergencies.

Stretch Marks Fade

Stretch marks can be faded by massaging the skin around them. These scars, also known as *striae*, result from major weight changes and/or hormonal shifts during and after pregnancy. Elevated hormone levels seem to damage collagen—a fibrous protein found in skin.

Theory: Massaging healthy skin near stretch marks pushes collagen into their borders, helping to fill in the scars. It also stimulates collagen synthesis.

Also helpful: Exercise, which improves muscle tone and lowers body fat.

Joshua L. Fox, MD, medical director, Center for Laser and Cosmetic Surgery, New York City.

Help for Women with Facial Hair

Vaniqa, an FDA-approved prescription cream, slows hair growth in 60% of women who use it twice daily.

Important: It is not a cure, but an adjunct to shaving, tweezing, waxing, electrolysis and/or laser therapy.

Caution: Pregnant and breast-feeding women should not use Vaniqa.

Possible side effects: Burning, stinging. *Cost:* $50 for a 30-gram tube (two-month supply). Vaniqa is a "cosmetic drug," so insurance coverage is unlikely.

Deborah S. Sarnoff, MD, associate clinical professor of dermatology, NYU Medical Center, and cosmetic dermatologist in private practice in New York City and Long Island.

Related Useful Sites

Employment

☐ Best Jobs USA
www.bestjobsusa.com

A terrific place to search not only for a new job, but to learn about all aspects of your job search, including the best places to live and work, a schedule of current industry trade shows and the online version of *Employment Review,* a great publication to help you manage all aspects of your career.

☐ Hard@Work
www.hardatwork.com

This site offers information and guidance for all employees. *The Watercooler* is the place for discussion groups. Talk about what's happening in your own career, and learn about the latest developments in workplace issues. *Stump the Mentor* offers practical suggestions for career questions and problems. *The Rock Pile* offers case studies to help people deal with career crises.

Business

☐ Entrepreneur.com
www.entrepreneurmag.com

For small-business people who want to meet others in their fields or industries. A variety of bulletin boards, including such specific areas as hot business opportunities, marketing strategies, home-based business trends and opportunities.

☐ Entrepreneurial Edge
www.lowe.org

An information toolbox for entrepreneurs, small-business owners and home-based office workers. Main feature: A vast searchable database of electronic documents, Web links and books on starting or operating a business. Also includes a long list of published small-business resources and a discussion group.

☐ entreworld.org
www.entreworld.org

A wealth of helpful articles and resource lists for existing and aspiring entrepreneurs. Attractively designed and easy to navigate, the site is sponsored and managed by the nonprofit Kauffman Center for Entrepreneurial Leadership.

☐ Franchise Direct
www.franchisedirect.com

This site offers a comprehensive franchise opportunity listing, providing views, news and advice to entrepreneurs and franchisers alike. You can select from a list of available opportunities and read detailed descriptions of the businesses, their financial situations and what's involved in becoming a franchisee. You'll also find insightful tips in assessing franchises and how to minimize your risk.

☐ Small Business Administration
www.sbaonline.sba.gov

Informative site from US Small Business Administration (SBA). *Angel Capital Electronic Network (ACE-Net)* database puts small businesses looking for capital together with potential investors. *Starting Your Business* has information on relevant workshops, publications and videos, SBA services such as counseling, even shareware. *Financing Your Business* gives information on many loans, financial and technical assistance programs. Also: Hot buttons for *Disaster Assistance, Business Cards* (leave 'em or search 'em) and *Property for Sale.* Lots more here.

☐ Small Business Advisor
www.isquare.com

This site contains a heavy dose of promotional material for business books, services, etc., most of which are not unique to the voluminous world of business publications. However, link to the newsletter page for current and back issues of the on-line newsletter *The Small Business Advisor.* It contains a substantial amount of helpful information for small-business owners, including tax advice, financing strategies, marketing tactics and business computing.

☐ Small Business Taxes & Management
www.smbiz.com

This is the Web version of *Small Business Taxes & Management,* which provides tax news and guidance to small- and medium-sized companies. Useful: Reference tables feature corporate and individual tax rates, links to helpful IRS sites and frequently used tax forms.

Family and Education

Family Time

www.familytime.com

Here's a great place for tips on how to get your stressed-out and busy family highly organized. Once you register (for free) you can take advantage of the calendar, shopping list, address book, recipes and much, much more.

Kaplan

www.kaptest.com

The Kaplan Educational Center site offers practice tests and tips for careers as diverse as accounting, law, medicine and nursing. There's even a whole section on how to reduce anxiety on test day. Also, useful information on financial-aid packages.

KidNews

www.kidnews.com

Great news service for kids and teachers. Stories on the site can be used at no charge, and anyone can submit a story. Read or submit articles in several categories, including news, features, profiles, creative, goodies, sports or reviews. KidNews also offers a *PenPal* section and *Cool Hangouts*. Also, links to other kids' sites.

KidsCom

www.kidscom.com

A very colorful interactive site for kids ages 4 to 15. Follow an action-adventure series, communicate with computer pen pals around the world, discover new crafts and games, including fun ones on Internet safety.

Safe Within

www.safewithin.com

This site contains the information you need about how to keep you and your loved ones safe. There are eight different sections, including pet safety, child safety, travel safety and senior safety.

Advice about Love

http://homearts.com/depts/family/advicef4.frm

Here's a great place to take those "Mars/Venus" questions. Choose a category and subject (e.g., *The Single Life/Relationship Troubles*) and you'll be directed to lots of links that will help you with your love life.

Index

garlic in preventing, 6
stages and grades of, 4–5
treating, 4–6
Prostate pain, relief of, 330
Prostate removal, sex and, 330
Prostate specific antigen (PSA), blood
test for levels of, 4
Protein, osteoporosis and, 18
Pseudoephedrine (Sudafed) for sinusitis,
55
Psoriasis, smoking and, 8
Psychological stress, curbing, in
preventing heart attacks, 9
Pumpkin seed *(Cucurbita pepo),*
benefits of, 76

Q

Qualified personal residence trust, 200

R

Radiation
coronary arteries and, 12
for prostate cancer, 5
Raloxifene (Evista) osteoporosis and, 19
Real estate, investments in, 163–64
Rebates, credit card, 92
Recipes, alcohol in, 65
Reflexology, hand, 79–80
Reiki, benefits of, 78
Relationships, improving, 333
Rental car, saving on, 182
Repetitive stress injuries, exercise and,
69
Resedronate (Actonel), osteoporosis
and, 19
Respiratory disorders, exercise and, 69
Restless legs syndrome, relief from, 49
Retirement, transitioning in, 195
Retirement community, finding right,
193–94
Retirement funds, drawing on, 129–30
Retirement plans. *See also* Investments
brokerage options on 401(k), 190
collecting all benefits, 190–91
divorce and, 193
filing extension for, 128
401(k) in, 189–92
hidden costs in 401(k), 190
interest-only loans in, 193
IRA distribution, 189
personal asset protection, 202–4
protecting IRA beneficiaries in,
188–89
Roth IRAs in, 187–88
Social Security and, 192
steady income and, 88–89
stress and, 193
wills in, 204
Reverse mortgages, 89
Revocable living trusts, 206–8
Revocable trusts, 206
Rizatriptan (Maxalt) for migraines, 50
Roaches, getting rid of, 247
Road rage, 311
Roth IRAs, 125, 187–88
Roulette, 233

S

Safety. *See also* Fraud; Scams; Theft
car, 240, 241
food, 314
gas grills and, 312
hotel cribs and, 315
household, 311–12
improved lighting and, 312–14
jumping from runaway car, 309–10
lightning and, 314
road rage and, 311
St. John's wort
birth control pills and, 330–31
surgery and, 35
Sales reps, success secrets for, 295
Salt
effect on bones, 20
osteoporosis and, 18
Satellite television, saving on, 177–78
Saunas, exercise and, 73
Savings, credit versus, 92
Savings bonds, leaving to charity, 208
Scams
avoiding, 315–17
e-mail, 319
Sciatica, therapy for, 81
S corporation, 299
Sebum, 26
Securities
writing off worthless, 125–27
Selective estrogen receptor modulators,
osteoporosis and, 19
Selective serotonin reuptake inhibitors
(SSRIs) for chronic fatigue, 48
Seniors. *See* Elderly
Senior Softball World Series, 229
Separation, taxes and, 141–43
Seratonin-2 agonists for migraines, 51
Sertraline (Zoloft) for chronic fatigue, 48
Severance, employee, 283
Sex, practicing safe, 330
Sex life
arthritis and, 334
exercise and, 333
jump starting, 327–29
prostate removal and, 330
seniors and, 329
Shellfish, benefits from, 61
Shopping, Web, 297–98
Shoulders, sore, reflexology for, 80
Side air bags, 241
Sigmoidoscopy, 32
Simvastatin (Zocor) for cholesterol, 23
Sinusitis, preventing, 55–56
Sinus surgery for sinusitis, 55–56
Sleep. *See also* Insomnia
in improving relationships, 333
problems with, 54–55
Sleep apnea, snoring and, 41, 47–48
Small stocks, investments in, 148–49
Smoking. *See also* Nicotine
avoiding, in preventing cancer, 3
methods for quitting, 7–8
osteoporosis and, 18
psoriasis and, 8
Snoring, sleep apnea and, 41, 47–48
Social Security
checking benefit statement in, 192
taking payouts, 192

tax-saving strategy, 124
Sodium, cutting back on, in preventing
heart attacks, 9
Soft drinks, osteoporosis and, 18
Sole proprietorship, 298–99
Sore throats, atypical esophageal reflux
and, 40–41
Soy foods, benefits of, 78–79
Soy milk, calcium and, 64–65
Specialists, getting appointment with, 39
Spike lavender for bronchitis, 84
Stairways, hidden hazards in, 311
Stockbrokers, dealing with
unscrupulous, 165
Stock options, need for professionals
and, 148
Stock redemption agreements, 211
Stocks. *See also* Investments
biotech, 148, 160–61
business-to-business technology, 148
small, 148–49
value, 158
Stomach
air travel and problems with, 221
causes of upset, 51–52
reflexology for upset, 80
Strength training. *See* Weight lifting
Streptokinase (Streptase), dangers of, 15
Stress
chronic fatigue and, 48
errors in tests for, 33
vitamin C and, 12
workplace, 325
Stretch marks, 334
Stroke-reducing nutrients, 70
Strokes
exercise versus, 71–72
fruits in preventing, 60–61
preventing, 16–17
vegetables in preventing, 60–61
Sumatriptan (Imitrex) for migraines, 50
Sunscreen, discarding old, 15
Surgery
children and, 34–35
herbs and, 35
penile enlargement, 329
prostate, 4–5
Viagra and, 35
Syndrome X, heart attacks and, 10–11

T

Tax-deferred account, moving funds to,
160
Tax-deferred property, 90
Taxes. *See also* Internal Revenue Service
(IRS)
alternative minimum, 133
avoiding, on mutual fund, 127–28
breaks in
on business loans, 138
for home owners, 118
business entities and, 298–300
charity donations and, 143
credits on
for adoption, 110
for children, 110
for dependent care, 110
earned income, 138–39